PRIME·TIME Hits

Television's Most Popular Network Programs

1950 TO THE PRESENT

SUSAN SACKETT

BILLBOARD BOOKS   An imprint of Watson-Guptill Publications/New York

For Galen, who is part of the 21st century's
next generation of television viewer-users,

And for Gene, who had already been there (and beyond)
in his mind, and will always live in mine.

Research Assistant: Marcia Rovins
Editor: Tad Lathrop
Senior Editor: Paul Lukas
Book and Cover Design: Bob Fillie, Graphiti Graphics
Cover Illustration: Carmine Vecchio
Production Manager: Hector Campbell

Copyright © 1993 by Susan Sackett

First published 1993 by Billboard Books, an imprint of Watson-Guptill
Publications, a division of BPI Communications, Inc., 1515 Broadway,
New York, NY 10036.

Library of Congress Cataloging-in-Publication Data
Sackett, Susan.
     Prime-time hits: television's most popular network programs,
1950 to the present/Susan Sackett
        p.   cm.
     Includes index.
     ISBN 0-8230-8392-6
     1. Television programs—United States—History.
2. Television programs—United States—Awards. I. Title.
PN1992. 3. U5S23   1993
791. 45' 75' 0973—dc20   93–1508
                                                      CIP

Manufactured in the United States of America
First Printing, 1993
1 2 3 4 5 6 7 8 9 / 99 98 97 96 95 94 93

Page 1, clockwise from top left: Sid
Caesar, Dean Martin, Sharon Gless,
Raymond Burr

Page 3, center: Ed "Kookie" Barnes;
clockwise from top left: Richard Boone,
Lucille Ball, Clayton Moore, Milton Berle

Page 99, center: Buddy Ebsen; clockwise from top left: Diahann Carroll, Vincent Edwards, Eva Gabor, Dan Blocker

Page 169, center: Henry Winkler; clock-
wise from top left: Telly Savalas; Farah
Fawcett-Majors; Carroll O'Connor,
Redd Foxx

Page 267, center: Ted Danson; clockwise from top left: Lisa Bonet, Don
Johnson, Bruce Willis, Roseanne Arnold

Page 331, center: Bob Saget; clockwise
from top left: Candice Bergen, Dixie
Carter, Tim Allen, Robert Stack

ACKNOWLEDGMENTS

The best part of writing a book, as with any job, is getting to work with other people. In a nonfiction book such as this, the most important of those people has always been my research assistant. Marcia Rovins was a godsend on my first book for Billboard/Watson-Guptill (*The Hollywood Reporter Book of Box Office Hits*), and I knew I could count on her to come through for me again on *Prime-Time Hits*. She has my deepest gratitude, as always.

I would like to thank the many talented people who took time from their hectic lives to spare me some moments and share their experiences with me. Thank you, Gary Owens, Elinor Donahue, Margaret Loesch, Vin Di Bona, George Schenck, Frank Cardea, and Gary Grossman. Also thanks to Carl Kugel and Darlene West-Ramos for support; Cheryl Blythe, Carol Aerenson, John Felz, Don McCulloch, and Chuck Southcott for further research assistance; the kind people working at the Academy of Television Arts and Sciences Library; Ivan Snell, Jr., for allowing me access to his *TV Guide* collection; Mark Hahn for his support during my Bad Computer Days; Darlene Lieblich at Fox Broadcast Standards, who was able to answer my every question (well, almost); Dawn Roddenberry and Richard Compton for friendship and encouragement; and my friend and TV writing partner Fred Bronson, for patience, love, and support.

I also want to thank my friends at Billboard Books, particularly Senior Editor Paul Lukas; Bob Fillie, the book's designer; and Hector Campbell, the production manager.

Finally, my deepest gratitude to my editor, Tad Lathrop, who believed in this book from the start and encouraged me to find a way to make it work. What a treat it is to work with an editor as fine as Tad.

CONTENTS

THE 1970s

INTRODUCTION

My first experience with television was very much like that of Richie Cunningham in "Happy Days." One day when I was about six, my father brought home a huge piece of furniture with a small piece of glass embedded in the front and no legs to support it. He took it into our living room and placed it on top of the even larger Emerson radio set, which made a perfect stand for this box called a "television." After plugging it in, he turned it on. Then we waited. And waited.

Those early TV's took forever to warm up, but when they finally did, there was sudden magic. Little black-and-white people sang and puppets played and I was enthralled. Soon all the kids in my Bridgeport, Connecticut, neighborhood were basking in the glow of the tiny seven-inch screen as we watched "Kukla, Fran and Ollie," "Howdy Doody," and my favorite, "The Stu Erwin Show" (I admired Jackie Erwin's pigtails and soon began growing my hair, too). And when it was turned off, I remember racing to the back, waiting for my new "TV friends" to emerge and play with me (Well, I *was* only six).

Although I may not have understood the principles of television, I was completely hooked after my first experience with the medium. I began writing letters to my favorite characters. I sent an invitation to Jackie Erwin, (and the future Zelda on "Dobie Gillis"), asking her to my eighth birthday party. Sheila James, who played the little girl on the show, sent me a card all the way from Hollywood—how she got my invitation I'll never know—and 40 years later, when I finally met her, I was able to thank her for it. On trips to nearby New York City, I dragged my mother to the NBC studios at Rockefeller Center, where we took the behind-the-scenes tour time and again, year after year, right up until I finished high school and moved to Florida. I never tired of learning new things about this magical world.

When I graduated from the University of Florida, I took a "sensible" position as a schoolteacher, but I longed to work in Hollywood. So three years later, I left my cushy job in Miami for the unknown, drove across the country, and landed work at, of all places, NBC in Burbank. Six years later I had the good fortune to work for one of the true geniuses in television—Gene Roddenberry, the creator of "Star Trek." Knowing Gene changed my life. I was able to work with the man who fashioned my favorite show (by then it had been cancelled) and later the spinoff series "Star Trek: The Next Generation." Our relationship lasted 17 years, and then Gene died in 1991. I still miss him terribly.

Which brings us to the present and this book. Having already written *The Hollywood Reporter Book of Box Office Hits*, I felt it was only natural that a companion book based on television hits should follow, especially since I had worked in the television industry for over 20 years. But there would have to be some adjustments. Where that book had used 1939 as the starting point for the hit films to be discussed, this one would have to begin much later; although television had been around for years, it wasn't until 1950 that TV became a practical reality for the average family. That year was also the starting point for complete Nielsen listings, which served as the source for the all-important yearly top 10 lists, the basis for my writing.

In the early years of TV, there were many ratings companies keeping track of how well shows were doing; AC Nielsen, Arbitron, Trendex, and others all reported to the networks, which, based upon the popularity of a program, knew how much to charge advertisers. Network television really exists for this primary purpose; entertainment is only secondary. And of course, should a show do really poorly and be lacking in advertising support, it goes down the tubes, so to speak—it's cancelled. This, of course, is an oversimplification, but that's basically how it works.

In compiling the list of the 166 top 10 hit shows included in this book, I used the rankings as given by the AC Nielsen company. Each television season runs from the fall to the following spring. All of the top 10 shows for each season from 1950 onward are covered here, right up through the 1991–92 season, which had the most current complete rating list available at publication time. If a show was ranked in the top 10 more than once—like "I Love Lucy" or "Gunsmoke" or "The Cosby Show"— it appears in this book in the year it *first* debuted in the top 10, even if it ranked lower that year than in subsequent years. If a series went on to a higher ranking in a later year, that "peak position" is shown at the beginning of the show's list of credits. A complete listing of all top 10 shows for the last 43 years is included for reference.

A lot has happened during those 42 years. I've got a bigger television now and I know that the people don't live in the back of the set. My tastes have changed, too—I still enjoy family shows like the old "Stu Erwin" series, but I'm more fickle and my favorites are likely to change annually. Right now they include "Murphy Brown," "Northern Exposure," "Empty Nest" (my dogs love Dreyfuss—they think he lives in the back of the set), and, of course, "Star Trek: The Next Generation," and not just because I've been lucky enough to have written for that show. Next year, who knows?

The future of television is changing so rapidly that current rating systems may become outmoded. In the early 1990s there were already plans for fiber optics to digitally carry hundreds, perhaps thousands, of channels laden with movies, shopping channels, sports, weather, and interactive TV, along with dozens upon dozens of other choices. As of this writing, the Big Four networks (Fox's FBC has definitely proved itself worthy of playing in the big leagues) only grab about 60 percent of the available television audience, leaving a huge 40 percent of the viewing public to turn their attention elsewhere.

One thing is certain. Television will continue to be an extension of our lives in the future as never before, with the promise of wondrous new "happy days" ahead of us.

SUSAN SACKETT
Studio City, California
April, 1993

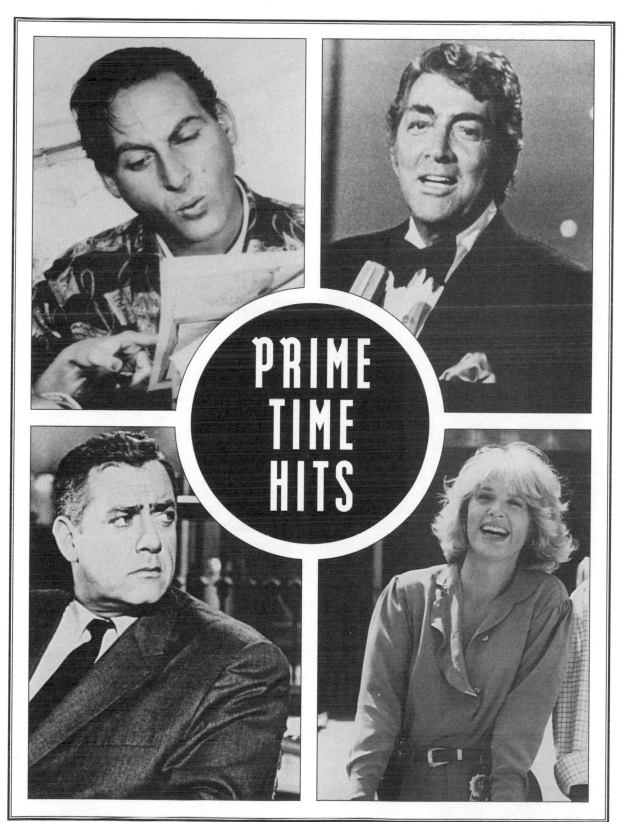

PRIME
TIME
HITS

"Say kids, what time is it?" While it may have been "Howdy Doody Time" for the members of that show's Peanut Gallery, it was the Golden Age of Television for the rest of the TV audience, or so it is widely believed.

Television first gained mass acceptance in the 1950s, and at that time it drew from previously established sources of entertainment for much of its programming. Former vaudevillians hastened to adjust their acts to accommodate the new medium with comedy/variety shows. Live theater came to home audiences in the form of new TV anthology series.

Much of television in the '50s was nothing more than an outgrowth of radio in the '40s. Even the best-loved, most popular series of the 1950s (and probably of all time), "I Love Lucy," was based on a radio show.

Another staple of radio, the quiz show, made the transition to television and created enough of a sensation to cause movie attendance to drop from 82 million in 1946 to only 46 million in 1955.

The quiz show scandals burst that bubble a few years later. The second half of the decade was dominated by westerns, at first recycled from old movies (like "Hopalong Cassidy"), but later featuring originals like "The Rifleman" and "Have Gun, Will Travel." By 1958, over 31 of the 60 weekly prime-time shows were saddling up each week, planting seven of these firmly in the top 10 for that year.

If, as someone once said, the test of a really great show is its ability to weather reruns, then perhaps the nostalgic '50s truly were television's Golden Age. "I Love Lucy," "The Ed Sullivan Show," "Alfred Hitchcock Presents," "Gunsmoke," and "You Bet Your Life" (the original Groucho Marx version) were all over the dial in the early 1990s, and a proliferation of videocassettes attested to their enduring popularity.

Return with us now to those thrilling days of yesteryear...

TEXACO STAR THEATER

There was never any question about whom or what the "star" in the title referred to. Although the show was initially called the "Texaco Star Theater," it soon became apparent that Milton Berle, a.k.a. Mr. Television, a.k.a. Uncle Miltie, was the real galactic core around which all other celestial bodies revolved. Within two years of his television debut, Berle had stolen more than just the jokes he claimed to have purloined for his routines—he had captured the hearts and fierce loyalty of America's early television viewers.

When "Texaco" premiered on Tuesday, June 8, 1948, the format was strictly vaudeville, a bill of dancers, jugglers, acrobats, guest stars, and sketches—in short, it was simply a video version of the already successful radio show that Berle had been doing for ABC on Wednesday nights. In the 1948–49 season, he did 39 radio shows for ABC and the same number of TV shows for NBC—78 live shows in one season. In 1949 Berle gave up his radio show entirely, and by the start of the new decade, Berle was the king of all he surveyed from his television throne.

His show's unprecedented popularity had some unanticipated side effects. The city of Detroit was baffled when the reservoir water levels dropped each Tuesday evening shortly after 9:00 P.M. An investigation revealed that Detroit's citizens were waiting until Berle was off the air to go to the bathroom; the simultaneous flushing of thousands of toilets created havoc with Detroit's water works. In addition, restaurants and bars across North America began to lose patrons—until they caught on and installed TVs for their customers to watch "Texaco Star Theater."

Berle is credited with being responsible for the staggering rise in television sales of the late '40s and early '50s: in 1948, 975,000 TV sets were manufactured; by 1950 the number of TV households had reached 3.8 million, the majority of which were tuned faithfully to Berle each week; and by 1951 he was seen in 6.8 million homes—a number equivalent to an audience of about 60 million today.

What was it about this man and his personality that made him such a television sensation?

Born Milton Berlinger on July 12, 1908, Berle began his career as a child comic (thanks to a pushy stage mama) and silent screen actor before taking to the stage, nightclubs, and radio. By the time NBC offered him "Texaco Star Theater," he was wise enough to demand and receive creative control. He belonged to several unions and on occasion even ran the cameras. "I was a perfectionist," he wrote in his autobiography. "[I] couldn't leave anything alone, couldn't let myself trust anyone completely to get something done exactly the way I wanted it. So I ran like a maniac all week, directing when we had a director, getting into the dance blocking when we had a dance director, setting shots for the camera men, giving readings to actors, demanding costume changes, light changes—hell, I got into everything."

One of the first things Milton Berle did was to surround himself with other talented people, from the weekly quartet of "Men from Texaco" clad in service station attire singing the show's intro ("Oh we're the men from Texaco, we work from Maine to Mexico...") to the vaudeville cigar-chomping old-time sidewalk pitchman Sid Stone ("Tell ya what I'm gonna do") to the nerdy Arnold Stang. But mostly people tuned in to see Milton do the same "shtick" week after week. "Good evening, ladies and *germs*!" he'd intone. Inevitably, someone in his audience would cackle uncontrollably. "Hey lady, don't lay an egg!" he'd implore. Then he'd duck-waddle all over the stage on his ankles, or take a pie in the face (or, in a running gag, a chalky powder puff whenever he uttered the word "makeup!"). And at least once during the show—in a characterization that became his trademark—he'd appear in drag. This was not an effeminate routine; Berle simply would appear in a dress and high heels, makeup, outlandish Carmen Miranda headdresses, and feather boas. The audiences always roared their approval.

By the 1950–51 season, the third for "Texaco Star Theater," Uncle Miltie's salary had jumped from $1,500 a week to $11,500 a week. But the star was dissatisfied with NBC because the network refused to film the series, adhering to their

CREDITS

PRODUCERS: Ed Cashman, Arthur Knorr, Edward Buzzell, Donald O'Connor, others. DIRECTORS: Ed Cashman, Gregg Garrison, Sid Smith, others. WRITERS: Milton Berle, Bobby Gordon, Danny Shapiro, Coleman Jaacoby, Arnie Rosen, Goodman Ace, others. HOSTS: Milton Berle, Jimmy Durante, Donald O'Connor.

EMMYS

Best Kinescope Show (1949), Most Outstanding Kinescope Personality–Milton Berle (1949).

Mr. Television himself—yes, that's Milton Berle in drag (center), flanked by French singer Jean Sablon (left) and actor Victor Moore and comedienne Gracie Fields.

policy of making only kinescopes.* Berle was aware that three-camera filming was becoming the way to go in those early days, pioneered by Lucille Ball and others, but the network refused to yield. Instead, they offered Berle an exclusive "lifetime" contract that would run for the next 30 years—until 1981—at $200,000 per year. He signed, reluctantly, but years later had it renegotiated to allow himself more freedom.

By the fall of 1951, Berle was beginning to feel the effects of three solid years of doing a live revue each week. He insisted on, and was granted, every fourth week off. Unfortunately, this was the beginning of the end for him as the King of Television. Ratings eventually declined, the show slipping from first place in 1950 to 20th by June of 1952.

"Texaco Star Theater" was punched up for the 1952–53 season, but the corsets and custard pies were gone. Despite the talents of comedy writer Goodman

Ace, the new format with a toned-down Berle was far less successful. "I played a character named Berle who was caught up weekly in the trials and tribulations of putting on a television show...The only trouble was that I was not the Milton Berle of the crazy costumes and all the zany shticks my audiences had come to expect. I was everybody's straight man," Berle wrote in his autobiography. And while the "Texaco Star Theater" continued until 1956 with such weekly guest hosts as Jimmy Durante, Donald O'Connor, and Mitzi Gaynor, Milton Berle himself later segued to "The Buick-Berle Show" in 1953 (see page 40).

---

* A kinescope is produced by placing a film camera in front of a television set and filming the live broadcast as it appears on that television, resulting in a rather poor-quality copy generally not suitable for future rebroadcasts, i.e., reruns. And no reruns equalled no residuals for the disgruntled Berle.

FIRESIDE THEATRE

NUMBER 2, 1950–51

One of the earliest successful anthology series, NBC's "Fireside Theatre" went on the air in 1948 and for the first couple of years presented two 15-minute dramas in its 30-minute time slot. By the fall of 1950, however, the show settled into what became its routine for the duration of the series—one 30-minute teleplay.

Under the guidance of television pioneer Frank Wisbar, "Fireside Theatre" became a testing ground for innovative drama. Wisbar, the show's director and producer for the first five years, was a Lithuanian-born newspaperman, playwright, and moviemaker who had worked with television for Germany in the late 1930s, installing the new viewing equipment in Hitler's airplanes. He later fled to Washington, where he served Uncle Sam during World War II, then migrated to Hollywood after the war. His stories ran the gamut from Chaucer's "Pardoner's Tale" and Bret Harte's "Miggles" to stories based on articles in the *Saturday Evening Post*.

At first he tried using motion picture stories. "Bang! They went off in our faces," he once said. Radio plays and some off-beat stories also fell flat. "The shows I thought were artful were just arty, and I got no response." He also tried "message" stories. "I used to love to attack, to be vitriolic," he continued. Among some of the more memorable shows:

■ "The Bunker" (written by Frank Wisbar), set during Hitler's last hours, and dubbed "a slick offering" by *Variety*, the program recreated what might have transpired in the Fuehrer's underground headquarters as the Russian forces stormed Berlin.
■ "Threshold" (written, produced, and directed by Frank Wisbar), the story of a professor who refuses to bow to totalitarian force.
■ "The Devil's Due," an adaptation of Washington Irving's story "The Devil and Tom Walker," the tale of a man who made a deal with the Devil in order to get rid of his wife.

■ "The Golden Ball" (written, produced, and directed by Frank Wisbar), the story of a paralytic who was miraculously cured.

Many of the stories had almost science fiction or fantasy premises that seemed to foreshadow television's years-in-the-future "Twilight Zone," for example:

■ "The Bed by the Window" (written, produced, and directed by Jack Bernhard), the story of an old folks' home where one man who had the bed by the window described the beauty of the outdoors to another who coveted this prized bed; the envious man caused the death of the man in it—only to discover when he was given this bed that it faced a solid wall.
■ "Anniversary" (written and directed by John Reinhardt), the story of a young wartime RAF fighter pilot who was killed the day before his first wedding anniversary, but was seen to return to keep his date with his wife the next day. Later that night the wife was killed in a bombing raid and never knew that her husband had been killed the day before.
■ "Germelshausen," based on an old German legend about a buried city that rose to the surface every 100 years.

From the beginning "Fireside Theatre" received critical acclaim, but what is especially noteworthy is that the *commercials* were also considered fair game for reviewers. In the early days of television, as with radio, networks didn't sell time to dozens of advertisers—the sponsors were large corporations who owned these shows outright and packaged the entire half-hour complete with their commercials. No doubt potential viewers were relieved to read the following, from an early review in *Variety*. "P & G [Proctor and Gamble] plugs, also on film, occupied the usual opening, middle and closing positions and did an adequate huckstering job on Crisco, Ivory and Duz."

CREDITS

EXECUTIVE PRODUCERS: Frank Wisbar, others. PRODUCERS: Frank Wisbar, John Reinhardt, Jack Bernhard, John Housman, others. DIRECTORS: Frank Wisbar, John Reinhardt, Jack Bernhard, William C. Menzies, others. WRITERS: various.

Because "Fireside Theatre" was done on film (with the exception of a few experimental live shows in the beginning), the sponsors were able to resell the programs into early syndication; by 1951 many were recycled and sold to local sponsors, popping up all over the dial under various titles such as "Royal Playhouse," "Blue Flame Theatre," "Your TV Theater," "Crest Theater," "Family Theater," and "Snowcrop Matinee Theatre" (Snowcrop was the name of an orange juice company).

In the fall of 1952, Frank Wisbar began appearing on camera to introduce each episode; he was followed for two seasons by actor Gene Raymond, and miscellaneous other talent introduced the show during the 1954–55 season.

Then in 1955, in the show's seventh year of production, Jane Wyman became permanent hostess. (Coincidentally she was president of the company that produced the series.) The title was immediately changed to "Jane Wyman Presents the Fireside Theatre," and she was set to star in 14 of the 34 half-hour episodes. The series was produced with taste and a high budget. The first season's shows featured such guest stars as Carolyn Jones, Charles Coburn, Fay Wray, Chuck Connors, and Jack Kelly. The following year the title was changed to simply "The Jane Wyman Theatre." Miss Wyman continued to host the show until 1958, when it began a healthy cycle of reruns.

Ratings of "Fireside Theatre" remained strong for several seasons, with the show in the top 10 through 1954. But by then audiences' tastes were shifting away from anthology drama and it dropped to 20th place, then 24th for the next year. Yet despite the lag in ratings, the quality of the programs never really dropped off; ABC even brought back some of the reruns in 1963 for a summer replacement series under the title "Jane Wyman Presents."

Jane Wyman, hostess of "Fireside Theatre."

PHILCO TELEVISION PLAYHOUSE

NUMBER 3, 1950–51

If the '50s were the Golden Age of Television, then "Philco Television Playhouse" was a solid 24-carat nugget. From the moment it hit the airwaves, "Philco" established a precedence that was seldom equalled.

This live dramatic anthology series was the brainchild of Fred Coe, one of television's most eminent pioneers. In 1948 Coe was a 29-year-old producer/director grounded in the classics courtesy of Yale Drama School. Being young and enthusiastic didn't hurt when he set his sights on the new medium of television. With Coe as producer and sometimes director of "Philco Television Playhouse," the television audience could look forward to quality drama each Sunday night at 9:00.

The series premiered on October 3, 1948, with "Dinner at Eight," by Edna Ferber and George S. Kaufman, pared down to the one-hour format by Sam Carter. " 'Philco Television Playhouse' is bigtime video thesping, unquestionably the most ambitious and successful attempt yet to capture full-bodied legit production for the tele-screen," enthused *Variety*.

During the first few seasons, however, all did not go smoothly for Coe and Co. Alarmed at the possibility that this upstart medium would siphon off ticket-buying movie audiences, the heads of Hollywood's major motion picture studios cried "foul." Since the programs were being done live in New York while simultaneously being recorded on kinescope for later broadcast on NBC's nine other affiliated stations, the movie moguls promptly dubbed these kinies "film." A 35-millimeter print was the same as a 16mm kinie in their (legal) opinion, and the threat of lawsuits from movie studios who owned the film rights to these plays (and were panicked over the new medium's competition) became a serious worry for Coe.

He sidestepped the issue for the first year by either optioning plays or using ones in the public domain.

"That first year we did a lot of shows that we *could* do," he said. " 'Cyrano' with Jose Ferrer, a few plays that were available because they hadn't been tied up by films...and a couple of Shakespearian dramas."

Later the format was changed to a sort of "book-of-the-week club," dramatizing a published novel each week. But it soon became apparent that boiling novels down to 60 minutes was a nearly impossible task for the writers. Coe began searching for writers who could not only adapt other people's writings, but had intriguing original ideas of their own. Such heavyweights as Paddy Chayefsky, Horton Foote, Gore Vidal, Delbert Mann, and Arthur Penn were all enlisted to supply material for the show.

In one year Chayefsky penned nine teleplays for Coe, including the much-lauded "Marty," a script finished weeks earlier than Chayefsky had intended, due to pressure from Coe. "Marty" aired on May 24, 1953, and starred Rod Steiger and Nancy Marchand. It was a modest drama about a young butcher whose mother was intent on his seeking a wife. No one, least of all Chayefsky, could have predicted what was to follow. In 1955 a film version was made, starring Ernest Borgnine and Betsy Blair. Produced by Harold Hecht, it won Oscars for Best Picture and Best Director (Delbert Mann). Borgnine took home the Best Actor award, and Chayefsky won an Academy Award for Best Screenplay.

Another success came with Horton Foote's "A Trip to Bountiful." In 1985 Foote's second cousin, Peter Masterson, directed a motion picture entitled "The Trip to Bountiful." The film starred Geraldine Page, who walked away with an Academy Award for her performance. Foote's screenplay based on the television drama won him a Oscar nomination for Best Screenplay Based on Another Medium.

The acting in "Television Playhouse" was also top-notch,

CREDITS

CREATOR/PRODUCER: Fred Coe.

DIRECTORS: Fred Coe, Delbert Mann, Arthur Penn, others.

WRITERS: Paddy Chayefsky, Horton Foote, Gore Vidal, Sumner Locke Elliot, others.

GUEST STARS: Steve McQueen, Joanne Woodward, Walter Matthau, E. G. Marshall, Eva Marie Saint, John Cassavetes, others.

Lee Grant and Eli Wallach in "Shadow of the Champ."

featuring old-timers and newcomers alike. Peggy Wood, Lillian Gish, Grace Kelly, Joanne Woodward, Leslie Nielsen, Maureen Stapleton, Sidney Poitier, E. G. Marshall, Eva Marie Saint, and John Cassavetes all appeared on the "Playhouse" over the course of its seven-year run.

Because of the nature of live television, there were, of course, some on-air disasters. On one show actress Kim Hunter was doing a flashback scene in which she and the leading man were killed in an automobile accident. When they completed the scene, someone in the control booth gave the order to release the two actors so they could get to their next scene. But the camera was still on them, and America watched as two "dead" people got up and walked away from the accident. Another time, the show was running too long and the director decided to cut a scene. The floor manager was ordered to tell the actors their scene would be eliminated and they would cut directly to a scene involving a nun. Somebody forgot that the mike from the booth to

the floor was "open," and Fred Coe's voice was heard over the airwaves shouting, "Get the nun on—get the nun on...*get the damn nun on!*"

In 1951 the show acquired a new sponsor and became known as the "Philco-Goodyear Television Playhouse," with each manufacturer alternating weeks of sponsorship. Although the quality was maintained, the ratings fell off due to the plethora of new and varied programming on television.

Fred Coe's name was so closely associated with the show that one reviewer called it the " 'Phil-Coe' Television Playhouse." But unfortunately for that show, at the end of 1954 NBC decided to move him to "Producers' Showcase," a series which featured dramatic specials such as "Peter Pan" and "The Petrified Forest." And in the following year, 1955, Philco ended its sponsorship and was replaced by Alcoa as alternating sponsor. Eventually Alcoa assumed sole sponsorship, and telecasts continued until the fall of 1957. But without Fred Coe, it really wasn't the same series.

YOUR SHOW OF SHOWS

NUMBER 4, 1950–51

Sid Caesar (right), with Imogene Coca.

Television's very first "cult" show was born on February 25, 1950. This remarkable variety show owed its huge success to the talents of two special people in front of the camera, in addition to the efforts of a behind-the-scenes support team that read like a veritable "who will be who" of the late 20th century's most creative minds.

Max Liebman was the producer responsible for bringing this 90-minute variety show to television. Liebman, who emigrated to America from his native Vienna in his youth, established himself as a producer of vaudeville shows for a summer resort in the Poconos in Pennsylvania. His biggest discovery there was Danny Kaye.

After moving on to Hollywood to produce films for Kaye, Leibman continued to scout talent and spotted Sid Caesar in a revue in Florida. Soon afterwards Liebman was introduced to an advertising executive named Sylvester "Pat" Weaver (younger readers are probably more familiar with his famous daughter's name—Sigourney), whose client, Admiral (a television manufacturing company), was looking for a vehicle to sponsor so it could promote its product. In 1949 Weaver hired Liebman to produce the "Admiral Broadway Review," starring Sid Caesar. A year later Weaver, now an NBC vice-president, had Liebman rework this show and presented it to television audiences as "Your Show of Shows."

The series was an instant hit, with its rapid pace of humorous sketches, song-and-dance routines, and the zany, freewheeling *live* antics of Caesar and company.

And what a company it was. "Your Show of Shows" was blessed with an unparalleled number of gifted stars and writers. Caesar himself was one of the truly great comics of the century. Born May 8, 1922, Sid was the son of Austrian-Polish Jewish immigrants. As a youngster in his native Yonkers, New York, he studied the saxophone, but his talents for acting and especially mimickry soon became apparent (he honed his skills at dialect imitation by listening to the speech patterns of the many foreign patrons of his father's restaurant). He later performed at the obligatory borscht belt hotels in the Catskill Mountains, which saw the likes of nearly every young stage hopeful before he or she moved on to the "big time."

In "Your Show of Shows" Caesar was off the wall, taking sketches beyond their written limits when it suited him. He participated in every writing session and pushed the writers, gaining a reputation for being explosive. "Sure, I used to try to start things," he said in *TV Guide*. "I did it on purpose to get them thinking, to get myself thinking. Once I start to spout material, I try to go at it from every angle, get things going that way. It's better if you argue about it a little. One idea leads to another."

Caesar was the centerpiece of "Your Show of Shows," but nearly equal credit must go to his partner, Imogene Coca. The chemistry between these two people was so perfect, many thought they were a married couple (they weren't). Coca had a background in stage and was mainly a song-and-dance woman. Often there would be an elaborate dance number written in which Coca would begin what appeared to be a legitimate routine, only to have it disintegrate into the physical comedy for which she was particularly gifted.

Other cast members of note were Howard Morris and Carl Reiner. Both went on to successful careers, particularly Reiner, who later created "The Dick Van Dyke Show."

Live TV constantly put Caesar to the test as the master of the ad-lib. One week very nearly turned to disaster for him when he found himself dressed in the wrong outfit. He was attired in a leopard loincloth and high-laced Roman sandals for what he thought was a circus sketch. Just before he was to go on, he spotted Carl Reiner and Howie Morris on stage in business suits. Producer Liebman had forgotten to tell Caesar about his switching the two sketches. When the commercial ended, Sid grabbed a sport coat and put it on over his leopard loincloth, still wearing the gold lame sandals. "Without hesitation, I ran out, as though nothing was wrong," he said. "There I stood, shirtless, a leopard-skin loincloth showing under a sport jacket, complete with Roman sandals. In short, your typical business executive. The audience roared. Carl, not knowing what to do, asked me why I was wearing the funny shoes. All I could manage was, 'Well, you know how sometimes you get a present and feel obligated to wear it at least once? And besides, it looked like rain this morning!'"

It must have been frustrating for the writing staff to have a loose cannon like Sid Caesar doing their material. But it certainly didn't hurt their careers. The writers were young and enthusiastic, and a baptism by Caesar helped launch many of the entertainment field's best writers. Woody Allen, Neil Simon, Mel Brooks, Larry Gelbart ("M*A*S*H"), and Bill Persky and Sam Denoff ("The Dick Van Dyke Show") were all staff writers sharpening their skills on "Your Show of Shows."

By 1954 the ratings had slipped, and "Show of Shows" was no longer in the top 25. The final show aired on June 5, 1954, 160 performances after the series began. The cast and crew parted company, off to pursue their separate careers. Sid Caesar starred in "Caesar's Hour," with Howard Morris and Carl Reiner continuing as second bananas and Nanette Fabray and later Janet Blair playing his wife. The program lasted three years. Meanwhile, Imogene Coca got a show of her own, but it survived only one season.

In 1973 Liebman took some of the series' best comedy sketches and released them theatrically. Check video stores for *Ten From 'Your Show of Shows.'*

CREDITS

CREATOR/PRODUCER: Max Liebman. DIRECTORS: Max Liebman, Nat Hiken ("You'll Never Get Rich"). WRITERS: Mel Brooks, Neil Simon, Woody Allen, Mel Tolkin, Lucille Kallen, Larry Gelbart, others. REGULARS: Sid Caesar, Imogene Coca, Carl Reiner, Howard Morris, Bill Hayes, Bambi Linn and Rod Alexander (dancers), others.

EMMYS

Best Variety Show (1951, 1952), Best Actor—Sid Caesar (1951), Best Actress—Imogene Coca (1951).

THE COLGATE COMEDY HOUR

NUMBER 5, 1950–51

Dean Martin (left) and Jerry Lewis.

During its five-year run, "The Colgate Comedy Hour" racked up more firsts for NBC than most networks see in five decades. It was the first commercial series to originate from Hollywood (September 30, 1951), it offered the first network colorcast (November 22, 1953), and it was the first TV series for a number of famous personalities, such as Eddie Cantor, Fred Allen, Abbott and Costello, Bob Hope, Donald O'Connor, Jimmy Durante, Gordon MacRae, and a young comedy team called Martin & Lewis.

Dean Martin and Jerry Lewis first joined forces in

1946 and became overnight sensations, appearing on stage, in numerous nightclubs, and on film, radio, and records; they also made regular appearances on Ed Sullivan's "The Toast of the Town" television series on CBS. NBC saw the duo as a possible answer to Sullivan and tapped them to alternate as hosts of the "Comedy Hour" (and they did eventually make a large dent in Sullivan's ratings).

Their initial trepidation was that they would use up all of their best material if they hosted the show every week. "I resisted television because I didn't want to be eaten alive by the very nature of the industry," said Lewis in a 1992 Disney Channel special, "The Golden Age of Comedy—The Kings of Comedy." "Before we would be through with a year's work in television, they would have eaten up everything we would have written in four years and then some." So the pair agreed to host every four to six weeks. Over five years they hosted the series 28 times; most people still think of Martin & Lewis when they think of "Colgate Comedy Hour."

Because the show was live, ad-libs abounded. The two broke character constantly and talked in asides to the audience, letting them "in" on things, using their talents and basic instincts to get laughs. And they were a perfectly mated pair. "It was as though twins were born, separated at birth, and found each other 25 years later," Jerry Lewis said. "While (Dean) was 10 years my senior, he knew when I was going to breathe. I knew when he was going to turn his head."

Much of their comedy was physical: Jerry playing a chorus of "Lady of Spain" on a set of bedsprings while mugging for the camera; or Dean shaving in a "mirror," only his reflection was Jerry (the old Harpo Marx routine); Jerry as a limp, rubber-bodied marionette. Jerry was always the underdog, and "an underdog is always sweet," Lewis said about his character. He took pratfalls, did impersonations, and almost always put away his partner, who, because he was laughing, often had difficulty continuing with the live sketch as scripted. There were rewrites right up until air time, usually because Dean and Jerry kept improvising new material.

The show had its share of running gags, too. At any time during a routine, Jerry, playing his man-child character in an adolescent's voice, would suddenly blurt out, "I like it, I like it!," and the audience would howl. There was a gag in which all kinds of things would come out of a suitcase—clothes, hot dogs, a midget, a rabbi. They did variations on this routine with picnic baskets producing an entire grocery store's worth of goodies, and a briefcase variation which provided enough books to open a library.

"The thing that Dean and I had was love for one another that we allowed an audience to see," Lewis stated. "The love was my hero worship for him. His love was me, the kid brother." But eventually the love came to an end. The team's last appearance on "The Colgate Comedy Hour" was on November 13, 1955. A year later they released their final film together (*Pardners*), then went their separate ways. Fans were heartbroken, predicting doom for both, but the talented performers proved they knew what they were doing. Jerry Lewis went on to star in many popular films, and

while he was a moderate success in his homeland, by the 1970s he was considered an icon in France. Lewis eventually had two TV shows of his own, "The Jerry Lewis Show" (ABC, September–December 1963) and another version by the same title, which ran on NBC from 1967 to 1969. For several subsequent decades he became best known for the annual Jerry Lewis Telethon, in which he raised millions of dollars for the Muscular Dystrophy Association.

Dean Martin's career also took off, and he became a famous singer and actor; in 1965 he had his own hit television series (see page 150).

In addition to the Martin & Lewis co-hosting of "The Colgate Comedy Hour," there was another famous partnership of co-hosts: Abbott and Costello. At the same time, the pair was also starring in their own syndicated 30-minute comedy show, which produced 52 episodes from 1951 to 1953. This team, too, had a falling out, culminating with Lou Costello's exiting the "Comedy Hour." The shock of their breakup reportedly put Bud Abbott in the hospital. They never settled their differences, and at the time of his death in 1959, Costello was suing Abbott for $222,000 in unpaid royalties.

Another memorable and beloved host was Eddie Cantor. The banjo-eyed comic had already had a lengthy and successful career when he became an alternating host of the "Comedy Hour" when it premiered in 1950. But his health was failing, and in September 1952 Cantor suffered a heart attack immediately following one of his performances. He was forced to curtail his appearances, but returned the following year and did one more season.

By 1953 the producers had begun to vary the format of the program and toss in the occasional musical comedy, such as "Roberta" (with Gordon MacRae) and "Anything Goes" (with Ethel Merman and Frank Sinatra). Still the show remained in the top 10 through the 1954 season. Then in 1955 the name of the series was changed to the "Colgate Variety Hour," but the format was far afield of the original intent. The last program aired on December 25, 1955.

The series had a brief resurrection in 1967, produced by George Schlatter. The new version had guest stars Edie Adams, Mel Brooks, Shelley Berman, Phyllis Diller, Nanette Fabray, Bob Newhart, Carl Reiner, Nipsey Russell, Allan Sherman, and Rowan and Martin–and this was all for the first show. The revival didn't last more than a season, but Schlatter came back the following year with two of the stars, Rowan and Martin, in a show of their own, called "Laugh-In" (see page 154).

CREDITS

PRODUCERS: various. DIRECTORS: Bud Yorkin, others. WRITERS: Norman Lear, others. HOSTS (ROTATING): Dean Martin, Jerry Lewis, Bud Abbott, Lou Costello, Eddie Cantor, Fred Allen, Spike Jones, Jackie Gleason, Donald O'Connor, Bob Hope, Ray Bolger.

EMMYS

Best Male Star of Regular Series–Donald O'Connor (1953).

GILLETTE CAVALCADE OF SPORTS

NUMBER 6, 1950–51

Boxing was the mainstay on the "Gillette Cavalcade of Sports."

"Cavalcade of *Sport*," singular, would have been a more appropriate title, since only one sport was ever a part of this "cavalcade"—boxing. Heavyweights, middleweights, lightweights, welter, feather, bantam, fly—the series ran the gamut. It also had a lot to do with sales of television sets in those early days, especially to bars where watching the Friday night fights took on ritualistic overtones.

One of the earliest successful commercial network television shows, "Cavalcade of Sports" premiered on Friday evening, September 29, 1944, and lasted 16 years. It originally was broadcast locally in New York, but by 1946 the "Cavalcade" went national on NBC and two years later picked up a permanent sponsor, Gillette. "Look sharp! Feel sharp! Be sharp!" the sponsor urged in harmonized song at the beginning of each fight, and millions of boxing fans sang along each week with the Gillette parrot, "To look sharp, every time you shave..." Then it was on to the main event, with ringside announcer Jimmy Powers describing the weekly bout. Initially, the fights originated from Madison Square Garden, but as television became more sophisticated the show went on the road to broadcast top bouts from around the country.

Everything on early television came under the scrutiny of reviewers, and boxing was no exception. Pity the poor TV critic who found himself having to find something to say about a boxing match as television fare. One such critic for *Variety* (Sept. 12, 1951) managed to say this: "Camera coverage, except for a minor lapse at the moment [Walter] Cartier scored his TKO in the eighth round, was good...In the eighth round, however, when Cartier unexpectedly carried the fight into a near corner of the ring, the cameras were just a trifle slow into moving over with the action." No instant replays in those days. The reviewer also went on to express his enjoyment of the animated commercials for razors and blades.

By 1954 the bouts were being broadcast in glorious (and gory) living color. On March 26, 1954, "Gillette Cavalcade of Sports" became the first sporting event to utilize NBC's new $600,000 mobile color unit.* *Variety*'s reviewer had trouble seeing the advantages of color in fights: "Tint adds virtually nothing to boxing, if this was any criterion; to put it positively, it subtracts, since b&w is sharper and, curiously, stronger in the flesh dimensions...When caller Jimmy Powers mentioned that Scholz' eye was blacking up, it was not observable, nor was there any confirmation by a viewer that any blood-letting was going on." How lamentable that the camera didn't zoom in for a close-up of some poor boxer's eye closing up, or of the drip of bright red blood as it poured from a nice, deep gash. Obviously, color television's days were doomed, at least from *Variety*'s perspective.

Actually, it was the weekly boxing matches that were doomed. "Gillette Cavalcade of Sports" was only one of many boxing programs presented by all the networks, with a fight available for viewing six nights a week during the sport's TV heyday. However, by 1960, the public's taste for gore (*Variety* notwithstanding) had diminished, and the "Gillette Cavalcade of Sports" presented its last broadcast in June 1960. And four years later, in 1964, the last regular network boxing series went off the air.

---

*The only previous use of the new mobile unit had been at the Tournament of Roses Parade in Pasadena on New Year's Day, 1954.

CREDITS

PRODUCERS: Jack Mills, Bill Garden, others. DIRECTORS: Jack Dillon, Jack Mills, others. ANNOUNCER: Jimmy Powers.

EMMYS

Best Sports Program (1954).

THE LONE RANGER

NUMBER 7, 1950–51

A fiery horse with the speed of light, a cloud of dust, and a hearty hi-yo Silver! The Lone Ranger! With his faithful Indian companion, Tonto, the daring and resourceful masked rider of the plains led the fight for law and order in the early West. Return with us now to those thrilling days of yesteryear. The Lone Ranger rides again!

—OPENING VOICEOVER

It has been said that the test of a true connoisseur of classical music is someone who can listen to the opening strains of Rossini's "William Tell Overture" and not think of the Lone Ranger. But for anyone born in the first half of the 20th century, and for many a fan of the Masked Man who caught the numerous reruns of the program during the latter half of the century, this will forever be an impossibility.

The television version of "The Lone Ranger" had roots running back nearly two decades. Created in 1933 by Fran Striker and George Trendle, the program ran for 16 years as a successful radio show before making its TV debut in 1949. Clad all in white (good guys always wore white in those days, with the exception of Hopalong Cassidy), the backstory concerned John Reid, the only one of six fictional Texas Rangers, including Reid's brother, who had survived a massacre. Reid was saved by an old childhood friend, a Mohawk Indian named Tonto (played by Jay Silverheels, who himself was part Mohawk). Reid vowed revenge against the gang that murdered the Rangers. Tonto suggested Reid disguise himself with a mask made from his murdered brother's black vest. After rounding up the gang members, Reid and his trusty horse Silver, along with Tonto aboard Scout, rode off into weekly sunsets in pursuit of justice.

The format for television was kept virtually intact after the transition from radio. Co-creator Trendle, who was also one of the show's producers, laid down the law when it came to the Lone Ranger's characterization. In a *Newsweek* interview at the time, he said that he "intended to give the youngsters a great deal of action and excitement without arousing unwholesome desires and

instincts...to teach patriotism, tolerance, fairness, and a sympathetic understanding of fellow men and their rights and privileges." A tall order, but to make sure his hero wouldn't corrupt the kids, Trendle had a list of dos and don'ts for his radio and TV writers:

"The Lone Ranger believes that our sacred American heritage provides that every individual has the right to worship God as he desires.

"The Lone Ranger never makes love on radio, television, in movies, or in cartoons.

"The Lone Ranger is a man who can fight great odds, yet take time to treat a bird with a broken wing.

"The Lone Ranger never smokes, never uses profanity, and never uses intoxicating beverages.

"The Lone Ranger at all times uses precise speech, without slang or dialect. His grammar must be pure. He *must* make proper use of 'who' and 'whom,' 'shall' and 'will,' 'I' and 'me,' etc.*

"The Lone Ranger never shoots to kill. When he has to use guns, he aims to maim as painlessly as possible.**

"Play down gambling and drinking scenes as far as possible, and keep the Lone Ranger out of saloons. When this cannot be avoided, try to make the saloon a cafe–and deal with waiters and food instead of bartenders and liquor."

While this might have made the Lone Ranger sound like a candidate for sainthood, it also helped keep the program high in the ratings, both on radio and during its TV run. And it wasn't just for the kids, either. Surveys showed that 52 percent, or slightly more than half the audience, was composed of adults.

Who was that masked man, anyway? Clayton Moore, of course, who starred as the Lone Ranger for all but two years of its network run (with John Hart hiding behind the mask from 1952 to 1954). It is said that he adopted a lifestyle similar to that of his character. In 1979, however, the Wrather Corporation, owners of the copyrighted character, was about to release a new film version of "The Lone Ranger," with a different actor

CREDITS

CREATORS: Fran Striker, George W. Trendle. PRODUCERS: Jack Chertok, George W. Trendle, Sherman Harris, Harry Pope. WRITERS: Fran Striker, George Seitz Jr, others. CAST: *John Reid/Lone Ranger* (Clayton Moore, John Hart), *Tonto* (Jay Silverheels).

starring. They decided that Moore could no longer appear in public as the Lone Ranger, and the court ordered him never to appear in his mask again. The heartbroken Moore, who for years made personal appearances at his own expense urging youngsters to lead clean, well-behaved lives, did the only thing he could—he obeyed the law. However, he also found some cool wraparound shades that looked like a mask, and continued to appear in public as the man who had once played the Lone Ranger. The public championed their hero, and finally, in 1985, the lawyers withdrew their complaint, and the Lone Ranger rode again.

Following the ABC network run from 1949 to 1957, the program went into syndication with over 200 half-hour episodes. In 1966, a cartoon version was introduced on CBS for Saturday mornings. Both programs are still occasionally seen in syndication today.

---

* Tonto, however, seemed exempt, opting to begin most sentences with "Me," as in "Me see man do bad thing."

** One of the reasons for his trademark silver bullets was that silver is a precious metal that served to remind him to shoot sparingly and always remember the high cost of human life.

ARTHUR GODFREY'S TALENT SCOUTS

NUMBER 8, 1950–51

Arthur Godfrey.

Among the mainstays of radio had been the "amateur hour" programs that presented new entertainment hopefuls for the first time, with the winners receiving prizes and, if they were lucky, their "big break." It was only a question of time as to when this genre would make it to the new medium of television.

Audiences didn't have to wait long. Early in 1948, Ted Mack brought the "Original Amateur Hour" to the short-lived DuMont television network. Not to be outdone, CBS soon readied its own version of a talent contest, hosted by a cocky, freckle-faced, "boy-next-door type"—with an attitude.

Arthur Godfrey had been on radio as a commentator since 1929. In 1945 he won the hearts of audiences when, as a special reporter at the funeral of President Franklin D. Roosevelt, he broke down and cried on the air. "Arthur Godfrey and His Friends" debuted the following year, and it wasn't long before he became the first personality to have *two* top-rated TV shows running simultaneously. He also had a morning talk show, one of the first ever on television, called "Arthur Godfrey Time." He even had a short-lived show in 1950 called "Arthur Godfrey and His Ukulele." "The Old Redhead," as Godfrey was called, was ubiquitous.

Godfrey hosted "Talent Scouts" for 10 years. The format had a twist: instead of just bringing out the nervous showbiz-hopeful, as was done by Ted Mack and others, Godfrey's format added scouts—highly respected professionals who supposedly had made "discoveries" of new, young talent. Actually, most of these aspiring singers/dancers/whatevers were semi-professional already. The format was further enhanced by having the studio audience vote for their favorite of the day via the "applause meter." Among Godfrey's and his scouts' many discoveries were Pat Boone, the McGuire Sisters, the Chordettes, and Carmel Quinn. All later became regulars on "Arthur Godfrey and His Friends" (see page 28).

Others who went on to fame and fortune after appearing on "Talent Scouts" included Connie Francis (who in 1950, at the age of 13, appeared singing and playing the accordion), Rosemary Clooney, Tony Bennett, Steve Lawrence, Al Martino, Leslie Uggams, the Diamonds, Roy Clark, and Patsy Cline. His staff missed a few, though. Both Elvis Presley and Buddy

Holly failed to score high marks at their auditions and never had a crack at the applause meter.

No applause meter was needed to confirm the success of "Arthur Godfrey's Talent Scouts." The show was an unqualified hit from the first broadcast, and by 1951 it climbed to the top of the Nielsen ratings. The *Variety* reviewer for the premiere episode (Dec. 8, 1948), was awestruck: "Whatever the indefinable quality that has skyrocketed Arthur Godfrey into the coast-to-coast bigtime...it's been captured in spades on video*...As far as Lipton, the sponsor, is concerned, this one's in the tea bag."

The real draw was essentially Godfrey himself. Whenever the host took a week off and brought in a "name" vacation replacement (like Steve Allen, Herb Shriner, and Joe E. Brown), the ratings inevitably dipped until Godfrey returned. He would mug, grimace, and gesture throughout the shows, leaving his radio audiences bewildered, but the TV audience couldn't get enough of his warmth, whether pitching new talent or his sponsor's products ("Lipton, the *brrrisssk* tea!").

Godfrey had a reputation for being hot-headed and unpredictable, and true to form, he managed to give the CBS folks a good scare one summer night in 1953. On August 17 of that year, he surprised the entire nation, as well as the people at CBS, when he decided to cancel the talent and the scouts at the last minute (remember, these shows were *live*). He made headlines when he replaced that evening's show with an impromptu version of his daytime show, "Arthur Godfrey's Friends," corralling the McGuire Sisters and Marion Marlowe, among others, at the last minute. It seems Godfrey got a peek at that evening's talent during the dress rehearsal, as was his custom, and decided that the performances were substandard. CBS's switchboard lit up with callers volunteering their own talent if Godfrey needed them to help out.

The show continued to be among the top 10, along with "His Friends," until 1954, when newer TV programs began to garner more attention. The last telecast was on July 21, 1958.

---

*A word to the VCR generation: In the early days, the term "video" was simply synonymous with television and had nothing to do with yet-to-be-invented videotape or cassettes.

CREDITS

TOP 10 PEAK: No. 1, 1951–52.
PRODUCERS: Irving Mansfield, Jack Carney, Art Carney, Larry Puck, others. DIRECTORS: Robert Stevens, David Rich, others. WRITERS: various. HOST: Arthur Godfrey. ANNOUNCER: Tony Marvin.

HOPALONG CASSIDY

NUMBER 9, 1950–51

Matinee idol William "Bill" Boyd was an unlikely role model for television's first generation of young children. The tall, handsome, silver-haired Boyd had been acting in films since 1919, but was "discovered" by Cecil B. DeMille in 1926. It was DeMille who gave Boyd leading roles in his extravaganzas *The Volga Boatman* (1926) and *King of Kings* (1927). But Boyd's career floundered in the early 1930s. Then in 1934 producer Harry Sherman bought the screen rights to six of Clarence E. Mulford's books about a cattleman named Hopalong Cassidy. He offered Boyd, who by now was playing heavies, the role of the lead villain. Boyd, however, managed to convince Sherman not to use his first choices of James Gleason or David Niven in the role of "Hoppy," and insisted on playing the part himself.

Boyd's life at this time wasn't exactly exemplary; the actor had a reputation for fast living and wild spending. Before Sherman granted him the plum role, he made Bill Boyd swear off his heavy boozing and womanizing. Boyd agreed, and incorporated the changes in his own life into the Hoppy characterization. As originally conceived by Mulford, Hopalong Cassidy was an illiterate, "Tobacco-chewin', hard-drinking', able-swearin' son of the Old West who got his nickname because of a limp." Bill Boyd changed all of that, transforming his character into a straight-shooting, upright knight of the range who'd sooner kiss his white horse Topper than smooch with the ladies. By the second film, even the limp was gone, the explanation being that the "wound" had healed.

The first movie, *Hop-a-long Cassidy*, was released in 1935, and over the next 13 years a total of 66 motion pictures based on the cowboy's exploits were made. At first Boyd was uneasy around horses and had to have a stunt double, but he grew to love playing Hopalong once he learned to ride. "It's like a vacation," he once said. "I ride my horse 'Topper,' chase rustlers and outlaws, shoot my six-shooters, and do the things that every kid—and man, too—in America would want to do."

In 1948 Boyd set his sights on the next logical step for Hoppy—television. Always a gambling man, he hocked everything to purchase the TV rights to the films and his character. In that same year, he sold the first package of "Hopalong Cassidy" television episodes–edited-down versions of his films—to New York's local station WNBT. They were an overnight success; a year later the series aired nationwide, and by 1950 his show was ranked in the top 10.

For TV broadcast, his movies were chopped down to a length of one hour (and later in syndication they were cut even further, into 30-minute episodes). Bearing in mind that television screens were really tiny in those days (average: 10 inches), it was easy to find scenes to cut. The wide, sweeping chase scenes were almost entirely eliminated, with most of the action confined to scenes that could be viewed without eyestrain. Yet not too much emphasis was put on closeup shots either, since the cowpokes still had to be seen on horseback.

In the first year, a narration by Boyd was added, along with an occasional new scene in case the viewers recognized these re-edited films. When the movie supply ran out and the audience clamored for more, an additional 50 new episodes were shot. A new sidekick was added, too. Edgar Buchanan played Hoppy's buddy Red Connors. (Buchanan later co-starred in his own series in the 1960s as Uncle Joe on "Petticoat Junction"—see page 122.)

In January 1950, at the height of his popularity, Hopalong made two debuts—on the radio and in a comic strip. The Sunday afternoon broadcast over the Mutual radio network was heard on a total of 496 stations by an audience estimated at 25 million. And the comic strip appeared in 50 newspapers around the country. Hoppy also

---

CREDITS

CREATOR: Harry "Pop" Sherman. BASED ON: The series of novels by Clarence E. Mulford. PRODUCERS: William Boyd, Toby Anguist. DIRECTORS: various. WRITERS: various. CAST: *Hopalong Cassidy* (William Boyd), *Red Connors* (Edgar Buchanan). SIDEKICKS (FROM FILMS): Jimmy Ellison, George "Gabby" Hayes.

reached the public via comic books, records, and 50 different novelties.

Children worshiped Hoppy, and the character became TV's first merchandising phenomenon. Fortunately, Bill Boyd had the foresight to retain the merchandising rights. While kids gobbled up items licensed with the Hopalong Cassidy name (like bubblegum cards, juvenile cowboy outfits, bedsheets, and wallpaper), Boyd prospered. The show and merchandising tie-ins made him a multimillionaire. He eventually sold out his stock of films, and the rights, for a reported $70 million, and retired comfortably to Dana Point, Calfornia, where he lived with his fourth wife, actress Grace Bradley. He died in 1972 at the age of 74.

Bill Boyd's last romp atop Topper (for the TV cameras, at least) came on December 23, 1951. After that, the show appeared in syndication and enjoyed further popularity until the mid-'50s and the advent of the "adult" western.

William Boyd.

MAMA

NUMBER 10, 1950–51

Mama and Papa: Peggy Wood and Judson Laire.

I remember...my big brother Nels, my little sister Dagmar, and of course Papa. But most of all, I remember Mama.

—Opening Voiceover

By the time "Mama" came to television in 1949, millions of Americans were already familiar with the Norwegian family Hansen from the autobiographical book *Mama's Bank Account* by Kathryn Forbes, which became the basis for the successful stage play, musical, and motion picture called *I Remember Mama*. It is not difficult to understand the saga's popularity. Just as today's audience seems to have romanticized the "golden," family-oriented decade of the '50s, the audience of the mid-20th century waxed nostalgic over this dramedy* that harkened back to a simpler era still—the turn of the century.

The first successful television situation comedy/drama had a simple format. What it amounted to basically was "Mother Knows Best" (before "Father" hit the airwaves), but in a family setting where love and mutual respect were at the core. Yes, Mama and Papa were immigrants to the New (and often bewildering) World, and ya, by Yimminy, they spoke with accents, but their kids—100 percent American born—never made fun of their parents and never thought that they knew better than their elders.

"Mama" was not the first ethnic comedy to reach television. An earlier, very similar program called "The Goldbergs," featuring a humanly warm, immigrant *Jewish* family, had flourished on the radio for 20 years before producer Gertrude Berg brought it to TV only six months before "Mama." The comparisons were inevitable. The show was dubbed " 'The Goldbergs' with a Norwegian accent" by some. Even CBS executives themselves were known to refer to "Mama" as "The Scandanavian Goldbergs."

Both shows featured a strong female lead character, central to the story. Both also had women producing the program—Gertrude Berg for "The Goldbergs," and Carol Irwin for "Mama"—practically unheard of in those non-liberated early days of television. And probably not coincidentally, both shows had the same sponsor—General Foods. What the "Goldbergs" was doing for Sanka, "Mama" was now duplicating for General Foods' "good to the last drop" Maxwell House. In fact, the commercials were so well integrated into the scripts that audiences didn't seem to mind the pitches, which came at the beginning of the 30-minute program and at show's end, in Mama's kitchen where the coffee pot was always warm and bubbling and ready for the whole ensemble to gather 'round.

But it wasn't the coffee klatches that kept people tuning in week after week for eight years. The success of "Mama" was due in large measure to the broad appeal of sympathetic, well-cast characters brought home by the excellent writing, directing, and acting.

Starring in the title role was Peggy Wood, already a veteran of 40 years on the stage by the time she was cast as the grandmotherly, down-to-earth, good-humored Mama. It would have been hard to picture anybody else in the role (although Irene Dunne did a memorable turn in the film version).

Each supporting cast member seemed well-suited to his or her part. Particularly notable was Dick Van Patten, who at age 20 was cast as the 17-year-old son, Lars, and who for several years had the producers and sponsors on edge while they worried constantly over his draft status (the Korean War was raging, but Van Patten was not called.) Years later Van Patten would make his mark on television as the middle-aged father in "Eight Is Enough."

Three child actresses played the part of the irrepressible youngest daughter, Dagmar. Initially, the part went to Iris Mann, but she was soon replaced by Robin Morgan, who continued until the last year when Toni Campbell took over. In a quote in *The Great TV Sitcom Book*, Robin recalled the difficulties of doing a live show each week: "When one of my wobbly baby teeth fell out in the middle of a show, I worked its loss into the plot. When an adult colleague's eyes glazed over with dialogue amnesia (no TelePrompTers for us), one had to rescue the victim and save the continuity." She also recalled seeing the first cow-milking of her life, 15 floors above Manhattan (where the show originated) when nature's urges interrupted a dress rehearsal for the annual Christmas show, "The Night the Animals Talked."

It was amazing that the show lasted as long as it did. Peggy Wood once recalled, "Nobody at CBS ever really expected the show to be a success. One of the network bosses said at the beginning, 'I give it a fast eight weeks.' We outlasted *him* by a good seven years." But in 1956, CBS announced it was cancelling the program, prompting a flood of letters, phone calls, and protests. People felt as if the door had been closed on some old family friends, and the outcry was enough to motivate CBS to bring the show back in December, this time on film on Sunday afternoons. The revised program ran only three more months, with the final episode airing in March 1957.

---

*Drama-comedy; "sitcom" somehow seems too frivolous for "Mama."

CREDITS

Producer: Carol Irwin. Directors: Ralph Nelson, Don Richardson. Writers: Frank Gabrielson, others. Cast: *Mama*—Marta Hansen (Peggy Wood), *Papa*—Lars Hansen (Judson Laire), *Nels* (Dick Van Patten), *Katrin* (Rosemary Rice), *Dagmar* (Iris Mann, Robin Morgan, Toni Campbell), *Aunt Jenny* (Ruth Gates).

I LOVE LUCY

NUMBER 3, 1951–52

"Lu-u-u-cy! You have some 'splaining to do!" Lucille Ball and Desi Arnaz.

She was known by the title "Queen of the Bs" when, sometime in the 1940s, the former model and ingenue's career began to flounder and she found herself lacking for juicy movie roles.

Early in that decade Lucille Ball had married a Cuban bandleader named Desiderio Alberto Arnaz y de Archa III, better known to the world as Desi Arnaz. By the end of the 1940s, Lucille Ball and Desi Arnaz were struggling to keep their marriage afloat in a stormy sea. Then the ever-resourceful Lucille had an idea. In an effort to strengthen her marriage, she would bring her successful radio show, "My Favorite Husband," to television. And she would replace her radio co-star, Richard Denning, with real-life husband Desi.

Not on my network, was the reply of CBS chieftain William Paley. Nobody, he thought, would believe a typical American housewife in a domestic-comedy series married to a hot-blooded Latin bandleader. Undaunted, Lucille and Desi put together a stage act and toured the United States in the summer of 1950. When rave notices followed, Lucy stormed into Paley's office. "The public believes we can be husband and wife," she insisted. Paley relented and allowed them to do their pilot film, and the rest, as everyone who owns a television set knows, is history.

"I Love Lucy" was without a doubt the most successful television show of all time. Over 40 years after its 1951 debut it was still on the air, and it was said that at any given moment, someone somewhere in our "global village" had a TV set tuned to "I Love Lucy" reruns.

The premise of the show was simple: Lucy Ricardo, a stage-struck housewife, lived in a New York apartment with her bandleader husband, Ricky Ricardo. For balance, Lucy was given a next-door neighbor/best friend, Ethel Mertz (Vivian Vance), who was married to Fred (William Frawley). The Mertzes were the Ricardos' landlords, but more importantly, the couple acted as foils for Lucy's foibles and antics.

And, of course, it was Lucy's clownings, muggings, and pratfalls that kept this "situation-slapstick" (as *Newsweek* once called it) at the summit of the ratings for six years. Naturally, the show had a script, written each week by the same team of three writers—Jess Oppenheimer, Bob Carroll, and Madelyn Pugh—who had done Lucille's radio series earlier. But as Lucille herself once said, "We never see them. We never discuss anything with them...After two readings we get on our feet and throw the scripts away."

And thanks to Lucy's ad-libbing skills, there were scores of memorable moments in the 179 episodes. Whether it was getting hit with pies and seltzer, cramming her face and hat with chocolate candy, trampling a vat of grapes, downing bottles of "Vitameatavegamin" ("Do you poop out at parties? The answer to all your problems is in this bittle lottle!"), or stealing John Wayne's footprints from in front of Grauman's Chinese Theater, there was no scene that Lucille Ball did not make uniquely her own. Take, for example, the scene where she met William Holden for the first time in a 1955 episode. "I was disguised in a putty nose so [he] wouldn't recognize me. I lit a cigarette, and the end of my nose caught fire, so I put it out in a cup of coffee," said Lucy. "The audience was hysterical —but not nearly as hysterical as I was: setting fire to my nose was an accident!"

The most memorable moment of the series has long been acknowledged as the arrival of Lucy's baby. In the most widely heralded birth in television history, Lucille Ball's timing was, as always, impeccable.

In 1952 Lucille was pregnant with the couple's second child, and to cope with her ever-expanding waistline, it was decided to incorporate her condition into the show's storyline. Lucy was now "expecting" (TV censors in those days considered the word "pregnant" a big no-no). She was to have her real baby by caesarean section on January 19, 1953—a Monday night, an "I Love Lucy" night. With that in mind, the show was written to have Lucy's TV baby arrive on that evening's episode. Since the series was filmed several weeks in advance, there was no problem. On the big night, 54 million Americans tuned in to learn that Lucy Ricardo had a boy. And that night Lucille Ball Arnaz appropriately enough delievered a baby boy too, Desiderio Alberto Arnaz IV. In April 1953 Lucy graced the cover of the first edition of a new publication, *TV Guide*, while her baby became an important character on the show,

played at first by twins, and later by Richard Keith as "Little Ricky." (The first and only time the Arnaz' real son appeared on the show was the last "I Love Lucy" episode, in 1957.)

From the beginning both Lucille Ball and Desi Arnaz realized the potential of being able to rerun their program. The old kinescopes, with their fuzzy images and poor sound quality, were out of the question. So Desilu, the production company which they had set up, devised another plan. In what was to set the pattern for nearly all future sitcoms, they recorded "I Love Lucy" on three film cameras. To do this, they converted an old film studio into a theater with bleachers for a live audience. Then, as the show was performed, it was simultaneously recorded on film by all three cameras. Later it could be edited using some footage from each of the three cameras (close-ups, medium shots, wide-angle shots). The format is still used today, the only difference being the more frequent utilization of tape, rather than film.

"I Love Lucy" remained firmly atop the Niesen ratings charts until it went off the air in 1957. By then, it was becoming difficult to maintain the pace, plus the "Love" part of the title was by now meaningless. The couple finally split, and they were officially divorced on May 4, 1960. Meanwhile, their production company, Desilu, had expanded considerably. The company was responsible for producing such programs as "Mission: Impossible," "Star Trek," and "The Untouchables." In 1962 Lucille, now married to production executive Gary Morton, bought out Desi's interests in the company for $3 million. In 1967 she sold off Desilu's assets, including the old RKO lot where she once was the B-movie queen, for nearly six times that amount in Gulf and Western stock, and the lot became part of an expanded Paramount Pictures.

After 1957 there were no more "I Love Lucy" episodes, but there were several "Lucille Ball–Desi Arnaz Shows," hour-long specials about the travels and travails of the Ricardos and Mertzes.

Lucille Ball continued to work in television over the next several decades. She returned in "The Lucy Show" (1962–68—see page 116), "Here's Lucy" (1968–74—see page 160), and finally the short-lived "Life with Lucy" (1986). She died on April 26, 1989, the last surviving member of the original "I Love Lucy" gang of four.

CREDITS

TOP 10 PEAK: No. 1, 1952–53.
CREATORS: Lucille Ball, Desi Arnaz, Jess Oppenheimer, Bob Carroll, Madelyn Pugh. PRODUCERS: Jess Oppenheimer, Lucille Ball, Desi Arnaz. DIRECTORS: Marc Daniels, William Asher, others. WRITERS: Jess Openheimer, Bob Carroll, Madelyn Pugh. CAST: *Lucy MacGillicuddy Ricardo* (Lucille Ball), *Ricky Ricardo* (Desi Arnaz), *Ethel Mertz* (Vivian Vance), *Fred Mertz* (William Frawley), *Little Ricky Ricardo* (Richard Keith/Keith Thibodeaux).

EMMYS

Best Situation Comedy (1952, 1953), Best Comedienne—Lucille Ball (1952), Best Series Supporting Actress—Vivian Vance (1953), Best Actress, Continuing Performance—Lucille Ball (1955).

THE RED SKELTON SHOW

NUMBER 4, 1951–52

For 20 years Red Skelton was the clown prince of television. Although some might call him a comedian or comic, Skelton himself would be the first to agree that his true stage persona was indeed that of a clown. It should come as no surprise, then, to learn that Skelton was simply carrying on the family tradition. His father Joe was a circus clown and roustabout in the glorious tradition of early 20th-century circuses. The real surprise, however, is that Richard "Red" Skelton (the nickname, obviously, was for the colorful thatch atop his head) never met his father. Joe Skelton was an alcoholic who died just three months before Red's birth.

As a child, Red idolized the father he never knew and sought to emulate him. But he soon realized that life under the big top was not his calling, and he made his career move to the vaudeville stage, film (he appeared in 36 movies, including *Having Wonderful Time* with Lucille Ball), and later radio.

By 1951 he had been clowning around on radio for 10 years when NBC offered him his own television show. On radio he had developed a whole repertoire of characters that were just perfect for this visual medium—in fact, it's hard to imagine how radio audiences could have appreciated this man with the rubber legs and elastic face. The move to TV was a wise one; "The Red Skelton Show" (later "The Red Skelton Hour") became a television fixture for the next 20 years, one of the most successful variety shows in TV history.

With Red Skelton, NBC (and two years later, CBS) got a whole gallery of memorable characters while only having to pay one performer. A favorite among Red's creations was the half-bum, half-clown "Freddie the Freeloader." The character was an audience pleaser, as were such others as Clem Kadiddlehopper, Sheriff Deadeye, San Fernando Red, Cauliflower McPugg, George Appleby, the Mean Widdle Kid—the seemingly endless list even included two seagulls, Gertrude and Heathcliffe. Frequently the show ended with Skelton doing a Freddie the Freeloader mime number called "The Silent Spot," utilizing the medium of television, and Skelton's special talents, to their fullest visual potential.

In addition to Skelton's clowning antics, his shows included name guest stars, dance acts, and musical numbers, packing a lot of entertainment into the one-hour format. Yet ironically, while "The Red Skelton Show" was in the top 10 for so many years, it always seemed to come under harsh criticism from reviewers. For the premiere show, *Variety* noted that "He's a terrif (sic) bet for TV but that he needs more production and imagination for his show. Comedian played almost the entire 30 minutes before a blank curtain, scoring with his mugging, slapstick and some okay material based on the many zany characters he's created in radio...it's doubtful that even Skelton can get away with that for a 39-week season." Well, scenery was added and he did get away with it, in fact, for 20 seasons. The following year *Variety* decided to take on Skelton's personae: "While these characters stood Skelton in good stead for years in radio, TV's intimacy makes them no longer welcome." And even the

CREDITS

TOP 10 PEAK: No. 2, 1966–67.
PRODUCERS: Red Skelton, Cecil Barker, others. DIRECTORS: Seymour Burns, others. WRITERS: Red Skelton, Will Fowler, Sherwood Schwartz, Jesse Goldstein, Dave O'Brien, others. CAST: The Skylarks, The David Rose Orchestra, The Alan Copeland Singers, The Tom Hansen Dancers. GUEST STARS: Ed Sullivan, Rocky Marciano, Marie Wilson, Don Drysdale, Liberace, Harpo Marx, Mahalia Jackson, Shirley Temple, The Beach Boys, Audrey Meadows, Bobby Darin, Eve Arden, Robert Stack, Gig Young, Peter Graves, Jerry Lewis.

EMMYS

Best Comedy Show (1951), Best Comedian—Red Skelton (1951), Outstanding Writing Achievement in Comedy—Sherwood Schwartz, Dave O'Brien, Al Schwartz, Martin Ragaway, Red Skelton (1960). In 1986 Red Skelton received the ninth annual ATAS Governor's Award.

switch from live to film was panned: "The way the switch to film knocked off Skelton's spontaneity—which actually is one of the comic's chief claims to fame—left little for home viewers even to chuckle about." Year after year the critics kept after poor Red: "Red Skelton isn't going to make it in his new time-new day-new network without an uphill fight." "His Freddie the Free Loader (sic) was strictly an unfortunate fellow *sans* the deep sympathy accent that would warm viewers to his series of plights." "Skelton has in recent outings developed an irritating habit of breaking up at his own jokes, often before he has finished them, and of going out of character in his skits." Etc., etc.

Meanwhile, Skelton was undeterred by all this; his show was always in the top 25, frequently in the top 10, reaching as high as the number two spot in the Nielsens for a couple of years. He switched networks after the first two seasons, from NBC to CBS, and stayed with "The Big Eye" until 1970, when he did a brief and final show back at NBC. The time periods were often switched, and the show's length varied from 30 to 60 minutes. But somehow, even after all the shuffling around, Red Skelton's loyal audience always managed to find him.

Unfortunately, it was the same audience that had found him originally and had stuck with him for many of the 20 years of his show. While the ratings were sensational, the demographics were not. Skelton had refused to contemporize his show, never allowing hard rock acts or young starlets to appear. Thus NBC, anxious to attract a younger audience of twentysomethings (Skelton's average viewer age was 35), finally cancelled the show in 1971.

Red Skelton was in retirement during the early 1990s, but continued to prove his talents by painting. His canvases of clowns, many of which bear a striking resemblance to a certain red head, have become collectors' items selling worldwide for considerable sums.

Red Skelton (left), with Tennessee Ernie Ford.

ARTHUR GODFREY AND HIS FRIENDS

NUMBER 6, 1951–52

Arthur Godfrey.

It could have been called "The Year of the Redheads." Three of television's top 10 shows featured strong, red-headed personalities as their stars—Lucille Ball ("I Love Lucy"), Red Skelton ("The Red Skelton Show"), and "Arthur Godfrey and His Friends," starring none other than the man who in fact called himself "The Old Redhead." And of all these people, Arthur Godfrey seemed to most exemplify the fiery personality so often thought to typify carrot-tops.

"Arthur Godfrey and His Friends" went on the air in 1949, shortly after his success with "Arthur Godfrey's Talent Scouts" (see page 18). By 1951 both were in the top 10 ("Talent Scouts," in fact, was at number one), and both stayed comfortably ensconced in the Nielsen top 10 for many years.

Godfrey started with a circle of regulars on his broadcast. But over the course of the next 10 years, many in this assortment of singers, ukulele players, and what have you, would become ex-"Friends" at the whim of Godfrey.

Among his "Friends" were singers Marion Marlowe, the McGuire Sisters, lei-clad Hawaiian singer/uke strummer Haleloke (pronounced Ha-lee-**low**-kee), and Julius LaRosa. (Godfrey himself fancied the ukulele and often strummed a tune while offering his his trademark greeting, "Howa'ya, Howa'ya, Howa'ya!")

But his relaxed style belied a temper just below the surface. On October 19, 1953, on his live show (some estimated he once had a combined audience of 82 million for his two CBS shows), Godfrey shocked his viewers with his introduction of singer-regular Julius LaRosa. "You're doing pretty good, aren't you? Getting big money in nightclubs, and so forth. This show must be a pain in the neck to you." A baffled LaRosa sang his song, then stood hangmouthed as Godfrey announced in front of millions: "Thank you, Julie. And that, folks, was Julie's swan song." Godfrey told the press he decided on making the dismissal public because "I hired him on the air, I educated him on the air, and so I fired him on it."

Yet despite the reputation Godfrey was gaining as

fire-happy, his loyal audiences hung on, even as a running feud with the press ensued. Godfrey made another faux pas when he buzzed a New Jersey airport in his DC-3 and had his pilot's license suspended for six months. The press had a field day.

The firings continued. The Chordettes were suddenly let go in 1953, and orchestra leader Archie Bleyer was released in 1954. He soon married one of the Chordettes, founded the Cadence record label, and pushed their recording of "Mr. Sandman" to the top of the charts. Bleyer later discovered Andy Williams and the Everly Brothers, so in a sense it was fortuitous for Archie Bleyer that Godfrey let him go.

By April of 1955 there were more firings–this time the wholesale dismissal of Marion Marlowe, Haleloke, the Mariners, and three writers. Following the latest purge, Marlowe and Haleloke both enjoyed a flurry of engagement dates and adulation by a sympathetic public, but eventually they faded into obscurity.

There were some regulars who managed to hold onto their jobs throughout the Godfrey purges. The McGuire sisters, who were "discovered" on "Arthur Godfrey's Talent Scouts," scored top 10 hits with "Sincerely" and "Sugartime" in the mid-1950s and stayed with Godfrey until 1957. Other Godfrey discoveries included singer/future Miss America Anita Bryant, singer Pat Boone, and Japanese singer Miyoshi Umeki. Only Tony Marvin went the whole nine yards, or nine and a half years.

One of Godfrey's sponsors had been Chesterfield cigarettes, and like the good host that he was, he enthusiastically touted his sponsor's product on the air. That is, until he got cancer and had a lung removed in 1959. He fought the illness, gained back his health, and did one season as a co-host on "Candid Camera" (1960–61), thereafter making only rare appearances on television. His radio show continued until 1972, and he did a guest appearance on TV's "The Love Boat" as late as 1979. During his last years he became an advocate of environmental issues. He succumbed to cancer in 1983.

CREDITS

TOP 10 PEAK: No. 3, 1952–53.
PRODUCERS: Jack Carney, others.
DIRECTORS: Robert Bleyer, others.
WRITERS: various. REGULARS: Janette Davis, Archie Bleyer's Orchestra, The Mariners, The Chordettes, Haleloke, Frank Parker, Marion Marlowe, Julius LaRosa, Lu Ann Simms, The McGuire Sisters, Carmel Quinn, Pat Boone.
ANNOUNCER: Tony Martin.

THE JACK BENNY SHOW

NUMBER 9, 1951–52

Jack Benny and Don Wilson.

"Well!"

No other comedian could put away an audience so easily by uttering just one word. Jack Benny did it for 16 years on the radio, and when he set his sights on television, he did the same for TV audiences.

Born Benjamin "Benny" Kubelsky on St. Valentine's Day, 1894, he originally studied to be a concert violinist, then discovered his true calling of comedy and turned to the vaudeville circuit. He eventually acquired his own radio show in 1932, where he developed his repertory cast, most of whom continued with him when he made the transition to television.

On radio and later TV, Jack Benny played the same character—a self-deprecating skinflint. He mastered

the art of comic timing and made deadpan silences his trademark. The longest laugh in the history of radio came during this now-famous routine:

> BURGLAR
> Your money or your life!

No response from Jack. After a long pause, during which the audience began to giggle:

> BURGLAR
> Well?
>
> JACK
> I'm thinking it over!

The audience went crazy, the laughter lasting several minutes. The gag was later repeated on television, where it was also a hit.

The miserly image of Jack was, of course, a fiction, merely part of his persona. "The best humor I can possibly get is out of a stingy [character]," Jack once said. "You can go as wild as you want. The audience has a point of reference; everybody knows somebody who's real tight." In real life, however, Jack was noted for his exceptional philanthropy, due in part to the fact that he had to overcompensate to play down his reputation.

Jack was one of the few comedians who could regale an audience with the use of just three fingers aside his cheek. He didn't tell jokes; he *was* the joke. Asked why the use of three fingers, Jack replied, "Because three fingers are funnier than four."

The format of "The Jack Benny Show" changed little throughout the years. The thinly disguised variety show revolved around a comedian named Jack Benny who had a weekly show to produce, and along the way there were always problems involving his "cast members," who happened to be the same as the real cast. (George Burns, Jack's best friend, used a similar format for "The George Burns and Gracie Allen Show.")

The Jack Benny Show cast consisted of his wife, Mary Livingstone, who always played Jack's *girlfriend*, since he felt he could get more laughs out of situations that way; Dennis Day, the Irish tenor who somehow managed to work his singing into the show's comedy sketch; Don Wilson, Jack's corpulent announcer; and Eddie Anderson as Rochester, Jack's ever-patient valet/butler. Anderson was one of the first black performers to hold a steady job in the early days of television, and the writers often gave him the punchline at the expense of Benny:

ROCHESTER
Boss, you'd better buy another tube of toothpaste. The last one's run out.

JACK
What are you talking about? There must be another squeeze in it.

ROCHESTER
Look, I didn't mind when you had me squeeze it with a nutcracker day before yesterday.

I didn't mind when you sent me down to Union Station yesterday and had me put it in front of the train. But this is it. I refuse. I won't do it.

JACK
Rochester!

ROCHESTER
All right, all right! But that's the last time I'm asking Don Wilson to sit on it.

Another regular was the late Mel Blanc, most noted for being the voice of Warner Bros. cartoon characters Bugs Bunny, Daffy Duck, and Elmer Fudd. Blanc played several characters on the show, including a sleepy Mexican* and Professor LeBlanc, Jack's long-suffering violin instructor.

Actually, Jack's inability to play the violin was also part of his comic shtick. In reality, Benny owned a Stradivarius and practiced two to three hours a day. Occasionally he treated audiences to some of his musical talent, as in the case of a serious concert he worked into one show in 1953. According to the *Variety* review, "CBS quotes [concert violinist Yasha] Heifetz as saying the comic has 'beautiful fingering and bowing.' He's no Heifetz...but he handled the instrument competently."

"The Jack Benny Show" was seen as a series of 10 specials in 1951 and 1952. From 1953 to 1959, the show was seen on alternate weeks, then went weekly in 1959 until leaving the air in 1965. It was always in the top 20, and usually made the top 10. In the 1990s Benny's early radio shows could still be heard in many areas of the country, and his television shows continued to be shown to a new generation of viewers in syndication on cable.

In 1974 Jack Benny was set to star in his first film in many years, *The Sunshine Boys.* But he was ill with cancer and died shortly before filming began, at the age of 80—er, 39.**

————
*One of the few racial stereotypes of the program, this was still acceptable in the politically incorrect 1950s. Although there were "fat" jokes at the expense of Don Wilson, there were, mercifully, never any racist remarks in connection with the Rochester character.

————
**Jack's best friend, George Burns, was enlisted to fill his shoes and subsequently won the Oscar for Best Supporting Actor.

CREDITS

PRODUCERS: Ralph Levy, Hilliard Marks, Seymour Berns, Irving Fein, Fred DeCordova (future producer of "The Tonight Show"). DIRECTORS: Ralph Levy, Fred DeCordova, Bud Yorkin, others. WRITERS: Sam Perrin, George Balzer, Milt Josefsberg, John Tackaberry, Al Gordon, Hal Goldman. CAST: Jack Benny, Mary Livingstone, Eddie "Rochester" Anderson, Don Wilson, Mel Blanc, Dennis Day, Frank Nelson.

EMMYS:

Best Continuing Performance (Male) in a Series by a Comedian, Singer, Host, Dancer, M.C., Announcer, Narrator, Panelist, or Any Person Who Essentially Plays Himself—Jack Benny (1957); Best Comedy Series (1958–59, 1960–61); Best Actor in a Leading Role (Continuing Character) in a Comedy Series— Jack Benny (1958–59); Best Writing of a Single Program of a Comedy Series—Sam Perrin, George Balzer, Hal Goldman, and Al Gordon (1958–59, 1959–60); Outstanding Directorial Achievement in Comedy—Ralph Levy and Bud Yorkin (1959–60).

YOU BET YOUR LIFE

Say the secret "woid" and the duck will come down and pay you $100. It's a common woid, something you see every day.

With those "woids" Groucho Marx would launch into the quiz segment of television's most successful game show, "You Bet Your Life." Yet in the truest sense, the program wasn't really a game show, but a showcase for the incredible talent of Groucho.

Julius "Groucho" Marx and his zany brothers, Harpo, Chico, and Zeppo (the fifth brother, Gummo, was their manager), had made some of the wackiest slapstick movies of the 1930s, but during the '40s their popularity declined. In 1947, Groucho's friend John Guedel (producer of Art Linkletter's "House Party") approached Groucho with an offer to do a radio quiz show. "How soon can I start?" replied the desperate Groucho. Three years later, they made the inevitable move to television.

The format was a natural: Groucho, *sans* the painted eyebrows and moustache from his films, perched atop a stool ("I'm the highest paid stool pigeon in the U.S.," he quipped), puffing his cigar, and hurling barbs and witticisms at the hapless contestants for several minutes before starting the actual quiz. The question-and-answer session was really the least interesting part of the show; what kept audiences coming back for more was the host. The game was merely an excuse for him to chat with people—always an amusing, mismatched man and woman, with the attractive female receiving the brunt of Groucho's sexist (though 1950s-acceptable) humor. "I focus on the guests," Groucho told *Newsweek*. "I let them talk until they get confused. Then I move in. I don't prod. When some contestant puts his foot in his mouth, I just push it in a little further." Although Groucho was a whiz at ad-libs, the show was carefully scripted. Groucho's remarks and "ad-libs"

appeared on an overhead monitor, and when he seemed to be rolling his eyes skyward bemusedly, he was really reading his next zinger.

A team of 12 talent scouts would spend weeks on the road searching for these contestants. Occasionally they were showbiz hopefuls, such as Phyllis Diller, who made her TV debut on "You Bet Your Life." A young Candice Bergen, General Omar Bradley, and heavyweight boxing champ Rocky Marciano all took turns at being insulted by the Quizmeister. In the late '50s, a young contestant announced that he was a writer working on a novel. His name was William Peter Blatty, and the novel, published years later, was *The Exorcist*.

In order to avoid interrupting Groucho when he was "on a roll," the show was filmed for one hour (in Hollywood) by *nine* cameras, then edited down to fill the 30-minute time period. Groucho was noted for his blue, off-color humor, most of which was ad-libbed despite the script, so heavy editing was always mandatory. Occasionally, however, he was able to shine through. A contestant once told Groucho that he and his wife had 16 children. "Why do you have so many children?" Groucho asked. "Because I like my wife," replied the contestant. Groucho then shot back, "I like my cigar too, but I take it out sometimes!" Or take the time a clergyman appeared as a contestant:

GROUCHO
I understand that men of the cloth are not of great means. How can you afford a vacation here on the West Coast?

CLERGYMAN
Well, Groucho, I just had a windfall.

GROUCHO
Oh? Have you tried Alka Seltzer?

Eventually Groucho would get down to the business at hand and play the actual quiz. Contestants

---

CREDITS

TOP 10 PEAK: No. 3 (tie), 1953–54. PRODUCER: John Guedel. DIRECTORS: Robert Dwan, Bernie Smith. WRITERS: various. HOST/QUIZMASTER: Groucho Marx. ANNOUNCER: George Fenneman.

EMMYS:

Most Outstanding Personality— Groucho Marx (1950).

Groucho Marx.

started off with $100 in cash, then wagered amounts of it on the questions, sight unseen; no one actually had to bet his or her life, although a few probably felt like they had after taking it on the chin from Groucho. The contestants weren't necessarily mental powerhouses, which was always something of a treat to Groucho. "We don't have to have brains on our show," he said. "The stupider the better, just as long as they can talk. Anyway, the encyclopedic mind gets pretty dull." And whenever a couple lost all their money, Groucho would always bail them out by awarding $50 for the correct reply to the the self-answering question, "Who was buried in Grant's tomb?"

"You Bet Your Life" was seen on NBC from 1950 until 1961. In 1980 MCA syndicated a new version of the show starring Buddy Hackett, but it was pulled after only a few months. Then in 1992 the show was revived again, this time starring Bill Cosby. Amid much fanfare and ballyhoo, "You Bet Your Life" was syndicated to hundreds of markets across the United States. The media attention it generated seemed fit for something just short of the Second Coming. Reviews were all raves; success was inevitable, based primarily on the popularity of the show's star. The format was basically the same, with one subtle change: the secret-word duck, which had borne a strong resemblence to Groucho, complete with moustache, eyebrows, and cigar, was changed to a black goose, à la the Cos. But soon all bets were off, as the syndications ratings didn't deliver and the series was cancelled after one season. It seemed to prove the words that Groucho's announcer, George Fenneman, used each week in the show's opening: there was just no comparison to "The one—the only—GROUCHO!"

DRAGNET

NUMBER 4, 1952–53

This is the city. Los Angeles, California. I work here. I carry a badge. My name's Friday. The story you are about to see is true; the names have been changed to protect the innocent.

With this introduction, Jack Webb set the stage each week for his no-nonsense, soft-spoken character, Los Angeles Police Sergeant Joe Friday, to round up the bad guys and bring them to justice. This he did on and off for 21 years (including three years in radio) on "Dragnet," the most successful crime drama of all time.

Jack Webb was the man behind Joe Friday's Badge 714. A homely, crew-cut man with loving-cup ears, he seemed an unlikely sex symbol, yet during the heyday of "Dragnet" he received thousands of letters from amorous females. He also amassed a pile of fan mail from actual police officers complimenting him on the show's inspiring authenticity.

From the start, this realism was exactly what Jack Webb had intended to capture. A former World War II bomber pilot, Webb had taken to radio announcing after the war, landing his own show in San Francisco. Eventually he made his way to Los Angeles, where he had minor roles in a few movies. In 1949 he was appearing in the film *He Walked by Night*, in which he played a police lieutenant. On the set he met the technical advisor, a Los Angeles detective sergeant named Marty Wynn. "Why don't you do a real story about policemen?" Wynn asked Webb, who had been producing his own radio shows. Intrigued, Webb asked to tag along on calls with Wynn and his partner. By listening to the police radio's unemotional reports of crime, he began to learn the lingo of the profession.

Webb's first incarnation of "Dragnet" debuted on NBC radio in the summer of 1949. The show, which Webb claimed to have created "because I was starving and had to keep the wolf from the door," was slated to be only a summer replacement. But as Webb labored over his creation, the show began to catch on. Within two years it was the most popular show on radio. By 1952 Jack Webb, like so many others of that era, had made the transition to television.

The tube proved a natural medium for Webb's style. He became the master of the close-up shot, which helped provide the authenticity for which he strove. Webb produced, wrote, directed, and starred in the series, basing each episode on real cases from the files of the Los Angeles Police Department. It was a nonviolent show—few fistfights, fewer bullets, very few words. "We just want the facts, ma'am," deadpanned Joe Friday, and the expression became a national catch phrase. Webb portrayed police work realistically, homing in on the plodding, exhausting, and dangerous aspects of the job. "We're trying to play fact and not fiction," Webb said. "We try to make cops human beings, guys doing a job for low pay, but we're trying to get away from the 'dumb cop' idea. They aren't dumb; they're pretty smart. The average law officer has a handful of law books in the back of his car. The officer's job is not to make an arrest, but get a conviction."

To that end, Sergeant Joe Friday and his partner (Ben Alexander as Officer Frank Smith for six years; Harry Morgan as Officer Bill Gannon later on) always got their man or woman, and we always learned of their punishment:

"A trial was held in and for the county of Los Angeles. In a

CREDITS

TOP 10 PEAK: No. 2, 1953–54. CREATOR: Jack Webb. PRODUCERS: Jack Webb, others. DIRECTOR: Jack Webb. WRITERS: Jack Webb, Ben Alexander, others. CAST: *Sgt. Joe Friday* (Jack Webb), *Officer Frank Smith* (Herb Ellis, Ben Alexander), *Officer Bill Gannon* (Harry Morgan). GUEST STARS: Raymond Burr (playing a mad bomber in the first episode), Milburn Stone, Martin Milner, Lee Marvin, Leonard Nimoy (playing a juvenile delinquent in 1954), Carolyn Jones, Veronica Cartwright.

EMMYS

Best Mystery, Action, or Adventure Program (1952, 1953); Best Mystery or Intrigue Series (1954).

moment, the results of that trial." (Break for commercial.) Close-up of the suspect, looking like a deer caught in headlights: "The suspect was found guilty of (name of crime) and is now serving a zillion years in the state penitentiary in San Quentin." Cue the music: *dum da dum dum*.

The "Dragnet" theme, written by Walter Schumann, had a popularity of its own, inspiring two hit records in 1953: a rendition by Ray Anthony and His Orchestra, and a satirical version by humorist Stan Freberg, which reached number one and sold over a million records ("The legend you are about to hear is true; only the needle should be changed to protect the record.").

"Dragnet" ran from December 1951 until September 1959 and was simultaneously syndicated under the title "Badge 714." It left the air and returned in 1967 with Friday's new partner (Officer Gannon) and a new title—"Dragnet 1967." Each year thereafter until the

show's cancellation, the year became an adjunct to the title, ending with "Dragnet 1970."

In 1987 a feature film version paired Dan Aykroyd as Friday's nephew and Tom Hanks as his partner. The movie was actually a send-up of the Webb original, played strictly for laughs. Harry Morgan made a guest appearance as Gannon, now an L.A.P.D. captain.

From 1989 to 1990 a new syndicated "Dragnet" series ran for 52 episodes. It had an all-new cast and characters, but failed to perform well in the ratings.

In the early 1990s 22 of the original "Dragnet" episodes were in syndication on the Nostalgia Channel. Others not in syndication were held by Mark IV Limited, Webb's production company. Over the years Webb produced several other series, including "Pete Kelly's Blues," "Hec Ramsey," "Emergency," and the heir apparent to "Dragnet"—"Adam 12" (see page 188). Webb died in 1982, at the age of 62.

Jack Webb, in the sunglasses and white shirt, was most famous for starring in "Dragnet," but here he also directs a scene.

THE BUICK CIRCUS HOUR

NUMBER 6, 1952–53

On October 7, 1952, NBC began broadcasting a new live program every fourth Tuesday in the same time slot that was normally held down by "Texaco Star Theater" (see page 4), thereby giving Milton Berle some well-deserved time off.

The new program was called "The Buick Circus Hour," and it starred Joe E. Brown as the centerpiece, an Old Clown who befriended the show's lead character, a young singer. The series was actually one continuous story—a *nighttime* soap opera, if you will, in an era when such things didn't exist. The Clown became friends with a nightclub singer named Kim O'Neill, played by Dolores Gray, who had fallen in love with the owner of the circus, Bill Sothern (John Raitt). O'Neill joined the circus in order to be near the object of her affection; Sothern, meanwhile, had lived an adventuresome, extravagant life and had no intention of being tied down. The storyline followed the Clown's efforts to bring the two lovebirds together, with the conflict arising from the clash of personalities under the big top.

This circus setting of the series gave the show its production numbers, with clowns, jugglers, side shows, live animals, and other acts spicing up the weekly love story. Even the incorporation of the Buick commercials had a circus theme: on one occasion clowns put the Buick through a test, riding it over a succession of logs. Frequently the plot got lost amid this (literal) three-ring circus atmosphere.

CREDITS
PRODUCER: John C. Wilson. DIRECTORS: John C. Wilson, Frank Burns. WRITERS: Anita Loos, Jerry Seelen. CAST: *The Old Clown* (Joe E. Brown), *Bill Sothern* (John Raitt), *Kim O'Neill* (Dolores Gray). RINGMASTER/COMMERCIAL ANNOUNCER: Frank Gallop.

Guest stars appeared from time to time; Milton Berle gave up his night off to make an appearance. Other guests included Paul Winchell and Jerry Mahoney, a very popular ventriloquist act of the 1950s. Comedian Bert Lahr, the Cowardly Lion from the feature film *The Wizard of Oz* (1939), appeared a couple of times, and Wally Cox, '50s television's Mr. Peepers, popped in to do a couple of sketches.

Joe E. Brown, the Old Clown who tied it all together, was perfectly cast. Known for his Grand Canyon-sized mouth, which stretched into an infinite ear-to-ear grin, the actor/comedian had been in show business since he ran away from home to join the circus in 1901, at the age of nine. He learned clowning and mastered the art of pantomime, but also did some turns as a trapeze artist and acrobat. He was a familiar face to audiences when "Buick Circus Hour" appeared, thanks to the many films he made in the '30s and '40s, among them *The Circus Clown* (1934), *A Midsummer Night's Dream* (1935), *Wide Open Faces* (1938), *Shut My Big Mouth* (1942), and the hit musical film *Show Boat* (1951).

The show reached its happy, inevitable conclusion (girl gets boy) on June 16, 1953.

Joe E. Brown went on to do several more movies until his death in 1973; they included *Around the World in 80 Days* (1956), *Some Like It Hot* (1959), and *It's a Mad, Mad, Mad, Mad World* (1963).

Joe E. Brown.

GANGBUSTERS

One of the most popular forms of television of the late 1980s and early 1990s was "reality" programming. Shows like "Unsolved Mysteries" and "America's Most Wanted" fired the imagination of the American public with the possibility that they might help catch a criminal or solve a mystery. Most of the audience, however, was unaware that these programs had their roots in a radio/television show dating back more than a half century.

The original "Gangbusters" program made its debut on the radio in 1937 and continued in that medium for 20 years. In March 1952 the show began its transition to television and was an immediate success. The series presented, on film, documented stories of actual crimes based on the files of FBI and local and state law enforcement agencies. Phillips H. Lord, the writer and creator of "Gangbusters," narrated the stories and offered up-to-the minute clues on wanted criminals. At the end of the show, still photographs of a criminal were shown and a complete description was provided. The audience was then told to phone local police, the FBI, or "Gangbusters" (although there were no toll-free 800 numbers in those days) if they had any idea of the person's whereabouts. Over the years, this "most wanted" feature of the show resulted in the apprehension of several hundred criminals.

The stories themselves were intriguing. One episode explored the "Man from Mars," an actual police case in San Gabriel, California. It was classic reality programming, filmed on location using the stores that were the real scenes of the crime, along with the police officer involved in the case who actually shot the "Man from Mars." The nickname referred to the costume worn by a murderer who escaped from prison, hid out in sewers, and terrorized San Gabriel with holdups and murders. A different, three-part episode concerned the case of Willie Sutton, the criminal who masterminded one of the largest jewelry store robberies of all time and later escaped from Sing Sing prison. As with modern programs of this type, the show used actors to dramatize the heist.

The series took off like, well, gangbusters. The critics reluctantly admitted that it had all the trappings of a success. *Variety* at first bemoaned the fact that it was "just one more show [on] the long list of hackneyed and trite cops-'n'-robbers mellers [*Variety*-ese for "melodramas"] on TV," but admitted, "through the competent work of producer-director Richard Bare, [the show's creator Phillips H. Lord] has come up with one of the better produced TV film series on the airwaves. With the exception of some antiquated stock shots, which made for a phony opening, the show perked along at an acceptable speed and, since this type of stereotyped drama obviously hasn't yet worn out its welcome, the series should gain a sizeable audience."

"Gangbusters" alternated with "Dragnet," primarily because Jack Webb needed time to build a sufficient stockpile of episodes, and it certainly benefited from being in that particular time slot. Webb even appeared at the end of each telecast to plug the following week's episode of "Dragnet."

Almost as soon as it began, the "Gangbusters" television run ended. The final episode aired on Christmas Day, 1952, when the show was at the height of its popularity. It was probably the highest rated series ever to be cancelled in the history of television. The reason for its demise? Jack Webb now had enough "Dragnet" episodes in the can for weekly broadcasts, so tobacco company Liggett and Myers, which bankrolled both series, pulled the plug on "Gangbusters." The series continued on radio until 1957.

CREDITS

CREATOR: Phillips H. Lord.
PRODUCER/DIRECTOR: Richard Bare. WRITER: Phillips H. Lord. NARRATOR: Phillips H. Lord. CAST: various.

Myson Handley and Joyce Jameson.

THE BUICK-BERLE SHOW

NUMBER 5, 1953–54

Milton Berle.

When the ratings of "Texaco Star Theater" began slipping in 1952 (see page 4), the format of the show was changed. New writers were hired by the network. The team was headed by Goodman Ace, a successful radio writer. (One of his staff writers was Selma Diamond, who decades later became known to audiences as the sandpaper-voiced "Selma Hacker" on "Night Court" [see page 310].)

The show's changes saw the demise of host Milton Berle's freewheeling vaudeville style in favor of a more structured situation comedy. In the tried-and-true formula that had worked so well for George Burns and Jack Benny, Berle now played the harried star of a television variety show who was subjected to the eccentricities of his staff and guests. New cast regulars included Ruth Gilbert as his secretary, Max, and the bespectacled nerd Arnold Stang as Francis the lovestruck (with Max) stagehand. Young ventriloquist Jimmy Nelson, along with his dummies Danny O'Day and Farfel (the latter a talking dog), replaced Sid Stone in the commercial pitches.

In the following year, 1953, the show lost its sponsorship by Texaco. The new sponsor was Buick, which immediately co-joined its name to Berle's in the title. Audiences, however, did not take to these changes for "Uncle Miltie." After an initial rush in the ratings, the show's popularity slacked off. Buick jumped ship in 1955 and went over to the more popular "Jackie Gleason Show" (number two compared to Berle's number 11 at the end of the 1954–55 season).

Meanwhile, Berle signed on with Whirlpool and Sunbeam, for 1955–56; fortunately, the new sponsors did *not* change the show's name to the "Whirlpool-Sunbeam-Berle Hour." Instead, it was simply called "The Milton Berle Show," now broadcast in color from Hollywood.

For the last season, the show added a number of guest stars and worked the skits around them. Particularly memorable was the guest on the final show, on June 14, 1955. A young, nervous Elvis Presley delighted the audience, although he bewildered the *Variety* reviewer, who noted: "Elvis Presley was on hand to please his fans with his usual frenetic song stylings. There were a couple of skits between Berle and Presley

involving the latter's strange fascination for the younger generation, which certainly added no value to the program."

Apparently not; even the appearance of Elvis couldn't save "The Milton Berle Show." NBC cancelled the series, partially due to the competition from the CBS show "You'll Never Get Rich," starring Berle's old buddy, Phil Silvers. After 366 weekly one-hour live shows (of which Berle missed only one—June 16, 1954, the night after his mother died), Berle was told he could now rest. But his "retirement" was short-lived. He needed to work, and after a two-year hiatus, he returned to television in October 1958 as the host of "Milton Berle Starring in the Kraft Music Hall." At least this time his name was above the sponsor's.

This show was seen for 30 minutes on Wednesdays, live from Hollywood, but after 39 programs, TV's potential Mr. Wednesday Night was still its former Mr. Tuesday Night when the program was cancelled in May 1959. To Milton Berle, it was like having his air supply cut off. NBC, however, honored its long-term contract and found a vehicle for him: hosting "Jackpot Bowling Starring Milton Berle." He was now playing second fiddle to a bowling ball—quite a comedown for the man once known as "Mr. Television." That show went off the air the following spring, and it was five more years before Berle found another TV series. He obtained a release from his NBC contract and returned in September 1966 in an all-new "Milton Berle Show" on ABC, a 60-minute variety show that included Bobby Rydell and a group of go-go dancers in an effort to capture a young audience. It didn't, and the show was cancelled by the following January, this time falling victim to competition from another "Uncle"—it seems the TV audience preferred "The Man from U.N.C.L.E." to Uncle Miltie.

Despite these setbacks, Milton Berle's career never faltered. He appeared in films and guested on many television shows over several subsequent decades. As his late wife Ruth put it, "The world's greatest love affair is not Romeo and Juliet, but Milton and show business."

CREDITS

PRODUCERS: Milton Berle, others. DIRECTORS: Greg Garrison, Milton Berle. WRITERS: Goodman Ace, Jerry Seelen and Phil Charig, Aaron Ruben, Selma Diamond, Jay Burton, Bill Manhoff, Nate Monaster, Buddy Arnold, Al Schwartz. REGULARS: Milton Berle, Ruth Gilbert, Arnold Stang, Jimmy Nelson. GUEST STARS: Margaret Truman, Gertrude Berg, Frank Sinatra, Tallulah Bankhead, Martha Raye, Eddie Cantor, Phil Harris, Mickey Rooney, Esther Williams, John Wayne, Elvis Presley.

FORD TELEVISION THEATRE

NUMBER 7, 1953–54

Perhaps it was just a matter of time. Television in the 1950s was awash in a sea of "Theaters" and "Playhouses," all bankrolled by major corporations: Kraft, Philco, Armstrong, Goodyear, Texaco, General Electric, U.S. Steel, as well as "Fireside Theatre," added to the profusion. And all were ranked in the Nielsen top 25. So it seemed inevitable when "Ford Television Theatre," after five years as a television staple, was suddenly catapulted into the Nielsen top 10.

The anthology series matched the quality of the others play for play, week for week. Premiering in October 1948 with "Years Ago," starring Raymond Massey, the series presented many prestigious dramas. Initially, "Ford Theatre" (named after the car, not the place where Abraham Lincoln was assassinated) aired for one hour once a month on CBS, but by the second season the show was on biweekly. The original focus was on Broadway plays, and since the broadcast was live from New York, the show utilized Broadway talent. Some of the earliest presentations were "Joy to the World," with Eddie Albert and Janet Blair (November 1948); "Outward Bound," with Lillian Gish, Freddie Bartholomew, and Nina Foch (March 1949); "One Sunday Afternoon," with Burgess Meredith and Hume Cronyn (May 1949); "Twentieth Century," with Fredric March, Lilli Palmer, and E. G. Marshall (October 1949); "Alice in Wonderland," with Jack Lemmon as *both* Tweedledee and Tweedledum (December 1950); and Lillian Gish again in "Spring Again."

The series left CBS and took a hiatus from June 1951 until it was picked up by NBC in October 1952, where it became a 30- rather than 60-minute presentation. The October 8 "premiere" starred Will Rogers, Jr. and Marguerite Chapman in "Life, Liberty and Orrin Dooley." Rogers played the role of a GI returning to his Oklahoma farm after a stretch in the Korean War, enrolling in a grammar school for some "larnin' " but falling for the schoolmarm instead. Plays were now

CREDITS

PRODUCERS: Garth Montgomery, others. DIRECTORS: Marc Daniels, Franklin J. Schaffner, Robert Stevenson, others. WRITERS: various.

filmed by Screen Gems, the fledgling television arm of Columbia Pictures, which would eventually become one of the strongest providers of TV product.

Other famous folk who starred in "Ford Theatre" were Howard Duff and Angela Lansbury ("The Ming Lama"), Shelley Winters in her TV debut in "Mantrap" (co-starring Jerry Paris, who later became a top TV director), Peter Lawford and James Whitmore in "For Value Received," and Thomas Mitchell in a number of plays. Many actors and actresses made their first television appearances on this show, including Judy Holliday ("She Loves Me," November 1949), Ernest Borgnine ("Night Visitor," April 1954), and Vince Edwards ("Garrity's Sons," March 1955). Other debutants included Robert Young, Donna Reed, Tab Hunter, Ann Sheridan, and Roger Smith. And Ronald Reagan and his wife Nancy Davis made their first professional appearance together in "First Born" (February 1953).

Marc Daniels directed the series each time it appeared on CBS. Daniels later became the director of "I Love Lucy," and in the late 1960s he directed many episodes of "Star Trek."

Following Daniels' exit from the show, Franklin Schaffner took over for a couple of seasons. Schaffner directed a lot of early television, won several Emmys, then went on to a successful film career that included *Planet of the Apes* (1968) and *Patton* (1970), for which he won the Academy Award.

Later episodes were helmed by British director Robert Stevenson, who directed most of the popular Disney films of the '60s and early '70s, including *The Absent-Minded Professor* (1961) and the Academy Award-winning movie *Mary Poppins* (1964).

NBC cancelled "Ford Television Theatre" in September 1956, after a four-year run. A month later the series was picked up on ABC, where it continued in the half-hour format until the final episode of the series aired in July 1957.

Angela Lansbury and Howard Duff in "The Ming Lama."

THE JACKIE GLEASON SHOW

NUMBER 8, 1953–54

And awa-a-ay we go! —JACKIE GLEASON

He drank 100-proof "coffee" and loved pizza for breakfast. He created enough of his own characters to populate a small town. And he brought cheer to television audiences for more than 20 years with hardly a letup.

Herbert John "Jackie" Gleason grew up in Brooklyn, New York, the son of poor parents; his father abandoned the family when Jackie was eight, so his mother took a job dispensing tokens in the subway. He entered show business by the usual route—vaudeville, nightclubs, the stage. He plunged headlong into the fledgling medium of television as the original Riley in "The Life of Riley" (1949), but was soon replaced by the film version's star, William Bendix. Undaunted, Gleason returned to familiar territory and brought his nightclub act to television's stepchild network, DuMont.

His "Cavalcade of Stars"—he was most of them—gave him the perfect arena in which to develop the characters that would be with him for most of his performance career: Reggie Van Gleason III, the upper-crust playboy; the Poor Soul, born under an eternal black cloud; Charlie the Loudmouth; Joe the Bartender; and one Ralph Kramden. It was on "Cavalcade" that Gleason first breathed life into the character for which he would most be remembered and loved.

When CBS made a bid for "Cavalcade of Stars" they hit the jackpot. At last they had an answer to NBC's ever-popular Milton Berle. "The Jackie Gleason Show" premiered in September 1952, and by 1955 it had climbed to second place in the ratings, right behind "I Love Lucy," giving CBS the number one and number two spots.

The show's success was due in no small part to the talents of Gleason, who, like Berle, was ubiquitous. He wrote, acted, arranged the lights and microphones, and even got in the hair of the director. He was noted for his non-rehearsal of the show over the protests of his cast members, preferring to rewrite the script right up until showtime.

His photographic memory of last-minute changes usually didn't fail him, and he expected no less of his fellow performers. One time, however, he slipped up and was saved by the quick thinking of Art Carney. Gleason, as "Honeymooner" Ralph Kramden, exited through the bedroom door, followed by wife Alice (Audrey Meadows). The script called for them to return to the scene immediately, but Gleason had disappeared, leaving Alice to go looking for him while Art Carney was left alone on the stage in front of live-TV cameras. Without skipping a beat, Carney strolled over to the icebox and found an orange. Then he sat down at the kitchen table and for the next two minutes peeled that orange until Gleason, who had wandered off to get a tissue to mop his brow, returned to the set. It was one of TV's funniest live moments.

Live TV also had more serious disadvantages, exemplified by the night in 1954 when Jackie Gleason slipped on stage during a comedy sketch and broke his leg. At first the audience thought it was part of the routine, but the reality of the situation soon became apparent. Fortunately, it was towards the end of the show, and the cast and crew managed to cover while Gleason was rushed off to the hospital. Guest hosts filled in for many weeks until

---

CREDITS

TOP 10 PEAK: No. 2, 1954–55. EXECUTIVE PRODUCER: Jack Philbin. PRODUCERS: Jack Hurdle, Ronald Wayne, others. DIRECTORS: Frank Satenstein, Frank Buneta, others. WRITERS: Marvin Marx, Walter Stone, Leonard Stern, others. THEME: "Melancholy Serenade," written by Jackie Gleason. REGULARS: Jackie Gleason, Art Carney, Audrey Meadows, Joyce Randolph, Frank Fontaine, Sheila MacRae, Jean Kean, The June Taylor Dancers.

EMMYS

Best Supporting Actor–Art Carney (1953, 1954, 1955), Best Supporting Actress in a Regular Series–Audrey Meadows (1954), Special Classification of Individual Achievement–Art Carney for "The Jackie Gleason Show" (1966–1967; 1967–1968).

Gleason, still recovering and sporting a cast on his leg, was able to return. His movement was slowed down considerably, but his wit was intact.

The initial run of "The Jackie Gleason Show" was on CBS from September 1952 until June 1955, when Gleason was offered a contract that would eventually total $11 million to produce his "Honeymooners" as a series on its own—in effect, television's first spin-off.

"The Honeymooners" was originally a very small segment of "Cavalcade of Stars" and later "The Jackie Gleason Show." Its roots harkened back to Gleason's working class upbringing. Bus driver Ralph Kramden (Gleason) was an Everyman, a poor working stiff brimming with ideas for get-rich-quick schemes that always backfired. He shared a small flat in Brooklyn (their furniture consisted primarily of an icebox and kitchen table) with his long-suffering wife Alice (Audrey Meadows). His buddy was neighbor Ed Norton (Art Carney), a "sanitation engineer" (read: sewer worker) and the perfect foil for the star; Norton made up for his lack of smarts in his loyalty to best friend Ralph. Ed's wife Trixie (Joyce Randolph) was to Alice what Ethel Mertz was to Lucy Ricardo in "I Love Lucy"—neighbor, confidante, co-frustrated housewife—although she was never featured as prominently.

"The Honeymooners" would eventually reach cult status. Fans, numbering in the millions, watched the original 39 1955–56 episodes in reruns ad infinitum. Thousands joined a fan club called R.A.L.P.H. (Royal Association for the Longevity and Preservation of "The Honeymooners") and held conventions where they recited choruses of buzzwords from the series, like "One of these days, Alice, *pow*! Right in the kisser," and "You wanna go to the moon, Alice?" In 1985 Gleason released close to 80 film clips known as the "lost" episodes —footage from the kinescopes of the live "Honeymoon" sketches first performed as part of the old "Jackie Gleason Show." Fans embraced this discovery as if it were the unearthing of a 10th Beethoven symphony.

Surprisingly, the original "Honeymooners" broadcasts never fared this well. The ratings were not what was expected, and by 1957 CBS had abandoned the "Honeymooners" in favor of new entries of "The Jackie Gleason Show," with *all* his familiar characters returning for two more years.

During the early '60s, Gleason hosted "Jackie Gleason and His American Scene Magazine," with a new cast of regulars along with old favorites like Frank Fontaine (Crazy Guggenheim) and the June Taylor Dancers. Then in September 1966 "The Jackie Gleason Show" moved to Miami Beach, Florida, so Jackie could indulge his addiction to golf. Along with this move came a rebirth of "The Honeymooners"—still a series within a series—recast with Sheila MacRae now playing Alice and Jane Kean as Trixie. The show was taped in color, and remained a Saturday night staple until 1970. Gleason continued to appear in films and television until his death in 1987.

Jackie Gleason as Joe the Bartender.

THIS IS YOUR LIFE

NUMBER 10, 1953–54

From Debbie Reynolds's appearance on "This Is Your Life."

Imagine you go to the theater to see a play. The lights dim, you settle into your seat, ready for a pleasant evening's entertainment. Suddenly, the houselights come up, brighter than ever; someone rushes down the aisle and confronts you with a microphone while cameras are poking into your face. Surprise! You're about to have your private life laid bare before millions of people. Live, from (Hollywood or New York), *this is your life*!

Audiences loved the "surprise party" shtick of this show that each week tricked and trapped unsuspecting people, mostly celebrities, into tripping down memory lane. All sorts of long-forgotten school teachers, childhood friends (or enemies), kids, pals, in-laws, and business associates were paraded before the weekly victim, who generally smiled cordially throughout what sometimes was an ordeal.

The brainchild of Ralph Edwards, who was also the emcee, "This Is Your Life" had been on the radio since 1948. The show grew out of a stunt performed on Edwards' radio show, "Truth or Consequences." When the U.S. Army asked Edwards to help boost morale in paraplegic soldiers, he selected a despondent young GI and hit on the idea of presenting his life on the air, integrating his happier past with the promise of a hopeful future. Among the people brought to the mike were the boy's old track coach and the head of his draft board. As luck would have it, the gimmick worked. Two years later, the rehabilitated soldier was wheeled into the studio by his new bride. Edwards recalled it as one of the most emotionally satisfying moments of his career: "I told him, 'Here's your year's rent, and here's your key. Come and get it.' And he got up and walked to the mike. It was the greatest thrill I ever had. The crowd stood up and cheered. I knew then and there that there must be a show in this sort of thing."

Indeed there was. Audiences ate up its soppy sentimentality. On television too, it was a resounding hit, tying with the well-established "Colgate Comedy Hour" for 10th place in its second season.

Many celebrities took turns being set up for the surprise. Among the familiar names were Bob Hope, Stan Laurel, Marilyn Monroe, Jack Benny, George Burns, Nanette Fabray, Bette Davis, Lilly Pons, Red Nichols,

Phil Harris, and Eddie Cantor. Cantor was one of the few people who had to be told in advance, since producers feared for his heart condition. Occasionally unknowns were among those honored, usually saintly people who had founded orphanages or rescued drowning victims.

Most guests reacted with the appropriate astonishment and enthusiasm. One night in 1959, though, Ralph Edwards finally met with disaster. His subject was Lowell Thomas, the globe-trotting writer and newscaster. After being surprised at a banquet at New York City's Astor Hotel, Thomas just would not play along. "This is a sinister conspiracy," he muttered to the TV cameras. Edwards tried to recover with "I'm sure you're going to be very happy as your life goes by." Thomas snapped back, "I doubt that very much." As the show plodded along things progressed from bad to worse. "I happened to be there the night you got your very first radio contract. Do you remember?" prodded actress Beulah Bondi. "No, I don't," Thomas replied flatly. Edwards became flustered as the show went off track and commercial cues were missed; at one point Edwards had to ask, "Are we on?" Thomas suffered through every minute, stating, "My first thought was, 'Where can I vanish?' It's the kind of thing I would have gone off on an expedition to avoid."

"This Is Your Life" remained on NBC until 1961. Ralph Edwards became a successful producer of many game shows, including "It Could Be You," "Name That Tune," and "The Cross-Wits." He was also responsible for bringing the popular daytime show "The People's Court" to the air.

Edwards revived "This Is Your Life" again in 1971–72 in a syndicated version. In 1983 Edwards again resurrected the show for syndication, with Joseph Campanella hosting. Then in 1987 Ralph Edwards hosted two "This Is Your Life" specials. Each featured two honorees, Betty White and Dick Van Dyke on the first, and Tim Conway and Barbara Mandrell on the second. In addition, reruns of the original series have been shown frequently on cable TV's American Movie Classics channel. (Although the show was done live, film copies were preserved, since each guest received a film of his or her appearance as a memento.)

CREDITS

CREATOR/PRODUCER: Ralph Edwards. PRODUCERS: Axel Gruenberg, Alfred Paschall, others. DIRECTORS: Axel Gruenberg, Dick Gottlieb, others. WRITERS: various. HOST: Ralph Edwards. ANNOUNCER: Bob Warren.

EMMYS

Best Audience Participation, Quiz, or Panel Program (1953, 1954).

THE TOAST OF THE TOWN

NUMBER 5, 1954–55

He couldn't sing or dance. He didn't tell jokes. And he often forgot the names of the acts on his show. But audiences adored him, and for 23 years Ed Sullivan was a permanent fixture on Sunday night television.

An impresario with a keen eye for talent, Ed Sullivan had been a sportswriter and syndicated columnist for the New York *Daily News* when CBS nabbed him to host "The Toast of the Town," the mother of all vaudeville shows. For his first outing, June 20, 1948, this 20th-century P. T. Barnum presented nine different acts (on a total budget of $1,350*), including a young Italian singer and his Jewish partner, fresh from the borscht belt—Dean Martin and Jerry Lewis. They split a welcome $200 for their efforts and rejoiced that success was at hand. A tradition had begun: over the next two decades an appearance by up-and-coming young performers on "Sullivan" usually signaled they had *arrived*.

If Ed Sullivan was personally lacking in talent, he made up for it in the performers he presented. The "Great Stone Face" amassed over 20,000 acts during the run of his show. Singers, dancers, tumblers, plate-atop-stick jugglers—all vied for the honor of appearing on Ed Sullivan's "really big shew." Rudolf Nureyev might be slated to follow a trained poodle act; opera diva Maria Callas could have been triumphant at the Met, but she might serve as a warm-up act for Sullivan's favorite little mouse-puppet, Topo Gigio. All were equally loved by Sullivan ("Let's re-e-ally hear it for them!").

In late 1954 the show's name was changed from "The Toast of the Town" to "The Ed Sullivan Show," which people had been calling it all along.

Sullivan is probably best remembered for two of his discoveries, both in the newly emerging Age of Rock.

In the fall of 1956, he reintroduced Elvis Presley to the American public. Presley had made other TV appearances, but his career's future was cemented after his "Sullivan" bow. And Ed, ever the Irish Catholic prude, was taken aback by the gyrations of "The Pelvis." For his next two appearances, the cameras were permitted to photograph the King from the waist up only.

In 1964 Ed Sullivan (who professed to dislike rock and roll) again made history by bringing the Beatles to American television. The American success of the "Fab Four," already a phenomenon in Europe, was no accident. Months ahead of the group's "Sullivan" appearance, the U.S. audience had been seeded with promotional gimmicks, from a massive push on the Beatles' latest single, "I Want to Hold Your Hand," to the distribution of posters, bumper stickers, and buttons imploring young fans to "Be a Beatles Booster." When the Lads from Liverpool finally appeared on the show, the audience, mostly young girls, screamed so loudly they drowned out the music and had to be shushed by Ed. Another Sullivan success story.

Over the years, there were many other discoveries. In the early '50s he spotted 10-year-old Itzhak Perlman perched atop crutches (he'd suffered from polio) and playing the violin, and he immediately signed him up; 17-year-old Liza Minnelli, in 1963, proved she was more than just Judy Garland's kid. The Rolling Stones, the Jackson Five, and the Doors all stepped out on Sullivan's stage. Before going on, the Doors had promised not to use the lyric, "You know we couldn't get much higher" from their popular song, "Light My Fire," which Sullivan found offensive; but the group reneged and was not invited back.

Ed Sullivan showcased more borscht belt performers than the well-known Grossinger's resort: Myron Cohen made 41 appearances; Wayne and Shuster headlined 53 times; and Jackie Mason appeared numerous times until the much-publicized falling out following Mason's giving Sullivan "the bird" on national television. Mason thought it was funny; Sullivan did not and lambasted him publicly. (Years later they would settle their differences.) Elvis's suggestive hip

---

CREDITS

TOP 10 PEAK: No. 2, 1956–57.
PRODUCERS: Ed Sullivan, others.
DIRECTORS: various. WRITERS: various. HOST: Ed Sullivan.

EMMYS

Best Variety Series (1955), Special Emmy Award to Ed Sullivan (1971).

Ed Sullivan with the Beatles.

movements, deodorant ads, cleavage, obscene gestures—all were banished from "The Ed Sullivan Show."

Big Name Talent abounded, sandwiched in between the sword swallowers, ventriloquists, and pandas on roller skates. At one time or another Sullivan presented Margaret Truman, Humphrey Bogart, Walt Disney, Bob Hope (in his first TV appearance), Charles Laughton, Liberace, Barbra Streisand, Jayne Mansfield (playing the violin), and Lauren Bacall (reciting "Casey at the Bat"). He showcased dozens of black performers at a time when this was not commonly done—entertainers like Sammy Davis, Jr., Ella Fitzgerald, Duke Ellington, Pearl Bailey, George Kirby, and Lena Horne.

With so many acts over so many years, it is not surprising that Sullivan sometimes got confused. Once he had the Supremes on, praised them lavishly, then forgot the group's name, mumbling lamely, "Here are the girls." Joan Rivers recalled that her first appearance in 1966 was an accident: "Right before the show they had been pitching Johnny Rivers to him, and he went on the show and said, 'Next week, Joan Rivers!' So I was on the show by mistake." He introduced Roberta Sherwood as Roberta Peters, and some New Zealand natives became "the fierce Maori tribe from New England." The oft-befuddled host once mangled a pitch on behalf of the tuberculosis drive as "Good night and help stamp out TV." And after Sergio Franchi sang on

the 1965 Christmas show, Sullivan implored, "Let's hear it for the Lord's Prayer!" "An error now and then makes me human," countered Sullivan. "I think people identify with me. I'm not a performer, I'm a host. Sort of like some ordinary guy from Iowa who somehow met someone famous and is throwing a party for his friends and says, 'Hey, look who I got!'"

The party was finally over in 1971, after audiences' tastes had changed and "The Ed Sullivan Show"—which at one time ranked second in the Nielsen ratings—had slipped out of the top 20. CBS cancelled the show. Too upset to do a big finale, Sullivan chose a rerun for his final show (by then the show had been done on tape for many years) featuring Carol Channing, Robert Klein, and Gladys Knight. The last bit featured Ed's faithful little Italian mouse, Topo Gigio, saying "Kiss-a me goo' night, Eddie." Over the next few years Sullivan did a number of specials, including a 25th anniversary show in 1973. He died of cancer in 1974.

In the early '90s there was a resurgence of interest in "The Ed Sullivan Show." "The Very Best of the Ed Sullivan Show" was released in a series of videotapes, and reruns of edited shows were syndicated on late-night television.

---

*Two decades later, an hour's worth of "The Ed Sullivan Show" ran the network $372,000.

DISNEYLAND

NUMBER 6, 1954–55

Before it was "The Happiest Place on Earth," "Disneyland" was only a television series; the theme park in Anaheim, California, was still under construction. And it was no accident that both shared the same name, and the same godparent, Walt Disney.

At a time when most motion picture studios were shunning telelvision, fearful of the impact the medium would have on their theatrical product, Walt Disney embraced it. In 1954 he premiered his weekly television series called "Disneyland." At the same time, construction was underway for an $11 million, 270-acre amusement park surrounded by orange groves in an area 45 minutes south of Los Angeles. Both were considered risks, which delighted the visionary man who would become "Uncle Walt" to several generations of children.

"Disneyland," the television program, like the Anaheim theme park, had four "lands" in which adventures took place on a rotating basis: Adventureland, Frontierland, Tomorrowland, and Fantasyland. Each land featured a different kind of program, and to explain the new series, Walt Disney himself appeared as the series host on the very first "Disneyland" program, October 27, 1954.

Initially, the creator of the world's best-loved rodent, Mickey Mouse, was reluctant to appear on camera and worried about his voice. "It cracks," he complained. "I have a little laryngitis because I smoke too much. And I talk too much; all day long I'm talking in meetings and wherever I go. I have a nasal twang, a Missouri twang." But Walt (he always insisted that people call him "Walt," never "Mr. Disney") was persuaded to host the first "Disneyland" show, establishing a precedent for all future TV series produced by his company.

In the opening "Disneyland" program, he used almost the entire hour to explain what the future shows would be like—perhaps the first TV series to start with a program explaining itself. Audiences learned that "Adventureland" would offer filmed stories both fictional and educational; "Tomorrowland" might tell stories of space travel years before America was poised to launch its first national space program; "Fantasyland" would feature mostly animation—the cartoons for which the Disney studios were celebrated; and "Frontierland" would offer stories about early American history.

During the first year "Disneyland" presented "Operation Undersea," probably television's first "infomercial." It was an hour-long behind-the-scenes documentary/trailer for Walt Disney Productions' upcoming film, *20,000 Leagues Under the Sea*, and the Television Academy deemed it worthy of an Emmy Award. The series was also liberally sprinkled with the studio's backlog of films, such as *Alice in Wonderland*, *So Dear to My Heart*, *Treasure Island*, *Wind in the Willows*, and *Nature's Half Acre*, as well as original films like the impressive *Man in Space*, prepared with technical advice by rocket scientists Willy Ley and Wernher von Braun.

But nothing fired the public's imagination like Walt's man from Frontierland—Davy Crockett.

Walt had been contemplating doing a series of shows based on legendary American heroes—Johnny Appleseed, Daniel Boone, Mike Fink, and Davy Crockett. Crockett was first on the drawing board, and Walt began searching for the right actor to play the hero. He screened the science-fiction film *Them* to check out its lead, James Arness, but when six-foot-five-inch Fess Parker appeared in a scene, he shouted, "That's our Davy Crockett!"

The saga of Davy was initially aired in three parts: "Davy Crockett, Indian Fighter" (December 15, 1954); "Davy Crockett Goes to Congress" (January 26, 1955); and

---

CREDITS

Top 10 Peak: No. 4, 1955–56.
Executive Producer/Host: Walt Disney. Producer: Bill Walsh.
Directors: various. Writers: various.

EMMYS

Best Variety Series Including Musical Varieties (1954), Best Individual Program of the Year—"Operation Undersea" (1954), Best Action or Adventure Series (1955), Best Producer, Film Series—Walt Disney (1955).

"Davy Crockett at the Alamo" (February 23, 1955). After the first part aired, Davy's theme song, "The Ballad of Davy Crockett," was released, and an entire generation of coonskin-capped kids ran around singing "Davy, Davy Crockett, king of the wild frontier!" The song soared to number one for 13 weeks, selling 10 million records. Davy Crockett merchandise filled whole warehouses as raccoons fled for their lives to avoid the coonskin cap craze. Everything from Davy Crockett lunchboxes to bunk bed sets ("with scenes of Davy in action on the mattress," enthused one unwitting radio announcer) helped make up a $400,000 deficit Walt had incurred in bringing the Crockett films to television. The studio later spliced the footage together into an 80-minute feature film that earned a theatrical profit of $2.5 million.

A fourth entry in the TV saga, "Davy Crockett and the River Pirates," was aired in December 1955 in an attempt to recapture the public's interest in a craze that had already peaked.

"Disneyland" was the most innovative television program to date, and boosted by such successes as "Davy Crockett," it sent ABC's sagging ratings soaring as the network's first genuine hit. The series ran on ABC until the fall of 1958, when it moved to NBC as "Walt Disney's Wonderful World of Color" (see page 164).

In 1966 Walt Disney succumbed to lung cancer, at the age of 65.

Ed Sullivan (left), Walt Disney, and friends.

THE GEORGE GOBEL SHOW

NUMBER 8, 1954–55

George Gobel, with Peggy King.

"Tonight, I, oh, perhaps I should introduce myself. I'm George...er, George...George...Isn't that funny? Faces I remember real good, but names—believe thee me! See, that's why I have this wristwatch: 'To George, the adorable man I love and cherish, the father of my children, the light of my life, from your loving, adoring wife, Mrs.'–continued on watchband–'Alice Gobel.' Of course! That's it, George *Gobel*. I'd know me anywhere."

In 1954 such casual utterings each Saturday night by a five-foot-five-inch, 138-pound crew-cutted man captured the attention and adoration of the American television audience. George Gobel, a self-effacing comic and guitar-strumming singer, seemed an unlikely candidate for a television success story. And it was even more baffling when he garnered the Emmy for Outstanding New Personality in 1954, since "Old Lonesome George," as he liked to call himself, had been in show business since 1927.

Billed as "Little George Gobel," young George had started as a singer in radio at the age of eight. At 12, he was a regular performer on WLS-Chicago's "Barn Dance." After serving in the Army Air Force in World War II, Gobel developed his standup routine, appearing in nightclubs and on early TV shows like "The Garry Moore Show" and NBC's "Saturday Night Revue" in 1953 and 1954.

By the end of 1954, NBC had decided it was time for George Gobel to go solo and gave him his own program to showcase his talents. George continued his persona of the bewildered, henpecked nebbish, whose favorite expression was "Well, I'll be a dirty bird!"

"The trouble with me is, people don't remember who I am," he said in *Time*. "When I go to a party, nobody says hello; but when I leave, everybody says goodbye." Nobody, including George, could pin down his style. "I don't think it's like anybody else's," he said. "I didn't think about it until other people started describing it. They describe it in so many ways, I get kind of mixed up. I guess it's offbeat, casual. I get a line I figure will be funny or not, and I don't try to figure it out."

In the show's simple format, he merely walked out and started to tell stories in his Midwestern accent. One typical example went as follows: "It's interesting how I got to be called George Gobel. One day Dad called all 16 of us children into the living room and said,

'OK, now, which one of you kids wants to be George Gobel?' I wanted to be Douglas Fairbanks, Jr. But that was already taken." Or this one: "The National Safety Council predicted there would be 407 accidents due to careless driving over the holiday weekend, and so far only 209 have been reported. Now, some of you folks just aren't tryin'."

Given such non-side-splitting examples, it is hard to cite the reason for Gobel's meteoric rise to the heights of TV popularity. Certainly there were funnier folk on the tube.

His producer/head writer, Hal Kanter (who would one day be executive producer of "All in the Family"), attributed Gobel's success to his honesty. "This guy always tells the truth, no matter what," he once said. Like the time one of the show's sponsors, Dial Soap, announced a jingle contest in which the big winner would receive either $25,000 in cash or the income from a producing oil well. After the commercial, Gobel stood in front of the camera and leveled, "I think it's only fair to tell you about that oil well contest—a lot of people are going to lose."

Part of the show's format involved sketches that revolved around George and his wife, "spooky old Alice." (George's real-life wife didn't seem to mind his using her name.) Alice was played by Jeff Donnell (yes, Jeff was a woman), and later by Phyllis Avery. Another regular on the variety/comedy show (1957–58) was Eddie Fisher, whose show alternated with Gobel's. Each star occasionally visited the other's show. Other regulars over the years were singer Peggy King, Joe Flynn, Anita Bryant, the Modernaires, and Harry von Zell.

For his final season, Gobel moved to CBS (October 1959 to June 1960), but by the end of the '50s, the popularity of "The George Gobel Show" had begun to wane, largely thanks to the new wave of adult westerns. George continued to earn a living as an occasional actor on assorted series and specials, while deriving a nice income from "Leave It to Beaver," which was filmed by his own production company. In the 1970s Gobel became a regular on the hit daytime game show "Hollywood Squares." In 1982 he had a continuing role as the drunken Mayor Otis Harper, Jr., on the sitcom "Harper Valley P.T.A."

George Gobel died as the result of complications during heart bypass surgery in 1991, at the age of 71.

CREDITS

PRODUCERS: Hal Kanter, Al Lewis, Alan Handley, Bill Burch, Will Roland, Fred De Cordova, others. DIRECTORS: Bud Yorkin, Richard McDonough, Fred De Cordova, others. WRITERS: Hal Kanter, Harry Winkler, Everett Greenbaum, Howard Leeds, Elton Packard, Jack Brooks, Milton Rosen, Norman Lear, others. REGULARS: George Gobel, Peggy King, The John Scott Trotter Orchestra, Eddie Fisher, Jeff Donnell, Phyllis Avery, Joe Flynn, Anita Bryant, Harry von Zell. GUEST STARS: Fred MacMurray, Vaughn Monroe, Fran Allison, Janis Paige, Jack Carter, Johnny Mathis, Jim Backus, Richard Greene, Henry Fonda.

EMMYS

Most Outstanding New Personality— George Gobel (1954), Best Written Comedy Material—James Allardice, Jack Douglas, Hal Kanter, Harry Winkler (1954).

DECEMBER BRIDE

NUMBER 10, 1954–55

Spring Byington.

That most venerable of clichés, the mother-in-law joke, got its own show on television back in 1954. But within a few months of its premiere, "December Bride" proved that it was more than a one-joke show. It was witty and clever and for the first time ever presented an aging woman as someone capable of *personhood*.

Familiar to audiences as a star of stage and screen, the actress playing the older lady who hoped to be a bride in the *winter* of her life was ironically played by a woman named Spring. What's more, Lily Ruskin, played by Spring Byington, was actually well-liked by the son-in-law and daughter (actors Dean Miller and Frances Rafferty) with whom she lived.

Lily was usually engaged in some do-good project, creating a total mess of it but tying up all the loose ends by the show's finale. Along the way she proved that older people could be self-sufficient, cheerful, and open-minded, far from the stereotype audiences might have expected. And, indeed, she won the hearts of her TV audience as well as those of her suitors, among whom were Lyle Talbot, Regis Toomey, and Paul Cavanaugh.

Spring Byington, who was in her late 60s when she starred in "December Bride," described her character in *Time*: "Lily hasn't lost her appetite for life and is now free to do ridiculous things. She can play with life much more because she is mature of heart. She isn't stopped because other people are not doing it. She drives to Mexico alone. If something appeals to the mature person, if there is no really cogent reason for not doing it, let us do it, let us not be bound by hidebound convention." And Byington herself had much in common with her alter ego: "TV keeps me young because it keeps me busy, keeps my mind alert, my senses sharp and my interest up," she said.

According to the show's creator/writer/producer, Parke Levy, the message of "December Bride" was "that a woman can be attractive to men regardless of her age. It makes every dame* over 45 think she's still desirable."

Levy had originally created the show for the radio in the early '50s, basing the character on his own mother-in-law. When he proposed the program to various producers around Hollywood, no one wanted Spring Byington to recreate her original role, so Levy took his idea to Desi Arnaz at Desilu Productions. Desi not only bought the show with Byington, but managed to get the program on the CBS schedule right after his own "I Love Lucy." With the strong lead-in of "Lucy," the show could not fail.

Although the series was basically a "slice of life," viewers reacted strongly when the story became too close to real life. About 100 letters a day were received by the show's producers, highly critical whenever the story overstepped the boundaries of '50s morality. Levy commented, "Once we played a scene that showed Frances Rafferty and Dean Miller in twin beds. Dean got out of his bed and went over to Frances. He never touched her, but we got all sorts of audience squawks asking us to keep the show out of the bedroom." (In fact, it was years before television even hinted that people did anything in bedrooms but sleep. The TV "code," originating from the old Hayes Office that policed motion picture guidelines in the '30s and '40s, required that if a couple was shown in their bedroom, they must have twin beds; if there was any interaction, one foot had to be on the floor at all times.)

One of the most memorable secondary characters from "December Bride" was the requisite next-door neighbor, in this case Pete Porter, played by Harry Morgan. Pete didn't understand the Henshaws' devotion to their mother-in-law, and found ample opportunity to trash his own: "When my mother-in-law was in San Diego, she walked out on the pier and the fleet refused to come in."

Pete was the neighborhood curmudgeon who also found nasty things to say about his wife, Gladys, whom we never saw. That is, until the characters were spun off into their own series. "Pete and Gladys" (the latter played by Cara Williams) went on the air in September 1960, a year after "December Bride" had completed its original run. Harry Morgan later segued from "Pete" into "Dragnet," as Jack Webb's partner (see page 34), and eventually co-starred as Col. Sherman Potter on "M*A*S*H" (see page 202).

---

*Levy made this statement in 1956, when the use of "dame" was tolerated.

CREDITS

Top 10 Peak: No. 5, 1956–57. Creator: Parke Levy. Producers: Parke Levy, Fred De Cordova. Directors: Jerry Thorpe, Fred De Cordova. Writers: Parke Levy, Lou Derman, Bill Davenport, Arthur Julian, various. Cast: *Lily Ruskin* (Spring Byington), *Ruth Henshaw* (Frances Rafferty), *Matt Henshaw* (Dean Miller), *Hilda Crocker* (Verna Felton), *Pete Porter* (Harry Morgan). Guest Stars: Rory Calhoun, Rudy Vallee, Joel Grey, Edgar Bergen, Frances Bergen, Zsa Zsa Gabor, others.

THE $64,000 QUESTION

NUMBER 1, 1955–56

You step into the isolation booth. Beads of sweat break out on your brow. The question is unlocked from its guarded vault and handed to the toothsome emcee. And now, for the big money, your question is this: In the summer of 1955, what quiz show rose from obscurity to the top of the Nielsens in only four months, leaving "I Love Lucy," "Ed Sullivan," and a host of other top shows in its wake, to become the most popular TV game of all time? Wait, now—don't answer just yet. This is a two-parter. Ready? What number one show would come crashing down from its mighty pedestal with a resounding thud just three short years after its debut?

The answer is, of course, "The $64,000 Question." But the *real* $64,000 question is: How?

The first runaway hit since Milton Berle's "Texaco Star Theater," this big-money quiz show was launched on CBS on June 7, 1955. Soon 84 percent of all TVs were tuned to the program each Sunday night; restaurants and movie theater owners closed up shop as they themselves went home to watch. Sales of the sponsor's products soared; nary a tube of Revlon's "snow peach" lipstick could be found as store shelves were emptied by eager viewers.

The format of the quiz was uncomplicated. Based on an old radio show called "Take It or Leave It," whose grand prize was $64, the game called for contestants to answer increasingly difficult questions while their winnings continued doubling (after $512, the amounts were rounded off to the nearest thousand); a streak of 11 correct questions brought the grand prize of $64,000. Along the way, plateaus were reached; once a contestant passed the $8,000 mark, a losing answer would automatically bring a consolation prize of a Cadillac car. (Multiply these amounts by five, and you'll get some idea of just how huge these prizes in mid-1950s, pre-inflation dollars would be today.)

Contestants were Everyman and Everywoman types, based on the sponsor's belief that the audience would readily empathize with a shoe salesman who knew grand opera, a grandmother who knew all about baseball, or a U.S. Marine who could correctly name all the dishes on the menu at the dinner King George VI served to the President of France in 1939. (After correctly identifying the dishes as consommé, quenelles, filet de truite saumonée, petits pois à la françaises, sauce maltaise, and corbeille, accompanied by Chateau d'Yquem and Madeira Sercial, Richard S. McCutchen became the first person to win the grand prize.)

Among the contestants were a few famous names. Child star Patty Duke appeared as an expert on music; Jack Benny went on as an authority on the violin, although he quit after the first question, opting to keep the $64. And Randolph Churchill, son of Prime Minister Winston Churchill, blew it after just two questions, failing his English history question about the derivation of the word "boycott."

But the most famous alumna of this quiz show was a struggling 27-year-old Ph.D., psychologist Joyce Brothers. After deciding she and her husband could use the money, they did a scientific analysis of the show, determining what specialty might be acceptable to the show's producers. "It finally got down to a choice between prizefighting and plumbing. Prizefighting seemed more interesting," declared Dr. Brothers in a *TV Guide* interview. She studied non-stop for three months, won a spot on the show, and became the second person to take home the grand prize.

What she didn't know was that she was chosen by the producers as someone they were sure would *lose*. "I didn't know there was anything wrong with the program; then I found out later...the producers at the time were worried about people winning too much and were looking around for a big loser. They picked me for the patsy, and far from helping me, they ignored me entirely. From the $16,000 question—'Who was the referee in the long-count fight between Dempsey

CREDITS

CREATOR: Louis G. Cowan.
EXECUTIVE PRODUCER: Steve Carlin.
PRODUCERS: Joe Cates, Mert Koplin. DIRECTORS: Joe Cates, Curt Steen. HOST: Hal March.

EMMYS

Best Audience Participation Series (1955).

Hal March welcomes Mabel Morris to the set of "The $64,000 Question."

and Tunney?' [Dave Barry]—the questions were purposely designed to get me off."

Quiz/game shows soon spread faster than poison ivy, and by 1956 the networks were weighted down by the likes of "High Finance," "Giant Step," "Can Do," "The Big Surprise," "The $64,000 Challenge," and "Twenty-One." It was this last one that would usher in the genre's downfall.

Accusations of game show double-dealings began to circulate in 1957, when a player on "Dotto" claimed his opponent had a notebook full of answers given to her by the producers. When they tried to buy him off, he instead took his story to the New York State Attorney General's office.

Then later that same year, Herbert Stemple, a contestant on "Twenty-One," cried foul, claiming he was told to take a dive so that the more charismatic Charles Van Doren could surface a winner. The show's producers, Barry and Enright, tried to sue Stempel for libel, but the whistle was now being blown with increasing frequency.

The New York City District Attorney convened a grand jury in August 1958. Although many witnesses perjured themselves with lies and cover-ups, the truth eventually emerged: quiz shows had been rigged all along. Some, like Dr. Brothers (she would go on to fame as a TV celebrity and syndicated columnist), were on the up-and-up, but others had been coached and/or supplied the answers. Patty Duke broke down in tears, telling the jury how the whole thing had been prearranged by her agent.

The sponsors said it was all in the name of drama and entertainment, and anyway, there were no laws prohibiting the fixing of quizzes. But the networks had had enough. Just as quickly as the big-money quiz shows had appeared, they vanished. "The $64,000 Question" aired its last show to a disillusioned, drastically diminished audience on November 2, 1958. It would be some time before game shows reemerged on network television, closely scrutinized by the network's broadcast standards departments. And never again would they become weekly fare in prime time.

THE MILLIONAIRE

NUMBER 9, 1955–56

Marvin Miller.

In 1955 Americans seemed fascinated with the idea of vicariously getting rich quick. If people dreamed of what it would be like to win $64,000, their fantasy lives went into overdrive when contemplating what they would do with the really big bucks being handed out on a fictional television program called "The Millionaire."

Partially inspired by the 1932 Paramount film *If I Had a Million*, "The Millionaire" was an anthology series of different weekly dramas with three continuing cast members.

John Beresford Tipton (the name was a composite of producer Don Fedderson's home town, his wife's home town, and his lawyer's first name) was the unseen multi*billion*aire whose doctors had ordered him to take up a hobby for relaxation. He decided on chess—human chess—and each week he would be seen (or rather, his hands or back would be visible) at his desk in his mansion, Silverstone, on his 60,000-acre estate. There he would manipulate chess pieces around a board while telling his executive secretary about the person whom he had selected to be the next recipient of his gift of one million dollars. And since he was playing God, he set the rules for his little game: the recipient had to agree to keep mum on the source and size of the bequest (the exception was that he or she could share the secret with a significant other). Billionaire Tipton then sat back and watched his little drama unfold.

The other two continuing cast members were Tipton's banker, played by Roy Gordon, who supplied the cashier's checks in the rags-to-riches turnovers, and Marvin Miller as Tipton's faithful retainer, Michael Anthony, who was assigned the task of presenting the actual check to the recipient. There was also one uncredited regular "cast member"—producer Don Fedderson's wife, Tito, who did a walk-on in virtually every installment.

The format provided for a broad spectrum of weekly dramas. Bundles were handed out with equal panache to housewives, criminals, widows, and burlesque queens. How the nouveaux riches reacted to or were affected by their windfalls then became the basis for the evening's episode. (What was surprising was how the details of the inheritance could remain a secret. Sudden wild spending ought to have at least raised a

few eyebrows, and in today's world might arouse suspicions of illicit endeavors.)

The show was a huge success with the '50s audience. Tipton apparently had a bottomless pocketbook and handed out those seven-figure checks for five seasons.

Marvin Miller, the actor who played the discreet personal secretary who delivered the big check weekly to Tipton's latest heir, had been a well-known actor in films of the 1940s and '50s. His specialty was portraying a wide range of nationalities, including Asians. Before he appeared on "The Millionaire," he was a regular on the children's TV series "Space Patrol," where he showed up weekly in various disguises. During the five and a half years he spent as gofer to his fictional millionaire boss, Miller received numerous requests for checks for a million dollars. He replied by sending each person a "check" for "a million dollars' worth of good luck." Following his seemingly minor part on "The Millionaire," Miller found himself typecast, with few new roles coming his way. He eventually turned to voiceover work and could be heard in a number of Saturday morning cartoons like "The Famous Adventures of Mr. Magoo" and "Fantastic Voyage." He was also the narrator for the original "FBI" tele-series. Miller died in 1985.

Although we never learned what actor actually sat in the chair of John Beresford Tipton, the show's producers revealed who spoke the part: the deep voice was that of a well-known Hollywood announcer, Paul Frees.

The series ran on CBS from January 1955 until September 1960, then went into daytime reruns until 1963. It was also syndicated under the title "If You Had a Million."

In 1978 CBS revived "The Millionaire" in a "Tuesday Night Movie"—actually a pilot for a potential new series. The two-hour film featured Robert Quarry as Michael Anthony, who doled out the checks in three separate plots. Guest stars included Martin Balsam, Eddie Albert, John Ireland, Ralph Bellamy, Jane Wyatt, and William Demarest.

The revised series never made it to the CBS lineup, perhaps because the very similar "Fantasy Island" was already such a huge success on ABC. As *Variety* put it, " 'The Millionaire' seems to have been to the bank one time too many."

CREDITS

PRODUCER: Don Fedderson.
DIRECTORS: various. WRITERS: various. CAST: *Michael Anthony* (Marvin Miller), *The Banker* (Ray Gordon), *John Beresford Tipton* (the voice of Paul Frees). GUEST STARS: Carolyn Jones, Martin Milner, Celia Lovsky, others.

I'VE GOT A SECRET

One of the most long-lived game shows of all time, "I've Got a Secret" had its own skeleton in the closet: it was cancelled in its initial run—in 1952—after only 13 weeks.

The original format had host Garry Moore decked out as a judge in a courtroom setting, with the guest in the defendant's dock and panelists approaching the bench like lawyers. By the second week, CBS had wisely burned the sets and abandoned the format in favor of the more familiar panel-show set. It still didn't click with viewers, but after the show's initial cancellation, CBS decided to bring it back for another round. It survived 15 years plus a couple of later revivals, one of TV's most successful game shows ever.

Mark Goodson and Bill Todman were pioneers in the TV game show industry. They knew a good thing when they saw it, and when Allan Sherman and Howard Merrill came to them with their idea for "I've Got a Secret," the producers grabbed it, paying each creator off with a flat $100. Sherman later signed on as the show's associate producer, but he became better known in the 1960s for his hit record albums, including *My Son, the Folk Singer* ("Hello Mudduh, Hello Fadduh...").

The show's format was based on an old parlor game called "Secret, Secret, Who's Got the Secret?" Four celebrity guest panelists would try to guess secrets of various contestants by cross-examining them. If the guests stumped the panel, they carted away an incredible $80 for their efforts. Obviously, this wasn't "The $64,000 Question." The games were played strictly for laughs and entertainment, with such secrets as "My husband snores," "I am Garry Moore's wife," or "Henry Ford once cranked my car." One guest's secret was that he collected string, and he proudly exhibited seven miles of it. "Is this your hobby?" asked Moore. "Oh no, sir," the string collector

replied. "This is my *secret*. My hobby is collecting lead pencils."

Back in 1954 the producers learned that England's Roger Bannister had cracked the four-minute mile. They flew him across the Atlantic to be a guest and reveal this "secret," but upon arriving and learning the show had commercial sponsors, he quickly turned around and headed back home. It seemed that Bannister would lose his "amateur" standing with the Amateur Athletic Union if he appeared on sponsored shows. The 2,000-mile trip back to England established another record for Bannister: the longest distance ever travelled to avoid appearing on a panel show.

Based on incidents like these, the show's producers soon discovered that it was better entertainment to create secrets for celebrity guests than to depend on the general public as possible sources, and "I've Got a Secret" began to take on the appearance of a contrived stunt show. In 1959 comic Johnny Carson was invited by the show's producer to shoot an apple off Garry Moore's head as his "secret." During rehearsal, working with a wooden dummy, Carson's aim was somewhat short of William Tell's. Moore, needless to say, wasn't wild about the idea and insisted on being protected by an inch-thick transparent shield. The only mishap during the actual taping of the show was the dripping of the apple juice into his left eye after Carson successfully hit his target.

Moore wasn't always so lucky. The program's writers went to great lengths to set him up for all sorts of "secrets." On one show he wrestled an alligator; on another a nine-year-old girl hit a golf ball off his nose. One time the blindfolded panelists were to guess what guest Don McNeill was doing: bouncing eggs on a rubber mat without breaking them, as Moore caught each one and slipped it into his pocket. After the gag was over, Moore rose to bid farewell to his guest, and panelist

CREDITS

TOP 10 PEAK: No. 5, 1957–58.
CREATORS: Allan Sherman, Howard Merrill. PRODUCERS: Mark Goodson, Bill Todman, Chester Feldman, others. DIRECTORS: various. WRITERS: various. HOSTS: Garry Moore, Steve Allen, Bill Cullen. PANELISTS: Bill Cullen, Kitty Carlisle, Henry Morgan, Faye Emerson, Jayne Meadows, Betsy Palmer, Bess Myerson, Elaine Joyce, Richard Dawson, others.

Garry Moore (left), with guest Curtis Hamill.

Henry Morgan crept up behind Moore and gave his pocket a good squeeze.

Other set-up "secrets" included Ernest Borgnine posing as a cab driver in a rented taxi and chauffeuring panelist Jayne Meadows to work; Jackie Cooper telephoning Ms. Meadows for a date; and actor Ronald Reagan making nine different entrances onto the show's set. Paul Newman disguised himself and headed out to the ballpark so he could sell hot dogs to panelist Henry Morgan and then make such a "secret" claim on the show that evening. Morgan didn't recognize Newman, but many fans at the ballpark did. By the time he was able to make his pitch to the unsuspecting Henry Morgan, Paul Newman had sold $25 worth of franks.

Although there were many combinations of stars and guests on the panel, by 1958 the regulars included Henry Morgan, Betsy Palmer, Jayne Meadows, and Bill Cullen. Faye Emerson and Bess Meyerson also took turns as frequent panelists.

Garry Moore hosted the program from 1952 until 1964; from 1964 to 1967 Steve Allen assumed the hosting chores, and he also did a stint as host of the 1972 syndicated version. In 1976 Bill Cullen, a former panelist, took up the hosting reins with a panel featuring Henry Morgan, Elaine Joyce, Phyllis George, Pat Collins, and Richard Dawson.

In 1992 the Carsey-Werner Company, which had just resurrected "You Bet Your Life" with Bill Cosby, announced plans to produce and distribute a new incarnation of "I've Got a Secret." No host had yet been set, and it was slated for a fall 1993 premiere in syndication. But its future seemed doubtful when "You Bet Your Life" got the axe in the spring of 1993, since the two series were meant to be "piggybacked" in syndication.

GENERAL ELECTRIC THEATER

NUMBER 3, 1956–57

What most people remember about "General Electric Theater" (which had its initial run on CBS from 1953 till 1962) is not the fine made-for-television plays it presented, or its honor roll of guests, including many Academy Award winners who starred in the productions. No, what the program is best remembered for is its host. Yet the man selected to introduce "General Electric Theater" almost didn't get the job because back in the 1940s he had bitten the hand of television, the hand that now wanted to feed him.

In 1954 "G.E. Theater" signed Ronald Reagan to take on the hosting and occasional guest-starring chores for the series. The move shocked his friends. "I remember Ronnie telling all of us not to join TV because it was the enemy of the movies," recalled Ann Sheridan. "Next thing, he was on 'G.E. Theater,' with his contact lenses, reading the commercials."

The man who would become the 40th president of the United States had a change of heart, embraced television, and went to work touting lightbulbs. Between Sunday night television appearances, Reagan toured the country as a P.R. representative for G.E., visiting the company's 135 plants and addressing over 250,000 workers. His talks hit on the blessings of free enterprise and the evils of big government. It was a warm-up act for what would later be his greatest performance of all.

"General Electric Theater" was the last of the great theatrical anthology series to make the top 10. And it did it the easy way—with top talent starring in top productions written by top dramatists. Many actors as reluctant as Reagan to appear on the "boob tube" eagerly changed their tune for a chance to appear in this prestigious series.

Bette Davis, for example, made her television debut on March 10, 1957, in a story called "With Malice toward One." It was a polished yarn about a spinster who was an accountant by day and a romance novelist by night. One of her stories ended with a fictional writer shooting a fictional publisher. That same book was attacked by a handsome publisher at a summer workshop, who said that the climax was unrealistic. In response, Davis's romance-writer character bought a gun and threatened the publisher with murder, then acknowledged the hoax as a means of making her point—that the story was plenty realistic. Bette Davis

was the 18th Academy Award winner to appear on the series, and she received rave reviews for her performance.

In December 1957 another well-known movie actor made his TV dramatic debut: Fred Astaire appeared in a comedy piece called "Imp on a Cobweb Leash." It was a rarity for Astaire since the renowned hoofer did no dancing in the story; instead, he demonstrated his flair for comedy. Both audience and producers were delighted with the results and invited Astaire back for more. In "Man on a Bicycle" he played a luxury-loving opportunist who attempted to help a young French childcare worker.

Other stories included "The Girl with the Flaxen Hair," starring Ray Bolger, the story of a lovelorn accounting clerk attracted to a department store saleslady; Tony Curtis in "The Stone," in which Curtis played the biblical David in his run-in with the giant Goliath; "Robbie and His Mary," a dramatization of the romance between Scottish poet Robert Burns and Mary Campbell; and "New Girl in His Life," starring John Forsythe and Noreen Corcoran. Forsythe and Corcoran teamed up for their own series ("Bachelor Father") shortly after this pilot was aired as an episode of "General Electric Theatre" on May 26, 1957.

One of the more controversial episodes starred black entertainer Sammy Davis, Jr., in a story called "Auf Wiedersehen." At the time it was filmed—in 1957—Sammy was having a much-publicized relationship with a white star, Kim Novak. Although the relationship later ended, G.E. was concerned about the effect Davis's appearance might have in the South (which represented 63 percent of its market). They decided to shelve Sammy Davis's episode. Only after his agent threatened to expose G.E.'s bigotry did they (reluctantly) allow the episode to air. It proved to be one of the best-received of the entire series.

"General Electric Theater" continued its fine dramatic presentations until 1962. It returned to the air in 1973, when General Electric produced a series of occasional dramatic "specials" under the title "G.E. Theater," also airing on CBS. The teleplays, ranging in length from one hour to 90 minutes, included "I Heard the Owl Call My Name" and "Tell Me Where It Hurts."

CREDITS

PRODUCERS: Gil Ralston, Arthur Ripley, Mort Abrahams, William Frye, others. DIRECTORS: Sheldon Leonard, Boris Sagal, others. WRITERS: various. HOST: Ronald Reagan (1954–62). GUEST STARS: Broderick Crawford, Bette Davis, Charles Laughton, Fred Astaire, Sammy Davis, Jr., Lou Costello, Jonathan Harris, Raymond Massey, Robert Loggia, Steve Allen, Jayne Meadows, Lauren Chapin, Ronald Reagan, Nancy Davis, others.

EMMYS

Best Writing in Drama, Original Teleplay, a Single Program, Comedy or Drama—Fay Kanin, "Tell Me Where It Hurts" (1973–74).

Host Ronald Reagan, well before his Teleprompter days, reviews a script with Joan Crawford.

ALFRED HITCHCOCK PRESENTS

NUMBER 6, 1956–57

Alfred Hitchcock had been thrilling and chilling film audiences for 28 years when Lew Wasserman, head of MCA-Revue TV (later Universal), approached the portly British director with an offer to do a weekly television series. Hitchcock politely declined. He was doing quite nicely, thank you, producing films.

But Wasserman was unrelenting. He knew it was logical for "Hitch" to move from cameo appearances in his own films to the hosting of TV suspense melodramas like those that had appeared frequently on "Kraft Television Theatre," "Philco TV Playhouse, "Ford Theatre," and other anthology series. Hitch could use his favorite stars, Wasserman said; he could oversee the selection of scripts and even direct a few each season; and best of all, he could take a check to the bank each week for $129,000 (less taxes). The suspense was over; Hitchcock signed.

Each week, Hitchcock provided the prologue and epilogue to the story. A line-drawn silhouette of his caricature was soon filled by the penquinesque bulk of the series host, synchronized to the sound of Gounod's "Funeral March of a Marionette." (Hitchcock selected the now-familiar theme, which he recalled hearing as background music for the F.W. Murnau 1927 silent film, *Sunrise*.) "Good e-e-vening," Hitchcock intoned with a voice that seemed to come from a mouth crammed with mashed potatoes. Then, with a deadpan delivery, he set up the story for the night. He might be standing next to a torture rack: "This is called a rack. It is a type of medieval *chaise longue*. The victim lies down and his limbs are fastened to these rollers at each end. The body is then stretched to and past the breaking point. They were quite droll in those days." Clearly, his tongue was planted somewhere in his cheek, along with those potatoes.

He would then launch into "a word from our sponsor," Bristol-Myers, who was not immune to the wit of the "Master of the Macabre." At first the sponsor was flabbergasted at his lack of proper respect. But before long they began to appreciate the light-hearted knocks. "My guess is that the sponsor enjoys my lack of obsequiousness, but in the beginning they had difficulty in getting used to my approach and they took umbrage at my less than worshipful remarks," Hitchcock stated. "However, the moment they became aware of the commercial effects of my belittling—they took a look at their sales charts—they stopped questioning the propriety of my cracks."

The show originally ran in a 30-minute format on CBS from 1955 to 1960. For the next two years it appeared on NBC (1960–62). It then expanded to "The Alfred Hitchcock Hour" and returned to CBS from 1963 to 1964, moving back to NBC from October 1964 to its conclusion in the fall of 1965.

Over the 10 years of the series' first run (it later was in syndication on cable television), there were dozens of memorable episodes, each with an O. Henrian irony awaiting the entranced audience at show's end. The premiere episode, "Revenge," was a typical Hitchcock-directed effort. It starred Vera Miles as a woman recently released from an insane asylum. One afternoon her husband returns from work, and she claims she's been attacked by a stranger. Later, on a car trip, she points to a man and cries, "That's him! That's the one who did it!" Her outraged husband promptly kills him. A short time later, as they drive along, she points to yet another man, and with the same conviction, shouts, "There he is! That's the man!" Whoops.

"Breakdown," which first aired on November 13, 1955, was directed by Hitchcock and

CREDITS

EXECUTIVE PRODUCER: Alfred Hitchcock. PRODUCER: Joan Harrison. DIRECTORS: Alfred Hitchcock, others. WRITERS: Francis Cockrell, Stirling Silliphant, Roald Dahl, others. HOST: Alfred Hitchcock. GUEST STARS: Vera Miles, Joseph Cotten, Jessica Tandy, William Shatner, Werner Klemperer, Jack Albertson, George Peppard, Audrey Meadows, Claude Rains, Bill Mumy, John Forsythe, others.

EMMYS

Best Teleplay Writing (Half Hour or Less)—James P. Cavanagh, "Fog Closes In" (1956); Best Direction (Half Hour or Less)—Robert Stevens, "The Glass Eye" (1957).

starred Joseph Cotten as a man who chastises his employee for crying on the job. Later, Cotten's character is about to be pronounced dead. He's alive, the audience knows he's alive, but he's totally paralyzed—only his tear ducts are functioning. ("Look!" cries the doctor. "Those are tears! He's alive!")

Murder was a staple of the Hitchcock bag of tricks, and one of the best-remembered episodes is "Lamb to the Slaughter," starring Barbara Bel Geddes, who offs her policeman-husband with a frozen leg of lamb, then serves it up to the investigation team, who unwittingly and happily munch away on the murder weapon. By clueing in the audience, Hitchcock effectively made us all accomplices, something with which the television censors were not pleased. In the epilogue, Hitchcock usually had to inform the audience that the wrongdoer eventually got caught; in this case, he said that the murderer tried the same trick on her next husband, but she had forgotten to pay the electric bill and was apprehended in the act since the lamb had thawed and was too soft to be of any "good."

An award-winning episode called "The Glass Eye" starred Jessica Tandy and William Shatner. The story involved a lonely spinster who falls for a ventriloquist, only to eventually learn that she's hopelessly in love with the life-sized dummy. (The title came from the glass eye she accidentally lifted when the dummy fell apart in her hands.) The director, Robert Stevens, won an Emmy for his efforts.

Alfred Hitchcock died in April of 1980, but in 1985 he was seemingly resurrected to host a new version of "Alfred Hitchcock Presents." Thanks to the process of computer colorization, clips of his original black and white appearances were color-enhanced and edited into the new series, which consisted of color remakes of some of the original scripts, plus all-new episodes. No doubt about it—Hitch would have been pleased to have been the first dead man to host a television series.

Barbara Bel Geddes, from the "Lamb to the Slaughter" episode of "Alfred Hitchcock Presents."

GUNSMOKE

NUMBER 7, 1956–57

From left: Milburn Stone, Amanda Blake, James Arness, and Dennis Weaver.

In 1952 programming executives at CBS radio found themselves with a gap in their nighttime schedule. Several months before, two young writers named Norman Macdonnell and John Meston had proposed a series called "Jeff Spain." It would be an "adult" western, with realistically behaving, *human* characters. They made up a list of don'ts: No one would be allowed to say "sidewinding varmint"; no one would carry two guns slung low on the hip; no one would have a favorite horse, much less one that did tricks. Unfortunately, no one at CBS thought much of the idea, until there was a sudden opening in the schedule. "Jeff Spain," now renamed "Gunsmoke," was rushed into production, with mellow-voiced William Conrad reading the role of the show's hero, Marshal Matt Dillon.

So successful was the radio oater that two years later CBS began laying plans to bring "Gunsmoke" to television. They enlisted Macdonnell and Meston to help launch this new series and began casting about for someone to replace Conrad, who was deemed too bulky, short, and balding to be a television hero. (Conrad, of course, went on to star in his own series, "Cannon" and

"Jake and the Fat Man," proving that indeed he was hero material.) John Wayne was on everyone's A list, but the "Duke" declined. He did, however, have a young actor under contract whom he felt would be perfect for the role—a six-foot-seven-inch man by the name of James Arness. Until that time, Arness's only claim to fame had been his role as a towering monster uncovered from the arctic ice in *The Thing* (1951) and an appearance as a giant carrot in the B-movie *Them* (1954). Despite those iffy credits, Jim Arness was reluctant to sign for the series, afraid that a role in a TV western would ruin his budding career. But Duke finally persuaded him to step into the boots of the marshal of Dodge City, and he even introduced the series' first 30 minute episode on September 10, 1955.

"Gunsmoke" shot to the top of the rating charts, and within the first two years it reached the number one spot, where it stayed for many years. It would prove to be television's most successful drama of all time, with a continuous first run of nearly 20 years.

One of the reasons for the show's success was the fact that it was character-oriented, rather than a shoot-'em-up. The central figures in the "morality plays" produced each week were real people who happened to reside in a western frontier town of the 1880s. Matt Dillon (Arness) was the marshal, a towering man (one director had to stand him in a hole in order to get his head in the picture) who was stern yet vulnerable, tough yet tender.

A loner and a bachelor, Dillon's "family" consisted of his friends and associates in Dodge City. Miss Kitty was played by throaty Amanda Blake. In the radio series it had been clearly established that she was a working girl, the town prostitute. But televison of the '50s, being somewhat more subtle, made her the Long Branch saloon keeper. If she was also a madam, it was kept under wraps, and there was never so much as a kiss between Miss Kitty and her implied main squeeze, Matt Dillon. "When I first started," said Amanda Blake in *TV Guide*, "a reporter asked me what Kitty was, anyway? I said, 'Why, she's a tramp.' I thought it was common knowledge. But CBS screamed. I almost lost my job." Miss Kitty never spoke of her love for Dillon, generally expressing her fondness for him with her oft-repeated catchphrase, "Be careful, Matt." The only physical contact between the two occurred once when Miss Kitty fainted and Matt picked her up. Arness commented on the reason for the platonic relationship: "People like Westerns because they represent a time of freedom. A cowboy wasn't tied down to one place or to one woman...[They] certainly don't want to see a U.S. Marshal come home and help his wife with the dishes."

Dennis Weaver played the role of Chester Goode, Matt Dillon's obsequious, hobbling deputy who spoke with a twang and always called him "Muster Dellon." Weaver stayed with the series until 1964, when he moved on to shows of his own, including "Gentle Ben" and "McCloud." He was replaced by Ken Curtis, who became Matt's new sidekick, Festus Haggen, and the character fulfilled a similar function in the "Gunsmoke" family, providing comic relief.

Rounding out the main cast was Milburn Stone as Dr. Galen "Doc" Adams, the town's crusty physician whose main source of income seemed to be from Matt Dillon— Doc dug enough bullets out of Dillon's "flesh wounds" to open his own lead mine.

In 1961 "Gunsmoke" expanded from 30 minutes to a full hour format. Its ratings continued to be strong, but by 1967 they had begun to sag. In February of that year, the network announced the cancellation of "Gunsmoke." But there was a public outcry, and the show was saved through the personal intervention of board chairman William S. Paley. The show was given a new night—Mondays, where it again rose in the Nielsens. But by 1975, although it was still among the top 30, CBS decided the audience was too old demographically. After 20 years of 156 halfhour and 356 one-hour segments, the network finally cancelled the longest running drama in the history of television.

In 1987 "Gunsmoke" rose from Boot Hill in a CBS movie special, "Gunsmoke: Return to Dodge." Series producer John Mantley and frequent director Vincent McEveety returned, along with regulars Jim Arness and Amanda Blake (Weaver was not available and Milburn Stone had died back in 1980). It was successful enough to warrant another return to the Old West in 1990, with Arness again strapping on the guns for "Gunsmoke: The Last Apache." No other original cast members appeared; sadly, Amanda Blake had succumbed to AIDS.

CREDITS

TOP 10 PEAK: No. 1, 1957–58. CREATORS: Norman Macdonnell, John Meston. PRODUCERS: Norman Macdonnell, John Mantley, others. DIRECTORS: Vincent McEveety, others. WRITERS: various. CAST: *Marshal Matt Dillon* (James Arness), *Dr. Galen "Doc" Adams* (Milburn Stone), *Miss Kitty Russell* (Amanda Blake), *Chester Goode* (Dennis Weaver), *Festus Haggen* (Ken Curtis), *Quint Asper* (Burt Reynolds). GUEST STARS: Darryl Hickman, John Carradine, Sherry Jackson, Kurt Russell, Diane Ladd, Claude Akins, Morgan Woodward, Robert Lansing, Ricardo Montalban, Jack Elam, Slim Pickens, Earl Holliman, Ken Olandt, Michael Learned.

EMMYS

Best Dramatic Series with Continuing Characters (1957); Best Supporting Actor, Continuing Character, in a Dramatic Series—Dennis Weaver (1958–59); Outstanding Performance by an Actor in a Supporting Role in a Drama—Milburn Stone (1967–68).

THE PERRY COMO SHOW

NUMBER 9, 1956–57

Perry Como.

Dream along with me, I'm on my way to a star!
—PERRY COMO, IN OPENING SONG

An ex-barber from Canonsburg, Pennsylvania, Perry Como had been singing popular hit songs for years on his own radio show when NBC decided to give him a television version of the program. In 1948 Como began a thrice-weekly, 15-minute show called "The Chesterfield Supper Club," which became "The Perry Como Show" in 1950, moving over to CBS. Then in 1955 NBC wooed the dreamy-voiced Como back into the fold, with the intention of giving CBS and its new "The Honeymooners" program a run for their money. The ploy worked, and Perry Como went on to become the season's "newest" sensation.

His singing style was his trademark: casual, relaxed, comfortable as an old sock. He was so laid back, someone once coined the expression "*Como*-tose" to describe him. *Time* magazine said he was so relaxed "that he sometimes gives the impression of being made of sponge rubber with a core of Seconal."

Perched atop a stool, dressed in an old golf sweater, the man was anything but a dynamo, and yet people adored him. They called him "Mr. Nice Guy," and he was. "Perry is heaven, just heaven," frequent guest star Patrice Munsel enthused in *Newsweek*. "He is completely and totally secure. The scenery can fall down and the guest can blow all his lines, but Perry is smart enough to let the audience in on the fluffing. He knows that the worst thing is to have an audience embarrassed for you." Rosemary Clooney, who had been given her first real break by Como in the '40s, agreed. "He's always the same: gentle, sweet, ready to help...I don't think Perry ever had a guest who didn't want to come back."

His show was an instant hit. Nobody could quite explain why. "Radio and TV seem to be my medium," the equally puzzled star admitted. "If you get lucky and do what people like, then you last. It's like shooting craps with the dice loaded. I guess we've proven that we've got the right formula." Dinah Shore pointed out, "What makes Perry's show a lasting success and why he can go as long as he wants to is his great outgoing warmth. He also seems to have some great inner strength. He's a strong, quiet man like Gary Cooper or John Wayne."

He had a smooth baritone voice to match his easygoing disposition. Fans, entranced by what they saw and heard on the tube, wanted more of Como, and gobbled up his records. When he introduced "Round and Round" on his show, audiences loved it, a recording was released, and the week of April 6, 1957, it soared to the top of the *Billboard* charts. In 1958 "Catch a Falling Star," another song that premiered on his program, became the 13th of his hits to go over the million mark.

Fans began flooding the network with so many letters with requests for songs that the show's writers worked in a bit around his mailbag: "Letters! We get letters! We get stacks and stacks of letters! 'Dear Perry, would you be so kind, to fill a request and sing the song I like best?'"

Como was assisted in his weekly series by a core group of talented singers and dancers, and guest stars were pressed into service in the comedy sketches written by veteran TV writer ("The Milton Berle Show") Goodman Ace. "The whole show is written, but it doesn't sound as though it is," Ace admitted. "It's much more difficult to write this easy kind of comedy. We never go in for the great big joke—the big yuk. Perry knows that his audience will shy away from anything that isn't just plain nice and friendly."

Although Como never changed his singing style to the more contemporary rock and roll, he was always open to the inevitable changes in musical tastes. In fact, many early rock and roll performers appeared as his guests on the program, among them such stars as the Everly Brothers, Fats Domino, Paul Anka, Fabian, Frankie Avalon, and Bobby Rydell.

In 1961 "The Perry Como Show" became "Perry Como's Kraft Music Hall," but it was virtually the same show, with most of the supporting regulars continuing on with him. New additions included Kaye Ballard and Don Adams, who would eventually get shows of their own, and Paul Lynde, who later became the popular center square on the long-running game show "The Hollywood Squares."

After 1963 Perry cut back his schedule to only a few specials per year, including Christmas shows, which continued into the 1980s.

CREDITS

PRODUCERS: Lee Cooley, Robert S. Finkel, others. DIRECTORS: Gray Lockwood, others. WRITERS: Goodman Ace, Jay Burton, Mort Green, George Foster, others. REGULARS: Perry Como, The Ray Charles Singers (*not* the famous rhythm and blues singer/pianist), The Peter Gennaro Dancers, Frank Gallop, Ed Herlihy, The Mitchell Ayres Orchestra, Kaye Ballard, Don Adams, others. GUEST STARS: Rosemary Clooney, Frankie Laine, Irene Dunne, Sal Mineo, Patience and Prudence, Carol Channing, Isaac Stern, Ethel Merman, Jack Carter, The Mills Brothers, Ginger Rogers, Robert Preston, Maureen O'Hara, Shelly Berman, Arnold Palmer, Gary Player, Jack Nicklaus, others.

EMMYS

Best Male Singer (1955); Best MC or Program Host, Male or Female (1955); Best Male Personality, Continuing Performance (1956); Best Performance by an Actor, Continuing Character, in a Musical or Variety Series (1958).

THE DANNY THOMAS SHOW

NUMBER 2, 1957–58

Entertainer Danny Thomas had built his career on the nightclub circuit and, briefly, in films. Then he set his sights on television and spent two years, from 1950 to 1952, as rotating host of NBC's "All Star Revue." But the work wasn't fulfilling and Thomas denounced the medium as a "workplace for idiots." He returned to the road and nightclub work, but within the year he found himself dining on sour grapes, tired of being away from home so much.

In 1953 he began developing a television project for ABC. He was working closely with writer Mel Shavelson, pleading for him to devise something that would allow him to stay in Los Angeles, at home with his family. "I was away on the road so much that they hardly knew me," he wrote in his 1991 autobiography. "They called me 'Uncle Daddy.' I didn't know my girls' dress sizes, and I wanted my son to know me as something more than a telephone pal." That was it! Shavelson leaped to his feet. The concept for their new show had just been born.

Thomas's wife, Rose Marie, had no trouble coming up with the title: "Make Room for Daddy." Thomas explained that while he was on the road, his daughters slept in the couple's bedroom, filling his drawers with their clothing. Whenever "Daddy" returned to town, the children had to shift bedrooms to "make room for daddy."

In the show's format, as with so many shows in the 1950s, Danny Thomas played a character that was loosely based upon himself. His alter ego was named Danny Williams (after his real-life brother William), and he was, not surprisingly, a nightclub entertainer who struggled to maintain a normal family life while engaged in his showbiz career. "I had finally found a way to stay home with my family," Thomas wrote, "by doing a show about me and my family." Jean Hagen was cast as Danny's wife, Margaret (Thomas's own daughter's name—later nicknamed Marlo), and the kids were 11-year-old Sherry Jackson as Terry (the name of another of Thomas's real-life daughters) and seven-year-old Rusty Hamer as Rusty. (Imaginative character names were not Thomas's strong suit.)

At the end of the third season, Jean Hagen announced she'd had it and was leaving the show. Despite two Emmy nominations, she was tired of playing fourth fiddle to Danny and the kids. What to do? For the first time ever, a leading lady was killed off.

"Mommy's gone to heaven," little Terry and Rusty were told as the show went into its fourth season. During that year, its final one on ABC, Marjorie Lord was introduced, first as Rusty's nurse when he contracted measles, then as Danny's fiancée. But there would be no wedding at season's finale—Ms. Lord herself was engaged to be married, and actors being such a superstitious lot, she refused to be married twice in the same year, claiming it was bad luck.

"Make Room for Daddy"—at the end of the 1956–57 season the show was redubbed "The Danny Thomas Show"—ran on ABC for four seasons, and although nostalgically remembered today, it was a resounding flop in the ratings, ranking *11th from the bottom* of 118 shows.

At the beginning of the 1957 season, the rechristened show was set for a move from ABC to CBS. However, CBS board chairman Bill Paley began to get cold feet and tried to find a way out of airing this "turkey." But the sponsors were more powerful in those days, and they wanted this series slated for the slot in which they had purchased time—Monday nights at 9:00. Fortunately for CBS, Paley's hands were tied.

In the premiere episode, in October 1957, Danny Williams was married to his new bride, who arrived complete with adorable five-year-old stepdaughter Linda, played by the precocious Angela Cartwright.

CREDITS

CREATORS: Danny Thomas, Mel Shavelson, Lou Edelman. PRODUCERS: Danny Thomas, Lou Edelman, Sheldon Leonard, Charles Stewart, Jack Elinson. DIRECTORS: Bill Asher, Sheldon Leonard, Danny Thomas. WRITERS: Mel Shavelson, Chuck Stewart, Jack Elinson, others. CAST: *Danny Williams* (Danny Thomas), *Margaret Williams* (Jean Hagen), *Kathy Williams* (Marjorie Lord), *Rusty Williams* (Rusty Hamer), *Terry Williams* (Sherry Jackson, Penney Parker), *Linda Williams* (Angela Cartwright), *Uncle Tonoose* (Hans Conried), *Gina* (Annette Funicello).

EMMYS

Best Actor Starring in a Regular Series—Danny Thomas (1954), Best Situation Comedy Series (1954), Best Direction in Comedy—Sheldon Leonard (1956, 1960–61).

Rusty Hamer and Sherry Jackson help the star celebrate the 100th episode of "The Danny Thomas Show."

Suddenly the show took off, an instant top 10 ratings hit. The series had found its audience, which would remain loyal throughout the duration of the show.

There would be many changes over the years. The children gradually outgrew their parts. Terry was shipped off to school, then returned, played by a different actress (Penney Parker); new regulars came and went. One of the most beloved was Danny's Lebanese Uncle Tonoose, played by Hans Conried. Throughout it all, Danny Thomas remained a stalwart anchor. But by 1964 he too was burned out and decided to call it quits.

There were a couple of reunion shows. A special, "Make More Room for Daddy," aired on NBC in 1967, in which Rusty, newly graduated from college, enlisted in the army and married the colonel's daughter. A 60-minute special, "Make Room for Granddaddy," ran on CBS on September 14, 1969, and reunited Thomas, Marjorie Lord, Angela Cartwright, Rusty Hamer, and Hans Conried, along with guests Don Rickles and Tim Conway. It became a pilot for a 1970–71 series of the

same title, which was picked up by ABC. The show introduced Danny's "grandson," played by Michael Hughes.

By this time Danny Thomas had become a television production executive, and during the next two decades his company turned out a number of hit shows, including "The Andy Griffith Show" (a spin-off of "The Danny Thomas Show"—see page 100), "The Dick Van Dyke Show" (see page 120), "Gomer Pyle, USMC" (see page 128), and "The Mod Squad." His daughter, Marlo, became famous in her own show, "That Girl," while son Tony Thomas became a well-known producer, whose company, Witt-Thomas Productions, was responsible for the hit shows "Golden Girls" (see page 304) and "Empty Nest" (see page 324).

In 1991 Danny Thomas made a rare guest appearance on his son Tony's production "Empty Nest," in which he played an aging physician. A week later the world was stunned and saddened to learn that the man who had once despised television, yet had brought so much to it, was dead of a sudden heart attack at the age of 79.

TALES OF WELLS FARGO
NUMBER 3, 1957–58

Dale Robertson.

For those people born after 1962, when this series went off the air, "Tales of Wells Fargo" was *not* a show about ATMs, CDs, safe deposit boxes, and home mortgage loans. Long before they became the local Wells Fargo Bank branch down on the corner (in most western states), the firm of Wells Fargo owned a stagecoach line in the 1860s. Their job was to see that gold and other valuables made it to their destinations in the Old West—sort of like today's armored trucks. (Over a century later Wells Fargo Bank remained proud of that early image and even used stagecoaches in their commercials.) Perhaps it was inevitable that these heroic folk would become the subject of a television western series during that genre's heyday.

When "Tales of Wells Fargo" premiered in March of 1957, a mid-season replacement for a long-forgotten NBC show called "Stanley,"* critics assailed it with a fury. Although "Tales" had a headstart on the onslaught of westerns (correctly) predicted for the new season, *Variety* wrote, "It's doubtful whether the jump on the others will prove of any value. This Revue (MCA) series is strictly formula, with none of the characterization or human values that have embellished the better class of TV westerns to date." In other words this was a lowbrow western, a throwback to the days of "The Lone Ranger" and "Hopalong Cassidy." That it could succeed against the current trend of "adult" westerns was inconceivable.

Nevertheless, that is exactly what "Wells Fargo" did. With only one continuing character, troubleshooter Jim Hardie, played by Dale Robertson, the series assured folks that the mail and gold got through safely week after week.

Robertson was a stroke of casting genius. Born in Harrah, Oklahoma, Dayle LyMoine Robertson earned a Silver Star during World War II and was the consummate athlete. He was voted Most Outstanding Athlete in college for his performance in football, basketball, and baseball. He dropped the "y" in his first name and entered films in 1949, where he soon became known for his macho image. He particularly excelled at horsemanship, racing quarter horses for a hobby.

Yet at first he turned down the chance to star in "Wells Fargo." "I thought there were going to be too many westerns on TV," he said. "I knew of about one hundred unsold test films for western series. Besides,

I had my sights on something else. I was up for 'Perry Mason.' Unfortunately, they didn't want to make Mason the kind of character I talk like." He wisely accepted, but not, however, before securing almost 50 percent ownership in the series. And as for the show's lack of sophistication, Robertson told *Time* magazine, "The adult westerns are dishonest. All that conversation is just a cheap, underhanded way of makin' up for the lack of a good story."

Apparently the viewers agreed with him. Although the show was surrounded by a field of adult oaters, "Tales of Wells Fargo" became the second-highest ranked western series of the 1957–58 season, right after "Gunsmoke." With all the angst being proffered by the others, gunfights and fistfights were somehow a welcome respite. The show's lack of pretension may have been the very reason for its success. Even *Variety*, a few years after its scathing initial review, was forced to admit that the series "didn't tax the grey matter too much and dished up enough fisticuffs and gunplay to keep the viewers of the purple sage content. Film work is clean and sharp and the half-hour seems to clip by at a steady trot...Robertson was given ample opportunity to show his mettle in a barroom brawl and a shoot-out with the tough guys. A 30-minute western doesn't need much more."

Maybe not, but during its sixth season, the producers made that oft-fatal error: they decided the series was due for a change. The show, now filmed in color, was given a new time slot, moving from the familiar Monday night at 8:30 to Saturday nights at 7:30 for a full hour so it could compete with "Perry Mason." Jim Hardie now had an extra half hour to fill, so they gave him a ranch, some permanent sidekicks (Jack Ging, William Demerest), and a number of lady friends (Virginia Christine, Mary Jane Saunders, Lory Patrick). Bad move. The public didn't cotton to their hero's settlin' down to this domestic life. In 1962 NBC did what all those gol dang varmints couldn't— they cancelled "Tales of Wells Fargo" and sent the stagecoach and its escort Jim Hardie riding off into the sunset.

> ### CREDITS
> PRODUCERS: Nat Holt, Earle Lyon. DIRECTORS: Earl Bellamy, others. WRITERS: various. CAST: *Jim Hardie* (Dale Robertson), *Beau McCloud* (Jack Ging), *Jeb Gaine* (William Demerest), *Ovie* (Virginia Christine), *Mary Gee* (Mary Jane Saunders), *Tina* (Lory Patrick).

---

*"Stanley," a live comedy from New York, starred Buddy Hackett, Paul Lynde, and Carol Burnett. It was on the air from September 1956 to March 1957.

HAVE GUN, WILL TRAVEL

NUMBER 4, 1957–58

...Paladin, Paladin, where do you roam?
—OPENING THEME SONG

He looked like the heavy. Dressed all in black (good guys, with the exception of Hopalong Cassidy, you'll recall, *never* wore black), packing a six-shooter in a holster that bore the image of a white chess knight, Paladin, a "paragon of chivalry" (as dictionary-defined), was no ordinary hero. This knight of the Old West handed out business cards: "Have Gun, Will Travel, Wire Paladin, San Francisco."

The card contained no telegraph or fax number, of course. But Paladin always informed his potential clients that he resided in Frisco's classy "Hotel Carlton." There he spent the other half of his double life; when he wasn't championing the cause of righteousness, he was a mysterious loner. Yet he could also be a charmer with an eye for the ladies. He quoted Keats, Shelley, and Shakespeare, read newspapers in Chinese, and enjoyed haute cuisine and vintage wines with fine bone china and crystal stemware.

But it wasn't just the ladies of old San Francisco who were fond of Paladin. (Was this his first name or his last?) When the prairie dust cleared from the stampede of westerns competing for their share of television's Nielsen ratings, "Have Gun, Will Travel" was standing tall in the saddle. The first year it was aired it hit fourth place, and for the next three years it settled into a comfortable third.

Richard Boone, the six-foot-two-inch actor selected for the role of Paladin, was a seventh-generation nephew of frontiersman Daniel Boone (and a distant cousin of singer Pat). His looks were as rugged as the hinterlands his famous ancestor had once explored, giving him an almost sinister quality that magnetized fans. He had become known as "Dr. Konrad Styner" on the TV series "Medic" (NBC, 1954–56), but there was no comparing the two characters. Boone himself described both his personae: "I guess the word for Dr. Styner was 'objective.' But this Paladin is no mere observer. He's a participant who lives like a king, with a need to make the most of every moment, whether he's drinking a glass of wine or hunting somebody down...People *like* Paladin. He's an intriguing sort of guy with an air of mystery about him."

Even as viewers were taking an immediate liking to their new hero, critics at first seemed baffled. " 'Have Gun, Will Travel' makes no pretense at being an 'adult western,'" wrote the reviewer for *Variety* just after the first episode aired. "It's strictly an actioner. There's no overlying psychological motif—it's strictly business." Obviously some observers did not know what to make of this new hero who was as quick with a quotation from the classics as he was with his Colt .45. It didn't take long for people to see that this indeed *was* an adult western. In fact, with "Have Gun, Will Travel," the TV western really came of age.

Richard Boone had signed only a five-year contract, and by the end of the 1961–62 season he was beginning to suffer burnout. "Every time you go to the well," said Boone, "it's a little further down. The show has carried one or two seasons too long." So at the end of the season, he announced that he would pack up his chessmen and calling cards and ride off into the sunset. Of course, what he really wanted to do was *direct*. (Doesn't everyone?) "It's the director who has all the fun. Any time a camera is involved," said Boone, "it's the director who tells the story, more than the writer, producer or anybody else. And that's what I want to do." He had already directed 26 episodes of "Have Gun" during the first five years of the series, and was ready to move on to bigger things. CBS, however, was able to sign Boone for a final sixth year before he moved on.

"Have Gun, Will Travel" served as a springboard for some of the finest talents in television. The show's head writer was Gene Roddenberry, who later went on to create two series of his own, "The Lieutenant," and the one for which he will always be remembered best— "Star Trek." The producer and occasional writer of "Have Gun," Sam Rolfe, later created the cult series "The Man from U.N.C.L.E." And actress-turned-director Ida Lupino honed her directorial skills on "Have Gun" at a time when there were very few women directors in Hollywood. She later went on to become one of the industry's top TV directors.

In 1962 Duane Eddy recorded an instrumental version of the show's theme music, "The Ballad of Paladin," written by Johnny Western, Richard Boone, and Sam Rolfe. Eddy's RCA recording reached number 33 on the *Billboard* charts.

CREDITS

Top 10 Peak: No. 3, 1958–59.
Producers: Sam Rolfe, Frank R
Pierson, others. Directors:
Richard Boone, Ida Lupino,
Andrew V. McLaglen, others.
Writers: Gene Roddenberry,
Sam Rolfe, Shimon Wincelberg,
Harry Julian Fink, others. Cast:
Paladin (Richard Boone), *Hey
Boy* (Kam Tong), *Hey Girl* (Lisa
Lu). Guest Stars: Jack Lord,
Martin Balsam, Robert Blake,
Martin Gabel, George Kennedy,
William Conrad, James Mitchum,
others.

Richard Boone.

THE LIFE AND LEGEND OF WYATT EARP

NUMBER 6, 1957–58

Long live his fame, long live his glory, and long may his story be told!

—OPENING THEME SONG

"The Life and Legend of Wyatt Earp" had the distinction of becoming TV's first "adult" western, premiering on ABC on September 6, 1955, four days ahead of CBS's "Gunsmoke." It took two years for "Wyatt Earp" to finally crack the top 10 (no mean feat, since by that time there were nearly 30 westerns on TV). What turned the trick was the show's individuality.

From the start, the creators of "Wyatt Earp" knew they would need something more than a gun-toting marshal taming the wild frontier, so they aimed for authenticity. The series used the historical biography *Wyatt Earp*, by Stuart N. Lake, as the bible for Frederick Hazlitt Brennan's scripts. Lake had known the real Wyatt Earp, a U.S. marshal who was born in 1848 and survived the bullets of the Old West until 1929. The biographer spent the last four years of Earp's life with him while working on his biography, which became a major sourcebook for westerns during the next three decades. In the interest of further authenticity, Lake was retained as a technical advisor by the show's producers.

The series star, rugged ex-marine drill instructor Hugh O'Brian, spent seven months reading and studying Lake's biography of Earp before the show began filming. "He's a controversial character who has been depicted as everything from saint to devil, lawman to bully, loquacious to taciturn," said O'Brian. "I'm convinced that he was a thoroughly honest man, righteous and utterly fearless. He was also just. In two hundred gunfights, he killed only four men. He had a wonderfully subtle sense of humor, and was essentially an easy-moving, relaxed type of guy. But he could tense up like a coiled spring, and he had fabulous reflexes. You stay alive through two hundred gunfights, and you've *got* to have fabulous reflexes!"

Impeccably dressed in frock coat, ruffled shirt, flowered silk vest, string tie, and black sombrero, the six-foot, 180-pound O'Brian actually bore a close resemblance to the real Earp (minus the original's handlebar moustache). Every effort was made to maintain authenticity, right down to the Buntline Specials—the Colt .45 guns with the extra-long barrels that the real Earp had custom-made. Horseback riding, however, was kept to a minimum; according to a Hollywood riding instructor charged with training actor O'Brian for the series, "That boy can't ride nothin' wilder'n a wheelchair."

Maybe not, be he knew how to manage a buck. He owned a percentage of the series and invested wisely in such business interests as a building-equipment firm, a company that rented guns to TV westerns, a hotel, and a line of men's toiletries. His personal income was estimated at more than half a million dollars for 1959, a veritable fortune in those days.

The storyline throughout the series largely adhered to the real Earp's exploits. The first season saw Wyatt Earp becoming sheriff of Ellsworth, Kansas. By the second year of the show, he'd moved on to Dodge City, the same lawless town Matt Dillon was striving to clean up over on rival network CBS (no references were ever made to the fictional Dillon and Co.). By the last two seasons of the show, he'd reformed Dodge and set his sights on Tombstone, where there was still plenty of life and legend left. Drawing on the historical "gunfight at the O.K. Corral," the final two seasons depicted Earp trying to rid Tombstone and Arizona Territory of the notorious Clanton gang. The finale, a five-part story, concluded with the famous shootout, complete with Doc Holliday and Earp's brothers, Virgil and Morgan, in which they finally routed the Clantons. It was the first time a television series was completely and neatly wrapped up with a conclusion (on September 26, 1961, six years and 266 episodes after it first went on the air).

The theme music for "The Life and Legend of Wyatt Earp" was the only TV theme at that time written by one of Hollywood's best-known composers, Harry Warren, who was famous for "Jeepers Creepers," "We're in the Money," "I Only Have Eyes for You," "You Must Have Been a Beautiful Baby," and "That's Amore." The lyrics ("Wyatt Earp, Wyatt Earp, brave courageous and bold...") were written by Harold Adamson, who also wrote the lyrics to the "I Love Lucy" theme.

Hugh O'Brian.

CREDITS

CREATOR/EXECUTIVE PRODUCER: Lou Edelman. BASED ON: *Wyatt Earp*, by Stuart N. Lake. PRODUCERS: Robert F. Sisk, Roy Rowland. DIRECTORS: Frank McDonald, Roy Rowland, Paul Landres. WRITER: Frederick Hazlitt Brennan. CAST: *Wyatt Earp* (Hugh O'Brian), *Bat Masterson* (Mason Alan Dinehart III), *Doc Holliday* (Douglas Fowley, Myron Healy), *Shotgun Gibbs* (Morgan Woodward), *Sheriff Johnny Behan* (Lash La Rue, Steve Brodie).

THE RESTLESS GUN

NUMBER 8, 1957–58

He doesn't look so restless here: John Payne.

In March 1957 John Payne introduced his character of Vint Bonner, the sympathetic working cowhand, on "The Schlitz Playhouse of Stars." The CBS anthology drama series had already been responsible for one successful series pilot, "A Tale of Wells Fargo," starring Dale Robertson, which had aired during the same season. The pilot for "The Restless Gun" was called "Sixshooter," and when it ran on CBS that night, it was already in the NBC fall lineup.

John Payne, a six-foot-three-inch, 195-pound, rugged (was there any other kind?) hero-type, starred as an itinerant cowpoke who would spend six months in one town and a year in another, constantly moving around the West, trying to stay one step ahead of his reputation as the fastest gun in those parts. Obviously it was Vint Bonner, more than his gun, that was restless. The poor guy would have loved to settle down, but his meanderings were necessitated by his shooting prowess; nobody wanted him around, so off he'd go to find work as a ranch hand, cattle drover, or whatever.

But his reputation seemed greatly exaggerated. Essentially a quiet, idealistic man, he really detested gunfighting and downplayed this skill as much as possible. As Vint put it, "I ain't a killin' man." Payne expressed it somewhat more eloquently: "I can be a fast draw when the script calls for it," he told *TV Guide*, "but we don't concentrate on it. People sort of naturally gravitate toward Bonner when they've got problems, and Bonner tries to solve them as best he can. If there is such a thing as a next-door neighbor in a western, that's Vint Bonner."

John Payne had built his reputation in motion pictures, but not as a western hero. His early career saw him starring in several Hollywood musicals with Betty Grable while under contract with 20th Century Fox, and by the time he was signed for "The Restless Gun," he had 80 films under his belt, only six of which were westerns.

When John Payne set his sights on a television series, he knew he wanted one thing: control. Payne was the series' executive producer, occasional writer, star, and narrator. He retained 50 percent of the rights for his company, Window Glen Productions. He invested his earnings in California real estate before the boom of the '70s and '80s, and it made him a rich man. Payne seemed to have a gift of foresight. Long before the advent of cable TV, he found himself a lone voice in the wilderness when he was convinced that what was then called "pay TV" was the wave of the future. "The producer who says pay TV isn't coming," he said in a 1958 *TV Guide* interview, "is like a man sitting on a railroad track insisting that the steam engine bearing down on him from just one mile away isn't an engine at all and that he can sit there as long as he wants to."

The other producer of the series was David Dortort, who also wrote many of the episodes. Dortort would go on to become the producer of his own western series, "Bonanza." Not surprisingly, he saw opportunities for his future program in the pool of talent being used for

CREDITS

CREATOR: Frank Burt. EXECUTIVE PRODUCER: John Payne. PRODUCER: David Dortort. DIRECTORS: James Neilson, Edward Ludwig, others. WRITERS: David Dortort, David Victor, John Payne, Christopher Knopf, others. CAST: *Vint Bonner* (John Payne). GUEST STARS: Jack Elam, Claude Akins, Denver Pyle, Dan Blocker, Rip Torn, Paul Fix, Lurene Tuttle, Chuck Connors, Corey Allen, Ray Teal, Peggy Castle, others.

"Restless Gun." One of the show's more frequent guest stars was Dan Blocker, who played mostly heavies (no pun intended). Blocker, of course, would become the jovial Hoss Cartwright on "Bonanza." Dortort also cast Ray Teal as a sheriff in "Restless Gun" and liked his portrayal so well he cast him in "Bonanza" as Sheriff Roy Coffee, a part Teal held down for 10 years.

Then there were the guest stars, an incredible number of whom went on to have their own series. Both Chuck Connors and Johnny Crawford made (separate) appearances during the first season of "The Restless Gun." The pair co-starred in "The Rifleman" beginning in 1958. Other guests who eventually starred or co-starred in their own series were Claude Akins ("Lobo," "Movin' On," "B.J. and the Bear"), Ellen Corby ("The Waltons"), Irene Ryan ("The Beverly Hillbillies"), Edgar Buchanan ("Petticoat Junction"), and Robert Blake ("Baretta"). Many well-known theatrical film stars also appeared as guests, including James Coburn, Tom Tryon, and John Carradine.

In 1958 NBC offered Payne a chance to expand the series from 30 minutes to a one-hour format, but he turned the network down. The program ran for two years, from 1957 to 1959, and with a small total of 77 episodes, was seen for only a season in syndication (on ABC) following cancellation.

WAGON TRAIN

NUMBER 2, 1958–59

Robert Horton (left) and Ward Bond.

Ward Bond was a football player for the University of Southern California in 1928 when director John Ford tapped him and a young lad named John Wayne to star in a film called *Salute*. The three struck up an immediate friendship; in the decades to follow Bond and Wayne would often be cast as sidekicks in Ford's films. By the time Ford directed Bond in his 1950 film *Wagonmaster*, the actor had played supporting roles in over 200 movies, including nearly 150 westerns, among them *The Big Trail* (1930), *Dodge City* (1939), *Virginia City* (1940), and *Fort Apache* (1948).

Wagonmaster became the inspiration for the television series "Wagon Train." The basic premises were closely allied. The movie concerned cowhands who join a wagon train headed for Mormon country in Utah, while the TV series had California as the final destination. In both versions, Bond played the stalwart wagonmaster, leader of a chain of "prairie schooners" crossing America's western frontier in the post-Civil War era.

Beginning in September 1957 the wagons left St. Joseph ("St. Joe"), Missouri, and rolled across the American plains, mountains, and television screens for eight years. Ward Bond played Major Seth Adams during the first four seasons, until his death in 1960. His wagonmaster characterization was one of a no-nonsense leader on these westward treks, week after week blending strength and maturity with compassion. *Time* magazine described him as "fatherly one minute, the next he is roaring like a mule with colic. An extrovert's extrovert, he has a grin like a Texas river, a mile wide and an inch deep, and a laugh that can shatter a klieg light." Bond had a tough-as-nails temperament, which was readily apparent when he broke his hip on the set after a horse backed into him. He hollered for his Scotch and milk (the milk was for his ulcer, he said, the Scotch for him), and he returned to the set by the next day. But he tempered his bellowings with a set of old-fashioned values and a soft spot for kids. When he first signed for the series he showed concern for the show's format. "Nobody is going to make me play a story with a degenerate in it. Not on a TV show that children are watching."

Co-starring for the first five years was Robert Horton, who played the wagon train's tough scout. To get a feel for the role, Horton drove his car cross-country, from St. Joe to California, before starting work on the series. He had strong feelings about the way he played his character, Flint McCullough. "Why should I act like a movie cowboy? I'm *not* a movie cowboy," he

said, "and most of the real cowboys of 1870 weren't either. They were from the East, and a lot of them were well-educated."

According to *Newsweek*, there was no love lost between Bond and Horton (who wanted meatier roles), and there were frequent flare-ups on the set. To relieve the stress, horseplay was encouraged. "If you don't have fun," said Bond, "it ain't worth doing for *any* money...We got the best damn crew in show business...It would be impossible to do what we do in five days if we didn't. We don't have time to sit around looking for motivation and all that stuff. But, by God, we have fun!"

In 1960 Bond died of a sudden heart attack while preparing for a personal appearance. The following season a new wagonmaster took over the reins when John McIntyre won the role of Chris Hale. McIntyre had appeared as Detective Lieutenant Dan Muldoon on TV's *Naked City*. Now he led the pioneers across the trails and up to the top of the Nielsen charts. "Wagon Train" had reached the number two spot by 1958, the year after its premiere, and it held down that position (right behind the number one "Gunsmoke") until the 1961–62 season, when it finally made number one.

In that same year (1962), Robert Horton, anxious to spread his wings and declaring he would have no more of westerns, left the wagons for what he hoped would be greener pastures. It wasn't the best of career moves; his next series would be another western—"A Man Called Shenandoah" (1965–66).

Actually, "Wagon Train" never really depended too much on its leads. The show focused more on the weekly guest characters, played by some of Hollywood's finest actors. Each week's episode would bear the title of that character: "The (character's name) Story." These people encountered by the wagon train brought their lives, loves, conflicts, and travails to the trail. Characterization was strong; sophisticated emotional outpourings and dramatically revealing byplay, rather than flying bullets, usually solved the situations. Of course there were the occasional gunfights necessitated by the genre, but these were usually downplayed.

In 1963 the series completed its run on NBC, pulled up stakes, and set out for the unknown territory of a new network. On ABC the episodes were expanded to 90 minutes for the final season (1964–65), but the ratings had been slipping since the show's peak back in 1962. After 440 episodes, the wagons halted once more in California, their journey done at last.

CREDITS

TOP 10 PEAK: No. 1, 1961–62.
PRODUCERS: Richard Lewis, Howard Christie, others. DIRECTORS: various (including an episode by John Ford). WRITERS: various. CAST: *Major Seth Adams* (Ward Bond), *Flint McCullough* (Robert Horton), *Chris Hale* (John McIntyre), *Bill Hawks* (Terry Wilson), *Charlie Wooster* (Frank McGrath), *Kate Crowley* (Barbara Stanwyck). GUEST STARS: Ernest Borgnine, Marjorie Lord, William Bendix, Debra Paget, Mickey Rooney, Joseph Cotten, Vera Miles, Tommy Sands, others.

THE RIFLEMAN

NUMBER 4, 1958–59

Chuck Connors (right), with Johnny Crawford.

Unlike so many popular TV westerns of the day, "The Rifleman" had no opening jingle for audience sing-a-long identification.

While the series' setting and trappings were in keeping with the '50s' western craze, its popularity relied almost completely on the strong family appeal of its ongoing storyline: a single-parent family struggling to survive in the late 1800s.

Lucas McCain (Chuck Connors) was a widower and homesteader settled down to ranching life in North Fork, New Mexico. While he tried to instill strong moral values in his young son, Mark (Johnny Crawford), assorted thugs, drunks, and killers provided the lesson *du jour*. This was due in part to the ineptitude of the town marshal, Micah Torrance (Paul Fix), who constantly had to rely on the services of McCain and his amazing skill with a specially rigged rifle.

Lucas McCain could have been the National Rifle Association's poster child. He toted a full-length .44-40 1892 Winchester carbine with a hair-trigger lever action that fired off a round every three-tenths of a second.

Fortunately Chuck Connors (yes, he looked *rugged*) topped out at six feet, five-and-a-half inches, just the right height to spin the rifle's barrel under his arm without it scraping his armpit. It was for this ability that Lucas McCain billed himself as "the fastest man with a rifle." Not too many people gave him an argument.

A rifle had also played an important role in Chuck Connors's casting interview.

Connors got his start in the field of sports, and after finishing a stint in the army back in 1946, he played basketball for the Boston Celtics. "I was far from being the world's greatest," said Connors. In fact, he soon moved on to major league baseball, playing for both the Chicago Cubs and the then-Brooklyn Dodgers. He played heavies in TV westerns before he was called to interview for the lead in "The Rifleman."

"When I came in," said Connors, "the producer picked up a rifle and heaved it at me across the room. I grabbed it and started to heave it back to him. They wanted to see how I handled a rifle." Well enough to land the job, as it turned out.

Like so many other westerns of its era, "The Rifleman" began as a pilot incorporated into another series, in this case "Dick Powell's Zane Grey Theater" on CBS. That series was the all-time spin-off champion, eventually spawning *seven* westerns, including "The Rifleman" and "Wanted: Dead or Alive." "The Rifleman" arrived on rival network ABC in the fall of 1958 and

zoomed to the number four position in the ratings. Its ratings began to sag by 1962, despite occasional attempts to spice thigs up by introducing a love interest for Lucas. But it seems more likely that ratings dropped because the boy was beginning to outgrow his part and lose his young audience.

Johnny Crawford began playing Mark McCain at the age of 12 and was heralded as one of the finest child actors around (he specialized in crying on cue). He had spent six months over at Walt Disney Studios sporting Mouseketeer ears on "The Mickey Mouse Club," where the lad had demonstrated his talents as a hoofer and singer. He was thrilled to land the part of Mark and, since he was a baseball buff, worshiped former baseball player Chuck Connors. He had planned a career as an actor, but after "The Rifleman" wrapped in 1963 after 168 episodes, he found that casting calls were rare, and the 17-year-old Crawford drifted towards other areas. At one point he joined a rodeo.

"I enjoyed the anonymity of being a real cowboy on the circuit," he said in *People*. "I was tired of the fame." He also pursued an interest in music and did quite well with several best-selling records, including "Cindy's Birthday" (number eight in 1962) and "Your Nose Is Gonna Grow" (number 14 in that same year). During his 20s, roles became scarcer. In the early '90s he was concentrating on his music, hoping to cut an album with his group, Johnny Crawford and His 1928 Jazz Orchestra, while supplementing his income by running an antique auto rental business. He admitted surprise at how many fans the series seemed to have retained: "I guess it has sort of a timeless appeal, and I think that that is more because of the relationship between the father and the son than the relationship between the Rifleman and his rifle...I hope."

For 30 years following "The Rifleman," Chuck Connors continued to be saddled with that association. Asked whether or not this surprised him, the actor replied, "No it doesn't surprise me. It was a very fine, well-written character by Sam Peckinpah, and if you're being typecast at all, and most of us are, that's a great way to be typecast. So 'The Rifleman' is still popular with a lot of people, and I'm proud to be associated."

In 1990 Chuck Connors and Johnny Crawford were reunited (in different roles) as guest stars in an episode of "Paradise," a CBS western series that starred Lee Horsley.

Chuck Connors died of lung cancer in 1992. He was 71.

CREDITS

CREATOR: Sam Peckinpah. PRODUCERS: Jules Levy, Arthur Gardner, Arnold Laven. DIRECTORS: Joseph H. Lewis, Arnold Laven, others. WRITERS: Sam Peckinpaw, Robert Culp, others. CAST: *Lucas McCain* (Chuck Connors), *Mark McCain* (Johnny Crawford), *Marshal Micah Torrance* (Paul Fix), *Miss Milly Scott* (Joan Taylor), *Lou Mallory* (Patricia Blair), *Sweeney* (Bill Quinn), *Hattie Denton* (Hope Summers). GUEST STARS: Dennis Hopper, Leif Erickson, Martin Landau, others.

MAVERICK

NUMBER 6, 1958–59

Nachez to New Orleans, livin' on jacks and queens,
Maverick is a legend of the West.
—Opening Theme Song

In 1867 a Texas cattle owner made an unconventional decision. In an era when every self-respecting cattleman marked his calves with a searing red-hot iron in an effort to curtail rustlers, Samuel A. Maverick (1803–1870) refused to perform such a cruel act. As a result of this bold deviation from western norms, a new word entered the English lexicon: "maverick," defined by Webster as "an unbranded animal, a motherless calf, and an independent individual who does not go along with a group or party."

Sam Maverick, 19th-century cattleman, may be a hero to animal rights activists, but his television namesake was anything but a hero. When the series "Maverick" was first created back in 1957, it was originally planned as just another western, Warner Bros.' latest entry into the sagebrush fray. The character of Bret Maverick was to be a card shark who took his "work" seriously. But the series' star, James Garner, soon found that he just couldn't play the part with a straight face, a problem that turned out to be a boon: Garner's talent for comic acting was more than a little responsible for the incredible ratings success that "Maverick" ultimately achieved. It wasn't long before the series, a maverick in its own right, gained a reputation for being a western send-up, rather than a straight-faced western.

Garner played Bret Maverick (the hero was named for both the historical cattleman and creator/producer Roy Huggins's son Bret) as an untrustworthy, self-centered antihero who couldn't ride very well, couldn't shoot straight, and would rather run than fight. James Garner contended that "Maverick" was derivative of the 1945 film *San Antonio*,

even attributing his wardrobe to that movie. He dressed like a western dandy, he said, because "they used stock shots from the [Errol] Flynn movie, so my clothes had to match up," even claiming that some of his outfits were the same ones worn by Flynn.

Producer Huggins furnished all the show's new writers and directors with the series' bible, a "Ten Point Guide to Happiness," which included the following reminders:

- "Heavies in 'Maverick' are always absolutely right. And they are always beloved to someone."
- "In the traditional western story, the situation is always serious but never hopeless. In a 'Maverick' story the situation is always hopeless, but never serious."
- "The cliché flourishes in the creative arts because the familiar gives a sense of comfort and security. Writers and directors of 'Maverick' are requested to live dangerously."

Even with these illuminating guidelines, Huggins had his share of script problems. "I wasn't able to get stories out of conventional westerns," he told *Newsweek*. "They just didn't fit." To overcome this obstacle, he turned to the classics, doing western versions of everything from Shakespeare's "Othello" to Robert Louis Stevenson's "The Wrecker." "The secret is to take them in the spirit of larcenous affection instead of with awe and trepidation," Huggins said.

Eventually the stories began to parody television itself. An episode called "Gun Shy" featured an inept Marshal Mort Dooley with his limping deputy, Clyde, and a saloon keeper named Amy. Another, "Three Queens Full," lampooned "Bonanza" with a character named Joe Wheelright living on the Subrosa Ranch. "Dragnet" also fell

CREDITS

Creator: Roy Huggins.
Executive Producer: William T. Orr. Producers: Roy Huggins, Coles Trapnell, William L. Stuart. Directors: various. Writers: various. Cast: *Bret Maverick* (James Garner), *Bart Maverick* (Jack Kelly), *Beau Maverick* (Roger Moore), *Brent Maverick* (Robert Colbert), *Samantha Crawford* (Diane Brewster), *Dandy Jim Buckley* (Efrem Zimbalist, Jr.). Guest Stars: Whitney Blake, Ray Teal, Adam West, Troy Donohue, others.

victim to the spoofing, with Garner doing a deadpan narration, à la Joe Friday.

While production values were high, the producers found almost from the beginning that they were always behind schedule. To compensate, in the second season they introduced a brother for Bret—Bart Maverick, played by Jack Kelly. Two film crews worked simultaneously, shooting two different stories, one involving Bret, the other brother Bart (and on occasion, both). These were then shown on alternate Sunday nights, allowing much-needed time to finish each episode.

Jack Kelly's popularity never rose to the level of Jim Garner's, which presented a problem when Garner walked off the show in 1960 in a contract dispute. Garner eventually won his case, but meanwhile "Maverick" was one brother short. In the fall of 1960, Roger Moore (later the star of TV's "The Saint" and filmdom's James Bond movies) was cast as English cousin Beauregard Maverick. Beau and Bart alternated during the 1960–61 season. Then in the spring of 1961, yet another "long lost" brother, Brent (Robert Colbert), was introduced. Like the others, he never quite gained the popularity that Bret had enjoyed, and ABC finally cancelled the series in 1962 (perhaps because they ran out of names starting with "B" for new Maverick relatives).

James Garner didn't work much in TV for the 11 years after he left "Maverick"; he had a starring role in a short-lived western series called "Nichols" (1971–72), then found another niche for himself as Jim Rockford in "The Rockford Files" (1974–80), playing a sort of modern Maverick. But the original Maverick character continued to beckon; in 1979 Jim Garner and Jack Kelly guested in a made-for-TV movie, "The New Maverick." The film introduced a nephew, Ben (they found another "B" name after all!), and launched a spin-off series called "Young Maverick," starring Charles Frank and Susan Blanchard. The series lasted only a couple of months, however, before it was cancelled. In 1981 ABC again attempted a revival

of the series, now titled "Bret Maverick," in which Garner reprised his role of Bret. But as with many sequels, it didn't survive and was pulled after one season. (NBC showed reruns of "Bret Maverick" during the summer of 1990.)

In 1992 Warner Home Video released two episodes apiece of three western series of the '50s and '60s: "Cheyenne," "Bronco," and "Maverick." The

James Garner (top) and Jack Kelly.

"Maverick" video, priced at $14.95, featured "Duel at Sundown," with Clint Eastwood, and "Shady Deal at Sunny Acres," with Efrem Zimbalist, Jr.

Also in 1992 Warner Bros. announced plans for a theatrical version of "Maverick" to star Mel Gibson. James Garner had agreed to perform an unspecified role. No date was set for the release of the film, to be directed by Richard Donner.

THE REAL McCOYS

NUMBER 8, 1958–59

When "Grandpappy Amos and the girls and the boys of the family known as the Real McCoys" left their home in the hills of West Virginny and headed for Californ-eye-ay, television found Nielsen space for some corn among the oats. Westerns were still king, but soon country corn would rule. Debuting in October 1957 on ABC, "The Real McCoys" would become the prototype for a bumper crop of imitators in the 1960s, including "The Andy Griffith Show," "Petticoat Junction," "Green Acres," and its most obvious progeny, "The Beverly Hillbillies."

The success of "The Real McCoys" lay in its brilliant casting of Walter Brennan as Grandpa Amos McCoy, the chicken-walking, arm-flapping, cantankerous grand-pater familias of his pack o' young'uns. The premise, of course, was "fish out of water," or you can take the bumpkin out of the country, but you can't take the country out of the bumpkin. And Brennan was the quintessential bumpkin—he'd been playing more or less the same part in the 300-odd films he'd appeared in since 1925. "I started playing old men when I was 32," said Brennan in a *Newsweek* interview, "because I got my teeth knocked out in a mob scene. One day the casting director says: 'We need an old man.' He looked at me, and I've been an old man ever since." Brennan was the first male three-time Oscar winner (*Come and Get It* [1936], *Kentucky* [1938], and *The Westerner* [1940]) when he made the transition to television.

When "The Real McCoys" premiered, critics didn't cotton to it. *The New York Times* proclaimed it was "for anyone who wants his corn as high as an elephant's eye," and *Variety*, which said the show's chief saving grace was Walter Brennan, judged it to be "strictly Ma and Pa Kettle stuff... there's a lot of banter of marriage at 13, water wearing away the skin, and other 'Tobacco Road' lingo."

On that subject, there was certainly no mistaking the dialogue for Shakespeare. "Kids won't learn English from this series," Brennan said, "but this is one show that won't teach them better ways to ruin the furniture or throw food."

Although initially pleased to be the star of this series, which revolved around his character, Brennan continually tried to quit the show throughout its six-year run, protesting that he didn't know how to do comedy; but each year viewers thought otherwise, sending the series to as high as number five in the 1960–61 season. (In the last season, Brennan finally managed to secure a deal for only 16 out of 26 episodes.)

The other actor who is best remembered in "The Real McCoys" is Richard Crenna, who had been the original pubescent, squeaky-voiced Walter Denton on radio and TV's "Our Miss Brooks." He played Amos's grandson, Luke McCoy, newly wed to Kate "Suger Babe" McCoy, and together they looked after his orphaned sister, "Aunt" Hassie, and 11-year-old brother, Little Luke. Crenna eventually went on to star in some high-quality television series, like "Slattery's People" and "Centennial." In the '90s he was still in demand both as an actor and top director.

In 1962 "The Real McCoys" switched networks, moving from ABC to CBS, which had bought the series for a reported price of $7.5 million. That same season saw CBS adding "The Beverly Hillbillies" to their lineup. At the end of the season, "The Real McCoys," which had been penciled in for a seventh year, was abruptly cancelled. Said a CBS executive, "It's because of the fatigue factor. If a show begins to wear thin on the ear and eye, you don't just say, 'Well, the tread is thin, but I'll wait till next year to buy new tires.' You change now and avoid a blowout." The only blowout, however, would appear to be the one the Beverly Hillbilly Clampetts caused the McCoys. Seems thar jest weren't room enuf fer all them hill folk on that thar CBS network.

CREDITS

TOP 10 PEAK: No. 5, 1960–61.
CREATORS: Irving and Norman Pincus.
EXECUTIVE PRODUCER: Irving Pincus.
PRODUCERS: Danny Arnold, Charles Isaacs. DIRECTORS: Sheldon Leonard, Hy Averback, Richard Crenna, others.
WRITERS: Bill Manhoff, Jack Elinson, Chuck Stewart, others. CAST: *Grandpappy Amos McCoy* (Walter Brennan), *Luke McCoy* (Richard Crenna), *Kate McCoy* (Kathy Nolan), *Hassie McCoy* (Lydia Reed), *Little Luke McCoy* (Michael Winkleman), *Pepino Garcia* (Tony Martinez). OTHER REGULARS: Andy Clyde, Madge Blake, Joan Blondell, James Lydon, Lloyd Corrigan, Willard Waterman, others.

From left: Walter Brennan, Kathy Nolan, Lydia Reed, and Richard Crenna.

FATHER KNOWS BEST

NUMBER 6 (TIE), 1959–60

"Here's Robert Young!..." the unseen announcer told viewers, week after week, and the proud papa stood with his family while the anonymous voice introduced his wife, their brood, and the actors who played them. For nine prime-time years (and umpteen more in reruns) TV watchers welcomed the Andersons into their homes. They were America's Everyfamily, the image of the ideal family at the time: stereotypically Waspish, with one working father, one homemaker mother, a teenage daughter and son, a cuddly little girl.

Were members of the TV audience really all white, Wasp, and just so darn nice back then? Despite what some modern politicians might like to envision for America today, the truth is that there weren't a lot of families like the Andersons of Springfield in the 1950s. What "Father Knows Best" presented was a *paradigm*, its characters cast from perfect molds. People could look at this brood and reach for, but never quite grasp, the cozy world of Anderson-ville.

But audiences certainly loved reaching. Jim Anderson was actually *employed*— rare for TV fathers of the '50s; he also didn't bellow or rule with a fist of iron. He and his wife Margaret tried to set examples for their children; they weren't particularly preachy, and neither was the show. Each week's story was a gentle lesson in the art of attaining adulthood while learning to respect other people, beginning at the family level. The Andersons' three adorable children never had pimples, periods, or drug problems. They never even used the toilet— it took the arrival of Archie Bunker to bring that experience to the tube. They never had knock-down, drag-out fights with their parents. The family members had a deep abiding love and mutual respect for one another. If there

was a certain naiveté about all this, well, these were the '50s after all, the golden years of television innocence.

When Robert Young starred in the radio version of the series, which began in 1949, it was originally titled "Father Knows Best?" with a question mark. Fictional fathers of the day tended to be dweebs, and it was assumed that this characterization would be used in this series. Wrong. This father was neither a "Life of Riley" klutz nor a "Dagwood Bumstead" bumbler. Jim Anderson was a mature, responsible parent who had both feet firmly planted, an ideal father who counseled and advised his kids.

When the series moved over to CBS-TV in September 1954 after five years on the radio, Robert Young was the only original cast member to make the transition. The warm domestic sitcom (the emphasis was more on the "sit" than the "com") didn't do much for CBS's ratings, and after the first year they decided to cancel the series. That network would also have to learn a lesson from Father: following a flood of mail from outraged viewers, NBC picked up the series for the next three years. By 1958 CBS had mended the error of its ways and bought back "Father Knows Best"; it remained on the network's schedule until 1960, when Robert Young took stock of the fact that he'd been a role model and father image over the course of three decades, and enough was enough. The series continued in prime-time reruns for another two years on NBC and then segued to ABC for yet another season of prime-time reruns. In 1977 NBC presented a made-for-TV movie, "The Father Knows Best Reunion." The audience was brought up to date on the lives of the Andersons since the '50s: the nest was now empty; Betty was a widow with

CREDITS

PRODUCER: Eugene B. Rodney. DIRECTORS: William Russell, Peter Tewksbury, various. WRITERS: Roswell Rogers, others. CAST: *Jim Anderson* (Robert Young), *Margaret Anderson* (Jane Wyatt), *Betty "Princess" Anderson* (Elinor Donahue), *James "Bud" Anderson, Jr.* (Billy Gray), *Kathy "Kitten" Anderson* (Lauren Chapin).

EMMYS

Best Actor in a Comedy Series— Robert Young (1956, 1957), Best Actress in a Comedy Series—Jane Wyatt (1957, 1958–59, 1959–60), Best Direction of a Single Program of a Comedy Series—Peter Tewksbury (1958–59).

two children, Bud was in a troubled marriage, and Kathy was in a relationship with an older, divorced man. The times, they had a-changed.

In the 1990s the original series enjoyed a resurgence of popularity; the 203 episodes were screened in cable reruns—on the Family Channel, of course.

What became of the Andersons after their years in Springfield?* Robert Young went on to star in the role of another warm father figure, the family doctor of "Marcus Welby, M.D." (1969–76), became a pitchman for Sanka Coffee, and overcame a 30-year battle with alchohol addiction. Jane Wyatt went from playing a generation's understanding mother figure to becoming a cult star after accepting the role of Amanda, Mr. Spock's mother, on "Star Trek." A popular guest at the numerous "Star Trek" conventions, Wyatt became known to young fans for her "marriage" to a Vulcan; few of those same fans remembered her as Robert Young's TV wife. Elinor Donahue, who played the

Andersons' teenage daughter, Betty, starred as the mother on the Fox-TV series "Get a Life" (1990–92). Later she worked on several other Fox series, including "Herman's Head" and the cartoon show "Eek the Cat." "Fox has become my network," laughs Donahue. "It tends to be where I work the most." Billy Gray, who played the young son, Bud, had few fond memories of the TV series, arguing that the "dialogue, the situations, the characters were all totally false." He left the acting profession and became a champion dirt bike rider and race car driver in the late 1970s. Lauren Chapin overcame a drug addiction, resurfaced as a born-again Christian, and continued to do occasional acting roles.

---

*A popular setting for TV shows, Springfield represents Anytown, U.S.A. There are no fewer than 13 Springfields in different states across the U.S., including the one that is now home to that '90s TV family, "The Simpsons."

From left: Elinor Donahue, Robert Young, Lauren Chapin (in front), Jane Wyatt, and Billy Gray.

77 SUNSET STRIP

NUMBER 6 (TIE), 1959–60

Edd "Kookie" Byrnes.

koo·kie*kü-kē*\ *adj (1959): having the character-
istics of a kook: CRAZY, OFFBEAT*
—WEBSTER'S DICTIONARY

Has it only been 34 years since the word "kookie"
entered our lexicon? Although the dictionary doesn't

defer to the word's actual source, there is no doubt that
Kookie was one of the first superstars to come out of
television, and he appeared on the series "77 Sunset
Strip."

In the 90-minute pilot episode, the character of the
parking lot attendant named Kookie was nohwhere to

be seen. Edward (Edd) Byrnes, the man who would become the series' runaway teen-heartthrob star, was originally cast in a one-shot part, playing a killer "with considerable skill and conviction" according to a *Variety* review. By the time the series was reworked, the 25-year-old Byrnes found himself a permanent cast member—right behind top-billed Efrem Zimbalist, Jr., and Roger Smith.

Setting a pattern that would continue for decades to follow, the studio initially failed to recognize the star power of the supporting character named Gerald Lloyd Kookson III, a.k.a. Kookie. (Other second bananas who zipped past their higher-billed co-stars to achieve superstardom include Leonard "Mr. Spock" Nimoy of "Star Trek," Henry "Fonzie" Winkler, and Michael J. Fox of "Family Ties.") Until Kookie caught on, ABC spent much misdirected effort in promoting the show's main lead, handsome, debonair Efrem Zimbalist, Jr. (better remembered by younger audiences of the '90s as the father of Stephanie, who starred in "Remington Steele"). The Warner Bros. publicity department busily cranked out press releases touting the middle-aged actor as television's answer to Clark Gable, citing his impeccable taste in clothing, his rugged profile, his happy family, and his theatrical performances of Shakespeare, Ibsen, and Noel Coward. Television audiences collectively yawned. All the public wanted was more of Kookie.

He was the prototype for Fonzie (of the '70s' "Happy Days")—a hip, cool, rebel *sans* cause, the kind of man your mother warned you about. Teenagers dug him like crazy, man. In less than a year following the 1958 debut of "77 Sunset Strip," the ratings, which originally showed only a 19.4 percent viewing audience, soared (by mid-1959) to a 38 percent Nielsen share, making it the leading program in its time period and tying with "Father Knows Best" for the number six spot, giving ABC a much-needed hit.

Not a moment was to be wasted. Warner Bros. tore up the old press handouts and began to market their newfound treasure, who by now was receiving more fan mail than any other star on the lot. They searched for a gimmick with which to promote the young lad. In the pilot episode, the nervous actor had affected a mannerism of constantly combing his wavy hair. This shtick carried over into his characterization of Kookie, the car jockey at Dino's, next door to the private-eye offices at "77 Sunset Strip." Fans were enthralled, mailing him combs by the hundreds. It wasn't difficult to imagine

this prop as the focal point of a song by Byrnes, and a recording was rushed into production. "Kookie, Kookie (Lend Me Your Comb)" (as implored by a teenaged Connie Stevens) soared to number four in the *Billboard* listings. It was full of Kookie jive-talk, like "I've got smog in my noggin" (I'm losing my memory) and "Baby, you're the ginchiest" (you're the coolest). In fact, most of Byrnes's dialogue in the series consisted of Kookie-isms—phrases like being "buzzed by germsville" (put into the hospital), "mushroom people" (people who come out at night to party), and "stabling a horse" (parking a car). "I never talk that way," said Byrnes in *TV Guide*, "and the only way I can keep those speeches in my head is to learn them word by word."

Byrnes, who had first appeared on TV as an Indian in a skit with Joe E. Brown on "The Buick Circus Hour" for $125, enjoyed his skyrocket to success. But eventually he found himself typecast, and after the series' cancellation in 1963, he had a tough time getting work. He did a number of "spaghetti" westerns (filmed in Italy) in the '70s, and appeared in the hit movie *Grease* (1978). He later enjoyed a revived career as a guest actor on various TV series of the '90s.

The cast's two other leads tried to jump on the recording bandwagon; Roger Smith's album *Beach Romance* quietly bombed, and Efrem Zimbalist, Jr.'s single of "Adeste Fideles" in English and Latin fell short of starting a stampede to record stores. Warner Bros. had modest success with a release of the jazzy soundtrack of "77 Sunset Strip."

By the 1963–64 season, the series was in serious trouble. In an attempt at revitalization, the format was punched up—nearly always the harbinger of a death knell. William Conrad was brought in as producer/director, the co-leads of Roger Smith and Edd Byrnes were dropped, and Zimbalist was left to solo as a serious Phillip Marlow-esque globetrotting gumshoe, complete with voiceover à la Raymond Chandler. There were cameos by dozens of "names," including Burgess Meredith, Peter Lorre, Wally Cox, William Shatner, Kennan Wynn, Ed Wynn, Walter Slezak—and that was just in the season's opener. But none of this helped. By February 1964 the show was "splitsville." (Reruns continued from April until September of that year). "77 Sunset Strip" passed into television history, but would always be remembered as one of the first television shows to create a star-legend.

As Kookie would say, "Crazy, Daddy-O!"

CREDITS

PRODUCERS: Roy Huggins (pilot), Howie Horwitz, Fenton Earnshaw, William Conrad. DIRECTORS: various. WRITERS: various. CAST: *Stuart Bailey* (Efrem Zimbalist, Jr.), *Jeff Spencer* (Roger Smith), *Gerald Lloyd "Kookie" Kookson III* (Edd Byrnes), *Roscoe* (Louis Quinn), *Suzanne* (Jacqueline Beer). OTHER REGULARS: Byron Keith, Richard Long, Robert Logan, Joan Staley, plus "crossover" stars from other Warner Bros. private-eye TV shows (Connie Stevens, Anthony Eisley, Troy Donahue, others). GUEST STARS: Ray Teal, The Mary Kaye Trio, Kathleen Crowley, Chad Everett, Dawn Wells, Richard Conte, William Shatner, others.

THE PRICE IS RIGHT

NUMBER 8, 1959–60

Spanning five decades, "The Price Is Right" is television's longest-running game show. It first appeared as a daytime entry in 1956 on NBC, and it had the distinction of airing at one time or another on all three major networks—NBC, ABC, and CBS. The series had numerous hosts, announcers, and models. But most people know it for its main *raison d'être*—it gave away fabulous prizes, including the always-desirable *brand new car!*

"The Price Is Right" debuted before the notorious quiz-show scandals of the late '50s and, with the industry smarting from such ignominy, sailed blissfully unscathed through those troubled waters. If there were any charges of rigging leveled at "Price," it managed to thwart them successfully, one of the reasons for its staying power.

In 1956 "The Price Is Right" began as a daytime entry, and by 1957 it was also on the evening lineup, where it resided until 1963, switching to ABC for one more year (1964). The host was the bespectacled and bow-tied Bill Cullen. He had been emceeing game shows since 1946, starting with radio's "Winner Take All." Throughout his career, he appeared on at least 25 different series—radio and television, daytime and nighttime. Always in demand, he could be seen on all three networks during one season in the mid-1960s: on "Eye Guess" on NBC, "The Price Is Right" on ABC, and "I've Got a Secret" on CBS.

One of the secrets of his success was his constant awareness that the game's the thing. "It's great to be witty and funny," he said, "but a host should never distract a contestant from winning money."

"The Price Is Right" began as a panel show. Four contestants, seated on stage, bid on such items of merchandise as stoves and refrigerators. But unlike the way the game was later played, contestants could make three bids, in increasing intervals of $50. At any stage a contestant could elect to "freeze." (Anyone who bid higher than the value of the item automatically lost.)

CREDITS

CREATOR: Bob Stewart.
PRODUCERS: Bob Stewart, Mark Goodson, Bill Todman, Jay Wolpert, Frank Wayne, others.
DIRECTORS: Max Miller, Mark Breslow, others. WRITERS: various.
HOSTS: Bill Cullen, Dennis James, Tom Kennedy, Bob Barker.
ANNOUNCERS: Don Pardo, Johnny Gilbert, Johnny Olson, Gene Wood, Rod Roddy, others.
MODELS: Beverly Bentley, Toni Wallace, Janice Pennington, Pamela Parker, others.

Those surviving got to go on to the showcase of pricey gifts, and in an era when materialistic values were just creeping into the American psyche, these prizes were lavish—Rolls-Royces, ferris wheels, sable coats, beach houses. They were often silly as well: a color TV with a live peacock as a color guide, a barbeque pit with a mile of hotdogs and a six-foot jar of mustard.

The home audience was also included, which accounted for much of the show's prime-time popularity. Viewers could send in their bids on special showcases. In the very first week, they overwhelmed the production staff with over 3.5 million postcards. Once, a 38-year-old home player from Brooklyn offered the show's mailroom staff a $2,000 bribe to select his as the winning card. Instead they called the cops, and when the suspect attempted to escape, he was shot and injured.

"The Price Is Right" left the ranks of prime-time fare in 1964, but Goodson-Todman, the show's producers, knew a good thing when they had it. In 1972 the series returned to CBS's morning lineup, now dubbed "The *New* Price Is Right," hosted by Bob Barker, where it rested at the top of the daytime ratings for over 20 years. A simultaneous prime-time-access syndicated version was also launched that year, with Dennis James. Later the show had a few other (brief) prime-time runs.

The series format underwent some changes. The contestants were now selected from the studio audience, four the first time, and invited to "Come on down!" to the stage, where they did their guessing. As on the original prime-time version, the audience urged them on with shouts of "Higher!" or "Lower!" The person coming closest to the actual price without going over then got to continue; others were called down to the stage one at a time after each game to join the remaining three players. Showcase prizes continued to be lavish, with trips, cars, and other luxury items abounding. And yes, the winners had to pay hefty taxes. Uncle Sam loves a winner, too.

Bill Cullen.

WANTED: DEAD OR ALIVE

NUMBER 9, 1959–60

Long after most people had forgotten the basic premise of "Wanted: Dead or Alive," they remembered the series for one thing—its star. Aloof, brooding loner Josh Randall, the bounty hunter and central character of the show, was portrayed by aloof, brooding loner Steve McQueen, on his way to becoming a Hollywood legend. "Wanted: Dead or Alive" was to be his proving ground.

The series was spun off from a Dick Powell-Four Star venture called "Trackdown," produced in 1957 by Vincent Fennelly. The "Trackdown" episode served as the new series' pilot centered around an Old West bounty hunter—a man who reaped a reward for tracking down outlaws. The actor Fennelly had in mind from the start was Steve McQueen. "I picked him because he was a little guy," said Fennelly in Malachy McCoy's *Steve McQueen: The Unauthorized Biography*. "You know, a bounty hunter is a sort of underdog. Everyone's against him except the audience. And McQueen was an offbeat guy. He wasn't the best-looking guy in the world, but he had a nice kind of animal instinct. He could be nice but with some hint of menace underneath."

At first McQueen was only mildly interested. He had his sights set on the big money he could make in feature films. But after looking over a script, McQueen decided to take on the character of Josh Randall.

In the sink-or-swim ocean of television westerns, each new series had to have its own special gimmicks, and "Wanted" had its share. Randall spoke infrequently and softly, and carried a .30–40 sawed-off carbine he called his "Mare's Leg." He focused more on the "alive" than "dead" aspect of the capture, and tried to apprehend rather than shoot his quarry. As an actor, Steve McQueen constantly strove to create a credible, realistic character. "I try to think what Randall would do in a situation," he said during the series' production, "and I also try to put in some of my own ingredients—what I would do." Despite the toughness that McQueen seemed to project, he was at heart a pacifist and built that element of his personality into his character. "I don't like fighting," he said. "I try to talk my way out of it if I can," and so did Randall.

His interpretation of his character led to "creative differences" with the producers of "Wanted: Dead or Alive." Several disputes ended with his walking off the set. "I fell out with the company over the interpretation of Randall," he explained. "One row was over my cowbow hat. They thought that all cowboys had shiny new saddles and that their hats were never crumpled. I quit and stormed out."

The series was nearing the end of its second season on CBS in 1960 when McQueen began making it clear that he was serious about wanting to be released from the contract so he could work in features. His previous films hadn't sparked much attention—things like *The Blob* (1958) and *The Great St. Louis Bank Robbery* (1959). But following his first true taste of success in *The Magnificent Seven* (1960), a promising career in feature films loomed, and he was beginning to receive many offers. McQueen had several fights with the series' producers over script content and character development. More tantrums followed. His agent urged him not to walk out, with the familiar warning, "You'll never work in Hollywood again." At one point when he was beginning to feel pressured, almost cornered, he booked tickets to Australia for himself and his wife, planning on moving to the outback to become a sheep farmer. He would quit acting, he decided, rather than compromise his values.

Following meetings with Four Star production executive Dick Powell, he was given more control over his character, and McQueen stayed with the series for another season, finally leaving in 1961. The last telecast of the series was in March of that year, after 94 episodes had been filmed.

In 1987 Rutger Hauer starred in a theatrically released version of the TV series. The title was the same—*Wanted: Dead or Alive*, with Hauer playing Nick Randall, grandson of Josh. It updated the concept to include the CIA's pursuit of Arab terrorists, but it bombed at the box office.

CREDITS

CREATOR/EXECUTIVE PRODUCER: Vincent Fennelly. PRODUCERS: John Robinson, Ed Adamson. DIRECTORS: Thomas Carr, Donald McDougall, others. WRITERS: various. CAST: *Josh Randall* (Steve McQueen), *Jason Nichols* (Wright King). GUEST STARS: Michael Landon, Nick Adams, Richard Eyer, Paul Burke, James Coburn, others.

PERRY MASON

NUMBER 10, 1959–60

According to his creator, Erle Stanley Gardner, Perry Mason was "the greatest of all criminal lawyers, real or fictional, living or dead." A person could be standing over a dead body, smoking gun in hand, yet the audience knew from the minute Perry took this person's case that his client was innocent, a victim of circumstantial evidence. Before the final commercial, Perry's client would be exonerated in a climactic courtroom scene in which the true killer, inevitably nailed by Mason, would break down in a sobbing confession.

When Gardner created Perry Mason in 1932, he could not have imagined that 60 years later, audiences would still be enjoying the exploits of his brainchild. His original novels were translated into several motion pictures, and a radio series of over 3,000 episodes ran from 1943 to 1955. When the series moved to television, the radio program, which had always put more emphasis on romance than mystery, changed its name to "The Edge of Night," and continued as a soap opera until 1984.

No one exemplified Gardner's image of Perry Mason more than Raymond Burr. To the public, he *was* Perry Mason. Yet he almost didn't get the role. When the producers were casting the original TV series in 1957, their first choice was Fred MacMurray. But MacMurray turned down the role because he didn't want the work load of an hour-long weekly drama. Raymond Burr, who had played mostly heavies in his career (the murderer in Hitchcock's *Rear Window*; the "Human Bomb" in the first episode of "Dragnet"), actively lobbied for the part of Mason, even going on a crash diet in order to look the part (Perry Mason was described as big, but not fat). Finally they agreed to test the persistent Burr, whom they had had in mind for the role of

D.A. Hamilton Burger. Creator Erle Stanley Gardener took one look at Burr's screen test, yelled "That's him!" and that was that.

The thankless job of playing Mason's nemesis, "Ham" Burger, went to William Talman, and it is usually (and erroneously) reported that in nine years of going one-on-one with the fabled Perry Mason, the beleaguered district attorney never won a case (and even more surprisingly, he never lost his job). But that is not technically correct. Mason actually lost *one* case during the series' 271 episodes—a client refused to reveal evidence that would have saved her.

From the start, Burr was dedicated to the role. Before filming began, he spent months absorbing the atmosphere of courtrooms, judges' chambers, sheriff's stations, and jails. He even went so far as to hole himself up in an office/bedroom just off the "Perry Mason" set so he could arise at 5:30 and memorize his legal speeches. He saw his role almost as a crusade for the legal profession. "I speak for world peace through law," he told a *TV Guide* interviewer. "I'm a kind of one-man lobby for the legal profession. I believe that the world will either destroy itself or learn how to settle things by law. So it becomes the world's most important profession. Perry may be a white knight on a horse, but he is accepted. He gives millions of people an awareness of what the law is and the tremendous need for it. It's not very often that a person is given the opportunity to use his personal image to do so much good in the world."

"Perry Mason" continued to solve cases until 1966, when CBS finally cancelled the show. That last first-run episode was called "The Case of the Final Fade-Out," and Erle Stanley Gardner did a rare cameo as the judge. But the

---

CREDITS

TOP 10 PEAK: No. 5, 1961–62.
CREATOR: Erle Stanley Gardner.
EXECUTIVE PRODUCER: Gail Patrick Jackson. PRODUCERS: Ben Brady, Arthur Marks, Arthur Seid, others. DIRECTORS: Arthur Marks, Richard Donner, others. WRITERS: various. CAST: *Perry Mason* (Raymond Burr), *Della Street* (Barbara Hale), *Paul Drake* (William Hopper), *Hamilton Burger* (William Talman), *Lt. Tragg* (Ray Collins), others. GUEST STARS: Walter Pidgeon, Bette Davis, Robert Redford, Ryan O'Neal, Leonard Nimoy, David McCallum, others.

EMMYS

Best Actor in a Dramatic Series— Raymond Burr (1958–59, 1969–61), Best Supporting Actress in a Dramatic Series—Barbara Hale (1958–59)

Raymond Burr, with Barbara Hale.

series refused to fade out. In 1973 someone at the network decided that what CBS needed for its new fall lineup was an all-new version of "Perry Mason." In fact, they called it "The New Perry Mason." But the only thing new was the casting—the slim Monte Markham as an athletic Mason, plus a whole new lineup of actors replacing those who had played the original roles for nine years. The public would have none of it. After one season, "The New Perry Mason" was history.

Then a strange thing happened. It could have been called "The Case of the Series That Refused to Die." In 1985 NBC acquired the rights to the series and began programming a number of "reunion" movie specials. "The Return of Perry Mason" was 1985's highest-rated made-for-TV movie and spawned a whole new series. Raymond Burr was coaxed out of a well-earned retirement in which he was raising sheep, poultry, and orchids on his 40-acre farm. He reluctantly returned as the invincible barrister, with Barbara Hale reprising her role as Mason's gal Friday, Della Street. The telefilms

became so popular that NBC began programming them on a regular basis, with new episodes still being broadcast every few months in 1993. The series still used the familiar format, complete with the opening theme music by Fred Steiner and the picture of a courtroom setting the stage for the drama that was about to take place. Each situation still presented lots of suspects, with Perry's client always number one on the list.

Part of what kept the show alive for so long was the presentation of three or four possible suspects and the inevitable unmasking of the real culprit in a final courtroom scene. Sixty years after its inception, the formula that Erle Stanley Gardner established showed no signs of failing. But it was Raymond Burr, even more than Perry Mason's creator, who would always be associated with that character. In 1993, at the age of 76, he was as convincing as ever in the role of the world's most famous lawyer. As Della Street put it in 1992's "The Case of the Heartbroken Bride," "You never change, Perry Mason. You only weather."

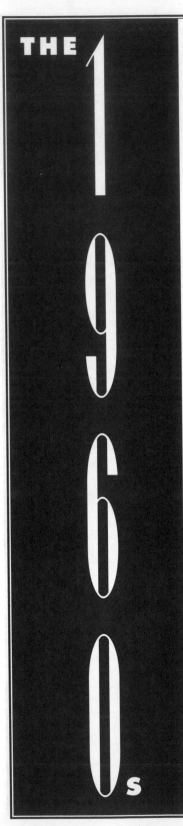

THE 1960s

If the '50s were "fabulous," the '60s could only be dubbed "silly." Cowboys were still reaching for the sky and top 10 ratings, but witches, monsters, Munsters, Martians, and a man who thought he was a bat were giving chase. And their southern cousins were soon a-hankerin' for some o' them Nielsen ratin's.

"The Beverly Hillbillies" premiered in 1962, with spin-offs and clones and down-home series taking to TV like boll weevils to cotton. By the end of the decade, television was in hillbilly heaven—its acres were green and its junctions sported petticoats. Television earned the dubious nickname "rube tube," while CBS, which ran most of the rural programming, was dubbed the Country Broadcasting System.

It wasn't all fun and cornpone, though. The decade of the '60s was one of the saddest times in United States history; assassinations of beloved leaders, the so-called "living-room war" in Vietnam, protest marches, and unrest in the cities all had a sobering effect. At the height of the mayhem, television countered with shows like "Rowan & Martin's Laugh-in," which helped the TV audience keep its sense of humor.

By now television was the province of the entire world— the Global Village was under construction. And in 1969 the medium took one small step for humankind as a family when 720 million people around the world watched Neil Armstrong and Edwin Aldrin walk on the moon that belonged to everyone. The best things in life—including television—were still free, at least for the time being.

THE ANDY GRIFFITH SHOW

NUMBER 4, 1960–61

Mayberry, North Carolina. A sleepy, dusty southern town circa 1960. Andy Taylor's the sheriff, justice of the peace, newspaper editor, and the town's most eligible widower. That's his young son, Opie, the cute, freckled-faced boy who's just lost his baby teeth. It's tough being a single parent and role model to the boy, but Andy's got plenty of help. There's Aunt Bea, of course, whose matronly wisdom is second only to her prize-winning apple pie. And there's the always cheerful Barney Fife, Andy's cousin/deputy sheriff, who keeps a bullet for his gun in his shirt pocket "just in case." Then there are the Pyle boys, Gomer and Goober, a couple o' kind-hearted local yokels who always have a friendly word.

This may seem like a dubious scenario for a success-ful television series, but successful it was. "Rural" was in, although "The Andy Griffith Show" was anything but the cornpone of "The Real McCoys" or "Green Acres." The people of Mayberry were genuine, believ-able folk with countrified, albeit Waspish, values. Viewers seldom saw African-Americans, Jews, Hispanics, or other ethnic types, but no one seemed to mind. For eight years audiences empathized with Andy's attempts to raise his boy while this offbeat slice of southern Americana paraded through his life.

"The Andy Griffith Show" was partly the brainchild of Sheldon Leonard, who created the pilot for the series as an episode of "The Danny Thomas Show" (airdate: Feb. 15, 1960). In that show, Danny got arrested while driving through a small southern town. The sheriff, of course, was Andy Taylor, and naturally all was solved within 30 minutes, just in time for the final commercial.

But most of what went into the creation of Mayberry, North Carolina, U.S.A., can be attributed to one person only: Andy Griffith.

In a sense, Griffith grew up in Mayberry, but it was really called Mt. Airy. Set in the northwest corner of North Carolina at the foot of the Blue Ridge Mountains, award-winning "All-American Town" Mt. Airy sowed its seeds deep within Griffith's psyche when he was just a lad about Opie's age. Griffith found a way to bring his bucolic roots and southern drawl into a characterization that made the series one of television's biggest prime-time hits.

Perhaps it was because this was a quieter time in American history—the Eisenhower years were over, the tumultuous '60s were just beginning. Perhaps it was due to the folksy characters we all would have liked to have had for friends or neighbors. Whatever the rea-son, the series was a resounding success, continually listed high among the top 10 shows during its first run.

Twenty-five years after departing the prime-time air-waves, "The Andy Griffith Show" was still going strong, supported by a cult following. With more than five mil-lion Americans tuning in the series on a daily basis (syndicated, mainly on TBS), it was one of the three most watched shows on U.S. cable TV in 1992. Then

---

CREDITS

TOP 10 PEAK: No. 1, 1967–68. CREATORS: Sheldon Leonard, Andy Griffith. EXECUTIVE PRODUCER: Sheldon Leonard. PRODUCERS: Aaron Ruben, Bob Ross, Richard O. Linke. DIRECTORS: Sheldon Leonard, Bob Sweeney, Aaron Ruben, Richard Crenna, Lee Phillips, others. WRITERS: Jack Elinson and Charles Stewart, David Adler, Ben Gershman and Leo Solomon, others. CAST: *Andy Taylor* (Andy Griffith), *Barney Fife* (Don Knotts), *Opie Taylor* (Ronny Howard), *Aunt Bea Taylor* (Frances Bavier), *Gomer Pyle* (Jim Nabors), *Goober Pyle* (George Lindsey), *Floyd Lawson* (Howard McNear). OTHER REGULARS: Elinor Donahue, Hope Summers, Aneta Corsaut, Hal Smith, Jack Dodson, Paul Hartman, Betty Lynn, Jack Burns. GUEST STARS: Bob Denver, Jesse White, Edgar Buchanan, Jackie Coogan, Buddy Ebson, Alan Hale, Jr., Bill Bixby, Barbara Eden, Michael J. Pollard, Sterling Holloway, Rance Howard, Clint Howard, Don Rickles, Jerry Van Dyke, Rob Reiner, Jack Albertson, Teri Garr, others.

EMMYS

Outstanding Performance in a Supporting Role by an Actor—Don Knotts (1960–61, 1961–62, 1962–63, 1965–66, 1966–67), Outstanding Performance by an Actress in a Supporting Role in a Comedy—Frances Bavier (1966–67).

there was the "Andy Griffith Show" Rerun Watchers Club, founded in 1979, with 650 chapters and over 20,000 members strong. These self-styled fans, sort of small-town "Trekkies," were like junkies when it came to their favorite series. They attended conventions, held chapter meetings, recited dialogue, swapped trading cards, and spent lots of money on calendars, books, and souvenirs. Imagine a 23-karat gold-rimmed, limited-edition plate featuring Sheriff Andy Taylor for just $29.50; or there's *Aunt Bea's Mayberry Cookbook*, published by Rutledge Hill Press, chock full of mm-mm-good down-home cookin'—things like Aunt Bee's Fried Chicken, Grandma's Biscuits, and Opie and Leon's Buttermilk Pie (Ron Howard's favorite when he was a little boy, according to his mother when she submitted the recipe).

"The Andy Griffith Show" was no Johnny-come-lately to popularity. When CBS finally cancelled it in 1968, it was ranked in the number one spot, only one of two series in TV history to end its run while it was on top ("I Love Lucy" was the other). By that time, Andy Griffith had decided it was time to move on. "Well, it's been awfully good," he said at the big farewell bash CBS threw for the crew. "It's been the best eight years of my life. I'll see ya again." (He did, of course.) Others in the cast had by then either moved on or were ready to make the move. Jim Nabors (Gomer Pyle) had already been spun off into his own series, "Gomer Pyle, USMC"; Ronny Howard had grown from a kindergartener to a teenager in high school—a role he would soon play to perfection in "Happy Days." Don Knotts (Barney Fife) would eventually have his own series, "The Don Knotts Show" (1970–71). What's more, CBS had wasted no time in preparing for the future. Reruns of all 249 episodes of "The Andy Griffith Show" were being shown under the title "Andy of Mayberry," while a brand-new series was already poised and ready to roll that fall—"Mayberry R.F.D." starring Ken Berry (see page 156).

It was Thomas Wolfe, another famous North Carolinian, who said, "You can't go home again," but in 1986 the denizens of Mayberry did their best to prove him wrong. A made-for-television movie, "Return to Mayberry," saw Andy Taylor returning to the town to run for sheriff after all those years, only to discover that

Barney Fife was also in the race. Ron Howard (by then a top producer/director) also returned, as did originals Aneta Corsaut (Helen Crump) and Betty Lynn (Thelma Lou). Even Gomer and Goober were there. (Missing were Howard McNair as Floyd, who died in 1969, and Frances Bavier as Andy's beloved Aunt Bea, who was too ill to appear and passed away a short time later.) And, *gaw-lee!*—it was the highest-rated movie of the

Andy Griffith and Ron Howard.

entire 1985–86 season. Surrounded by his former co-stars, the now gray-haired patriarch of Mayberry reflected on the glory days of the town: "Those were the best years of my life," he mused.

An "Andy Griffith Show Reunion," with most of the surviving cast members, aired in February 1993. It presented memorable moments from the series with black and white and color clips from favorite episodes of each actor.

RAWHIDE

NUMBER 6, 1960–61

Head 'em up. Move 'em out.
— OPENING TO "RAWHIDE"

Getting cattle from point A to point B seems an unlikely premise for a hit western, but that's exactly what "Rawhide" did for seven years, week after week on CBS (from January 1959 to January 1966). Obviously, there was more to it than that. With bullets ricocheting across America's television screens on almost an hourly basis, this series perhaps more than any other had *authenticity* as a main ingredient. It also had fine production values. And it didn't hurt that it had actor Clint Eastwood along for the cattle drive each week.

"Rawhide" was loosely based on the diary of a real-life cattle drover who lived in the 1860s. Although his accounts may have been the original fodder for the show's stories, there certainly was a good amount of story content attributable to the imaginations of the writers. But this series always *felt* more realistic than most. The "Rawhide" cowboys (in the literal sense of the word) had dust on their clothes and boots; they sweated and most likely stank; they dressed the way men dressed on a cattle drive along the Sedalia Trail from North Texas to the Kansas beef markets. The show's fine direction and camera work did much to convey the message that life on the trail was a daily struggle for survival. Even the need for water became a story point to hammer home. In emphasizing the lack of water along the trail, one drover exclaimed: "The man was sure right when he said, 'If he owned Texas and Hell, he'd rent out Texas and live in Hell.'"

Heading 'em up week after week was the seldom-recalled hero of this saga, Gil Favor, played by Eric Fleming. He was a man's man, a born leader with but one purpose: bringing in the cattle. Each week's show opened with a different, brief

narration by Favor, to set the tone: "It sounds simple when you start up," he proclaimed in one voiceover. "Get the herd to Aboline. Before you're halfway there, the cattle are the least of your worries. I know. Gil Favor, Trail Boss." Those other "worries" usually came in the form of stampedes, would-be rustlers, Indian raids, stagecoach encounters, and all the usual events one might meet in a life that was truly one of the hardest a person could wish for.

Gil Favor had help, of course. His second-in-command, trusted scout Rowdy Yates, was played by Clint Eastwood, and the series became his springboard to fame. In true Hollywood style, Eastwood was cast in the part after he was spotted by one of the producers in the CBS commissary. "I was the dumb sidekick, the one who wasn't too swift, the one with a little slack lip," Eastwood reminisced in the *Los Angeles Times*. "They were fun years, and they were frustrating, too. I grew to hate exposition and lots of dialogue because on 'Rawhide' we had to explain everything in the dialogue...It was frustrating, too, because I wanted to direct a show or two, but they always found some excuse for me not to. I was pigeonholed as an actor. It was pretty restrictive, but I sure learned a lot."

One of the things Eastwood learned was that he wanted to be a movie actor. During the series' hiatus, he spent some time off in Italy, making "spaghetti" westerns, including *A Fistful of Dollars* (1964) and *For a Few Dollars More* (1965). Eastwood's success coupled with his desire to play a more important role in "Rawhide" resulted in the departure of Eric Fleming from the show in 1965. Fleming, too, had set his sights on moviemaking, but instead met with tragedy: while he was on location in Peru the following summer filming a new adventure

---

CREDITS

PRODUCERS: Charles Marquis Warren, Vincent M. Fennelly, others. DIRECTORS: Ted Post, Thomas Carr, Others. WRITERS: various. CAST: *Gil Favor* (Eric Fleming), *Rowdy Yates* (Clint Eastwood), *Pete Nolan* (Sheb Wooley), *Wishbone* (Paul Brinegar), *Jim Quince* (Steve Raines), *Jim Scarlett* (Rocky Shahan), *Harkness "Mushy" Mushgrove* (James Murdock), *Jesus Patines* (Robert Cabal). GUEST STARS: Barbara Stanwyck, Buddy Ebsen, James Coburn, Burgess Meredith, Barbara Eden, others.

---

series, his canoe tipped over in the swift current of the Huallaga River and he drowned. Eventually the producers agreed to let Eastwood, as Yates, take over as trail boss for the final season (1965–66). Others in the cast included country singer Sheb Wooley as Pete Nolan (Wooley earned fame for his bizarre hit song, "Purple People Eater"), Paul Brinegar as Wishbone the cook, and Steve Raines as Jim Quince, the latter two regulars appearing in nearly all of the series' 144 episodes.

One of the memorable aspects of "Rawhide" was its theme music, the whip-cracking "rollin', rollin', rollin'" tune recorded by Frankie Laine. The music was by Dmitri Tiomkin, a noted composer of motion picture soundtracks. Although his work was not limited to western themes, they were among his most memorable scores. Some of them included *Duel in the Sun* (1947), *Red River* (1948), *High Noon* (1952), *Giant* (1956), and *The Alamo* (1960). The unforgettable lyrics by Ned Washington ("move 'em on, head 'em up, head 'em up, move 'em on") were much parodied, even three decades later. Example: a 1992 commercial for Old El Paso food sauces urged viewers to "pour 'em on, eat 'em up, eat 'em up, pour 'em on."

Meanwhile, "Rawhide" kept them dogies rollin' right along into syndication and on to videocassettes, which CBS issued beginning in 1991 with their "Rawhide" Collector's Edition. No doubt their sales slogan was, "Move 'em out!"

Clint Eastwood (left) and Eric Fleming.

CANDID CAMERA

Courtesy of Photofest

Allen Funt readies a trap with Larraine Day.

Smile! You're on "Candid Camera!"

Before there was a "Candid Camera," there was a "Candid Microphone." Allen Funt, a onetime gag writer for radio's "Truth or Consequences," discovered his secret formula for the "Candid" programs while he was stationed at an army base in Oklahoma during World War II. Charged with doing a radio show concerning servicemen's gripes, he noticed how his subjects froze when confronted with a microphone, so he found a way to conceal it and banish their inhibitions. He later parlayed this into the successful above-named radio show which originated in 1947. In 1948 he started a TV show, "Candid Mike," which became the prototype for the now-familiar "Candid Camera."

For years his series ran on early television as a segment on other programs, most frequently on "The Garry Moore Show." Then in 1960 the show was finally given its own spot on CBS, where it consistently rated in the top 10.

The format was simple, yet ingenious: people were caught in the act of being themselves. A camera was hidden from the view of the person being set up, often just a few inches from their faces. Scenarios running from the sublime to the ridiculous were devised. The "victim" was caught in Allen Funt's snare with inevitably hilarious results. And along the way, some really strange things happened: a clothing salesman produced a tongue depressor to examine a customer's throat; animals talked; a sign on the road read, "Delaware Closed Today" (motorists asked, "Is Jersey open?").

At first Allen Funt appeared in all the stunts himself. He recalled only one bad experience: once, when he was portraying an over-zealous barber, the customer, tired of being harangued into having services he didn't want, grabbed a razor and chased Funt around the shop for five minutes. Funt said it was the only time in thousands of stunts that he was ever threatened with violence.

"Candid Camera" became so ingrained in American culture that people began to assume that wherever Funt went, his camera followed. On one occasion in the 1960s, he was a passenger on a plane that was hijacked, and the passengers jumped up and cheered, assuming—incorrectly—that it was a television stunt.

The show was one of the first successful "reality" programs. "At its best," said Funt, "it gets down to what people are really like. It's as close to ordinary people as television has come up with yet." For 11 years producer Funt had four crews working five days a week, filming up to 60 people a day for potential shows. By 1985 he figured he had recorded about 1.4 million people. (Not all were used, of course.)

Of all the stunts he pulled, the one the public recalled most fondly ("and I don't understand why," said Funt) was the one called "Talking Mailbox." Funt described it in a *Psychology Today* interview as follows: "We put a microphone and a speaker in a mailbox in New York City and had it talk to people passing by. Most are cynical at first, but soon they are carrying on a conversation with the box, answering questions about where the mailman is and lifting the lid so that the box can get a better look at them. The best part occurs when a tough old-timer challenges the box by threatening to call a cop. The mailbox persuades him that it means no offense. Convinced that this really is a special experience, the old timer calls another passerby over to talk to it. Despite his urging, the box won't say a word. The next 10 seconds of silence get some of the biggest laughs of anything we've ever done."

Another well-remembered segment was "the car with no engine." A car with no engine under the hood was rolled down a hill to a gas station, and the driver asked the attendant to change the oil and then headed for the restroom. When she returned, he told her the car didn't have an engine. She told the bewildered attendant that a joke's a joke and that he'd better put it back under the hood by the time she returned from the restroom again.

The gags didn't always work. Most of them were filmed in New York City, where the series was based, and New Yorkers (being New Yorkers) aren't apt to notice very much. Once Funt and his crew had a knight in full armor emerge from a sewer manhole, and most people simply passed him by without so much as a curious glance.

"Candid Camera" enjoyed a healthy seven-year run on CBS, then was abruptly cancelled in 1967. Later, Allen Funt brought the concept back in numerous incarnations, including a syndicated version in the 1970s, a Playboy cable channel rendition in the mid-1980s, and a gaggle of "theme" specials for CBS, including the December 1987 "Candid Camera Christmas Special," "Candid Camera: Eat! Eat! Eat!" (January 1989, co-hosted by Allen and his son, Peter Funt), "Candid Camera on Wheels" (May 1989), "Candid Camera...Funny Money" (January 1990), "Candid Camera...Smile, You're on Vacation" (April 1990), "The Candid Camera Comedy Shopping Spree" (May 1990), "Candid Camera...Physical Fitness" (May 1990), "Candid Camera Goes to the Doctor" (September 1990), and "Candid Camera...The Sporting Life" (November 1990).

In 1991 a new "Candid Camera" series with Funt serving as producer and Dom DeLuise signed up as host was making the rounds in syndication. In the era of fast food and "sound bites," adjustments had to be made. Where the original segments ran an average length of five minutes, they now averaged half that time in the new series.

Shorter segments were not the only consequence of changing times. Funt claimed it was "harder to deceive people now. They are more know-ledgeable about technology, more sophisticated about their rights, more cynical and assertive and, of course, sensitized to the 'Candid Camera' type of experience."

So be on the alert, but don't be surprised if someday somebody steps up to you and says, "Smile! You're on 'Candid Camera!'"

CREDITS

Top 10 Peak: No. 2, 1962–63. Creator: Allen Funt. Executive Producer: Bob Banner. Producers: Allen Funt, Julio DiBenedetto, Bob Shanks. Directors: Julio DiBenedetto, Lou Tyrrell, others. Writers: various.* Host: Allen Funt. Guest Hosts: Arthur Godfrey, Dorothy Collins, Durward Kirby, Bess Myerson, others.

---

*At one time the writing staff boasted William Saroyan, who was in trouble with the income tax board and needed to find a way to earn some quick money. He was paid $5,000 a week for his trouble.

THE UNTOUCHABLES

NUMBER 8 (TIE), 1960–61

Television critics decried it as too violent. Italian-American groups denounced it as racist. Nevertheless, "The Untouchables" lived up to its title and continued to entrance the American television audience for four seasons on ABC, from 1959 to 1963.

Originally appearing as a two-part episode of "Desilu Playhouse" in the spring of 1959, "The Untouchables" was based on the career of Eliot Ness, a U.S. federal agent, and starred Robert Stack as the stone-faced, robotic Ness. He had been a last-minute choice when producer Desi Arnaz learned only hours before filming was to begin that Van Johnson, the man he had signed to play Ness, wanted double the salary he'd been offered. Cameras were ready to roll as Desi hurriedly thumbed through the *Academy Players Directory* searching for an instant replacement. It took some incredible persuasion on the part of Arnaz, but Stack was on the set the next morning at six o'clock.

Until he filmed the "Desilu Playhouse" drama, Robert Stack had done only limited television work. He was, after all, a veteran of over 30 successful motion pictures. He agreed to do the "Playhouse" part, thinking it would end there. But the night the show aired, an ABC program executive, desperate for something unique for the 1959 fall lineup, spotted the potential in a full-time "Untouchables" TV series. Arnaz agreed, but Stack wasn't interested. "TV series was a dirty word," he said in a *Los Angeles Times* interview. "At that time, television series were for people who were out of work and couldn't get a job in the movies." Again, the Cuban producer used his powers of persuasion, promising that "The

Untouchables" would be a first-class endeavor. Stack relented, and the series became an instant hit.

Arnaz kept his promise, and production values were incredibly high. Attention to authenticity contributed to the look and feel of the show. The wardrobe, the props, and the cars all helped depict the 1930s era with accuracy. Two full-time researchers were employed to check guns, clothing, and furniture. Newspapers of the period were specially printed in a local shop. And the studio parking lot looked like an antique auto dealership. Robert Stack believed, in fact, that among the determining factors in making the show a hit were the old cars. "We had a black Pierce Arrow with those wonderful headlights coming out of the fenders," Stack said in a CNBC interview with Dick Cavett. "You could take it down a dark alley at night with the garbage cans and the guys with the machine guns, and there was more suspense...the best actor we had was that Pierce Arrow."

The first few years of the series concentrated on the historical aspects of Ness's attempts to reel in Al "Scarface" Capone, and because of the number of Italian mobsters involved, there was a brouhaha concerning the overemphasis on criminals with Italian surnames. Frank Sinatra, Senator John Pastore, even Cardinal Spellman all began to put pressure on the show's producers. The Liggett and Myers Tobacco Company dropped sponsorship after their product was effectively boycotted. Al Capone's widow brought a $1.5 million suit against the show (which was heavily insured for libel), claiming they used his name without obtaining permission.

CREDITS

EXECUTIVE PRODUCER: Quinn Martin, Jerry Thorpe, Alan Armer. PRODUCERS: Charles Russell, Josef Shaftel, others. DIRECTORS: John Peyser, Stuart Rosenberg, others. WRITERS: various. CAST: *Eliot Ness* (Robert Stack), *Agent Martin Flaherty* (Jerry Paris), *Agent William Youngfellow* (Abel Fernandez), *Agent Enrico Rossi* (Nicholas Georgiade), *Frank Nitti* (Bruce Gordon), *Al Capone* (Neville Brand). NARRATOR: Walter Winchell. GUEST STARS: Nehemiah Persoff, Norman Fell, Elizabeth Montgomery, Peter Falk, Robert Redford, Robert Duvall, William Bendix, Barbara Stanwyck, William Bendix, Lloyd Nolan, Telly Savalas, Cloris Leachman, Vic Morrow, others.

EMMYS

Outstanding Performance by an Actor in a Series, Lead or Support—Robert Stack (1959–60).

Robert Stack.

In truth, the series had always shown Ness grappling with a number of gangsters such as George (Bugs) Moran, Vincent (Mad Dog) Coll, and Kate (Ma) Barker, none of whom were the real Ness's quarry. But the producers yielded to the pressure, and by the second year, Eliot Ness had stopped his relentless pursuit of Capone, Lucky Luciano, Frank Nitti, and others in favor of less ethnic sounding, fictitious criminals named "Smith," "Jones," and "Grant." Bending to pressure, Arnaz announced that there would be no more fictional hoods with Italian names; there would be more stress on the law-enforcement role of Ness's right-hand man in the show, Agent Rossi, and more emphasis would be placed on the contributions made to American culture by Americans of Italian descent. The tobacco industry, it seems, proved Ness's most formidable opponent of all.

By the fourth year, much of what had given the show its impetus had been so watered down that the series had lost its appeal. At the same time, the production schedules had become grueling. "We would work all night," said Robert Stack. "The camera operator died

after the third year of a coronary. I hemorrhaged my vocal cords and everybody was ill. At the end, we were supposed to do a fifth year and I said, 'There is nothing left.' "

After 114 episodes, G-man Ness appeared to have routed his last mobster. But in the summer of 1987, Eliot Ness and his Untouchables were resurrected for a feature-length motion picture. The Brian DePalma film version of *The Untouchables* starred Kevin Costner as a more humanized Ness, while the film's violence made the original TV series look like a romp through a daisy field. It was a resounding hit at the box office. Motivated by the resurgence of interest in Eliot Ness, NBC brought back Robert Stack (whom they had under contract for "Unsolved Mysteries"—see page 342) for one more time in a 1991 TV movie, "The Return of Eliot Ness." Set in 1947, the story had Ness coming out of retirement to clear the name of a murdered Untouchable.

A new series from Paramount Pictures, shot on location in Chicago, went into syndication in 1993.

BONANZA

NUMBER 2, 1961–62

"Another western is just what Saturday night television needs least, and that's what 'Bonanza' appears to be—just another western."

Calling "Bonanza" a "longshot...without a fresh twist to distinguish it," the reviewer for *Variety* couldn't have been further off the mark. He thought the show would soon be history, and indeed it would, but not the kind he envisioned.

Within a year of its September 1959 premiere, "Bonanza" was moved to its permanent Sunday night berth on NBC; within another year it was ranked number two, and for most of its long prime-time run, the series would battle it out with "Gunsmoke" for the title of the most popular western ever made for television. Just another western, indeed.

What "Bonanza" brought to the genre was a de-emphasis on shootouts and gunfights and more emphasis on the American dream: home, family, traditional values. By now the central characters have, of course, become legendary, and the series has been dubbed into dozens of foreign languages; rare is the person who doesn't know of the Cartwrights of the Ponderosa ranch.

"Bonanza" was created by David Dortort, who had made his mark as producer of the hit series "The Restless Gun" (see page 78). When he began casting for Ben Cartwright and his three sons, he knew exactly what he was looking for. The patriarch of the Cartwright clan had to be a strong father figure. "Father always turns out to be a fool," Dortort said in *TV Guide*. "On TV it's mother who really knows best. Ben Cartwright is *not* a blithering idiot, but someone his three sons can respect." He spotted Lorne Greene in an episode of "Wagon Train," and the actor who had once been the "Voice of

Canada" for the Canadian Broadcasting Company became head of the Ponderosa.

Dortort was familiar with Dan Blocker from his work on "The Restless Gun," and the 275-pound actor, who had been teaching school in Texas only a few years before, became the middle brother, Hoss.

Michael Landon's biggest claim to fame until that time had been the lead in *I Was a Teenage Werewolf* (1957), but Dortort had worked with him on "Restless Gun," admitting he'd made a mistake by killing him off in the pilot. He rectified the error by assigning Landon the role of Little Joe Cartwright.

The fourth role to be cast was that of the eldest brother, Adam, for whom he selected Pernell Roberts, an unknown New York actor. His choices were to prove propitious, with all but Blocker (who died suddenly of a heart attack in 1972) eventually starring in series of their own.

Each actor brought a special quality to his character. Ben (Lorne Greene) was the founder of the Cartwright dynasty, a widower three times over (each of his sons' mothers had met a tragic death while their sons were still infants). He had better luck when it came to eking out a living. His "bonanza" came from a silver strike in the Comstock Lode, a vein that brought untold riches to those lucky enough to make such a strike in the mountains near Virginia City, Nevada, in the 1860s.

Adam (Pernell Roberts) was the serious, stable, older brother; dressed all in black, he became a sex symbol to college coeds in the audience, who spent Sunday nights gathered in dormitories for a glimpse of this most mysterious of the Cartwrights.

CREDITS

TOP 10 PEAK: No. 1, 1964–65. CREATOR: David Dortort. EXECUTIVE PRODUCER: David Dortort. PRODUCERS: Dortort, Richard Collins. DIRECTORS: various. WRITERS: various. CAST: *Ben Cartwright* (Lorne Greene), *Adam Cartwright* (Pernell Roberts), *Hoss Cartwright* (Dan Blocker), *Little Joe Cartwright* (Michael Landon), *Hop Sing* (Victor Sen Yung), *Sheriff Roy Coffee* (Ray Teal), *Candy* (David Canary), *Dusty Rhoades* (Lou Frizzel), *Jamie Hunter* (Mitch Vogel), *Griff King* (Tim Matheson). GUEST STARS: Yvonne De Carlo, Herschel Bernardi, Telly Savalas, Tommy Sands, Charles Ruggles, Bonnie Bedelia, Inger Stevens, Jack Carson, Ruth Roman, Howard Duff, others.

Hoss (Dan Blocker) was a mountain of a man who played a gentle, jovial giant. He was easily distinguished by his broad grin and 60-gallon hat.

Little Joe (Michael Landon) was the baby of the family, both figuratively and literally. He began as a 22-year-old with handsome, boyish looks and little experience. By the time the series had run its course in 1974, Landon had directed over a dozen episodes, written several more, and of course co-starred in all of them. His success story would be one of the most often told in television as he continued producing, directing, writing, and acting in his own series over the next three decades, working right up until his untimely death at the age of 54 in 1991.

Americans remained faithful to "Bonanza" throughout its long run, despite the changes wrought by the latter years. Pernell Roberts left the series in 1965, reportedly tired of the weekly grind. He didn't land much work, though, until 14 years later, in 1979, when he starred in his own series, "Trapper John, M.D." David Canary was introduced in 1967 as the ranch hand Candy. Some other new characters came on board in the early 1970s.

By the time NBC's longest-running series (14 years,

440 episodes) was cancelled in 1973, the ratings had finally dropped off. It was due in part to the death of Dan Blocker, though the series was also suffering from the competition on Tuesday night, where it had been re-slated to run against ABC's movies and CBS's successful "Maude" and "Hawaii Five-O."

There was a 1988 spin-off movie entitled "Bonanza: The Next Generation." It was intended as a pilot for a sequel series, and starred John Ireland as the deceased Ben Cartwright's brother Aaron (Lorne Greene had died before filming began) and Michael Landon, Jr., as Little Joe's son, Benji. When that didn't sell, creator/producer David Dortort began anew in 1992 with a first-run series called "Bonanza: Legends of the Ponderosa." In that one, Michael Landon, Jr., still played the son of Little Joe, and Ben Johnson starred as an old friend of Ben Cartwright. The young heir to the late Michael, Sr., was set to write and direct several of the initial 26 episodes. " 'Bonanza' was where my father got all of his breaks and wrote and directed and learned his craft," said Michael, Jr. NBC planned to air part of the series in November 1993 as a two-hour movie titled "Bonanza: The Return." If successful, the network had plans for two more movies and possibly a full series.

From left: Dan Blocker, Lorne Green, Pernell Roberts, and Michael Landon.

HAZEL

**Shirley Booth poses atop a power mower for a "Hazel" publicity shot.
Note what appears to be a label still tagging the mower.**

This series could have been titled "Hazel Knows Best." Hazel was the name of the Baxter family's housekeeper, and there was never any doubt about who ran the household. Throughout every crisis—and viewers could count on at least one a week—Hazel took charge, generally over the protests of her long-suffering employers.

The series actually began as a popular Ted Key cartoon in *The Saturday Evening Post* 19 years earlier, and in 1961 Hazel became one of only a handful of cartoon characters ever to receive shows of their own. It wasn't a western, a spy thriller, or a cop show, and most critics panned it royally. "The comedy is so banal and so shamelessly contrived that it can only be exasperating to the adult mind, particularly when the laugh-track finds hilarity in everything from the movement of an eye muscle to the merest complication of plot," wrote the reviewer in *Variety*. Adding insult to injury, he went on to say that " 'Hazel' is grossly unworthy of its star, Shirley Booth." The attitude was slow to die. Years later, critics were still decrying Booth's defection to TV, in one case stating, "Miss Booth playing Hazel is roughly tantamount to John Barrymore playing Henry Aldrich, but probably no one could play it better."

On that account, at least, he may have been right.

Shirley Booth had had a long and illustrious career on the Broadway stage, along with a few choice roles in film, when she was tapped for the role of the dominating maid who habitually preempted her boss's authority. She had won both the Tony and Oscar awards for her stage and screen portrayals of Lola Delaney in 1950s productions of "Come Back, Little Sheba," as well as the New York Drama Critics Award and the Cannes Festival acting award. She had also been the original Dolly Levi in the movie *The Matchmaker* (1958), the prototype for the musical "Hello, Dolly!" But critics have been known to be wrong, and this time Shirley, like her character Hazel, was right as usual. The TV character became her most memorable performance, and when she died in 1992 at the age of 94, the four-time Emmy Award winner was most fondly remembered not for her well-deserved stage and screen accomplishments, but for her role as Hazel.

Don DeFore played attorney George Baxter, the supposed head of the family. Hazel had no compunction about meddling in his business affairs, and he seemed resigned to being second-in-command of his home life. During the 1940s and 1950s DeFore had played mostly supporting roles, typically as a sweet but gullible bumpkin. He spent six years, from 1952 to 1958, as Ozzie Nelson's next-door neighbor, Thorny Thornberry, before landing the opportunity to play the hapless George Baxter.

The series only reached the top 10 in its first season, a comedy respite from all the flying bullets of TV's ever-popular westerns. For four years the format remained basically the same, with George and Dorothy Baxter struggling to raise their adorable little boy, Harold. Then someone noticed that Hazel was a white maid working for an all-white family in an all-white neighborhood. Social conscience was just beginning to creep into the early 1960s, and "Hazel" needed a little push to get with it. The show got it when the NAACP threatened a nationwide boycott of Ford, which sponsored the series, and more black actors were hired.

After four seasons on NBC, the format of "Hazel" was abruptly changed. Viewers learned that George Baxter had left for "an assignment" in the Middle East, leaving Hazel and George's son Harold (who stayed behind to finish high school, it was explained) to move in with George's brother Steve, a real estate salesman. Unfazed, Hazel continued doing what she did best, meddling in the lives of those she worked for, proving that she knew best. The series' producers were not always right, however. Besides the format change, the show also got a new network, CBS, where it survived for only one season.

CREDITS

EXECUTIVE PRODUCER: Harry Ackerman. PRODUCER: James Fonda. DIRECTORS: William D. Russell, others. WRITERS: William Cowley, Peggy Chantler, others. CAST: *Hazel Burke* (Shirley Booth), *George Baxter* (Don DeFore), *Dorothy Baxter* (Whitney Blake), *Harold Baxter* (Bobby Buntrock), *Rosie* (Maudie Prickett), *Harvey Griffin* (Howard Smith), *Steve Baxter* (Ray Fulmer), *Barbara Baxter* (Lynn Borden), *Susie Baxter* (Julia Benjamin). GUEST STARS: Ann Jillian, Rosemary DeCamp, John Archer, Virginia Gregg, others.

EMMYS

Outstanding Continued Performance by an Actress in a Series, Lead—Shirley Booth (1961–62, 1962–63).

DR. KILDARE

NUMBER 9, 1961–62

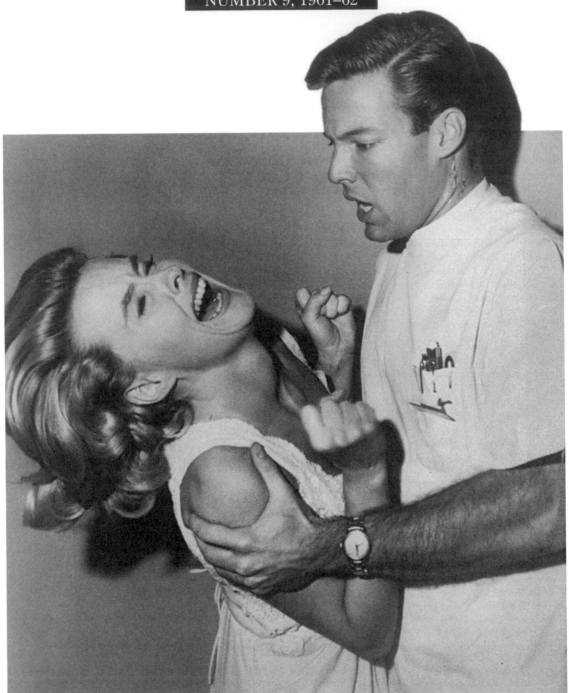

Richard Chamberlain, with guest star Dina Merrill.

In 1938 MGM acquired the rights to novelist Max Brand's creation, *Dr. Kildare*, and began a series of more than a dozen successful movies based on the characters of a medical intern and his mentor. Lew Ayres starred as the young Dr. Kildare, while Lionel Barrymore played the crusty senior Dr. Gillespie. When they decided to translate the concept to television, the studio ordered up a pilot which enlisted the original actor, Lew Ayres, to play a more mature Kildare. According to executive producer Norman Felton, "The result was a clinical sort of film, too much like a documentary." It was a resounding failure. Felton did a second pilot, hiring veteran actor Raymond Massey, famed for his portrayal of Abraham Lincoln, to play the wise Dr. Gillespie.

Locating just the right person for the role of young Kildare was a bit more of a challenge. At least 35 actors read for the part, including William Shatner. Shatner, in fact, was the top contender when he decided to accept another offer—"For the People" (and when that was quickly cancelled, he found himself being offered the Captain's chair in a new series called "Star Trek"). Finally producer Felton allowed a nervous young actor named Richard Chamberlain to read. Until then, Chamberlain had done only a few minor roles in TV, and had recently been collecting $38 a week at the unemployment office. "He had the physical appearance that we wanted. We decided to let him try the pilot film."

Apparently he had the physical appearance that the audience wanted. The series became one of those overnight hits all producers dream about, and Chamberlain found himself the object of 80 million admirers around the globe. He was mobbed wherever he went by throngs of squealing women who wanted to know more about his, not Kildare's, bedside manner.

But it was more than Chamberlain's boyish blond looks that attracted viewers and the 4,500 fan letters a week; Dr. Kildare was an idealist, a medical crusader, and a virtual boy scout. This latter aspect of his character frustrated Chamberlain. "He is good, high-minded, trustworthy, loyal, kind, warm-hearted, friendly, sincere, and chaste," said the actor in the *Saturday Evening Post*. "He also is nobler than humans prefer other humans to be. If I were to mold Kildare, I would make him more subject to faults and weaknesses—like the rest of us. I might even have him pinch a nurse or two." Horrors. What would Dr. Gillespie think?

Despite Chamberlain's image of his character, the show's producer David Victor declared in *Newsweek*,

"We stress reality. If we can achieve only 75 percent drama to keep the reality, then we achieve only 75 percent." The reality wasn't the blood-and-guts type that would be portrayed a decade later on "M*A*S*H," but rather the human-interest kind reflected in the relationship between Dr. Gillespie and his protege Dr. Kildare. They had a father-son sort of intimacy, which was stressed more than the doctor-patient relationships. The stern but concerned Gillespie was always prodding, pushing his charge to strive just a little more. "Being the best at something you love—that's important," instructed Gillespie.

"Dr. Kildare" was the forerunner of an epidemic of medical series (another hit, "Ben Casey," premiered within four days of "Kildare"). The show had a successful five-year run, but by 1966 Richard Chamberlain was almost relieved when the program wasn't renewed. He blamed the decline in ratings on the show's shift in emphasis away from the Kildare-Gillespie conflict. "It was wonderful at first," he said. "The relationship between Kildare and Dr. Gillespie interested me. But as time went on, it became more and more an anthology show, and the guest stars became more and more important. They ran out of arguments...At the end I couldn't find anything new to say with the character. I had worn out every facet."

Indeed, the producers had shifted the series away from its main characters in favor of the illnesses and problems of the "guest" patients, even serializing some 30-minute episodes during the final season, rather than continuing with the one-hour format that had worked so well until then. NBC finally cancelled the series in the fall of 1966 after 192 episodes. Richard Chamberlain, who at one time was concerned that the bubble would burst and he'd be back on the unemployment line, proved he had staying power and became the "king of the miniseries" in the 1970s and 1980s, starring in such successful epics as "Centennial," "Shogun," and "The Thorn Birds."

In 1972 MGM tried to resuscitate the series in a new incarnation called "Young Dr. Kildare," starring Mark Jenkins as Kildare and Gary Merrill as Gillespie. The half-hour series was videotaped and had a brief run in syndication.

In 1992 Boardwalk Entertainment, a New York-based development firm, announced plans to produce the 55-year-old Max Brand classic once again after obtaining rights from the creator's estate. The firm's executives were planning a series of episodes in the style of the recent updates of "Perry Mason" and "Columbo."

CREDITS

CREATOR: Max Brand. EXECUTIVE PRODUCER: Norman Felton. PRODUCERS: David Victor, others. DIRECTORS: various. WRITERS: various. CAST: *Dr. James Kildare* (Richard Chamberlain), *Dr. Leonard Gillespie* (Raymond Massey), *Nurse Zoe Lawton* (Lee Kurtz), *Dr. Simon Agurski* (Eddie Ryder), *Dr. Thomas Gerson* (Jud Taylor). GUEST STARS: Beverly Garland, Jack Weston, Charles Bronson, Stanley Adams, Walter Matthau, Rosemary DeCamp, James Mason, others.

THE BEVERLY HILLBILLIES

NUMBER 1, 1962–63

Come 'n' listen to my story 'bout a man named Jed...
—OPENING THEME SONG

Accompanied by banjo twangs, so began "The Ballad of Jed Clampett," the theme song for "The Beverly Hillbillies," and for nine years America listened to and watched this man from the Ozarks. Jed, of course, along with his seemingly inbred relatives, had struck "black gold," "Texas tea," so he did what "The Real McCoys" had done five years before him: "loaded up the family and moved to Beverly" in a 1921 flatbed truck, like rich Joads from *The Grapes of Wrath*, driving to the Promised Land.

If Californ-y was becoming overrun with rubes, so were the Nielsens, and CBS had its own gusher in the form of a genu-wine ratings hit. In a television record that has yet to be equalled, "The Beverly Hillbillies" pumped itself straight to the top within three weeks after its premiere, stayed in the number one position for two years, and remained a Nielsen top-tenner for several more years.

The critics were aghast. From the moment it aired, "The Beverly Hillbillies" was pronounced a piece of hopeless TV trash. "If television is America's vast wasteland, the 'Hillbillies' must be Death Valley," sniffed one critic. "Too absurd to be even slightly amusing," sighed another. "At no time does it give the viewer credit for even a smattering of intelligence," wailed *Variety*. Only the *TV Guide* reviewer had the guts to admit, "The single, simple, and to some people outrageous fact is that 'The Beverly Hillbillies' is funny." Folks thought so too, giving it some of the highest-rated half-hours in TV history; in fact, the most watched 30-minute episode of all time was

the "Hillbillies" segment in which Granny mistook a kangaroo for a giant jack rabbit.

Producer Paul Henning created the series and wrote most of the episodes. When he first thought of a locale for the *nouveaux riches* Clampetts, Hemming "tried to think of an upbeat setting. At first I thought we'd go to New York," Hemming said, "and then I thought, why go to New York when Beverly Hills is a few blocks away and it's just as classy." It was the American Dream that somehow became the American Nightmare, these po' folk making good and living in La La Land.

Humor was derived from the naiveté-cum-wholesomeness of the bumpkin Clampett clan: Jed, the patriarch with a simple manner but a quick mind; Granny, superstitiously clinging to the old ways, who could serve up a mean possum-innards stew; Elly May, virginal but on the cutting edge, her brain as precariously put together as the rope that belted her jeans; and Jethro, equally pure with a boyish mind trapped in the body of a hunk of a man. His unworldliness was incredible, as demonstrated by a scene at a hotel:

CLERK
You've got a surprise coming to you: your suite.

JETHRO
So are you, ma'am.

Years later, scholars would attempt to analyze the series for its social content and underlying themes, but creator Hemming explained, "I wasn't writing it with any hidden meanings attached other than those basic virtues of honesty and caring. I was just trying to make the show funny."

The show's success continued to baffle the experts. What *was* so darn funny about "The Beverly

---

CREDITS

CREATOR: Paul Henning. EXECUTIVE PRODUCER: Al Simon. PRODUCER: Paul Henning. DIRECTORS: Joe Depew, others. WRITERS: Paul Henning, Mark Tuttle, others. CAST: *Jed Clampett* (Buddy Ebsen), *Granny Daisy Moses* (Irene Ryan), *Elly May Clampett* (Donna Douglas), *Jethro Bodine* (Max Baer, Jr.), *Milburn Drysdale* (Raymond Bailey), *Jane Hathaway* (Nancy Kulp), *Mrs. Margaret Drysdale* (Harriet MacGibbon), *Cousin Pearl Bodine* (Bea Benaderet). GUEST STARS: Paul Lynde, Frank Wilcox, Louis Nye, Sharon Tate, Phil Silvers.

Max Baer Jr., Buddy Ebsen, and Irene Ryan.

Hillbillies?" Perhaps it was the fact that the characters never seemed to change, living an eternally-Ozark existence. The Clampetts may have settled in Beverly Hills, but as Granny once put it, "Dirt is dirt." They continued to hunt for their dinner; they grazed their critters on the lawn and watered them in the "cee-ment pond." They never threw any business Gucci's way either, preferring their old duds to shopping for new ones on Rodeo Drive.

The only time the formula was tampered with was at the beginning of the sixth season. Where do we go now? the producers asked. Someone had the idea—an old one—of taking the show to Europe. So Jed became heir to a castle and the clan went off to England for a change of venue. Later they returned to their proper roots, where, they realized, they really did belong: not in the mountains of Arkansas, but in their true home, the hills of Beverly.

The series was cancelled in 1971. A 1981 TV movie, "The Return of the Beverly Hillbillies," guest-starred Werner Klemperer.

A "Beverly Hillbillies" film was planned for release sometime in 1993. Twentieth Century Fox said the picture would possibly star Buddy Ebsen, now age 85, playing the widowed Jed Clampett finally getting remarried. Others tentatively signed included Lily Tomlin as Miss Hathaway and Cloris Leachman as Granny. It seemed certain that the movie would have no trouble finding an audience. More than 30 years after its premiere, "The Beverly Hillbillies" was still attracting 60 million viewers a week from its syndication in 55 U.S. cities. In addition, it was being broadcast in numerous countries the world over, and was being dubbed into native languages.

Wonder how the Japanese say, "Y'all come back now, heah?"

THE LUCY SHOW

NUMBER 4 (TIE), 1962–63

Vivian Vance and Gale Gordon flank the star of "The Lucy Show."

Americans had been Lucy-less for a year (see "I Love Lucy"—page 224) when their favorite redhead returned to the CBS airwaves in October 1962 with a new series. Where other stars needed their full names in their series' titles (e.g., "The Danny Thomas Show," "The Andy Griffith Show," "The Red Skelton Show," and "The Jack Benny Show") there could never be any doubt who the star of "The Lucy Show" was. There was only one Lucille Ball, and America still loved her.

This time she did it alone. In the new series' format, Lucy played a widowed mother with two children who shared her Connecticut home with friend Vivian Vance (whose character was appropriately named Viv), a divorcée with a son of her own. The comedy, loosely based on the book *Life Without George* by Irene Kampen, centered on the two women and their hare-brained attempts to get rich or find men—not much substance, but dynamite in the hands of these two old teammates. Very often the humor was physical, as in one oft-remembered scene concerning stilts and a bunk bed.

What seemed to be missing was a male foil for Lucy's humor, but the situation was quickly remedied with the addition of longtime pal Gale Gordon. Lucy's first choice for Fred Mertz in "I Love Lucy" had in fact been Gordon, but he was already involved with "Our Miss Brooks" (as Principal Conklin). During the "I Love Lucy" series he had made a couple of appearances as Mr. Littlefield, Ricky's stodgy boss at the Tropicana Night Club. On "The Lucy Show," he parlayed that attitude into the character of Theodore J. Mooney, president of the Danfield First National Bank. By the second season, Lucy was working part-time for the long-suffering Mr. Mooney.

The 1965 season opener found Lucy now residing in San Francisco to start a new life. Amazingly, Mr. Mooney was also transferred to a local bank, where Lucy now continued working for her nemesis. Vivian Vance, however, had decided she'd had enough, making only rare appearances by "flying out" from Connecticut. A new best friend was added, Mary Jane Lewis, played by Mary Jane Croft, a longtime personal friend of Lucy's.

There had been a bitter divorce from Desi Arnaz in 1960; Lucy remarried to TV executive Gary Morton, and by 1962 things had cooled off enough for Lucy and Desi to settle their differences for the sake of the business. Although Desi produced the new series at first, he eventually sold his interest of 300,000-plus shares in Desilu studios to his ex-wife for $2.5 million, making her the only female head of a major independent studio in the history of Hollywood.

For someone whose high school drama coach once told her parents, "She's too shy and reticent to put her best foot forward," she'd come a long way. The woman who would by 1968 command the world's largest TV-producing facility with an annual gross business of over $20 million once confessed that as a newly-arrived Goldwyn Girl in Hollywood of the 1930s, "I was Miss Nervous. I was terrified by strange people who kept telling me I lacked poise." That same woman who became the queen of the small screen and the most beloved comedienne in American history overcame her fears and never stopped learning from people. In an interview taped in 1985 she generously shared credit for her success with her live audiences: "A little bit of America was in every seat," she said, "and they were our barometer as to what was funny and what wasn't. Now, you've got to learn from that every week for 20 years or more."

In September 1968 "The Lucy Show" metamorphosed into "Here's Lucy" (see page 160).

CREDITS

BASED ON: *Life Without George*, by Irene Kampen. EXECUTIVE PRODUCER: Desi Arnaz. PRODUCERS: Elliott Lewis, Jack Donohue, Thommy Thompson. DIRECTORS: Jack Donohue, Maury Thompson. WRITERS: Bob Carroll, Madelyn Martin, Bob Weiskopf, Bob Schiller, Jerry Belson, Gary Marshall, Perry Grant, Dick Bensfield, others. CAST: *Lucy Carmichael* (Lucille Ball), *Vivian Bagley* (Vivian Vance), *Theodore J. Mooney* (Gale Gordon), *Chris Carmichael* (Candy Moore), *Jerry Carmichael* (Jimmy Garrett), *Sherman Bagley* (Ralph Hart), *Mary Jane Lewis* (Mary Jane Croft), *Harrison Cheever* (Roy Roberts). GUEST STARS: Carol Burnett, Buddy Hackett, Hans Conried, Jack Benny, Bob Hope, Tammy Grimes, Milton Berle, Danny Kaye, Arthur Godfrey, Danny Thomas, Dean Martin, George Burns, others.

EMMYS

Outstanding Continued Performance by an Actress in a Leading Role in a Comedy Series —Lucille Ball (1966–67, 1967–68).

BEN CASEY

NUMBER 7 (TIE), 1962–63

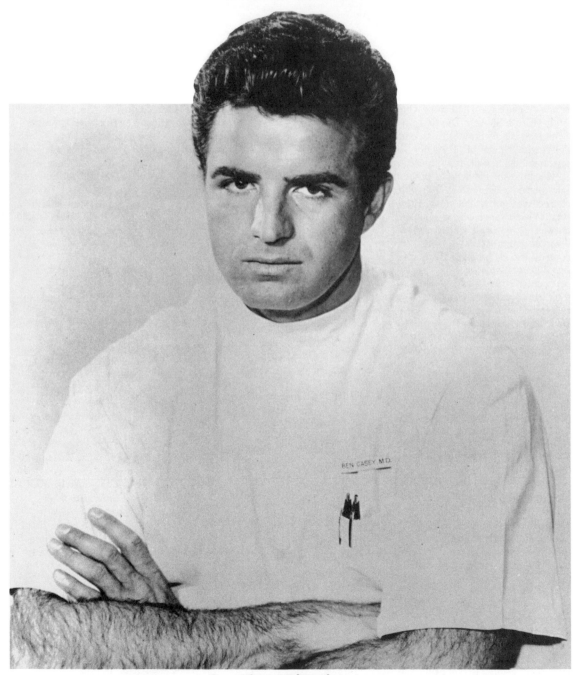

Vincent Edwards.

Within four days of the premiere of "Doctor Kildare" on NBC, "Ben Casey" presented his medical credentials on rival network ABC. And although "Kildare" was more of an overnight success, "Casey" soon built a strong following and managed to achieve high ratings by its second year.

The two medical shows were as dissimilar as their protagonists. Kildare was blond, boyish, upbeat. Casey was darkly hirsute, masculine, and brooding. Blair General, where Kildare wore his always-immaculate intern whites, was a spotlessly gleaming facility; County General Hospital, home to chief resident in neurosurgery Ben Casey, was more institutional, more angular, filmed in contrasting lights and shadows.

Then there were the attitudes. Kildare didn't have one. Casey had enough for both. Arms firmly folded across his chest (*New York Times* critic Jack Gould quipped, "Edwards has exhausted all conceivable methods of folding his arms"), tunic shoulder buttons undone (his mode of dress started a fad among teenage girls, who bought "Ben Casey" shirts by the thousands), the sardonic neurosurgeon bullied patients and colleagues alike. There was never any doubt that Ben Casey was an Angry Young Doctor. Nor was there any doubt that he was just about the most skilled neurosurgeon in the country, where, it seemed, an astonishing number of people needed to have their heads operated on.

Although the Kildare phenomenon provoked more fan response, with Dick Chamberlain's mail out-pulling Vince Edwards's three to one, "Ben Casey" appealed more to the intelligentsia and to urban viewers, attracting an audience of 32 million a week. The show's enormous popularity was evidenced in a *TV Guide* poll that designated Edwards as "favorite male performer" of the 1961–62 season, and the show as "favorite new series." Nurses were among his staunchest viewers. In New York City's St. Vincent's Hospital, for instance, where the curfew for student nurses was 10:30 P.M., on nights when "Ben Casey" was on duty (the show aired from 10 to 11 the first and last two years of its six-year run), regulations were relaxed so the medical professionals could stay up till he grimaced his last grimace.

Like so many success stories in television, Edwards almost didn't get the part. The creator of "Ben Casey," James Moser, who had had a popular TV medical series in the late '50s with "Medic," starring Richard Boone, had auditioned over 100 actors and still hadn't found his

Dr. Casey. "Then one day Vince came in," said Moser. "He had the build, he had the look. All I thought was, 'If only he can act.'" In Edwards's early years the young Italian actor had been an avid admirer of Marlon Brando, and he would hang around backstage when Brando was performing *A Streetcar Named Desire* on Broadway in the late '40s, hoping some of Brando's style would rub off on him. Apparently, it worked. Moser had been looking for a combination of surliness and conviction, exactly what he found in the brooding portrayal by Edwards.

Like Dr. Kildare, who had Dr. Gillespie for a mentor, Ben Casey found his guru in Dr. David Zorba, the hospital's chief of neurosurgery. Sam Jaffe, a munchkin-like man with a twinkling eye and candyfloss hair who had once played the title role in *Gunga Din* (1939) in little more than a diaper, was the antithesis of Ben Casey— warm, patient, all-wise, all-caring. He also had the good sense to see beyond Casey's gruff facade to the true humanitarian he alone knew lived somewhere just below that unbuttoned tunic. Jaffe had also played the wise High Lama in the film *Lost Horizon* (1937), so the part of savvy Dr. Zorba seemed right up his alley. And unlike so many of his fellow performers from motion pictures, he had no qualms about working in television. "This is the age of anxiety," Jaffe said in *Newsweek* in 1962. "It's the age of neurosis and people need help. Who can help people? The doctor. A doctor has something to say to people, something they want to hear." The icing on the cake for Jaffe was that he could work with his wife, Bettye Ackerman, who played anesthetist Dr. Maggie Graham on "Ben Casey."

The series ran for five years on ABC, and by March of 1966 Ben Casey had stitched up his last patient. "When 'Casey' finally ended," said Vince Edwards, "it was like the end of a five-year run on Broadway. Oh, it wasn't really a drag. The first two years were exciting, the third less so, the fourth and fifth just hard work, and anybody who says different is a damn liar. But it gave me a shot at directing, ten shows, and that ain't bad."

Even though he hung up his stethoscope, Edwards had no problems reviving the role for a 1988 reunion TV movie called "The Return of Ben Casey." In the syndicated film viewers learned that the 60-year-old doctor was now chief of neurosurgery at County General.

In the early 1990s the original series found a new audience in reruns on the Nostalgia cable channel.

CREDITS

CREATOR: James E. Moser. EXECUTIVE PRODUCER: James E. Moser. PRODUCERS: Matthew Rapf, Fred Frieberger, John Meredyth Lucas, others. DIRECTORS: Sidney Pollack, Marc Daniels, Vince Edwards, others. WRITERS: James E. Moser, various. CAST: *Dr. Ben Casey* (Vince Edwards), *Dr. David Zorba* (Sam Jaffe), *Dr. Maggie Graham* (Bettye Ackerman), *Dr. Ted Hoffman* (Harry Landers), *Nurse Wills* (Jeanne Bates), *Orderly Nick Kanavars* (Nick Dennis). GUEST STARS: Patty Duke, Jerry Lewis, Robert Loggia, Margaret Leighton, James Farentino, Kim Stanley, others.

EMMYS

Outstanding Single Performance by an Actress in a Leading Role—Kim Stanley, (1962–63).

THE DICK VAN DYKE SHOW

NUMBER 9, 1962–63

Dick Van Dyke and Mary Tyler Moore.

As first conceived, "The Dick Van Dyke Show" might have been called "The Carl Reiner Show." When Reiner, a former writer for Sid Caesar's "Your Show of Shows," began formulating his idea for a semi-autobiographical comedy in 1958, he saw himself as the focal point of the show. He would play a writer working for a tyrannical boss, an over-the-top version of Sid Caesar himself (who was known to take meetings sitting atop a gold throne), and surrounded by a team of other writers, including a knockoff of Selma Diamond, one of Reiner's actual coworkers on "Your Show." Part of the show would center on the suburban home life of the writer/hero, who, like Reiner, lived in New Rochelle, New York.

A pilot was made in which Reiner himself starred as Rob Petrie, Barbara Britton played his wife, Morty Gunty and Sylvia Miles played the other comedy writers, and Jack Wakefield played the comedian boss. Titled "Head of the Family," the pilot was aired in the summer of 1960. But Reiner had trouble finding a sponsor for his show; the problem, it turned out, was not the concept, but Reiner himself. He set ego aside, listened to the advice of producer Sheldon Leonard, and caught a performance of Dick Van Dyke in Broadway's *Bye Bye Birdie*. Thus was born "The Dick Van Dyke Show."

No lead actor could have been more suitable. From the moment Van Dyke made his entrance during the opening credits (sometimes he tripped over the ottoman, sometimes—gotcha!—he didn't), he owned the show. The man with an elastic face and limbs that seemed to be minus some sort of skeletal structure (who once admitted, "When I was a child I looked exactly like Stan Laurel") clowned, stumbled, and pratfell his way through 158 episodes, much to the delight of audiences. The show, in fact, was recorded in front of a live audience, and the laughter was often so raucous that portions had to be edited out for the sake of belief. Yet the first season was greeted with critical blahs and the sponsors nearly dropped the show. It was saved when the Television Academy sent them their wake-up call by bestowing several Emmy nominations on Van Dyke and company.

And what a company it was. The series divided neatly into two hemispheres: the world of Rob Petrie's (Van Dyke's) work at "The Alan Brady Show," and his home life in New Rochelle with his beautiful wife Laura (TV's first truly sexy wife) and their son Ritchie. In another stroke of casting luck, Mary Tyler Moore had won the co-starring role of Laura Petrie because she'd missed out on the role of Danny Thomas's daughter in "The Danny Thomas Show" a few years earlier. When casting for Laura, executive producer Thomas remembered the actress who had been too mature to play his kid. She hadn't had much luck in show business; the young actress's biggest parts so far had been as the "Happy Hotpoint" elf (she sold ovens) and as the disembodied legs of switchboard operator Sam in the 1957–60 crime drama "Richard Diamond, Private Detective."

As Laura Petrie, Mary Tyler Moore brought her own touches to the character. Before the actress took up housekeeping, no self-respecting TV housewife would be caught dead doing the laundry without her high heels, evening gown, and basic pearls. But Mary felt silly. "I suggested to Carl [Reiner] that when I vacuum the rug, I wear pants," she said. "I couldn't imagine putting on a little dress for that." In the spring of 1965, *Time* magazine reported, "Mary Tyler Moore has helped make capri pants the biggest trend in U.S. casual attire." She also had a fountain of talent. "Mary was 23 when she started the show, and she'd never done any comedy at all," Van Dyke said. "Boy, did the talent spring out of her." Together, Moore and Van Dyke had something that every show strives for between its leads: chemistry.

The other setting for the series, the offices of "The Alan Brady Show" where Rob Petrie (the original Carl Reiner character) was head writer, had an equally potent mixture of talented actors. Reiner had now recast himself as Alan Brady; in essence he was now the Sid Caesar–like star of a comedy show. His chief flunky was his hapless brother-in-law, Mel Cooley (Richard Deacon), and Rob Petrie's two comedy-writing assistants were the man-crazed Sally (Rose Marie) and Buddy (Morey Amsterdam), a man who could evoke laughter by merely mentioning his wife's name (Pickles). All in this ensemble cast were masters of the ad lib, and their talents contributed to the vast success of the series. "Some of our funniest shows came from our worst scripts," Van Dyke admitted. One of his favorite episodes was "It May Look Like a Walnut," a sci-fi parody in which Danny Thomas played a walnut-eating alien from the planet Twilo with an eye in the back of his head and no thumbs. "It was the most fun to do," Van Dyke told the *Los Angeles Times*. "We wanted to do a dream sequence that was totally bizarre and kind of a horror thing. We all kind of pitched in on it and came up with the idea. Carl came up with the idea of using Danny Thomas. I don't know why it struck us so incredibly funny that the invader from outer space looked like Danny Thomas."

"The Dick Van Dyke Show" was never out of the top 20 in its entire five-year run. No wonder, then, that CBS was thrown into a tailspin when, in 1966, producers Carl Reiner, Sheldon Leonard, and Danny Thomas announced that this would be the show's last season. In 1961 they had made a pact with the cast that they would do exactly five years' worth of episodes and no more. "We wanted to quit while we're still proud of it," Van Dyke said.

The series had one of the most successful runs in syndication of any comedy show; during the early 1990s, it was the cornerstone of "Nick at Nite" on the Nickelodeon cable channel. Van Dyke, in fact, was named "chairman" of Nick at Nite and did commercials on the importance of "preserving our television heritage." And although the original cast was reunited for the first time since 1966 in the 1992 edition of HBO's "Comic Relief," Van Dyke insisted there were no plans for any reunion specials. "Tom Wolfe was right," he said. "You can't go back."

CREDITS

TOP 10 PEAK: No. 3, 1963–64. CREATOR: Carl Reiner. EXECUTIVE PRODUCERS: Sheldon Leonard, Danny Thomas. PRODUCER: Carl Reiner. DIRECTORS: Sheldon Leonard, Carl Reiner, John Rich, Jerry Paris. WRITERS: Carl Reiner, Bill Persky, Sam Denoff. CAST: *Rob Petrie* (Dick Van Dyke), *Laura Petrie* (Mary Tyler Moore), *Alan Brady* (Carl Reiner), *Sally Rogers* (Rose Marie), *Buddy Sorrell* (Morey Amsterdam), *Ritchie Petrie* (Larry Matthews), *Mel Cooley* (Richard Deacon), *Jerry Helper* (Jerry Paris), *Millie Helper* (Ann Morgan Guilbert), *Stacy Petrie* (Jerry Van Dyke). GUEST CAST: Danny Thomas, Ken Berry, others.

EMMYS

Outstanding Writing Achievement in Comedy—Carl Reiner (1961–62, 1962–63, 1963–64, 1965–66), Sam Denoff, Bill Persky (1963–64, 1965–66); Outstanding Comedy Program (1962–63, 1963–64, 1965–66); Outstanding Directorial Achievement in Comedy—John Rich (1962–63), Jerry Paris (1963–64); Outstanding Continued Performance by an Actor in a Comedy Series, Lead—Dick Van Dyke (1963–64, 1964–65, 1965–66); Outstanding Continued Performance by an Actress in a Comedy Series, Lead—Mary Tyler Moore (1963–64, 1965–66); Outstanding Program Achievement in Entertainment (1964–65).

PETTICOAT JUNCTION
NUMBER 4, 1963–64

From left: Bea Benaderet, Gunilla Hutton, Linda Kaye Henning,
Lori Saunders, and guest stars Eva Gabor and Eddie Albert.

It didn't take creator/producer Paul Henning long to spin off another hit series from his number one powerhouse, "The Beverly Hillbillies." Within a year of its premiere (1962), he hit the airwaves with yet another dose of corn syrup. This time, he yanked Cousin Pearl Bodine (actress Bea Benaderet) out of Beverly Hills, renamed her Kate Bradley, and set her amid a group of down-home folk in Hooterville, somewhere in the boondocks of America...home to "Petticoat Junction." Soon the public would be getting quite fat on its steady diet of cornpone on CBS—by now nicknamed the Country Broadcasting System.

Bea Benaderet played Kate, owner of the Shady Rest Hotel, but she spent more time keeping an eye on her buxom daughters (the name *Hooter*ville was probably not intended as a pun) and her neighbors. "Petticoat Junction" referred to the point on the Hooterville railroad line where the young ladies hung their petticoats (young ladies *wore* petticoats in those days) over the sides of the water tank in which they skinny-dipped. So much for the cultural sights of Hooterville. There was a running story line about the steam-driven train, too, and Kate was constantly running up against Homer Bedloe, vice president of the railroad, who wanted to scrap the Hooterville–Pixley train and terminate its two engineer employees.

CREDITS

CREATOR: Paul Henning. EXECUTIVE PRODUCER: Paul Henning, Charles Stewart. PRODUCERS: Paul Henning, Dick Wesson. DIRECTORS: Richard Whorf, Richard Bare, Ralph Levy, others. WRITERS: Paul Henning, Charles Stewart, others. CAST: *Kate Bradley* (Bea Benaderet), *Uncle Joe Carson* (Edgar Buchanan), *Billie Jo Bradley* (Jeannine Riley, Gunilla Hutton, Meredith MacRae), *Bobbie Jo Bradley* (Pat Woodell, Lori Saunders), *Betty Jo Bradley* (Linda Kaye Henning), *Charlie Pratt* (Smiley Burnette), *Floyd Smoot* (Rufe Davis), *Homer Bedloe* (Charles Lane), *Steve Elliot* (Mike Minor), *Dr. Janet Craig* (June Lockhart). GUEST STARS: Eddie Albert, Eva Gabor, others.

Critics were underwhelmed by all this. *Time* magazine wrote: "Apparently, the networks just take it for granted that any six fools and a can of laughter will win high ratings. Paul Henning...is obviously attempting to corner corn. He has produced another CBS comedy called 'Petticoat Junction,' a kind of Hickadoon through which runs an old steam train called the Hooterville Cannonball. The railroad company is threatening to put the train out of service. Why bother? The Nielsen Limited is barreling up the track the other way." Of course, *Time* was way off track on that one.

One of the notable things about this series was its frequently changing cast. Bea Benaderet (Kate Bradley), who had played Blanche Morton on "The

George Burns and Gracie Allen Show" when Paul Henning was that series' head writer, had also once been up for the part of Ethel Mertz on "I Love Lucy" (she had been Lucille Ball's first choice). And from 1960 to 1964 she was the voice of Betty Rubble on "The Flintstones." In the fall of 1968, she succumbed to lung cancer at the age of 62. The cast and crew of "Petticoat" were saddened by her sudden death, and a replacement was never found.

A motherly character—Dr. Janet Craig, the town physician—was created to fill the void. At the same time, June Lockhart, the mom on "Lassie" and mother to the Space Family Robinson on "Lost in Space," had just lost her job when "Space" was cancelled. "I wrote Paul and said I was looking for a series. I don't know why actors have to play it so coy," she said, "when they are 'at liberty.'" Henning was thrilled and gave her the role of Dr. Craig. "She said she was out of her silver-lamé tights and looking for work...I've been a fan of hers since 'Lassie.' I was the only one who liked her better than the dog."

The daughters, Billie Jo, Bobbie Jo, and Betty Jo (one wonders if there is a mandate somewhere that southern names must end in "Jo"), were played by an assortment of lithesome young actresses over the seven years of the series. There were three actresses for Billie and two for Bobbie (only one for Betty, Paul's daughter—Linda Kaye Henning). No one seemed to notice. The 1968 season saw the addition of a handsome young pilot who crashed his plane outside of Hooterville and was nursed back to health by the girls, eventually marrying Betty Jo.

In 1965, two years after the premiere of "Petticoat Junction," Paul Henning did it again. He spun off the spinoff, begetting "Green Acres" (see page 140), yet another successful countrified sitcom.

In 1970 CBS finally derailed the old Hooterville Cannonball after the ratings started slipping. The 148 episodes were still being syndicated in reruns in 1993.

MY FAVORITE MARTIAN

NUMBER 10, 1963–64

"My Favorite Martian" was in the vanguard of a new genre, the fantasy-sitcom. Its roots lay in the '30s' and '40s' series of *Topper* features (which had already been translated into a delightful TV series that ran from 1953 to 1955); its future would include the talking horses, twitching noses, and blinking genies of "Mr. Ed," "Bewitched," "I Dream of Jeannie," and many others.

The premise was "a fish out of water." In this case, the water was on another planet—Mars. In the opener, a Martian archeologist crash-landed his flying saucer on Earth, a loathesome planet he was studying. "Earth's all right for a visit but I wouldn't want to live here," he informed the audience in the show's first week. Tough. He was here for the duration, at least until cancellation of the series, which CBS hoped wouldn't happen for a long, long time. He was "adopted" by a young reporter who had to stay mum on the story of the century and closet the alien as his "Uncle Martin" (like "Martian"—get it?). This was difficult, since Uncle Martin had some special "talents." Just behind his head were two retractable rabbit-ear antennae, which when extended provided him with his superpowers, the usual things like flying, telepathy, talking to animals, and invisibility.

Sounds pretty hokey, but it was incredibly well-received by audiences and critics. *Variety* noted, "It has a basic appeal for both young and adult alike," calling the show "delightfully funny." Bill Bixby played the "nephew," Tim O'Hara, a perfect straight man to the eccentric Uncle Martin, who at times resembled a male Gracie Allen. (Tim: "Come on, Uncle Martin. I'm serious." Martin: "I'm Uncle Martin.") In fact, the show resembled "The George Burns and Gracie Allen Show" in many ways, since Gracie herself seemed to be from some other world, totally bemused by planet Earth.

The puckish Martian invader was aptly played by Ray Walston, who came to the part with some experience: he'd played another impish character with superpowers, the Devil, in the 1955 stage and 1958 screen versions of *Damn Yankees*. Decades later he began a career comeback at age 78, playing guest roles in "Star Trek: The Next Generation," and he had a recurring role as Judge Bones on the CBS series "Picket Fences." But he will be identified with the role of Uncle Martin the Martian long after the many others in his extensive career are forgotten.

Bill Bixby didn't seem to have any problems with typecasting after starring as the nephew in this series. He worked steadily in TV, playing the lead in a long string of successful TV series, most notably "The Courtship of Eddie's Father" (1969–72), "The Magician" (1973–74), and a fantasy-drama in which *he* was empowered—"The Incredible Hulk" (1978–82). In the early '90s he became a sought-after director of film and especially TV sitcoms, such as "Blossom."

"My Favorite Martian" utilized Hollywood wizardry to get the special effects that the genre demanded. The antennae, for instance, were operated by a remote button controlled by Ray Walston. If the scene called for him to fly, he "flew" via a harness device similar to the one used to fly Mary Martin in *Peter Pan*.

Jack Chertok was the creator and producer of "My Favorite Martian," and the success of the series prompted then-chief of CBS, Jim Aubrey, to assign Chertok another series. In 1964 he created a fantasy comedy featuring a female "alien," really a robot named Rhoda with special abilities. "My Living Doll" starred Bob Cummings and Julie Newmar. Mercifully, this sexist comedy (she was programmed to do *anything* she was told) survived only one season.

The gimmick of "My Favorite Martian" wore thin after its third season, and in 1966 it was cancelled before Uncle Martin was able to phone home.

In 1973 CBS dusted off the concept and aired a Saturday morning animated spinoff, "My Favorite Martians," featuring the voice of Jonathan Harris (star of "Lost in Space"). It included additional passengers stranded on Earth with Uncle Martin: his nephew Andy and their dog, Oakie Doakie. The series ran for two years.

CREDITS

CREATOR/PRODUCER: Jack Chertok. DIRECTORS: Sheldon Leonard, John Erman, others. WRITERS: various. CAST: *Uncle Martin the Martian* (Ray Walston), *Tim O'Hara* (Bill Bixby), *Lorelei Brown* (Pamela Britton), *Harry Burns* (J. Pat O'Malley), *Detective Bill Brennan* (Alan Hewitt), *Police Captain* (Roy Engle). GUEST STARS: John Considine, Arlene Martell, Ann Marshall, others.

Ray Walston.

125

BEWITCHED

NUMBER 2, 1964–65

Elizabeth Montgomery, Dick York, and family.

For eight years, Samantha Stephens twitched her pert, upturned little nose and television audiences were "Bewitched." The simplest of all the premises of the fantasy-sitcom shows started with a question in late 1962 posed by Screen Gems vice-president William Dozier, who asked a fellow executive at lunch one day, "What if..." (all great ideas begin with those two words; it's written down someplace) "What if we did a series about a pretty young witch married to a 'straight' husband, who didn't know when he married her that she was a witch?" (The idea was not that unusual—there were a few successful 1940s theatrical films based on that premise , including *I Married a Witch* with Veronica Lake.) Several meetings and many years later, a pilot script was commissioned from Sol Saks.

Actress Tammy Grimes was approached to play the lead role of what was now called "Bewitched," but she turned it down because she wasn't sure it was right for her. In addition, she wanted numerous rewrites, and so on. As luck would have it, the actress Elizabeth Montgomery and her husband-to-be, director William Asher, were searching for a property that they could work on together. After reading the pilot script, Liz could hardly contain her excitement. "This is a series I just must do, that's all," she told Dozier. Her husband would direct the series, and Liz would star as the witch who just wanted to be a normal '60s housewife. As part of the deal, she also managed to retain 20 percent of the profits; Tammy's loss turned out to be Liz's $6-million-plus gain over the years in reruns.

"Bewitched" was an instant hit, ranking at number two for its first season (right behind "Bonanza") and remaining in the top 10 for several seasons thereafter. In essence, it was a one-joke show, but that didn't stop people from wanting to see what antics Samantha and her even witchier mother, Endora (Agnes Moorehead), would pull each week. Director Bill Asher described the series as a mirror of his own philosophy of life and marriage when he told *TV Guide* in 1967, "The show portrays a mixed marriage that overcomes by love the enormous obstacles in its path. Samantha, in her new role as housewife, represents the true values in life. Material gains mean nothing to her. She can have anything she wants through witchcraft, yet she'd rather scrub the kitchen floor on her hands and knees for the man she loves. It is emotional satisfaction she craves." Pretty '60s stuff, to be sure, but that basically defined good witch Samantha.

Comedy entered the picture through the constant interference by that other '60s cliché, the meddling mother-in-law. The running joke of that era was that every man envisioned his mother-in-law as a witch, but Darrin Stephens, the advertising executive newly wed to Samantha, hit the jackpot with Endora. At various times, Samantha found herself having to undo her mother's spells, which transformed the witch-pecked Darrin into every four-legged, scaled, or feathered creature imaginable. Endora was hopeless; she never used Darrin's real name, but preferred to add insult to injury by calling him *Durwood*.

Samantha broke her self-inflicted vow of witchery abstinence at least three times per show, because it was just too tempting to twitch her nose and—voilà!—the dishes were done, the laundry was folded, the kitchen was spotless, or her husband was human again.

If there was a certain amount of silliness to all this, it was a clever bit of television magic (made more believable with exceptionally well-done special effects) that cast an entertaining spell over audiences year after year. And those audiences were willing to accept anything, not even questioning the sudden switch in actors playing Samantha's husband after five years. Darrin Stephens was originally played by Dick York, but in 1969 he quit the show to deal with an addiction to painkillers he'd been using since sustaining a serious back injury 10 years earlier while filming a western. When "Bewitched" aired its first show of the new fall 1969 season, there was Samantha smooching with a new Darrin played by Dick Sargent, and no one seemed to notice. Was it one of Endora's spells? Had Samantha done something to him? No explanation was ever offered.

Beginning with the show's second season, the couple became parents of a baby girl, Tabitha. Rarely do children in sitcoms age in real time; writers usually foreshorten childhood so they can hire older kids to read the lines. Not so with "Bewitched." The year after Tabitha was "born," she was one year old, played by a set of interchangeable twins (California has laws about infants working under hot lights for more than a few minutes). By the time Tabitha was two, in 1966, the Murphy Twins, Erin and Diane, were switching off as the toddler who had inherited her mother's talents (but not yet skill) in witchcraft. However, the Murphys were fraternal rather than identical twins, and as their differences became apparent, one twin, Erin, was selected to solo. A young "warlock" son, Adam, was added to the brood in 1969.

In 1972 the series was sagging in the ratings when someone trotted out the old idea of "Let's take the show on the road, preferably to Jolly Olde England, where there are castles," a last-gasp attempt that usually signals an imminent finale for a series. Sure enough, "Bewitched" had run out of spells when it was finally cancelled in 1972 after a healthy eight years on ABC. Its 306 episodes were later seen regularly in syndication.

In 1977 a spinoff called "Tabitha" was launched by ABC, with Lisa Hartman playing the role of the bewitching daughter. Original Tabitha Erin Murphy claims she was not used because she was still too young to play the now-older young lady. The show ran one season. In 1992 Erin Murphy was conducting acting workshops and had been approached to do a possible new series, "Bewitched Again."

CREDITS

CREATORS: William Dozier, Sol Saks. EXECUTIVE PRODUCER: Harry Ackerman. PRODUCERS: Danny Arnold, William Froug, William Asher, others. DIRECTOR: William Asher, others. WRITERS: various. CAST: *Samantha Stephens/Serena** (Elizabeth Montgomery), *Darrin Stephens* (Dick York, Dick Sargent), *Endora* (Agnes Moorehead), *Maurice*** (Maurice Evans), *Tabitha Stephens* (Erin and Diane Murphy), *Adam Stephens* (David and Greg Lawrence), *Larry Tate* (David White), *Gladys Kravitz* (Alice Pearce, Sandra Gould), *Aunt Clara* (Marion Lorne), *Uncle Arthur* (Paul Lynde), *Esmerelda* (Alice Ghostley), *Doctor Bombay* (Bernard Fox), *Betty* (Marcia Wallace). GUEST STARS: Jack Warden, Robert Q. Lewis, others.

EMMYS

Outstanding Performance by an Actress in a Supporting Role in a Comedy—Alice Pearce (1965–66), Marion Lorne (1967–68); Outstanding Directorial Achievement in Comedy—William Asher (1965–66).

---

*Serena was Samantha's mischievous identical cousin.

**Maurice was Samantha's father, played by a noted Shakespearean actor.

GOMER PYLE, U.S.M.C.

NUMBER 3, 1964–65

Jim Nabors.

Shazam, shazam, shazam!
—GOMER PYLE, WHEN EXCITED

If it hadn't been for his asthma, Jim Nabors might still be living in his native Sylacauga, Alabama, eking out some meager living down home. But in 1958, after attending the University of Alabama, he decided to head for the somewhat dryer climate of Los Angeles, where by day he worked as an apprentice film cutter and by night sang in his booming baritone at a club called the Horn. It was there that he was spotted by comedian Bill Dana, then head writer for "The Steve Allen Show," and he made a few appearances on that series. One night Andy Griffith dropped by to catch his act at the Horn, and the two good ol' country boys got to talkin' between songs. Andy liked what he heard and offered him a walk-on in his CBS series, "The Andy Griffith Show." Nabors said he felt "as nervous as a cat in a room full of rocking chairs," but Griffith put his mind at ease, assuring him that "all I had to do was act like one of those fellows down home who sit around the gas pump reading comic books."

It wasn't long before the bumbling, hayseed gas jockey, Gomer Pyle, was spun off into his own CBS series. Folks just sort of took kindly to the childlike innocence that poured out of Gomer's lopsided mouth. And the military seemed like a good place to send him; the genre was gaining in TV popularity and it would open up innumerable comedy opportunities. Of course, a good straight man was necessary, and Pyle was given one in the form of his Marine Corps sergeant, Vincent Carter, aptly played by Frank Sutton.

There was a perfect chemistry between the bumpkin character of Gomer and the seemingly tough-as-nails sergeant. Frank Sutton himself had been an army buck sergeant in World War II who took part in 14 assault landings in the Pacific, but at heart the man who grew up in country towns in Kentucky and Tennessee was a pacifist. He brought some of that soft touch to Seargent Carter, too. "Carter sees something of himself in Gomer," he said in *TV Guide.* "Gomer only sees the good parts of Carter. Gomer is all good. I worry about leaning too heavily on him. Yet when I go on a real marine base the privates always come up to me and say, 'Why don't you deck him?'...Playing Sergeant Carter is a gas! He's larcenous, jealous, egocentric. Yet when the time comes to do a brutal or sadistic thing, he cops out; he can't do it."

The series ran from 1964 to 1969, always in the Nielsen top 10. Then in 1969 Jim Nabors was offered a different kind of series, one with his own name in the title: "The Jim Nabors Show." It was every entertainer's dream, and so, with "Gomer Pyle, U.S.M.C." second from the top in the ratings, he decided it was time to call a halt to the Marine Corps and move on.

Nearly everyone in the cast of "Gomer Pyle" would eventually co-star on another series. Frank Sutton and Ronnie Schell (Private Duke Slatter) appeared regularly on Jim's variety show, which lasted until 1971; Ted Bessell (Private Frank Lombardi) and Schell also starred in "That Girl"; Allan Melvin (Sgt. Charles Hacker) appeared on "All in the Family"; and William Christopher (Private Hummell) became Father Mulcahy on "M*A*S*H."

Following "The Jim Nabors Show," Nabors co-starred with Ruth Buzzi in a children's series, "The Lost Saucer" (1975–76) and had his own syndicated talk show in 1978. He was featured in the film *The Best Little Whorehouse in Texas* (1982) and appeared in the reunion show, "Return to Mayberry," in 1986. But it was Jim Nabors' powerful baritone voice that created a whole separate career for him. After the Gomer years, he recorded over a dozen hit albums and had 16 singles on the charts. In 1992 he was living in Hawaii, coming over to the mainland for occasional concert and club dates.

CREDITS

TOP 10 PEAK: No. 2, 1965–66. CREATOR: Aaron Ruben. EXECUTIVE PRODUCERS: Sheldon Leonard, Aaron Ruben. PRODUCERS: Ed Feldman, Aaron Ruben, Jack Elinson, others. DIRECTORS: Coby Ruskin, John Rich, others. WRITERS: various. CAST: *Pvt. Gomer Pyle* (Jim Nabors), *Sgt. Vincent Carter* (Frank Sutton), *Pvt. Duke Slater* (Ronnie Schell), *Pvt. Frankie Lombardi* (Ted Bessell), *Pvt. Lester Hummel* (William Christopher), *Corp. Charles "Chuck" Boyle* (Roy Stuart), *Bunny Olsen* (Barbara Stuart), *Sgt. Charles Hacker* (Allan Melvin), *Col. Edward Gray* (Forrest Compton). GUEST STARS: Pat Morita, Robert Hogan, others.

THE FUGITIVE

NUMBER 5, 1964–65

"The Fugitive" was the original cliffhanger television series, a format that had worked well in serialized Saturday afternoon matinees at the movies but had never been successfully attempted in weekly episodic TV.

The "fugitive" was Dr. Richard Kimble, a man arrested, tried, and convicted of a murder he did not commit. In the first episode, he returned to his home to find his wife dead, the victim of a burglary attempt; he also saw the suspect—a one-armed man—fleeing the scene. Unable to prove otherwise, Kimble was convicted of her murder and sentenced to die. Enroute to prison, the train derailed and Kimble made good his escape. He was free, but only as long as he could stay one step ahead of his pursuer, the police lieutenant from hell who was determined to bring him to justice.

Over the course of 120 episodes, Dr. Richard Kimble, played by David Janssen, garnered a wide following as he moved from town to town, odd job to odd job, story to story. In a sense, the series was a throwback to the anthology series of the 1950s, with new stories and casts each week, anchored by the fugitive himself, who quickly became entangled in the lives of the people he met. Each week he assumed a new identity and a new career, and whenever possible, he helped those who were in trouble. Sound familiar? Although the resemblance to a 1990s series on NBC is most likely coincidental, there is an uncanny similarity between "Quantum Leap" and this classic '60s series. Although "Leap" protagonist Sam Beckett was not on the lam, each week he found himself taking on a new persona, often working at some new job, and generally performing good deeds, ever hopeful that he would soon be returning home.

Audiences adored "The Fugitive," which premiered on ABC in 1963, and by its second season the series hit the top 10. People seemed to get a vicarious thrill from watching their hero narrowly miss being caught. It seemed to touch an untapped part of the human psyche, one's worst nightmare vividly realized (and in full color, by the third season). "Kimble has a preoccupation that almost everyone has," said David Janssen, "that paranoid feeling of being falsely accused." Or possibly the fear that if you look over your shoulder, someone might just be gaining on you.

So great was the appeal of "The Fugitive" that an inevitable spate of imitations soon hit the air, shows like "Run for Your Life" and the short-lived sitcom "Run, Buddy, Run," and even a Saturday-morning canine version called "Run Joe Run."

After four years David Janssen decided to call it quits. In that amount of time, the fugitive had been blinded by an explosion, run down by a car, knocked unconscious 10 times, and stabbed four times; he had survived 30 fights, three concussions, eight gunshot wounds (they were all "flesh wounds"), and several illnesses, including acute cases of amnesia and pneumonia. He had variously been employed as a truck driver, chauffeur, delivery man, merry-go-round operator, sail mender, bartender, fruit-picker, janitor, orderly, assistant veterinarian, and invalid sitter. The writers most often selected "Jim" as the alias of choice, with surnames generally of Anglo-Saxon derivation, like Lincoln, Fowler, Russell, Wallace, McGuire, and Corbin. And although Dr. Kimble managed to escape the relentless pursuit of the obsessed Lieutenant Gerard, he was unjustly arrested, or nearly so, a dozen

CREDITS

CREATORS: Roy Huggins, Quinn Martin. EXECUTIVE PRODUCER: Quinn Martin. PRODUCERS: Alan Armer, others. DIRECTORS: various. WRITERS: various. CAST: *Dr. Richard Kimble* (David Janssen), *Lt. Philip Gerard* (Barry Morse), *Donna Taft* (Jacqueline Scott), *Helen Kimble* (Diane Brewster), *Fred Johnson, the One-Armed Man* (Bill Raisch). NARRATOR: William Conrad. GUEST STARS: William Shatner, Mickey Rooney, Melvyn Douglas, Ossie Davis, Brian Keith, Vera Miles, Ed Begley, James Doohan, Howard Da Silva, others.

EMMYS

Outstanding Dramatic Series (1965–66).

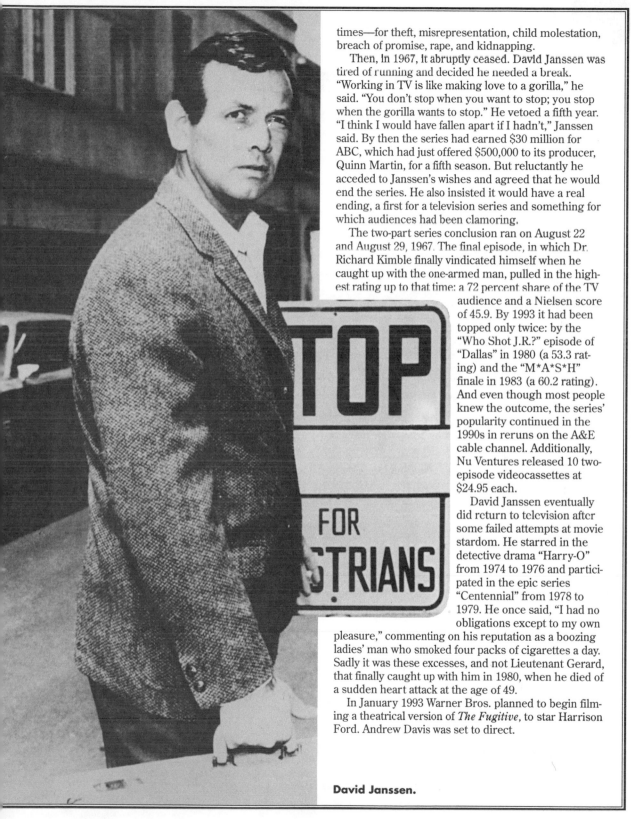

times—for theft, misrepresentation, child molestation, breach of promise, rape, and kidnapping.

Then, in 1967, it abruptly ceased. David Janssen was tired of running and decided he needed a break. "Working in TV is like making love to a gorilla," he said. "You don't stop when you want to stop; you stop when the gorilla wants to stop." He vetoed a fifth year. "I think I would have fallen apart if I hadn't," Janssen said. By then the series had earned $30 million for ABC, which had just offered $500,000 to its producer, Quinn Martin, for a fifth season. But reluctantly he acceded to Janssen's wishes and agreed that he would end the series. He also insisted it would have a real ending, a first for a television series and something for which audiences had been clamoring.

The two-part series conclusion ran on August 22 and August 29, 1967. The final episode, in which Dr. Richard Kimble finally vindicated himself when he caught up with the one-armed man, pulled in the highest rating up to that time: a 72 percent share of the TV audience and a Nielsen score of 45.9. By 1993 it had been topped only twice: by the "Who Shot J.R.?" episode of "Dallas" in 1980 (a 53.3 rating) and the "M*A*S*H" finale in 1983 (a 60.2 rating). And even though most people knew the outcome, the series' popularity continued in the 1990s in reruns on the A&E cable channel. Additionally, Nu Ventures released 10 two-episode videocassettes at $24.95 each.

David Janssen eventually did return to television after some failed attempts at movie stardom. He starred in the detective drama "Harry-O" from 1974 to 1976 and participated in the epic series "Centennial" from 1978 to 1979. He once said, "I had no obligations except to my own pleasure," commenting on his reputation as a boozing ladies' man who smoked four packs of cigarettes a day. Sadly it was these excesses, and not Lieutenant Gerard, that finally caught up with him in 1980, when he died of a sudden heart attack at the age of 49.

In January 1993 Warner Bros. planned to begin filming a theatrical version of *The Fugitive*, to star Harrison Ford. Andrew Davis was set to direct.

David Janssen.

PEYTON PLACE

NUMBER 9, 1964–65

"She felt her knees beginning to give under her, and still he kissed her, holding her upright with his hands tangled in her hair. When he lifted his bruising, hurtful mouth at last, he picked her up, carried her to the car, and slammed the door behind her."
—*PEYTON PLACE*

Today, there are several dozen romance novels a month published with writing like this, all jockeying for space as they jam countless bookstalls across five continents. But when Grace Metalious penned these words in her 1956 novel sensation, *Peyton Place*, it set tongues to wagging and censors to banning. Her book was considered scandalous filth, and although it was banned in Providence, Omaha, Ft. Wayne, and the entire country of Canada, it managed to sell more than 300,000 hardback and 9 million paperback copies when it first hit the stands, surpassing even the venerated *Gone with the Wind* to become the best-selling novel of the 20th century to that date. Inevitably, the book was made into a movie, and it was not long before it was turned into a television series.

"Peyton Place," as it first appeared on television, ran from the fall of 1964 until the summer of 1969. It had the distinction of being the first nighttime soap opera, a 30-minute program on ABC spread out over two nights a week. It was the "continuing story," as the announcer informed us at the start of each program, of a mythical seacoast town in the state of New Hampshire, but one suspects it could have been set anywhere. It drew an audience the way a freeway pileup draws gawking rubberneckers: 60 million people watched during its best run,

which happened to be the Thursday night edition during the first year (it aired on Tuesday and Thursday at 9:30 P.M.).

The show's creator and producer, Paul Monash, spoke in loving terms about his series when he told an interviewer from *The New York Times* that the original book (which he despised) had been "a negativistic attack on the town, written by someone who knew the town well and hated it. Ours is a love affair with the town...The general feeling we have of the town is of people evolving toward the light." Initially, it was too bland for the *New York Times* reviewer, who after viewing the premiere declared, "The sanitized derivation from the late Grace Metalious' novel will undoubtedly be greeted with understandable dismay by some viewers who will wonder where TV will descend next."

Perhaps it seemed sanitized in the first few episodes, but one would be hard-pressed to find the heliotropism so lovingly described by Monash.

Americans eagerly tuned in to catch the plethora of murders, separations, divorces, illegitimate births, wife beatings, drunkenness, blackmail, rape, incest, nymphomania, and good old-fashioned sex—lots of sex. The denizens of Mr. Peyton's town were obsessed with it, it seemed.

The show was noted for its cast, one of the largest ever assembled for a television series, with over 100 recurring roles. "Peyton Place" launched the career of Mia Farrow, who played teenager Allison MacKenzie for the first two years, then left the series and never looked back as her film career soared. Her love interest

---

CREDITS

CREATOR/EXECUTIVE PRODUCER: Paul Monash. BASED ON: *Peyton Place*, by Grace Metalious. PRODUCERS: various. DIRECTORS: various. WRITERS: various. CAST: *Constance MacKenzie* (Dorothy Malone), *Dr. Michael Rossi* (Ed Nelson), *Allison MacKenzie* (Mia Farrow), *Rodney Harrington* (Ryan O'Neal), *Leslie Harrington* (Paul Langton), *Betty Anderson* (Barbara Parkins). GUEST STARS: Gail Kobe, Mariette Hartley, Kent Smith, John Kerr, Lana Wood, Diana Hyland, Percy Rodriguez, David Canary, Bruce Gordon, Lee Grant, Leslie Neilsen, Ruby Dee, Robert Hogan, Florida Friebus, Gena Rowlands, Dan Duryea, Leigh Taylor-Young, Susan Oliver, Barbara Rush, others.

EMMYS

Outstanding Performance by an Actress in a Supporting Role in a Drama—Lee Grant (1965–66).

on the show was Rodney Harrington, played by Ryan O'Neal, and he too went on to a successful movie career. Nearly every working actor in Hollywood managed to appear in the nighttime soap, including some long-overdue black actors.

In 1968 producer Paul Monash decided it was time a black family settled in Peyton Place. Naturally, this being the '60s, the members of that family were the most beautifully dressed, well-educated people in the county. The father was a neurosurgeon. (In a town the size of Peyton Place, population 10,000, just how many people did they think needed brain surgery?) But Percy Rodriguez, who played the part of Dr. Harry Miles, was delighted with his role, even if it suggested tokenism. "Let us say if I am to be regarded as a symbol," he said, "let it be for some good. I want to reach the children, to motivate them. If adults disagree, shame on them."

By this time the show's ratings were in trouble, and nothing seemed to help. In its heyday, "Peyton Place" had been seen *three* nights a week, but by the fall of 1968, it had sunk to number 82 in the Nielsens. The producers admitted it was time to tie up as many loose ends as possible and end the series, which aired its last episode in June 1969. But it resurfaced for several more go-rounds of lust and mayhem. In 1972 it was revived as a spinoff daytime serial, "Return to Peyton Place," for a run of two years (the previously dead-and-buried Martin Peyton was resurrected in this version). Again, many cast members were reunited for a 1977 TV movie, "Murder in Peyton Place," in which intrigue surrounded the deaths of Rodney Harrington and Allison MacKenzie. (This film can occasionally be found on TBS.) In 1985 this New England mill town without pity surfaced yet again in "Peyton Place: The Next Generation," another made-for-TV movie. Nine of the original cast, including Dorothy Malone, Tim O'Connor, and Barbara Parkins, made appearances in the film, which can occasionally be seen on local channels.

Ed Nelson, with guest star Gena Rowlands.

COMBAT!

NUMBER 10, 1964–65

When "Combat!" premiered on ABC in 1962, the echoes of the last gunfire of World War II could still be faintly heard in the memories of audience members who had witnessed the final surrender of the Germans only 17 years before. To the war's veterans, it was recent nostalgia; for the youth in the audience, many of whom would soon be facing a war of their own in an increasingly visible place called Vietnam, it was a sort of morbid curiosity that held their fascination.

"Combat!" did not glorify war, however; it didn't splash the small screen with hour after hour of blood, guts, and pounding artillery fire. To be sure, there were the requisite battle scenes, but the series excelled at bringing the war down to a personal level.

The central characters were the two leaders of a U.S. Infantry platoon, K Company: Lt. Gil Hanley (Rick Jason) and Sgt. Chip Saunders (Vic Morrow). Each week they and the regular members of their platoon managed to dodge booby traps, mine fields, and enemy bullets, frequently emerging behind enemy lines in post-D-day French Normandy. If the series was burdened by any plot device, it was the necessity of getting our heroes out alive each week so the show could continue. The audience knew this had to be, and it softened the suspense, one of the serious handicaps of an action-adventure series built around continuing characters.

The stories took full advantage of the medium of television to tell the small story, the human one. Story lines might deal with the relationships with the French patriots whose land was occupied, or with raw recruits terrified by their first confrontation with the enemy and death. An episode could involve the safe evacuation of elderly people from their ancestral farm, or getting aid for a wounded comrade while trapped behind enemy lines—poignant dramas in which war was neither glorified nor hellish, just extant (albeit hazardous to normal life).

The war drama became a familiar fixture of 1960s television, although not to the degree that westerns had been for the '50s. Series like "The Gallant Men," "The Lieutenant," "Rat Patrol," "Twelve O'Clock High," and the comedy "Hogan's Heroes" were in every network's kit bag. "Combat!" had the distinction of being the only war drama to make it into the top 10, a fact that could be attributed in part to the excellent production values of the MGM-produced show. The series added a dimension of realism by putting its cast through a boot camp before production began. The merging of the black and white production (it didn't switch to color until its last season) with actual stock footage from World War II completed the effect.

When not on location in the San Fernando Valley (doubling for French farm country), the show was shot on the MGM back lot. Many of the same sets were seen repeatedly: a certain courtyard, a familiar farmhouse, an arched bridge used so frequently it was dubbed "The 'Combat' Bridge" when seen in other concurrent MGM efforts (like "The Man from U.N.C.L.E."), and an endless succession of French villages that were systematically and routinely blown up as the series continued over the course of five years. As Vic Morrow noted, "We shot up Lot Two pretty good, then moved on to Lot Three. When we get through decimating this—well, I figure the Thalberg [MGM Administration] Building is next."

CREDITS

EXECUTIVE PRODUCER: Selig J. Seligman. PRODUCERS: Gene Levitt, various. DIRECTORS: Robert Altman, Ted Post, various. WRITERS: Richard Matheson, Bob and Esther Mitchell, various. CAST: *Lt. Gil Hanley* (Rick Jason), *Sgt. Chip Saunders* (Vic Morrow), *Caje* (Pierre Jalbert), *Pvt. William G. "Wildman" Kirby* (Jack Hogan), *Littlejohn* (Dick Peabody), *Doc Walton* (Steven Rogers), *Doc* (Conlan Carter), *Pvt. Braddock* (Shecky Greene), *Pvt. Billy Nelson* (Tom Lowell). GUEST CAST: Rance Howard, Theodore Bikel, Dennis Weaver, Bill Bixby, Beau Bridges, Alfred Ryder, Joseph Campanella, Frank Gorshin, Tommy Sands, Andrew Prine, John Cassavetes, Fernando Lamas, Rip Torn, others.

Vic Morrow.

Although Rick Jason was the ostensible star of the series, many in the audience were drawn to its ruggedly handsome co-star, Vic Morrow, who played Sgt. Chip Saunders. Morrow had first attracted attention in the 1955 movie *The Blackboard Jungle*, as a knife-wielding juvenile delinquent. He left film for television, and did many guest shots, including an episode of "Bonanza" in 1960 in which he rescued Ben and Adam Cartwright from a lynch mob. Critics praised his excellent work. Wrote *Variety*, "If the series must have continuing heroes, it could hardly hope for a more perfect star than Morrow, who not only looks the part of the youthful but seasoned squad leader but also has the acting range to do full justice to a good script."

During the '70s Vic Morrow appeared in several TV movies and mini-series, including a supporting role in the historic mini-series "Roots." But it is primarily his tragic death that most people remember today. While on location in Southern California filming the 1982 feature *Twilight Zone: The Movie*, Morrow was killed in a freak helicopter accident. Two children in the scene also perished in the tragic mishap. The incident gained further notoriety when the film's director, John Landis, was indicted for involuntary manslaughter. A jury later acquitted him of all charges.

"Combat!" was still showing nightly in reruns on the Nostalgia cable channel in 1993, as well in syndication on various local stations.

BATMAN

NUMBERS 5 AND 10, 1965–66

With a ZAP! POW! and CRUNCH! "Batman" became the first and only television series in history to finish the season holding down *two* positions in the top 10 simultaneously. Holy Nielsens!

In January 1966 this "camp" show pitched its tent in America's living rooms and within weeks created the phenomenon known as Batmania. Yet the series almost didn't make it onto the airwaves. When preview audiences gave it the lowest rating of anything ABC had ever tested, the network executives were glum; had they not already bought the project, it would have ended up in the bat guano pile.

Fortunately for ABC, "Batman" was an unqualified hit. Long before Warner Bros.' dark, brooding films of the late '80s and early '90s, this version of the characters created by Bob Kane in 1939 was a Crayola comic book that took full advantage of living color, fast pacing, humorous dialogue, stylized directing, and formula format. The show was serialized over two nights: Wednesday was cliffhanger night, with the Caped Crusader and Robin the Boy Wonder usually in the clutches of the villain-of-the-week, about to be done in; Thursday was the more popular of the two nights, for good reason: the Dynamic Duo had to be rescued and the story tidied up. (They were and it was.)

Then there were the gimmicks. There were written labels on everything from the Batpoles (appropriately marked ACCESS TO BATCAVE VIA BATPOLES), which were separately marked "Bruce" and "Dick" (Batman's and Robin's alter egos, Bruce Wayne and Dick Grayson), to the Batphone, to the Hyperspectographic Analyzer and the Chemo-electric Secret Writing Detector and the Electronic Bugging Devices in the Batcave. There were lots of batgadgets like the Intergalactic Recorder, the Terrestrial Scanner, the Interdigital Batsorter, and the Atomic Batpile, source of power for the Batmobile, a souped-up Lincoln Continental circa 1966 with the equivalent price tag in those days of a Rolls Royce—$30,000.

If all this sounds a bit, well, batty to anyone who has never seen the show, rest assured it was all in good fun. Executive Producer William Dozier (co-creator, with Sol Saks, of "Bewitched") admitted he too was baffled when first approached by then-vice-president of ABC-TV development, Doug Cramer, to do a series based on the comic book. There had been 15 Saturday serial films in the '40s, but he had somehow missed them and in fact had never even heard of the Dynamic Duo. " 'Batman' was simply not in my ken," he said. "I have always been associated with loftier projects*...I bought a dozen comic books and felt like a fool doing it. I read them, if that is the word, and asked myself 'What do I do with *this*?' Then I hit on the idea of camping it." It worked, and adults enjoyed it on that level, while the youngsters took it to be high adventure—the perfect family show.

Every actor in Hollywood lobbied for a part in the series. Frank Sinatra reportedly was furious when he didn't land the role of the Joker (the part went to Cesar Romero instead). Burgess Meredith played another

---

CREDITS

BASED ON CHARACTERS CREATED BY: Bob Kane. EXECUTIVE PRODUCER: William Dozier. PRODUCER: Howie Horwitz. DIRECTORS: various. WRITERS: various. CAST: *Bruce Wayne/Batman* (Adam West), *Dick Grayson/Robin* (Burt Ward), *Alfred* (Alan Napier), *Police Commissioner Gordon* (Neil Hamilton), *Police Chief O'Hara* (Stafford Repp), *Aunt Harriet Cooper* (Madge Blake), *Barbara Gordon/Batgirl* (Yvonne Craig). GUEST STARS: *The Penguin* (Burgess Meredith), *The Joker* (Cesar Romero), *The Riddler* (Frank Gorshin, John Astin), *Catwoman* (Julie Newmar, Lee Ann Meriweather, Eartha Kitt), *The Black Widow* (Tallulah Bankhead), *Egghead* (Vincent Price), *Dr. Cassandra* (Ida Lupino), *Falseface* (Malachi Throne), *The Sandman* (Michael Rennie), *The Puzzler* (Maurice Evans), *Mr. Freeze* (George Sanders), *Ma Parker* (Shelley Winters), *Clock King* (Walter Slezak), *The Minstrel* (Van Johnson), *The Siren* (Joan Collins), *Shame* (Cliff Robertson), *Louie the Lilac* (Milton Berle), *The Bookworm* (Roddy McDowall), *King Tut* (Victor Buono), *Minerva* (Zsa Zsa Gabor), plus Leslie Parrish, Ethel Merman, Terry Moore, Jim Saint John, Lesley Gore, Glynis Johns, Rudy Vallee, Roger C. Carmel, Anne Baxter, Edward Everett Horton, Howard Duff, Harvey Lembeck, Liberace, David Wayne, Carolyn Jones, Joan Crawford, and others.

Holy publicity shot! Batman (Adam West), Robin (Burt Ward), and friends—uh, make that enemies.

memorable villain, the Penguin (Batman creator Bob Kane claimed to have received the inspiration for the Penguin off a pack of Kool cigarettes, which featured Willie the Penguin in its ad campaigns); one writer likened Meredith's portrayal to "a crazed FDR" (referring to the way he held his cigarette holder and wore a monocle, not his waddling around and quacking.) A character called Egghead was played by Vincent Price, who was forced to wear a bald cap and recite bad dialogue. They had to drill a hole in the back of the cap so the perspiration could drain out and be blotted. "It was miserable," he recalled. Virtually every line he had to deliver was a pun, like "Oh, I am egg-static!" and "We will remove their masks and egg-spose their faces to the public." Puns, in fact, were part of the shtick. One character, a good guy, was named Pat Pending; he was the world's richest inventor.

Unlike the popular *Batman* movies of the '90s, the TV series played up the superhero's sidekick, Robin (the Boy Wonder), who was given to spouting epithets beginning with "Holy"—for example, "Holy Houdini!" when Commissioner Gordon disappeared, or "Holy Sewer Pipe!" when he saw the Riddler emerge from a manhole.

All this (and more) kept people tuning in each week to the "same bat time, same bat channel" for one bat season, at least. But by the second year, the gimmick had worn thin. So the producers did the thing that usually spells batcurtains for success: they changed the show's format. The series went to only one night a week, and they added a Caped Crusaderette in the form of Batgirl (Yvonne Craig) to assist the Dynamic Duo (now renamed the Terrific Trio). Holy Cancellation! The same Nielsens that had been his for the taking now plunged lower than the Batcave.

Was this the end of our heroes? Not for long. In the 1970s there were a couple of animated Saturday morning cartoon series featuring Batman and the voices of stars Adam West and Burt Ward. Then in 1989 the *Batman* film was released. Holy Box Office Hit! The film, which played it straight, without campiness, became one of the top releases of all time. A 1992 sequel, *Batman Returns*, did only so-so, unable to approach the Batmania generated by the first film.

In the fall of 1992, Fox Children's Network introduced a new "Batman," produced by Warner Bros.' animation division. According to Fox Kids Network president Margaret Loesch, the series was "an animated drama, not a traditional cartoon. It has a very strong 'film-noir' look, a dark, brooding tone to it. It's highly stylized, and the action and very effective storytelling make it a real departure from traditional animation, which is more gag- and less story-oriented." Not only was it Fox Kids' highest-rated series, it was the highest-rated children's series on TV.

---

*Could he have been referring to "Bewitched," the series he co-created with Sol Saks at Screen Gems?

HOGAN'S HEROES

NUMBER 9, 1965–66

Riding the crest of a wave of World War II nostalgia in television programming, "Hogan's Heroes" featured those nutty Nazis up to their old tricks again. The premise for this series sounds like a bad joke, but television audiences were already becoming fans of a "war can be fun" cycle of TV shows. "McHale's Navy" had been on since October 1962, and "The Wackiest Ship in the Army," "Mr. Roberts," and "Hogan's Heroes" all premiered in the same week in September 1965.

Derived from the stage play/motion picture *Stalag 17,** a serious drama with comic overtones, "Hogan's Heroes" was a comic farce about a POW camp, a concept made somehow more acceptable by the length of time—two decades—that had passed since the war. With the emphasis on upbeat comedy, CBS even went so far as to hire noted humorist Stan Freberg to write a clever commercial. The man who would one day pen the classic prune commercial, "Today the pits, tomorrow the wrinkles," touted "Hogan's Heroes" with: "If you liked World War II, you'll love 'Hogan's Heroes!'" CBS was inundated with calls and eventually pulled this ad of questionable taste.

The series had the distinction of outraging Jews and the American Nazi Party alike; representatives of both groups agreed the show was a mockery of history, but of course for different reasons. *Variety*, however, had high praise for the series, remarking that "there seems to be a desire to soften the brutal memories of the conflict by making all the Nazis endearingly stupid and the prisoners an ingenious bunch who live it up at their captor's expense," and called Bob Crane's portrayal of the American POW's leader, Col. Hogan, "refreshing." *TV Guide* also lauded the series, saying, "The bad guys are Chaplinesque embodiments of authoritarian absurdities—a barking, *heil*ing, goose-stepping batch of uniformed robots, pompous asses, bootlickers, toadies, cowards, and dupes. It's a funny, nonoffensive show, and its real theme, as Bob Crane sums it up, is: 'Look how clever the Allies are!'"

Series star Bob Crane was under strict orders from the show's executive producer, Edward Feldman, not to camp it up. "Eddie made it clear to me that I absolutely must not play Hogan as a buffoon," he said. "I play him seriously, as a hero, as a leader who can inspire other men to keep fighting, even when behind bars.

Colonel Hogan and his merry band of POWs spent six years—one more than the actual war—incarcerated in Stalag 13. The term should actually be used loosely; they managed to turn the camp into a giant piece of Swiss cheese and could have left at any time. But Hogan and the boys were actually charged with a serious mission: aiding the Allies while "based" at the German POW camp. Not that anything could go seriously wrong. The camp was run by the most inept caricatures of German officers ever seen. Hogan's counterpart, Colonel Klink (even his name sounded dumb), was the most incompetent camp commandant the world had ever seen. Werner Klemperer played the hapless commander, while his bumbling oaf of an assistant, Sgt. Schultz, was played by John Banner. Ironically, both Klemperer and Banner had fled the Nazis prior to World War II, emigrating to the safe haven of the United States. Banner, an Austrian Jew whose entire family was wiped out by the Nazis, insisted "Schultzy" wasn't one of the "heroes." "I would

---

CREDITS

EXECUTIVE PRODUCER: Edward H. Feldman. PRODUCERS: various. DIRECTORS: Gene Reynolds, Edward H. Feldman, others. WRITERS: Lawrence Marks, others. CAST: *Col. Robert Hogan* (Bob Crane), *Co. Wilhelm Klink* (Werner Klemperer), *Sgt. Hans Schultz* (John Banner), *Louis LeBeau* (Robert Clary), *Peter Newkirk* (Richard Dawson), *Sgt. James Kinchloe* (Ivan Dixon), *Sgt. Richard Baker* (Kenneth Washington), *St. Carter* (Larry Hovis), *Helga* (Cynthia Lynn), *Hilda* (Sigrid Valdis), *Col. Crittendon* (Bernard Fox). GUEST STARS: Nina Talbot, Steward Moss, Gavin MacLeod, others.

EMMYS

Outstanding Performance by an Actor in a Supporting Role in a Comedy—Werner Klemperer (1967–68, 1968–69).

refuse to play a sympathetic Nazi," he said. "I see Schultz as the representative of some kind of goodness in any generation." Schultz, terrified of being sent to the Russian front, was noted for the line, "I know *nussing*, nussing!"

A couple of the "heroes" went on to bright careers. Richard Dawson, who played the resourceful Englishman Peter Newkirk, became well-known in the '70s for hosting the popular game show "Family Feud." Robert Clary as the Frenchman Louis LeBeau went on to star in "Days of Our Lives," and Ivan Dixon, the African-American who played Sgt. James Kinchloe for five of the series' six years, later became a successful television director.

The series' star, Bob Crane, did not fare so well, and his life had a tragic ending. His television career floundered after "Hogan's Heroes," but he refused to go back to his morning L.A. radio roots even after being

offered $300,000 a year to do a daily show. In 1978, while starring in a play in Scottsdale, Arizona, the actor was bludgeoned to death as he slept in his apartment. Several suspects were questioned but released for lack of evidence. Then, in 1992, the case was reopened when, based on some "new" evidence, a suspect was finally arrested. The outcome was still pending at the end of the year.

After six seasons, the series had managed to hold on to its high ratings (although it was only in the top 10 during the 1965–66 season), but by then it was getting almost impossible to wring any more laughs out of the concept, and the series left the air in 1971, sending 168 episodes off to rerun land, where they can be seen to this day.

———————————

*It took a successful plagiarism lawsuit by playwrights Donald Bevan and Edmund Trzinski to get that point across.

Bob Crane (left) and John Banner.

GREEN ACRES

NUMBER 6, 1966–67

"Green Acres" was one of the last television series to be derived from a radio show. In 1950 Jay Sommers had created "Granby's Green Acres," a radio comedy about a city slicker who pulled up stakes and wife and headed for the country. The concept was itself derivative; Fred MacMurray and Claudette Colbert had played transplanted city folk who took up chicken farming in the 1947 movie *The Egg and I*. In 1965 Sommers refashioned his radio series and approached Paul Henning, producer of "The Beverly Hillbillies" and "Petticoat Junction," with his updated ideas. Henning had been given carte blanche by Jim Aubrey at CBS to program whatever he wanted, sight unseen. He gave Sommers' show a "Petticoat Junction"/Hooterville setting, in essence creating a spinoff with its own spin, a sort of reverse "Beverly Hillbillies." Hennings went even further, "cross-pollinating" (as he called it) the three shows, the first producer to have characters from several shows likely to pop in on any one of those shows.

Eddie Albert played the gentleman farmer Oliver Wendell Douglas, a lawyer who preferred to enjoy "the chores!" and "fresh air!" rather than languish in the city rat race. Eva Gabor was cast as Lisa, his socialite wife who "got allergic smelling hay." Too bad. She was his wife, it was the unliberated '60s, and off she went, negligees, feather boas, diamonds, and all, so she could be with her hubby and his hayseed friends.

Eva Gabor, youngest of the three Hungarian-born Gabor sisters (Zsa Zsa and Magda were the others), was not Jim Aubrey's cup of goulash; he feared people would be turned off by her thick accent, dahlink. But Henning pointed out that Desi Arnaz had been even less intelligible and he'd done okay, so Aubrey and CBS relented. Eva recalled that those were "the happiest six years of my life. It was the only time in my long

career that I was grounded. I was in one place for six years and it was a joy."

That place was Pixley, complete with all its assorted rubes, con artists, and crazy characters. There was even a pig, Arnold, played by a succession of porkers, and all but the first year's Arnolds were females (they were easier to work with). Arnold even had his/her own fan clubs on college campuses across the nation, and he/she won two "Patsy" awards, a kind of Emmy for animal actors. The rapid turnover in Arnolds was necessary because once the pigs matured and passed 200 pounds (fully grown sows weigh 900 pounds, boars 1,000), they lost their cuteness. And thankfully none was ever turned into pork chops; the owner/trainer couldn't stand to part with his critters.

But the main humor came from the culture clash of city meets country, plus a touch of Gracie Allen-ish farmer's-wife humor with a Hungarian accent. Take this dialogue exchange, for instance, after Oliver discovered that his alfalfa field was at last blooming:

LISA
Vat do ve do with falafel?

OLIVER
Alfalfa. It's fodder for the animals.

LISA
But vat about da mother?

OLIVER
Mother? No, no, Lisa. Fodder is what animals eat.

LISA
Dey eat dere father? How terrible!

Obviously it wasn't meant to be Shakespeare, which is of course why fans adored this sort of silly banter and pushed "Green Acres" into the top 10 by the second year of its run. Eddie Albert believed the show was

CREDITS

CREATORS: Jay Sommers, Paul Henning. EXECUTIVE PRODUCER: Paul Henning. PRODUCER: Jay Sommers. DIRECTORS: Richard Bare, others. WRITERS: Jay Sommers, Dick Chevillat. CAST: *Oliver Wendell Douglas* (Eddie Albert), *Lisa Douglas* (Eva Gabor), *Mr. Haney* (Pat Buttram), *Eb Dawson* (Tom Lester), *Hank Kimball* (Alvy Moore), *Fred Ziffel* (Hank Patterson), *Doris Ziffel* (Barbara Pepper, Fran Ryan), *Sam Drucker* (Frank Cady), *Newt Kiley* (Kay E. Kuter), *Alf Monroe* (Sid Melton), *Ralph Monroe* (Mary Grace Canfield).

Goodbye, city life: Eva Gabor and Eddie Albert.

"a comment on how insane our society is. The writing was very light and very weird," he said in *People*, "but it had a profound base under it that none of us knew." He went on to mention that "a professor once told me students see it as surrealistic. He said, 'The comedy is like *Pickwick Papers* or *Gulliver's Travels* or Voltaire. It's so far out that it becomes truth, deep truth."

In 1971 CBS decided to clean (farm)house, and axed virtually every country series in their lineup, including "Green Acres." But the series always had a strong following, and 22 years after cancellation, Cable's Nickelodeon was rerunning the series' 170 episodes from time to time, as were many local stations.

Following "Green Acres" Eva Gabor made numerous guest appearances on series like "The Love Boat" and "Fantasy Island," but ended up spending most of her time supervising her corporation, Eva Gabor International, the largest wig manufacturing company in the United States. And Eddie Albert was farming his own "green acre" at his home where he grew veggies and claimed that drinking his own fresh carrot juice each day helped keep him 84 years young.

In 1990 the whole gang returned (except for Hank Patterson as Mr. Ziffel, Arnold's "father," who died in 1975) for a TV reunion movie called "Return to Green Acres." Eddie Albert, then 82, and Ms. Gabor, close to 70 at the time, seemed to have barely aged as they were reunited in the CBS special with all the old gang: store owner Sam Drucker; handyman Eb Dawson; con man Mr. Haney (we never learned his first name); Alf and Ralph, the dense pair of sibling carpenters; and talkative agricultural representative Hank Kimball.

DAKTARI

NUMBER 7, 1966–67

Ross Hagen, with Judy the Chimp and Clarence the Cross-Eyed Lion.

Ivan Tors was a producer with a penchant for animals. The Hungarian-born playwright/screenwriter/director first entered television in the early 1950s and is nostalgically remembered for such shows as "Science Fiction Theater" (1955–57), television's first anthology sci-fi series; "Sea Hunt" (1957–1961), the underwater adventure that made Lloyd Bridges a star; "Flipper" (1964–68); and "Gentle Ben" (1967–69).

In the early '60s, Tors teamed up with animal behaviorist Ralph Helfer to build a permanent animal compound for training and filming animals for Hollywood productions. One of their first efforts was a 1965 movie developed by Tors and actor Marshall Thompson called *Clarence the Cross-Eyed Lion*. After the film proved its popularity at the box office, the two decided to develop it into a TV series, "Daktari," which had a successful run on CBS from 1966 to 1969. In the series, Thompson played the title role of Dr. Marsh Tracy, the "Daktari" (Swahili for "doctor") in charge of the Wameru Study Center for Animal Behavior. But the opening credits, played over rhythmic tribal-like music, drew attention to the real stars of the show: the animals. We saw an elephant with a bandaged toothache being led to the compound, along with Judy the Chimp and the irrepressible Clarence, the aforementioned strabismic feline who started it all.

The series was filmed at a 260-acre compound built by Tors and Helfer called Africa U.S.A. It was located about 40 miles north of Los Angeles in Soledad Canyon. At one time the ranch housed over 600 largely uncaged performing animals, including many exotic cats like lions, cheetahs, leopards, and tigers, plus boa constrictors, rhinos, zebras, elephants, hippos, giraffes, and baboons. Each one was "affection trained"—a term coined by Helfer to mean praise for good behavior rather than punishment for undesirable efforts. The compound was even open to the public on weekends for tours. Unfortunately, Africa U.S.A. endured severe floods in the spring of 1969, forcing its closure.

The partnership with Tors was dissolved later that year, and Ralph Helfer established his own compound in the hills north of Los Angeles county. Years later he was still training animals for film and TV and offering

CREDITS

CREATORS: Ivan Tors, Marshall Thompson. EXECUTIVE PRODUCER: Ivan Tors. PRODUCERS: Leonard B. Kaufman, others. DIRECTORS: Paul Landers, Marshall Thompson, others. WRITERS: Bob Lewin, Malvin Wald, others. CAST: *Dr. Marsh "Daktari" Tracy* (Marshall Thompson), *Paula Tracy* (Cheryl Miller), *Hedley* (Hedley Mattingly), *Jack Dane* (Yale Summers), *Mike* (Hari Rhodes), *Bart Jason* (Ross Hagen), *Jenny Jones* (Erin Moran), plus *Clarence, the Cross-eyed Lion*, and *Judy the Chimp*, as themselves.

classes at local colleges so the public could learn about his efforts in this fascinating endeavor. While not training, Helfer continued to travel to Kenya, Africa, where he was working to save the animal population from extinction.

On the series, Clarence didn't do all his own stunts; this pampered, overgrown pussycat had his own stand-in. Major, another Helfer-trained feline, doubled for Clarence whenever there were any trucks involved in the scenes, since Clarence spooked at the sight of these vehicles. Major even had his own makeup artist who applied cosmetic scarring like Clarence's so that he would resemble the star when photographed in closeups.

Even though the old Hollywood bromide warns actors, "Never work with children or animals; they'll upstage you every time," Cheryl Miller didn't seem to mind playing second fiddle to the big cat and the chimp with the high I.Q. The then-24-year-old actress who played the teenaged daughter of Daktari got her training by working with Ralph Helfer and the beasts for four weeks before the first cameras ever rolled on the movie that led to the series. During her sojourn on the show, she wrestled leopards, rode a one-and-a-half-ton white rhino, wound a five-foot African rock python around her neck, and allowed a scorpion to walk on her hand. She landed the job because, as Helfer put it, "She wasn't one of the sweaty-palmed ones. The animals know." Ivan Tors agreed. "She had the basic chemistry. You either like animals or you don't."

Marshall Thompson, who starred as the veterinarian and also directed many of the episodes, had previously appeared in more than 30 films, including *Battleground* (1949) and *To Hell and Back* (1955). After "Daktari" he spent some time in Africa producing, directing, and acting in a documentary series, "Orphans of the Wild." In 1989 Thompson left Africa and returned to Michigan, where he lived in retirement until his death in May 1992 at the age of 66.

In 1993 "Daktari" was still being seen in reruns on cable's TNT channel. And *Clarence the Cross-Eyed Lion* was available for rental at video stores to keep the youngsters entertained.

THE LAWRENCE WELK SHOW

NUMBER 10 (TIE), 1966–67

Wunnerful, wunnerful!   —LAWRENCE WELK

He had only a fourth-grade education and spoke English with a thick German accent that belied his North Dakota birthplace, yet he went on to become one of the most beloved figures in television through five decades. "The Lawrence Welk Show" began its weekly appearances on the tube in 1955 as a summer replacement. The show ran on Saturday nights on ABC for 16 years, following which Welk produced new episodes in first-run syndication on more than 250 stations, until 1,542 performances later, on February 25, 1982, he produced his last show.

The format was basically an old-fashioned dance party, complete with long gowns, popping champagne corks (his orchestra was known as the Champagne Music Makers, among other nicknames), polkas, and waltzes.

Lawrence Welk resisted attempts to modernize his repertoire, claiming great difficulty in comprehending the Beatles' music and remaining true to his own style. "You have to play what the people understand," he said. (Or at least, what he himself understood.)

To Welk, the audience came first. He knew his fans were older women and mothers with middle-American values, and he proclaimed, "We try to please our audience. We try to bring it some joy, happiness, and relaxation and always to be in good taste—the kind of entertainment that should come into the home."

Occasionally his early-20th-century, prudish farmland upbringing got the better of him, as when he fired Alice Lon, one of the Champagne Ladies used for window dressing on the show, in a dispute over the length of her hemlines. Welk was very strict in his dress code. The popular Lennon Sisters, a singing sisters act that began when the girls were preteens and teenagers and continued until all

were well into their 20s, ran into similar difficulties. Dianne Lennon recalled the bandleader insisting they wear crinolines and puffed sleeves even as young adults; Kathy remembered a similar brouhaha over the time they wore—gasp!—modest, one-piece bathing suits for a pool sequence. "Mr. Welk got more letters than you could believe afterwards from people asking him how he could have allowed our legs to be shown on television," she said. "He came to us with those letters and said, 'I told you!' And he told the wardrobe people never to put us in bathing suits again." She also recalled the group finally quit in 1967 when, after 10 years, he refused to pay them more than scale—$210 apiece per week. "No act is worth a penny over scale to me," he told them. The Lennon Sisters eventually had their own show, "Jimmy Durante Presents the Lennon Sisters," from 1969 to 1970, in which they earned *$12,500* a week, and they appeared as regulars on "The Andy Williams Show" from 1970 to 1971.

Welk was still fondly remembered by his former protégés when he passed away in 1992 at the age of 89. One of the earliest Champagne Ladies, Roberta Lynn, also had warm memories of Welk, and nostalgically recalled his accent getting him into trouble on occasion. "If you're going to do an impersonation of Lawrence Welk," she said, "every 'b' is a 'p.' My name was 'Roperta,' and it was the 'poys in the pand.' And because of this, he would say things that came out a little different. Here's how he introduced one of the shows—I think it was our first television show. He said, 'Good evening mine friends, and welcome to our very first teewee show. Here from the *peautiful* Aragon *Pallroom* tonight, we got the Champagne Lady, Ro*perta* Lynn, and all the *poys* in the *pand*, and we got a new arrangement in the key of 'chee.' Okay, *poys*, I want you all to *pee* on your toes now. Ah-one an' ah-two...'"

After the show went out of production in 1982, Welk continued to

---

CREDITS

EXECUTIVE PRODUCER: Sam Lutz. PRODUCER/DIRECTOR: James Hobson. WRITERS: various. HOST: Lawrence Welk. REGULARS: "Champagne Ladies" Alice Lon and Norma Zimmer, The Lennon Sisters (Dianne, Peggy, Kathy, Janet), Pete Fountain, [former Mousketeer] Bobby Burgess, dozens more.

plow his money back into his various financial enter-
prises. His corporation, Teleklew Inc., managed today
by his son, Larry, Jr., deals in music publishing, record-
ings, and real estate, including the Lawrence Welk
Resort (a 1,000-acre complex in Escondido in northern
San Diego County), a mobile home park near
Palm Springs, and an office and apart-
ment complex in Santa Monica.
A museum and theater at the
Lawrence Welk Resort in
Escondido draws busloads
of tourists daily.

"The Lawrence Welk
Show" ran on ABC from July
1955 until September 1971,
when the network dropped
the broadcasts, claiming its
audience was "too old." This
was probably true, since the

sponsors at the time were Geritol and Sominex. Welk
responded by continuing to tape shows and syndicating
them in 250 markets around the country, more than
had aired his show on ABC. The program never missed
a week of air time, with the exception of the week following President Kennedy's assassination in 1963,
until production ceased in 1982.

By the '90s, the shows had been
repackaged and sold to the Public
Broadcasting Service (PBS),
which aired them on 270 of its
outlets across the country, with
contracts continuing through
1993. It did well, outranking
"Nova," one of PBS's highest-
rated series, and continued to
attract many new fans. Now
that's truly "wunnerful, wunnerful."

Lawrence Welk.

THE VIRGINIAN

NUMBER 10 (TIE), 1966–67

Doug McClure.

When you call me that, smile!

In fact, that oft-quoted line was never uttered in the television series derived from Owen Wister's 1902 novel *The Virginian*.

In the original novel, Trampas, the local bad man, accused the title hero (he was never given a proper name) of cheating at the poker table while simultaneously impugning his ancestry, following which our hero laid his Colt .45 pistol on the table and uttered the above, now-immortal line. Gary Cooper recreated that famous scene in his 1929 film version of *The Virginian*, one of several motion pictures to be made of the famous novel.

By the time the book became the rough blueprint for a television series, however, things had changed. The Virginian was still a lonesome cowboy, settled down to life as the foreman of the Shiloh Ranch in Medicine Bow, Wyoming, in the late 1880s. But Trampas was not vanquished in a gun duel, as he was in the original novel; as played by Doug McClure, he was now the headstrong young cowhand/assistant foreman. And although in the novel the Virginian actually settled down to married life with Molly Wood, a New England schoolteacher whom he had rescued from a marooned stagecoach, the Molly of the TV series, a newspaper publisher played by Pippa Scott, would actually be gone after the program's first season (1962–63).

It seems only natural that the translation of this novel to a weekly 90-minute episode—really more like a series of movies completed in eight days each—would have to take these assorted liberties with the concept. The original pilot for "The Virginian," in fact, was about as far from the final concept as the producers could get.

In 1958 James Drury was cast in the role of the Virginian in an episode of a now-forgotten anthology series called "Decision" (a three-month-long summer replacement for "The Loretta Young Show"), which aired the pilot as one of its weekly dramas. Four years later the pilot was picked up as a regular series, and fortunately Drury was no longer decked out in the "western dandy" duds that he had worn in the "Decision" episode: shiny hunting boots, skin-tight pants, lacy cuffs, and with a tiny pistol at his side.

James Drury had played some minor roles in film in the 1950s when the young actor was signed to an MGM contract, and by the end of that decade he had begun appearing in many television westerns, including "Gunsmoke," "The Rebel," and "The Rifleman." He gained a reputation for being something like his character while working on the series: an intensely private person with a bit of an air of mystery about him. He was also known for being temperamental, once refusing to be photographed or interviewed for a *TV Guide* article unless the piece was only about him and unless he alone was on the cover. He was reportedly moody and difficult on the set. But Drury, temperamental as he might of been, was nothing compared to his co-star, Lee J. Cobb, who played Judge Henry Garth, first owner of the Shiloh Ranch.

From the start, Cobb made it quite plain that he did not enjoy working in weekly television. He had been essentially a movie actor, and he groused his way through four seasons of the series, admitting at one time, "I'm ashamed of [the series]," then adding, "Well, you know, there is an awful lot of money involved."

Cobb also complained bitterly when the guest stars were given juicier roles while the series' regulars seemed to be relegated to becoming bit players. By 1966 Cobb had had it and, unsurprisingly, he quit as soon as his contract ran out, continuing to concentrate on various films like *Mackenna's Gold* (1969) and *The Exorcist* (1973) until his death in 1976.

Over the course of its nine years, "The Virginian" (retitled "The Men from Shiloh" for its final season [1970–71]) utilized virtually every western plot ever conceived. And with a lengthy 90 minutes to fill each week, it wasn't easy for the show's writers to continually come up with fresh ideas for Drury and company. There were tried-and-true chestnuts about outlaws stampeding the honest rancher's cattle, the pretty gal who runs the ranch after dad is mysteriously murdered, the dastardly character about to foreclose on the mortgage—melodramatic story lines like these were to be found week after week (and sometimes, all in the *same* week), while new characters regularly drifted in and out of the Shiloh "family."

Actors like Lee Majors and David Hartman would even go on to star in series of their own. And although the production values on "The Virginian" were consistently top-notch, with better-than-average camera work and music, the series eventually ran out of steam and ratings until NBC finally cancelled it in 1971. And when they did, nobody smiled.

CREDITS

BASED ON CHARACTERS CREATED BY: Owen Wister. EXECUTIVE PRODUCER: Frank Price, others. PRODUCERS: various. DIRECTORS: various. WRITERS: various. CAST: *The Virginian* (James Drury), *Judge Henry Garth* (Lee J. Cobb), *Trampas* (Doug McClure), *Molly Wood* (Pippa Scott), *Emmett Ryker* (Clu Gulager), *Betsy* (Roberta Shore), *Randy Garth* (Randy Boone), *John Grainger* (Charles Bickford), *David Sutton* (David Hartman), *Jim Horn* (Tim Matheson), *Roy Tate* (Lee Majors), *Col. Alan MacKenzie* (Stewart Granger), others. GUEST STARS: Hugh O'Brian, Colleen Dewhurst, Sonny Tufts, Leslie Nielsen, Angie Dickinson, Warren Oates, Charles Bronson, Ralph Bellamy, others.

FAMILY AFFAIR

NUMBER 4 (TIE), 1967–68

Anissa Jones and Johnnie Whitaker.

With divorce more prevalent in the late 1960s than ever before in American society, single-parent families on television series were becoming the "in" thing. Programs like "The Lucy Show," "Julia," "The Ghost and Mrs. Muir," "The Doris Day Show," "Bachelor Father," and even "Bonanza" presented homes where one parent, either divorced or widowed, was saddled with the task of raising kids without the support of a spouse. "Bachelor Father," which ran from 1957 to 1962, in fact bore a strikingly ancestral resemblance to "Family Affair," which was even cited by *Variety* as "an outright steal." While most would not be so bold as to accuse the show's creators of any such impropriety, "Family Affair" did indeed border on the derivative.

For starters, there was the swingin' bachelor uncle whose life was disrupted when he found himself a father surrogate to an instant family of orphaned kids. (Okay, "Bachelor Father" only had *one* teenage daughter to raise, while "Family Affair" had a teenage daughter plus two cuddly kidlets, ages seven and nine). Each show had a gentleman's gentleman of foreign origin to guide the bachelor through this ordeal—Peter Tong (Chinese) in "Bachelor Father" versus Mr. French (English) in "Family Affair."

CREDITS

CREATOR: Edmund Hartman, Don Federson. EXECUTIVE PRODUCER: Don Federson. PRODUCER: Edmund Hartman. DIRECTOR: Charles Barton. WRITERS: various. CAST: *Bill Davis* (Brian Keith), *Mr. French* (Sebastian Cabot), *Buffy* (Anissa Jones), *Jody* (Johnnie Whitaker), *Cissy* (Kathy Garver), *Emily Turner* (Nancy Walker).

But if the premises were interchangeable, that is where the similarities ended. "Family Affair" had a completely different treatment of the concept, and it worked splendidly. Casting played a large part in the success of this series, which was in and out of the Nielsen top 10 during the course of its five-year run on CBS. Brian Keith played the bachelor father-figure, the kids' uncle who begrudgingly agreed to rear his inherited family. He groused and grumbled, but he proved his mettle as a parent despite his ineptitude. Sebastian Cabot was cast as the stuffy English butler with the soft interior. Mr. French was perplexed by children, remarking in the first episode, "In England we have only two stages—infancy and manhood." He was the last person one would expect to be sucked in by the youngsters, but that's exactly (and predictably) what happened. The teenage daughter, played by Kathy Garver, was lost in all of this, a perky 19-year-old U.C.L.A. coed who didn't seem to mind being upstaged by the little ones at every turn. But the show's main

draw were the two most adorable children to walk in front of a camera since Shirley Temple's Good Ship Lollipop last docked in port.

Anissa Jones and Johnnie Whitaker were nine and seven years old, respectively, when they first displayed their freckles and dimples for the American audience. They played the twins, Buffy and Jody, who were supposed to be six in the first season. Whitaker had acted in films and TV since he was three, building a reputation on his ability to cry on cue. He had worked with Brian Keith in the movie *The Russians Are Coming, The Russians Are Coming* (1966), and it was Keith who suggested Johnnie for "Family Affair." The children became best friends and, as required by California law, attended school together three hours a day on the set while working. (Their teacher had at one time taught both Shirley Temple and Jane Withers.)

The series had originally been conceived as an adult show with kids in it, but it didn't take long for the network to realize that the series had great kid appeal. Both Jones and Whitaker quickly became the darlings of the CBS eye. The network rushed "Mrs. Beasley" dolls (Buffy's favorite toy) into production so that every little girl in America could have one; Anissa Jones recorded her voice to go with a Mattel "Buffy" doll, and she also endorsed a line of children's clothing, something she learned to loathe, since, in order to show them off, the producers insisted she still dress in those same cutesy dresses when she was already 13.

By 1971 the adorable moppets had turned into average teenagers, and CBS decided the series had run its course. Brian Keith later starred in the TV drama "Hardcastle & McCormick" (1983–86) and was constantly seen in film and television. Sebastian Cabot hosted the TV anthology series "Ghost Story," and died of a stroke in 1977. Johnnie Whitaker starred in the Saturday morning kids' series, "Sigmund and the Sea Monsters" (1973–75), and was featured in several Walt Disney productions. In 1992 he worked as a computer consultant and still did an occasional role in a film or TV show. Anissa Jones' career fizzled when she hit her teen years; she was found dead of a drug overdose in her California home in 1976 at the age of 19.

THE DEAN MARTIN SHOW

NUMBER 8, 1967–68

Everybody loves somebody sometime...
—OPENING SONG

Dino Crocetti, the son of an Italian barber from Steubenville, Ohio, didn't learn to speak English until he was five. By the time he was in his 50s, he was pulling down an annual salary larger than that of any performer to that time in the history of show business.

Dean Martin (he changed his name twice, the first time to Dino Martini) had a number one hit record ("Memories Are Made of This") early in 1956. Bolstered by this success, he split with his comedy partner, Jerry Lewis, that same year (see page 12) to strike out on his own. "When we broke up," he said, "people kept whispering behind my back that I was finished, that Jerry had been carrying me. This hurt me. It also scared me. I knew I could always make a living as a singer, but I wasn't sure whether I could stay in the big time." He was partly right. His movie career floundered for a couple of years, but he finally caught the attention of critics in the film *The Young Lions* (1958), and had another number one hit record in 1964, "Everybody Loves Somebody," which became his signature song.

Martin's popularity prompted NBC to book him as a guest host on "The Hollywood Palace," a last-gasp vaudeville-format TV series that featured different stars hosting each week. Only after his idol, Bing Crosby, took a turn on the series did Dino agree to do the show. Pleased with his performance, NBC wanted to spin him off into his own TV vehicle, "The Dean Martin Show." But by that time Martin wasn't particularly interested. He'd tasted success; his career was well on track, and he'd had the experience of the weekly television grind, thank you very much. It wasn't something he lusted after. "When the idea was brought to me," he told *TV Guide*, "I thought it was so crazy that I made a farce of it. First, I asked a ridiculous sum. Then I said I wanted to own the package 100 percent after the first showing of the series. I also said I wanted to work Sunday only, and I reserved the right not to sing on the show if I didn't want to. What I asked should have been thrown back into my face, but the network accepted it—and it was lucky for me, because the show has done wonderful things for my records and it has given me a recognition that one doesn't get from movies." "The Dean Martin Show" premiered on September 16, 1965, amid rumors, which Martin vehemently denied, that he agreed to do the series because Lewis's show had failed.

By now Dean Martin had created a character for himself, which became the focal point of the show. He played the boozing, broad-chasing stumblebum, a lovable lush who flubbed cue cards and sleepwalked through his show. Although there is nothing funny about the disease of alcoholism, in those days people thought this was hilarious. "I drink moderately," Martin would announce. "I have a case of Moderately in my dressing room!" Or "Every time I sit down, my housekeeper slips a coaster under me," and "My doctor told me to take a little drink before I go to bed. Do you know I find myself going to bed nine or ten times a night?" NBC warned him against using so many drunk jokes during

CREDITS

EXECUTIVE PRODUCER: Hal Kemp. PRODUCER/DIRECTOR: Greg Garrison. WRITERS: Paul Keyes, Harry Crane, Richard Eustis, Al Rogers, Treva Silverman, Ed Weinberger, Norm Liebmann, Rod Parker, others. HOST: Dean Martin. REGULARS: The Golddiggers, The Ding-a-Lings, Dan Rowan and Dick Martin, Dom DeLuise, Lou Jacoby, Kay Medford, The Sid and Marty Krofft Puppets, others. GUEST STARS: Frank Sinatra, Diahann Carroll, Jan and Dean, Bob Newhart, Danny Thomas, Eddie Fisher, Steve Allen, Jack Jones, Buddy Hackett, Peggy Lee, Dorothy Provine, Juliet Prowse, Jimmy Stewart, Orson Wells, Buddy Ebsen, Shecky Greene, Lena Horne, Zero Mostel, Goldie Hawn, Dennis Weaver, Joey Bishop, Red Skelton, Ruth Buzzi, Charles Nelson Reilly, Art Carney, Petula Clark, Liberace, Gene Kelly, Rodney Dangerfield, others.

his first season, but gave up after no one complained.

Martin had an aversion to rehearsals. "They wanted me there three days to rehearse," he protested. " 'Why three days?' I asked. 'So we can learn everything without the cue cards,' they said. I say, if cue cards are there, why not use them?" On the day of taping, Dino would do one run-through, reading the jokes on the cards but not doing them. And some gags, which he read perfectly at the rehearsal, he would pretend he couldn't make out during the taping, squinting at the cue cards, blowing lines on many, ad-libbing "blue" remarks on others. It was all part of his shtick, of course, and the audience (if not the NBC censors) loved his casual approach, his double-entendres, and the scantily clad ladies with whom he surrounded himself.

There were two groups of leggy girls associated with "The Dean Martin Show": the Golddiggers, the only chorines ever to get their own TV series (during their hiatus from Dean's show—"Dean Martin Presents the Golddiggers"), and the Ding-a-Ling Sisters, whose name should give an indication of Martin's attitude towards women. Indeed, his lecherous remarks and demeaning treatment of women in the peace-marching '60s found NBC a prime target for protesters, who picketed NBC for several (unsuccessful) weeks. Dean and the writers went right on making sexist remarks, as in this sketch between Dean and guest Steve Lawrence:

Dean Martin.

DEAN (GLANCING OUT AN
AIRPLANE WINDOW AT THE GROUND)
What's that down there—mountains?

STEVE
No—Raquel Welch lying on her back.

Fairly harmless stuff, but still typical of the attitude promoted by the show.

In 1973 the series' title was changed to "The Dean Martin Comedy Hour," but by 1974 the show had finally run its course. One of the segments, the "celebrity roast," was spun off into a series of occasional specials on NBC with Martin acting as the "roastmaster"; they continued until the 1980s.

In 1976 Dean Martin appeared with Jerry Lewis for the first time in 20 years, on a Muscular Dystrophy Telethon in Las Vegas. The long-overdue reunion was engineered by mutual friend Frank Sinatra. In the early 1990s, although basically retired, Martin occasionally turned up in a TV guest appearance.

NBC SATURDAY NIGHT AT THE MOVIES

NUMBER 10, 1967–68

Imagine a time with no VCRs, no cable channels with HBO, Showtime, the Movie Channel, or Cinemax. Home video hadn't been invented, so if you wanted to see a movie, you had two choices: you either went out to the theater and saw whatever flick was in current release, or you stayed home and watched the 87th running of John Ford's *Stagecoach* or some other ancient cinematic classic that had long since been relegated to the graveyard of TV. Then, in 1961, the movies, which had always disdained television, found that what goes around comes around. NBC premiered a new series called "NBC Saturday Night Movie."

It was the first time a network aired first-run Hollywood films in prime time on a weekly basis. Movies had, of course, been on TV since the early days, but they were always from the 1930s or '40s, black and white, and shown from a glitchy print. Sometimes they were classics, usually they were turkeys, and they were never shown in prime time on a network; movies were things run by local channels because they were cheap. But with this new NBC series, people could finally settle in with a box of homemade Jiffy Popcorn (the kind you made on the stove in an aluminum pan included with the kernels) and watch a movie in the comfort of their living rooms. Viewers were delighted to know that if they missed seeing a recent, highly touted film in the theaters, they would have another chance at it in a few years (three or four years was then considered "recent"), when it would make its way to television. And the price was always right.

It didn't take long for NBC to add another weekly movie night. For the 1963–64 season, the network added "NBC Monday Night Movie," beginning at 7:30 P.M.; from 1964 to 1965 there was the "NBC Wednesday Night Movie" at 9:00; and in 1965 there was an "NBC Tuesday Night Movie." ABC jumped into the film feeding frenzy in 1964 with "ABC Sunday Night Movie," while CBS added its own "CBS Thursday Night Movie" in 1965 and a "CBS Friday Night Movie" in 1966. By 1968 there was a different "Movie" on each night of the week, with the pie sliced this way: ABC had Sunday and Wednesday; NBC aired films Monday, Tuesday, and Saturday; and CBS held down Thursday and Friday.

"NBC Saturday Night Movie"—the name underwent periodic changes to either "NBC Saturday Night at the Movies" or simply "Saturday Night at the Movies"— became a prime-time hit in the 1967–68 season, many years after the series premiered. This was doubly sweet for the happy executives at that network because the competition was particularly stiff that season, with the films scheduled opposite "The Lawrence Welk Show" on ABC and "Hogan's Heroes" on CBS for the all-important first 30 minutes, and later opposite the popular "Petticoat Junction" and "Mannix" on CBS, and the not-so-popular "Iron Horse" and something called "ABC Scope" on ABC.

No doubt it was the quality of the movies and the big-name stars that grabbed the attention of the audience. Films shown on television for the first time included *Never on Sunday* (1960), with Greek star Melina Mercouri; *The Chalk Garden* (1964), with Deborah Kerr, Hayley Mills, and John Mills; two Alfred Hitchcock thrillers—*Marnie* (1964), with Tippi Hedren and Sean Connery, and *The Birds* (1963), with Rod Taylor and Tippi Hedren; the classic *Saratoga Trunk* (1945), with Ingrid Bergman and Gary Cooper; *No Man Is an Island* (1962), with Jeffrey Hunter and Marshall Thompson; *Flower Drum Song* (1961), with Nancy Kwan, James Shigeta, and Miyoshi Umeki; *Freud* (1962), with Montgomery Clift, Susannah York, and Larry Parks; *Bus Riley's Back in Town* (1965), with Michael Parks, Ann-Margret, and Janet Margolin; *Strange Bedfellows* (1964), with Rock Hudson, Gina Lollobrigida, and Gig Young; and *What a Way to Go!* (1964), with Shirley MacLaine, Paul Newman, Robert Mitchum, Dean Martin, Gene Kelly, Bob Cummings, and Dick Van Dyke.

With every network now programming movies, Hollywood was rapidly depleting its supply of first-run films. Although the network "Movie" trend continued well into the '90s, in the late '60s the networks began developing a new genre of television programming, the "made-for-TV" movie, to take up the slack. The networks' seasonal line-ups of hit films were also peppered with original TV movies, several of which became pilots for new series.

Jeffery Hunter, in *No Man Is an Island*.

ROWAN & MARTIN'S LAUGH-IN

NUMBER 1, 1968–69

Sock it to me!   —JUDY CARNE

A man with his hand cupped over one ear nuzzled the oversized microphone. "From beautiful downtown Burbank," he intoned, "it's 'Rowan & Martin's Laugh-In!' " For the next hour, people sat glued to their television sets, afraid to move lest they miss one of the 300 or more jokes written by a team of 16 writers, hurled at the viewers scattergun fashion in various blackouts, one-liners, sketches, and yes, even painted on gyrating, boogalooing bodies.

There were name games: "If Shirley Temple Black had married Tyrone Power, she'd be Shirley Black Power," and "If Jan Sterling had married Phil Silvers, divorced him, and married Robert Service, she'd be Jan Sterling Silvers Service." There was graffiti (sometimes painted on bodies): "Forest fires prevent bears," and "Little Orphan Annie—call the eye bank." And in the show's weekly running gag, the ever-unsuspecting Judy Carne was splashed with a water bucket after delivering her "sock it to me" catch phrase.

Part *Hellzapoppin'* burlesque, part TV's "That Was the Week That Was," yet uniquely its own, "Laugh-In" first aired as a pilot/special in the fall of 1967 to enough critical raves for NBC to rush the series into production as a mid-season replacement for the sagging "The Man from U.N.C.L.E." "What we did," explained producer/creator George Schlatter, "was take all the known forms of television, which were basically *Hellzapoppin'*, [Ernie] Kovacs, Milton Berle, and Steve Allen, and tighten it and make it just the joke—not the setup, not the payoff, but just the joke."

Funnymen Dan Rowan and Dick Martin, who had first impressed NBC in 1965 when they worked as summer replacements for Dean Martin, anchored the series with their straight man/Gracie Allen-esque routines, but it was the rat-a-tat-tat humor that kept most people tuning in. As Dick Martin explained in *Time* magazine, "Nobody's going to appreciate everything on our show. But if one gag goes completely over your head, there'll be another along in a few seconds that cracks you up and leaves somebody else just looking and saying 'Humph!' "

"Laugh-In" created its own lexicon of catch phrases:

"Sock it to me," "You bet your sweet bippy," "Look that up in your Funk and Wagnalls," Arte Johnson's German-accented "Verrry interesting," and "Here come da judge" (made popular by Pigmeat Markham and perpetuated on the series by Sammy Davis, Jr., in judge's robes and wig).

There was an all-star cast, except that they were all-unknown in those days. Goldie Hawn, the 22-year-old, body-painted, buck-toothed, blonde giggler was perhaps the most successful. Gary Owens tells how Goldie "would break up very easily. Many times the writers would write dirty things into the cue cards, and she wouldn't know it. She was expecting something else, so that's where they would get the giggle from." She may

---

CREDITS

CREATED BY: George Schlatter, Dan Rowan, Dick Martin. EXECUTIVE PRODUCERS: George Schlatter, Ed Friendly, Dan Rowan and Dick Martin. PRODUCERS: George Schlatter, Paul Keyes. DIRECTORS: various. WRITERS: Paul Keyes, Digby Wolfe, others. CAST: Dan Rowan, Dick Martin, Gary Owens, Ruth Buzzi, Henry Gibson, Larry Hovis, Arte Johnson, Jo Anne Worley, Judy Carne, Goldie Hawn, Pigmeat Markham, Dick Whittington, Chelsea Brown, Alan Sues, Dave Madden, Tiny Tim, Teresa Graves, Lily Tomlin, Johnny Brown, Richard Dawson, Patti Deutsch, Sarah Kennedy, Willie Tyler and Lester, others. GUEST STARS: Barbara Feldon, Buddy Hackett, Sheldon Leonard, Lorne Greene, Richard M. Nixon, John Wayne, Flip Wilson, Zsa Zsa Gabor, Bob Hope, Hugh Hefner, Debbie Reynolds, Peter Sellers, Johnny Carson, Raquel Welch, Jill St. John, Otto Preminger, Walter Matthau, others.

EMMYS

Outstanding Musical or Variety Program (Special) (1967–68), Outstanding Musical or Variety Series (1967–68, 1968–69), Outstanding Individual Achievement (Special Classification)—Arte Johnson (1968–69), Outstanding Directorial Achievement in Variety or Music, Series—Mark Warren (1960–71).

have played a dum-dum, but she had smarts when it came to her career. Goldie left the show in 1969 to star in the movie *Cactus Flower*, won an Academy Award, and never looked back.

Lily Tomlin became famous as Ernestine, the telephone operator locked in a 1940s time warp. She snorted like a sow in heat, waited "one ringy-dingy, two ringy-dingies," then asked, "Have I reached the party to whom I am speaking?" She brought along her own repertoire of kookie characters, including Edith Ann, the little girl in the oversized rocking chair. Tomlin later starred on Broadway and in hit films like *All of Me* (1984).

Other well-remembered regulars on the series included Ruth Buzzi, Arte Johnson, Henry Gibson, Judy "Sock it to me" Carne, Eileen Brennan, Jo Anne Worley, Richard Dawson, and Gary Owens. Gary recalls that "Ruth and I were the only two who did every show. Ruth and myself, and Dan and Dick did all 140 hours of the show." Gary spent most of the series with his hand cupped over his ear, the "guy in another dimension," as he recalls being described by George Schlatter. "I was one of the very few who ever got to say my name; it would be 'Morgul as the friendly Drelb,' and 'yours truly, Gary Owens.'" Eventually NBC invited Owens to put his ear print in cement in the NBC parking lot, but he laments the day it happened, "February 9, 1971, the day of the [7.1] earthquake, and there's a big crack in it!"

The series' enormous popularity had famous people clamoring to appear as guests on the show (and for a scale fee of only $240). Perhaps the most remembered was Richard Nixon, who uttered those now-famous four words, "Sock it to *me*?" (and eventually the nation did). John Wayne appeared in an Easter Bunny suit, but his vanity got the best of him when he did a Gary Owens impression and refused to wear Gary's trademark glasses. Gary recalls, "He didn't want to be seen in glasses because I think he equated glasses with age, but his comment was, 'I didn't think anyone would recognize me with glasses on.'"

"Rowan & Martin's Laugh-In" was oft-copied, but never equalled. "Hee Haw" openly admitted that the

series was a country cuzzin to "Laugh-In." "Turn On," a much-ballyhooed clone from George Schlatter, lasted exactly one episode on ABC February 5, 1969. It was immediately cancelled when the sponsor dropped it due to too many sexual innuendoes. And "Laugh-In" itself had its own spin-off in "Letters to Laugh-In," a show hosted by Gary Owens in which viewers were invited to submit jokes. (The "winner" received "seven action-packed days in beautiful downtown Burbank.")

As the newly discovered talent moved on to their newly discovered careers elsewhere, the ratings began to drop off, and by 1973 the show was history.

The "Laugh-In" crew. In the front row are Dick Martin (left) Dan Rowin (right), flanking guest John Wayne.

In 1979 George Schlatter tried to capture lightning in a bottle for a second time, with a new version simply titled, "Laugh-In." It aired as a series of NBC specials during the 1977–78 season, but paled in comparison to the original. Then in 1979 someone pointed out that one of the unknowns in the 1977 cast was Robin Williams, who by then had a hit series in "Mork & Mindy." So NBC dusted off the specials and aired them during the summer of 1979, hoping to capitalize on Williams's fame.

In 1993 George Schlatter produced a two-hour "Laugh-In's 25th Anniversary Special." The February broadcast featured clips from the original series, as well as special appearances by members of the original cast (with the exception of Dan Rowan, who had passed away in 1987).

MAYBERRY R.F.D.

NUMBER 4, 1968–69

After eight years of doing "The Andy Griffith Show," the series' namesake wanted out of the weekly grind of TV. The executives at CBS were frantic; "Andy" was television's number one rated series and they were reluctant to part with this cash cow. No problem—Andy found a way for them to have their hoecake and eat it, too. He devised a new series to take its place and had no trouble selling the network on the "sequel" that would retain the same folksy quality and understated humor of its progenitor. According to Richard Linke, the executive producer (along with Griffith), "They [CBS] were buying a winning team."

"Mayberry R.F.D." (that's a postal abbreviation meaning rural free delivery) was more than just a spinoff of "The Andy Griffith Show"—it was a virtual clone, with only Andy Taylor and Barney Fife as the missing links. The series even had Andy and Barney as occasional visitors to town, along with Andy's new bride (played by Aneta Corsaut). There was a new male lead, Ken Berry, in the role of Sam Jones, yet another widowed parent raising a small boy (Buddy Foster, brother of actress Jody) on his own. The other new character was Arlene Golonka as Sam's romantic interest, Millie Swanson. The rest were mainly familiar faces. Aunt Bea (Frances Bavier) simply shifted jobs from housekeeping for Andy to assisting Sam on his farm residence. She stayed two seasons, then left the series and was replaced by Alice Ghostley. Other regulars who hung around the Mayberry scene were George Lindsey as Gomer Pyle's cousin Goober, Jack Dodson as county clerk Howard Sprague, and Paul Hartman as Emmett Clark, the fix-it

shop owner. It was business as usual in Mayberry.

The character of Sam Jones differed from Andy Taylor in that he wasn't the sheriff. He was a gentleman farmer who, soon after arrival in the Mayberry area, was elected to the Mayberry Town Council. Actor Ken Berry had played the bumbling captain on "F Troop" from 1965 to 1967, so he was a familiar face to audiences. He managed to work his friendly, bumbling "F Troop" style into "Mayberry."

The emphasis, though, was more on human nature than on broad humor, with an occasional episode containing a good dose of pathos. For example, when Goober wanted to ask Millie to the Harvest Ball he asked Sam to write the invitation for him. She went to the dance with Goober, but when he saw Sam and Millie dancing together, he realized they were meant for each other, and in a poignant, bittersweet speech admitted, "There's a look that passes between them, and you can see it all the way across the dance floor. She'll never have that look for me. Maybe some day some other girl will, but not Millie."

Yet as warm and human as the characters were, the star of the show—the link that kept the two series connected— was actually Mayberry, the town itself. It was still a nice place to visit, and a nice place to live. The audience thought so right up until CBS decided that it was time to cut the corn out of its weekly diet, and purged all of its countrified series that were deemed "demographically undesirable." But the series survived in reruns for 20 more years, and in 1993 could be seen weekdays on cable's TNT channel.

> **CREDITS**
>
> CREATED BY: Andy Griffith.
> EXECUTIVE PRODUCERS: Andy Griffith, Richard O. Linke.
> PRODUCER: Bob Ross. DIRECTORS: various. WRITERS: various. CAST: *Sam Jones* (Ken Berry), *Aunt Bea* (Frances Bavier), *Goober Pyle* (George Lindsey), *Howard Sprague* (Jack Dodson), *Emmett Clark* (Paul Hartman), *Millie Swanson* (Arlene Golonka), *Mike Jones* (Buddy Foster), *Aunt Alice* (Alice Ghostley). GUEST STARS: Andy Griffith, Don Knotts, Ronnie Howard, Aneta Corsaut, Maudie Prickett, others.

Ken Berry and Arlene Golonka.

JULIA

NUMBER 7, 1968–69

During the latter part of the 1960s, television began to reach the age of maturity. No longer was TV an exclusive whites-only club; advertisers, aware that the 22 million black people in the United States had considerable purchasing power, began appealing to their equal-opportunity pocketbooks. In 1965 Bill Cosby became the first black to co-star in a dramatic series without playing a butler or servant. By 1968, of the 56 nighttime dramatic shows, 21 had at least one regular black performer. There were three variety shows hosted by blacks; at least five TV shows had black writers (up from only one in the previous year), and two black directors had earned their Guild cards. The reasons commonly given for these remarkable (and they were remarkable in those days) changes were the success of Bill Cosby in NBC's "I Spy," the pressures of social change, and the assassination of the Rev. Martin Luther King, Jr. Sociologists, in fact, were scrambling to bring into focus all the reasons for TV's sudden rush to "black gold."

Whatever the reason might have been, 1968 was truly a watershed year in the history of African-Americans in television. And at the forefront was not only a black, but a woman: singer Diahann Carroll, who will forever be remembered as the first black to star in her own series. This landmark show premiered on NBC September 17, 1968, and was immediately subjected to a barrage of criticism.

"Julia" may have been black, but the lead character—an air force widow raising her button-cute six-year-old alone (her husband had been shot down over Vietnam), living in an all-white luxury apartment complex, wearing fine, expensive clothes, surrounded by white friends and white co-workers—was decried as being non-representative of black society. True, there were some confrontations with racism on the show, but bigotry was thinly veiled. People seemed to go out of their way not to notice her skin color, as in this

exchange over the telephone between Julia and her employer-to-be:

JULIA
Did they tell you I'm colored?

DR. CHEGLEY
Mm, what color are you?

JULIA
W-why, I'm Negro.

DR. CHEGLEY
Oh. Have you always been a Negro, or are you just trying to be fashionable?

The series' beautiful star, Diahann Carroll, found herself inundated with so much mail she hired two full-time assistants just to handle the tidal wave of questions like: "Don't you realize you're letting the white community get away with murder by not insisting it address itself to the black male?" "How do you reconcile Julia's lavish life-style with her nurse's salary?" "Do you know how many black nurses there actually are in America?" "Is there any truth to the rumor that Julia's going to have a white boyfriend?" "Don't you feel guilty about doing this show?" The fact that Carroll had no decision-making power didn't seem to matter; she was still held personally responsible for the show's short-comings. "Why are we singled out as a TV show?" she angrily asked in *Time* magazine. "The fact that the show went on the air at all is a plus, and a plus long overdue. Somebody decided, 'Let's have a black lady starring on TV in 1968'—in *1968*. Why not attack *that*? That it took so long? Isn't that an outrage?"

Diahann believed that too many critics mistakenly judged the program as a documentary or social tract rather than for what it was—a sitcom (thankfully without laugh track) that was about as true to life as other TV series.

CREDITS

CREATOR/PRODUCER: Hal Kanter.
DIRECTORS: Hal Kanter, others.
WRITERS: Hal Kanter, others.
CAST: *Julia Baker* (Diahann Carroll), *Dr. Morton Chegley* (Lloyd Nolan), *Corey Baker* (Marc Copage), *Earl J. Waggedorn* (Michael Link), *Marie Waggedorn* (Betty Beaird), *Hannah Yarby* (Lurene Tuttle), *Paul Cameron* (Paul Winfield), others.

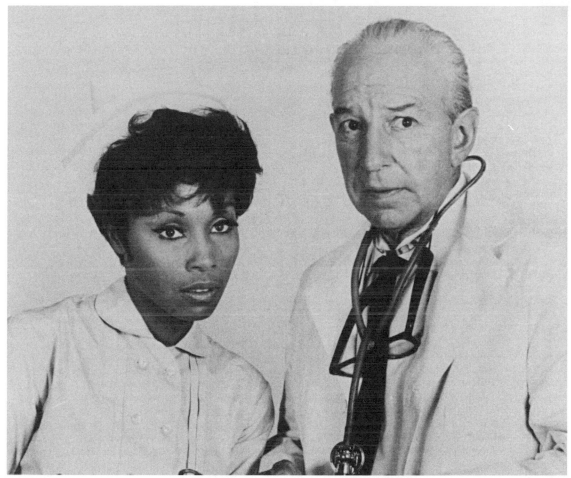

Diahann Carroll, with Lloyd Nelson.

The series' creator, Hal Kanter, felt that the racial aspect was only incidental. During the first season of the show he explained in *Time*: "To me, the news is that a Negro family is featured, and they're not choppin' cotton and they're not on relief, but they're part of what some people consider the mainstream of American life." The series went out of its way to spotlight black people who were fully assimilable—the sort of blacks who, as one critic noted, "could move into your neighborhood and not disturb you at all." Kanter, in fact, saw "Julia" as "some sort of apology for a lot of the things we had done on 'Amos 'n' Andy.'"

For years after the show's run, Diahann Carroll continued to be put on the defensive about the character she created. When a 1992 documentary, "P.O.V.: Color Adjustment," appeared on PBS, produced by black filmmaker Marlon T. Riggs, she found herself on the hotseat 24 years later, still defending "Julia." "She was about entertaining the American public, and Kanter wanted an American black woman that was part of what

the television scene was at that time," she said. "It was single mothers; they were all attractive and learning about being in the workplace. Some of them were raising children, and most of them didn't have husbands. I think Hal did a hell of a job."

The viewers did too, and the series became a ratings hit. But in 1971, after three years, Carroll decided to ask for a release from her contract. "I was exhausted," she admitted in her 1986 autobiography. "I had had, to put it simply, enough...[When] the show went off the air, I remember feeling so relieved, so free. I was emotionally drained...I had had fun, I had done good work, and I hoped that I had made some inroads in television for other black actors. But enough was enough." Carroll eventually did return to television, first in 1976 as the hostess of the short-lived "Diahann Carroll Show," then as the stylish and scheming businesswoman Dominique Deveraux in the continuing nighttime drama, "Dynasty," and most recently in a recurring guest role on "A Different World."

HERE'S LUCY
NUMBER 9, 1968–69

In the fall of 1968, CBS's "The Lucy Show" (see page 116) segued into "Here's Lucy" with barely a bat of Lucille Ball's famous false eyelashes. In 1967 Lucy had sold her interest in Desilu Studios to Gulf & Western, then the parent company of Paramount Pictures, for $17 million. Desilu was incorporated into the Paramount fold, where Lucy and her husband/executive producer Gary Morton continued filming her series under its new title.

The format was revamped, but Lucille still played Lucy, a wacky, befuddled carrot-top with a predilection for slapsticky trouble. In "Here's Lucy" she was the well-meaning secretary to the president of the Unique Employment Agency ("Unusual jobs for unusual people"); that prexy just happened to be her brother-in-law, played by Lucy's favorite TV nemesis, Gale Gordon. In what was fast becoming television's most common family situation, she was a widowed mother raising her two teenage kids, played by her real-life children, Desi Arnaz, Jr., and Lucie Arnaz. Vivian Vance had bowed out of this one, but made occasional guest appearances.

The employment agency setting provided the chance for Lucy to get involved in all sorts of antics. In one story, Lucy became secretary to an actress (Shelley Winters) who ate too much. To help her control her weight, Lucy consumed everything in sight. In another episode, Lucy substituted for her daughter as a rock and roll singer; in yet another, she accidently grabbed the wrong suitcase at the airport and was mistaken for a spy.

Perhaps the best-remembered (and funniest) segment was the night Elizabeth Taylor and Richard Burton came to call. Lucille Ball had tried for months to get them to appear on the show, but there had been too many schedule conflicts. Then, 10 days before they were set to film the first show of the 1971 season, the Burtons gave them the green light. By that time, all the season's scripts were prepared and the writers had long since departed. With time running out, Lucy succeeded in landing original "I Love Lucy" writers Bob Carroll, Jr., and Madelyn Davis, who were in semi-retirement (thanks to their healthy residuals). They managed to come up with a script in the requisite 10 days, and it was a real gem.

The scenario involved a routine in which Lucy managed to get Elizabeth Taylor's 69-carat diamond ring* stuck on her finger. At a press conference, Lucy hid behind a curtain, while Liz unveiled the ring—on Lucy's arm, which poked through the curtain and masqueraded for Taylor's own arm. It was one of television's most memorable sight gags.

By 1971 Desi, Jr., had left the show to attend college, and although he made some guest appearances, there was less emphasis placed on the children and home life and more on special guest stars. One of the guest celebrities was Jack Benny, who dictated his life story to Lucy, his temporary secretary, while she portrayed all of the women in his reminiscences.

During the 1972–73 season, Lucille Ball broke her leg while skiing at Snowmass, Colorado, and the writers incorporated her accident into the season's scripts. Forced to remain in a cast, she played all 24 episodes either in bed, in a cast, or in a wheelchair. Desi, Jr., pulled himself away from his studies to cover for his injured mother whenever he could.

The 1973–74 season was the show's last one, the writers having devised just about every Lucy situation imaginable for the talented comedienne. Lucy left the weekly airwaves, but never retired. She did a number of specials and returned in a dramatic role in the critically acclaimed 1985 made-for-TV movie, *Stone Pillow*, in which she played a street person. In 1986 she had a last crack at television in a series called "Life with Lucy," co-starring her old friend Gale Gordon. For the first time ever, audiences didn't seem to love Lucy, at least not an old Lucy trying to perform the young antics she had always soared in. The show's 75-year-old star was an embarrassing flop, but it wasn't her fault—the material simply wasn't right for her. ABC pulled the series after less than two months.

That series proved to be her final curtain call. Lucille Ball died in 1989 at the age of 77. She will always be remembered as television's most beloved comedienne.

---

* Elizabeth refused to use a prop ring, costing the show $1,500 a day for extra insurance plus six security guards to ensure the million-dollar diamond's safety.

CREDITS

TOP 10 PEAK: No. 3, 1970–71.
EXECUTIVE PRODUCER: Gary Morton. PRODUCERS: Tommy Thompson, Cleo Smith. DIRECTORS: Jerry Paris, Coby Ruskin, others. WRITERS: Milt Josefsberg, Ray Singer, Bob Carroll, Jr., Madelyn Davis, others. CAST: *Lucille Carter* (Lucille Ball), *Harrison Otis Carter* (Gale Gordon), *Kim Carter* (Lucie Arnaz), *Craig Carter* (Desi Arnaz, Jr.), *Mary Jane Lewis* (Mary Jane Croft). GUEST STARS: Elizabeth Taylor, Richard Burton, Flip Wilson, Lloyd Bridges, Danny Thomas, Sammy Davis Jr., Danny Kaye, Ginger Rogers, Helen Hayes, Vivian Vance, Ann-Margret, Johnny Carson, Joe Namath, David Frost, others.

Keeping things all in the family (from left): Lucie Arnaz, Lucille Ball, and Desi Arnaz, Jr.

MARCUS WELBY, M.D.

NUMBER 8, 1969–70

He was warm, personable, had a terrific bedside manner, and even made housecalls. He was the perfect family doctor (even his name was perfect: Welby—"well be"), a throwback to the days when doctors treated people, not illnesses, and offered more than the "take two aspirin and call me in the morning" prescription. "Marcus Welby, M.D.," as played by Robert Young, might have been titled "Doctor Knows Best," for along with a friendly smile and a cure, there was always a bit of warm, fatherly advice for his patients. (And best of all, he never seemed to present a bill.)

Doctor Welby was a G.P. (general practitioner), a medical term that disappeared around the same time doctors stopped using leeches. Today he would be called an internist, but the meanings are the same. He treated every illness known to humankind, from the usual aches and pains to bad trips on LSD (the rage in the late '60s and early '70s). "We don't treat fingers or skins or skulls or bones or lungs," he declared in the first episode, which aired in September 1969 on ABC. "We treat people." He was assisted in his practice by the youth-appealing character of Dr. Steven Kiley, played by James Brolin, who made his house calls on a motorbike.

To research the part, Robert Young spent time talking to doctor friends and reading non-technical medical books. And ensuring the series' authenticity was a team of medical consultants, members of the Physicians Advisory Committee of the American Medical Association, which had been set up to advise TV and movie medical productions back in 1955. These physicians were in big demand around the beginning of the '70s, when a spate of television doctors ruled the airwaves. In addition to "Marcus Welby, M.D." there were "The Bold Ones" on NBC, which premiered the same week as "Marcus," and "Medical Center" on CBS, which debuted a week later. ("Marcus Welby" was the fastest out of the starting gate, however, and hit number one in its second year.) Series creator/executive producer David Victor, formerly of "Dr. Kildare," was very concerned about authenticity and welcomed the medical advisors. "I realize my responsibility very fully," he said. "To be correct only helps the story."

This was apparent when the show went too far in describing a new treatment for Rh-factor difficulties in babies. "We took too much dramatic license in our interpretation," said Victor. The episode was already in the can when Victor ordered scenes reshot to comply with the AMA's advice. And based on its diligence in striving for accuracy, the AMA presented "Marcus Welby, M.D." with a special achievement award at its annual convention in June 1970.

The emphasis was less on illnesses and more on the people suffering from them. "What we do are stories about people, people who have something wrong," said Victor. "The guy that can fix it happens to be a doctor." Story lines encompassed such scenarios as a lawyer with a terminal disease who refused to cut back on his work load; a mother with an ulcer brought on by rearing her retarded daughter without any help; and a bride-to-be who was diagnosed with leprosy (now called Hansen's Disease). And there were the formerly taboo topics: in a medium that once forbade the use of the

CREDITS

TOP 10 PEAK: No. 1, 1970–71. CREATOR/EXECUTIVE PRODUCER: David Victor. PRODUCER: David O'Connell. DIRECTORS: various. WRITERS: various. CAST: *Dr. Marcus Welby* (Robert Young), *Dr. Steven Kiley* (James Brolin), *Consuelo Lopez* (Elena Verdugo), *Myra Sherwood* (Anne Baxter), *Kathleen Faverty* (Sharon Gless), *Janet Blake Kiley* (Pamela Hensley). GUEST STARS: Susan Strasberg, Lew Ayers, Tom Bosley, Susan Clark, Cloris Leachman, William Schallert, Diana Muldaur, Pernell Roberts, Clint Howard, Carmen Zapata, Beverly Garland, others.

EMMYS

Outstanding Dramatic Series (1969–70), Outstanding Continued Performance by an Actor in a Leading Role in a Dramatic Series—Robert Young (1969–70), Outstanding Performance by an Actor in a Supporting Role in Drama—James Brolin (1969–70).

James Brolin, as Dr. Steven Kiley, with guest star Carrie Snodgrass.

word "pregnancy," we now had people suffering from venereal disease, sexual impotence, drug addiction, and unwanted pregnancies.

One episode, first aired on February 20, 1973, had gay rights activists crying "foul," and rightly so. The story dealt with homosexuality, but Dr. Welby treated it like an illness. This might have been in keeping with the character of the kindly old doctor, who was pushing 70, came from the "old school" of thinking, and was subject to the ignorances and prejudices of his generation. But none of that was mentioned in the script, in which Welby tried to convince the "patient" that his homosexuality was imagined, not real, and that he was on a self-destructive path.

The series served to introduce actor James Brolin, Welby's aforementioned long-haired motorcycle-jock medical partner. He was definitely an asset in drawing the younger fans, and each week Drs. Welby and Kiley paid a housecall on an estimated 40 million viewers. Brolin told a *TV Guide* interviewer why he thought viewers were so attracted to medical shows: "Grownups, like children, like to be frightened," he postulated. "Kids go for monsters and horror creatures. Adults go for cancer and brain tumors. You would guess that people would want to turn away from life's ugliness, but a human is funny. He is the only animal that likes to scare himself." Executive producer David Victor, however, saw it differently: "The medical show is the most basic format. All of us are aware of our mortality," he told *TV Guide*. "We identify immediately with a medical situation...Secondly, a doctor in a medical story can bring a matter to a logical conclusion. He gives antibiotics, or performs surgery, and makes something happen. The viewer understands it clearly and actually learns while he is being entertained."

"Marcus Welby, M.D." kept right on entertaining for nine years, until the series was cancelled in 1976. In May 1984 the good doctor was brought out of retirement for a reunion ABC movie special, "The Return of Marcus Welby, M.D." Elena Verdugo returned as Welby's nurse, Consuelo Lopez, but the telefilm was minus Dr. Kiley, who was "practicing in New York City" (actually, James Brolin was busy on another series—"Hotel"). It was intended as a pilot for a new series which never materialized. In December 1988 "NBC Monday Night at the Movies" presented "Marcus Welby, M. D.—A Holiday Affair," which followed the widowed doctor's meanderings through Europe, where he found a new romance. There he treated a blind ballet star. Quite a distance to go for a house call.

WALT DISNEY'S WONDERFUL WORLD OF COLOR

NUMBER 9, 1969–70

The world is a carousel of color...
—OPENING THEME SONG

Programs from Walt Disney had been a weekly staple of television since the first "Disneyland" series went on the air in 1954 (see page 50). By 1958 the series had switched titles to "Walt Disney Presents," and it continued to offer quality family entertainment on ABC—in black and white. Then in 1961, the man dubbed the "Showman of the Century" brought his series to a new network and gave it a face lift.

Retitled "Walt Disney's Wonderful World of Color," the program was still seen by most viewers in basic black and white, since there were few color sets available for average consumers at a price they could afford. NBC had plans to change all that, with "World of Color" serving as a partial catalyst. NBC's parent company was RCA, which happened to be in the fore when it came to manufacturing color TVs, and which also happened to be the co-sponsor of the new Disney series. Promoting its own product on its own show would benefit both. (Eastman Kodak, a manufacturer of cameras and film, was the other sponsor, equally poised to take advantage of this excellent opportunity to push its product in color.) However, it wasn't until the end of the decade that the price of color sets dropped to a point at which the general public could afford them; by that time, the competition in the color TV market had broadened to include Japanese-manufactured, solid-state, "instant-on" sets, a giant stride in color TV technology.

Along with the proliferation of sets came the long overdue recognition of "The Wonderful World of Color"—the only show with "color" in the title. Not surprisingly, a Disney series entered the top 10 for

the first time since the coonskin-capped Davy Crockett and his pals rode across the screen in 1955.

The series had changed little in the ensuing years; the "Disneyland" format of the four lands (Fantasyland, Frontierland, Adventureland, and Tomorrowland) was gone, but the weekly anthology series still served up fantasy, adventure, and all the rest, including a number of Disney movies, educational episodes, nature films, and so on. All the usual Disney schmaltz was there too, as in "The Hound Who Thought He Was a Raccoon," the heart-tugging story of a lost puppy adopted and raised by a raccoon. How the Disney cinematographers were able to coax such extraordinary performances from their animal actors is anybody's guess.

There were also Disney theatrical films, recycled and broken down episodically to fit the weekly format, generally airing in several parts. These included *Summer Magic* (1963), with Disney's child-actress discovery, Hayley Mills, along with Dorothy McGuire and Burl Ives; *Those Calloways* (1965), starring Brian Keith, Walter Brennan, Linda Evans, and Brandon de Wilde in the story of a backwoods New Englander fighting to preserve a lake as a bird sanctuary; *The Monkey's Uncle*, with Disney perennials Tommy Kirk and Annette Funicello in this sequel to 1964's *The Misadventures of Merlin Jones*.

In addition to recycled Disney movies, there were original productions: "The Legend of Sleepy Hollow," based on the Washington Irving novella and narrated by Bing Crosby, who also sang two songs; "The Legend of El Blanco," an engaging story about a white horse believed to have magical powers; "The Legend of the Boy and the Eagle," a Hopi Indian tale that blended wildlife and human live action with the usual spectacular

CREDITS

EXECUTIVE PRODUCERS: Walt Disney (died in 1966), Ron Miller. PRODUCERS: various. CO-PRODUCER: Roy Disney. DIRECTORS: various. WRITERS: various. HOST: Walt Disney. NARRATOR: Dick Wesson. GUEST STARS: Roger Mobley, Edmond O'Brien, Harvey Korman, Victoria Shaw, Hayley Mills, Burl Ives, Dorothy McGuire, Tommy Kirk, Annette Funicello, Leon Ames, Brian Keith, Vera Miles, Walter Brennan, Linda Evans, others.

EMMYS

Outstanding Program Achievement in the Field of Children's Programming (1962–63).

Disney outdoor cinematography (no doubt selling lots of those color sets); and "The Not So Lonely Lighthouse Keeper," the tale of a sweet old salt who happily tended an isolated lighthouse until he lost his job to automation. The latter had plenty of Disney-esque anthropomorphic critters (most notably a ram, a pelican, and a sea lion) tossed into the story, making it part narrative, part nature study.

In 1972 the title was changed to "The Wonderful World of Disney," and in 1979 the series again underwent a title change, this time to "Disney's Wonderful World." Two years later, in 1981, NBC decided not to renew the series, which had been suffering from the competition of CBS's "60 Minutes." But CBS then signed a deal with Disney Studios for a series simply titled "Walt Disney," which ran until 1983. The show was off the air for two and a half years, until in 1986 ABC picked up the ball; they rechristened this latest version "The Disney Sunday Movie," now introduced by Disney president Michael Eisner. The program consisted mainly of original, made-for-TV movies, and received critical acclaim if not the undying adulation of the TV audience, perhaps because ABC slotted it against the CBS "60 Minutes" powerhouse. In 1988 the show was passed to NBC again, which still insisted on running what was now titled "The Magical World of Disney" on Sunday nights opposite "60 Minutes." That incarnation ran until 1990.

In 1993 the good folks at the Walt Disney Company were concentrating on programming for cable's Disney Channel, and seemed to be taking a breather from one of the longest-running (albeit multi-titled) series in production almost four decades after "it all began with a mouse" back in Disneyland in 1954. And reruns of some of the early "Disney" series from the '50s and '60s were being shown on the Disney Channel in 1993 as well.

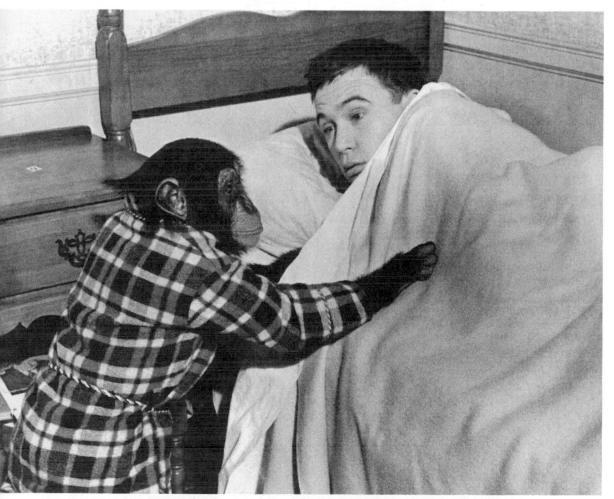

Among the theatrical film releases to appear on "Walt Disney's Wonderful World of Color" was *Monkey's Uncle*, starring Tommy Kirk.

THE DORIS DAY SHOW

NUMBER 10, 1969–70

"I knew Doris Day before she was a virgin."

So claimed humorist Oscar Levant, referring to the purer-than-pure characters Doris portrayed in a string of '60s films in which her dialogue was mostly limited to the words "No!" and "Not until we're married!" Over the course of her career, she starred in more than 40 films and accrued a pile of money, thanks to the careful management of her husband/agent Marty Melcher. Or so she thought.

In 1968, six months before her television series premiered, Melcher died from bacterial endocarditis, leaving Doris a 44-year-old widow with a broken heart and a pile of unpaid taxes. It seems he had been badly advised and had blown her fortune. Yet she was truly grief-stricken over the loss of her beloved husband of 17 years and admitted, "I couldn't even bring myself to face the fact that I was supposed to begin work on my new television series—the last deal Marty had made for me before he passed on."

It was her son, Terry Melcher (by her first marriage and whom Marty had adopted), who urged her to work—for therapy as much as for the badly needed money. Six weeks after Marty's death she filmed the first segment of her first (and only) television series. Her son Terry assumed what would have been his stepfather's role and, at the age of 26, became executive producer of the show. (Melcher, a well-known record producer, was responsible for such number one hits as the Byrds' "Mr. Tambourine Man" [1965] and "Turn, Turn, Turn" [1965], and the Beach Boys' "Kokomo" [1988].)

As series go, this one is remembered for having more format changes than any other show in TV history—a total of

CREDITS

EXECUTIVE PRODUCER: Terry Melcher. PRODUCERS: Jack Elinson, Norman Paul, others. DIRECTORS: Bob Sweeney, Coby Ruskin, Denver Pyle, Marc Daniels, others. WRITERS: Jack Elinson, Norman Paul, Laurence Marks, others. CAST: *Doris Martin* (Doris Day), *Buck Webb* (Denver Pyle), *Billy Martin* (Philip Brown), *Toby Martin* (Todd Starke), *Myrna Gibbons* (Rose Marie), *Michael Nicholson* (McLean Stevenson), *Ron Harvey* (Paul Smith), *Angie Palucci* (Kaye Ballard), *Louis Palucci* (Bernie Kopel), *Cy Bennett* (John Dehner), *Jackie Parker* (Jackie Joseph), *Willard Jarvis* (Billy DeWolfe), *Dr. Peter Lawrence* (Peter Lawford), *Jonathan Rusk* (Patrick O'Neal).

four over the course of its five-year run on CBS. In the first season, Doris played a widowed woman raising two children alone—not exactly an original concept. Her character, Doris Martin (why do stars always want their characters to have their own first names?), decided to leave the Big City and move to the country to raise her kids on her father's ranch, where she became a sort of "Doris of Mayberry." But at the end of the first season (1968–69), Doris Day, who by now had worked through most of her grief, began to take more of an interest in the show. "I sensed that the concept of the show was all wrong," she said. "I was supposed to be living on a farm in the country and I realized that people wanted to see me in the city, wearing pretty clothes and getting involved with sophisticated people. So I made up my mind toward the end of that first year that the setting of the show would have to be shifted to San Francisco. I felt that that's what Marty would have done."

In the second season, Doris Martin decided to work in the Big City—we learned it was San Francisco—and she commuted to her job as executive secretary to Michael Nicholson, editor of the fictional *Today's World* magazine. It was during this season that the ratings began to climb, eventually placing the series in the Nielsen top 10 (with strong Monday night lead-ins from "Gunsmoke," "Here's Lucy," and "Mayberry R.F.D."—in positions two, four, and six, respectively). The show seemed to be perfectly on track, but at the end of season two, there was a third format change.

In the opening episode of season three (1970–71), Doris Martin decided to uproot her family once more and head for full-time life in San Francisco; her father stayed back on the ranch. This move may have been a wise one; although it didn't help in the ratings—she wouldn't make the top 10 again—it may have saved the show from the bucolic-plague axe that felled all the CBS rural sitcoms around that time. Doris, her kids, and the family sheepdog all lived over Pallucci's Italian Restaurant, and a couple of wacky Italian neighbors (played by Kaye Ballard and Bernie Kopell) were added to the show's cast.

Things seemed to be going well when, once again, the format was changed. In the most amazing metamorphosis of all, Doris Martin was now a *single* career woman (à la Mary Tyler Moore), with no kids, no father, no dog, a new boyfriend (Peter Lawford), and a much more exciting job as a reporter for her magazine. Not a word of explanation was given for this remarkable alternate universe in which Doris seemed to have landed. This format remained intact until the series' demise, in 1972.

After that, Doris Day eschewed television. By the 1990s she had left the Hollywood scene and was living on the Northern California coast. A lifelong devotee of animal causes, she volunteered her time for animal welfare. She was president of the nonprofit Doris Day Pet Foundation, which rescued stray and injured dogs and cats, spayed or neutered them, and attempted to find good homes for these creatures.

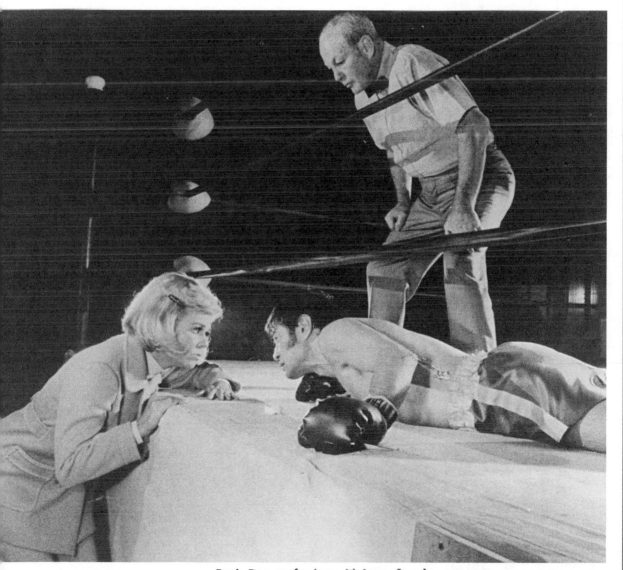

Doris Day conferring with Larry Storch.

THE 1970s

In the 1970s, television came of age—the Age of Lear. "All in the Family" may have caught viewers by surprise, but once this Pandora was let *into* the box, there was no turning back. With the arrival of Norman Lear, TV's Age of Innocence was at an end.

Along with Lear's adult comedies came an era of television permissiveness. A company called Home Box Office—better known today as HBO—began broadcasting via newly laid cable in 1972, delivering uncut theatrical releases—four-letter words, nudity, and all—directly into people's living rooms.

From the early years of television, the networks all subscribed to something called the "Television Code," a mechanism for industry self-regulation instituted by the National Association of Broadcasters, a throwback to the old Hayes Office (which acted as a watchdog for movies during the 1930s and '40s). Then, in 1975, the NAB implemented "family viewing time," which meant that programs airing between the hours of 7:00 and 9:00 P.M. Eastern Standard Time had to be suitable for all-family viewing. Thus the situation comedy—"sitcom"—reached the apex of its popularity in this decade, with nine out the top 10 shows fitting into that category in 1978. Crime, however, still paid big bucks from sponsors, and that genre flourished in the 9 to 11 PM lineup. The legacy of the "family hour" continued in the early '90s; although there were no formal guidelines, most of the networks still tacitly adhered to it.

The 1970s were also marked by the birth of a new genre—the miniseries. In 1977 Alex Haley discovered his "Roots," and several of the series' eight parts became the highest-rated TV broadcasts of all time.

If the '70s decade was the Age of Lear, it was also the Age of Leer. "Jiggle" shows like "Charlie's Angels" and "Three's Company" reached their peak at the end of this decade. And just emerging was the genre that would dominate the '80s—the prime-time soap opera, spearheaded by a show called "Dallas."

THE FLIP WILSON SHOW

NUMBER 2, 1970–71

**Flip Wilson
as Geraldine.**

Bill Cosby had been the first black man to co-star in a TV drama series ("I Spy," 1965–68); Diahann Carroll had been the first black woman to get her own sitcom ("Julia," 1968–71); and in 1970 Flip Wilson became the first black to host a successful variety series.

Four years earlier, Flip had been a hit as a guest on NBC's "The Tonight Show Starring Johnny Carson." In the years that followed, he appeared several more times on Carson's show, often guest-hosting; he also made appearances on "The Ed Sullivan Show," "Rowan and Martin's Laugh-In" (where he helped perpetuate the "Here come da judge" routine), "The Carol Burnett Show," "The Dean Martin Show," and others. In 1969 NBC gave him his first opportunity to solo, in a special "Flip Wilson Show," with guest stars Jonathan Winters, Arte Johnson, Andy Williams, and Jackie DeShannon. It was lauded by viewers and critics alike, and in the fall of 1970, "The Flip Wilson Show" premiered as a regular weekly series on NBC.

It was a tough season for any variety series, let alone one hosted by a black man. The genre was one of the most popular of the day, with 16 comedy-variety shows on the three networks that season. But variety series had also been suffering from a high mortality rate, with shows hosted by Jerry Lewis, Judy Garland, Frank Sinatra, Pat Paulsen, and Phyllis Diller among the many casualties.

Flip was extraordinarily talented, however, and he was blessed with an equally skilled producer in Bob Henry, who had worked with Nat "King" Cole on his variety series in 1957. Why did Flip succeed in a medium where the extraordinarily popular Cole had failed? "What killed us was that black was not beautiful in those days, and Madison Avenue wouldn't go out and sell us," the producer said in *TV Guide*. "We had a low budget, few big guest stars and no sponsors...Flip, on the other hand, can do almost anything, and he comes along at a time when black is *in*. There's a solid black market in this country today, and Madison Avenue even uses Flip to do suntan lotion commercials for *white* people."

CREDITS

EXECUTIVE PRODUCER: Monte Kay. PRODUCER: Bob Henry. DIRECTOR: Tim Kiley. WRITERS: Flip Wilson, Herbert Baker, Hal Goodman, Larry Klein, Bob Weiskopf, Bob Schiller, others. HOST: Flip Wilson. GUEST STARS: David Frost, James Brown, The Muppets, Lucille Ball, Ed Sullivan, The Osmonds, Jack Benny, Pearl Bailey, Buddy Hackett, Ruth Buzzi, Richard Pryor, Tony Randall, Lena Horne, others.

EMMYS

Outstanding Variety Series (1970–71); Outstanding Writing Achievement in Variety or Music, Series—Herbert Baker, Hal Goodman, Larry Klein, Bob Weiskopf, Bob Schiller, Norman Steinberg, Flip Wilson (1970–71).

Flip (born "Clerow") Wilson was one of 24 children, 18 of whom survived. His father split when he was seven, and young Clerow later spent time in foster homes, running away 13 times. A stint in the Air Force, where he entertained his fellow troops, earned him his moniker for his flippant attitude and humor. Nightclub work and occasional appearances on TV shows followed, until the dates on the "Tonight Show" set him on his climb to the top.

Like Jackie Gleason and Jonathan Winters before him, Flip Wilson carried a whole busload of characters he created for himself. He is probably best remembered for the sassy, sexy, drag characterization of Geraldine, who wore fishnet hose on shapely, enviable legs, had a boyfriend named "Killer," and always fell back on the line, "The Devil made me do it." "She" created another expression that became popular in the '70s when she informed her admirers that "What you see is what you get."

His other well-known character was the Reverend Leroy, known as "Rev," a hip-talking minister of the "Church of What's Happening Now." One week he told his "parishioners" that a combination beach party/baptism had been called off. "The oil slick got in the way," he announced. Another time he complained that the Brotherhood and the Sisterhood were having difficulties getting along. "During rehearsals of 'Angels on Parade,'" he said, "there'll be no more harp-snatchin', wing-pinchin' or cloud-peakin'." "Every black person has known a Reverend Leroy," Flip said. "I met mine when I was nine and I was the best testifier in our little church."

Flip Wilson proved he was the best in the race for the Nielsens when he stayed in the top 10 for two seasons in a row, and reached as high as number 12 in the third season of the series. But by the fourth year, "The Waltons" on CBS was giving him a real run for his money, and his show dropped out of the top 20. NBC cancelled the series in 1974. In later years Wilson made guest appearances on specials and variety shows, and he returned to television for a season in "Charlie and Company" (1985).

IRONSIDE

NUMBER 4, 1970–71

Raymond Burr.

For years people had been accosting Raymond Burr, requesting autographs, then politely saying "Thank you, Mr. Mason."

After nine years as Perry Mason, the world's most astute attorney, Burr had become familiar to millions of fans who instantly identified him with that role. Then, six months after that series ended its original run in 1966, Ray Burr returned to television in the role of a new character. Would he be able to pull it off, or was he forever typecast?

"Ironside" premiered as a pilot/telefilm in March 1967 and instantly sealed Burr's future success in a different role. This time, Burr played Robert T. Ironside, the semi-retired San Francisco chief of detectives, who was put in a wheelchair in the pilot (and kept there for the remainder of the series) by the bullet of an attempted assassin. He remained an advisor to the police force and set up house-keeping on the third floor of their headquarters, where he waged war on crime with the aid of three assistants—a white man, a black man, and a police-woman.

"In 'Ironside,'" Burr explained, "I've switched from the defense to the prosecution...There's more latitude for showing a human being because he is not tied down to a courtroom."

Throughout all the years he was working on "Perry Mason," and during part of the time he worked on "Ironside," Burr continued to show concern for his fellow human beings. He made 12 trips to Korea and a dozen more to Vietnam to boost morale in servicemen there. He did this without publicity—for personal reasons, not to help boost ratings. "He always preferred to listen to our gripes rather than gab about Perry Mason," one gunner told *TV Guide*.

Burr always took his work seriously. When he was playing Perry Mason, he spent his down time address-ing law groups, hoping to promote world peace through law. After spending some time in Ironside's wheelchair, he turned his efforts towards the special needs and problems of paraplegics, speaking to groups of disabled veterans on weekends.

Don Mitchell played Mark Sanger, Chief Ironside's "legs," his assistant who also helped him in and out of his redesigned, wheelchair-accommodating "paddy wagon" (complete with Rolls Royce engine). At first, the role smacked of tokenism in an age when it was

becoming *de rigueur* to have a black for appearances' sake. Mark Sanger was a reformed juvenile delinquent, and Mitchell seemed to relish playing the street tough, rejoicing in the chance to be one of the few black men in important roles on '60s television so perhaps "some little black kid could see a black face on television that wasn't swinging from a vine," he said, "and that's impor-tant. I grew up without it."

Mitchell did an outstanding job with the character, and the producers allowed Ironside's assistant to evolve to police officer, law student, and eventually a full-fledged attorney near the conclusion of the series' eight-year run.

The female member of Ironside's support team was Policewoman Eve Whitfield, played by Barbara Anderson. It was her first major television role, and it brought her an Emmy for Best Supporting Actress in the 1967–68 season. She left the series in 1972 and went on to other successful work in television, including a recurring role on "Mission: Impossible" as well as guest spots on other television series such as "Night Gallery" and "Hawaii Five-O."

In 1972 "Ironside" was used to promote another series. In a two-part episode begun on "Ironside," the chief's other assistant, Detective Sergeant Ed Brown, played by Don Galloway, was hit by a sniper's bullet and faced the same pos-sible paralysis and wheelchair confinement as Ironside. The doctors who treated him on the Thursday night episode of "Ironside" didn't resolve the problem until the following Tuesday night, when "The Bold Ones" premiered its fall season with the conclusion of Thursday's "Ironside" cliffhanger. This pioneering "marriage" of two NBC shows would eventually become a fairly common prac-tice in the industry and was still in existence in the 1990s, such as when "Empty Nest" concluded its story on "The Nurses."

"Ironside" didn't make the Nielsen top 10 until the third year of its run, and it flirted with the ratings list in the subsequent years, reaching as high as number 10 in the 1972–73 season. But by 1975 the premise had worn pretty thin and the series was cancelled. Raymond Burr returned to television and became a hit all over again in remakes of "Perry Mason" (see page 96), although it's fair to assume that autograph-seekers were no longer referring to him as "Mr. Mason."

CREDITS

CREATOR. Collier Young. EXECUTIVE PRODUCERS: Frank Price, Cy Chermak. PRODUCERS: various. DIRECTORS: various. WRITERS: various. CAST: *Chief Robert T. Ironside* (Raymond Burr), *Policewoman Eve Whitfield* (Barbara Anderson), *Det. Sgt. Ed Brown* (Don Galloway), *Mark Sanger* (Don Mitchell), *Policewoman Fran Belding* (Elizabeth Baur), *Commissioner Dennis Randall* (Gene Lyons), *Lt. Carl Reese* (Johnny Seven), *Diana Sanger* (Joan Pringle). GUEST STARS: Wally Cox, Kim Darby, Joseph Campanella, Vera Miles, Slim Pickens, Dane Clark, David Hartman, Vic Morrow, E. G. Marshall, Norman Alden, Carolyn Jones.

EMMYS

Outstanding Performance by an Actress in a Supporting Role in a Drama—Barbara Anderson (1967–68).

ABC MOVIE OF THE WEEK

NUMBER 6, 1970–71

A throwback to the days of anthology series like "Philco Playhouse" and "G.E. Theater," "ABC Movie of the Week" presented a new made-for-TV 90-minute movie each Tuesday night from 1969 until 1975. It added one on Wednesday night from 1972 to 1975 (appropriately renaming the show "ABC Tuesday Movie of the Week" and "ABC Wednesday Movie of the Week") and ran another on Saturdays from 1971 to 1974 as the "ABC Movie of the Weekend" and "ABC Suspense Movie."

At first these features were not quite up to theatrical standards, yet they were somehow better than the average television fare. But over time they began to improve in quality, until top writers and stars were competing for a chance to appear in them. Occasionally, ABC would sneak in a pilot for a possible TV series to see what kind of ratings it would generate. Most didn't make it onto the regular schedule, but many were big hits and were then included in the network's series lineup.

Several films earned Emmy awards for the writers or actors involved. The most memorable was probably "Brian's Song," which first aired in December 1971. The story concerned the real-life friendship between Chicago Bears running back Gale Sayers, played by Billy Dee Williams, and Brian Piccolo, played by James Caan in a pre-*Godfather* TV appearance.

Other movies of note included:

- "The Over-the-Hill Gang" (October 1969), with Pat O'Brien, Walter Brennan, Chill Wills, Edgar Buchanan, Jack Elam, Andy Devine, Gypsy Rose Lee, and Kris and Rick Nelson, a spoof of the popular western genre. A sequel was made the following year (November 17, 1970) called "The Over-the-Hill Gang Rides Again," with Fred Astaire now added to the cast.
- "Gidget Grows Up" (December 1969), starring Karen Valentine, Edward Mulhare, Paul Petersen (of "The Donna Reed Show" fame), Paul Lynde, and Bob Cummings;
- "The Journey of Robert F. Kennedy," a February 1970 documentary written by Arthur Schlesinger, Jr., and narrated by John Huston;
- "The House That Would Not Die" (1970), a thriller starring Barbara Stanwyck and Richard Egan;
- "Maybe I'll Come Home in the Spring" (February 1971), starring Jackie Cooper, Eleanor Parker, and Sally Field (then noted for *Gidget* and "The Flying Nun") in her first non-comedy role;
- "Divorce His/Divorce Hers," a 1973 TV-movie starring Richard Burton and Elizabeth Taylor.

Among the pilot films to air on "Movie of the Week" was "Alias Smith and Jones," a lighthearted western starring Peter Duel and Ben Murphy as bank robbers trying to go straight. The series premiered in January 1971 and ran through January 1973. (Peter Duel committed suicide in December 1971; the character was then played by Roger Davis.) Another successful pilot was "The Night Stalker," a tale of a vampire and the newspaper reporter who hunted him down. The subsequent series "Kolchak: The Night Stalker" premiered on ABC in September 1974, starred Darren McGavin, and ran for a year.

CREDITS

TOP 10 PEAK: No. 5, 1971–72.

EMMYS

Outstanding Writing Achievement in Drama, Original Teleplay, Special—Tracy Keenan Wynn and Marvin Schwartz, "Tribes" (1970–71); Outstanding Performance by an Actor in a Supporting Role in Drama—Jack Warden, "Brian's Song" (1971–72); Outstanding Writing Achievement in Drama, Adaptation—William Blinn, "Brian's Song" (1971–72); Outstanding Single Performance by an Actress in a Leading Role—Cloris Leachman, "A Brand New Life" (1972–73); Outstanding Performance by an Actor in a Supporting Role in Drama—Scott Jacoby, "That Certain Summer" (1972–73).

Peter Duel (left) and Ben Murphy, appearing in "Alias Smith & Jones."

HAWAII FIVE-O
NUMBER 7, 1970–71

Jack Lord.

Television cop shows that are filmed on location in the beautiful tropical isles of Hawaii can usually be counted on to bring in high ratings. Who doesn't enjoy watching gently blowing palm fronds and turquoise-blue waves caressing warm sunny beaches? Throw in a few bikini-clad beach bunnies and let the crimes begin. A-*lo*-ha!—instant hit. CBS has always led the pack as the network with the highest number of Hawaii-based series. Before there were the '80s hits of "Magnum, P.I." and "Jake and the Fatman" there was the mother of all island cop shows, "Hawaii Five-O," which holds the record as the longest-running crime series on television to date. ("Dragnet" also ran 12 seasons, but not consecutively.) And, of course, it was the first TV series to be filmed entirely on location in Hawaii.

A fictitious branch of the Hawaii State Police, "Hawaii Five-O" was headed by Detective Steve McGarrett and his crack team of crimebusters. Although Hawaii's lush scenery was arguably the star of the series, Jack Lord, who played McGarrett, insisted that there were no stars other than himself—all other cast members and guests were merely "featured players." Lord had a reputation for difficulty on the set, brought on by his relentless pursuit of perfection and his extensive technical knowledge. Directors complained they couldn't direct him—he directed himself. He also gave suggestions to the people in charge of lighting and cinematography, thus earning himself the nickname of "the Lord." He reportedly rewrote his CBS biography, altering the year of his birth; if true, it would have made him seven years old when he graduated from John Adams High School in Queens, New York. His rewrite bore the mark of his own style of prose, describing himself as "tempered in the crucible of the New York stage...a highly disciplined product of the theater, steeped in the art of acting...and [he] possesses a striking facial bone structure for which the cameras have an affinity." (No mention was made of his modesty or jovial personality.) Fellow "Five-O" cast and crew sidestepped this self-styled, stonefaced over-achiever who dabbled in art, wrote books and poetry, and at one time (following the series' conclusion) was considering running for governor of Hawaii.

James MacArthur was the series co-star, and in truth he *was* the co-star, although Jack Lord would only allow his credit to read "with," not "co-starring." MacArthur

was pleased to have finally made a name for himself apart from his renown as Helen Hayes' son and the second banana in a string of Disney adventure yarns like *The Light in the Forest* (1958), *Third Man on the Mountain* (1959), *Kidnapped* (1960), and *Swiss Family Robinson* (1960). He abandoned his movie career for the "Five-O" series, steeling himself against Jack's lording it over him. His character, Danny Williams, was nicknamed Danno, as in the series' most famous buzzwords, uttered at the end of each episode by McGarrett: "Book 'em, Danno!"

Detective Steve McGarrett's nemesis was another lord—a crime lord named Wo Fat (played by Khigh Dhiegh) who had ties to the Red Chinese. Like Holmes's Moriarity, Wo Fat continued to hound McGarrett for all 12 seasons, beginning with the first episode in 1968, when this Fu Manchu clone had McGarrett trussed up in diving gear, blindfolded, gagged, locked in a soundproof room, and submersed in water. Naturally he escaped (or it would have been television's first one-episode drama series), and Wo Fat became a recurring character who didn't meet his doom until 284 hours later, on April 5, 1980, at the series' conclusion.

In between bouts with Wo, McGarrett helped rid the Islands of murderers, spies, gambling syndicates, drug smugglers, bunco artists, and enough criminals to make most tourists forswear any thoughts of a Hawaiian holiday. The Chamber of Commerce, in fact, had some trepidation for precisely this reason, but soon learned that such fears were unfounded when tourism figures swelled, thanks to the boost from that gorgeous scenery.

"Hawaii Five-O" enjoyed high ratings throughout most of its run, placing as high as number three during the 1972–73 season. The show also produced a hit theme song, popularized by the Ventures in 1969 when the instrumental hit number four on the *Billboard* singles chart.

In 1992 plans were announced by producer Steve Tisch for a feature film version of "Hawaii Five-O," due for release late in 1993. Jack Lord, who retired from acting after "Five-O," was living a fairly reclusive life in Hawaii and was not expected to reprise his role, although a cameo appearance in the film was considered a possibility.

CREDITS

TOP 10 PEAK: No. 3, 1972–73.
CREATOR: Leonard Freeman. EXECUTIVE PRODUCERS: Leonard Freeman, Leonard Katzman. PRODUCERS: Bob Sweeney, Bill Finnegan, Philip Leacock, Richard Newton, others. DIRECTORS: various. WRITERS: various. CAST: *Det. Steve McGarrett* (Jack Lord), *Det. Danny "Danno" Williams* (James MacArthur), *Det. Chin Ho Kelley* (Kam Fong), *Det. Kono Kalakaua* (Zulu), *Governor Philip Grey* (Richard Denning), *Wo Fat* (Khigh Dhiegh). GUEST STARS: Loretta Swit, Nina Foch, Andy Griffith, Barry Atwater, Dana Wynter, Bert Convy, George Chakiris, Richard Masur, Adam Arkin, Elaine Joyce, Dane Clark, Sal Mineo, Nehemiah Persoff, William Windom, John Byner, Marc Singer, Mel Ferrer, Harold Gould, John Colicos, France Nuyen, others.

MEDICAL CENTER

NUMBER 8, 1970–71

America continued its love affair with hypochondria with the advent of "Medical Center," yet another doctor series featuring a health care professional as a surrogate father. In this case, Dr. Paul Lochner was the kindly physician who headed up University Medical Center, a fictitious complex in Los Angeles that bore a strong resemblance to UCLA Medical Center. Breaking the "Dr. Kildare"/"Ben Casey" mold, this series' white-haired senior doctor wasn't saddled with an intern or resident under his tutelage; his younger counterpart was a seasoned doctor who by the show's second year was the director of the student health service.

James Daly played the senior physician. He came to television with a long resume of Broadway appearances and films, including *The Court-Martial of Billy Mitchell* (1955), *I Aim at the Stars* (1960), and *Planet of the Apes* (1968). His work in TV included roles on prestigious series like "Hallmark Hall of Fame" (for which he won an Emmy) and "Omnibus." "Star Trek" fans will recall his guest-starring role in the episode "Requiem for Methuselah." "One reason I took this series," he told *TV Guide* during the second year of filming "Medical Center," "is that when you do a role, to do it right you have to learn about it. I became a Civil War buff when I had to play General Lee, and you can imagine the reading I did when I played Henry Adams and Mark Twain. You start on a book to get some insight into the character you're supposed to become and you end up reading everything you can get your hands on...I'm having lunch with the chief of staff of the UCLA Medical Center. What does the man do? What is he like? What exactly does the job consist of? What's the quality of his life? All that is important."

Chad Everett, on the other hand, knew perfectly well that the purpose of his character was to build a strong

female audience, a role he had little difficulty fulfilling with his dark, dimpled good looks. Still, he longed for the days when he had been a co-star on the 1963 western, "The Dakotas." "I could be a big sex symbol," Everett said, "but with the white coat and stethoscope I can't be as animal as in a pair of tight Levis with a gun slung low on my hip."

Everett, who was born Ray Cramton, was one of several stars "invented" by agent Henry Willson. It was Willson who had named Tab Hunter and Rock Hudson, "great marketing names," said Everett, who admitted, "I feel more like a Chad than a Ray." His agent was also cautious enough to ensure Everett's future, securing him 10 percent ownership of "Medical Center," and at least 75 percent of the dialogue in each episode, and Everett admitted to counting his lines to be certain of this total.

Like "Marcus Welby, M.D." (which premiered the day before "Medical Center," September 23, 1969), this series had a medical advisor on staff to ensure accuracy. This was vital in a series that focused on people whose problems arose from their developing the "disease of the week." Phrases like "aortic stenosis," "massive pulmonary embolism," and "periarteritis nodosa" contributed to the series' medi-babble and kept hypochondriacs scrambling for their medical dictionaries. Creator and executive producer Frank Glicksman insisted in *TV Guide* that his show was different, however, because "what we do is to tell a good basic human story, in which the disease more or less is incidental...only when we have the plot lines all drawn do we sit down and find a disease to go with the story. The human body is very cooperative. It always comes up with something." Stories dealt with all the former television taboos; CBS's

CREDITS

CREATORS: Frank Glicksman, Al C. Ward. EXECUTIVE PRODUCER: Frank Glicksman. PRODUCER: Al C. Ward. DIRECTORS: various. WRITERS: various. CAST: *Dr. Paul Lochner* (James Daly), *Dr. Joe Gannon* (Chad Everett), *Nurse Chambers* (Jayne Meadows), *Dr. Jeanne Bartlett* (Corinne Camacho), others. GUEST STARS: O.J. Simpson, Cicely Tyson, Ed Asner, Percy Rodriguez, Carol Lawrence, Tyne Daly, William Windom, Susan Oliver, James Shigeta, Julie Harris, Steve Forrest, Gale Sondergaard, Monte Markham, Joan Van Ark, Robert Reed, others.

James Daly (left) and Chad Everett.

censors were kept busy with their blue pencils, but once the floodgates were opened, in poured tales of abortion, drug addiction, venereal disease, impotence, artificial insemination, and rape. "You couldn't believe the dos and don'ts—mostly don'ts—that the network threw at us until they saw we were beginning to develop healthy ratings," said James Daly.

Two pilots for potential spinoffs were incorporated into "Medical Center" as episodes of the series. An episode called "The Choice" aired on February 9, 1972, an MGM spinoff pilot for a series to be titled "Family Practitioner." It starred Monte Markham, who would have the title role in the remake of "Perry Mason" in 1973, and Tyne Daly, who happened to be James Daly's daughter. Markham showed up again as a staff surgeon in a 1974 episode of "Medical Center." In March 1976 the producers tried again with a potential spinoff called

"Angel's Nest," the story of a barely surviving San Francisco street clinic. The episode starred Scott Hylands, Philip M. Thomas, and William Redfield, but it was labeled "a dud" by reviewers, and the series never materialized.

The ratings for "Medical Center" were in the top 10 for only one season, then began to slip; by 1976 CBS had decided to retire this longest-running medical series in prime time television. (With 144 episodes completed, the series outlasted "Marcus Welby" by four months.)

James Daly, who had once spent seven years on the road as a spokesman for Camel cigarettes, died of a heart attack two years after the series was cancelled, at the age of 59. Two of his children—Tyne Daly ("Cagney and Lacey") and Tim Daly ("Wings")—went on to successful acting careers.

THE FBI

NUMBER 10, 1970–71

ABC had been programming "The FBI" on Sunday nights against CBS's "Ed Sullivan" and NBC's "Walt Disney" shows since 1965. By 1970, this action series had found an audience of 40 million viewers, mostly male, who were tired of jugglers, acrobats, and dam-building beavers. The five-year-old series was suddenly a top 10 hit—a feat which would not be repeated in the series' nine-year run.

The Quinn Martin Production (which was proudly announced at the start of each episode by an anonymous, booming voice) had the potential for lots of blood-'n'-guts violence, but much of the bloodletting was done off-camera. There were, however, loads of car chases. Odd thing about those car chases. All of the cars—driven by bad guys and agents alike—were Fords. Not so odd, actually, since the series was sponsored by Ford (in direct challenge to NBC's Sunday night hit, "Bonanza," brought to you by Chevrolet). Directors were instructed to include in their camera angles, whenever possible, the company's logo as it appeared emblazoned somewhere on the car.

The series was touted as being based on actual cases from the files of the real Federal Bureau of Investigation in Washington, D.C., and therefore it strove for authenticity. The technical advisor and the show's leading proponent was none other than then-FBI-head J. Edgar Hoover. Although there had been at least one radio show ("The FBI in Peace and War") based on Bureau cases, there had been no television series prior to the debut of "The FBI" in 1965. Yet according to Hoover, he had received more than 600 proposals for potential TV series. Some, he claimed, were from friends; others bore the endorsement of influential people in government and industry. "We knew that a less than

first-rate program could cheapen the FBI's name and have an adverse effect upon its image," he said.

In 1964 he was again approached, this time by Warner Bros. and Quinn Martin. There had been a successful feature produced by the same studio in 1959, *The FBI Story*, starring Jimmy Stewart and Vera Miles, and Hoover had been favorably impressed. He decided to give this new TV proposal his full endorsement, while retaining rights of approval with respect to (1) scripts—to ensure accuracy and present the FBI in a positive image; (2) casting—he insisted, for example, that actors cast in the role of FBI agents look the part; and (3) sponsorship—Hoover wanted to be sure no political candidate or party placed a commercial during the show's hour, or it might appear to be a de facto endorsement.

During preproduction, the show's producer, production manager, story editor, and casting director toured the FBI's facilities in Washington, D.C., to help them get the "feel" of the Bureau and its personnel, meeting with employees and soaking up all the background Hoover felt was necessary to produce the series. A month later, the art director visited the headquarters in order to plan the design of the sets back on a California sound stage. And Efrem Zimbalist, Jr., who starred in the series as Inspector Erskine, took a crash course on the FBI firearms ranges and in the laboratory and identification divisions, and conferred at length with Hoover himself. Commented Hoover in *TV Guide*, "We fully understood that 'The FBI' was to be a dramatic, rather than a documentary, program. However, we wanted each episode to be grounded firmly on fact and to portray the Bureau's jurisdiction, procedures, and techniques as authentically as possible."

CREDITS

CREATOR/EXECUTIVE PRODUCER: Quinn Martin. PRODUCERS: Charles Larson, Philip Saltzman. DIRECTORS: various. WRITERS: various. CAST: *Inspector Lewis Erskine* (Efrem Zimbalist, Jr.), *Arthur Ward* (Philip Abbott), *Barbara Erskine* (Lynn Loring), *Agent Tom Colby* (William Reynolds), *Agent Chris Daniels* (Shelly Novak), *Agent Chet Randolph* (Anthony Eisley). NARRATOR: Marvin Miller. GUEST STARS: Lee Meriwether, Jeffrey Hunter, Dina Merrill, Robert Blake, James Daly, Diane Baker, Martin Sheen, Joan Van Ark, Frank Converse, David Soul, Nancy Wilson, Hal Linden.

Many telecasts closed with a short segment admonishing viewers to be on the lookout for desperadoes from the FBI's "most wanted" list. But despite all the genuflecting mandated by the Bureau's chief honcho in Washington, the show was basically a cops-and-robbers opus, good guys versus bad guys, rounded up by the straight-laced Inspector Erskine.

ABC cancelled the series in 1974, after a healthy nine-year run of 234 episodes. In 1981 a new series titled "Today's FBI" starred Mike Connors (formerly of "Mannix") in an updated version of the original. It even aired in the same Sunday-night time period. But after a year spent rounding up those guilty of murder, kidnapping, extortion, and the usual crimes, the series was cancelled. A 1991 entry titled "FBI: The Untold Stories" showed more promise; at least it had been renewed for a second season in 1992. This one was an anthology series, without a leading continuing character, with the exception of Pernell Roberts ("M*A*S*H," "Trapper John, M.D.") as host/narrator. The series had actors dramatizing actual cases from the FBI files, but in keeping with the trend in reality shows, there were also interviews with real-life law-enforcement officials involved in the investigations.

William Reynolds (left) and Efrem Zimbalist, Jr.

ALL IN THE FAMILY

NUMBER 1, 1971–72

Clockwise from top left: Rob Reiner, Sally Struthers, Carroll O'Connor, and Jean Stapleton.

CREDITS

CREATOR: Norman Lear. BASED ON: "Till Death Do Us Part" (BBC Television). EXECUTIVE PRODUCERS: Norman Lear, Bud Yorkin, Mort Lachman, Hal Kanter. PRODUCERS: various DIRECTORS: John Rich, others. WRITERS: Norman Lear, others. CAST: *Archie Bunker* (arroll O'Connor), *Edith Bunker* (Jean Stapleton), *Gloria Bunker Stivic* (Sally Struthers), *Mike Stivic* (Rob Reiner), *Lionel Jefferson* (Mike Evans), *George Jefferson* (Sherman Hemsley), *Louise Jefferson* (Isabel Sanford), *Henry Jefferson* (Mel Stewart), *Irene Lorenzo* (Betty Garrett), *Frank Lorenzo* (Vincent Gardenia), *Stephanie Mills* (Danielle Brisebois), others.

EMMYS

Outstanding Comedy Series (1970–71, 1971–72, 1972–73, 1977–78); Outstanding Continued Performance by an Actress in a Leading Role in a Comedy Series—Jean Stapleton (1970–71, 1971–72, 1977–78); Outstanding Continued Performance by an Actor in a Leading Role in a Comedy Series—Carroll O'Connor (1971–72, 1976–77, 1977–78, 1978–79); Outstanding Directorial Achievement in Comedy, Series—John Rich (1971–72), Paul Bogart (1977–78); Outstanding Writing Achievement in Comedy Series—Burt Styler (1971–72), Michael Ross, Bernie West, Lee Kalcheim (1972–73), Bob Weiskopf, Bob Schiller, Barry Harman, Harve Broston (1977–78); Best Supporting Actor in Comedy—Rob Reiner (1973–74, 1977–78); Outstanding Supporting Actress in a Comedy Series—Sally Struthers (1978–79).

...Gee, our old La Salle ran great...
—OPENING THEME SONG

He called his wife "dingbat" and his son-in-law "meathead." He was an equal-opportunity bigot, a no-holds-barred conservative, a last-gasp holdout of an endangered species. Twenty years earlier audiences would have nodded in sympathetic agreement with his beliefs, laughing with him rather than at him. But the *vox populi* had been heard, and Archie Bunker's voice was crying alone in the Queens, New York, wilderness.

The series could have been called "Father Knows Nothing." Archie (played by Carroll O'Connor) was an antihero, and creator Norman Lear and his writing staff went out of their way to portray him as a metaphor for the Old Ways; the times, they had a-changed, and while Archie-the-throwback pined for Glenn Miller, Herbert Hoover, and his old sedan, the world was rushing past him in a kaleidoscopic revolution of youth.

To be sure, Archie did have his adherents in those who still clung to the same values as he, and regardless of their political and social belief structures, viewers couldn't help feeling just a tinge of sympathy for Archie despite his malaprops, his abusiveness, his racism. Lear saw to that by making him more human than any television character before him. This man actually went to the toilet (which he pronounced "terlet"), something that viewers couldn't have imagined of, say, Robert Young or Jane Wyatt. (Archie, in fact, made TV safe for the sound of the first toilet flush ever heard on television.) He also belched and did countless other things that normal, breathing humans do. His language mocked anyone who was not a card-carrying White Anglo-Saxon Protestant. For the first time, televison audiences heard racial epithets in abundance; street terms like "spade," "spic," "hebe," "dumb Polack," "coon," and "bleedin' heart liberal pinko atheist" came pouring out of Archie's blue-collared throat.

Sympathy for Archie was aroused not by his grousing and raving but by his love of home and hearth. Archie truly loved his ding-batty wife Edith (Jean Stapleton), and he adored his "Little Girl," his married daughter Gloria (Sally Struthers). His son-in-law, Mike "Meathead" Stivic (Rob Reiner), was the perfect antithesis to Archie as he continually tried to keep his father-in-law from becoming too right-wing.

The series had a mid-season (January 12, 1971) premiere. It opened with a disclaimer: "The program you are about to see is 'All in the Family.' It seeks to throw a humorous spotlight on our frailties, prejudices, and concerns. By making them a source of laughter we hope to show—in a mature fashion—just how absurd they are." Yet in spite of this "warning," those who tuned in to the first episode of this landmark television event were still caught off balance by it. People asked themselves, Did I really see what I thought I just saw on *television*? The CBS switchboard braced itself for an electronic meltdown; it never materialized, although some buzzing ensued around the water cooler the next morning among those who did see the first episode.

The series didn't really get under way until the following fall, when it began the first full season of its eight-year run. The program started slowly in the Nielsens, exactly as producer Norman Lear had expected. "We were a brand-new show, practically unheralded," Lear said in *TV Guide*, "and you can imagine how our uncensored dialogue sounded to people who'd just been snickering over 'Hee Haw.' If we baffled them, they had a choice of powerhouse movies to switch to on NBC and ABC. But I knew we were going to be talked about. When word-of-mouth began to spread, we'd begin to climb."

Much word of mouth came in the form of rave reviews. " 'All in the Family' is not just the best-written, best-directed, and best-acted show on television," gushed *TV Guide*, "it is the best show on television." By the end of the first full season, "All in the Family" had zoomed to number one, a position it held for five firm years, changing the future of television sitcoms forever.

Lear believed that Archie's popularity stemmed from his basic lovability. In one segment, Gloria became pregnant, then miscarried. The father-daughter scene at the end was so touching, many in the studio audience were in tears. In another episode, Archie confessed to crying while watching the movie *Love Story*. It was this flip side of Archie that kept audiences watching.

"All in the Family" gave rise to three spinoffs: "Maude," in 1972 (see page 194); "The Jeffersons," in 1975 (see page 212); and "Gloria," starring Sally Struthers, which ran from 1982 to 1983. Archie Bunker's household evolved over the years: Gloria and Mike moved out in 1975 and had a child; the Bunkers took in a Puerto Rican boarder for a while; Archie changed jobs and bought a bar, Archie's Place. In 1979 Jean Stapleton left the series (as had Sally Struthers and Rob Reiner), the name was changed to "Archie Bunker's Place," and her character was written out by doing the heretofore unthinkable in sitcom—she was killed off with a stroke. The series continued under its new name and format until 1983. In 1991, reruns of "All in the Family" were seen in prime time for the first time in 12 years when the episodes were paired with a new Norman Lear series, "Sunday Dinner"; surprisingly, the reruns of "All in the Family" brought in higher ratings than the new series, which was cancelled after only one month.

"All in the Family" made stars of its mostly unknown cast. Carroll O'Connor went on to star in "In the Heat of the Night" (NBC from 1988 to 1991; later on CBS); Jean Stapleton appeared frequently in dramatic television and on stage; Rob Reiner followed in his father Carl's footsteps and became a director, helming several hit feature films; and Sally Struthers starred in "Gloria," guest-starred on television, and led charity appeals for the Christian Children's Fund.

SANFORD AND SON

NUMBER 6, 1971–72

Redd Foxx (seated) and Demond Wilson.

The perfect companion piece to Norman Lear and Bud Yorkin's "All in the Family," "Sanford and Son" bowed in 1972 and was described by some as an "All in the Black Family." Some saw the curmudgeonly character of Fred Sanford, played by Redd Foxx, as a black mirror image of Archie Bunker, and indeed he did have his moments of racial bigotry, as in this dialogue:

POLICEMAN (INVESTIGATING A BURGLARY)
Were they colored?

SANFORD
Yeah. (Pause.) White.

POLICEMAN
Do you want to go to the hospital?

SANFORD
I can't waste three days.

POLICEMAN
It only takes a few minutes.

SANFORD
It only takes *you* a few minutes. It takes us three days in the waiting room.

But the basic running story line focused more on the generation gap/father-son conflict: Fred Sanford, the elderly junkman portrayed by the not-so-elderly Foxx (he was 49 at the beginning of the series), versus Lamont, the "Son" in the title, representing the younger generation, a man trying to leave the rat's nest of his childhood, marry, and strike out on his own. At such moments, his old man would usually grab his chest, roll his eyes skyward, and speak to his dear, departed wife: "Elizabeth! I'm comin' to join you, Elizabeth!" And Lamont would of course agree to stay a bit longer.

Lear and Yorkin had optioned the rights to a British series about a Cockney junk dealer and his offspring called "Steptoe and Son," which had been running on the BBC for 10 years. They shot a couple of pilots for their American version, with no luck selling it. Then Lear, Yorkin, and their partner Aaron Ruben (who produced "The Andy Griffith Show" and created its spinoff, "Gomer Pyle, U.S.M.C."—see pages 100, 128) had the idea of making the junk dealer and his son black, and the project began to gel. In New York they talked to actor Cleavon Little, who had just won a Tony for his role in the Broadway hit *Purlie*. Little was unavailable, but he did have an idea. "You know who you ought to get for the old man?" he said. "Redd Foxx!" The

idea hadn't occurred to any of the producers. Foxx was known for his "black and blue" humor, with his mostly four-letter vocabulary imparting a definite emphasis on the blue.

Redd Foxx was born John Elroy *Sanford*—hence the show's title. When starting out in the business, he landed a job as a dishwasher in a Harlem restaurant. There he worked under the name of Chicago Red (for his red hair) alongside another man known as Detroit Red (also for his red hair). Detroit's real name was Malcolm Little. Later he changed it to Malcolm X, while John Sanford/Chicago Red would become Redd Foxx ("Eight letters so it fits nice on a marquee"). "Chicago Red was the funniest dishwasher on earth," Malcolm X would one day write. Foxx perfected his routines in Harlem bars and came up the hard way, at one time spending 95 days in jail for stealing food (the charges were never proved and later dropped). He teamed up with Slappy White and played the "chitlin circuit" of black clubs. Later he struck out on his own.

During the 1974–75 TV season, with "Sanford and Son" in its customary number two position in the Nielsens, Foxx had a run-in with NBC concerning, among other things, the lack of a window in his dressing room. The studio had given him a cubbyhole of a room, with no sunlight. When the network stood its ground, Foxx withheld his services. The first two episodes of the season had him "out of town." The ratings plummeted, and the unfavorable publicity about his lack of a window created enormous public sympathy, putting pressure on NBC until they finally yielded to Foxx's demands. He got his window, a shiny new golf cart for getting around NBC's long halls, a salary increase, and a percentage in the series.

By 1977 both Foxx and his co-star Demond Wilson had had enough of the series, and it wasn't renewed. A 1977 spinoff, "The Sanford Arms," starring most of the supporting cast who were still around, proved a flop and was cancelled after only a month. In 1980, another spinoff, "Sanford," did star Redd Foxx, but not Demond Wilson. It ran from March 1980 till July 1981.

In 1991 Redd Foxx was starring in a new CBS sitcom, "The Royal Family." On the afternoon of October 11, he suddenly clutched his heart and keeled over on the set. His co-star Della Reese at first thought he was just clowning around, doing the old "Elizabeth, I'm coming to join you" routine. But this time, the heart attack was real, and he never regained consciousness. Redd Foxx died that evening at the age of 68.

CREDITS

TOP 10 PEAK: No. 2, 1972–73.
CREATED BY: Norman Lear, Bud Yorkin, Aaron Ruben. EXECUTIVE PRODUCER: Bud Yorkin. PRODUCERS: Aaron Ruben, Saul Turteltaub, Bernie Orenstein. DIRECTORS: various. WRITERS: various. CAST: *Fred Sanford* (Redd Foxx), *Lamont Sanford* (Demond Wilson), *Grady Wilson* (Whitman Mayo), *Julio Fuentes* (Gregory Sierra), *Melvin* (Slappy White), *Bubba* (Don Bexley), *Rollo Larson* (Nathaniel Taylor), others. GUEST STARS: Sheldon Leonard, Greg Morris, Barbara Rhoades, Merv Griffin, Steve Lawrence, Eydie Gorme, others.

MANNIX

NUMBER 7, 1971–72

Mike Connors, with Gail Fisher.

In the late 1960s, television was under heavy criticism for its gratuitous violence. Producers were taking considerable flack from consumer watchdog groups urging viewers to boycott sponsors of overly violent programming. Yet in 1967, Bruce Geller, who a year earlier had brought "Mission: Impossible" to the airwaves, introduced a new and heavily violent cop show to television.

Critics immediately decried it, although the violence was nothing like that in, say, "The Untouchables." "Mannix" wasn't wall-to-wall bullets; there were shootings, certainly, but more and more the drama seemed to turn to chases—by foot, car, and helicopter. Eventually, critics threw up their hands and let the bullets fall where they may. By the fourth year, the series had built enough of a following to place it firmly in the Nielsen top 10, especially when CBS switched the series from Saturday night at 10:00 to Wednesday night at 10:00 (opposite ratings lightweights "Man and the City" on ABC and "Night Gallery" on NBC).

"Mannix" (his first name was "Joe," but "Mannix" had a better ring to it for a series title) began with a gimmicky format in its first year. Mike Connors, who had played the lead in the series "Tightrope" from 1959 to 1960, starred as the iconoclastic detective working for a buttoned-down, high-tech agency known as Intertect. In the pre-Computer-Age year of 1967, this agency prided itself on taking a mega-bite out of crime. Mannix, however, did not approve of the electronic miracle of computerization, and preferred to do his crimebusting the old-fashioned way—with fisticuffs and guns. The producers apparently agreed. By the 1968–69 season, Intertect and its mainframe were erased from memory; Mannix was on his own.

Well, almost. He now had a gal Friday named Peggy Fair. Fair was black, an irony the producers hadn't noticed when they created the character. "Gail was chosen from 18 girls, black and white, who tried out for the role," said executive producer Bruce Geller in *TV Guide*. "The part was by no means locked in for a Negro. Some people flatten out on the screen, and others jump right out at you. Once we saw her, we decided on her immediately." Gail Fisher was delighted to win

the role and did not feel it was a token part. "I think I'm on there doing a very good job—talented and sexy," the actress said when first cast.

Mannix continued to solve crimes while a team of writers busily cranked out the fast-paced stories long on brawling and body count and short on extended dialogue. One of the writers, Harold Medford, told *TV Guide* that although he was pleased to be working on the series, he had his doubts about the literary value of a show like "Mannix." "The whole concept is hogwash," he said emphatically. "A real private eye is a sleazy character who works divorce cases. Mythic or not, I rather like Joe Mannix, who is non-Mike Hammer. Physical, sure, but also a kind of gentleman, and not in the bogus sense of a Philo Vance or an Ellery Queen."

The actor playing Mannix was an Armenian-American named Kreker Ohanian, who had the good sense to realize an acting career would benefit from a name change. As Mike Connors, he entered television in the early 1950s, appearing in anthology dramas such as "Schlitz Playhouse" and in minor parts in westerns like "Maverick" and "Cheyenne." His big break was receiving the starring role as the undercover agent in "Tightrope." "Mannix" followed seven years later, and during its eight-year run, Connors was nominated for an Emmy four times. In 1981 he returned to television in the role of Ben Slater in "Today's FBI."

By 1993 he was mostly retired, although he did make occasional guest appearances in TV movies.

The noteworthy music for "Mannix" was composed by Lalo Schifrin, who also penned the memorable theme music for "Mission: Impossible," which was on the *Billboard* Hot 100 chart for 14 weeks in 1968.

"Mannix" continued to attract a faithful audience until 1975, when it slipped from the top 25 in the Nielsens, and CBS cancelled the series. The final ignominy came when an area of Paramount Studios that housed the outdoor sets for the series—a charming little village near the main gate of the studio that had been dubbed "Mannix Square"—was torn down the following year to make way for a new parking lot.

CREDITS

EXECUTIVE PRODUCER: Bruce Geller. PRODUCERS: Ivan Goff, Ben Roberts. DIRECTORS: various. WRITERS: Harold Medford, Chester Krumholz, Stephen Kandel, Cliff Gould, Ed Adamson, John Meredyth Lucas, others. CAST: *Joe Mannix* (Mike Connors), *Lou Wickersham* (Joseph Campanella), *Peggy Fair* (Gail Fisher), *Lt. Adam Tobias* (Robert Reed). GUEST STARS: Kim Hunter, Barbara Anderson, John Colicos, Celeste Yarnall, Darren McGavin, Dane Clark, Guy Stockwell, Eddie Egan, Rip Torn, Larry Storch, others.

ADAM 12

NUMBER 8 (TIE), 1971–72

One Adam 12, One Adam 12: See the man...
—Squad-Car Radio Dispatcher

It could have been titled "Son of Dragnet." Created in partnership by Jack Webb, originator of the top 10 series "Dragnet" (see page 34), "Adam 12" incorporated all the elements that Webb was famous for; it was a realistic cop show with believable people pursuing the daily lives of Los Angeles cops. The title referred to the identification number of the black-and-white squad car driven by the two officers as they cruised the L.A. streets, keeping them free of crime. (In the mythical world of television, anything's possible.)

Executive producer Webb even went to the trouble of hiring a real L.A.P.D. employee to record the voiceovers heard by the officers in their squad car. When audiences heard communications between the dispatcher and the officers on the road, the voice was supplied by Shaaron Claridge, who recorded her authentic sound once a week before working her regular job at the local police station. "We knew that no professional performer could begin to duplicate [Shaaron's] delivery, so we chose her," said Webb. "Aside from adding what we believe to be a great, authentic sound to 'Adam 12,' Shaaron makes certain that the calls are spoken in the proper radio-communications jargon."

When it came to casting, Webb knew he wanted a young rookie paired with an older, wiser partner in this police drama/"buddy" series. A 26-year-old actor named Kent McCord was already under contract to Universal, the studio producing the series, plus he had played a rookie cop in a "Dragnet 1968" segment. He was quickly cast as Officer Jim Reed. But finding the proper man for the older lead was a bit more difficult. He had to be physically right, tough enough to play a strong veteran officer but nonetheless attractive and sympathetic. Someone suggested Martin Milner, who was then age 40, still youthful and wholesome, yet had a quality of maturity.

Milner had been playing the "boy next door" type since he was 14, when he was cast as one of the sons in the movie *Life with Father* (1947). He met Jack Webb a few years later, when he was 18, while working with him in the 1951 film *The Halls of Montezuma*. Later Webb used him in the "Dragnet" radio series, where the youngster even played the parts of older characters, since he couldn't be seen. Eventually Milner landed the co-lead in the popular TV series "Route 66," spending four years behind the wheel of a shiny Corvette sports car until the show went off the air in 1964. In 1968 he found himself back behind the wheel in "Adam 12," only this time it was a police squad car. One of the reasons Jack Webb knew he would be right for the part was Milner's experience driving for the cameras. Milner himself told Webb, "I'm probably the best in the business at hitting camera marks while driving. With all my experience, I can pull right into a close-up."

In a show like "Adam 12," which depended on teamwork, it was vital that the two lead actors not only get along, but like each other. No matter how good actors are, the camera is not always fooled. Luckily, they hit it off almost from the start. According to a *TV Guide* interview with the show's executive producer, Herman Saunders, Martin Milner was extremely likeable. "Marty's the cement that holds it all together," he said during production of the 1973 season. "He's got an even temperament; he thinks...surprisingly, he's got a wry comedic

CREDITS

CREATORS: Jack Webb, Robert A. Cinader. EXECUTIVE PRODUCER: Jack Webb. PRODUCERS: Robert A. Cinader, James Doherty, Herman S. Saunders, others. DIRECTORS: Jack Webb, Joseph Pevney, Chris Nyby, others. WRITERS: various. CAST: *Officer Pete Malloy* (Martin Milner), *Officer Jim Reed* (Kent McCord), *Sgt. MacDonald* (William Boyett), *Officer Ed Wells* (Gary Crosby), *Dispatcher (voiceover)* (Shaaron Claridge), others. GUEST STARS: Benny Rubin, Edd Byrnes, Mickey Dolenz, Jayne Meadows, June Lockhart, others.

Martin Milner (left) and Kent McCord.

sense and will break everyone up with a Don Rickles-type insult line just when tedium and frayed nerves are setting in. Most important, he and Kent *really* like each other. That's a necessary ingredient in all successful shows. It comes through on the screen and it makes the audience like *them*. I think that's the main reason we get as high as number two in the Nielsen ratings and why this crazy little show might go on as long as 'Dragnet' did."

Kent McCord agreed. "There isn't a day I don't learn something from Marty and [that] he doesn't make me laugh." The two got on so well they even took vacations together with their families. Milner and McCord got together later to do a film — not an "Adam 12" reunion, but the first original made-for-TV movie for the Nashville cable channel, called "Nashville Beat," which aired in 1989.

"Adam 12" had a healthy run of seven years, airing its last episode of summer reruns in August 1975 (and last original episode in May of that year). Ironically, the final new episode contained a pilot for a potential spinoff series, one of two proposed to the networks during the course of "Adam 12." The first one aired in March 1974 in an episode guest-starring Frank Sinatra, Jr., and Sharon Gless, who were to be stars of the new series, "Fraud." When that didn't sell, Webb tried again in May 1975, introducing in the last episode of the series a new potential spinoff called "Dana Hall." Again no sale.

In the 1989–90 season an updated, syndicated version of the series called "The New Adam 12" distributed 52 episodes. The show was recast with new officers but the same format, although a new, spiffier black-and-white car was used.

FUNNY FACE

NUMBER 8 (TIE), 1971–72

Sandy Duncan.

In the late 1960s, CBS programming executive Fred Silverman caught 22-year-old Sandy Duncan in an obscure off-Broadway play called *Your Own Thing*. He was struck by her Audrey Hepburn poise, her Katharine Hepburn mannerisms, her Carol Burnett comic timing, and her Debbie Reynolds energy. "This is a kid who will merchandise her own vitality," he is reported to have said. "We must sign this remarkable girl!" Soon afterwards, CBS finalized a contract with Duncan and developed a series to showcase her talents. The show was called "Funny Face," a loose adaptation of the 1927 Broadway musical with Fred and Adele Astaire and the 1957 film of the same name, starring Fred Astaire and Audrey Hepburn.

"Funny Face" turned out to be CBS's fastest rising new series of the 1971–72 season. Critics deplored the show's format and scripts, but sang hosannas to its blonde, freckle-faced, bouncy star, Sandy Duncan, who seemed to have invented the word "perky." Audiences also warmed to the Texas-born actress with a flair for comedy who easily rose above the mediocre material. Her show, positioned as it was between "All in the Family," "The New Dick Van Dyke Show," and "The Mary Tyler Moore Show," was soon beginning to outdraw these other sitcoms. Sandy Duncan was not just in the Nielsen top 10; this was the hottest show of the season, and she had a good shot at making number one. Then tragedy struck.

It began with a series of headaches Sandy Duncan suffered. At first doctors thought they were due to stress from the pressures of big-time TV and her unraveling marriage. They were wrong. Duncan was being told by doctors to "be patient." She was, but the pain continued. Doctors took x-rays, which disclosed a walnut-sized tumor pressing on the optic nerve, but couldn't determine its severity. Cortisone was prescribed for what doctors hoped was just an inflammation of the optic nerve. The headaches persisted, Sandy's left eye began bulging, and her weight dropped to 86 pounds. Finally, the doctors agreed they had no choice but to operate. The young actress sailed through it, but lost the vision in her left eye. Her first

thoughts were about her burgeoning career: Was she going to be horribly disfigured, causing audiences to shun her? When she learned that there had been no muscle damage, she brightened. "I am grateful that the eye movement has not been affected," she said with amazing bravery, optimism, and cheer for someone who had undergone such serious brain surgery.

It was too late, however, to save her show; the promise of number one glory never had a chance to materialize. With Sandy Duncan taking time to recuperate, the series was cancelled in December 1971 after only 13 episodes.

A year later, CBS was willing to try again. But someone forgot to look in the rule book under "Success, Not Tampering With." They took the character Sandy had been playing and completely changed her. The newly revamped "Sandy Duncan Show" was a dismal failure and was yanked from the CBS lineup within three months.

Sandy Duncan managed to survive it all. She went on to a successful Broadway career, where she appeared in a number of musical revivals of such shows as "The Music Man," "The Sound of Music," "The Boy Friend," and "Peter Pan."

In 1987 Sandy was again given her own series, this time through a fluke. In 1986 Valerie Harper had begun starring in an NBC series called "Valerie." A year later she left the show over contract disputes. NBC decided to continue the series, now retitled "Valerie's Family," although there was no one named Valerie in sight (creating a lot of puzzlement among new viewers). Sandy Duncan was cast in the lead, playing Valerie's divorced sister-in-law. When the contract dispute deadlocked, Valerie's character was killed off, leaving Sandy (playing Sandy Hogan) in charge of what was now called "The Hogan Family."

In September 1990 the series changed networks, from NBC to CBS, and for the next year, Sandy Duncan finally got to star on that network for the first time since the 1972 fiasco. "The Hogan Family" was cancelled in the fall of 1991. In 1993 Sandy Duncan continued to work in television, and was frequently seen in commercials for "Wheat Thins" and other Nabisco products.

CREDITS

CREATOR/PRODUCER: Carl Kleinschmitt. EXECUTIVE PRODUCER: Jerry Davis. DIRECTORS: Hal Cooper, others. WRITERS: Bob Rodgers, others. CAST: *Sandy Stockton* (Sandy Duncan), *Alice McRaven* (Valorie Armstrong), *Kate Harwell* (Kathleen Freeman), *Pat Harwell* (Henry Beckman), *Maggie Prescott* (Nina Talbot). GUESTS: Tom Bosley, Danny Spelling, others.

THE MARY TYLER MOORE SHOW

NUMBER 10, 1971–72

Mary Tyler Moore, flanked by future spinoff stars Cloris Leachman (left) and Valerie Harper.

Who can turn the world on with her smile?
—OPENING THEME SONG

The perfect series for the newly liberated woman of the '70s, "The Mary Tyler Moore Show" celebrated single womanhood, working womanhood, and living-on-your-own womanhood. During the first few years of the show, the opening song did not begin with the above words; instead, each week's credits showed a nervous thirtysomething woman driving from Somewhere to the Big City (we learned, surprisingly, it was not New York or L.A., but Minneapolis), alone, starry-eyed, while the lyrics asked the musical question, "How will you make it on your own?" and ended with the doubt resolved—"You're gonna make it after all."

But was there really any doubt Mary would make it? CBS certainly had its questions before the series went on the air in 1970. The network brass wanted to make her a divorcée, not a sexually liberated single woman; a compromise was struck, and as the series opened, Mary Richards (Mary Tyler Moore's character) was just recovering from a failed "relationship." Then there was the concern about the casting of her support group. None of these people were *comedians*, the execs complained; this show was supposed to be a *comedy*. How could it ever work?

That proved to be the least of CBS's worries. Casting, it turned out, had produced the strongest ensemble of players in television, a roster that today reads like a TV who's who. Before the series filmed its last episode (before a live studio audience) in 1977, two of the series' actors, Valerie Harper and Cloris Leachman, would be spun off into shows of their own— "Rhoda" and "Phyllis," respectively.

Nearly all of the others would go on to star or co-star in their own series. Ed Asner, as Mary's gruff boss Lou Grant, eventually got his own spinoff show. Ironically, "Lou Grant" (1977–82) became a drama, not a comedy, when that fictional producer of Channel 12's "Six O'Clock News" (Mary was the associate producer) returned to his roots as a hard-boiled newspaperman. Gavin MacLeod, who played Mary's fellow newswriter Murray Slaughter, eventually got his own show, and *ship*—he went on to become Captain Stubing of "The Love Boat" (1977–86—see page 268). Ted Knight, the narcissistic news anchor Ted Baxter on "MTM," starred in two versions of "The Ted Knight Show" and the Nielsen hit "Too Close for Comfort" (see page 272). Betty White, Channel 12's sex-crazed "Happy Homemaker," became one of the leads in "The Golden Girls" (see page 304). She and Georgia Engle (who played Ted Baxter's wife, Georgette) also appeared together in "The Betty White Show" (1977–78). John Amos, who played Gordie Howard, the weatherman (and one of the few blacks in the series), left early to co-star in "Good Times" (see page 216).

With so much talent around, it might seem that a kind of ego gridlock would develop. Not so with this series. "As long as it's a good show," said Moore in *Newsweek*, "I don't care who the star is. Sure, I get itchy if I'm not featured after four or five segments, but when one character at a time is featured, the audience gets to know him and care for him." Surrounding herself with so much talent, Moore realized, could only reflect well on her. "My forte is not being funny," she said, "but reacting in a funny way to those around me."

The producers were well aware of this. According to a *TV Guide* interview with co-creator/writer/producer Allan Burns, "We firmly resist Mary doing zany things just to get laughs. She never tramps out wine grapes with her bare feet or gets mixed up in the chorus line at the Copacabana. We start with an everyday premise recognizable to everyone and assume reasonable intelligence on the part of our characters. Mary is a possible person—a woman reacting in a basically womanly way. We surround her with possible people." Valerie Harper, who played the sharp-tongued Rhoda Morgenstern, agreed. "What cracks me up is that she is never 'the star.' She insists on being a fellow player."

Still, there was enough spotlight left for Mary herself; she was the one who ultimately became America's sweetheart. Ms. Richards may have lost her virginity, but she still had that childlike innocence audiences longed for. Yet on occasion Mary was indeed a woman with "spunk." (On her first interview with Mr. Grant, he informed her, "You've got spunk. I hate spunk.") She even spent some time in jail in one episode, when she refused to reveal her information sources. Picture the perfectly coiffed, bright eyed, optimistic Mary as she entered the slammer, tossed in a cell with some "ladies of the evening." She not only kept her cool but also shrugged off a fellow inmate's comment, "What are you in for? Impersonating a Barbie Doll?"

For seven wonderful years, America (and the many countries around the world where the series was shown) welcomed this group of characters into their homes on Saturday nights. Then in 1977 Ms. Moore herself decided it was time to sign off from the WJM newsroom. The series concluded its 136th and final episode with the new station owners having decided to fire everyone but the photogenic Ted Baxter. One by one the characters all left the newsroom to go their separate ways; finally it was Mary's turn. Singing "It's a Long Way to Tipperary," she switched off the light and exited the newsroom for the last time. The set went coal-black, a touching moment in which we, the audience, suddenly realized we'd seen the final moment.

While so many of her fellow players went on to hit series, Mary Tyler Moore had not scored one of her own by the early 1990s. She appeared in a number of highly acclaimed feature films, including *Ordinary People* (1980), but three "comeback" series—"Mary" (1978), "The Mary Tyler Moore Hour" (1979), and "Mary" (1985–86)—were disastrous flops. Her original hit series, however, continued to appear in syndicated reruns, notably on Nickelodeon's "Nick at Nite," which occasionally screened "Mary-thons" of the best episodes. And CBS filmed a 90-minute retrospective that aired in 1991 and was later rerun; in it, the original cast reunited to reminisce about the series' seven-year run.

CREDITS

TOP 10 PEAK: No. 7, 1972–73. CREATORS/EXECUTIVE PRODUCERS: James L. Brooks, Allen Burns. PRODUCERS: David Davis, Ed. Weinberger, Stan Daniels, others. DIRECTORS: Jay Sandrich, Hal Cooper, others. WRITERS: James Brooks, Allen Burns, Bob Ellison, Treva Silverman, Ed. Weinberger, Stan Daniels, others. CAST: *Mary Richards* (Mary Tyler Moore), *Lou Grant* (Ed Asner), *Ted Baxter* (Ted Knight), *Rhoda Morganstern* (Valerie Harper), *Murray Slaughter* (Gavin MacLeod), *Phyllis Lindstrom* (Cloris Leachman), *Gordon Howard* (John Amos), *Georgette Franklin Baxter* (Georgia Engel), *Sue Ann Nivens* (Betty White), *Bess Lindstrom* (Lisa Gerritsen), *Ida Morganstern* (Nancy Walker), *Martin Morganstern* (Harold Gould), *Marie Slaughter* (Joyce Bulifant), others. GUEST STARS: Robert Hogan, Beth Howland, Penny Marshall, Henry Winkler, John Ritter, Louise Lasser, Craig T. Nelson, others.

EMMYS

Outstanding Performance by an Actor in a Supporting Role in Comedy—Ed Asner (1970–71, 1971–72, 1974–75); Outstanding Performance by an Actress in a Supporting Role in Comedy—Valerie Harper (1970–71, 1971–72, 1972–73); Outstanding Directorial Achievement in Comedy Series— Jay Sandrich (1970–71, 1972–73); Outstanding Writing Achievement in Comedy Series—James L. Brooks and Allan Burns (1970), Treva Silverman (1973–74), Ed. Weinberger and Stan Daniels (1974–75), David Lloyd (1975–76), Allan Burns, James L. Brooks, Ed. Weinberger, Stan Daniels, David Lloyd, Bob Ellison (1976–77); Outstanding Continued Performance by an Actress in a Leading Role in a Comedy Series—Mary Tyler Moore (1972–73, 1973–74, 1975–76); Outstanding Performance by an Actor in a Supporting Role in Comedy—Ted Knight (1972–73, 1975–76); Actress of the Year, Series—Mary Tyler Moore (1973–74); Best Supporting Actress in a Comedy—Cloris Leachman (1973–74); Writer of the Year, Series—Treva Silverman (1973–74); Outstanding Comedy Series (1974–75, 1975–76. 1976–77); Outstanding Continuing Performance by a Supporting Actress in a Comedy Series—Betty White (1974–75, 1975–76); Outstanding Single Performance by a Supporting Actress in a Comedy Series—Cloris Leachman (1974–75).

MAUDE

NUMBER 4, 1972–73

God'll getcha for that. —MAUDE

Tall, basso-profundo-voiced, ballsy, self-assured, "right-on Maude" was anything but a typical television house-wife. Audiences were first introduced to Edith Bunker's cousin Maude in an episode of Norman Lear's "All in the Family" (see page 182), when she came to nurse the ailing Edith and stayed to curse the railing Archie. She was the antithesis of everything he stood for, a female Archie Bunker from an alternate universe. He was ultra-conservative; she, ultra-liberal. He was blue-collar and lower-middle-class; she liked her collar white and her class upper-middle. But if truth be told, both were cut from the same cloth, a tightly wound bolt labeled "stubborn," and neither would have made a good candidate for assertiveness training, since they would surely have known more than the instructor.

Bea Arthur played the "enter-prisin' socializin', everything but compromisin' " liberal from hell, whose favorite curse for anybody who crossed her was, "God'll getcha for that!" Norman Lear knew he wanted Bea for the role of Archie Bunker's nemesis, having been struck by a performance she gave 17 years earlier in an off-Broadway revue. "So many people in this business are carbons of other people," Lear said in *TV Guide*, "but Bea is an absolute original...When we decided to bring in a relative who hated Archie, we knew we needed some-body very strong to stand up against Carroll O'Connor, and we never thought of anybody but Bea." Lear tailored the character of Maude to fit Arthur, sending writer/producer Rod Parker to her house to get her input and feelings on a variety of sub-jects. So it wasn't coincidental that

Bea Arthur and Maude Findlay had some things in common. "In some ways, I *am* Maude," Arthur told *TV Guide*. "Like her, I'm a liberal—sometimes a pretty mis-guided liberal, I suppose. It just eats me up when I see somebody being dishonest; I'm the sort of person who goes through life taking landlords to small-claims court."

After her two visits to the Bunker household, Lear decided it was time for Maude Findlay to have a show of her own, so she was spun off into a new series called—what else?—"Maude." (Eventually, "Maude" would spin off a grandchild of "All in the Family"—"Good Times," starring Maude's maid, Florida [Esther Rolle]; see page 216.) We learned that Maude was on her fourth husband, her daughter Carol was on her first divorce, and her conservative neighbor Dr. Arthur Harmon (played by Conrad Bain) and his wife Vivian (Rue McClanahan) were on their first—and hopefully last—Maude, since although there was a good-neighbor policy, she wasn't easy to take.

The viewers knew from the start that there was something different about this show. The subject matter was, to say the least, controversial. In the first season the series fea-tured a two-part episode called "Maude's Dilemma," aired on November 14 and 21, 1972. The theme was abortion, although this was not a new area for TV. In 1964 a woman on the soap "Another World" had an "illegal operation," but Maude was the first prime-time lead character to have this opera-tion that was not yet protected by *Roe v. Wade* (that decision was still a year away). The public reaction was milder for these episodes' first air-ings than it was when they were rerun the following August. The

CREDITS

CREATOR: Norman Lear, Rod Parker. EXECUTIVE PRODUCERS: Rod Parker, Hal Cooper. PRODUCERS: Charlie Hauk, others. DIRECTORS: various. WRITERS: various. CAST: *Maude Findlay* (Beatrice Arthur), *Walter Findlay* (Bill Macy), *Carol* (Adrienne Barbeau), *Phillip* (Brian Morrison, Kraig Metzinger), *Dr. Arthur Harmon* (Conrad Bain), *Vivian Harmon* (Rue McClanahan), *Florida Evans* (Esther Rolle), *Henry Evans* (John Amos), *Mrs. Naugatuck* (Hermione Baddeley), *Chris* (Fred Grandy), *Bert Beasley* (J. Pat O'Malley), *Victoria Butterfield* (Marlene Warfield).

EMMYS

Outstanding Lead Actress in a Comedy Series—Beatrice Arthur (1976–77).

Bea Arthur and Bill Macy.

ratings went through the Nielsen ceiling the first time the shows aired, propelling the series to number one for the two weeks and guaranteeing a position of number four for the season. At the same time, the November broadcasts brought nearly 7,000 letters of complaint. By the time the shows were scheduled for rebroadcast the following August, the United States Catholic Conference had organized a protest. Of the 217 CBS affiliates, 39 chose not to broadcast the episodes, and seven sponsors pulled their ads. This time, *17,000* letters of protest poured in. Yet viewership actually increased for the rebroadcasts, giving the show a 41-percent share. If the program was so offensive, why did almost 65 million people tune in?

Other controversial episodes dealt with Maude's husband Walter and his problems with alcoholism, and Maude's discovering she had manic-depressive illness and needed to take the drug lithium. The latter was a simplistic two-part story developed by Norman Lear, based on a member of his own family who had had favorable results with lithium. The script was thoroughly researched by doctors at Harvard, who alerted the CBS affiliates to brace themselves for phone calls; 35 of the affiliates ran public service spots telling viewers where to get help.

But "Maude" was not just social commentary or a public service; at heart, it was a comedy. Maude's acid tongue generally delivered the wittiest lines, as in her retort in one episode when asked the source of a black eye: "I was jumping rope—without a bra." When Maude became the first prime-time character to decide to undergo a face-lift, she voiced her need by saying she felt "Like an old hen with a turkey's neck and crow's feet—I could be the centerfold for the Audubon Society." Bea Arthur was planning to undergo a face-lift along with her character, but her Beverly Hills surgeon refused, telling her to come back in a few years since there was nothing wrong with her. So Maude was transformed with tape and makeup, while Arthur held off for several years.

By 1978 many in the cast were ready to move on. Adrienne Barbeau, who played daughter Carol, had been given less and less to do each year, and the others felt the same. Bea Arthur admitted, "One can only live with the same character for so long, and it is time for both of us to take a rest...We've accomplished what we set out to accomplish...for the first time we presented somebody who wasn't just a bubblehead out to get laughs. For the first time, issues were dealt with, thoughts were exchanged. I think we made television a little more adult, I really do."

Right on, Maude.

BRIDGET LOVES BERNIE

NUMBER 5 (TIE), 1972–73

Meredith Baxter and David Birney.

196

One of the longest-running comedies ever to play on Broadway, *Abie's Irish Rose* had 2,327 performances following its debut in 1922. The immensely popular play became the basis for a 1927 novel, a 1942 radio program, and even a 1946 movie. All that was left, of course, was a television series. And CBS saw to that in 1972, when it premiered "Bridget Loves Bernie."

Loosely based on *Abie's Irish Rose*, "B Loves B" was the story of an ethnic intermarriage. Bernie Steinberg, a nice Jewish boy, was a New York cab driver/writer-wannabe whose parents owned a delicatessen. The object of his affection was Bridget Theresa Mary Colleen Fitzgerald, a *shiksa*, which is Yiddish for beautiful, blonde, blue-eyed, Irish Catholic girl complete with adoring, rich, country-club-member parents. And thereby hangs a tale, which is to say, this was a one-joke series. Naturally, Bridget and Bernie got married, and ran into all sorts of in-law troubles; along the way, the show reworked every imaginable ethnic cliché. Bridget had a brother who was a priest; Bernie had an Uncle Moe. Bridget had a delicate gentile stomach; Bernie's mom stuffed it with matzo ball soup. When her daughter-in-law got sick, she asked her family wistfully, "Why couldn't that wonderful girl throwing up in the bathroom be Jewish?" And just in case viewers tired of the war of the Irish roses, Bernie had a best friend to keep things kosher, a man who was— you guessed it—black.

CBS chose the perfect time slot for the series when it premiered in the fall of 1972: this hunk of corned beef was sandwiched right between megahits "All in the Family" and "The Mary Tyler Moore Show." "If they ran mouse races after 'All in the Family,'" said actor David Birney, "people would leave their sets on. That means the pressure of a large audience is on us, behooving us to be good."

The series was the highest-rated new show of the season, with about 30 million viewers, but within a few months, writers were having difficulty coming up with fresh humor. References to problems that plague most interfaith marriages, like birth control, abortion, and the religious upbringing of the kids, were avoided or deleted from scripts. By December, the emphasis had been placed squarely on the two main characters.

Meredith Baxter was 25 at the time she landed the role of the Irish colleen Bridget (Baxter herself was Protestant). The daughter of television actress Whitney Blake, she had appeared in TV and films; her most recent role before being cast in "B Loves B" was playing the big sister of the boy who owned the rats in the 1972 horror movie *Ben*.

David Birney, on the other hand, *was* Irish (also Protestant), but he had been living in New York long enough to soak up some Jewish culture. "Lenny Bruce summed it up," Birney said in *TV Guide*. "'If you live in New York, you're Jewish.' I haven't tried to act Jewish for the show, but I've used the city to give me the feel of urban toughness that I need for Bernie Steinberg."

Despite the show's popularity, Birney was tough on Bernie. "A guy who drives a fleet cab doesn't use it as his own personal car; and people who own a successful delicatessen don't live behind it; that's right out of the '40s."

Bridget kept right on loving Bernie until they were cancelled at the end of the first season. CBS cited the ratings as the official reason, but they had been consistently high, and many felt the decision was due to pressure from Jewish organizations protesting the glorification of mixed marriages. The series became a "one-season wonder," and was gone by the fall of 1973.

Bridget and Bernie, however, kept right on loving. The program was noted for being the first TV series to show a couple cuddling in bed; the pair liked it so much they started an off-camera romance that eventually led to Meredith and David tying the knot. The marriage lasted a bit longer than the series, but it too was cancelled, late in the 1980s, and Meredith Baxter-Birney (who by then had gone on to fame as Michael J. Fox's mom on "Family Ties"—see page 294) dropped the hyphenated surname. It seemed Meredith no longer loved Bernie, er, Birney.

CREDITS

BASED ON: *Abie's Irish Rose*, by Anne Nichols. EXECUTIVE PRODUCER: Douglas S. Cramer. PRODUCERS: Arthur Alsberg, Don Nelson. DIRECTORS: various. WRITERS: various. CAST: *Bridget Fitzgerald Steinberg* (Meredith Baxter), *Bernie Steinberg* (David Birney), *Walter Fitzgerald* (David Doyle), *Amy Fitzgerald* (Audra Lindley), *Father Mike Fitzgerald* (Robert Sampson), *Sam Steinberg* (Harold J. Stone), *Sophie Steinberg* (Bibi Osterwald), *Uncle Moe Plotnick* (Ned Glass), *Otis Foster* (William Elliott), *Charles the Butler* (Ivor Barry).

THE NBC SUNDAY MYSTERY MOVIE

NUMBER 5 (TIE), 1972–73

At the time "The NBC Sunday Mystery Movie" became a Nielsen top 10 entry, it consisted of four rotating series under one umbrella title. They were "Columbo," "McCloud," "McMillan and Wife," and "Hec Ramsey."

"Columbo" was the oldest of these series. In the mid-1960s, NBC commissioned a package of movies for television to be made under the working title of "Project 120" (for 120 minutes). The title was later changed to "World Premiere Movies," and one of these films, produced by Universal in 1966, was called "Prescription Murder," adapted from a stage play by Richard Levenson and William Link. Their leading character was based in part on the police detective in Dostoyevski's *Crime and Punishment*. In "Prescription Murder," a wealthy psychiatrist who murdered his wife was dogged by a bumbling, rumpled detective named Columbo. Based on this drama, NBC, in partnership with Universal, produced a second pilot film, "Ransom for a Dead Man," which starred Peter Falk as Lt. Columbo. His first name was never given. (His wife, however, did have a first name—Kate. Although we never met her during the "Columbo" series, she later received her own spinoff, "Kate Loves a Mystery." The series ran from February to December, 1979.) It was this second pilot that sold the show to NBC, and it was the most successful hit of the "Sunday Mystery Movie" quartet.

On the stage, the role of Columbo had been played by Thomas Mitchell, and the producers had tried to get Bing Crosby, a close approximation of Mitchell, for the TV lead. But Der Bingle wasn't interested—he was 67 years old and happier playing golf—and the role eventually went to Peter Falk. In "Columbo," it was never a question of "whodunit"—we learned that in the first five minutes of the show. The murderer was always an intelligent, well-dressed, well-spoken, generally wealthy person. Columbo stuck to him like a flea on a dog. In his trademark disheveled trenchcoat, he always had the

suspect believing he/she was getting away with the crime, until right before the final commercial, when Columbo would make a false exit from the room, return, shake his head, and ask "just one last question" or inform his quarry that "There's just one little thing bothers me." He was apologetic yet smooth, and the villain, usually speechless, often saluted the brilliant but klutzy detective.

Columbo proved to be a born-again favorite. In 1989 Universal dusted off its "Columbo" property and pressed Peter Falk back into service, rumpled raincoat and all (his raincoat, in fact, looked like it hadn't been to the cleaners in the 12 years since he had left the air.) ABC aired these new episodes several times throughout the year as part of an "ABC Mystery Movie" series, which was still being produced during the 1992–93 season.

Dennis Weaver as McCloud.

"McCloud" first appeared in 1970 as part of an NBC parent show called "Four-in-One," yet another rotating series, with "Night Gallery," "The Psychiatrist," and "San Francisco International" making up the remainder of that set. In 1971 McCloud, already a familiar face to viewers, moved from "Four-in-One" to "The NBC Mystery Movie" (seen on Wednesdays from 1971 to 1972, and on Sundays thereafter).

Dennis Weaver played the lawman from Taos, New Mexico, who came to New York to study the big-city ways of police work. In the Big Apple he was under the tutelage of Police Chief Peter B. Clifford, played by J.D. Cannon. He also had a continuing romantic interest in Chris Coughlin, played by Diana Muldaur.

Familiar to audiences as the gimpy deputy Chester in "Gunsmoke," Weaver had a hard time shaking that image, even after two interim series—"Kentucky Jones" in 1964–65, and "Gentle Ben" from 1967 to 1969. But eventually audiences embraced Deputy Marshal Sam McCloud, although there was no revival of the character after the series left the air in 1977. Weaver subsequently served for two years as president of the Screen Actors Guild, and in the 1990s could be seen in Southern California doing commercials for Great Western Bank (in western garb, of course), a role he took over from John Wayne after the Duke passed away.

"McMillan and Wife" was created especially for "NBC Mystery Movie." Rock Hudson played the Police Commissioner of San Francisco, a hands-on kind of guy who did all his own crime fighting—rather strange for a commissioner. And if he was elsewhere involved, his wife, played by Susan St. James, could usually be found pursuing the bad guys. It was Hudson's first venture into television, something the veteran of 58 movies had managed to eschew until then. But when asked about the differences between moviemaking and television filming, he found only one: "For television you work faster. What would take 10 weeks for a feature takes 10 days for the tube. Otherwise no difference," he said. (He would later star in two other series, "The Devlin Connection" and "Dynasty"—see page 276.)

In 1977 Susan St. James quit the series, so her character was killed (off-screen) in a car accident, and the series was retitled simply "McMillan." Nancy Walker, who played the McMillans' housekeeper (and simultaneously played Rhoda Morganstern's mom on "Rhoda" —see page 214) also left that year, and Martha Raye played the maid for the 1977 season, the series' final one.

The fourth series under the "NBC Sunday Mystery Movie" umbrella was "Hec Ramsey," added in the 1972–73 season. It starred Richard Boone, better known to television audiences as Paladin from "Have Gun, Will Travel" (see page 74). Boone played Hec Ramsey, a "modern," reformed gunfighter in turn-of-the-century Oklahoma, making this the only western in the group of four shows. Ramsey was the town's deputy sheriff who was hooked on the new-fangled crime-busting ways, like fingerprints (and even hoofprints), magnifying glasses, ballistics, and other scientific methodology. The series was a critical favorite; *Life* magazine called Boone "probably the best actor that ever happened to television," adding, "The older he gets, the more he seems a sort of Walter Cronkite with spurs." Unfortunately, viewers found this the least engrossing of the four shows, and "Hec Ramsey" was cancelled in 1974, after a two-year run.

Other series came and went as part of the "Sunday Mystery Movie." They included "Amy Prentiss," starring Jessica Walter (1974–75); "McCoy," starring Tony Curtis (1975–76); "Quincy, M.E.," starring Jack Klugman (1976–77); and "Lanigan's Rabbi," starring Art Carney (1977). Only "Quincy" became a popular success, running on its own after the cancellation of "The NBC Sunday Mystery Movie" in 1977. ("Quincy" ran until the fall, 1983.)

"COLUMBO" CREDITS

CREATORS: Richard Levinson, William Link. EXECUTIVE PRODUCERS: Richard Levinson, William Link, Dean Hargrove, Roland Kibbee. PRODUCERS: Douglas Benton, Robert F. O'Neill, Edward K. Dodds, others. DIRECTORS: Steven Spielberg, Nicholas Colasanto, others. WRITERS: Steven Bochco, others. CAST: *Lt. Columbo* (Peter Falk). GUEST STARS: John Cassavetes, Blythe Danner, Myrna Loy, Vera Miles, Jack Cassidy, Rosemary Forsyth, Martin Milner, Barbara Colby, Robert Conrad, Janet Leigh, William Shatner, others.

"McCLOUD" CREDITS

EXECUTIVE PRODUCERS: Leslie Stevens, Glen A. Larson. PRODUCERS: Dean Hargrove, Michael Gleason, others. DIRECTORS: Douglas Heyes, Russ Mayberry, Hy Averback, others. WRITERS: Douglas Heyes, Peter Allan Fields, others. CAST: *Deputy Sam McCloud* (Dennis Weaver), *Police Chief Peter B. Clifford* (J. D. Cannon), *Sgt. Joe Broadhurst* (Terry Carter), *Chris Coughlin* (Diana Muldaur). GUEST STARS: Sebastian Cabot, Peter Haskell, Susan Strasberg, Robert Hogan, Elisha Cook, Sharon Gless, Rick Nelson, Jackie Cooper, Stefanie Powers, Linda Evans, Shelley Winters, Barbi Benton, Leigh Taylor-Young, others.

"McMILLAN AND WIFE" CREDITS

EXECUTIVE PRODUCER: Leonard B. Stern. PRODUCERS: Paul Mason, others. DIRECTORS: John Astin, Robert Michael Lewis, others. WRITERS: Oliver Hailey, Steve Fisher, others. CAST: *Commissioner Stewart McMillan* (Rock Hudson), *Sally McMillan* (Susan St. James), *Sgt. Charles Enright* (John Schuck), *Mildred* (Nancy Walker), *Agatha* (Martha Raye), others. GUEST STARS: Cameron Mitchell, Sharon Acker, Eileen Brennan, John Astin, Roddy McDowall, Alex Karras, others.

"HEC RAMSEY" CREDITS

EXECUTIVE PRODUCER: Jack Webb. PRODUCER: Douglas Benton. DIRECTORS: various. WRITERS: various. CAST: *Hec Ramsey* (Richard Boone), *Sheriff Oliver B. Stamp* (Rick Lenz), *Amos B. Coogan* (Harry Morgan), *Norma Muldoon* (Sharon Acker). GUEST STARS: Stella Stevens, Steven Forrest, Stuart Whitman, Ruth Roman, Rita Moreno.

SERIES EMMYS

Outstanding Continued Performance by an Actor in a Dramatic Series—Peter Falk, "Columbo" (1971–72, 1974–75, 1975–76); Outstanding Writing Achievement in Drama Series—Richard L. Levinson and William Link, "Columbo" (1971–72); Outstanding Limited Series— "Columbo" (1973–74); Outstanding Lead Actress in a Limited Series—Jessica Walter, "Amy Prentiss" (1974–75); Outstanding Single Performance by a Supporting Actor—Patrick McGoohan, "Columbo" (1974–75).

THE WALTONS

NUMBER 2, 1973–74

Good night, John-Boy.   —CLOSING LINE

In a medium that liked its families upscale and wacky and its dramas action- or violence-packed, "The Waltons" was an unlikely candidate for a hit series. As CBS's Thursday night challenge to NBC's "The Flip Wilson Show" and ABC's "The Mod Squad," both popular series, this warm, wholesome, family-oriented show was given virtually no chance of survival beyond its first season. And its initial ratings seemed to prove the prognosticators right: "The Waltons" held down 59th place in the Nielsens for several weeks after its bow in the fall of 1972. But CBS stood firmly behind its program, even running ads in newspapers pleading, "Save the Waltons." That strategy, plus a certain amount of patience while the series found its audiences, paid off handsomely. By April of 1973 the series had reached 14th place; by the following season, it hit its highest position in the Nielsens—number two, right behind "All in the Family."

All in the Walton family, however, were nothing like the Bunkers. The members of the Walton clan were wholesome, poor-but-happy children of the 1930s' Great Depression era. The father was a quiet tower of strength, the mother a hard-working earth mom struggling to raise her family of Virginia hillfolk with extra helpings of love, while extolling the virtues of honesty, thrift, and kindness towards others. They were not hillbillies, these sturdy, realistic denizens of Walton's Mountain. The extended family included the brood of seven children plus Grandma and Grandpa Walton, all played by a huge cast who began as virtual unknowns.

The series had its antecedents in a novel by Earl Hamner, Jr., called *Spencer's Mountain*. The 1960 novel was semi-autobiographical, centering on the author's childhood in the Blue Ridge Mountains of Virginia. When

Warner Bros. bought the property for a film, the location was switched to the Grand Tetons of Wyoming, and Henry Fonda was cast in the role of the father. Hamner was less than thrilled with the big-screen treatment, which took severe liberties with his story. "Whatever it was the story had," he said, "they ruined."

But 10 years later Hamner decided to try again, this time with a made-for-TV movie called "The Homecoming—A Christmas Story." Henry Fonda was approached for the lead, but turned it down since the emphasis was on the son, John-Boy, rather than the father. The December 1971 TV movie starred Patricia Neal as the mother and Andrew Duggan as the father, while Edgar Bergen and Ellen Corby played the grandparents. Richard Thomas played the eldest son, John-Boy. The film was never intended as a pilot for a series, but that's exactly what it became. CBS was so pleased by the ratings of the virtually unpromoted movie that the network immediately began to plan a full series,

---

CREDITS

CREATOR: Earl Hamner, Jr. EXECUTIVE PRODUCERS: Lee Rich, Earl Hamner, Jr. PRODUCERS: various. DIRECTORS: various. WRITERS: Earl Hamner, Jr., others. CAST: *John Walton, Sr.* (Ralph Waite), *Olivia Walton* (Miss Michael Learned), *Grandpa Walton* (Will Geer), *Grandma Walton* (Ellen Corby), *John-Boy Walton* (Richard Thomas, Robert Wightman), *Mary Ellen Walton* (Judy Norton-Taylor), *Jim-Bob Walton* (David W. Harper), *Elizabeth Walton* (Kami Cotler), *Jason Walton* (Jon Walmsley), *Erin Walton* (Mary Elizabeth McDonough), *Ben Walton* (Eric Scott), *Ike Godsey* (Joe Conley), *Rev. Fordwick* (John Ritter), others. NARRATOR: Earl Hamner, Jr.

EMMYS

Outstanding Drama Series (1972–73); Outstanding Continued Performance by an Actor in a Leading Role, Drama—Richard Thomas (1972–73); Outstanding Continued Performance by an Actress in a Leading Role, Drama—Michael Learned (1972–73, 1973–74, 1975–76); Outstanding Performance by an Actress in a Supporting Role in Drama—Ellen Corby (1972–73, 1974–75, 1975–76); Outstanding Writing Achievement in Drama, Series—John McGreevey (1972–73), Joanna Lee (1973–74); Outstanding Continued Performance by a Supporting Actor in a Drama Series—Will Geer (1974–75); Outstanding Lead Actress for a Single Appearance in a Drama—Beulah Bondi (1976–77).

which went on the air the following season. This time, Earl Hamner, Jr., had creative control; he wrote many of the scripts and consulted on the others (he also narrated, lending a touch of authenticity).

The new cast retained only Richard Thomas as John-Boy, a few of the other child actors, and Ellen Corby as the grandmother. All the other roles were recast, and most of the actors remained in their parts for the series' entire nine-year run. During that time, viewers watched John-Boy grow up, finish high school and college, and move to New York, eventually to be written out of the show when Richard Thomas wanted to depart the

The Waltons.

series in 1977. The character was even recast for some guest appearances between 1979 and 1981 (with Robert Wightman playing the part), but fans mostly associated Richard Thomas with that role, one he was still remembered for years later.

Over the course of the series, the Walton children grew up, some married and moved away, and the lives of the actors unfolded along with those of their Walton counterparts. In 1992 Judi Norton (Mary Ellen) wrote and directed plays in Los Angeles; Eric Scott (Ben) was vice-president of marketing with a courier company; Jon Walmsley (Jason) was married to Lisa Harrison, who played John-Boy's girlfriend Toni Hazelton on the show; David Harper (Jim-Bob) was a scenic painter in L.A.; Kami Cotler (Elizabeth) was a graduate student at U.C.

Berkeley, studying to teach English; Mary Elizabeth McDonough (Erin) did occasional spots as a correspondent for "Entertainment Tonight"; and Richard Thomas, John-Boy himself, had a successful acting career, as well as a large brood of his own that included triplets. Ralph Waite, who played the father, made an unsuccessful bid for Congress in 1990 and continued acting, appearing as Kevin Costner's father in the 1992 film *The Bodyguard*. Michael Learned (mother Olivia Walton) continued her acting career, and at one point toured in a production of the play *Love Letters*. Ellen Corby suffered a stroke in 1976, and trooper that she was, she managed to make a few appearances in the series over the following years. Will Geer (Grandpa Walton) died in 1978, an event that was incorporated into a touching episode in which Grandpa had passed away.

The series discontinued its regular broadcasts in 1981, but there were several Walton "specials" over the next couple of years (televised, ironically, on NBC rather than CBS). "A Wedding on Walton's Mountain" aired in February 1982; "Mother's Day on Walton's Mountain" ran in May of that year, followed by "A Day for Thanks on Walton's Mountain" in November. Although there were no big "reunion" movies after those shows, most of the original clan were on hand in October 1992, when 6,000 fans converged on Schuyler, Virginia, the original home of Earl Hamner, Jr., for the opening of the Walton's Mountain Museum. Unfortunately, a Warner Bros. fire in late 1991 had destroyed most of the original "Waltons" sets, so the museum was able to display only replicas of the famous Walton kitchen, living room, and John-Boy's bedroom, along with some surviving memorabilia like John-Boy's eyeglasses.

During the 1992 presidential campaign, President Bush and the Republicans invoked the Waltons as exemplifying the "family values" he was trying to emphasize, saying he wanted to "make American families a lot more like the Waltons and a lot less like the Simpsons."* ("The Simpsons," an animated series, quickly filmed a retaliation episode detailing just how similar the two families really were, since both "spend a lot of time praying for the end of the Depression.")

In 1993 "The Waltons" was being aired on the Family Channel, where it was, no doubt, that cable channel's flagship program.

*It was indeed a strange campaign in which several television series were invoked—see "Murphy Brown" (page 332).

M·A·S·H

When CBS decided to turn Robert Altman's 1970 irreverent hit movie *M*A*S*H* into a weekly television series, the doomsayers predicted failure, especially when the series was to be categorized as a sitcom. It was long on *sit*, they were certain, but how could a series set amidst a war have any *com*?

At first it seemed they may have been right; the series was anything but a hit from the start, and CBS didn't help things any by continually shifting the 30-minute program to new times and dates during the first season. Then there were scathing reviews, like the one in *TV Guide* complaining that while the patients were sedated, "the rest of us, unfortunately, do not have the advantage of being anesthetized...The trouble is their locale and premise...Beware of a program whose title has asterisks between the letters." Well, *TV Guide* ate a humble TV dinner a few years later after the series, despite its shaky beginnings, became an unqualified hit.

"M*A*S*H," in fact, was a smash. The series focused on the antics of doctors, mostly civilians like "Hawkeye" Pierce (Alan Alda), who were trying to maintain their sanity in a military situation, only three miles from the front of the Korean War, which really wasn't a declared war at all, but rather a "police action." The setting was an unabashed parallel to the conflict then taking place in another Asian country at the time—Vietnam; "M*A*S*H" gave the writers and producers a perfect context in which to comment indirectly on that unpopular war. The series lasted for 11 years, eight more than the war in Korea, garnered an unprecedented 99 Emmy nominations, and created some of the best-loved and best-remembered characters ever seen on the tube.

The leader of the pack was Hawkeye, a character based on the original creator of "M*A*S*H" (an acronym for Mobile Army Surgical Hospital), surgeon-turned-novelist Dr. H. Richard Hornberger (pseudonym: Richard Hooker). The part had been played by Donald Sutherland in the movie, but Alda took his character and molded him into three dimensions, rather than just the womanizing, boozing prankster of the film. Alda emerged from the series a superstar; "M*A*S*H" was his training ground for writing and directing, as well as an extended opportunity to hone his acting skills. Other characters came and went, but Hawkeye was always at the heart of the series.

Most of the best episodes focused more on the ironic mirth sometimes found in war, rather than going for the

CREDITS

TOP 10 PEAK: No. 3, 1982–83. CREATORS: Gene Reynolds, Larry Gelbart. BASED ON: *M*A*S*H*, by Richard Hooker. EXECUTIVE PRODUCERS: Gene Reynolds, Larry Gelbart, Burt Metcalfe. PRODUCERS: John Rappaport, others. DIRECTORS: Gene Reynolds, Alan Alda, Jamie Farr, Burt Metcalfe, Harry Morgan, others. WRITERS: Larry Gelbart, Burt Metcalfe, John Rappaport, Dan Wilcox, Dennis Koenig, Thad Mumford, Karen Hall, Alan Alda, others. TECHNICAL ADVISOR: Dr. Walter Dishell. CAST: *Capt. Benjamin Franklin "Hawkeye" Pierce* (Alan Alda), *Capt. John "Trapper John" McIntyre* (Wayne Rogers), *Maj. Margaret "Hot Lips" Houlihan* (Loretta Swit), *Maj. Frank Burns* (Larry Linville), *Cpl. Walter "Radar" O'Reilly* (Gary Burghoff), *Lt. Col. Henry Blake* (McLean Stevenson), *Father Francis Mulcahy* (William Christopher), *Cpl. Maxwell Klinger* (Jamie Farr), *Col. Sherman Potter* (Harry Morgan), *Capt. B.J. Hunnicut* (Mike Farrell), *Maj. Charles Emerson Winchester* (David Ogden Stiers), *Dr. Sidney Freedman* (Alan Arbus). OTHER REGULARS: Bobbie Mitchell, Kellye Nakahara, Marcia Strassman, Patricia Stevens, Judy Farrell, Jeff Maxwell, Jan Jordan, Gwen Farrell, Rosalind Chao, others. GUEST CAST: Blythe Danner, Clete Roberts, others.

EMMYS

Outstanding Comedy Series (1973–74); Best Lead Actor in a Comedy Series—Alan Alda (1973–74, 1981–82); Actor of the Year, Series—Alan Alda (1973–74); Outstanding Directing in a Comedy Series—Jackie Cooper (1973–74), Gene Reynolds (1974–75, 1975–76), Alan Alda (1976–77); Outstanding Continuing Performance by a Supporting Actor in a Comedy Series—Gary Burghoff (1976–77), Harry Morgan (1979–80); Outstanding Writing in a Comedy Series—Alan Alda (1978–79); Outstanding Supporting Actress in a Comedy Series—Loretta Swit (1979–80, 1981–82).

"laugh every 28 seconds" normally demanded of standard sitcoms by the networks. Although there was a laugh track, the producers of "M*A*S*H" had a standing rule: No laugh track in the O.R. (operating room). At times, this series had overtones of the best of the medical dramas, although humor was ever-present, even as the doctors fought to save lives—and their own sanity.

There were any number of memorable shows over the course of the series' 255 half-hour episodes. Among the finest was one called "The Interview," written by Larry Gelbart. Filmed documentary-style in black and white, there was no story and only a partial script. In writing this episode, Gelbart first taped interviews with cast members responding in character to questions posed by newscaster Clete Roberts (who had actually done similar interviews in Korea). These became the basis for the script; however, Roberts also improvised when the show was actually filmed, and the actors responded with their own improvisations.

Another memorable episode involved the use of a ticking clock visible in the corner of the screen; while the show unfolded before us—as the doctors performed a tricky surgery—the viewers were made aware of the urgency as the clock ticked off in 30 minutes of real time.

Not all the fine shows had gimmicks, though. There were thoughtful episodes like "Comrades in Arms," written by Alan Alda, in which Hawkeye and Margaret "Hot Lips" Houlihan, normally friendly adversaries, found out that war makes for strange bedfellows, literally.

"M*A*S*H" was noted for its wonderful characters, a family that included several father-figures, like Col. Henry Blake (McLean Stevenson) and his successor (after Blake was killed off), Col. Potter (Harry Morgan), as well as Father Mulcahy (William Christopher), the kindliest celluloid priest since Bing Crosby wore a collar. There were Hawkeye's best friends, Capt. John "Trapper John" McIntyre (Wayne Rogers)* and, for eight subsequent years, Capt. B. J. Hunnicut (Mike Farrell). And there was Corporal Klinger (Jamie Farr), the "straight" drag queen, bucking for a Section Eight discharge. The problem was, no matter how many lace stockings and tight girdles Klinger wore with his assorted dresses and hats to try

to look crazy, he was always overshadowed by the ever-so-much-more-absurd war itself, next to which his crazy getup paled in comparison.

But like all good things, even a television war must come to an end. And so it was with "M*A*S*H." A final two-and-a-half-hour episode, "Goodbye, Farewell and Amen," aired on February 28, 1983. It proved to be the highest-rated program in TV history, with a 60.2 Nielsen rating and a 77 share, as millions of people tuned in to pay their final respects to one of television's major prime-time hits.

Alan Alda (left) and Jamie Farr.

Bolstered by the success of "M*A*S*H," CBS and 20th Century Fox decided to produce a sequel series, "AfterMASH." It followed Col. Potter, Max Klinger, and Father Mulcahy at a stateside civilian hospital. The series lasted a little more than one season—September 1983 to December 1984. After "M*A*S*H," there really wasn't much more people wanted to see.

In 1992 20th Century Fox spent $1.25 million for a massive restoration project to digitally remaster all 255 episodes of the series. Each filmed episode was color-corrected, scene by scene, and closed-captioning for the deaf was added for the first time.

In the 1990s "M*A*S*H" remained one of television's most popular syndication hits, with reruns scheduled well into the 21st century. In addition, Columbia House Video was selling cassettes of the episodes through a special club.

---

*Years later, "Trapper John, M.D." would become a spinoff series, with the part played by Pernell Roberts.

KOJAK

NUMBER 7 (TIE), 1973–74

Who loves ya, baby?   —KOJAK

A bald-headed, 50-year-old, overweight, six-foot-one-inch Greek with a thick New York accent would seem the least likely candidate for an international sex symbol. But that is what Aristotle "Telly" Savalas became when he was cast in the role of Lieutenant Theo Kojak, N.Y.P.D. Within two weeks of the "Kojak" debut in the fall of 1973, Savalas found himself mobbed whenever he ventured to his usual public haunts, like the racetrack.

Savalas, who didn't turn to acting until the age of 35, was the veteran of 32 movies and several television series, playing mostly heavies, when Abby Mann, creator and producer of "Kojak," sought him out in 1972. Mann hired Savalas for his telefilm "The Marcus-Nelsen Murders," which served to introduce the Kojak character (and incidentally won Mann a writing Emmy). But Savalas was not interested in being confined to what he saw as just another cop show. Mann prevailed upon the execs at Universal Studios to change his mind. "I chased him from Madrid to Rome to Paris to London," said Universal's Tom Tannenbaum. "He wasn't indifferent to the idea that became 'Kojak,' but he wouldn't sign anything except the dinner check." Eventually Telly was wooed by the CBS brass, with a good deal of brass finally going into the actor's paycheck, to the tune of $30,000 per week.

Following the success of "The Marcus-Nelson Murders," CBS ordered a full series of episodes of this cop show. With a tube full of detectives of all descriptions—fat, rumpled, Hawaiian, black, and paraplegic, just to name a few—what made CBS think this one would be different? The answer was the charismatic Telly Savalas in the lead role. "He's exciting, enormously talented, one of the most sensitive performers around," said Mann in *TV Guide*. "He has brute power, which he releases with no seeming effort. Yet gentleness and compassion underscore his style. And Telly's perfect for TV—he needs no preparation. He can spend 15 minutes phoning in horse bets, then walk on and instantly do the most delicate type of acting." Gambling, in fact, was one of Savalas's greatest pleasures. He reportedly once won $125,000 at baccarat in a London club, then turned around and lost $117,000 of it. Yet he left the club a happy man, $8,000 richer. And his passion for horse racing once saw him the owner of his own thoroughbred, a horse named Telly's Pop.

The "Pop" in the horse's name referred, of course, to one of Lt. Kojak's trademarks—his ever-present lollipop. It was a humanizing touch for this sharply-dressed, tougher-than-nails member of New York's finest, and the shtick added to the Kojak mystique while helping to increase his popularity abroad (not to mention boosting lollipop sales at home and overseas).

If "Kojak" became a surprise ratings hit in the United States, it was an equally surprising worldwide sensation. In Germany he was called "the lion without a mane." The Aussies called him the "lolly cop," and he was reported to be the favorite TV star of Queen Elizabeth II of England. In Japan, actor Shuichiro Moriyama, who dubbed the voice of Kojak into Japanese, shaved his own head in tribute to Kojak. And although the

---

CREDITS

CREATOR: Abby Mann. EXECUTIVE PRODUCERS: Abby Mann, Matthew Rapf, James McAdams. SUPERVISING PRODUCER: Jack Laird. PRODUCERS: Irv Wilson, Chester Krumholz, others. DIRECTORS: William Hale, Jeannot Szwarc, Telly Savalas, Robert Day, Charles S. Dubin, others. WRITERS: Abby Mann, Jack Laird, Steve Carabatsos, others. TECHNICAL ADVISOR: Burt Armus. CAST: *Lt. Theo Kojak* (Telly Savalas), *Frank McNeil* (Dan Frazer), *Lt. Bobby Crocker* (Kevin Dobson), *Det. Stavros* (George Demosthenes Savalas [Telly Savalas's brother]), *Det. Rizzo* (Vince Conti), *Det. Saperstein* (Mark Russell). GUEST STARS: Paul Anka, Rosey Grier, Suzanne Pleshette, Max Von Sydow, others.

EMMYS

Best Lead Actor in a Drama Series—Telly Savalas (1973–74).

series came under attack in some countries like Colombia, which accused it of exporting violence, most of the world adored the series and its star. "He's a nice guy in a violent world," said Savalas in *Newsweek*. "He's going to be tough, but he's going to use psychology. That is a great example for kids—that heroes are guys who use their heads. I love a man who walks away from an argument or violence."

After Telly Savalas had been playing the role of Kojak for a few years, he was asked whether he wanted to continue in the weekly drama. After all, he had had a successful film career, including an Academy Award nomination for *The Birdman of Alcatraz* in 1962, plus memorable parts in films like *The Greatest Story Ever Told*, the 1965 film in which he played Pontius Pilate (and first shaved his head), and *The Dirty Dozen* (1967). In 1974 he took home an Emmy for playing Kojak, and at that point CBS feared he might wish to leave the series. Savalas was by now identified with the role, so it was a tough call for him. "If they keep it elastic," he said, "I'll stay. If they make me a supercop, I'll quit. I won't stay one minute after it becomes boring. I revolt against monotony. This season [1975] is better than the first. I have women friends. I like the notion of a sex symbol at my age."

The series was eventually removed from the regular CBS lineup in 1978, after five years and 118 episodes (all of which were later seen in syndication). But in 1985 Savalas found that he still had what it took to be a sex symbol, when the sixtysomething actor was recruited for a new series of made-for-TV movies of "Kojak." These included "Kojak: The Belarus File" (1985) and "Kojak: The Price of Justice" (1987) for CBS, and a 1989 "ABC Saturday Mystery" episode of "Kojak" (the same revolving series that featured "Columbo," among others). Who loves him, baby? Apparently, the American public; in 1993 the end was nowhere in sight for this series.

Telly Savalas.

THE SONNY AND CHER COMEDY HOUR

NUMBER 7 (TIE), 1973–74

Salvatore Phillip Bono met Cherilyn Sarkisian LaPierre when he was a record promoter and she was an aspiring singer. They were married a short time later, in 1964; he was 29, the bride was barely 17. Within a year, the couple changed their names, first to Caesar and Cleo, then to the now-famous Sonny and Cher, and had their first hit record, a number one, four-million-copy bestseller called "I Got You, Babe."

Sonny adapted well to his Svengali-like role, and soon he and the shy Cher were cranking out some of the '60s' biggest pop-rock hits, like "All I Really Want to Do" and "Bang Bang." With the good times rolling, the two kids from poor backgrounds—as a child, Cher kept her soles attached to her shoes with rubber bands—began a spending binge, moving into a 22-room Bel Air, California, mansion and buying fleets of fancy automobiles and motorcycles. But by 1970, record fans had stopped buying their music. Sonny shrewdly appraised the situation and decided they needed to tour the nightclub circuit to regain their following.

Sonny adored working with live audiences, although it took some coaxing to get his diffident wife to go along with him. Eventually the two honed an act that put them back on the map. Guest shots on television followed, including a one-night stand as guest hosts on "The Merv Griffin Show" in 1971. Then-programming chief of CBS, Fred Silverman, caught their act and promptly signed them to a contract.

"The Sonny and Cher Comedy Hour" premiered as a summer replacement in August 1971. Audiences immediately warmed to the couple, who now did comedy sketches as well as songs. By the middle of the 1972–73 season, CBS had found a permanent berth for the duo; by the following year they had garnered enough of an audience to place their show in the Nielsen top 10.

The format consisted of the husband-and-wife team taking their gentle marital bickering out of their living room and into the audience's. The opening sequence always had putdown humor: Cher, usually clad in an exquisite, revealing Bob Mackie gown, needling her hapless hubby, and Sonny retaliating—all in fun, of course. Example: Sonny says he wants a new bed—he's tired of climbing into the upper bunk. Cher insults his short stature: "You'd need a ladder to climb into a lower bunk." Or Sonny zings one to Cher: "There's something I want to get off my chest, Cher—and onto yours." Oh yeah? Cher lobs one back: "Love means never having to say you're Sonny."

Fortunately, these opening segments didn't last too long, and the regular comedy sketches soon got under way. The best of these were "The Vamp," in which Cher portrayed notorious seductresses throughout history; "Sonny's Pizza," with Sonny playing a dimwitted pizzeria proprietor and Cher his lovely waitress, Rosa; "The Laundromat," with Cher as the tacky, leopardskin-clad housewife Laverne, sharing her problems with actress Teri Garr as her friend Olivia; and "Mr. and Ms.," a role-reversal spoof—"The continuing story of a liberated woman (Cher) and the sniveling coward who liberated her (Sonny)." The one-hour show always concluded with the couple

CREDITS

PRODUCERS: Allan Blye, Chris Beard. DIRECTOR: Art Fisher. WRITERS: Bob Arnott, George Burditt, Phil Hahn, Paul Wayne, Coslough Johnson, Bob Einstein, Steve Martin, Allan Blye, Chris Bearde, Earl Brown. REGULAR CAST: Sonny Bono, Cher Bono, Ted Zeigler, Chastity Bono, Freeman King, Peter Cullen, Steve Martin, Teri Garr, Billy Van, Bob Einstein, Shields and Yarnell, others. GUEST STARS: Harvey Korman, Robert Merrill, Carroll O'Connor, Glenn Ford, Gov. Ronald Reagan, The Jackson 5, Howard Keel, Wilfred Hyde-White, Larry Storch, Howard Cosell, Chuck Connors, Charo, Barbara Eden, Don Knotts, Wayne Rogers, Dinah Shore, The Smothers Brothers, Tony Curtis, Tony Randall, others.

EMMYS

Outstanding Directorial Achievement in Variety—Art Fisher (1971–72).

Sonny and Cher.

cuddling their bashful little girl, Chastity, while singing "I Got You, Babe."

The beat went on for two-and-a-half seasons. Then the Bonos announced to CBS executives that they were not only splitting up the act, they were splitting up, period. The show went off the air while each attempted separate variety shows. Over at ABC Sonny landed his own series called "The Sonny Comedy Revue." He got custody of some of the "Sonny and Cher Show" regulars, including Ted Zeigler, Freeman King, Billy Van, announcer Peter Cullen, and Teri Garr, who took over Cher's previous roles in "Sonny's Pizza" and other sketches. The series ran from September 1974 to December 1974. Cher's was called "Cher," and it ran on CBS from February 1975 to January 1976. Daughter Chastity Bono and Teri Garr appeared as regulars, along with Steve Martin, who had also been a regular on the original series.

Sonny without Cher? Cher without Sonny? What's a network to do? A business deal was struck: although the marriage was history, CBS pleaded for the two to reconcile for the sake of the series. In February 1976 "The Sonny and Cher Show" returned to the air. But there was nothing funny in their putdown humor. Who wanted to see an ex-couple fighting for real? With less-than-desirable ratings, the show was cancelled after only a year.

In November 1987 the former couple appeared together for a "Sonny and Cher" reunion, the first since their split, when as guests on "Late Night with David Letterman" they reluctantly sang "I Got You, Babe" for the first time in over a decade. In the intervening years Sonny had remarried, and in 1988 he was elected mayor of Palm Springs. And Cher had made a name for herself in motion pictures. Her acting career had seen her star in such highly praised films as *Silkwood* (1983), *Mask* (1985), and *Moonstruck* (1987), for which she received the Oscar as Best Actress.

CANNON

NUMBER 9 (TIE), 1973–74

For years William Conrad had made a living behind the camera. He had given up acting in 1956 to pursue a career as a producer and director on TV series like "Bat Masterson," "Naked City," "77 Sunset Strip," "Temple Houston," and "Gunsmoke." Conrad had an especially soft spot for the latter, since he spent nine years—from 1952 to 1961—as the unseen radio voice of Matt Dillon. He was also the unseen narrator on a variety of television productions that included the animated series "Bullwinkle" (1961–62) and the drama "The Fugitive" (see page 130). So when producer Quinn Martin called in 1971 to offer him a chance to star in a new series, his first inclination was to decline. Then William Conrad had a change of heart. The series, "Cannon," would be built around him, and he could help create the Cannon character. "I was worried," said Conrad in *TV Guide*, "before we made the pilot, whether after all those years

as a director and producer I could be detached from the production side. Well, I was so detached I was proud of myself. It's such a joy to sit on a set and not worry if the director is behind schedule. All I worry about is my work as an actor."

Hardly a candidate for stardom at age 51, Conrad was balding and fat. He actually preferred the term "fat" to the many euphemisms offered up by his press agents and studio publicists, who seemed to go out of their way to describe the star of "Cannon" as "portly," "corpulent," or "hefty." "There's nothing wrong with the word fat. If you're fat, you're fat," he declared. "I'm as healthy as I can be; I haven't felt so good in 20 years." When the series began in 1971, Conrad was an unlikely hero at five feet, nine inches, and 230 pounds. Two years later, with the show now a successful ratings hit, he was enjoying even more of the good life, with his

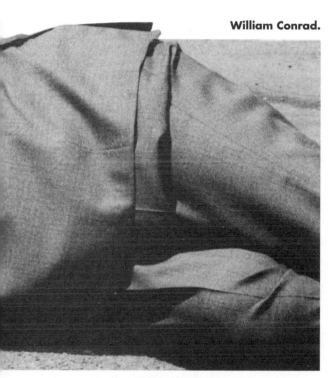

William Conrad.

Exacting fees from his well-heeled clients could take some interesting twists. Frank Cannon was established as a man of fine tastes in food and drink, a lifestyle he saw to it his clients helped perpetuate, as in one episode in which he was hired by a young boy's father to find the child's kidnappers:

> LASSITER
> Mr. Cannon, I'd like you to find the men who did this thing.
>
> CANNON
> I'm not sure you'll meet my price.
>
> LASSITER
> Name it.
>
> CANNON
> I did a little snooping, Mr. Lassiter. I checked your wine cellar. You've got four bottles of Lafitte Rothschild, 1949. They're the last in America.
>
> LASSITER
> You drive a hard bargain, Mr. Cannon.

William Conrad starred as Cannon for five years; the show was cancelled by CBS in 1976, after 124 episodes. Over the next several years, Conrad returned to doing voiceovers, including narration for "The Wild, Wild World of Animals" (1973–78), "How the West Was Won" (1977), and "Buck Rogers in the 25th Century" (1979–80).

In 1980 a "Cannon" made-for-television movie aired (it could hardly be called a "reunion," since Conrad was the only cast member). The film was called "The Return of Frank Cannon."

In 1981 Conrad starred in the short-lived TV series "Nero Wolfe," whose title character bore more resemblance to Cannon than to the Wolfe in the original Rex Stout novels.

The return of William Conrad took place in 1987, when the actor assumed a role perfectly designed for him in the CBS series "Jake and the Fatman" (hint: he didn't play the part of Jake). The seventysomething actor was as hefty, er, corpulent, uh, fat as ever and enjoying every minute of his popularity in the series, which continued until 1992.

weight pushing the 270 range. His explanation? "Like Topsy, I jes' growed...Nobody else seems to mind my size, so why should I?"

And indeed, nobody else did. Instead, Conrad's added visibility seemed to have boosted the series in popularity. In a television free-for-all that found dozens of gumshoes jockeying for shooting space (and high Nielsens), it wasn't easy to miss Cannon, even though he was yet another detective/private eye/ex-cop keeping the streets of Los Angeles safe for his wealthy clients. And although the show was violent—one episode had a man thrown out of a window, a young girl run over by a car, and a blow-torch attempt on Cannon's life—he usually managed to avoid violence and rarely used his gun, preferring to chase down the baddies in his behemoth Lincoln Continental.

CREDITS

CREATOR/EXECUTIVE PRODUCER: Quinn Martin. PRODUCERS: Arthur Fellows, Adrian Samish, Alan A. Armer, Harold Gast, others. DIRECTORS: George McCowan, Phil Leacock, others. WRITERS: Ed Hume, Robert Lewin, others. CAST: *Frank Cannon* (William Conrad). GUEST STARS: J.D. Cannon, Barry Sullivan, Keenan Wynn, Tom Skerritt, Sharon Acker, Larry Linville, Marj Dusay, Anne Baxter, Stefanie Powers, others.

CHICO AND THE MAN

It was one of television's greatest success stories. It was also one of its greatest tragedies. It began in the night-clubs of New York City, and it ended with a bullet.

Freddie Prinze (born Preutzel) was a product of the New York ghetto, a talented young man who billed himself as a "Hunga-rican" in his standup act—half Hungarian (his father), half Puerto Rican (his mom). Talent scouts spotted this handsome, puppyish (as his future co-star Jack Albertson would later describe him) comic doing his act at a New York improv club, and before he was 21, he was doing guest appearances on "The Tonight Show." From there, it was just a short hop to stardom when James Komack signed the young man to co-star in his upcoming NBC series, "Chico and the Man." "Freddie Prinze," enthused Komack, "is the best comic to come along in twenty years." But he would barely last another three.

When "Chico and the Man"—Jack Albertson played "the Man" of the title—hit the airwaves, audiences were charmed by the duo. The story line was familiar: Albertson's "Man," Ed Brown, was a crotchety old coot, the last Anglo holdout in an East Los Angeles Chicano (Mexican-American) neighborhood. In a way, he was NBC's second answer to Archie Bunker—a spare, since "Sanford and Son" was already doing that job so successfully. Enter Freddie Prinze, a.k.a. "Chico." He instantly glommed on to old Ed, promising undying friendship and abundant help in cleaning up Ed's neglected garage business in exchange for a partnership. "Take your flies and go," hurled the uninterested old white dude. Sorry. Chico was determined to turn Ed's life around for him. He stayed, and so did the audience. That is, until the protests started.

In a flurry of letters and picketing reminiscent of the flack surrounding

CREDITS

CREATOR/EXECUTIVE PRODUCER: James Komack. PRODUCERS: Alan Sacks, Michael Morris, Ed Scharlach, Jerry Ross, Charles Stewart. DIRECTORS: various. WRITERS: James Komack, Don Nicholl, Michael Ross, Bernie West, others. CAST: *Ed Brown* (Jack Albertson), *Chico Rodriguez* (Freddie Prinze), *Louis* (Scatman Crothers), *Mabel* (Bonnie Boland), *Mando* (Isaac Ruiz), *Della Rogers* (Della Reese), *Raul Garcia* (Gabriel Melgar), *Aunt Charo* (Charo).

EMMYS

Outstanding Lead Actor in a Comedy Series—Jack Albertson (1975–76).

"Bridget Loves Bernie," the Mexican-American community proclaimed the series an insult to all Americans of Mexican heritage. The show wasn't helped by racist lines like the above and other off-handed remarks like "This used to be a good neighborhood, when Mexicans knew their place—Mexico." Furthermore, the protesters argued, Prinze wasn't even Chicano, his accent was broad and overdone, and the show made too much use of the simplistic, bumbling, stereotypical Mexican "who must inevitably commit his dishonesties and stupidities only to be saved from himself by the condescending Anglo-American." So the producers did what had to be done—they fixed the show. They reshot some already-completed episodes, toned down the heavy ethnic insults, provided Chico with a "Hunga-rican" background to match Prinze's, gave Ed and Chico more of a father-son relationship with a generation gap rather than a culture gap at the heart of their conflict, and added a few Chicanos to the cast. The show was still a hit, although the ratings had dropped it down from its weekly number one position to a seasonal ranking of number three, still a respectable achievement for a new entry. But during the next season, the ratings plummeted, leaving "Chico and the Man" at 25th place by the end of 1975–76. Then it all came apart.

His series may have been floundering, but by January of 1977 Freddie Prinze was on top. He had become a showbiz phenomenon, even performing at the Inaugural Ball for President Jimmy Carter. But at 22 years of age, he was still too unsure of himself to handle it all. He had married 15 months earlier, fathered a child, Freddie, Jr., then just as suddenly found himself in a failed marriage. His wife wanted a divorce, his ex-manager successfully sued him for breach of

Freddie Prinze (left) and Jack Albertson.

contract, and he was doing drugs—cocaine, Quaaludes, alcohol. He talked about dying; he toyed with guns, one even accidentally discharging into a wall. On Friday, January 28, 1977, in the presence of his new manager, Marvin Snyder, he made a few phone calls; then, before Snyder could stop him, Prinze placed a gun to his temple and shot himself. He died 33 hours later. Despite everything, his mother insisted it was not intentional. "If anyone killed him," she said, "it was Hollywood." She filed suit and later won a verdict that awarded her $200,000 from Freddie's life insurance policy, the jury in essence agreeing that Freddie had been playing a prank with the gun when it went off, a result of his self-induced drugged state at the time.

"I think big! That's why I'm going to be a somebody!" Chico announced when he met the Man. If only Freddie had listened, that somebody might have been around a lot longer.

After Freddie's death, James Komack decided to continue the series in his memory. Although many critized the move as insensitive, Komack disagreed. "I

loved Freddie," he insisted. "I didn't continue 'Chico and the Man' strictly for selfish reasons. Besides protecting other people in the production, I didn't want the country to become eternal mourners." But although new members were added to the cast, including Della Reese the year before and a 12-year-old Chicano lad named Gabriel Melgar to play a younger sparring partner for Ed Brown, it just wasn't the same show. *Variety* said it best: "Without [Freddie Prinze], Jack Albertson is the sound of one hand clapping." In July 1978 the series aired its last episode.

Jack Albertson, who found new popularity, said at the time of the series' height, "One nice thing about achieving success at this age is that I have fewer years to become a has-been." He was 67 when the show debuted, and his performances would win him a Best Actor Emmy in 1976. Following the demise of "Chico and the Man," Albertson landed the role of Senator Kelley in a short-lived series called "Grandpa Goes to Washington" (yes, he was Grandpa). He died in 1981 at the age of 74.

THE JEFFERSONS

NUMBER 4, 1974–75

Well, we're movin' on u-up...
—OPENING THEME SONG

George Jefferson was Archie Bunker in blackface. Naturally, they both had the same father—Norman Lear. The Jeffersons were Archie's next-door neighbors on "All in the Family" (see page 182), although that show's viewers only met George's wife, Louise, for the first two years, since George, as bigoted against whites as Archie was against blacks, refused to set foot in the Bunker home for a long time. Then, in 1973, Norman Lear cast Sherman Hemsley in the role of George Jefferson; two years later Lear played mid-husband to yet another spinoff.

"The Jeffersons" premiered in January 1975 and ran for 10½ years on CBS, TV's longest-running prime-time black sitcom to date. It was an immediate hit, the first black sitcom since "Julia" (in 1968) to make it into the top 10 (it was decidedly more *com* than *sit*, unlike "Julia"). The series revolved around George Jefferson (Hemsley), a bigoted, loud-mouthed bully who barked at his wife and maid, despised his neighbors, and strutted like a peacock—in short, he was Archie Bunker's flip side. But George was a yuppie before the term was invented, and once he made a pile of money in the dry cleaning business (he owned a chain of stores), he left his Queens bunker for a "de-luxe apartment in the sky-y-y" over in Manhattan.

Sherman Hemsley was the total opposite of his character, and lest people confuse him with George, he was quick to point out that George's bark was really worse than his bite. "He's scared," explained Hemsley. "He uses his boastfulness to cover up a lot of

things." Hemsley came to acting late in life, after finishing a four-year enlistment in the air force in the late 1950s. He worked in local Philadelphia theater by night and spent his days as a letter carrier for the postal service. When he decided to try for the big time in New York, he made sure he'd lined up a postal job before tackling Broadway. Eventually he landed the part of Gitlow in the musical *Purlie*, where he was seen by Norman Lear, who remembered him in it when he was casting George Jefferson. Hemsley would go on to star in another successful series immediately after "The Jeffersons" left the air, when he played Deacon Frye in "Amen" (1986–91).

George's wife, Louise "Weezie" Jefferson, was played by Isabel Sanford, an energetic actress who was a good 21 years older than the actor who played her husband. She had spent 30 years in black theater, eventually landing supporting roles on Broadway in the 1960s. She then made her way to Hollywood, appearing in films like *Guess Who's Coming to Dinner?* (1967) and several TV series, including "Bewitched" and "The Mod Squad." and As George's wife, Louise was often forced to be the subject of his putdown humor, but she never had any trouble putting him right back in his place. Sanford saw similarities between herself and her character. "I don't think that Isabel Sanford is too different from Louise Jefferson," she said in an *Ebony* interview. "When I was with my husband, I was the boss. I mean, what *I* said would go. He may have thought he won, but I won every argument. And Louise does, too. She's the one who keeps George's feet on the ground. That's the way I was with my family."

CREDITS

TOP 10 PEAK: No. 3, 1981–82.
CREATORS: Don Nicholl, Michael Ross, Bernie West, Norman Lear. EXECUTIVE PRODUCERS: Norman Lear, George Sunga, Michael G. Moye. PRODUCERS: Jack Shea, others. DIRECTORS: various. WRITERS: various. CAST: *George Jefferson* (Sherman Hemsley), *Louise Jefferson* (Isabel Sanford), *Lionel Jefferson* (Mike Evans, Damon Evans), *Helen Willis* (Roxie Roker), *Tom Willis* (Franklin Cover), *Jenny Willis Jefferson* (Berlinda Tolbert), *Harry Bentley* (Paul Benedict), *Mother Jefferson* (Zara Cully), *Florence Johnston* (Marla Gibbs), others.

EMMYS

Outstanding Lead Actress in a Comedy Series—Isabel Sanford (1980–81).

The Jeffersons' son, Lionel, had been a friend of Mike Stivic on "All in the Family," and Mike Evans, who played Lionel, moved to Manhattan along with his "parents" when they were spun off. But Evans was involved with another show from the Lear factory, "Good Times," of which he was co-creator. The demands on his time were too much, and Evans asked to be freed from his "Jeffersons" contract. He spent four years away from the series while the role of Lionel was assumed by another actor, Damon Evans (no relation). Then, in 1979, he asked to return, and again played Lionel Jefferson. Audiences didn't seem to mind. Nor did Lionel's wife, Jenny, played by Berlinda Tolbert. Jenny was the daughter of the Jeffersons' next-door neighbors (who were, incidentally, television's first interracial couple), and in 1986 Jenny and Lionel were married. Yet she, like Samantha on "Bewitched," never seemed to notice that her husband had been switched to a new actor. Well, it *was* a fictional television show.

When George wasn't busy yelling at his wife or his neighbors, he chewed out his maid, Florence, played by Marla Gibbs. Like Sherman Hemsley (who once worked at the post office while he played theater), Gibbs was an actress who hedged her bets. For the first two years on "The Jeffersons," she held on to her job as a clerk with United Airlines, "just in case." She needn't

have worried. As it turned out, Gibbs stayed with the series all through its nearly 11-year run. In 1981 she was seen briefly in her own spinoff, playing the same character in a sitcom called "Checking In." It lasted only a few weeks (April 9–30, 1981), and she quickly got back her old job cleaning for the Jeffersons. Gibbs went on to become a highly successful producer and star of her own situation comedy, "227," which ran from 1985 to 1990.

By the early '80s, "The Jeffersons" had had an attitude adjustment. Racial jokes were no longer unique or timely. The series had mellowed, and so had George Jefferson. He ceased making jokes about playing "Pin the Tail on the Honky," Louise stopped saying "ain't" and using double negatives, and the references to Harlem and George's past life were almost totally gone. Michael G. Moye, the show's only black producer, admitted they were de-emphasizing racial and issue-oriented topics. "We don't go out of our way to look for black themes any more," he said. "We have a tremendous white audience, too." Maybe so, but the show seemed to have lost its soul. By 1985 there was really no place else to take "The Jeffersons." They not only had had their piece of the pie, they'd eaten it all. The show left the CBS lineup in July 1985, although it continued to be run in syndication.

From left: Isabel Sanford, Paul Benedict, and Sherman Hemsley.

RHODA

...New York, this is your last chance!
—OPENING VOICEOVER

Rhoda Morganstern was Mary Richards's best friend and upstairs neighbor on "The Mary Tyler Moore Show" for four seasons (see page 192). During the summer hiatus following the third season, Valerie Harper, the actress playing the plumpish, dumpy-shlumpy Rhoda, went to Weight Watchers and lost 30 pounds. Out went the fat jokes, although the producers did keep her in oversized sweatshirts for a while. But it was soon apparent to the series' creators, Jim Brooks and Allan Burns, that Ms. Morganstern's zaftig, 150-pound, ugly-duckling body had metamorphosed into that of a svelte Jewish swan in need of her own series. CBS agreed, and in the fall of 1974, Rhoda moved to "Rhoda."

The show's opening montage, complete with the title character's voiceover about her theretofore angst-ridden life, set the stage. Rhoda was now "on her own" —except she really wasn't. First she moved in with her plumpish, dumpy-shlumpy younger sister, Brenda (Julie Kavner). Then she moved in with her mom, Ida Morganstern, the quintessential chicken-soup-serving, husband-for-my-daughter-hunting Jewish mother, played to the hilt by Nancy Walker. In the eighth episode, all that changed. Having met the man of her dreams, Joe Gerard (David Groh), Rhoda had one of the biggest weddings ever thrown in TV land. Nielsen ratings went off the scale. Fans held mock "Rhoda and Joe" parties on The Big Night (October 28, 1974).

The series was hailed as the hit of the season. "It just may be the best thing to happen to Monday night since pro football," said *Time* magazine; "We doubt there's ever been a more successful spinoff in TV history," proclaimed *TV Guide*; *Variety* hailed "Rhoda" as "an instant hit, a well-conceived, well-written and well-executed sitcom that was off and running like clockwork from the opening minute...'Rhoda' is a can't-miss newcomer."

Much of the droll humor was to be found in the characters and their relationships to each other. Rhoda's self-deprecating putdowns ("I'm not married, I'm not engaged, I'm not even pinned. I bet Hallmark doesn't even have a card for me") were topped only by her classic yenta of a mother, Ida:

IDA
So how come you're not wearing a bra?

RHODA
Ma, I'm 33 years old.

IDA
That's all the more reason.

But it was hard to poke fun at this clearly attractive woman once she found love and marriage, so the writers tried a new tack. Kid sister Brenda was now the ugly duckling; she was, in essence, Rhoda: "My scale says 105—before I get the other leg on," moaned the terminally depressed kid sister.

Probably the most interesting character was one who was never seen—Carlton the Doorman. One of the show's writer/producers, Lorenzo Music filled in during rehearsals and eventually won the part, along with the hearts of viewers who roared whenever the voice of the always-inebriated Carlton came over Rhoda's and Brenda's intercom. "Hello. This is Carlton, your doorman," he would announce for the hundreth time, as if just introducing himself. The Carlton jokes soon became the highlight of the show. Example:

IDA (OVER INTERCOM)
There's a drunk in the lobby. You'd better tell the doorman.

RHODA
Ma, that *is* the doorman.

Eventually, the popular character was poised to be spun off into his own CBS cartoon series, to be called "Carlton Your Doorman." The character was (thankfully) sobered up for the kiddies, and the pilot, which aired on May 21, 1980, won an Emmy for producers Lorenzo Music and Barton Dean as Outstanding Animated Program—Special. However, it didn't sell as a series. Music continued to produce television shows, and he recorded many voiceovers (Garfield the Cat and the "crash-test" dummy, among others).

Nancy Walker (left) Valerie Harper.

Generally it takes several seasons for the lives of series characters to evolve. "Rhoda," on the other hand, seemed to be running on fast-forward. Soon after her marriage, she and hubby Joe were setting up housekeeping, again in sister Brenda's building. Soon they were having troubles in their marriage. Soon they were splitting up. By the beginning of the fourth season (1977), they were divorced and Rhoda was back in the wacky world of singledom. But the program's writers were never able to recapture the magic that all had felt at the beginning of the series, back when the reviews had all been raves. The excitement, like Rhoda's marriage, had fizzled. The series had a short fifth season, from September to December 1978, then was cancelled.

Most of the talented cast prospered in their careers following "Rhoda." Valerie Harper starred in her own series, "Valerie," from 1986 to 1987, but left over contract disputes while the show continued without her (and with a name change, first to "Valerie's Family," then to "The Hogan Family"). In 1990 she again returned to CBS, playing the lead in the short-lived comedy, "City" (January to June, 1990). The four-time Emmy winner continued to star in made-for-TV movies.

Julie Kavner, who played kid sister Brenda, became a regular on "The Tracey Ullman Show"

(1987–90). While she was on the series, she did the voice of an occasional cartoon character, Marge Simpson. When "The Simpsons" got their own prime-time series, Kavner continued as the voice of Marge (plus Marge's sisters and many others), and she received an Emmy for her vocal talents.

Nancy Walker first gained TV fame as Rosie the waitress in the Bounty paper towel commercials ("It's the quicker picker-upper"), which ran from 1970 to 1990. During the mid-'70s she simultaneously played Ida Morgenstern and Mildred the maid on "McMillan and Wife" (for which she received three Emmy nominations). She later went on to direct episodes of "The Mary Tyler Moore Show," "Rhoda," and "Alice." In 1990 she began playing another Jewish mother (ironically, neither she nor Valerie Harper was Jewish) in the Fox-TV series "True Colors." She was filming the final episode of "True Colors" in April 1992 when she died of lung cancer at the age of 69.

Beginning in 1993, "Rhoda" fans had a chance to catch the series on Nickelodeon's "Nick at Nite," which purchased 650 hours of programming from MTM's library, including episodes of "The Mary Tyler Moore Show," "Hill Street Blues," "Phyllis," "WKRP in Cincinnati," "Newhart," "The Betty White Show," and "St. Elsewhere."

CREDITS

CREATORS: James L. Brooks, Allan Burns.
EXECUTIVE PRODUCERS: James L. Brooks, Allan Burns, Charlotte Brown.
PRODUCERS: David Davis, Lorenzo Music.
DIRECTORS: various. WRITERS: various.
CAST: *Rhoda Morganstern Gerard* (Valerie Harper), *Brenda Morganstern* (Julie Kavner), *Ida Morgenstern* (Nancy Walker), *Martin Morgenstern* (Harold Gould), *Carlton the Doorman* (Lorenzo Music), *Joe Gerard* (David Groh), others. GUEST STARS: Jay Tarses, Tom Patchett, the cast of "The Mary Tyler Moore Show," others.

EMMYS

Outstanding Lead Actress in a Comedy Series—Valerie Harper (1974–75).

GOOD TIMES

NUMBER 7, 1974–75

**John Amos
and
Esther Rolle.**

"Good Times" was a spinoff of "Maude," which in turn was a spinoff of "All in the Family." All of these shows were in the family of series from Norman Lear's Tandem Productions. In "Good Times," television sitcom king Lear selected the character of Florida, Maude's maid, to solo. He took her out of Tuckahoe, New York, and sent her and her newly created family packing to the projects of Chicago, Illinois. The Evans family was poor, the father (whose name was changed from Henry to James for some reason when they moved) was unemployed, the kids were mostly wiseacres—and the audience was delighted. They quickly warmed to this black family of characters, and by the CBS series' first full season (the show began as a mid-season entry in February 1974), it established a record by being the second black series to make the Nielsen top 10 in the same season ("The Jeffersons" was holding down fourth place).

The series' success seemed to ride on the appeal of one character in particular, 18-year-old J.J., a rubber-mouthed toothpick played by 25-year-old Jimmie Walker. Television series have a way of making stars out of actors with a certain appeal for audiences, and it soon became apparent to the show's writers and producers that Walker (to use a term his character soon made a household word) was "dyn-o-mite!" Walker was no stranger to poverty; the young comic had come from a project in the South Bronx, New York, and parlayed his experiences into a standup nightclub routine that he had been doing for nearly seven years when he was tapped to play the eldest child in "Good Times."

But soon others in the cast became aware that Walker was having all the good times, and they wanted their share. In September 1975 *Ebony* magazine ran an article called "Bad Times on the 'Good Times' Set." It seemed that although the series had dealt with such subjects as juvenile alcoholism, gang violence, busing, menopause, blacks and hypertension, and blacks who rip off blacks, the cast was dissatisfied with the show's story content. Or so the public was led to believe. In truth, most of the problems stemmed from the fact that

Jimmie Walker was getting more than his share of the dialogue and too many close-ups. Rolle complained about J.J. to *Ebony*: "He's 18 and he doesn't work. He can't read and write. He doesn't think. The show didn't start out to be that...little by little...they have made him more stupid and enlarged the role...I resent the imagery that says to black kids that you can make it by standing on the corner saying 'Dyn-o-mite!' "

Walker quickly countered, reminding people that this was fiction, not a documentary. In an article he wrote for the *Los Angeles Times* in October 1992, he reminisced fondly and proudly about his role in the series: "If you look at the J.J. character in a time when more than 50 percent of inner-city youths are unemployed, he worked...He didn't do drugs, and talked friends out of doing them...J.J. wasn't involved in gang activities, and was shot for not joining a gang. Wow! Just like real life. His art won him many awards and later a job as a graphic artist."

Others weren't so thrilled. In 1976 John Amos (who had previously played Gordie, the weatherman on "The Mary Tyler Moore Show") left and was written out of the show, emphatically and terminally—they killed him off in an unseen car accident. Amos went on to star as the adult Kunta Kinte in the highly successful 1977 miniseries "Roots."

Meanwhile, a new husband was created for Florida. In early 1977, Moses Gunn was brought on board to play the part of Carl Dixon. But he didn't get much of a chance, because Ester Rolle quit before the 1977–78 season got under way. So they wrote her out of the series too, sending Florida and new hubby off on an extended honeymoon and placing J.J. and his jive talk in charge of the family, while the next-door neighbor became the family's surrogate mother. By the time Esther Rolle came to her senses and returned to the fold, it was too late to save the show. The show had dropped to 53rd place in the ratings, and by December 1978 the series was off the air. A final episode the following May attempted to tie up all the loose ends. But the good times were over for "Good Times."

CREDITS

CREATORS: Eric Monte, Mike Evans. EXECUTIVE PRODUCERS: Norman Lear, Allan Manings, Austin and Irma Kalish, Norman Paul. PRODUCERS: Jack Elinson, Gordon Mitchell, Lloyd Turner, Sid Dorfman. DIRECTORS: various. WRITERS: various. CAST: *Florida Evans* (Esther Rolle), *James Evans* (John Amos), *James ("J.J.") Evans, Jr.* (Jimmie Walker), *Thelma Evans* (BernNadette Stanis), *Michael Evans* (Ralph Carter), *Willona Woods* (Ja'net DuBois), *Carl Dixon* (Moses Gunn), *Nathan Bookman* (Johnny Brown), *Penny Gordon Woods* (Janet Jackson). GUEST STARS: Ralph Wilcox, Richard Ward, Derek Wells, others.

RICH MAN, POOR MAN

NUMBER 2, 1975–76

"Rich Man, Poor Man" was television's first hit miniseries, earning Nielsen ratings so high—averaging a 45 percent share of the television audience, or about 40 million viewers—that it overshadowed everything during the 1975–76 season, except for the top-ranked "All in the Family." It included a cast list that read like a "Who's Who" of Hollywood, earned 23 Emmy nominations, and won three Emmy Awards, all the while helping to make ABC the number one network for the season.

The series was based on Irwin Shaw's best-selling 1970 novel of the same name. The original hardcover edition had sold a respectable 92,000 copies when it was first published, and added a million and a half when it went to paperback. Following the success of the miniseries, *five million* more paperback copies were sold, and the book went through 39 printings, making the 66-year-old Shaw, who had received unfavorable reviews when the book was first published, a millionaire.

The series was nighttime soap opera at its best, full of the steamy sex scenes, violence, and lust for power that make the format such an audience-grabber. ABC invested $6 million in the production, the brainchild of then-ABC executive Barry Diller (who subsequently became head of Paramount, and later, Fox studios). The 752-page screenplay translated into 12 hours of footage, which ABC programming head Fred Silverman (formerly of CBS, later of NBC) inherited when Diller left the network. Silverman decided to slice it into nine weekly installments, which the series' executive producer Harve Bennett decried as "like a man who says this roast beef is magnificent, let's make sandwiches out of it." Nevertheless, it proved to be just the ticket for drawing a weekly audience. "Rich Man, Poor Man" premiered on Sunday, February 1, 1976, ran its second installment the following day (Monday, February 2), and thereafter appeared on successive Mondays, with a concluding two-hour program on March 22.

The story was not very original. It revolved around two Cain-versus-Abel brothers named Jordache (no, they didn't manufacture jeans)—one a nice guy, one a bum—and the girl they both coveted. The story began in 1945, concluded in 1965, and unfolded against a panorama of social issues like McCarthyism, the Korean War, Vietnam, campus riots, racism, and the sexual revolution.

With a series of this magnitude, the producers were convinced that only actors of marquee quality were right for the project, but with a TV budget this was impossible. So they took a chance and cast two unknown actors as the brothers. Peter Strauss played the "Rich Man," Rudy Jordache, who rose from his poor background to become a business and political maven. Strauss had appeared in the film *Soldier Blue* (1970) plus small parts on numerous TV series; following his starring role in "Rich Man, Poor Man," he (along with Richard Chamberlain) became known as the "king of the miniseries."

CREDITS

CREATOR: Barry Diller. BASED ON: *Rich Man, Poor Man*, by Irwin Shaw. EXECUTIVE PRODUCER: Harve Bennett. PRODUCER: Jon Epstein. DIRECTORS: David Greene, Boris Sagal. WRITER: Dean Reisner. CAST: *Rudy Jordache* (Peter Strauss), *Tom Jordache* (Nick Nolte), *Axel Jordache* (Ed Asner), *Julie Prescott* (Susan Blakely), *Mary Jordache* (Dorothy McGuire), *Willie Abbot* (Bill Bixby), *Duncan Calderwood* (Ray Milland), *Teddy Boylan* (Robert Reed), *Virginia Calderwood* (Kim Darby). GUEST STARS: Van Johnson, Steve Allen, Craig Stevens, George Maharis, Lynda Day George, Norman Fell, Talia Shire, Dorothy Malone, Kay Lenz, Murray Hamilton, Mike Evans, Dick Butkus, Fionnula Flanagan, others.

EMMYS

Outstanding Lead Actor for a Single Appearance in a Drama Series—Ed Asner (1975–76), Outstanding Single Performance by a Supporting Actress in a Drama—Fionnula Flanagan (1975–76), Outstanding Directing in a Drama Series—David Greene (1975–76).

The other brother, Tom Jordache, was cast with a virtual unknown. Nick Nolte's trouble-prone, good-hearted "Poor Man" may have died at the end of the 12-hour series, but the actor was resurrected at the box office and went on to become one of Hollywood's true superstars, appearing in such films as *North Dallas Forty* (1979) and *Down and Out in Beverly Hills* (1986). In 1991 he received a nomination for an Academy Award as Best Actor for his work in *Prince of Tides*, and in 1992 *People* magazine proclaimed him "Sexiest Man Alive" (readers are left to choose which one is the greater honor).

The third unknown was a woman who had mostly done modeling before being chosen for the female lead. Susan Blakely starred as the brothers' love interest. She also appeared in a number of "disaster" films of the '70s, including *The Towering Inferno* (1974) and *Airport '79: The Concorde* (1979). Ed Asner, who was simultaneously appearing as Lou Grant on "The Mary Tyler Moore Show" on CBS, took time out to portray the German-born father of the Jordache brothers, winning an Emmy for his memorable performance.

The series was so successful that a spinoff was created called "Rich Man, Poor Man, Book II" (retroactively making the first version "Book I"). Nolte, by this time, was busily making theatrical films, and his character, who had died at the end of the first "book," was not brought back. The weekly series premiered in the fall of 1976, with Peter Strauss returning as Senator Rudy Jordache. It wasn't nearly as popular as the original miniseries, and concluded in March 1977.

The original "Rich Man, Poor Man" series was repeated on ABC from May 1977 to June of that year, and was later aired in a marathon of episodes on the TNT cable channel, where it was likely that it would be repeated from time to time. Although it was not yet for sale in video stores, in 1992 the entire 12 hours was available to subscribers to a special video club.

Van Johnson (left) and Nick Nolte.

LAVERNE AND SHIRLEY

NUMBER 3, 1975–76

One, two, three, four, five, six, seven, eight.
Schlemiel, Schlimazel, Hasenpfeffer Incorporated. *

The surprise hit of the 1975–76 season was a female "buddy" series, "Laverne and Shirley." It was a spinoff of a better-known show, "Happy Days," which had been on the air for six years before introducing these two characters. "Laverne" soon outstripped its progenitor, placing higher in the Nielsens than the original.

"Happy Days" was set in Milwaukee of the 1950s, and in one episode viewers were introduced to a couple of really tough chicks who worked at the local brewery. It was implied that these ladies were no ladies; they were friends of "The Fonz," and they had "been around." ABC's executive in charge at the time, Fred Silverman, caught their act and decided there might be a series for these two characters. Instead of a pilot, he had the two actresses—Penny Marshall and Cindy Williams—film a 10-minute scene together. The scene was shot on a Friday night, edited on Saturday, shipped to New York for a viewing by the ABC brass on Sunday, and a series was ordered on Monday. Just to cement the characters, they guested a few more times on "Happy Days," making their effort a true spinoff.

The series didn't have much of a road map when it hit the air in January 1976, and according to Penny Marshall, "We worked it out as we went along—on-the-job training." The basic story line had Laverne and Shirley fulfilling their dreams by working as bottle cappers in the mythical Shotz Brewery in Milwaukee, sharing an apartment while husband hunting ("We're gonna do it!" went the opening theme song). The two were also purified for television's self-proclaimed "family hour"—there was no indication of hanky-panky, as there had been on "Happy Days." These two were definitely saving themselves for marriage. Well, Shirley was; Laverne was trying.

There was a palpable chemistry between the two actresses/characters, who were cited as blue-collar versions of Lucy and Ethel from "I Love Lucy." Much of the humor was physical; sight gags abounded. One of the most memorable of the show's 178 episodes involved the pair's getting locked out and stuck on the roof of their apartment. It was a perfectly choreographed, yet spontaneous-appearing scene involving the use of ropes and toilet plungers deployed like ski poles—a classic routine worthy of Lucille Ball and Vivian Vance themselves, and one that must be seen to be appreciated.

The pair was blessed with sitcom land's obligatory wacky next-door neighbors. These two, though, seemed like aliens from the Planet Weird. Lenny and Squiggy were played by real-life former college buddies Michael McKean and David Lander, who were originally signed to be writers on the show; eventually the writers persuaded director Garry Marshall to add these two characters to the cast. "We were the amyl nitrate twins," said Lander. "You pop us and laugh for two minutes." The pair had their own brand of success: a record album, "Lenny and the Squigtones," in 1979, and a line of Lenny and Squiggy dolls.

There can be little doubt that the casting of Penny Marshall as Laverne De Fazio was the result of nepotism, since her father, Tony Marshall, was the series' producer, while brother Garry was one of the executive producers and directors (later, sister Ronny Marshall Hallin became casting director). Penny had arrived in Hollywood reluctantly in the early '60s and received encouragement and a part (from big brother/producer Garry) as Jack Klugman's wacky secretary on "The Odd Couple." She admitted she was terribly insecure and flustered from the start. "In the beginning when I was doing 'The Odd Couple,'" Penny said, "there were times Jack Klugman would

---

CREDITS

TOP 10 PEAK: No. 1, 1977–78.
EXECUTIVE PRODUCERS: Garry Marshall, Thomas L. Miller, Edward Milkis. PRODUCERS: Mark Rothman, Lowell Ganz, Monica Johnson, Eric Cohen, Tony Marshall. DIRECTOR: Garry Marshall. WRITERS: various. CAST: *Laverne De Fazio* (Penny Marshall), *Shirley Feeney* (Cindy Williams), *Andrew "Squiggy" Squiggman* (David L. Lander), *Lenny Kosnowski* (Michael McKean), *Carmine Ragusa* (Eddie Mekka), *Frank De Fazio* (Phil Foster), *Mrs. Babish* (Betty Garrett), others.

From left: Cindy Williams, Eddie Mekka, and Penny Marshall.

literally have to pick me up and move me to my mark, because I was too petrified to walk. In those days, if I moved on stage, it was only to back into a wall."

Cindy Williams had a background in movies (along with Ron Howard of "Happy Days," she was one of the many talents to emerge from the George Lucas 1973 film *American Graffiti*). She had to be coaxed into doing a full TV series as Shirley Feeney after having done the bit on "Happy Days" as a favor to Garry Marshall. "I wasn't interested," she said, "because my movie career was going pretty well...but my manager convinced me that it wouldn't hurt my career, and ABC offered an amount of money I didn't know existed."

But as the years wore on, Cindy Williams began to feel like a gate crasher at a Marshall family reunion. She was sure her part was getting smaller, her work schedule tougher. "I've never been under so much strain, doing a weekly series," said the actress who was used to the leisurely schedule of film production. "It's the most brutal work I've done since working the midnight shift at the House of Pancakes." She was also tired of playing straightwoman to Penny, who seemed to be getting all the laughs. Back in 1976, when the show was young, she tried walking out. It lasted two days. Writers were fired, changes were made, Williams was happy. But by 1982 things were coming to a head. Williams was pregnant, and her pregnancy was duly

incorporated into the show's format. Shirley Feeney, former terminal virgin, was now Mrs. Shirley Feeney Meany, married to Walter Meany, an army medic stationed overseas. When she walked off the show, her character was shipped overseas, too. Suddenly "Laverne and Shirley" was just..."Laverne." It didn't work. Ratings fell, and the series was cancelled in May 1983.

A cartoon version of "Laverne and Shirley" ran on ABC on Saturday mornings from 1981 to 1982, which used the voices of the original cast. In the fall of 1982, the show was combined into "The Mork & Mindy/ Laverne & Shirley/Fonz Hour," which continued until the fall of 1983.

After the show was cancelled in 1983, Penny Marshall began a whole new career. She went on to direct such prestigious films as *Big*, with Tom Hanks (1988), *Awakenings* (1990), and the 1992 hit, *A League of Their Own*.

---

*At the beginning of each episode of "Laverne and Shirley," the two girls would skip down the street, chanting these words while doing a little jig. *Schlemiel* is a Yiddish word meaning fool or born loser; *schlimazel* is Yiddish for a chronically unlucky person, or again, a born loser; and *hasenpfeffer* is a kind of German rabbit stew. These were familiar street terms in Penny Marshall's native Bronx, New York. The significance was never explained, although it appears to stem from a childhood ritual, a secret pact of the kind kids often make, chanting important-sounding words.

THE BIONIC WOMAN

NUMBER 5, 1975–76

Lindsay Wagner, with Max the Bionic Dog.

ABC already had a hit series on its hands with "The Six Million Dollar Man" (see page 226), which had been running since January 1974, when it launched this companion piece, giving television a bionic couple of superheroes complete with super ratings. But "The Bionic Woman" almost didn't happen.

The character first appeared in an episode of "The Six Million Dollar Man"; she was a tennis pro who became the world's first bionic woman (TV sci-fi talk for part human, part machine) following a terrible skydiving accident. By the time she was put back together by the doctors, she could run faster than a cheetah, rip doors off cars bare-handed, and hear a pin drop—10 miles away.

Actress and bionic-to-be Lindsay Wagner was 26 years old when she first played this superwoman. A former teenage model and rock singer, Wagner landed a job as a Universal contract player in 1971, at age 22, for a mere $162 a week. She made occasional appearances in such shows as "Owen Marshall, Counselor at Law" and "The Bold Ones," along with a couple of movies.

One of those movies, *Two People* (1973), was seen by "Six Million Dollar Man" executive producer Harve Bennett, who remembered her and suggested that she be cast in the role of the bionic woman. In order to realize his vision, Bennett developed a two-part love story involving the bionic couple. They were midway through the shoot when Lindsay Wagner's Universal studio contract expired. Bennett saw to it that it was extended long enough to complete the episodes. Then Wagner's character, Jaime Sommers, died at the end of the two-parter, the result of failed bionics.

Meanwhile, ABC's audience, which had been slipping away during the 1974–75 season, suddenly stood up and took notice of the new character. Letters began to pour into Universal and ABC bemoaning the death of this sexy, leggy woman whom many were now comparing to Lauren Bacall. ABC insisted she be brought back from the dead for another two-parter. Since this was science fiction, a suitable rationale could easily be found for her resurrection: she was frozen at the moment of death (a bionic cryonic?) until new, non-rejecting parts could be prepared for her; then she would be restored to life.

ABC approved the story, but by the time they did, Lindsay, whose contract had again lapsed, had found herself a new manager who was demanding 10 times what the studio was offering. ABC insisted on using her and no one else. She got her price, the new episodes

CREDITS

CREATOR: Kenneth Johnson. BASED ON: *Cyborg*, by Martin Caidin. EXECUTIVE PRODUCER: Harve Bennett. PRODUCER: Kenneth Johnson. DIRECTORS: various. WRITERS: various. CAST: *Jaime Sommers* (Lindsay Wagner), *Oscar Goldman* (Richard Anderson), *Dr. Rudy Wells* (Martin E. Brooks), *Jim Elgin* (Ford Rainey), *Helen Elgin* (Martha Scott). GUEST STARS: Lee Majors, Dennis Patrick, others.

EMMYS

Outstanding Lead Actress in a Drama Series—Lindsay Wagner (1976–77).

kicked off the 1975–76 season, and the ratings showed a whopping 45 percent share of the audience.

An ecstatic ABC programming chief Fred Silverman came up with a suggestion for a spinoff series starring Lindsay Wagner, called, simply enough, "The Bionic Woman." Once again, Universal somehow allowed her contract to lapse. Only a year before, Lindsay Wagner had barely been able to pay her rent; by the time her manager had worked out a deal on "The Bionic Woman," she was signed for $500,000 a year in salary, plus a hefty percentage of the profits for any future "Bionic Woman" dolls.

Soon Lee Majors, star of "The Six Million Dollar Man," got word of Wagner's salary; it was $200,000 more than he was making—and he didn't have a doll, either. If he'd had a real bionic fist, he probably would have put it through the glass and chrome walls of Universal's "Black Tower" (corporate headquarters). Instead, he demanded (and received) a renegotiated contract. But the relationship between the two stars was as a cool as the steel in their bionic body parts.

"The Bionic Woman" debuted in January 1976 and was an instant hit, garnering more than 40 percent of the audience in its time slot and finishing ahead of its parent show at the end of the season. The series stayed on ABC until May 1977, when it was moved to NBC (while "The Six Million Dollar Man" remained with ABC). At the same time, the show introduced a new bionic character. Max, the bionic German shepherd dog, appeared in December 1977 in an episode intended as a pilot for a spinoff series revolving around this Rin-Tin-Tin impersonator. The pilot didn't sell, and "The Bionic Woman" ended its run in 1978 (as did "The Six Million Dollar Man").

There were two reunion movies following the series' conclusions. In June 1987 "NBC Sunday Night at the Movies" presented "The Return of the Six Million Dollar Man and the Bionic Woman." It was intended as a pilot for a new series, but it didn't sell.

The bionic folks returned in May 1989 for "The Bionic Showdown: The Six-Million Dollar Man and the Bionic Woman." The TV movie ended with a bionic engagement for the couple, hinting that there was the possibility of a bionic wedding in store during a future bionic episode.

Meanwhile, Lindsay Wagner kept herself busy earning a living as a car salesperson—she starred in a series of Ford commercials. So far she hasn't ripped the doors off any of the cars.

PHYLLIS

NUMBER 6, 1975–76

Cloris Leachman.

Poor Mary Richards—all her friends were leaving. First Rhoda was spun off into "Rhoda." Then, five years into the "MTM" series (see page 192), Mary's obstreperous landlady, Phyllis, starred in her very own sitcom. Everyone, it seemed, was splitting for Spinoff City.

Phyllis Lindstrom, the off-center, borderline-obnoxious landlady of Mary Richards (Mary Tyler Moore), seemed an unlikely candidate for her own comedy. The character was now a widow, raising precocious teenage daughter Bess, and minus her never-seen dermatologist husband Lars. While Rhoda headed east to New York, Phyllis struck out for the West Coast, landing in San Francisco and setting up housekeeping with, of all people, her disapproving mother-in-law and the woman's second husband, a judge. In fact, a whole slew of new characters peopled Phyllis's world. She even found a job, as an assistant to a photo-studio owner.

The series premiered in the fall of 1975 and was an immediate hit. Several things contributed to the series' overnight success. First, there was character recognition. Although basically an unsympathetic character, Phyllis was familiar to audiences from "The Mary Tyler Moore Show," and they were willing to give her a chance. Second, Cloris Leachman herself was a fine, four-time Emmy-winning actress who worked hard at bringing her character to life. "It's a tremendous kick for me," said the actress, who at 49 years old had finally been given her own series. "I want to do it all over again a million times. It's just like a tickle." Then there was the enviable time slot CBS gave the new entry: Monday night, sandwiched between superhits "Rhoda" and "All in the Family."

Also, the show's writing was excellent. The series represented a bold "first" for television: it was the first sitcom to tackle the problems of a middle-aged woman adjusting to widowhood. To flesh out Phyllis's character the writers decided to leave the self-indulgent Phyllis penniless, thanks to no life insurance from her deceased hubby; she also had no appreciable career skills, unless one counted her "uncanny knack for choosing just the right wine for dinner." "Phyllis is a somewhat eccentric, off-the-wall lady with totally inappropriate reactions to situations," said co-creator/writer/producer Ed. Weinberger. "There's a lot of

Cloris in Phyllis—an incredible, unpredictable spontaneity. Both will take on anything and do anything."

Cloris Leachman began her career as a teenager when she worked on local radio shows in her native Iowa. She studied drama at Northwestern University in Chicago, won a Miss Chicago beauty pageant, and was a runner-up in the Miss America Pageant in Atlantic City in 1946. From there it was just a short hop to New York City, where she entered the new medium of live television. She eventually moved to Hollywood, where she appeared in such series as "The Untouchables," "The Virginian," "The Donna Reed Show," and "Dr. Kildare." She received an Oscar for her performance in *The Last Picture Show* (1971), which she found time to film during her breaks from "The Mary Tyler Moore Show." No snob about the medium of television, Cloris was thrilled with the prospect of her own series, but was quick to point out that she was nothing like her ditsy alter-ego. "I've played this loony, crazy role lots of times and still do," she said. "But the true part of me is not like that at all. That's just what I show people. The true part of me, I think, is very serious." Cloris Leachman continued to work in television series in the '90s, often starring in miniseries and made-for-TV movies.

Four weeks into the filming of "Phyllis" the series was struck by tragedy. Barbara Colby, who had been playing the part of Phyllis's boss, Julie Erskine, was fatally gunned down by a vanload of thrill-seeking gang members. The grief-stricken cast and crew, in that time-honored tradition, vowed "the show must go on." The role was recast with Puerto Rican actress Liz Torres, who had understudied for Rita Moreno on Broadway, now playing Julie, owner of Erskine's Commercial Photography Studio.

Within a year, however, the producers decided to give Phyllis a new job, in the hope of regaining some of the ratings, which had begun to slip toward the end of the first season. She now worked as an administrative assistant to a member of the San Francisco Board of Supervisors and had a decidedly less acerbic personality. Other changes included a marriage for her mother-in-law's mother and for her daughter Bess. None of this helped. The ratings continued to plummet, and at the end of the 1976–77 season, the show was cancelled.

CREDITS

CREATORS/EXECUTIVE PRODUCERS/WRITERS: Ed. Weinberger, Stan Daniels. DIRECTORS: Jay Sandrich, others. WRITERS: various. CAST: *Phyllis Lindstrom* (Cloris Leachman), *Bess Lindstrom* (Lisa Gerritsen), *Julie Erskine* (Barbara Colby, Liz Torres), *Leo Heatherton* (Richard Schaal), *Audrey Dexter* (Jane Rose), *Judge Jonathan Dexter* (Henry Jones), *Mother Dexter* (Judith Lowry), others.

THE SIX MILLION DOLLAR MAN

NUMBER 9, 1975–76

Lee Majors.

Martin Caidin had tried unsuccessfully for years to have his novel *Cyborg* made into a television series. The idea was rejected by virtually every studio in town. Eventually, Frank Price at Universal optioned the book, but took on a different approach.

Price decided not to turn the novel into a series. "I gambled and talked ABC into letting us do the project as a Movie of the Week—nothing more," he said. When the movie that was planned as a one-shot was aired on March 7, 1973, it outdrew a Bob Hope special, something ABC had never achieved before.

The network was encouraged, but was willing to order only a limited number of "Six Million Dollar Man" episodes—90-minute movies, really—to be aired in the fall as a monthly feature of the Saturday night "ABC Suspense Movie." But soon ABC found itself with a hole in its sagging schedule on Friday nights; a weekly series of one-hour "Six Million Dollar Man" episodes was ordered up, and by January 1974 the show was part of the regular lineup.

The program built an audience slowly, and by 1975 its ratings were high enough to give the series a number nine rating in the Nielsens. Ironically, the series had already produced an offspring— "The Bionic Woman" (see page 222); the spinoff zipped past its parent the same year to land in the number five position, making the 1975–76 season a truly bionic success story for ABC.

The show that started it all was part science fiction, part fantasy entertainment, geared towards adults, but with a wide juvenile following. The main character, Steve Austin (Lee Majors), was an astronaut who had sustained near-fatal injuries in a plane crash during a training mission. Thanks to the miracle of modern techno-medicine, plus the six million big ones of the title, Steve returned to life a new man (literally).

Of course, cybernetic life was not without its price for Austin, who was now obliged to make good use of his new body parts (super speedy legs, a nifty super-arm, and an incredibly far-sighted bionic eye) for the organization footing the bill, the fictitious Office of Strategic Operations. Thus armed (and legged and eyed), Steve Austin, under the direction of the O.S.O., basically proceeded to save humanity and the planet in general for the next four years.

The public adored this new, cartoon-like superhero. Executive producer Harve Bennett (who had helped develop "Batman" back in the '60s, and would spend the '80s as executive producer/writer of *Star Trek* feature films) explained in *TV Guide* why he thought the

CREDITS

TOP 10 PEAK: No. 7, 1976–77.
BASED ON: *Cyborg*, by Martin Caidin. EXECUTIVE PRODUCERS: Harve Bennett, Glen A. Larson. PRODUCERS: Michael Gleason, others. DIRECTORS: various. WRITERS: various. CAST: *Col. Steve Austin* (Lee Majors), *Oscar Goldman* (Richard Anderson), *Dr. Rudy Wells* (Alan Oppenheimer, Martin E. Brooks). GUEST STARS: Lindsay Wagner, Darren McGavin, Martin Balsam, Britt Ekland, Earl Holliman, David McCallum, Carol Lawrence, John Saxon, others.

series filled a need in the American psyche: "I felt the time was right for the old-fashioned idealistic hero—like the Lone Ranger or Gary Cooper—who comes along to fight evil. But our guy couldn't be invincible like Superman. With all his powers, he had to be questioning, vulnerable and in jeopardy every so often—so that the audience would root for him and empathize with the human part of him."

One of the things Bennett did was to employ slow motion to film the superhero at his bionic best, coupled with special background music. It lent an air of credibility to Steve Austin's heroic feats, and the public began to take their bionics seriously, even sending suggestions to the show's producers, like "He should never sweat from his bionic right armpit."

For a while, Lee Majors, who played Steve Austin, performed acting chores that were themselves somewhat akin to bionic feats. He filmed the pilot movie for "The Six Million Dollar Man" while he was still co-starring in "Owen Marshall, Counselor at Law," and he continued filming both series for the remainder of the 1973 season. The actor dropped the "Owen Marshall" role as his bionic career began to take off. "I've advanced one banana at a time," Majors said in *TV Guide*. "On 'The Big Valley' I was fourth banana behind Barbara Stanwyck. On 'The Men from Shiloh,' I was third banana to James Drury and Doug McClure. On 'Owen Marshall,' I was second banana. And now, finally, I've made it to top banana."

In 1975 the series introduced Austin's female counterpart, Jaime Sommers (Lindsay Wagner), and by January 1976 she was up and (speed) running in a series of her own. In the second year of "The Bionic Woman," that show changed networks, from ABC to NBC. Both series were executive-produced by Harve Bennett and backed by Universal. The practice of "cross-pollination" so popular in the 1970s saw Lee Majors and Lindsay Wagner not only appearing in each others' shows from time to time, but shuttling back and forth between two different television networks—the first (and so far still the only) time this had been done in television on a regular basis.

In June 1987 a reunion movie called "The Return of the Six Million Dollar Man and the Bionic Woman" ran on "NBC Sunday Night at the Movies." It was intended as a pilot, but was not picked up. They tried again in May 1989 with another TV movie, this time called "The Bionic Showdown: The Six Million Dollar Man and the Bionic Woman." Like its predecessor, it was not turned into a series.

ABC MONDAY NIGHT MOVIE

NUMBER 10, 1975–76

Designed as a seasonal substitute for "ABC Monday Night Football," the "ABC Monday Night Movie" premiered in January 1970 and has continued on and off ever since. Films have included both made-for-TV movies as well as theatrical releases. Among the movies presented over the years have been:

- *Marilyn,* a 1963 documentary narrated by Rock Hudson, featuring film clips from Marilyn Monroe's movies, including footage from her last (and unfinished) film *Something's Got to Give.*
- *Woman Times Seven* (1967), starring Shirley MacLaine, Peter Sellers, Rossano Brazzi, and Robert Morley, a Vittorio De Sica-directed film with MacLaine portraying seven different types of women, some funny, some perceptive.
- *The Bliss of Mrs. Blossom,* a 1968 joint U.S.-British film with Shirley MacLaine and Richard Attenborough, a farcical comedy about the unfaithful wife of a brassiere manufacturer who hides her lover in their attic.

Many of the films offered were intended as pilots for future series. Some of the better ones, although unsold, included:

- "The Barbara Eden Show." Post–"I Dream of Jeannie," this starred Barbara as a harrassed young serial writer, and co-starred Joe Flynn and Lyle Waggoner.
- "Catch 22." Based on the novel of the same title, this adaptation of the antics of a company of fliers during World War II would have been ABC's answer to CBS's "M*A*S*H." It starred a young Richard Dreyfuss as Yossarian.
- "The Karen Valentine Show."

Having been a success as a young schoolteacher in "Room 222," Karen was given this chance for a series of her own in which she played a girl Friday at a public relations firm. Co-stars were Charles Nelson Reilly, Kenneth Mars, and Henry Gibson.

During the hiatus of "Monday Night Football" in 1976, "The ABC Monday Night Movie" made it into the top 10 for the first time, offering such films as "The Macahans," a pilot for "How the West Was Won" that starred James Arness, Eva Marie Saint, Richard Kiley, Bruce Boxleitner, Kathryn Holcomb, William Kirby Cullen, and Vicki Schreck. It was an ambitious attempt to return to the glory days of the western, with a narration by that ever-present voiceover artist, William Conrad. The film received excellent ratings when it aired on January 21, 1976. In 1977 a six-hour sequel was aired, but it was another year before ABC fully launched this series, with 20 more hours running from February 1978 to April 1979. The concept was loosely based on the 1963 John Ford-directed motion picture of the same name. The executive Producer was John Mantley, who had worked with Jim Arness in his "Gunsmoke" days.

Another of that year's films was "The Young Pioneers." Based on the book *Let the Hurricane Roar,* by Rose Wilder Lane, daughter of Laura Ingalls Wilder (author of the *Little House* books), this movie starred Linda Purl and Robert Hays and dealt with homesteading in the rugged Dakota territory of the 1870s.

Other 1976 movies included *On Her Majesty's Secret Service,* the 1969 hit James Bond film (with George Lazenby); *True Grit* (1969), with John Wayne and Kim Darby; and *Five Easy Pieces* (1970), starring Jack Nicholson.

CREDITS
TOP 10 PEAK: No. 3, 1976–77.

Jack Nicholson in *Five Easy Pieces.*

HAPPY DAYS

NUMBER 1, 1976–77

I found my th-rill...   —RICHIE CUNNINGHAM
Aaaay!   —FONZIE

In 1971 Garry Marshall wrote and produced a pilot that was originally called "New Family in Town." It didn't sell as a series, but did end up as a segment of "Love, American Style" in February 1972, retitled "Love and the Happy Day." It starred Ronnie Howard, Anson Williams, Marion Ross, and Harold Gould (as the father). Not a lot of people sat up and took notice. But a young director fresh out of film school did. His name was George Lucas, and years before he would become famous as the creator of *Star Wars* and its sequels, he directed a nostalgic movie called *American Graffiti* (1973), based on his own teenage years. It had certain similarities to the "Love, American Style" episode, including lots of rock and roll, vintage '50s cars, and one of its stars—Ronnie Howard.

The popularity of both Lucas's film and a concurrent hit Broadway musical called *Grease* attracted the attention of the ABC executives. Fifties nostalgia was in. Realizing what they had, ABC contacted Garry Marshall and asked him to revise his series. One of their requests was to incorporate a gang of greasers; Marshall balked, then gave them an alternative. He'd include one character to *represent* the wrong side of the tracks. He patterned this new character, Arthur Fonzerelli, hereafter known as "The Fonz" or "Fonzie," after "the only guy in my old neighborhood who had a motorcycle. This guy was cool...he very rarely spoke; he just kind of hovered. He'd nod a lot and he'd make guttural sounds—and everybody would get out of his way," Marshall later wrote in *TV Guide.*

CREDITS

CREATOR: Garry Marshall. EXECUTIVE PRODUCERS: Garry Marshall, Eddie Milkis, Tom Miller, Bob Boyett. PRODUCERS: various. DIRECTORS: Garry Marshall, Jerry Paris, others. WRITERS: various. CAST: *Richie Cunningham* (Ron Howard), *Arthur "Fonzie" Fonzarelli* (Henry Winkler), *Howard Cunningham* (Tom Bosley), *Marion Cunningham* (Marion Ross), *Potsie Weber* (Anson Williams), *Ralph Malph* (Donny Most), *Joanie Cunningham* (Erin Moran), *Arnold* (Pat Morita), *Al Delvecchio* (Al Molinaro), *Chachi Arcola* (Scott Baio), *Lori Beth* (Linda Goodfriend), *Ashley Pfister* (Linda Purl), *Heather Pfister* (Heather O'Rourke). OTHER REGULARS: Misty Rowe, Crystal Bernard, Cathy Silvers, Ted McGinley, others.

Fonzie was originally meant to be just another of the show's many characters who occasionally showed up, muttered a few lines, then faded into the background. "You're a side character," he told Henry Winkler, the New York Jewish graduate of Yale Drama School who'd won the part of the tough, leather-jacketed Italian biker. But the audience turned out to have an ongoing fascination with the Fonz, who was basically a nice guy for all his bravado, so ABC ordered Marshall to amplify the part. Suddenly, main character Richie Cunningham and his pals were relegated to the back burner. The Fonz moved into new digs above Mr. C's garage (he always referred to the Cunninghams as Mr. and Mrs. C) so he could become part of the "family," and the ratings obliged by shooting to the top. "Happy Days" went on the air in January 1974 and hit number one in the 1976–77 season, staying in the top three for the next three years.

Fonzie was rapidly becoming the star of the show. Henry Winkler's billing was upped to the number three spot in the credits, right behind Ron Howard (now grown up and no longer "Ronnie") and Tom Bosley (who had assumed the role of the father played by Harold Gould in the pilot). Eventually, Winkler received second-from-the-top billing, just nipping at Ron Howard's heels enough to make him nervous.

Around this time the network began to have thoughts about changing the title. "Fonzie's Happy Days," they thought, would tell it like it was. Ron pleaded with Garry Marshall not to change the show's name, and he agreed. ABC then suggested a Fonzie spinoff. Again, Marshall refused. Fonzie without Richie was like Tonto without the Lone Ranger...Mr. Spock without

Captain Kirk...They needed to play off each other or it wouldn't work. Instead, Marshall gave ABC a different spinoff, "Laverne and Shirley" (see page 220). (Eventually, Fonzie did get his own cartoon series, an ABC Saturday morning animated show called "The Fonz and the Happy Days Gang," which ran from 1980 to 1982, and then was incorporated into "The Mork & Mindy/ Laverne & Shirley/Fonz Hour" for an additional season.)

Over the course of the series' 11 years there would be many additions and replacements in the cast, as producers added things to keep the show fresh. Once, they even added a Martian. Robin Williams's performance as the alien Mork, half-scripted, half-improvised, was such a hit with the live studio audience that all 300 of them gave this newcomer an unheard-of standing ovation at the end of the taping. It wasn't long before Mork from Ork (sorry, Mars) was given his own spinoff, "Mork & Mindy" (see page 250).

Yet another spinoff was the result of Richie Cunningham's kid sister, Joanie (Erin Moran), reaching young adulthood. "Joanie Loves Chachi" (1982–83) was not as successful as the other two offspring, and stars Moran, Scott Baio (Chachi), and Al Molinaro (Al) returned to the "Happy Days" fold the following season.

By the 11th season, the fabulous '50s had given way to the not-so-interesting '60s, and the cast was ready to move on. The series aired its last episode in the spring of 1984.

"Happy Days" later took its place as a television classic. The Smithsonian Institution in Washington, D.C., requested Fonzie's leather jacket for its collection, where it took a place of honor with other television memorabilia like Archie Bunker's chair and the original 14-foot model of the Starship Enterprise. (If ABC had had its way, Fonzie would have worn a cloth jacket instead of his trademark leather one. Garry Marshall was hell-bent for leather; the network, concerned that this might foster juvenile delinquency, insisted Fonzie could wear it only when using his motorcycle. So Marshall had the bike in virtually every scene the Fonz appeared in—including indoors. Eventually the bike was phased out, but the jacket stayed.)

On March 3, 1992, most of the "Happy Days" cast was reunited for a television special featuring clips from the original series with commentary by the cast members. Many of these talented people had gone on to successful careers in entertainment. Ron Howard became a well-known film director of such hits as *Splash* (1984), *Cocoon* (1985), *Backdraft* (1991), and *Far and Away* (1992). Henry Winkler ended up working behind the camera with his own production company. He co-produced the TV series "MacGyver," among other projects. Tom Bosley played Sheriff Amos Tupper on "Murder, She Wrote" for many years and assumed the title role in the whodunit series "Father Dowling Mysteries." Marion Ross (Mrs. C.) appeared in the critically acclaimed series "Brooklyn Bridge."

From left: Donny Most, Henry Winkler, Anson Williams, Ron Howard.

CHARLIE'S ANGELS

NUMBER 5, 1976–77

From left: Jaclyn Smith, Kate Jackson, and Farrah Fawcett-Majors.

Sexism in television reached a new low in 1976 when Aaron Spelling's "jiggle" show, starring three curvacious, scantily attired females, hit the airwaves and sent shudders through the women's movement. "Charlie's Angels" rode the crest of the so-called "T & A" (for "tits and ass") genre, a last-gasp backlash from the male bastion that controlled creative decision-making in the industry. Ostensibly it was all in good fun, but the series only served to perpetuate the myth of women as sex objects, albeit popular ones.

The show centered around a harem of female detectives under the auspices of an unseen employer named Charlie (voiced by John Forsythe), with David Doyle cast in the role of the (figurative) eunuch who oversaw them. The basic premise was this: each week, each "Angel" was placed in jeopardy at least once per episode (a gimmick that was so important it was included in the show's bible). An unwritten law called for each lady to wear up to eight new outfits per

episode, along with trendy styles of hair and makeup, the rationale being that not only would the slavering men in the audience be checking in each week to see just how much they could see of each Angel, but the female viewers would hopefully be attracted to these outward trappings in an attempt to emulate America's hottest sex objects.

Somehow the formula worked. Somehow, 50 million voyeuristic Americans cheerfully tuned in to this mindless sexploitation week after week, making the series one of the highest rated in its premiere season, 1976.

The show was formulated in the mind of producer Aaron Spelling, who had made a name for himself throughout the '70s decade with series like "The Mod Squad" and "The Rookies." In fact, one of the performers in "The Rookies," Kate Jackson, helped devise this new program in which she would star.

Originally the series was to be called "Alley Cats," and the three heroines were to be leather-jacketed, karate-chopping toughs. Jackson recalled in *Time* magazine that during the filming of "The Rookies" she was pacing the floor in Spelling's office, giving him her input during a brainstorming session for his new creation. "Suppose these three girls work for this detective named...Harry," she recalled saying. "And then I saw the intercom on Aaron's desk, and I said, 'Suppose you never see Harry. He always calls them on the squawk box. And suppose instead of tough—mmm...' And then I saw a picture on the wall of three angels. 'Suppose they're, like, Harry's angels.' " Since there was already a series with "Harry" in the title ("Harry O"), they eventually settled on Charlie. ABC's new chief Fred Silverman loved the idea, and Kate Jackson immediately segued from "The Rookies" into the role of brainy Angel Sabrina.

Of the original three Angels, only Jaclyn Smith would last all five seasons. Kate Jackson soon got too demanding when she actually began thinking there should be some meaningful *dialogue* for her character; her requests got her canned at the end of the third season. She later starred in a number of television series, including the hit show "Scarecrow and Mrs. King," with Bruce Boxleitner.

Farrah Fawcett-Majors (she would soon drop the hyphenated surname after a divorce from "Six Million Dollar" husband Lee Majors) was perhaps the best-remembered Angel. She came to the series by way of her Ultra-Brite smile and Wella-Balsam-shampooed tawny mane and soon found herself in demand as a model. She quit the show after one season, became the star of a best-selling poster that highlighted two of her finer points, and later went on to star in a number of television miniseries, including the highly acclaimed "The Burning Bed."

With Farrah's departure, the series' producers began what became a frequent ritual of replacing fallen Angels. Cheryl Ladd won the role of the departed Fawcett's younger sister (the fact that she was the sister-in-law of the head of 20th Century Fox didn't hurt her any in getting the part). Kate Jackson was replaced by Shelley Hack, who a season later was herself replaced by Tanya Roberts.

Over the years the show's popularity declined, due in part to the wearing off of the novelty and despite an effort on the part of the producers to lighten up on the perceived S & M aspects of the series. Still, co-executive producer Leonard Goldberg recalled his favorite episode for *People* magazine in a 1986 interview; it was a first-season one called "Angels in Chains." "The *New York Times* ran a huge photo of the girls chained together wading through a swamp," he said. "The show got a 56 share. The rerun got a 52 share. I told Aaron we should just run it every week until it dropped below 40 and then make another show."

Aaron Spelling, who would go on to create a whole packet of escapist hits in the late '70s and early '80s like "The Love Boat," "Fantasy Island," "Hart to Hart," "Dynasty," and the '90s hit "Beverly Hills 90210," recalled thinking the show was purely "great camp. How can you really believe there were three young private detectives making $500 a week, wearing $10,000 Nolan Miller wardrobes and working for a man who was just a voice on the telephone?" he said in *People*.

"Female critics thought we were exploiting women, but you really can't have it both ways—scream that there's not enough women in TV, and when you put them on say, 'Well, what we really want to do is show them as brain surgeons or running for President.' We could never figure what the griping was about." And that, perhaps, summed up the trouble with the show.

The producers attempted to create a male version of the series when in April of 1980 they aired an hour-long spinoff pilot for a series called "Toni's Boys." Toni, played by Barbara Stanwyck, headed an investigatory team of three men (Stephen Shortridge, Bruce Bauer, and Bob Seagren). But the beefcake version wasn't convincing, and the pilot didn't sell.

The producers never did see any fault in their sexploitation, but fortunately the television viewers were a lot brighter than they were perceived as being. After five years they cried, "Enough!" The series had slipped from the top 10 to place 59th out of 65 shows, and CBS cancelled the series in 1981 after five years and 115 episodes.

Will there be a reunion movie? Creator Aaron Spelling said in a 1986 interview, "I'd pay each of them a million dollars to do a two-hour 'Charlie's Angels' reunion movie. But it would be very difficult to get any three of the four originals to do it." While so far there have been no takers for his offer, the three original Angels—Kate Jackson, Farrah Fawcett, and Jackie Smith—continued to have periodic get-togethers of their own, the three having remained good friends over the years. (Spelling did try again with a pilot for a Fox Network series, "Angels '88 [named for the year, not the number of Angels]. By 1993, however, it still hadn't been aired.)

CREDITS

TOP 10 PEAK: No. 4, 1977–78. CREATOR: Aaron Spelling. EXECUTIVE PRODUCERS: Aaron Spelling, Leonard Goldberg. PRODUCERS: Rick Husky, David Levinson, Barney Rosenzweig. DIRECTORS: various. WRITERS: various (reportedly a total of 75). CAST: *Sabrina Duncan* (Kate Jackson), *Kelly Garrett* (Jaclyn Smith), *Jill Munroe* (Farrah Fawcett-Majors), *Kris Munroe* (Cheryl Ladd), *Tiffany Welles* (Shelley Hack), *Julie Rogers* (Tanya Roberts), *John Bosley* (David Doyle), *Charlie Townsend's Voice* (John Forsythe). GUEST STARS: David Ogden Stiers, Diana Muldaur, Tommy Lee Jones, Don Gordon, Dean Martin, others.

THE BIG EVENT

NUMBER 6, 1976–77

Director Franco Zeffirelli instructs Robert Powell, playing the title role in "Jesus of Nazareth."

"The Big Event" was an NBC umbrella encompassing major television "events" such as the first-time airing of blockbuster movies, specials, and quality made-for-television films. It premiered in September 1976 with a double-header, the idea being to get viewers to leave that dial set to NBC all evening. The initial 90 minutes offered the first network airing of the hit 1974 disaster film *Earthquake* (complete with thundering soundtrack simulcast on local FM stations), which concluded the following week. The second half of the evening was "the party of a lifetime!" according to the NBC hype department. The program, "live from New York," first saluted an upcoming Muhammad Ali–Ken Norton fight with a party at Madison Square Garden. Then it shifted to George C. Scott emceeing festivities from Shubert Alley and Sardi's Restaurant, where he toasted the new Broadway season. The show ended atop the Gulf & Western Building for a shindig hosted by Lauren Bacall and Leonard Nimoy, who previewed new movies.

Events like this were hard to top, but NBC did its best, like offering the first-ever network broadcast of that 1939 classic movie blockbuster, *Gone with the Wind*. The film was shown over two nights to accommo-

date its length; it helped push "The Big Event" into the Nielsen top 10 and became the highest-rated single program in television history to that date. Other hit theatrical releases given first-time airings were the 1968 science fiction thriller *2001: A Space Odyssey*, and *The Godfather Saga*, an edited-for-television, 450-minute marathon containing parts of the first two Paramount Pictures *Godfather* releases (1972 and 1974) with added footage.

Documentaries were popular "Events," such as producer Greg Garrison's look at "The First Fifty Years" of NBC, with lots of vintage film clips. It was so well received (and he had so much leftover footage, even after the first 270 minutes aired in November 1976) that a year later he offered up 150 minutes more in "NBC: The First 50 Years—A Closer Look." Another three-hour documentary was boiled down from a number of *Life* magazine features into "*Life* Goes to the Movies," with lots of clips from the '30s through the '70s.

One of the finest made-for-TV movies of this series was offered over two nights in November 1976. "Sybil" starred Sally Field, fresh out of her "Flying Nun" habit and ready to soar in the promising acting career that awaited her. Here she played a woman stricken with multiple personality disorder; her characterization of the tormented Sybil Dorsett, based on an actual psychiatric case, would win her an Emmy. Joanne Woodward co-starred as her therapist, Dr. Wilbur.

Another outstanding made-for-TV movie was 1977's nine-hour, four-part miniseries/movie "Holocaust." It starred future Academy Award-winning actress Meryl Streep, and won eight Emmys.

The biggest "Big Event" for the 1978–79 season was the 25-hour adaptation of James Michener's western saga, "Centennial," starring Robert Conrad, Richard Chamberlain, Clint Walker, Raymond Burr, Sally Kellerman, and Chad Everett.

Other outstanding made-for-TV movies included "The Moneychangers," "Jesus of Nazareth," and "Tail Gunner Joe," starring Peter Boyle as Senator Joseph McCarthy.

This eclectic series also included "An Evening with Diana Ross," "The 'Father Knows Best' Reunion," and "The National Disaster Survival Test," a home-audience participation program.

The series continued sporadically through the 1980–81 season, occasionally airing "Big Events" on other weeknights, not just on Sunday. The last "Big Event" was seen in 1981.

EMMYS

Outstanding Special, Drama—"Sybil" (1976–77); Outstanding Lead Actress in a Drama Special—Sally Field, "Sybil" (1976–77); Outstanding Writing in a Special Program, Drama—Stewart Stern, "Sybil" (1976–77); Outstanding Lead Actor in a Limited Series—Christopher Plummer, "The Moneychangers" (1976–77); Outstanding Performance by a Supporting Actor in a Drama Special—Burgess Meredith, "Tail Gunner Joe" (1976–77); Outstanding Writing in a Special Program—Lane Slate, "Tail Gunner Joe" (1976–77); Outstanding Limited Series—"Holocaust" (1977–78); Outstanding Lead Actor in a Limited Series—Michael Moriarty, "Holocaust" (1977–78); Outstanding Lead Actress in a Limited Series—Meryl Streep, "Holocaust" (1977–78); Outstanding Single Performance by a Supporting Actress in a Drama—Blanche Baker, "Holocaust" (1977–78); Outstanding Directing in a Drama Series—Marvin J. Chomsky, "Holocaust" (1977–78); Outstanding Writing in a Drama Series—Gerald Green, "Holocaust" (1977–78).

THE ABC SUNDAY NIGHT MOVIE

ABC had been airing two-hour theatrical features on Sunday nights since September 1963. It wasn't long before the network began supplementing these with made-for-television movies.

The series lineup included several notable films:

■ *The Last Picture Show*, the 1971 film directed by Peter Bogdanovich, had an all-star cast that included Timothy Bottoms, Jeff Bridges, Cloris Leachman, Ben Johnson, Ellen Burstyn, Cybill Shepherd, Eileen Brennan, Clu Gulager, and Randy Quaid. This study of a small Texas town was based on the novel by Larry McMurtry. Cloris Leachman and Ben Johnson won Oscars for their performances, and model Cybill Shepherd made her screen debut in this film.

■ *The Heartbreak Kid* (1972), Cybill Shepherd's second film, was also featured. The Neil Simon comedy, directed by Elaine May, also starred Charles Grodin, Jeannie Berlin, Eddie Albert, and Audra Lindley.

■ *The Valachi Papers* (1972), a bloody (though toned down for TV) movie about Mafia life as seen through the eyes of Brooklyn mobster-turned-informer Joseph Valachi, starred Charles Bronson, Jill Ireland, Joseph Wiseman, and Lino Ventura.

■ *Can-Can*, the 1960 musical starring Frank Sinatra, Shirley MacLaine, Maurice Chevalier, Louis Jourdan, and Juliet Prowse, featured such Cole Porter favorites as "I Love Paris," "Let's Do It," "Just One of Those Things," and "C'est Magnifique."

Blockbuster hits airing during the 1976–77 season that helped push "The ABC Sunday Night Movie" into the top 10 included (in order of air date) *Lawrence of Arabia* (1962), *You Only Live Twice* (1967), *Butch Cassidy and the Sundance Kid* (1969), *Catch-22* (1970), *I Never Sang for My Father* (1970), *Patton* (1970), *Airport* (1970), *Jeremiah Johnson* (1972), *The Way We Were* (1973), *Live and Let Die* (1973), *The Paper Chase* (1973), *The Long Goodbye* (1973), *Thunderbolt and Lightfoot* (1974), and *The Stepford Wifes* (1975).

Priscilla Barnes (left) and Joan Collins in *The Wild Women of Chastity Gulch*.

BARETTA

NUMBER 8 (TIE), 1976–77

Detective David Toma was a real-life Newark, New Jersey, undercover cop. In 1973 his life and times were dramatized in a Universal television production called, appropriately, "Toma." At the end of the first year, Tony Musante, the actor playing the title character, decided he didn't like the grind of weekly TV; with the completion of the 22nd episode, he tendered his resignation. The series hadn't been a top 10 powerhouse, which was to be expected since it was slotted against "The Waltons," but it was pulling in a decent audience, and the shocked producers were frantic. Who quits a television show after just one year, especially when it's just been renewed?

They decided to salvage the Toma character, but with a few changes here and there. Actor Robert Blake was cast in the role, with the new series to be titled "Toma Starring Robert Blake." But the producers eventually decided to make a clean break of it; rather than spinning off Blake as the established character, they changed Toma's name to Baretta, changed his location to California, and gave him a cheap hotel room for digs; they also threw in a seedy pal for a best friend and a talking cockatoo named Fred. About the only similarities between the the two cops were that they were both Italian and both used disguises. Baretta was just as likely to nab the bad guy of the week wearing his old-woman disguise as he was to show up in blue jeans and T-shirt. He was a street cop, and he took his dress code to the streets, too.

Aside from the cocky cockatoo, the series was noted for its equally cocky lead actor. Robert Blake was no stranger to Hollywood. He'd begun at the tender age of two when his family moved west from Nutley, New Jersey. The toddler and his siblings entertained in parks while his father played

guitar and passed the hat. Later the youngster, still known by his given name, Mickey Gubitosi, became pal to Spanky McFarland in "Our Gang"/"Little Rascals" comedies. A few years later he moved on to a series of *Red Ryder* cowboy movies; he was Little Beaver in 32 of these films. In 1948 he won the role of a young Mexican boy who sold lottery tickets in the Humphrey Bogart classic, *The Treasure of the Sierra Madre*. By the '50s and '60s, Blake was appearing in classic early TV series like "Fireside Theatre," "Have Gun, Will Travel," "Bat Masterson," and "The Rebel." He regularly appeared on the 1963–64 series "The Richard Boone Show" as a member of the repertory cast.

Blake's biggest pre-"Baretta" break was when director Richard Brooks cast him in the role of the killer Perry Smith in his 1967 film *In Cold Blood*. More movie offers followed: *Tell Them Willie Boy Is Here* in 1969, and *Electra Glide in Blue*, the 1973 film in which Blake played a motorcycle cop. It was this last role that brought him to the attention of the producers of "Toma," who selected Blake only a month before shooting began. Once they decided to scrap the character entirely, the writers spent the next three weeks creating the new series character and format.

Tony Baretta's pet cockatoo garnered almost as much attention as the show's star. Fred, whose real name was Lala, was purchased from his native Hong Kong by renowned motion picture and television animal trainer Ray Berwick. When the bird arrived, he could only speak Chinese—not very helpful if he wanted a Hollywood career. But he soon caught on, and learned to squawk "Freeze" on cue—a valuable bit of vocabulary in a cop series. He also learned tricks like "steal Baretta's hat." Soon he had

---

CREDITS

CREATOR: Stephen J. Cannell. EXECUTIVE PRODUCERS: Bernard Kowalski, Roy Huggins. PRODUCERS: Jo Swerling, Jr., Ed Waters. DIRECTORS: Bernard L. Kowalski, others. WRITERS: Stephen J. Cannell, others. CAST: *Det. Tony Baretta* (Robert Blake), *Billy Truman* (Tom Ewell), *Inspector Shiller* (Dana Elcar), *Lt. Hal Brubaker* (Edward Grover), *Rooster* (Michael D. Roberts), *Fats* (Chino Williams), *Fred the Cockatoo* (Lala). GUEST STARS: Andrew Prine, Madilyn Rhue, Paul Williams, Kim Darby, others.

EMMYS

Outstanding Actor in a Drama Series—Robert Blake (1974–75).

Robert Blake, with Fred the Cockatoo.

learned "steal the show," as Fred/Lala became a star with a $1,000-a-week salary and his own stunt double (named Weird Harold). And just like so many other stars, the bird was known to get grouchy from lack of attention.

Fred was not the only one known for testiness on the Baretta set. Robert Blake's temperament was legendary. Producer Jo Swerling, Jr., quipped, "There is a love-hate relationship with Robert—we love him and he hates us." Executive producer Roy Huggins concurred. "Blake is unlike most actors," he said in *TV Guide*. "He won't even accept good material. He wants to change all of it to fit him. Sometimes we have to rewrite something that is very, very good because Blake says he has no feeling for it. I suppose that if you're willing to see a very good script put aside and a different one put in at the last moment, then Robert isn't difficult to work with." Whatever problems Blake may have had, his persistence paid off when he was awarded the Emmy in 1975 for Best Actor in a Drama Series.

Early in the series' three-year run, ABC was set to cancel "Baretta." They had a change of heart when Robert Blake won his Emmy; the ratings improved when the series moved to Wednesday nights, and in the 1976–77 season it tied for number eight in the Nielsen top 10. The show continued until June 1978, when its ratings again faltered and it was finally cancelled.

Robert Blake later starred in a number of television movies, and in 1985 he worked briefly in the series "Hell Town." But his personal life was becoming a hell of its own; close to a nervous breakdown, Blake quit the series after just 16 episodes, with the reluctant blessing of then-NBC head Brandon Tartikoff, to seek therapy for his emotional problems. By 1993 his old energy was back, and he was developing a crime thriller that he hoped to shoot as a feature film.

ONE DAY AT A TIME

NUMBER 8 (TIE), 1976–77

For the first 17 years of my life I was my father's daughter; for the second 17 I was my husband's wife. Now I have to find out who I am.
—ANN ROMANO

"One Day at a Time" was the philosophy espoused by Ann Romano, a thirtysomething divorcée who decided it was time to be her own person. Striking out on her own, she left her husband and moved to the Big City (in this case, Indianapolis) with her two teenaged daughters, vowing to raise them by herself while pursuing a career. The concept wasn't that drastic for the time; by December 1975, when the show premiered on CBS as a mid-season replacement, it was one of Norman Lear's less controversial ventures. Ann Romano wasn't the bigoted Archie Bunker; she wasn't the crusading Maude Findlay. She was merely representative of a growing number of people—not necessarily feminists—who found themselves in similar circumstances. Still, *Ms.* magazine asserted that " 'One Day at a Time' comes closer than anything...in sitcom to portraying a feminist point of view."

Shortly after the show went on the air, Norman Lear pointed out he was trying to do for the divorced woman what " 'All in the Family' did for the bigot—make her comedically respectable." According to producer Alan Manings, who co-created "One Day at a Time" with his actress wife, Whitney Blake, "Our divorcée is not a chicly-turned-out woman of the world...she is vulnerable and scared—like a woman stepping off a high diving board and suddenly realizing she doesn't know how to swim." Ann was a free spirit, albeit a scared one, but bolstered by familial love—an extended family that for a while included the obligatory wacky neighbor, plus the building "super," Schneider—Ms. Romano (as she insisted on being called) muddled through, one day at a time.

Along the way, there were the usual Norman Lear situations to be covered: abortion, religious cults, epilepsy, mental retardation, premarital sex for the teenage daughters—in fact, quite a number of the early episodes dealt with the sexual aspect of the girls' maturation. The director of the National Organization for Women at the time, Kathleen Bonk, even went so far as to voice her concern in their media-reform project: "The daughters have been portrayed in a much more traditional way than the mother, more the stereotype of teenage girls whose first thought is how to attract a boy and get a date to the dance. I like the series overall, but I think there's been an overemphasis on the girls' sexuality."

Ann Romano was played by Bonnie Franklin, a pixieish woman who was herself a 32-year-old divorcée when she began playing the role. Franklin had been performing since the age of nine, when she danced on "The Colgate Comedy Hour." She attended Smith College and graduated from UCLA. While still a student, she appeared in several episodes of "Gidget" and "Please Don't Eat the Daisies." Following a tour of the Orient for the USO in a production of *Carousel*, she headed for Broadway, where she had parts in *George M!*, *Dames at Sea*, and *Applause*. It was there that she met Norman Lear, who told her, "Don't take work till you hear from me." She ignored him and went off to Cincinnati to do *Oh! Coward*, when she got the call to star in the pilot for "One Day at a Time."

CREDITS

CREATORS: Alan Manings, Whitney Blake. EXECUTIVE PRODUCERS: Norman Lear, Alan Rafkin. PRODUCERS: Alan Manings, others. DIRECTORS: Alan Rafkin, Hal Cooper, others. WRITERS: Norman Paul, Jack Elinson, Alan Manings, others. CAST: *Ann Romano* (Bonnie Franklin), *Julie Cooper* (Mackenzie Phillips), *Barbara Cooper* (Valerie Bertinelli), *Dwayne Schneider* (Pat Harrington, Jr.), *David Kane* (Richard Masur). OTHER REGULARS: Mary Louise Wilson, Charles Siebert, Michael Lembeck, Nanette Fabray, Ron Rifkin, Glen Scarpelli, Shelley Fabares, Boyd Gaines, Howard Hessman.

EMMYS

Outstanding Directing in a Comedy Series—Alan Rafkin (1981–82), Outstanding Supporting Actor in a Comedy—Pat Harrington, Jr. (1983–84).

Mackenzie Phillips (left) and Bonnie Franklin.

As the series pressed on through the almost nine years of its existence, the characters and story line had to evolve to keep up with the cast's two teenagers, who were going through the usual problems of youth—and then some. The saddest and most publicized development was the drug problem experienced by Mackenzie Phillips, who played the older daughter, Julie.

Phillips had been raised during the "sex, drugs, rock and roll" subculture of the '60s. Her father was a Papa—John Phillips, of the singing group the Mamas and the Papas. She had smoked pot by the time she was 12 and was an alcohol abuser by age 14. Her acting career was in full swing, too—at 13 she landed a role in George Lucas's *American Graffiti* (1973) plus guest parts in numerous television series. Her career seemed on track when she signed to play Julie Cooper in "One Day at a Time."

Two years into the series, the producers began to notice a marked change in her behavior, coupled with weight loss and disorientation. Then one night in 1977, Phillips was found semiconscious on a West Hollywood street. She was charged with disorderly conduct under the influence of alcohol or drugs; later the charges were dropped when she completed a rehabilitation program. Although she missed only six weeks of work, she was fired from the series in 1980 when her physical deterioration began to show on camera. An addiction to cocaine and other drugs eventually led her to a rehab clinic in New Jersey (along with her father, who reportedly was addicted to heroin). She returned in 1981 and spent the next two years back on the series. But in 1983 she again showed signs of severe weight loss and exhaustion. The producers wrote her out of the show (the character suddenly up and left her husband and child), this time permanently.

The other sister was played by Valerie Bertinelli. After the completion of "One Day at a Time," she was nicknamed "The Queen of Sweeps" by the press for her ubiquitous presence in made-for-TV movies that usually aired during the key ratings periods known as "sweeps." Bertinelli starred in "Rockabye," "Child's Name," "Shattered Vows," and the Judith Krantz miniseries "I'll Take Manhattan" (1987). In 1990 she starred in her own short-lived sitcom called "Sydney," in which she played a private detective. She married rock star Eddie Van Halen, and they had a son, Wolfgang.

In 1984 Bonnie Franklin and Valerie Bertinelli announced that this would be their last season on the show, so the producers found a way to wrap it all up, with Ann and her new husband moving to London. Reruns of the series could later be seen occasionally in syndication and on TBS.

THREE'S COMPANY

NUMBER 3, 1977–78

"Three's Company," which premiered on ABC in 1977, was long on sexual innuendo. The jokes consisted mainly of double entendres having to do with sex—who was getting any, who wasn't. Remarkably, it seemed that no one was, not even Jack Tripper, a young man surrounded by feminine pulchritude. There he was, rooming with two luscious roommates—dark, intelligent, earth-mothering Janet, and bouncy, jiggly, bubbly, airheaded Chrissy Snow (even her name suggested she was a flake)—yet their relationships were always platonic. He knew, of course, that he'd never be able to convince his suspicious landlord of that fact (and thus could end up homeless, and worse, roommate-less), so instead he convinced his landlord, Stanley Roper, that he was gay, which at least was an acceptable situation as far as the landlord was concerned. Roper himself was the butt of many sex jokes—in fact, his wife thought he *was* a sex joke. You see, he was impotent. But that's another story; in fact, this guy got his own series so audiences could laugh at his "headaches" without interruption (see page 254).

Most people knew this wasn't Shakespeare. It wasn't even "All in the Family"; although the writers of that series helped create this project for ABC, its format, like "All in the Family," derived from that of another British ancestor, "Man about the House." But what made this series so popular was its star, Suzanne Sommers. She had begun her career as a model and had landed a few bit parts—the elusive blonde in the T-Bird in *American Graffiti* (1973), for example—before becoming one of 250 women who auditioned for the role of Chrissy.

After she won the part, people began to confuse the actress with the character. This was not one dumb bunny. The actress, who has authored several books, insisted, "I have a sexy quality about me that often makes people not take me seriously. I always have to overcome the dumb blonde stereotype." The producers refused to make changes in her character, to give her some depth, infuriating the actress. As she said in a *Ladies' Home Journal* interview, "When people looked at me, all they saw was the hair, the curves, the big bosom...a girl that was easy to sell to the public—cute and cuddly, and unthreatening because she was dumb. It was insulting."

In 1981 Sommers's husband, Alan Hamel, took over managerial chores from superagent Jay Bernstein, demanding that his wife/client now receive 10 percent profit participation (her face was plastered all over merchandise like Chrissy Snow dolls and lunchboxes) plus a salary increase—from $30,000 per episode to $150,000. Not surprisingly, the show's producers decided it was time for some Snow in Fresno—they shipped the character there, writing her out of the series. Over the remaining three years of the show, assorted blonde bimbo-types were brought in to replace her, but nearly a decade later, the only female with name recognition to emerge from "Three's Company" was still Suzanne Sommers. She went on to star in "She's the Sheriff" and the hit ABC show "Step by Step," co-starring Patrick Duffy. (And she'd be happy to sell you the secret of her successful bod: it's the Thighmaster, and she starred in the infamous infomercials pitching it.)

John Ritter played Jack Tripper; the name was a pun—his character excelled in pratfalls. And so did Ritter, the son of famed western singer Tex Ritter. "With comedy," said Ritter, "everything is timing. I follow my instincts and try not to go for the pratfalls but for the real humor. All my life, I've known that I could make people laugh. It's nice to be able to do

---

CREDITS

TOP 10 PEAK: No. 2, 1978–79.
CREATORS: Don Nicholl, Michael Ross, Bernie West. BASED ON: "Man about the House," by Johnnie Mortimer and Brian Cooke. EXECUTIVE PRODUCERS: Ted Bergmann, Don Taffner. PRODUCERS: Don Nicholl, Michael Ross, Bernie West. DIRECTORS: Bill Hobin, Dave Powers, various. WRITERS: various. CAST: *Jack Tripper* (John Ritter), *Janet Wood* (Joyce DeWitt), *Chrissy Snow* (Suzanne Sommers), *Stanley Roper* (Norman Fell), *Helen Roper* (Audra Lindley), *Ralph Furley* (Don Knotts), *Larry Dallas* (Richard Kline), *Lana Shields* (Ann Wedgeworth), *Cindy Snow* (Jenilee Harrison), *Terri Alden* (Priscilla Barnes).

EMMYS

Outstanding Lead Actor in a Comedy Series—John Ritter (1983–84).

that on a weekly basis and get paid for it." Ritter balked at any intimation that "Three's Company" was a one-joke show. "It's not about sex—that's cheap," he said in *TV Guide*. "It's about sexual tension, and Americans are used to that; the viewers know the difference." The Academy of Television Arts and Sciences certainly did—they awarded John Ritter the Emmy for Outstanding Lead Actor in a Comedy Series in 1984. Ritter remained in the public eye after "Three's Company"; in the 1992–93 season, he starred in the new CBS hit series, "Hearts Afire."

The third roomie, Joyce DeWitt (who played Janet Wood), was pegged as the dark, smoldering, quiet one. Along with Ritter, she stayed with the series all seven seasons. The actress dropped from sight after "Three's Company," pursuing ventures outside the entertainment industry, but in 1993 she was considering television and motion picture offers and planning a comeback.

With the departure of Suzanne Sommers, the ratings took a tumble, and the series was cancelled a few seasons later. A second spinoff series, "Three's a Crowd," starred John Ritter again in the Jack Tripper role, this time rooming with his true love. Like "Three's Company," the show was Americanized from a British predecessor— "Robin's Nest," in this case. The series lasted one year. In 1993, "Three's Company" could be seen in reruns on cable.

From left: Joyce DeWitt, John Ritter, and Suzanne Sommers.

60 MINUTES
NUMBER 4 (TIE), 1977–78

Since 1968, the sound of a ticking stopwatch has introduced television's oldest prime-time series still in production—"60 Minutes." Additionally, this "CBS weekly magazine" holds multitudinous records:

■ It has finished at number one in three decades, first in the 1979–80 season, the second time in the 1982–83 season, and now in the '90s, beginning in the 1991–92 season.

■ It has ranked in the Nielsen top 10 for 15 consecutive years, 11 of those in the top five.

■ It is the most-watched news program ever to run on television.

■ It has had the same executive producer since 1968, Don Hewitt, now age 69 (with no intention of taking an "early" retirement).

■ It has consistently picked off the competition like so many ducks in a shooting gallery.

Among the series "60 Minutes" has trounced in the fatal 7:00 P.M. Sunday-night time slot (its home since 1975) have been "The Wonderful World of Disney," "Cos," "The Hardy Boys/Nancy Drew Mysteries," "Out of the Blue," "A New Kind of Family," "Those Amazing Animals," "Code Red," "Here's Boomer," "Ripley's Believe It or Not," "Voyagers," "First Camera," "Silver Spoons," "Punky Brewster," "The Disney Sunday Movie," "Our House," "21 Jump Street," "Incredible Sunday," "The Magical World of Disney," "Booker," "True Colors," "Parker Lewis Can't Lose," "Hull High," "The Adventures of Mark and Brian," and "Eerie, Indiana." In 1993 "Life Goes On" was surviving on ABC, but just barely; it was taking a beating in the ratings by this bulwark of CBS television.

The show covered a vast range of topics, from toxic waste to the plight of the Palestinians to fraudulent organizations. Over the years "60 Minutes" blew the whistle on any number of crooks, rip-off artists, and con men (and women); the show championed justice, often stuck up for the underdog, and remained dramatically entertaining, thanks to its reality-programming format. But according to creator/executive producer Don Hewitt, the reason for the show's longevity and ongoing popularity could be summed up in the phrase "Tell me a story." "I think people are interested in stories, not issues," he said, "even though the stories may be about people coping with issues."

Profiles of famous (and infamous) people were part of the "60 Minutes" stock-in-trade. The series gave its audience intimate glimpses of celebrities like Johnny Carson, Vladimir Horowitz, Jackie Gleason (who challenged interviewer Morley Safer to a game of pool), and Paul Simon. Political figures were a mainstay of the show; Mayor Teddy Kollek of Jerusalem, former Soviet Union President Mikhail Gorbachev, Admiral Hyman Rickover (the father of the nuclear submarine), the Ayatollah Khomeini at the height of the Iranian hostage crisis, Ronald Reagan, George Bush, Bill and Hillary Clinton—all had heard those oft-dreaded words, "There's a crew here from '60 Minutes'!"

The series played host to a number of reporters known as "correspondents" throughout the years. Mike Wallace, who was with the series from the start, held the record as the longest-running member of this team. Among the others have been (in chronological order) Harry Reasoner, Morley Safer, Dan Rather, Ed Bradley, Diane Sawyer, Meredith Vieira, Steve Kroft, and Leslie Stahl. James Kilpatrick and Shana

---

CREDITS

TOP 10 PEAK: No. 1, 1979–80.
CREATOR/EXECUTIVE PRODUCER: Don Hewitt. PRODUCERS: Joe Wershba, Paul Loewenwarter, Grace Diekhaus, Philip Scheffler, Barry Lando, Igor Oganesoff, David Buksbaum, Imre Horvath, Harry Moses, Marion Goldin, William McClure, Joe DeCola, Al Wasserman, others. DIRECTORS: various. WRITERS: various.

EMMYS

Outstanding Achievement in Magazine-Type Programming, Individuals—Mike Wallace (1970–71, 1971–72, 1972–73); Outstanding Achievement for Regularly Scheduled Magazine-Type Programs (1972–73); plus dozens more.

Alexander were early sparring partners during a 1970s segment called "Point/Counterpoint," inspiring a famous "Saturday Night Live" routine between Dan Akyroyd and Jane Curtin ("Jane, you ignorant slut!").

In the 1980s a spot was added for Andy Rooney. As the show's resident curmudgeon, he reported in depth on such topics as advertising on license plates, varieties of telephones, and the relative attributes of different kinds of soap. His spots became so popular he wrote several books based on them. He got himself in hot water in December 1989 during a CBS news special when he cited "homosexual unions" as a cause of "self-induced" death among Americans, referring to the AIDS crisis. CBS suspended him for three months, but he was reinstated after three weeks when the program's ratings showed a sharp decline.

"60 Minutes" spawned a wealth of imitators. They included "20/20" on ABC (the most successful), along with its ABC stablemate, "PrimeTime Live," anchored by "60 Minutes" alumna Diane Sawyer, who joined the steadily climbing series in 1989. In addition, the various "reality" series such as "Inside Edition," "A Current Affair," and "Hard Copy" all owe a debt of gratitude to "60 Minutes."

With "60 Minutes" poised to celebrate its 25th anniversary in September 1993, the future continued to look promising. Executive producer Hewitt, when asked about the series' future, stated in a 1992 *Los Angeles Times* interview, "Will it live forever? Well, did you ever think Pan Am would disappear? *The Saturday Evening Post*?" Meanwhile, the stopwatch is still ticking...ticking...ticking...

Clockwise from left: Harry Reasoner, Diane Sawyer, Morley Safer, Mike Wallace, and Ed Bradley.

LITTLE HOUSE ON THE PRAIRIE

NUMBER 7, 1977–78

Laura Ingalls Wilder was past 60 in 1932 when she wrote *The Little House in the Big Woods*, the first of her series of children's books in the *Little House* series. She based the tales on her own childhood, when she and her parents struggled to survive a rugged prairie life in Walnut Grove, near Plum Creek, Minnesota. Late at night, hunkered down in their frontier house of the 1870s, her Pa would tell his young family stories and play the violin while wolves howled in the distance. She related stories of her impoverished but spiritually rich childhood to her own daughter, at whose insistence she finally wrote her series of children's books.

Forty years later, Ed Friendly, one of the creators of television's "Laugh-In," had the rights to these novels and was eager to bring the stories to television. Friendly shopped around his newly acquired property to all three networks, but because it was too tame—no car chases, no special effects—there were no takers. Perhaps, thought Friendly, the networks would consider it if the right star were part of the package.

Meanwhile, Michael Landon had wrapped his work in "Bonanza," and was deluged with offers: there were 36 detective series, six doctor shows, and one about an astronaut landing on the wrong planet. "They all were the worst kind of junk," said Landon. The actor narrowed his choices down to two: one concerned an investigative reporter who learned about crime from the inside, after having spent nine years in jail; the other was "Little House on the Prairie," brought to him by Ed Friendly.

"I couldn't make up my mind," said Landon in *TV Guide*. He came home one day and

found his 12-year-old daughter engrossed in the Wilder books. "Then I discovered that my wife, Lynn, had devoured them too when she was a girl, and was reading them again. I thought, 'How wonderful if parents and children can watch this series together—and maybe it would start the kids *reading* the books after seeing the episodes on television. Imagine a TV show that would make kids read?' So I went to NBC and told them 'Little House' was it."

The network ordered a pilot film made, which, if successful, would be expanded into a series. But from the start, there were "creative differences" between Landon and Friendly. Friendly was a purist, wanting the series to remain faithful to the Wilder books, with the kids dressed in tattered clothes and going barefoot, and Pa sporting the long beard which the original Charles Ingalls had worn; Landon was adamant about the dangers of young actresses going barefoot at the Simi Valley location strewn with glass, snakes, and other hazards, not to mention his unwillingness to hide his visage from fans who wanted to see Michael Landon's face, a boon to ratings. The network, of course, wanted those ratings, and before long Friendly departed the show altogether, leaving Landon in charge.

Landon soon set himself up as executive producer, star, director (one out of every two episodes), and writer (one out of three). "If Michael Landon bombs," he said, "I don't want anyone else to have to take the blame but Michael Landon." After the first few years of slow but steady growth (typical for dramatic shows, as opposed to instant-hit

---

CREDITS

CREATORS: Ed Friendly, Blanche Hanalis, Michael Landon. BASED ON: The *Little House* books, by Laura Ingalls Wilder. EXECUTIVE PRODUCER: Michael Landon. PRODUCERS: John Hawkins, Kent McCray, various. DIRECTORS: Michael Landon, others. WRITERS: Michael Landon, others. CAST: *Charles Ingalls* (Michael Landon), *Caroline Ingalls* (Karen Grassle), *Laura Ingalls Wilder* (Melissa Gilbert), *Mary Ingalls Kendall* (Melissa Sue Anderson), *Carrie Ingalls* (twins Rachel Lindsay Greenbush and Sidney Robin Greenbush), *Nels Oleson* (Richard Bull), *Harriet Oleson* (Katherine MacGregor), *Nellie Oleson Dalton* (Alison Arngrim), *Willie Oleson* (Jonathan Gilbert), *Isaiah Edwards* (Victor French), *Jonathan Garvey* (Merlin Olsen), *Andy Garvey* (Patrick Laborteaux), *Albert Ingalls* (Matthew Laborteaux), *Almanzo Wilder* (Dean Butler). OTHER REGULARS: Hersha Parady, Linwood Boomer, Wendy and Brenda Turnbeaugh, Ketty Lester, Lucy Lee Flippin, others.

That's Michael Landon up there, driving the wagon.

sitcoms), he godfathered the series straight into a prime-time hit. Over the years Landon gave something back, too. He would often give an assistant director an opportunity to direct, or see to it that an extra who wanted to get a SAG (Screen Actors Guild) card would get lines of dialogue, or that a women's costumer who came to him with a story idea not only was encouraged, but had her story idea bought, got help in writing it, and got on-screen writer's credit. Little touches like these were what made his crew (many of whom followed him from "Bonanza" and to his other series) one of the happiest and most loyal in Hollywood.*

"Little House" espoused Landon's strong family values; the Ingalls weathered lost crops, dire financial straits, fires, floods, and the onset of blindness in daughter Mary, but never lost their spirit while pulling together as a family.

Americans followed the Ingalls family as it grew over the nine years the series aired. There were births, marriages, and eventually even a title change for the series. In 1982 Charles and wife Caroline Ingalls bid farewell to their brood, now mostly grown, as the younger generation launched a series of their own—"Little House: A New Beginning." The show then followed Laura Ingalls, now Mrs. Wilder, and her husband Almanzo as they struck out on their own.

In 1981 Michael Landon created a similar series for his co-stars Merlin Olsen and Moses Gunn. Their show, "Father Murphy," was set in a prairie town not unlike Walnut Grove. That series ran until 1984.

"Little House" aired its last episode in March 1983. A series of three reunion movies ran from 1983 to 1984: "Little House on the Prairie: Look Back to Yesterday," "Little House: Bless All the Dear Children," and "Little House: The Last Farewell," in which they destroyed the town of Walnut Grove (in a spectacular blaze of glory) before unscrupulous land developers took over. It was indeed the final farewell to the popular series.

Michael Landon went on to create, produce, direct, and star in NBC's successful "Highway to Heaven" series, again with most of the "Little House" crew and former co-star Victor French. The series ran from 1984 to 1989. In 1991 he had sold a new series, "US," to CBS. He completed the pilot but became ill during the spring of that year with what proved to be inoperable pancreatic cancer. He died on July 1 at the age of only 53. The pilot for his last projected series aired on September 30, 1991.

At services for the actor, his son, Michael, Jr., eulogized him by saying, "My father left us with a legacy we will cherish from one generation to the next. His shows touched our hearts, our souls, and our minds. He taught us the value of life and the importance of family."

---

*A personal note: I frequently crossed paths with Mr. Landon when his office was above our "Star Trek" offices at Paramount Studios. He always had a huge smile on his face, always stopped to say hello to anyone nearby, and cheerfully posed for photographs with secretaries who brought cameras from home hoping for just such an occasion. He lit up the building when he entered just as surely as if someone had turned on a switch. In short, we all adored him.

ALICE

NUMBER 8 (TIE), 1977–78

Alice Doesn't Live Here Anymore was a highly acclaimed movie released by Warner Bros. in 1975. The film's lead, actress Ellen Burstyn, won an Academy Award for her portrayal of a New Mexico widow who, together with her young son, headed west in search of a singing career but found herself instead.

When CBS and Warner Bros. decided in 1976 to create a television series based on the popular movie, they made some changes. Most noticeably, the title was shortened to just "Alice." Central to both film and series was Mel's Diner, and only Alice and Mel survived the transition. As usually happens when a film is translated into a TV comedy (though the film was not a comedy), new characters were added. Alice was still a widow with a 12-year-old son named Tommy (Philip McKeon), but they were from New Jersey (to accommodate actress Linda Lavin's eastern accent) rather than New Mexico. Mel's Diner was still in Phoenix, and Mel himself was played by the same man who had created the role in the movie—Vic Tayback. Waitresses Flo (Polly Holliday) and Vera (Beth Howland) rounded out the cast.

At first, star Linda Lavin was hopeful that she'd get to sing on the show each week. But the producers decided that it would interrupt the flow of laughs if Alice were to suddenly burst into five minutes of song. They compromised: Linda Lavin sang the show's theme, "There's a New Girl in Town."

Lavin's Alice was a new breed of television female role model, a working gal in search of a career, rather than a husband—part Mary Tyler Moore, part Ann Romano (of "One Day at a Time"), yet somehow all Alice. Lavin herself was in awe of her own success. Her

background had been as an actress on the New York stage, where she'd appeared in such productions as Jules Feiffer's *Little Murders* and the musical *It's a Bird, It's a Plane, It's Superman*. She had a minor role as the female detective in the first season of "Barney Miller," but little else until "Alice." "I couldn't get arrested in television," she said on "Entertainment Tonight" in 1992. "I couldn't get a television commercial. I was too fat, I was too short, I was too dark. I couldn't get into television. So it never crossed my mind that this would be where my biggest success was."

During the nine-year run of "Alice," Lavin became an outspoken champion of the rights of blue-collar working women, just as Alice Hyatt had become a symbol for these workers. "She represented over 80 percent of the women who worked," said Lavin. During the show's second season, she received the Grass Roots Award from the National Commission on Working Women, and was still involved with this organization in 1993. "We present awards to those who have done the best work in documentary and real-life drama or fiction," she said, "based on the lives of working women in this country, what they do and what they are about. They are all 'Alice' and 'Alice' is all of them." Lavin was always outspoken during the show's run, addressing rallies in support of the Equal Rights Amendment. Lavin said of Alice, "She spoke through me and I could speak through her. The show became my commitment to reflect the truth of the times, as I believe television must." After "Alice" left the air, Lavin returned to Broadway, where she won the Tony Award for Neil Simon's *Broadway Bound*. Returning to Hollywood, Lavin starred in the ABC sitcom "Room for Two"

CREDITS

TOP 10 PEAK: No. 4, 1979–80. BASED ON: *Alice Doesn't Live Here Anymore*, by Robert Getchell. EXECUTIVE PRODUCERS: William P. D'Angelo, Harvey Bullock, R.S. Allen. PRODUCERS: Bruce Johnson, Madelyn David, Bob Carroll, Jr., others. DIRECTORS: various. WRITERS: Martin Donovan, Arthur Marx, others. CAST: *Alice Hyatt* (Linda Lavin), *Mel Sharples* (Vic Tayback), *Florence Jean "Flo" Castleberry* (Polly Holliday), *Vera Louise Gorman* (Beth Howland), *Tommy Hyatt* (Philip McKeon), *Belle Dupree* (Diane Ladd), *Jolene Hunnicutt* (Celia Weston), *Carrie Sharples* (Martha Raye). OTHER REGULARS: Charles Levin, Dave Madden, Marvin Kaplan, Duane R. Campbell, Ted Gehring, Tony Longo, Jonathan Prince, others.

beginning in 1991, in which she played another widow, this time a talk-show host.

"Alice" became a hit in its second season, and much of the success was due to the family of characters around which the show was based. Mel's Diner was their "home," and Alice, Flo, and Vera were the family "siblings." Mel, played by Vic Tayback, bore the brunt of frequent jokes about his cooking ability, or lack thereof. This running gag followed Tayback in his real life. "If I walked into a restaurant, the other diners would look around and say, 'I hope you're not cooking,'" the actor said in a 1985 interview. Based on this characterization, Tayback became the spokesman for Heinz 57 sauce in their "I used to be a lousy cook" commercials. The actor had played numerous supporting roles in such films as *Bullitt* (1968), *Papillon* (1973), and *The Choirboys* (1977) before landing the part of Mel Sharples in the film *Alice Doesn't Live Here Anymore*. Tayback, a heavy smoker, had triple bypass surgery in 1983, and died of a heart attack in 1990 at the age of 60.

Polly Holliday's character Flo was best remembered for her signature remark, "Kiss mah grits!" Like her character on "Alice," Holliday was southern-born

(Jasper, Alabama). She was knowledgeable about truck stops and diners too, since her father was a truck driver. She also had a Broadway background, and "Alice" was her first major television role. The character was later spun off into her own series, "Flo" (see page 262). Holliday was replaced on the show for a while with a similar character, Belle Dupree, played by Diane Ladd, the actress who had played Flo in the movie.

Beth Howland played the ditzy but lovable waitress Vera. Part Gracie Allen, part Edith Bunker, a bit of Marie Wilson of "My Friend Irma," she had a childlike innocence that played well off the gruffness of Mel, the intelligence of Alice, and the smart-aleck zinginess of Flo. Howland was the only one of the three women with a television background, having worked on "The Mary Tyler Moore Show," "The Rookies," and "Little House on the Prairie."

"Alice" aired its last new episode in March 1985. The series had a final episode in which Mel sold the diner and gave each waitress a bonus of $5,000, and Alice, after slinging hamburgers for nine years, took off for a gig in Nashville and her long-awaited singing career.

From left: Beth Howland, Linda Lavin, and Vic Tayback.

MORK & MINDY

NUMBER 3, 1978–79

In 1978, when the producers of ABC's "Happy Days" decided to create a spinoff series for a one-time character they had introduced on that show, they had no idea that the result would be something akin to Prometheus unchained. Robin Williams, set loose upon the world, exploded onto the television screen in his full, unrestrained, off-the-wall glory. His character was changed from a Martian to an Orkian (Mork from Ork), but it was Robin Williams himself who seemed to be the stranger from a strange land. Thankfully, he took viewers along to whatever planet his mind happened to visit each week and along the way gave ABC one of its most unusual overnight hits.

If you were lucky enough to get tickets to a "Mork & Mindy" taping—and this was no mean feat, since the line often snaked along the curb for hours at Paramount Studios—you were treated to pure, unleashed, uncensored Robin Williams, standup comic, who could easily have been working at the Improv or Comedy Store instead of on a soundstage surrounded by heavy overhead lights and multiple film cameras. There *was* a script to follow, but woe unto the director who tried. In one hour's time, Williams, his mouth spouting topical one-liners faster than an Uzi sprays bullets, could easily do hundreds of jokes, mostly improvised. One was in the presence of genius, and knew it. Some of the best things, of course, were completely unusable, since they might relate to any number of contemporary or controversial topics like drugs, politics, sex, and so on. Some of these were saved for a "blooper reel"—outtakes viewed by the cast and crew at Christmas parties. But the general public was never privy to these gems, most of which were deemed too risqué for

the public. The final season yielded this tame example:

INSTRUCTOR (GIVING MORK A DRIVING LESSON)
Depress the accelerator.

MORK/ROBIN (TO THE ACCELERATOR)
Have you seen our ratings?

The series did have a format, when it could be adhered to. Mork had arrived on Earth from his home planet to observe humans. He was befriended by an Earth woman, Mindy, and of course ended up living with her. Mindy (like Tim in "My Favorite Martian," to which this bears some similarity) had to hide Mork's otherworldliness and keep his identity a secret. Not easy, since he had some strange habits, like sitting on his head and drinking with his finger. Producer Garry Marshall said, "We had Mork drink with his finger so children would put their finger in their orange juice and parents would say, 'What are you doing?' And the kid'll say, 'Mork does that,' and the parents'll take a look at 'Mork & Mindy.' "

Each episode ended on a semiserious note, when Mork would don his red and silver metallic space suit and report back to Orson (his superior) in a commentary expounding on some newly learned aspect of the human condition. More often than not, it was a well-written observation that nonetheless seemed totally out of place in this comedy.

Robin Williams was the son of a Ford Motor Company vice-president. His father's dream called for his son to be a welder; Robin had other ideas, and attended Juilliard on a scholarship (where one of his teachers was John Houseman and his fellow classmate was

CREDITS

CREATED BY: Garry Marshall, Joe Glauberg, Dale McRaven. EXECUTIVE PRODUCER: Garry Marshall, Tony Marshall. PRODUCERS: Bruce Johnson, Dale McRaven. DIRECTORS: various. WRITERS: various. CAST: *Mork* (Robin Williams), *Mindy McConnell* (Pam Dawber), *Frederick McConnell* (Conrad Janis), *Cora Hudson* (Elizabeth Kerr), *Orson's voice* (Ralph James), *Eugene* (Jeffrey Jacquet), *Franklin Delano Bickley* (Tom Poston), *Remo Da Vinci* (Jay Thomas), *Jean Da Vinci* (Gina Hecht), *Nelson Flavor* (Jim Staahl), *Exidor* (Robert Donner), *Miles Sternhagen* (Foster Brooks), *Mearth* (Jonathan Winters).

Robin Williams and Pam Dawber.

Christopher "Superman" Reeve). He quickly moved from street mime to standup comic to small roles on television, including an ill-fated "Laugh-In" revival. In the decade after "Mork & Mindy" wrapped, Williams became a top film star, always in demand. Movies included *Popeye* (1980); *The World According to Garp* (1982); *Moscow on the Hudson* (1984); *Good Morning Vietnam* (1987); *Dead Poet's Society* (1989), for which he received a Best Actor nomination; *The Fisher King* (1991), with another nomination; *Hook* (1991); *Toys* (1992); and *Aladdin* (1992), as the voice of the Genie.

Poor Mindy, or rather Pam Dawber, the actress with the unfortunate fate of playing opposite the whirling dervish named Robin Williams; she turned in fine performances each week, but playing straight woman to a hyperkinetic scene-stealer like Williams is every actor's worst nightmare. Dawber managed to keep her cool, and her gentleness contrasted nicely with Robin's *mishegoss*, even if she was relegated to lines like, "Oh, *Mork*..." each time he went off the deep end. Dawber was frustrated by what amounted to a thankless role when, during the show's first season, she found herself being pushed more and more into the background. "I keep telling myself that I shouldn't be annoyed," she

told *TV Guide*, "that it's just my ego being hurt. But the facts are certainly there. Robin is really unique, and I wouldn't dare try matching him joke for joke. But nobody could. I'm not a comedienne anyway." Searching for something positive to say, Dawber added, "The way I see my Mindy role is that I'm sort of an anchor—someone to give the show breathing room as Robin goes through his antics." After "Mork & Mindy," Dawber starred in her own series, "My Sister Sam," from 1986 to 1988.

By 1981 the ratings were indeed depressing, the novelty having worn off. The producers decided to allow Mork and Mindy to marry and have a baby. The "baby" was played by Jonathan Winters (Orkans are born old and age backwards). Winters was Robin Williams's idol, and their scenes together were truly classic. Unfortunately, the audience didn't seem to care. At the end of the 1981–82 season, Mork bid Orson—and the audience—a final Orkian "Nanoo, nanoo."*

---

*Mork continued to be seen from 1982 to 1983 in the Saturday morning animated series, "The Mork & Mindy/Laverne & Shirley/Fonzie Hour," with Robin Williams and Pam Dawber supplying their characters' voices. Reruns of the 95 live-acted "Mork & Mindy" episodes were being aired in 1993 on Nickelodeon.

ANGIE

NUMBER 5, 1978–79

Garry Marshall's track record for sitcoms included such powerhouse hits as "Happy Days," "Laverne and Shirley," and "Mork and Mindy." When he first approached ABC in 1979 with his latest co-creation (with Dale McRaven), his title for the new series was "After Once upon a Time." He was met with blank stares, and finally explained that Angie was the second part of Cinderella. No way, said the network brass. Marshall would have to think up another title. "So I let my imagination soar," he said sarcastically, "and I came up with 'Angie.' "

"Angie" was blessed with a fine cast—stars Robert Hays, Doris Roberts, Debralee Scott, and Donna Pescow in the title role—plus a wonderful ABC time slot, between "Mork and Mindy" and "Barney Miller." So it was not surprising that this series, which premiered in February 1979, would become a prime-time hit. The question is, why was it only a one-year wonder?

It's a difficult question to answer. The story line concerned a modern Cinderella. Angie, a blue-collar waitress in Philadelphia, fell in love with and married a blue-blood Main Line pediatrician. Of course, she wasn't aware of his wealth at first, but soon after the show's first episodes the dirt-poor kid learned she'd hit the jackpot. Not the most original of concepts, and the potential for poor-little-rich-girl humor was soon exhausted.

Donna Pescow starred as Angie, the lovable, warm, Italian waitress who found her Prince Charming. She had received critical acclaim for her role in the John Travolta hit movie *Saturday Night Fever* (1979), playing the unrequited-love-struck disco groupie Annette. Executive producer Garry Marshall spotted her and knew the Brooklyn-born actress was perfect for the starring role in "Angie." The actress at first was flattered to be selected for the series, but baffled. "You saw

CREDITS

CREATORS: Garry Marshall, Dale McRaven. EXECUTIVE PRODUCERS: Bob Ellison, Dale McRaven, Thomas L. Miller, Eddie Milkis. PRODUCERS: Alan Eisenstock, Larry Mintz, Bruce Johnson. DIRECTORS: various. WRITERS: various. CAST: *Angie Falco Benson* (Donna Pescow), *Brad Benson* (Robert Hays), *Theresa Falco* (Doris Roberts), *Marie Falco* (Debralee Scott), *Joyce Benson* (Sharon Spelman), *Randall Benson* (John Randolph). OTHER REGULARS: Diane Robin, Tammy Lauren, Emory Bass, Valri Bromfield, Susan Duvall, Nancy Lane, Tim Thomerson.

me only in a dramatic movie," she told Marshall. "How do you know I can do comedy?" "Listen," said Marshall, "when you know, you know." In an interview with *TV Guide,* Marshall stated: "Donna is down-to-earth. "She wears well, she has a natural presence. Men like her, women like her. She's a nice person." Audiences liked her too, although the series lasted only a year and a half. Pescow—"My name rhymes with cow, as in moo"—later appeared in episodic television and on stage, including touring with the musical *A, My Name Is Alice.* From 1987 to 1991 she starred as Donna Garland in the syndicated sitcom "Out of This World," playing the mother of a teenaged daughter who was part alien (with a father from outer space).

Co-starring on "Angie" was Robert Hays, who was perhaps best remembered as the captain in the airport disaster spoofs *Airplane!* (1980) and its sequel, *Airplane II: The Sequel* (1982). Hays had worked in both film and television. His most recent series included the title role in the TV version of "Starman," which ran on ABC from 1986 to 1987, and the short-lived series "FM" from 1989 to 1990.

Doris Roberts played Angie's Italian mother who operated a newspaper stand. Roberts won an Emmy in 1983 as Outstanding Supporting Actress for her role in an episode of "St. Elsewhere." From 1983 to 1987 she played the part of secretary/part-time detective Mildred Krebs on "Remington Steele."

Debralee Scott played Angie's sister Marie in the series. She first appeared in television in "Welcome Back, Kotter," in which she played Rosalie "Hotsie" Totzie from 1975 to 1976. She later appeared in Norman Lear's controversial comedy, "Mary Hartman, Mary Hartman," playing the part of Mary's kid sister, Cathy Shumway.

The second season of "Angie" found the producers making changes to the format—so often a fatal mistake. They decided to move the newlyweds out from under the rich wings of the in-laws. Angie and Brad moved into a modest house—and right on out of the prime-time lineup. The series was cancelled in the fall of 1980.

The theme song from the series, "Different Worlds," was sung by Maureen McGovern and became a hit single.

From left: Doris Roberts, Donna Perscow, and Debralee Scott.

THE ROPERS

NUMBER 8, 1978–79

When the producers of "Three's Company" first offered the part of Stanley Roper, the libido-less landlord, to actor Norman Fell, he turned them down. "I didn't really like the part," said Fell. "I didn't see how Audra Lindley [as Helen Roper] and I could sustain a one-joke relationship based on our sexual incompatability and my impotence." Eventually he was persuaded that working steadily in a television series might be better than the alternative of holding out for the "right" script—which doesn't pay the bills.

Within a year of its debut in 1977, the "Three's Company" production team began to plan for a spinoff series that would star the Ropers. Once again, Norman Fell wasn't interested. "It took me long enough to get into a hit series," the actor told Fred Silverman, then-programming chief at ABC. "Now you want to put me in something else. So then we do 13 weeks and get cancelled, and I end up with nothing." Silverman persisted until, nearly a year and a half later, Fell relented.

"Three's Company" had been based on a popular English sitcom called "Man about the House" (see page 242). When the British version spun off its landlords into an even more successful comedy called "George and Mildred," the American production counterparts decided this would be just the thing for their landlords, too. A spinoff series, appropriately called "The Ropers," was given a go for six initial episodes. With the benefit of a strong lead-in from the progenitor series "Three's

Company," "The Ropers" bowed on March 13, 1979, to a 55 percent audience share, the second-highest series-premiere rating in history to that time. An ecstatic ABC ordered up a full season's worth of episodes to begin in the fall of 1979. Boosted by the premiere rating, the

(see page 242)

CREDITS

BASED ON: "George and Mildred," a BBC television series. EXECUTIVE PRODUCERS: Don Nicholl, Michael Ross, Bernie West. PRODUCER: George Sunga. DIRECTORS: various. WRITERS: Johnnie Mortimer, Brian Cooke (who created the British version), others. CAST: *Stanley Roper* (Norman Fell), *Helen Roper* (Audra Lindley), *Jeffrey P. Brookes III* (Jeffrey Tambor), *Anne Brookes* (Patricia McCormack), *David Brookes* (Vean Cohen), *Ethel* (Dena Dietrich), *Hubert* (Rod Colbin), *Jenny Ballinger* (Louise Vallance).

---

series soared into the Nielsen top 10 for the 1978–79 season, leaving "Three's Company" in its wake.

It really was a one-joke show. After selling their apartment building, the Ropers purchased a new townhouse. "Bedrooms don't interest Stanley," cracked Mrs. Roper when the agent gave them a tour of their new home. Mrs. Roper didn't interest him either. There was very little foundation for a marriage here, or for a television series. Within a season it was gone—a one-year wonder.

Norman Fell was a highly successful actor when he accepted the role of Stanley Roper. Although his name wasn't a household word (and he was often confused with look- and sound-alike Jack Klugman), he had been featured in such films as *Inherit the Wind* (1960), *It's a Mad, Mad, Mad, Mad World* (1963), *The Graduate* (1967), and *Catch 22* (1970). He co-starred with Burt Reynolds from 1970 to 1975 in the TV series "Dan August," and appeared in "Rich Man, Poor Man" (1976–77). "If you drained the energy out of Joey Bishop," wrote Robert MacKenzie in his review of "The Ropers" for *TV Guide*, "you would be left with something like Fell, who plays Roper with a glum wariness that can be funny."

Fell eventually did warm to his character, stating in *TV Guide* in early 1980, "I love Roper now because he's a complete ass. I've come to realize that he's a lot like Archie Bunker. But also he's a small man, a vulnerable human being, consistently at the bottom rung of the ladder—and like Charlie Chaplin's tramp, occasionally kicking the rich man in the pants. I think audiences like him because they can say, 'Here's a guy who's lower than we are.'" Unfortunately, the ratings had dropped off drastically by the end of the first full season (September 1979 to May 1980), and ABC chose not to renew the series.

From left: Jeffrey Tambor, Audra Lindley, Norman Fell, Jillian Kesner, and Lois Areno.

TAXI

The 1978–79 season was a unique one in the Nielsen top 10. Nine out of the 10 series making that honor roll were situation comedies, and seven of them aired on ABC, the network that had struck sitcom gold. With "Taxi," the network finally struck *class*. There were no jiggly-giggly girls, no spaced-out aliens, no throwbacks to the glory days of the '50s in the series. Instead, this was a show with meaning, thoughtfulness, and quite a bit of heart.

At the heart of "Taxi" was a creative team that had just come off one of the most successful series of all time. When "The Mary Tyler Moore Show" wrapped after seven seasons, the series' producers defected from MTM studios to Paramount Pictures, where they had a deal to develop a new television series. James L. Brooks, Stan Daniels, David Davis, and Ed. Weinberger (yes, there's a period after his first name) had been part of the moving force behind Mary, Lou, Ted, Murray, and Sue Ann (see page 192). Now, instead of an upscale newsroom, they wanted to try something different. "We felt we'd explored that world, but 'Taxi' was a blue-collar situation, and it was about guys. That really appealed to us."

"Taxi" took place at the headquarters of the fictitious Sunshine Cab Company in New York City, which could be compared to a modern Dante's Inferno. The boss, Louie (Danny DeVito), was a Dispatcher from Hell, and most of the cabbies considered this place a Limbo, a temporary place to work until their careers happened.

"Taxi" owed much of its "MTM" feeling of family to the incredible casting. Like Mary's group, nearly every actor associated with "Taxi" would move on to become a major star in film or television.

Judd Hirsch played Alex Rieger, the only cabbie in the group who was happy with his fate. "I'm the only one in ["Taxi"] who *admits* he's a taxi driver," said Hirsch. "I know the score. The others depend on me for reality, for honesty." Hirsch had starred in the TV series "Delvecchio" from 1976 to 1977. Following "Taxi" he appeared in several films, and was the star of the popular NBC series "Dear John" from 1988 to 1991 (Ed. Weinberger, an executive producer on "Taxi," was one of the show's producers).

Danny DeVito parlayed his role as nasty dispatcher Louie DePalma into a career. Louie was known for endearing lines like "I hope somebody slams the cab door on your nose and you sneeze and your head explodes." As the quintessential meanie, DeVito went on to star in such films as *Romancing the Stone* (1984); its 1985 sequel, *The Jewel of the Nile*; *Ruthless People* (1986); *Twins* (1989); and *Batman Returns* (1992). He also became a sought-after director, with credits that included *The War of the Roses* (1989) and *Hoffa* (1992), in which he also co-starred. He married actress Rhea Perlman, a frequent guest star on "Taxi" (she played

---

CREDITS

CREATORS/EXECUTIVE PRODUCERS/WRITERS: James L. Brooks, Stan Daniels, David Davis, Ed. Weinberger. PRODUCERS: Glen Charles, Les Charles. DIRECTOR: James Burrows. CAST: *Alex Rieger* (Judd Hirsch), *Louie DePalma* (Danny DeVito), *Elaine Nardo* (Marilu Henner), *Tony Banta* (Tony Danza), *Bobby Wheeler* (Jeff Conaway), *Reverend Jim Ignatowski* (Christopher Lloyd), *Latka Gravas* (Andy Kaufman), *Simka Gravas* (Carol Kane), *Zena Sherman* (Rhea Perlman), *John Burns* (Randall Carver). GUEST STARS: Ruth Gordon, Tom Selleck, Ted Danson, Tom Hanks, Penny Marshall, Martin Mull, Martin Short, Bubba Smith, Tom Ewell, Victor Buono, others.

EMMYS

Outstanding Comedy Series (1978–79, 1979–80, 1980–81), Outstanding Lead Actress in a Comedy, Single Performance—Ruth Gordon (1978–79), Outstanding Directing in a Comedy Series—James Burrows (1979–80, 1980–81), Outstanding Lead Actor in a Comedy Series—Judd Hirsch (1980–81, 1982–83), Outstanding Supporting Actor in a Comedy Series—Danny DeVito (1980–81), Outstanding Writing in a Comedy Series—Michael Leeson (1980–81), Outstanding Lead Actress in a Comedy Series—Carol Kane (1981–82, 1982–83), Outstanding Supporting Actor in a Comedy Series—Christopher Lloyd (1981–82, 1982–83).

Louie's girlfriend) before landing the role of Carla the barmaid in "Cheers."

Christopher Lloyd joined the cast in the second season as the loopy ex-hippie, Reverend Jim. Lloyd also had a motion picture career after "Taxi" disbanded, playing mostly spaced-out or outer-space weirdos. In 1982 he played Kruge, a Klingon captain in *Star Trek II: The Wrath of Khan*. He co-starred in all three *Back to the Future* films (1985, 1989, 1990). He also appeared as a "Toon" in *Who Framed Roger Rabbit* (1989) and as Uncle Fester in *The Addams Family* (1991).

Tony Danza played Tony Banta, a role tailored for the former fighter. Danza had been a middleweight

Banta. Two days before the shoot, they changed it to Tony Banta—it was a reflection on my acting ability. They were afraid I wouldn't answer!" Danza was another "Taxi" alumnus who found success following that series. He became the star of the top 10 hit show "Who's the Boss?" (see page 308), which ran from 1984 to 1992.

Andy Kaufman was another bizarre character in this strange collection. Apart from the series he had his own repertory company of characters, and he played all of them. Like a comic with a multiple-personality disorder, he seemed to be everyone but Andy Kaufman. One minute he was the popular host of "Saturday Night Live" inviting women on stage to wrestle with him (and seriously meaning it), the next he was lounge lizard Tony Clifton; he did a mean Elvis impersonation, and he did a character called "The Foreign Man." It was the latter that evolved into the Latka Gravas character on "Taxi"—an illegal alien of vague Central European origin, underscored by his own concoction of pseudo-foreign-speak. It may have sounded like baby talk, but audiences embraced it and understood exactly what he was trying to say. It worked so well they gave him a lady compatriot, expertly played by Carol Kane, who managed to catch on to his patter and convince us that she too was from...wherever Latka was from. Andy Kaufman died of cancer in 1984 at the age of only 35, an abrupt and sad ending to a promising career.

Back row, from left: Andy Kaufman and Christopher Lloyd; center row, from left: Danny DeVito, and Carol Kane; bottom row, from left: Tony Danza, Marilu Henner, and Judd Hirsch

For all its critical acclaim, "Taxi" was a one-year wonder, never again attaining Nielsen top 10 laurels. The ratings, in fact, were so low that in its fourth season, ABC cancelled the series. NBC seized the opportunity to keep the "Taxi" meter running, and aired the show during the 1982–83 season. But the series continued to draw low ratings—not helped by the network, which switched the show's week night three times and time slot four times—and "Taxi" was finally cancelled in 1983, right before winning three Emmys for its final season. The series can be found in syndicated reruns, and was recently made available for purchase through a video club.

boxer with a mediocre record of four wins and three losses when an independent producer saw him training in a Manhattan gym. He persuaded the young pugilist that his future lay in acting, not boxing, and encouraged Danza to enroll in drama classes. The character Danza played on "Taxi" was originally very different. "The script had called for 'Phil Ryan,' who was an Irish heavyweight," said Danza in a 1992 "Entertainment Tonight" interview. "So they met me, made it an Italian middleweight, and they changed the name to Phil

THAT'S INCREDIBLE!

NUMBER 3, 1979–80

People have always had a certain fascination with the bizarre, the dangerous, and the potentially fatal. Who has not rubber-necked at the site of a freeway accident, or sat glued to the eleven o'clock news watching voyeuristically as victims are removed from a freak airline disaster? Back in the late '70s, someone found a way to bring such fare to viewers on a weekly basis, on cue, and for very little money. The genre became known as "reality programming"; today it is often called "tabloid TV" for its resemblance to the sensationalism most frequently found in rags such as *The Enquirer* and *The Star*.

"That's Incredible!" was ABC's answer to a popular show on NBC called "Real People." But "Real People" searched out folks in America's heartland with interesting or amusing stories to tell, whereas "That's Incredible!" became a circus sideshow, a stunt extravaganza, often presenting "stories" of dubious taste. The show bowed in March 1980 to a furor in the press. "At least you can use those tabloid papers to line the cat box," moaned *TV Guide*'s reviewer Robert MacKenzie. "Incredible or Inexcusable?" asked *Newsweek*. "Incredible or Abominable?" echoed *Time*. "The worst brew of bad taste yet concocted by the network witches," shouted Morley Safer of "60 Minutes." "A hybrid of '60 Minutes' and 'The Gong Show' designed by a network Dr. Strangelove,' cried *People*.

The protests were not over the simple things done by sideshow freaks, such as the Chinese gentleman who put needles through his skin and hung weights from them, or the woman who covered herself with thousands of bees, or the man who suspended himself over a pool filled with hungry sharks. These were tame by comparison to the stunt setups that ran amok. To wit:

- Daredevil Stan Kruml dashed through a 50-yard-long tunnel of fire in a "flame retardant" suit. Inside the tunnel, the temperature had reached 1,700 degrees.

Kruml emerged from the inferno in twice the anticipated time, his fingers seared to stumps. His fee for this "stunt"? A mere $8,000, less $6,000 for expenses.

- Yet another daredevil, karate expert Steven Lewis, planned to hurl himself over two cars rushing toward him at 100 mph. He misjudged his cue, smashing his left foot through the first car's windshield. His leg reportedly rotated twice around his knee. From his hospital bed, the man said he planned to try the jump again as soon as he healed (despite talk of possible amputation), perhaps using a trampoline the next time.

- Gary Wells, hoping to be the next Evel Knievel, attempted a motorcycle jump over the fountains at Caesar's Palace in Las Vegas. As a crowd of 2,000 people watched in horror while cameras rolled, Wells lost control of his motorcycle, crashing into a concrete wall at 80 mph. Wells suffered a ruptured aorta along with severe pelvic, skull, and leg injuries.

All of these incidents occurred within the first year of the series, arousing the ire of the press and much of the public. Creator/producer Alan Landsburg, in the book *TV Turkeys*, commented defensively, "We are paying people reasonably well to go out and do incredible stunts for us...An unsuccessful stunt does our program no good. If it's gore, we don't show it." George Englund, the producer of the motorcyle-jumping fiasco (which did air) explained, "Everybody in this business caters to ratings. That's the business. They are reality shows and they go for the ratings. This isn't some deep seminar on American culture." Yet despite their protests, the producers began toning down the stunts by the second season and inserted a disclaimer that became a catch phrase for all shows of this type: "Kids, don't try this at home!" It was a sensible move on the part of the producers and ABC, who were already up to their necks in lawsuits from things like the above feats of not-so-derring-do.

CREDITS

CREATOR/EXECUTIVE PRODUCER: Alan Landsburg. PRODUCER: Woody Fraser. DIRECTOR: Arthur Forrest. WRITERS: various. HOSTS: John Davidson, Cathy Lee Crosby, Fran Tarkenton, Christina Ferrare, Tracey Gold.

Cathy Lee Crosby interviews Yogi Amrit.

Soon audiences were being treated to "tamer" stunts. In what may have been the beginning of the 1990s craze, a group of bungee jumpers hurtled themselves off the 1,000-foot bridge at Royal Gorge, Colorado; a paraplegic climbed the Himalayas in a wheelchair; a yogi survived confinement in a two-by-two-foot box lowered underwater; a blind girl became a track star, thanks to her use of radar; and a man juggled three whirring chainsaws. (Kids, don't try this at home!)

All this footage was aired before a studio audience and presented by three toothsome co-hosts, dimpled singer/talk-show host John Davidson, former football pro Fran Tarkenton, and actress Cathy Lee Crosby. Crosby herself came closest to being incredible—her résumé listed her as a tennis champion, trapeze artist, skydiver, and windsurfer, as well as "Wonder Woman." Crosby had starred in the title role in an ABC *Wonder Woman* movie back in 1984; she later turned down the part when offered the series lead (which went to Lynda Carter). "I love the show," Crosby said in defense of

"That's Incredible!" "It offers a better way of entertainment. Fran, John and I are like the Three Musketeers, encouraging people to develop their potential." Tarkenton concurred, saying, "We're doing positive, educational things...Human triumph means risk; this show celebrates human triumph on all levels." Davidson was more practical, appreciative of his steady job. Said the singer, "It's good exposure, only one day a week and a lot of money."

The series' initial appeal wore off, and after the first season the show never made it into the Nielsen top 10 again. But there was enough audience interest to keep the show going throughout most of the decade; after a four-year run (1980 to 1984), the series took a break, then returned in 1988 with John Davidson, Christina Ferrare, and Tracey Gold hosting what was now retitled "Incredible Sunday." The series also spawned a spinoff called "Those Amazing Animals," hosted by Burgess Meredith, who introduced the audience to such wonders as two-headed snakes, square-dancing spiders, and cannibalistic rats.

DALLAS

NUMBER 6, 1979–80

"Dallas" was an American saga of lust, greed, power, and sex—all the good stuff that viewers came to enjoy during its 13-year run. It was the first successful night-time soap opera since "Peyton Place" had appeared in the '60s, with a worldwide popularity that ran to 200 million viewers each year.

The series premiered on April 2, 1978, and was declared a loser by the press. "Prime time soap operas about the rich and powerful haven't worked all that well in the last few seasons," declared *Variety*. " 'Dallas' is just as dull and contrived as two recent Nielsen failures...so there's no reason to expect that its five episodes will fare any better this spring." Wrong. Although originally conceived as a limited series of five episodes, "Dallas" went on to produce *356* episodes over the course of the next 13 years. All shows should be such Nielsen "failures"; by the 1980–81 season, thanks to the invention of the season-end "cliffhanger," "Dallas" became the number one show in the country, and it held down the number one or two spot for the next five years.

This story of Texas oil-well millionaires began with a partnership between two wildcatting oil men, Jock Ewing and "Digger" Barnes. The partnership was dissolved 40 years earlier than the show's time frame, and Jock Ewing made off with most of the profits, as well as Barnes's true love, Ellie. The marriage produced three sons: J.R., the unscrupulous heir to the Ewing empire; Gary, who left the Ewing ranch, Southfork (and got his own spinoff series on "Knots Landing"); and Bobby, the "good" brother who married Pam, the daughter of Ewing rival Digger Barnes. Over the course of the series, the drama played out in the lives of these characters, their loves, their feuds, their sexual dalliances, their lust for each others' money and power and greed and...well, you get the picture.

The very first cliffhanger occurred at the end of the first full season, in the spring of 1979. "We made a conscious effort to do what no one had ever done before," said executive producer Leonard Katzman. "We wanted people to have something to think about over the summer." What they thought about was this: J.R.'s pregnant wife, Sue-Ellen, downed a bottle of vodka, swiped a car, and proceeded to wrap it and herself around a telephone pole. Would she live? Would the baby she was carrying live? Tune in next fall.

And viewers did. The cliffhanger worked so well, it became a rite of spring each year. The next season was the mother of all cliffhangers—"Who Shot J.R.?" The show ended the season on March 21, 1980, when someone pumped two bullets into black sheep J.R. Ewing. Although he was the man people "loved to hate," fans spent all summer arguing over who had done the dastardly deed. The answer was such a highly guarded

---

CREDITS

TOP 10 PEAK: No. 1, 1980–81. CREATOR: David Jacobs. EXECUTIVE PRODUCERS: Leonard Katzman, Lee Rich, Philip Capice, Larry Hagman. PRODUCERS: Peter Dunne, Jim Brown, Calvin Clements, Jr., David Paulsen, Arthur Bernard Lewis, Cliff Fenneman, Mitchell Katzman, Howard Lakin, Ken Horton. DIRECTORS: various. WRITERS: various. CAST: *J.R. Ewing* (Larry Hagman), *John "Jock" Ewing* (Jim Davis), *Eleanor Southworth Ewing (Miss Ellie)* (Barbara Bel Geddes, Donna Reed), *Bobby Ewing* (Patrick Duffy), *Pamela Barnes Ewing* (Victoria Principal), *Lucy Ewing Cooper* (Charlene Tilton), *Sue-Ellen Ewing* (Linda Gray), *Ray Krebbs* (Steve Kanaly), *Cliff Barnes* (Ken Kercheval), *"Digger" Barnes* (David Wayne, Keenan Wynn), *Gary Ewing* (David Ackroyd, Ted Shackelford), *Kristan Shepard* (Colleen Camp, Mary Crosby). OTHER REGULARS/GUEST STARS: Joan Van Ark, Martha Scott, Jared Martin, Susan Howard, Dennis Patrick, Morgan Woodward, Ted Gehring, Audrey Landers, Anne Francis, Monte Markham, Susan Flannery, Craig Stevens, Howard Keel, Morgan Brittany, Christopher Atkins, Glenn Corbett, Priscilla Presley, Alexis Smith, Dack Rambo, Barbara Carrera, George Chakiris, Marc Singer, Alejandro Rey, Steve Forrest, Leigh Taylor-Young, Howard Duff, Mark Lindsay Chapman, George Kennedy, Shannon Wilcox, Barbara Eden, others.

EMMYS

Outstanding Lead Actress in a Drama Series—Barbara Bel Geddes (1979–80).

secret that four different endings were actually filmed so that not even the cast knew the answer. When the resolution aired the following fall (November 21, 1980), CBS charged advertisers a record $500,000 for a 60-second spot, and 300 million people in 57 countries tuned in to find out that the shots heard round the world were fired by Kristin Shepard, J.R.'s scorned sister-in-law (Mary Crosby). The episode set a record as the highest-rated show in television history (surpassed later by the 1983 airing of the final episode of "M*A*S*H"), with a Nielsen rating of 53.3 and a 76 percent share of the audience—some 83 million Americans.

Other famous cliffhangers included a fire at Southfork (May 6, 1983), the shooting of Bobby in J.R.'s office (May 18, 1984), and Bobby's being killed by a speeding car. This last one was necessitated by the departure from the series of Patrick Duffy, who played Bobby Ewing. But after a year, Larry Hagman persuaded Duffy to return to the fold to help the sagging ratings. The problem was, how could the writers resurrect the late, departed Bobby? At the end of the season, on May 16, 1986, Pam entered the bathroom to find—"Good morning!"—Bobby, in the shower. All summer, fans' tongues were wagging (who was that man in Pam's shower who looked like Bobby?). Then in September they learned the answer. Pam had pulled a Rip Van Winkle: she had dreamed an entire season's worth of episodes!

Bobby was alive and well, but by this time the show's ratings were not. The solution to the Bobby situation had stretched the show's credibility beyond the audience's tolerance. The series continued for a few more years. There were fiery explosions, more power struggles for Ewing oil, oil spills, the deaths of Pam and of Bobby's new wife April, and on and on. By 1991 the show was ranked number 61 in the ratings, and like an oil well that's tapped out, CBS knew the series had run its course.

A final episode, which aired on May 3, 1991, had J.R. being shown what life would have been like if he had never been born, a kind of *It's a Wonderful Dallas*, with Joel Grey playing the part of the angel/tour guide. In the last scene, a depressed J.R. (the audience was depressed by this point too, after seeing all the misery he'd wrought) headed into the study, pulled out a revolver and...The camera cut back to Bobby in the hallway, who heard the sound of a shot being fired.

Thus ended "Dallas," with yet another cliffhanger. Did J.R. succeed in killing himself? Did he miss? Is he only wounded, waiting to come back in some future reunion movie? The producers aren't saying. Stay tuned.

Linda Gray, Larry Hagman, and Mary Crosby.

FLO

From left: Sudie Bond, Polly Holliday, and Lucy Lee Flippin.

When Polly Holliday was tapped to play the character of Flo on the Warner Bros. series "Alice," she purposely avoided seeing the film *Alice Doesn't Live Here Anymore*, on which the "Alice" TV series would be based.

"I didn't want to be influenced by what Diane Ladd had done in the picture [as Flo]," she said. Shortly after "Alice" went on the air in August 1976, the producers began talking about a "Flo" spinoff, just in case "Alice" failed. They seemed to think that the character might be better suited to the sitcom audience's taste for quirky characters. So "just in case," Holliday began to create a back-story for Flo, who at that time didn't seem to have much definition as a character.

Holliday, an Alabama State College graduate with a degree in music (she once taught classical piano), had also studied drama. One of the techniques she had learned as a student was something she called "puzzle-solving."

"I take the dialogue the writer has written on the page," she once explained, "and then I use my imagination to construct an entire background for the character—from birth to the present. I write it all down, as if I'm doing a novel."

Holliday applied this technique to her character, and what emerged was a fleshed-out Flo. Holliday based the accent on people she grew up with in Alabama; she projected three failed marriages for her character, including one to a racecar driver and another to a Bible salesman (and one Flo didn't want to talk about); she saw her as a high school dropout, with few job skills. And since she mothered the younger waitresses in "Alice," she assumed that Flo was an older sister in a large family.

By 1978 the "Flo" spinoff was a near-certainty, and Holliday put the finishing touches on her character. But she went a bit too far. She imagined Flo would return to her native Cowtown, Texas, settle in with her feisty mother and uptight sister, and then fall madly in love with a politician who gets elected governor. Flo would now be First Lady of Texas—a working-class misfit among the tony politicians at the state capital. Close, but no chili pepper. CBS hired a staff of full-time writers to help "conceptualize" the series, along with Holliday.

Several months later, they had a premise: Flo left Mel's diner for a promising new job as a hostess in a Houston restaurant. Before she reached her destination, however, she was waylaid by a flat tire just outside her hometown of Cowtown, Texas. She popped into a roadside café that she remembered from her younger days, and, on an impulse, bought the place. She named it "Flo's Yellow Rose," and slowly but surely began to transform this rundown roadhouse into the place of her dreams.

Along the way, she had to deal with a bartender who didn't like having a woman for a boss, a miserly mortgage holder, and her mother and sister, who pitched in to help make the place a success. Of course, the menu included a special "side dish" of Flo's signature phrase "Kiss mah grits," served unrequested whenever anyone crossed the tart-tongued but warm-hearted good ol' gal.

The series premiered in March 1980 and became an overnight ratings sensation. Thanks to a strong lead-in from "M*A*S*H," "Flo" soon outstripped its parent, "Alice," to land in the number one position each week until the end of its abbreviated season, a strong enough showing to give it an overall seasonal ranking of number seven.

With the series taking off, Polly Holliday was suddenly hailed as one of television's all-time great comediennes. "She is one of TV's truly funny women," said *Time*; *TV Guide* said, "Miss Holliday is a talented comedienne, a good line-tosser, and CBS was not slow to see that she needed room to spread out beyond 'Alice.'...Just go with the Flo."

But as flows go, "Flo" was soon gone. The fledgling program never seemed to find a stable home. At the start of the series' new season, CBS placed "Flo" opposite ABC's "That's Incredible!" and NBC's "Little House on the Prairie," both popular shows. Then the network tried moving the series to Saturday night opposite the newly emerging hit, "The Love Boat." A couple of months later, they shifted "Flo" to Tuesday at 8:30, opposite "Laverne and Shirley." None of this helped do anything but confuse the audience. Ratings plummeted, and by July 1981 CBS's bright new hit had been cancelled.

"Alice," however, continued until 1985, but unfortunately for Holliday, there was a new resident Flo-clone, Belle Dupree, played by Diane Ladd, who had played Flo in the original movie. So Polly Holliday was without a television home. After "Flo," the three-time Emmy nominee (twice for "Alice," once for "Flo") limited her TV appearances to guest-starring roles.

CREDITS

CREATORS: Harvey Bullock, Jim Parker, Pam Chais, Jenna McMahon, Dick Clair, Polly Holliday. EXECUTIVE PRODUCER: Jim Mulligan. PRODUCERS: Ron Landry, Tom Biener, George Geiger, Jerry McPhie. DIRECTORS: Marc Daniels, Dick Martin, Tony Mordente, Wes Kenny, Robert La Hendro. WRITERS: Dick Clair and Jenna McMahon, Stephen Miller, Robert Illes and James Stein, Coslough Johnson, John Boni, Phillip Harrison Hahn. CAST: *Florence Jean "Flo" Castleberry* (Polly Holliday), *Earl Tucker* (Geoffrey Lewis), *Farley Waters* (Jim B. Baker), *Mama Velma Castleberry* (Sudie Bond), *Miriam Willoughby* (Joyce Bulifant), *Randy Stumphill* (Leo Burmester), *Fran* (Lucy Lee Flippin), *Les Kincaid* (Stephen Keep). GUEST STARS: Forrest Tucker, Henry Jones, Barbara Babcock, Vic Tayback, Hoyt Axton (who also sang the theme, "Flo's Yellow Rose").

THE DUKES OF HAZZARD

NUMBER 9, 1979–80

Tire-screechin', car-crunchin' good ol' boys burst forth with a horn that blasted the strains of "Dixie" on CBS in the fall of 1979 and raced right to the number two Nielsen spot faster 'n a sheriff on the trail of moonshiners. Part rural comedy, part adventure, "The Dukes of Hazzard" co-starred two southern bubbas and a shiny orange car. And the car got most of the fan mail.

Burt Reynolds had helped popularize the rural backroads adventure genre in his hit 1977 movie *Smokey and the Bandit*. Film producer/director Gy Waldron saw the success of Reynolds's feature and quickly dusted off his 1974 film *Moonrunners*, an action comedy about modern-day bootleggers starring Robert Mitchum. It adapted perfectly to a TV format audiences would soon come to know as "The Dukes of Hazzard."

The Dukes were quintessential backwoods hayseeds, denizens of mythical Hazzard county "somewhere in the South." Each week cousins Bo and Luke Duke confronted the residents, who represented every clichéd southern character imaginable: cutoff-clad buxom babes whose IQs equalled their chest sizes; the dim-witted, pot-bellied sheriff; and the corrupt local political boss.

All of them took a back seat to the General Lee. This "character," a bright-orange, souped-up 1969 Dodge, actually received more than half of the show's 60,000 pieces of fan mail in its heyday, more than any of the actors in the series. Some of the young fans (most members of the audience were kids) asked for *autographed pictures* of the General Lee, and the producers obligingly had the car make tire-tread prints over its eight-by-ten glossies. There were dozens of General Lees used each season, since car

chases and the inevitable wrecks that followed took a high toll on these stunt cars—about three per episode were hauled off for scrap after the show's stunt drivers had had their way with them. Described by Warner Bros. in the General Lee's "official biography," the car was a 1969 Dodge Charger with a 440-cubic-inch Magnum V8 engine. It had racing numbers on the doors, a Confederate flag on the roof, and, of course, no emission control devices that would slow this muscle car down. The show's stars, Tom Wopat and John Schneider, drove all their own stunts except the ones that involved jumping or rolling. Schneider had even attended the Georgia School of High-Performance Driving nine years before landing the role of Bo Duke, just in case he should ever need such skills as an actor.

The human cast members at first didn't seem to mind playing second bananas to a car. Schneider, a native of Mount Kisco, New York, was residing in Atlanta mostly doing Coca-Cola commercials when the producers started their talent search for one of the series' leads. He arrived at the Atlanta audition in a dilapidated pickup, unshaven and toting a six-pack of beer. He propped his feet on the desk, drank the beer and told them he was from "Snailville." The producers bought his hick routine and signed him on the spot. Co-star Tom Wopat really was from farm country— Wisconsin, not rural Georgia— and had had experience on the Broadway stage, plus TV soap operas.

Some critics were surprisingly generous in their assessment of "The Dukes of Hazzard." *Variety* wrote: "What reads as perfectly dreadful on paper was accomplished on screen with a contagious rollicking quality, a fine

---

CREDITS

TOP 10 PEAK: No. 2, 1980–81. CREATOR: Gy Waldron. EXECUTIVE PRODUCERS: Paul R. Picard, Phillip Mandelker. PRODUCERS: Gy Waldron, Rod Amateau, Myles Wilder, Ralph Riskin. DIRECTORS: Rod Amateau, others. WRITERS: Gy Waldron, Myles Wilder, William Raynor, Leonard Kaufman, Martin Roth, Bruce Howard. CAST: *Luke Duke* (Tom Wopat), *Bo Duke* (John Schneider), *Daisy Duke* (Catherine Bach), *Uncle Jesse Duke* (Denver Pyle), *Sheriff Roscoe P. Coltrane* (James Best), *Jefferson Davis "Boss" Hogg* (Sorrell Booke), *Cooter* (Ben Jones), *Deputy Enos Strate* (Sonny Shroyer), *Deputy Cletus* (Rick Hurst), *Coy Duke* (Byron Cherry), *Vance Duke* (Christopher Mayer), *The Balladeer/Narrator* (Waylon Jennings, who composed and sang the title song).

From left: John Schneider, Tom Wopat, and Catherine Bach.

one year for "Dukes" merchandising. Their contracts had called for them to get five percent, and so far each had only received $16,000. Later, Schneider claimed that the walk-off was really over better scripts. The show was putting more and more emphasis on car chases, he explained. "It got to be like a comic strip, so that every 'Dukes of Hazzard' episode was so much like every other 'Dukes of Hazzard' episode that people would stop me on the street and ask, 'When are you going to finish the reruns and get back to new shows?' They were *watching* new shows." The producers rejoined with "We're not doing Proust or *Lysistrata*. We're only interested in the ratings." Warner Bros. countersued for $90 million, and the two leads quit. Bo and Luke were written out of the show, and a nationwide search for Duke lookalikes resulted in Byron Cherry and Christopher Mayer being hired from the more than 2,300 people who auditioned.

Cousins Coy and Vance were the new Dukes, but the fans didn't cotton to them. The ratings plunged to Number 30. Wopat and Schneider, unemployed actors, weren't faring too well, either. Both sides soon realized the error of their ways, and by February 1983, Warners, Wopat, and Schneider had dropped their respective lawsuits and countersuits and

sense of pace and self-deprecation and a sound track of sprightly instrumental country music that adds up to amusing blue-collar fun." Others criticized the show for its dialogue, or lack of it. *TV Guide* bemoaned lines like "Sure got ourselves in a heap o' trouble, cousin" (from Bo) and "You got that right" (Luke), and dubbed the series "moron heaven." Tom Wopat was quick to defend the show, saying "The critics forget that a very large percentage of the population of this country is not sophisticated and doesn't want to be."

In the spring of 1982, the series' two leads both walked off the show and filed suit for $25 million, claiming that the company had earned $190 million in just

resumed their collaborative relationship, with Cherry and Mayer becoming victims of TV politics—as far as the show was concerned, they were history.

The series was never able to regain the ground it had lost, although it continued cranking out new episodes for two more years, until it was cancelled in 1985. From February to November 1983, an animated Saturday morning series called "The Dukes" used the voices of Wopat and Schneider. A short-lived spinoff called "Enos" gave Sonny Shroyer as Deputy Enos Strate his own series (1980–81); after it was cancelled, Shroyer returned to "The Dukes of Hazzard" in 1982 till the end of the series.

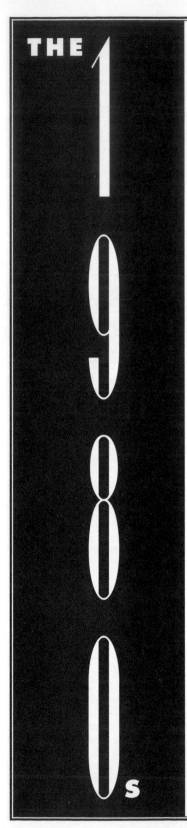

THE 1980s

he face of television was irrevocably changed during the 1980s. No longer monopolized by the Big Three networks, TV expanded to include a fourth network— Fox Broadcasting Company (FBC)—and a host of pay cable channels that provided entertainment and services. The television set itself became a tool, rather than a passive entertainment provider. While some viewers were still content to "vege out" on the sofa like "couch potatoes" (to use a descriptive phrase coined during the period), others hooked up TV "monitors" to video games and computers and began a process of interaction that, over the years, would become an increasingly important part of the TV experience.

But in the '80s the most revolutionary development came in the form of the VCR (video cassette recorder), which put control of television viewing squarely in the hands of the consumer. People watched what they wanted, when they wanted, choosing from an inventory of cassettes that included virtually every movie ever produced.

As if that weren't enough, a proliferation of cable channels offered an array of specialized entertainment and information choices. The channels included ESPN for sports, Lifetime for health and reruns of great shows like "LA Law" and "thirtysomething," E! for entertainment, the Comedy Channel for laughs, the Nostalgia Channel for oldies-but-goodies, plus the Discovery Channel, the Weather Channel, the Family Channel, the Travel Channel, C-SPAN, American Movie Classics, the Disney Channel, several shopping channels, and more. And one man—Ted Turner—brought viewers not one but *four* cable channels providing news, headlines, and movies.

The familiar network fare was still there, too. In the first half of the decade, the Nielsens were packed with cop shows, mysteries, and detective shows, plus nighttime soap operas like "Dallas," "Dynasty," "Falcon Crest," and "Knots Landing." New superstars emerged from the '80s, including Michael J. Fox, Tom Selleck, and (once again) Bill Cosby, the latter almost single-handedly resurrecting the dying genre of the TV sitcom. By 1986 sitcoms were again in vogue, holding down eight out of the top 10 positions. Television was once more a laughing matter.

THE LOVE BOAT

NUMBER 5, 1980–81

Come aboard; we're expecting you!
—OPENING SONG

When Douglas Cramer and partner W.L. Baumes acquired the rights to former cruise director Jeraldine Saunders' book, *The Love Boats*, they knew just what formula to apply to sell this as a television series to ABC. "You take 'Love, American Style'-type romances, interweave them on a luxury liner, get a regular cast of likable people, bring in lots of guest stars..." Sold. ABC ordered up a pilot after hearing just this much. Cramer knew that this was really just his old series, "Love, American Style," set afloat, with the difference being a core group of regulars to anchor each week's three stories.

It seemed simple, but it took three pilots to launch "The Love Boat" as a series. "The chemistry of the regulars was all wrong at first," said Cramer. The third pilot, however, was the charm. "The New Love Boat" aired on May 5, 1977, and introduced Gavin MacLeod, the former wisecracking Murray Slaughter of "The Mary Tyler Moore Show," as Captain Merrill Stubing. His casting proved to be the necessary final touch, and the series premiered that fall.

Critics ridiculed the new show, predicting it would sink faster than the Titanic. But they underestimated the power of love, and "The Love Boat" quickly torpedoed the competition, including the reigning queen of Saturday night, Carol Burnett. Audiences warmed to the floating parade of Hollywood's top stars, many of whom clamored to appear in one of the three weekly tales of love; the show's group of regulars seemed to click as well.

Bernie Kopell played the ship's doctor, who was ever-eager to make housecalls at the drop of a bikini. Kopell had been in television for years, playing everything from the leather-jacketed KAOS agent Siegfried on "Get Smart" to characters on "That Girl," "The Doris Day Show," and Mel Brooks's bizarre comedy, "When Things Were Rotten" (Kopell played Alan-a-Dale).

Ted Lange signed aboard as Isaac, "Your Ship's Bartender." Ted took his role so seriously he enrolled in bartending school for a 12-week course after receiving a letter from a fan accusing him of not knowing how to mix a proper martini. "I studied up on it," he said. "I had to. Just like I had to take fencing lessons when I did Shakespeare." Lest he be typecast, he added, "I saw myself as a bartender, but not servile. I wanted to project character, some warmth, not a black cliché."

Fred Grandy played the goofy and impetuous yeoman-purser "Gopher." Grandy, it turns out, was a Harvard graduate, *magna cum laude*, class of 1970. He stumbled into television by way of off-Broadway,

---

CREDITS

CREATORS: Douglas S. Cramer, W.L. Baumes. BASED ON: *The Love Boats*, by Jeraldine Saunders. EXECUTIVE PRODUCERS: Aaron Spelling, Douglas S. Cramer. PRODUCERS: Gordon and Lynne Farr, Henry Colman, others. DIRECTORS: Richard Kinon, Stuart Margolin, Alan Rafkin, Ted Lange, others. WRITERS: various. CAST: *Captain Merrill Stubing* (Gavin MacLeod), *Doctor Adam Bricker* (Bernie Kopell), *Burl "Gopher" Smith* (Fred Grandy), *Isaac Washington* (Ted Lange), *Julie McCoy* (Lauren Tewes), *Vicki Stubing* (Jill Whelan), *Judy McCoy* (Pat Klous), *Ashley Covington Evans* (Ted McGinley). GUEST STARS: Arte Johnson, Marion Ross, Bonnie Franklin, Meredith Baxter-Birney, Suzanne Somers, Jimmie Walker, Tom Bosley, Helen Hayes, Lillian Gish, Lew Ayres, Janet Gaynor, Douglas Fairbanks, Ginger Rogers, Ann Miller, Ethel Merman, Della Reese, Carol Channing, Florence Henderson, Charo, Bert Convy, John Ritter, Joyce DeWitt, Robert Walden, Ann Jillian, Donna Dixon, Hugh O'Brian, Jayne Meadows, Gene Rayburn, Jessica Walter, Samantha Eggar, Barbara Rush, Raymond Burr, Pearl Bailey, Steve Allen, Eleanor Parker, Ray Milland, Dick Martin, Stephanie Zimbalist, Bert Parks, Parker Stevenson, Rosey Grier, Eva Marie Saint, Soupy Sales, Susan Strasberg, Milton Berle, Barbara Billingsley, Mackenzie Phillips, Annette Funicello, Lilli Palmer, Telly Savalas, Jack Klugman, Susannah York, Priscilla Barnes, Loretta Swit, Marc Singer, Peter Barton, Colleen Dewhurst, John Davidson, Christopher Norris, Trevor Howard, Janet Jackson, and *hundreds* more.

commercials, and a couple of films. He would stay with the series throughout the entire nine-year cruise, but he later put his education to use. In 1992 Grandy won his fourth term as an Iowa congressman.

In 1979, 12-year-old Jill Whelan was added to the cast as Captain Stubing's daughter, Vicki. She played that role throughout her entire teenage life—not a bad one, since the cast and crew took an annual cruise themselves aboard one of the Princess Lines ships that plowed the waters off Mexico and/or Alaska. In 1993 Whelan was working as a production assistant at Madison Square Garden, where she helped set up acts, and she planned to produce projects of her own one day.

The ship's perpetually perky cruise director, Julie McCoy, turned out to be the only story without the happily-ever-after "Love Boat" ending. The actress playing Julie, Lauren Tewes, fought an addiction to cocaine throughout the seven years she was on the show, and suffered from emotional problems over her appearance and weight, her newfound stardom, and many of the difficulties Hollywood can present to the unprepared. She was also undergoing the breakup of her marriage, all of which contributed to her bent toward self-destruction. In 1984 the producers declined to renew her contract, instead adding a new cruise director, a Julie-clone named Judy McCoy. Tewes eventually overcame her addiction and returned for a two-hour special episode in November 1985. Later she appeared frequently in television commercials.

Over the course of the nine years, the show used more than 1,000 guest actors and actresses who romanced their way across the high seas (many were ABC stars on other shows that the network wanted to push). Lana Turner had the distinction of appearing as the one-thousandth guest in episode number 200,

which aired the first week of May 1985. The spot paid a hefty $25,000, a fee reserved for the show's top guests, not bad considering each show was divided into three 20-minute segments, with each guest usually only having to appear in one of them.

The show was filmed on a million-dollar set on a sound stage at 20th Century Fox, which duplicated the lounges, decks, and even the swimming pool of the real ships. But there was always an annual junket aboard the real thing. Paying passengers were given the choice of taking that cruise knowing there might be "inconveniences" involving the film crew and equipment; those who opted to cruise with the cast of "The Love Boat" (and there was always a waiting list) often found themselves being used as extras, and all passengers had the chance to mingle with their favorites as well as a "who's-who" roster of guest stars.

The series finally succumbed to the ratings crunch (plus they had used up every actor in Hollywood—Arte Johnson appeared so much they almost made him a regular). After the cancellation in 1986, there were three "specials" and a February 1990 reunion movie on CBS—"The Love Boat: A Valentine Voyage." In 1993 it seemed quite likely that there would be more reunions in the future.

Meanwhile, in 1993 Gavin MacLeod could be seen almost daily on various commercials touting Princess Cruises ("It's more than a cruise; it's the Love Boat"), the cruise line that had exclusive use of the licensed trademark "The Love Boat." He was also busy playing another captain, "Cap'n Andy," in the touring stage company of *Show Boat*.

While cruising was turning into the travel industry's hottest-selling vacation of the '90s, reruns of "The Love Boat" were steaming full-speed ahead in syndication.

From left: Ted Lange, Fred Grandy, Bernie Kopell, Gavin MacLeod, Lauren Tewes, and Jill Whelan.

HOUSE CALLS

Wayne Rogers (left) and Raymond Buktenica.

Another example of a television series derived from a movie, "House Calls" was based on the 1978 Walter Matthau film *House Calls*, a moderate hit at the box office. As a television series, however, this was just what Doctor Nielsen ordered. Premiering mid-season, the show garnered sensational ratings, especially during the slowest time of the year—the Christmas lull. Sandwiched between "M*A*S*H" and "Lou Grant," the series attracted a 35 percent share on Christmas Eve and a 37 on New Year's Eve. By its third week it was up to number 13 in the ratings; its first full season (1980–81) placed the show squarely in the top 10.

At first critics were, well, critical. They saw it as a rather tame sitcom about a bachelor with an eye for the ladies and his comely administrative assistant, but they liked the chemistry between these two characters, comparing them to Robert Wagner and Stefanie Powers (of "Hart to Hart") and even (in the opinion of executive producer Jerry Davis) to Cary Grant and Irene Dunne.

Wayne Rogers played the doctor who delighted in tickling the ladies' funny bones (or more, if they'd let him). He knew his way around a stethoscope from his three-year residency on "M*A*S*H" (1972–75). In that series he'd played Trapper John, a character who eventually got his own spinoff show called "Trapper John, M.D." But Rogers missed out on getting the part he had originated on television. Asked in *TV Guide* if he was disappointed, he replied, "Was Elliot Gould [Trapper John in the original movie version] disappointed? It's like originating a role in a Broadway play. Someone else eventually comes along and replaces you, and brings his own dimensions and character to the role. I'm delighted with the show and I wish them success, but I'm not sorry not to be in it." Rogers actually had several careers, so acting roles were only part of his concern. He had real estate holdings, corporate investments, condominiums, and a partnership in a Hollywood management firm. One of the most popular celebrity-hangout restaurants in Hollywood—the Columbia Bar and Grill—was owned by Rogers.

Lynn Redgrave starred opposite Rogers as his romantic interest. She was born into an acting dynasty, the youngest child of Sir Michael and Lady Redgrave (actress Rachel Kempson). Older siblings Vanessa and Corin entered acting while Lynn was still a growing child in England. And growing she was—she had a problem with weight control that eventually won her the lead in *Georgy Girl* (1966).

"Looking at my horrible, ugly bulk on that huge screen was the turning point of my life," she later admitted. "I never really had acknowledged my fatness before. Now I knew I *had* to diet and get thin." She did, and kept it off in the years that followed. In addition, she went on to become the spokesperson for Weight Watchers International, and wrote a book about her struggles called *This Is Living*.

After the birth of her third child in 1981, there were disputes between Lynn Redgrave and the show's producers that eventually made headlines. The actress claimed she was being harrassed for breastfeeding her baby on company time. That incident was resolved, but her salary demands were not. Her contract was not renewed; she appeared in eight episodes of the 1981–82 season, then was written out of the show (her character suddenly departed for England).

Redgrave was replaced by Sharon Gless, who was already under contract to Universal. It was painfully difficult for her to try to fill Redgrave's shoes; Lynn had been extremely well-liked by her fellow cast and crew and they weren't quick to accept a replacement into their ranks. It didn't matter. There was other trouble brewing. Wayne Rogers, who had profit participation and creative control in the series (he was involved in all production aspects, including scripts, editing, and casting) decided he wanted more than the $65,000 he was getting per episode. Universal and CBS decided differently. They cancelled the series at the end of the 1981–82 season. Sharon Gless immediately segued to "Cagney and Lacey" (see page 290). Wayne Rogers simply continued making money—in areas other than acting.

CREDITS

CREATORS: Max Shulman, Julius J. Epstein. BASED ON: *House Calls* (1978), by Shulman and Epstein. EXECUTIVE PRODUCERS: Jerry Davis, Arthur Gregory. PRODUCERS: Sheldon Keller, Bill and Kathy Greer, others. DIRECTORS: various. WRITERS: various. CAST: *Dr. Charley Michaels* (Wayne Rogers), *Ann Anderson* (Lynn Redgrave), *Jane Jeffries* (Sharon Gless), *Dr. Norman Soloman* (Ray Buktenica), *Dr. Amos Weatherby* (David Wayne), *Mrs. Phipps* (Deedy Peters), *Head Nurse Bradley* (Aneta Corsaut), *Conrad Peckler* (Mark L. Taylor).

TOO CLOSE FOR COMFORT

NUMBER 6, 1981–82

From left: Deborah Van Valkenburgh, Nancy Dussault, Audrey Meadows, and Ted Knight.

When "The Mary Tyler Moore Show" ended in 1977, virtually all the principals struck out on their own, landing in starring roles in new series (see page 192). For Ted Knight, who had played the loudmouth, buffoonish news anchor Ted Baxter, there was the promise of solo glory in "The Ted Knight Show." Unfortunately, the show lasted exactly six episodes, and then was felled by the cancellation axe.

Part of the problem was that Ted had become hopelessly typecast, forever associated with his characterization of Ted Baxter, a role that earned him two Emmy awards. "For a long time," said Knight in *TV Guide*, "*I* really didn't believe there was a Ted Knight. I thought Ted Baxter had swallowed him whole...No one seemed to remember anything I did before 'The Mary Tyler Moore Show' and a lot of people didn't seem to think I could do anything else."

Actually, Knight had had a lengthy career long before entering the world of television. Born Tadewurz Wladzui Konopka, the Connecticut native attended acting school on the East Coast. After graduation, he worked as a disc jockey, announcer, singer, ventriloquist, puppeteer, and pantomimist. He entered television in its early years, appearing in roles on such shows as "Lux Video Theatre," "The Lieutenant," "The Outer Limits," and "The Wild Wild West" before landing his job on "The Mary Tyler Moore Show." He also had a career doing voice work for a number of Saturday morning cartoons, including "Fantastic Voyage," "Journey to the Center of the Earth," and "Superfriends."

Eventually, ABC raided the British larder for yet another sitcom based on a British series—in this case one called "Keep It in the Family." Ted Knight was cast in the role of a conservative, middle-aged cartoonist who worked at home while his two daughters, striking out on their own, moved into the apartment downstairs. Thanks to a good time slot— "Three's Company" provided the lead-in—the series inched its way into the Nielsen top 10 by its second season. The show was a perfect companion piece to "Three's Company"; Knight represented

respectability, while his daughters were part of the jiggle set, the preceding show's forte. Upstairs, Henry Rush (Ted) and his pleasant wife Muriel (Nancy Dussault); downstairs, Jackie and Sara Rush, the fluff-brained sisters. When not bouncing across the set in short shorts or tight sweaters, the girls' dialogue filled in for them:

SARA
I can't help it if your boyfriends are attracted to me. When it comes to personality, I happen to be a 10.

JACKIE
When it comes to personality, you happen to be a 36C.

In 1983 the Rushes had a baby (whom they named Andrew) in an attempt to perk up the ratings, which were by now declining. Still, ABC cancelled the series at the end of the year. Then a strange thing happened. The producers of the show worked out a deal with Metromedia, a syndication distributor, whereby new episodes would continue to be produced in 1984. The new shows were offered to independent stations, and the show continued in production through September 1985.

Then, in a maneuver reminiscent of the old "Doris Day Show" (see page 166) the show's format was changed in April 1986 (after a brief hiatus), as was the title of the series. Now called "The Ted Knight Show," Ted still played Henry Rush and Nancy played wife Muriel, but the daughters were dropped in favor of the baby son Andrew and a new location. The family departed their San Francisco home for a house in Mill Valley and a new job (he bought a 49 percent interest in a newspaper). Henry's boss Monroe (JM J. Bullock) also made the transition, thus preserving some of the show's roots.

During the summer of 1986, Ted Knight became ill. The show was scheduled to begin production for a new season in the fall of 1986, but Knight died on August 26, before filming started.

CREDITS

CREATORS: Arne Sultan, Earl Barret, Brian Cooke. BASED ON: "Keep It in the Family," a Thames TV production created by Brian Cooke. EXECUTIVE PRODUCER: Arne Sultan, Aaron Ruben. PRODUCERS: Earl Barret, Jerry McPhie, Volney Howard, George Yanok. DIRECTORS: Will Mackenzie, Peter Baldwin, others. WRITERS: Arne Sultan, Earl Barret, Brian Cooke, George Yanok, others. CAST: *Henry Rush* (Ted Knight), *Muriel Rush* (Nancy Dussault), *Jackie Rush* (Deborah Van Valkenburgh), *Sara Rush* (Lydia Cornell), *Arthur Wainwright* (Hamilton Camp), *Monroe Ficus* (JM J. Bullock), *April Rush* (Deena Freeman), *Iris Martin* (Audrey Meadows), *Andrew Rush* (twins William Thomas Cannon and Michael Philip Cannon; Joshua Goodwin), *Lisa Flores* (Lisa Antille), *Hope Stinson* (Pat Carroll).

MAGNUM, P.I.

NUMBER 3, 1982–83

Every once in a while an actor emerges from the ranks of commercials and minor guest roles to become a superstar. For the decade of the '80s, that man was Tom Selleck. Described as the heir apparent to Clark Gable, Robert Redford, or Burt Reynolds, Selleck's charisma, matinee-idol looks, and overall Mr. Nice Guy image soon propelled the former huckster for Chaz men's cologne into the world of Hollywood stardom, in this case shifted about 3,000 miles west to Hawaii.

CBS had always had a soft spot for that tropical paradise. When "Hawaii Five-O" left the air in 1980, after 12 years of balmy breezes and swaying palms, the network brass was eager to fill the Hawaii gap, and "Magnum, P.I." seemed the perfect ticket. The series was offered to Tom Selleck, the six-foot-four-inch, 200-pound actor who had made more than 50 guest-starring appearances on television, including seven TV pilots that hadn't sold. He promptly turned it down. "I asked to have a look at the script," said Selleck in the *Saturday Evening Post*. "They showed it to me, and I didn't like it. As Magnum, I would be taking up where Sean Connery left off as Agent 007, with a Hawaiian setting thrown in for good measure. So I turned it down. I wasn't hungry." Producer Don Bellisario talked to him and agreed to redo the Thomas Magnum character, making him more down-to-earth, more vulnerable. He wouldn't be the owner of a huge Hawaiian estate; he'd be in charge of its security. The shiny red Ferrari wouldn't be his, either; it would belong to the owner, reclusive novelist Robin Masters, owner of the Robin's Nest estate. Magnum would speak in a slightly pubescent voice that cracked when he was excited (like Selleck himself), and he'd do occasional goofy things, like forgetting where he'd parked the car while trying to outrun the bad guys. Selleck agreed to the changes, signed, and became an overnight sensation. The series bowed in December 1980 and by its second season had risen to number three.

At first viewers tuned in for the usual reasons Hawaii-based shows were watched: beaches, babes, and bikinis, plus the requisite round of car chases, shootings, smuggling rings, drug busts, and all things popularized by "Hawaii Five-O" (see page 176). But soon the demographics began to show that "Magnum" appealed to *women*, not the normal audience for this type of series. They were tuning in to see just how many buttons this guy would undo on his trademark floral shirt (an item of apparel which went from geeky to "in" during the show's run), or to watch him shoehorn his lanky, leggy frame into the Ferrari convertible.

Tom Selleck was the first to deny his smoldering sex-symbolism. The Detroit-born future heartthrob moved with his family to Los Angeles when he was four. His father promised young Tom a gold watch if he refrained from drinking, smoking, or swearing until after his 21st birthday. Like his sister and two brothers, Selleck won the watch and continued to hold a conservative outlook on life similar to his parents'. A sports enthusiast, he attended USC on a basketball scholarship and made his first film appearance in 1970 with his teammates in a movie with Mae West (*Myra Breckenridge*). His first solo acting experience occurred on TV's "The Dating Game"; he was Bachelor Number Two, and he lost.

During each hiatus from "Magnum," Selleck found

CREDITS

EXECUTIVE PRODUCERS: Donald P. Bellisario, Glen A. Larson, Tom Selleck. PRODUCERS: J. Rickley Dumm, others. DIRECTORS: various. WRITERS: various. CAST: *Thomas Sullivan Magnum* (Tom Selleck), *Jonathan Quayle Higgins* (John Hillerman), *Theodore "T.C." Calvin* (Roger E. Mosley), *Orville "Rick" Wright* (Larry Manetti), *Mac Reynolds* (Jeff MacKay), *Lt. Tanaka* (Kwan Hi Lim), *Lt. Maggie Poole* (Jean Bruce Scott), *Agatha Chumley* (Gillian Dobb), *Assistant District Attorney Carol Baldwin* (Kathleen Lloyd), *"Icepick"* (Elisha Cook, Jr.), *Robin Masters' voice* (Orson Welles). GUEST STARS: Fritz Weaver, Robert Loggia, Frank Sinatra, Carol Burnett, Anthony Newley, Marcia Wallace, Gwen Verdon, Dana Delany, Tyne Daly, others.

EMMYS

Outstanding Lead Actor in a Drama Series—Tom Selleck (1983–84), Outstanding Supporting Actor in a Drama Series—John Hillerman (1986–87).

time to develop his movie career. He starred in *The High Road to China* (1983), *Three Men and a Baby* (1987), and *Mr. Baseball* (1992), to name just a few. His biggest disappointment was having to turn down director Steven Spielberg when offered the role of Indiana Jones in *Raiders of the Lost Ark* (1981) because of a conflict with the "Magnum" shooting schedule (the part went to Harrison Ford).

The show's central characters were really a triumvirate, three veterans of the Vietnam War who were there for each other then, and stood by one another back in Honolulu after the war ended. T.C., played by Roger

Tom Selleck.

Mosley, was a chopper pilot in 'Nam who parlayed that skill into Island Hoppers, a business offering flight-seeing trips around the Islands. It was hard to see how he made a living, though; his chopper was always broken, and when he could get it up and running, he was usually bailing out Magnum from some cliffhanging

situation. The third musketeer was Rick, who owned a local bar/disco/nightclub. He had a vaguely shady past that somehow led to his having underworld pals, like the notorious "Icepick." Larry Manetti played this role; he was mostly a third-wheel character, although on occasion he and some of Magnum's friends were the focal points of particular episodes.

John Hillerman completed the cast. For eight season viewers knew him as Higgins, the major-domo of Robin's Nest, a British braggadocio who was always reminiscing about "the time when I was climbing Mt. Everest" or some equally absurd adventure. He tolerated Magnum (who often addressed him as "Higgie Baby" just to annoy him) with gritted teeth and stiff upper lip, a kind of self-appointed conscience for the irresponsible, freeloading P.I. (private investigator). The byplay between these two opposites made for some of the show's best moments. Hillerman was actually born in Texas and the British accent was purely acting, a talent not lost on the Television Academy, which bestowed him with an Emmy.

There were many memorable episodes over the eight years. Outstanding ones included the time Magnum and a character played by Carol Burnett got locked in a bank vault; the hour-long stream-of-consciousness episode in which Magnum's surf ski got caught in an ocean current; the Vietnam War flashback sequences; and many more.

The series aired what the producers thought was its final episode at the end of the 1986–87 season, when Magnum died in a shooting and went to heaven. Fortunately, the series was picked up for another season— Magnum deserved a much better ending than this hokum, which was explained away by the "it was all a dream" ploy. The final episode of the 1987–88 season saw Magnum discovering his long-lost daughter and reactivating his navy commission, while Higgins revealed that he was actually the never-before-seen Robin Masters. Serious fans of the series doubted this—there were just too many indications to the contrary from eight years' worth of episodes. It seemed possible that a further clarification would be presented in a future reunion movie (there had been some serious speculation). Meanwhile, "Magnum, P.I." reruns were continuing in syndication in the 1990s.

DYNASTY

"Dynasty" was to be ABC's answer to CBS's prime-time hit, "Dallas." All the ingredients seemed to be there: the wealthy oil magnate, his loving bride, his bisexual son—just another typical dysfunctional family (was there any other kind in nighttime soaps?). Then, too, there was the fabulous wardrobe of gowns, furs, and jewels, along with the beautiful homes and cars. And there were the usual problems that seem to beset those suffering so under their burden of wealth: incest, murder, lust, and greed. The show debuted in January 1981, and after that first partial season, the series was all but ignored by the public. It was ranked number 45 and was sinking fast. Something was missing, something that would send the series in the opposite direction, towards its rightful place as a Nielsen top-tenner. That something was a bitch named Alexis.

"Dallas" had J.R. at its core; "Dynasty" would go one better with a villain*ess*, if only they could come up with the right person. The producers' first choice was Sophia Loren, but the glamorous Italian actress declined, saying her fans would never appreciate her in such a manipulative and cruel role. The next actress approached was Joan Collins. "No way," said Collins when offered the part by executive producer Aaron Spelling. Collins was abroad, basking in the warm Mediterranean sunshine when her agent called with the offer. "I wasn't inclined to go traipsing back to the U.S.A. again," she said. "Especially for some obscure TV series I'd never heard of." Eventually the British actress, who hadn't been working steadily in a while, was persuaded that the part of glamorous, sexy, deliciously bitchy Alexis was a good one, and she took the job. It turned out to be the role of a lifetime.

Set against the background of Denver, Colorado, "Dynasty" starred John Forsythe as Blake Carrington, the head of the Carrington clan (i.e., dynasty). His meager holdings included a large oil company, a stable of race horses, and a pro football team. His beautiful bride, Krystle (Linda Evans), a former secretary with his corporation, was fair-haired, fair-eyed, and pastel-clothed in soft, flowing, broad-shouldered outfits by designer Nolan Miller—the very vision of a glowing

angel. It didn't take too much thought on the part of the viewer to figure out that she was the good girl. Alexis Carrington Colby, on the other hand, was a former wife of Blake Carrington who was usually dressed in basic bitchy black—evil personified. She was the kind of gal who, when her husband-to-be (an archrival of Blake) had a heart attack during sex on their prenuptial night, worried that the wedding might be off and she would miss out on inheriting his millions. In fact, this incident became one of the show's trademark cliffhanger season endings, another concept that the series clearly lifted from "Dallas."

Alexis, she-devil that she was, just couldn't seem to keep her claws off Krystle. Over the years, viewers knew they could count on at least one good cat fight

---

CREDITS

TOP 10 PEAK: No. 1, 1984–85. CREATORS: Richard and Esther Shapiro. EXECUTIVE PRODUCERS: Aaron Spelling, Richard and Esther Shapiro. CO-EXECUTIVE PRODUCER: Douglas S. Cramer. SUPERVISING PRODUCER: Elaine Rich. PRODUCERS: Philip Parslow, others. DIRECTORS: Ralph Senensky, Gabrielle Beaumont, Philip Leacock, Don Medford, others. WRITERS: Richard and Esther Shapiro, Edward DeBlasio, others. CAST: *Blake Carrington* (John Forsythe), *Krystle Jennings Carrington* (Linda Evans), *Alexis Morell Carrington Colby Dexter Rowan* (Joan Collins), *Fallon Carrington Colby* (Pamela Sue Martin, Emma Samms), *Steven Carrington* (Al Corley, Jack Coleman), *Adam Carrington* (Gordon Thomson), *Cecil Colby* (Lloyd Bochner), *Jeff Colby* (John James), *Claudia Blaisdel* (Pamela Bellwood), *Andrew Laird* (Peter Mark Richman), *Sammy Jo Dean* (Heather Locklear), *Dominique Deveraux* (Diahann Carroll). OTHER REGULARS: James Farentino, Paul Burke, Michael Nader, Catherine Oxenberg, Karen Cellini, William Campbell, Rock Hudson, Ali MacGraw, George Hamilton, Ken Howard, Ted McGinley, Tracy Scoggins, others.

Linda Evans and John Forsythe.

between the adversaries per season. They fought in a lily pond, a mud puddle, a beauty parlor, and a burning cabin, and on one occasion engaged in a feather-filled pillow fight.

Other plot complications related to Blake Carrington's son, Steven. Was he or wasn't he gay? Even he didn't seem to know, but the actor playing him was fed up with the writers' unwillingness to commit one way or another and aired his feelings to the press. At the end of the 1982 season, Al Corley, who played Steven, wasn't invited back. We learned that Steven's face was destroyed in an oil rig explosion. But by the middle of the 1982–83 season, Steven was back, his bandages removed; through the miracle of modern medicine, he now had the face of actor Jack Coleman, who had been signed for the role. Steven Carrington eventually resolved his sexual ambiguity and decided he that was gay after all.

In 1984, actress Diahann Carroll, who had made television history when she became the first black to star in a sitcom ("Julia," see page 158), decided it was time for "Dynasty" to become integrated. She lobbied for a role on the show. "I want to be the first black bitch on television," she announced. And so she was. As Dominique Deveraux, an elegant nightclub owner, she gave Alexis a run for her money, but in a more catty way. And Dominique soon laid a bombshell on Blake: she was his long-lost half sister, the illegitimate daughter of their father.

And so it went, year after sudsy year. By 1989 the series had pretty much run its course in tandem with the end of the free-spending Reagan era. The series was cancelled without so much as a concluding episode. The unresolved cliffhanger in episode 217 left Blake shot, Krystle in a coma (off-camera, since Linda Evans had left the show already), and Alexis sailing over a balcony. "The way we were cut off was a disgrace," sighed John Forsythe. But wait. In 1991 ABC and Aaron Spelling brought the whole dynasty back for a reunion movie called "Dynasty: The Reunion" (clever, these titles). Nearly everyone returned, including Al Corley, the original Steve Carrington, who had made his peace with the producers. Blake recovered, Krystle recovered, Alexis recovered, and it was business as usual. Not all the threads were tied up, though—a powerful consortium was attempting to take over Blake's company, and the evil perpetrator escaped at the show's finale, leaving open the possibility of another reunion.

John Forsythe, meanwhile, starred in a 1992–93 series of his own, a political satire sitcom called "The Powers That Be." At 75 Forsythe was still a star; at that age not too many actors can make that claim, especially if the character is as virile as the show's Senator Powers, who had both a wife and a mistress—something Blake Carrington would certainly never do.

A spinoff series, "Dynasty II—The Colbys" (later shortened to simply "The Colbys") ran from November 1985 to March 1987.

SIMON & SIMON

NUMBER 7, 1982–83

At first glance, "Simon & Simon" might have seemed like just another detective-crime show, but this series was different. It was larger than its plots and car chases. It was a classic "buddy" series, with the emphasis on the caring relationship between the two principals, further strengthened by the fact that they were brothers.

When creator Phil DeGuere was casting for the two leads back in 1980, he had no trouble finding the actor who would play the preppie younger brother, A.J. CBS suggested he look at a young blond actor named Jameson Parker, whose credits had included some work in soaps plus episodes of "Family" and "Hart to Hart." "When he walked in," said DeGuere, "here was this intelligent, considerate, nice person who had the looks and charisma of a Robert Redford. I said to myself, 'He can't possibly act too.'" DeGuere screened Parker's "Hart to Hart" episode and was impressed enough (and wise enough) to hire him. The next step was not so easy; he needed to hire the other half of this brother act, and there had to be chemistry.

A number of men read for the part of older brother Rick Simon, but none of them clicked. Then DeGuere remembered testing Gerald McRaney for a TV film he had done called "The Gypsy Warriors" (McRaney had lost the part to Tom Selleck). McRaney had played mostly heavies, including rapists and murderers. As luck would have it, he happened to be on the Universal lot shooting an episode of "The Incredible Hulk" (playing a psychopathic cop) when DeGuere decided to "read" him during his lunch break. Jameson Parker was summoned to the studio to read with McRaney, and he arrived on his bicycle dressed in tennis shorts. It was hate at first sight between the two actors. "Here was this sort of rawboned, lanky, balding guy in a three-piece suit," said Parker in *TV Guide*. "I just had trouble seeing him in the part. Then he started reading, and every nuance of the humor was right there. It was apparent he'd been *born* to play Rick." "They played off each other so well," said DeGuere, "plus I think that they felt very comfortable in these roles."

The two actors' styles meshed so smoothly that in the years to follow, the various writers and directors would become frustrated by the pair's constant ad-libbing (some gags stayed, others were nixed). The two began socializing off-camera as well, taking trips with their families during the series' hiatuses.

With the leads cast, DeGuere shot a pilot for the series under its original title, "Pirate's Key." It was set in Florida, and it bombed. CBS decided to give the producer another chance; he moved the brothers' detective agency to a San Diego location and aired the new pilot in December 1981. For the rest of the season, the ratings were so low the show was constantly in danger of being cancelled. Then the network decided to give it a better time slot, piggybacked with their successful detective show, "Magnum, P.I." The two action-adventure-crime dramas made a perfect pair, and by the next season, "Simon & Simon" had made it into the top 10.

One of the reasons for the show's success seemed to be that the two Simon boys were brothers in their mid-30s who still respected their mother, an important character on the show. Mom Cecilia Simon (Mary Carver) often found herself inadvertently

CREDITS

TOP 10 PEAK: No. 5, 1983–84.
CREATOR: Philip DeGuere. EXECUTIVE PRODUCERS: Philip DeGuere, John Stephens, Richard Chapman. PRODUCERS: Mark Burley, Chas. Floyd Johnson, Michael Piller, others. DIRECTORS: Corey Allen, Vincent McEveety, others. WRITERS: Philip DeGuere, Richard Chapman, Michael Piller, others. CAST: *A.J. Simon* (Jameson Parker), *Rick Simon* (Gerald McRaney), *Cecilia Simon* (Mary Carver), *Downtown Brown* (Tim Reid), *Janet Fowler* (Jeannie Wilson), *Myron Fowler* (Eddie Barth), *Officer Nixon* (Scott Murphy), *Lt. Abby Marsh* (Joan McMurtrey), *Officer Susie* (Donna Jepsen). GUEST STARS: Peter Graves, Sharon Acker, June Allyson, Dee Wallace-Stone, Britt Ekland, Jean-Pierre Aumont, others.

involved in the boys' cases. Her addition to the cast helped pull ratings from the Midwest and South, where there was a strong sense of traditional family values. "I think there were many people out there who were craving a reinforcement of old values, family and otherwise," said DeGuere in *TV Guide*. " 'Simon & Simon' was reassuring to them. Watching it, you were laughing, and it was all very light, but some of the family stuff was right there, just beneath the laughs and the action."

Actor Jameson Parker was a lot like his character. He was brought up on the right side of the tracks, the son of a high-ranking U.S. diplomat. As A.J. Simon, Parker was supposed to be the younger brother, when in actuality he was less than a year younger than his on-screen partner. After "Simon & Simon" left the air, Parker starred in a number of made-for-television movies. He made headlines in 1992 when an irate neighbor shot him in a dispute over his dog and the neighbor's lawn. Although seriously wounded, he made a complete recovery, and the neighbor was arrested on attempted murder charges.

Gerald McRaney went on to star in his own series, "Major Dad," playing a straight-laced marine trying to raise a family of stepdaughters. A few years earlier, he had appeared on a couple of episodes of "Designing Women." He had designs on only one of them—Delta Burke, whom he married shortly afterwards.

In 1992 creator Phillip DeGuere filed a $31.2 million suit against Universal, claiming the studio cheated him out of his share of "Simon & Simon" net profits by overstating its costs and underreporting its revenues. Universal claimed that the series was still showing a $60.3 million net deficit. The case was still pending litigation at year's end.

"Simon & Simon" ran for seven years on CBS, frequently in the Nielsen top 10. In 1993 the series was still running in syndication.

Gerald McRaney (left) and Jameson Parker.

FALCON CREST

Robert Foxworth and Jane Wyman.

The basic premise of "Falcon Crest," companion piece to CBS's other nighttime soap opera hit, "Dallas," was the power struggle for the control of the family vineyard and winery, presided over by matriarch Angela Channing. While "Dallas" had oil, "Falcon Crest" had grapes; while the chief schemer of "Dallas" was J.R. Ewing, "Falcon Crest" had his female equivalent in Angela, "a strong-willed matriarch of a legendary vineyard—brooding in the mansion on the hill, empress of a vineyard kingdom but determined to enlarge her

power further still, even if it means driving her own nephew off his land," in the words of CBS and Lorimar Productions, the parent company.

Earl Hamner, who had brought his warm and wonderful family "The Waltons" to CBS several seasons earlier, claimed he got the idea for "Falcon Crest," a show about a decidedly dysfunctional family, from the life of one of his own ancestors who came from Italy to grow grapes for Thomas Jefferson. Although the 1980 pilot, called "The Vintage Years," was so bad it never actually aired, the series caught on nonetheless, thanks to its venerated star, Jane Wyman.

While the show was certainly about lifestyles of the rich and greedy, Wyman's character was not quite the villain that J.R. of "Dallas" was. Hamner himself had chosen the legendary actress, winner of an Academy Award for her portrayal of the deaf-mute rape victim in *Johnny Belinda* (1948). "We wanted a star of Jane's stature," said Hamner, "and certainly she comes from a legendary time in filmmaking." But he also wanted the audience to like the central character. "For all of her power and seeming ruthlessness," said Hamner of dowager Angela Channing, "the audience must *like* Angie—and who could not like Jane Wyman?"

The last time Jane Wyman had done television, she had starred and hosted her own 1950s anthology series, "Fireside Theatre" (see page 6), later changed to "The Jane Wyman Show." As with most performers who were used to the leisurely pace of feature films, she loathed the 16-hour days and frenetic pace of weekly television. "Falcon Crest" was her first series in over 25 years, and she soon became a star all over again at the unlikely age of 68.

Her co-star was Robert Foxworth, who played her nephew/nemesis, Chase Gioberti. Foxworth found fault with everything about the show, from the scripts to the dearth of location shooting after the first few years. It's a wonder he accepted the role at all. He had turned down the part of J.R. in "Dallas" before it was offered to Larry Hagman. "I didn't like the script or the concept," he said in *TV Guide*. Later he rejected the chance to star as Trapper John on "M*A*S*H." "You've got to be kidding," he told producer Gene Reynolds. "You can't make a half-hour sitcom out of a great movie." When he was offered "Falcon Crest," his first impulse was to say no once again. "I didn't care very much for the concept of the show," he said, "[but] I had already made two mistakes in turning down 'Dallas' and 'M*A*S*H' and, like baseball, I couldn't afford to take a third strike."

Even so, Foxworth found the scripts of "Falcon Crest" banal—and they were, chock full of the usual sudsy schemings and backstabbings, plus the earthquakes, gangland slayings, kidnappings, brain tumors, and comas that are the stock-in-trade of the genre. But at least Foxworth couldn't always find fault with the director; by the second season he was frequently sitting in the director's chair, prompting producer John Perry to comment (in the 1983–84 season), "They're among the best episodes we've ever done." His character was killed off at the end of the 1986–87 season when the actor decided he'd finally had enough sour grapes.

Rounding out the main cast was Lorenzo Lamas as Angela's grandson and chosen heir apparent, Lance Cumson. Lorenzo was the show's resident Latin hunk, and his pecs weren't lost on the female viewers who generally dominate the audience for this genre. The son of actor/director Fernando Lamas and Arlene Dahl, and the stepson of Esther Williams, Lorenzo appeared in a number of series and pilots while still a teenager in the late 1970s. Jane Wyman recalled that she was shooting a scene in 1958 for "The Jane Wyman Show" with Fernando Lamas. "Just before the second act," she said, "he got a phone call. He went crazy. 'It is a boy! I go now!' And that was the last I saw of him." Lamas, Sr., dashed off the stage to meet his baby Lorenzo for the first time. Twenty-five years later, all three would be working togther when he directed his son and former co-star Jane Wyman in an episode of "Falcon Crest."

By the eighth season, 1989–90, the producers decided the series needed a face-lift. The show had ended the previous season in 47th place in the Nielsens, trailing far behind the other two CBS/Lorimar soaps ("Dallas" and "Knots Landing"). The series took a much darker direction, with the battle for supremacy among the vintners of Napa Valley escalating into bizarre plot lines about international intrigue. Angela spent most of the season in a coma, and there were numerous stabbings and shootings and a drowning. CBS decreed this would be the last season for "Falcon Crest," now ranked number 68, and there was a concluding "they all lived happily ever after" episode in which Angela finally prevailed, along with her chosen heir.

CREDITS

TOP 10 PEAK: No. 7, 1983–84. CREATOR: Earl Hamner. EXECUTIVE PRODUCERS: Earl Hamner, Michael Filerman, Joanne Brough, Jeff Freilich, Camille Marchetta, Jerry Thorpe. PRODUCERS: Rod Peterson, Claire Whitaker, Ernie Wallengren, Greg Strangis, John F. Perry, Richard Gollance, Howard Lakin, Philip Parslow, Stephen Black, Henry Stern, Rena Down, Victoria LaFortune, Sheri Anderson. DIRECTORS: Jerry Thorpe, Jack Bender, Robert Foxworth, Fernando Lamas, others. WRITERS: various. CAST: *Angela Channing* (Jane Wyman), *Chase Gioberti* (Robert Foxworth), *Lance Cumson* (Lorenzo Lamas), *Maggie Gioberti Channing* (Susan Sullivan), *Tony Cumson* (John Saxon), *Cole Gioberti* (William R. Moses), *Victoria Gioberti Hogan* (Jamie Rose, Dana Sparks), *Julia Cumson* (Abby Dalton). OTHER REGULARS: Mel Ferrer, Margaret Ladd, Chau-Li Chi, Ana Alicia, David Selby, Roger Perry, Roy Thinnes, Lana Turner, Bradford Dillman, Maggie Cooper, Cliff Robertson, Raymond St. Jacques, Sarah Douglas, Gina Lollobrigida, Simon MacCorkindale, Parker Stevenson, Morgan Fairchild, Ken Olin, Apollonia, Cesar Romero, Celeste Holm, Henry Jones, Edward Albert, Kim Novak, Jane Badler, Marjoe Gortner, Robert Stack, Maggie Cooper, Rod Taylor, Gregory Harrison, Mark Lindsay Chapman, others.

THE A- TEAM

NUMBER 10   (TIE), 1982–83

From left: Dirk Benedict, Dwight Schultz, George Peppard, and Mr. T.

I love it when a plan comes together!
    —HANNIBAL SMITH, LEADER OF THE A-TEAM

In 1982, NBC head of programming Brandon Tartikoff caught the heavyweight title bout between Larry Holmes and Gerry Cooney. There he noticed a mountain of rippling black muscles known as Mr. T, fresh from his *Rocky III* film debut. When Tartikoff returned to his Burbank headquarters, he fired off a proposal for a new series to producer Stephen Cannell: "*Road Warrior, Magnificent Seven, Dirty Dozen,* 'Mission: Impossible,' all rolled into one, and Mr. T drives the car." Shortly thereafter, Stephen J. Cannell and Frank Lupo submitted their larger-than-life, live-acted cartoon called "The A-Team" for Tartikoff's approval, and NBC kicked off the series with its pilot on "NBC Sunday Night at the Movies" on January 26, 1983. The show soon began running weekly. Audiences took to this escapist, gratuitously violent series with glee; everyone, it seemed, wanted to be a part of the Team. Ratings shot the series to number three almost immediately, and the show finished its short first season at number 10.

The series is probably most remembered for its machine-gun-paced action. With explosions, weapons,

tanks, and jeeps flying through the air, it made the "Dukes of Hazzard" (to which it was initially likened) look like a Sunday drive through Pasadena. In fact, by the series' second year, it had come under official attack from the National Coalition on Television Violence, a Washington, D.C., watchdog group that actually sat and counted incidents of violence per show. "The A-Team" was found to have at least 34 offensive acts per hour (versus an average of seven on other prime-time series). An average episode might have such violent events as gunfights waged from an armor-plated bakery truck, a high-rise shootout with a helicopter, a stuntman falling seven stories from said high-rise into a swimming pool, plus the usual assortment of explosions and overturned vehicles.

David Hostetter, the Washington director of NCTV, said, "The program shows people resolving conflicts through violence, which is not an accepted or legal way in our society. The type of violence on 'The A-Team' is of a very dangerous nature in that no one gets hurt." His contention was that this could be harmful to children, "who can't discern fiction from reality." He wouldn't happen to have been speaking of the same children who had been enjoying *Grimm's Fairy Tales* for over a century, would he?—the ones where witches eat children and wolves swallow up old ladies, then have their stomachs sliced open? The fact is, children had absolutely no problem knowing that this was nothing more than a live-acted Saturday morning cartoon; after all, how many times had the Road Runner been bulldozed by Wylie Coyote, only to spring back to life? On "The A-Team," no one was ever killed or even shot. It was all in the interest of action and fun. Said Cannell, "It's a fantasy. 'The A-Team' is not to be taken seriously."

It should have been obvious to anyone paying attention that the characters were all larger than life. The premise had to do with four Vietnam servicemen who robbed the Bank of Hanoi at war's end, supposedly under secret orders. But they couldn't prove they were following orders, and they were being hunted by the government. With nothing to lose, they became vigilantes back in the States, champions of any underdog who could find them. It was highly formulaic: Act One set up the week's problem; in Act Two, the A-Team became involved; in Act Three, they set up their "Mission: Impossible"-like solution (e.g., a scheme to knock off the bad guys through an elaborate trap); and in Act Four, the plan was carried out. Week after week, the audience knew exactly what to expect and was never disappointed.

George Peppard played the Team leader, Col. "Hannibal" Smith. He was a master of disguise, one tough, cigar-chompin' cookie. Peppard was best remembered as the star of "Banacek" back in 1972–74; he had also been the first choice for the lead in "Dynasty," but after 16 days he was dropped from the pilot and replaced by John Forsythe, supposedly because of his tendency to want to direct the show (although Peppard claimed it was because the producers gave him notes on his acting). NBC took note and requested James Coburn be given the part of Hannibal; when he wasn't available, Peppard got the part.

The most visible and probably best-remembered member of the Team was Mr. T, a walking muscle machine with 35 pounds of gold chains around his neck. Born Lawrence Tero, T had been a professional wrestler before becoming a celebrity bodyguard in the mid-'70s for such notables as Michael Jackson, LeVar Burton, Muhammad Ali, and Leon Spinks. His first major starring role was as Clubber Lang, the boxing opponent of Sylvester "Rocky" Stallone in *Rocky III* (1982). His character on "The A-Team" was B.A. (for "bad attitude") Baracus. The producers in their wisdom

gave him an endearing weakness, however: B.A. was terrified of airplanes and flying in general and had to be slipped a mickey each week so the Team could get to its mission.

The person flying the planes was the cause of B.A.'s paranoia. "Howling Mad" Murdoch was more than just the Team's pilot; he was their certified wacko. Before they could proceed each week, pilot Murdoch had to be sprung from the insane asylum where he resided. (Why he kept returning there at mission's end is anybody's guess.) Dwight Schultz, an actor who had spent most of his acting career on the stage, played Murdoch. Following "The A-Team," Schultz appeared in several movies for television, as well as the 1989 theatrical film *Fat Man and Little Boy*. He had a recurring role on the syndicated television series "Star Trek: The Next Generation," playing the insecure Lt. Barclay.

Dirk Benedict played the Team member with the improbable name of Templeton Peck, nicknamed "Face," "The Face," or sometimes "Faceman." Most likely the moniker was for his extremely handsome visage. Face was a hustler who helped get whatever objects were needed for the mission; his skills and disguises were legendary. Benedict had co-starred in "Battlestar Galactica" prior to appearing on "The A-Team." The network objected to him as much as they did to Peppard, but Cannell hired him for the Team anyway.

There was a token female character along for the ride, but she really wasn't part of the Team. Amy Allen had hired them to help her in the pilot episode and stuck around after that. Her main functions were to tag along with them and look cute each week. Melinda Culea, the first actress to play this fluffy part, was dismissed after the first 10 episodes of the season when she had the audacity to ask that her role be expanded. An unhappy Team member was an ex-Team member. She was replaced in 1984 by Marla Heasley as Tawnia. She played tag-along too, but within a year the whole idea was dropped.

In 1986 Robert Vaughn was added to the cast as General Hunt Stockwell—an appropriate name, since he was hunting the A-Team. He captured them too, then put the Team to work for him as government agents.

The series was cancelled after four action-packed seasons and 128 episodes. Let's see...that's 128 times 34 acts of violence...which equals an active life in TV rerun syndication, where the show could still be seen in the 1990s.

CREDITS

TOP 10 PEAK: No. 4, 1983–84.
CREATORS/EXECUTIVE PRODUCERS: Stephen J. Cannell, Frank Lupo. PRODUCERS: Jo Swerling, Jr., John Ashley, Patrick Hasburgh, others. DIRECTORS: various. WRITERS: various. CAST: *Col. John "Hannibal" Smith* (George Peppard), *Sgt. Bosco "B.A." Baracus* (Mr. T), *Lt. Templeton "Face" Peck* (Dirk Benedict), *Capt. H.M. "Howling Mad" Murdock* (Dwight Schultz), *Amy Allen* (Melinda Culea), *Col. Lynch* (Lance LeGault), *Tawnia Baker* (Maria Heasley), *Gen. Hunt Stockwell* (Robert Vaughn), *"Dishpan" Frankie Sanchez* (Eddie Valez), *Carla* (Judy Ledford). GUEST STARS: William Windom, John Saxon, Melody Anderson, Felix Gonzales, Ron Palillo, others.

MONDAY NIGHT FOOTBALL

NUMBER 10 (TIE), 1982–83

For sports fans, Monday nights haven't been the same since ABC took football beyond beyond its traditional Sunday-afternoon slot.

In 1970, ABC spent a reported $8 million and took a giant risk when the network decided to bring what had been a weekend sport to prime time by creating "Monday Night Football." Some thought the network foolhardy. An NBC executive cautioned, "Football will work on weekends before viewers schooled in sports, but in the evening, trying to pull general audiences, it will fall on its helmet." Famous last words. The gamble paid off, and in the 1982–83 season, "Monday Night Football" became the first prime-time sports series in the Nielsen top 10 since "The Gillette Cavalcade of Sports" back in 1950 (see page 14). Twenty-three seasons later, it was still one of the most popular programs on television, having been on the air longer than any other prime-time show except "60 Minutes."

Football was a sport perfectly mated to television. It had action, drama, suspense, superstars, and personalities. And that was just in the booth. While celebrities like Joe Montana, Joe Namath, and O.J. Simpson were spilling their guts on the playing field, audiences were becoming equally enthralled with the banter and frequent bickering taking place in the broadcast booth between a team of three announcers, anchored by Howard "The Mouth" Cosell.

Howard Cosell was one of the original announcers of "Monday Night Football," signing on in 1970. From the start, ABC knew they had their hands full with this former New York lawyer who had turned to sports broadcasting in the mid-'50s. For one thing, he broke the unwritten broadcasters' taboo of never voicing a critique of the players. Cosell was opinionated, abrasive, sometimes funny, but more frequently controversial and prone to using vocabulary that would have sent people scurrying for their dictionaries had there not been a game at hand (he conveyed his ideas anyway). "He is overfull of himself and underfull of humor," wailed *TV Guide*. And his unbridled enthusiasm more than once jeopardized his career, like the time in 1983 when, referring to Washington Redskins' wide receiver Alvin Garrett, he excitedly yelled, "Look at that little monkey go!" Garrett happened to be black, and Cosell's choice of wording met with immediate criticism. And although Cosell insisted he only intended praise, it nearly cost him his job.

Yet despite all this, Cosell was a strong contributing factor to ABC's ratings. He continued in the booth until 1983, when he retired as "Monday Night Football" announcer. Some said "Good riddance," including *Variety*, which wrote, "Cosell had long since worn out his welcome and his act had become tired. Complaints that he made more of himself and his frequently ridiculous opinions were well founded." Maybe so, but Cosell's final season with "Monday Night Football" also happened to coincide with the first year the program made it into the Nielsen top 10. Cosell continued with "Monday Night Baseball" until his retirement in 1985.

The second announcer as part of the original three-man team in 1970 was Don Meredith. Nicknamed "Dandy Don," he had been an all-American in college and a star quarterback for the Dallas Cowboys from 1960 to 1968. His commentary was witty despite the obvious tension between him and Cosell. Meredith stayed with the series until 1973 but returned again in 1977, continuing to narrate until 1984.

Keith Jackson was part of the original triumvirate of announcers but was replaced by Frank Gifford in 1971. "Giff," like Meredith, had been an all-American at his college, the University of Southern California. After completing his education at USC, he entered the world of pro football in 1952 as the number one draft pick of the New York Giants, where he played for the next 12 years. Gifford held the record for longevity in announcing "Monday Night Football"—by 1993 he'd been with the series nearly 22 years.

Over the years, fans enjoyed seeing many sports legends serve as announcers, including Alex Karras (1974–76), Fran Tarkenton (1979–82), O.J. Simpson (1983–85), and Joe Namath (1985). No doubt there will be other superstars joining the announcing team in the future.

"NFL Monday Night Football" ("NFL" is frequently dropped from the title) was set to enter its 24th season in the fall of 1993. In 1992, aside from Frank Gifford, announcers included Don Dierdorf, who had been with the team in the booth since 1987, and Al Michaels, who had been doing play-by-play since 1986, when he took over that function from Gifford.

CREDITS

TOP 10 PEAK: No. 9, 1990–91.
EXECUTIVE PRODUCERS: Roone Arledge, others. PRODUCERS: Bob Goodrich, Ken Wolfe, others. DIRECTORS: Chet Forte, others.

EMMYS

Best Sports Personality—Frank Gifford (1977), Outstanding Sports Personality-Host—Al Michaels (1989, 1990).

KATE & ALLIE

NUMBER 8, 1983–84

Sitcoms seemed to be falling out of television favor in the early 1980s. The genre had peaked in the 1978–79 season, when nine out of the Nielsen top 10 shows were comedies. By 1982 the audience's preferences were leaning more towards action-adventure and detective shows. But in early 1984, a new, different kind of sitcom premiered on CBS; within two months it would become the only sitcom to make the season's top 10.

"Kate & Allie" was different because it was realistic. Neither Kate nor Allie jiggled or giggled; they weren't addle-brained fluff-heads, they weren't "Lucy" wackos, and they weren't just dumb wives or girlfriends. And they weren't space aliens or blue-collar bigots. Instead, they were two decidedly Wasp-ish women who had been high school buddies. Each had recently suffered through a divorce. To save on the high cost of living as well as to bolster each other, they and their combined three children moved into a Greenwich Village apartment. (And no, they weren't lesbians, either. CBS made that very clear, insisting that these two women's *single* beds in separate bedrooms be highly visible.) Allie managed the house while Kate was out there in the work force, an arrangement that worked better than many marriages do.

It was the perfect show for the times. The divorce rate was at its highest ever, with one out of two marriages splitting up. So it wasn't surprising that Sherry Koben, the series' creator, got the idea for "Kate & Alley" when she attended her high school's 10-year reunion and found herself surrounded by a sea of divorced women with children. While in past shows, unattached women raising children were always widows, this one

presented a scenario that a good percentage of viewers could relate to. "This is not a statement saying, 'Girls, leave the guys and go live with your best friend,'" co-star Susan Saint James, who played Kate, said in *People*. "Kate and Allie didn't plan this. It's just the best solution they could think of, and their friendship sustains them."

Remarkably, neither Jane Curtin, who played Allie, nor Saint James liked the idea of "Kate & Allie" when it was first presented to them. "I could relate to the problems of a divorced woman," said Saint James, having herself endured several failed marriages, "but I didn't want to play a show with glib kid actors." Curtin had other reasons. "All of the sitcoms I had loved took place outside the home. For 'Kate & Allie,' they wanted me to have two big kids. I didn't see myself as that maternal."

But the kids turned out to be pros, and over the course of the series' five-and-a-half-year run, several episodes were devoted exclusively to the problems of the rapidly maturing children.

The series' creative team always pointed out that one of the reasons for its success was that it was humor- rather than issue-oriented. "The show's not about women," Bill Persky, the director/executive producer, told *McCall's*. "It's about people, not sex or gender. We always find ways to make it funny *and* enlightening. But we never set out to do heavy themes or 'issue' shows. Our thinking always starts with 'This incident happened,' not with 'We have something to say.'" The comedy writing was gentle, subtle, and always clever. For example, when Allie's ex let the kids down on a long-promised

---

CREDITS

CREATOR: Sherry Kobin. EXECUTIVE PRODUCERS: Mort Lachman, Merrill Grant, Bill Persky, Saul Turtletaub, Bernie Orenstein. PRODUCERS: Bob Randall, Anne Flett, Chuck Ranberg. DIRECTORS: Bill Persky, others. WRITERS: Bob Randall, others. CAST: *Kate McArdle* (Susan Saint James), *Allie Lowell* (Jane Curtin), *Emma McArdle* (Ari Meyers), *Jennie Lowell* (Allison Smith), *Chip Lowell* (Frederick Koehler), *Charles Lowell* (Paul Hecht), *Ted Bartelo* (Gregory Salata), *Bob Barsky* (Sam Freed), *Lou Carello* (Peter Onorati).

EMMYS

Outstanding Lead Actress in a Comedy Series—Jane Curtin (1983–84, 1984–85), Outstanding Directing in a Comedy Series—Bill Persky (1983–84).

camping trip, Kate suggested she and Allie take the kids themselves:

ALLIE

But I'm not comfortable out-of-doors.

KATE

Just pretend the out-of-doors is a great big department store that sells animals, trees and dirt.

ALLIE

And snakes.

KATE

Designer snakes. Trust me.

The actresses playing Kate and Allie came from similar backgrounds, having both attended Catholic boarding schools when they were growing up. And although they weren't best friends like the characters they played, both had high regard for each other as actresses. "Working with Jane is pretty great," said Saint James in *McCall's*. "We both have the same work habits...Playing together is like a marriage. Because we have a contract, we're stuck with each other. And we stuck *with* each other," she said, referring to some of the difficult moments all series toss at their stars. Saint James, a 1969 Emmy winner for "The Name of the Game," had also played opposite Rock Hudson for five years in

"McMillan and Wife" (see page 198). Before "Kate and Allie," Jane Curtin was best remembered as one of the original cast members of NBC's "Saturday Night Live," which was her first big break; she got the job when she attended an open audition. Together, the two women had that rare, highly sought but seldom found chemistry that makes a series work, as did "Kate & Allie."

Over the years, the two women (along with their growing brood) continued to evolve. "Most sitcoms are based on the fact that the characters don't change," said Persky. "Our show is based on the fact that they do." The women held down different jobs, eventually opening their own catering business; the kids grew up and the older daughter left for college (around the same time the actress playing her did the same thing), and in 1988 Allie found a new love and was married.

After that, it was a stretch finding ways to keep the two women together. In the final season (1988–89), Kate moved into Allie's apartment to keep her company while her "weekend" husband was away on assignment Monday through Friday.

Susan St. James (left) and Jane Curtain.

HOTEL

NUMBER 9, 1983–84

Aaron Spelling had had great success with his romantic comedy/fantasy television shows. In 1977 he created a series of interwoven stories called "The Love Boat" (see page 268). The following year, he took that concept and placed a cast of romantics on "Fantasy Island," which premiered in 1978 and promised anyone that their dreams could come true, for a price. Then, in 1983, he again cloned his idea, this time setting his players into motion in "Hotel," a sort of landlubber's "Love Boat." It was based loosely on the Arthur Hailey bestseller of the same title, which had already been made into a theatrical movie in 1967. The Hailey concept itself had its roots in the 1932 film *Grand Hotel*, which opens with the famous lines, "Grand Hotel. People come and go. Nothing ever happens."

Fortunately for Spelling and for the audience, there were happenings aplenty. The premise was practically cut from the same sailcloth as that of "Love Boat": an anchoring cast, the routine parade of weekly big-name guest stars, the vacation setting—all were part and parcel of "Hotel."

For the original star, Spelling had a Really Big Name planned. Set to appear in her first weekly television series was Bette Davis. But Miss Davis was only able to film the series' pilot, which became the opening episode on September 28, 1983. She took ill shortly thereafter and was replaced by an actress who had spent much of her career following in Davis's footsteps. Anne Baxter was signed to play Victoria Cabot, the overseer of San Francisco's posh St. Gregory Hotel (a fictitious structure portrayed by footage of the Fairmont Hotel atop Nob Hill). Baxter had played Bette Davis's nemesis in *All About Eve* (1950), and in the 1971 stage version, renamed *Applause*, she played the role originated by Davis in the film. Ironically, she assumed the role intended for Davis in "Hotel."

The main character, however, was actually James Brolin, as hotel manager Peter McDermott. Brolin

hadn't done much television since his Emmy-winning role on "Marcus Welby, M.D." (see page 162). He was grateful, however, when that series ended in 1976. "That show took so long to die," he said later, "I was ready to shoot it in the head." In the intervening years he'd tried to make a go of a motion picture career, landing a few good parts such as that of Clark Gable in *Gable and Lombard* (1976) and a starring role in *The Amityville Horror* (1979). "I was getting along, doing this and that, a TV movie now and then," said Brolin in *TV Guide*, "but I wasn't having any fun. I didn't want to go back into weekly television." Then came the offer to do "Hotel." He was Aaron Spelling's first choice, but he wasn't particularly anxious to sign.

"But when I had read the last page [of the pilot script], I said: 'This is *good*. This is going to be a hit.'" When Spelling told him about the multiple guest stars, which meant less time for him to have to worry about being ready for the camera, he agreed to do the show.

Connie Sellecca co-starred as his beautiful assistant manager, Christine; later McDermott and Christine became "involved." Others in the regular cast included Shea Farrell as Mark Danning, director of guest relations; Nathan Cook as ex-con Billy Griffin, the chief of security; Heidi Bohay and Michael Spound as Megan and Dave Kendall, newlyweds who worked as desk clerk and bellhop; and Shari Belafonte-Harper, daughter of Harry Belafonte, as Julie Gillette, manager of hotel information.

In 1985 Anne Baxter died suddenly, and in a sentimental gesture, a portrait of her character was hung in the St. Gregory's lobby. The character was said to have died too, and the series took on overtones of a nighttime soap opera for a while when a battle for control of the hotel was waged among her heirs. Eventually Peter McDermott bought them out, and the squabbling, along with the series, came to a close in 1988.

CREDITS

CREATOR: Aaron Spelling. BASED ON: *Hotel*, by Arthur Hailey. EXECUTIVE PRODUCERS: Aaron Spelling, Douglas S. Cramer. PRODUCERS: E. Duke Vincent, Jerry London, Elaine Rich, others. DIRECTORS: various. WRITERS: John Furia, Jr., Barry Oringer, Andrew Laskos, others. CAST: *Peter McDermott* (James Brolin), *Christine Francis* (Connie Sellecca), *Victoria Cabot* (Anne Baxter), *Mark Danning* (Shea Farrell), *Billy Griffin* (Nathan Cook), *Dave Kendall* (Michael Spound), *Megan Kendall* (Heidi Bohay), *Julie Gillette* (Shari Belafonte-Harper), *Charles Cabot* (Efrem Zimbalist, Jr.), others. GUEST STARS: Lloyd Bochner, Morgan Fairchild, Jack Gilford, Shirley Jones, Lainie Kazan, Bill Macy, Erin Moran, Alejandro Rey, Pernell Roberts, Mel Torme, Arte Johnson, Liberace, Donald O'Connor, McLean Stevenson, Stewart Granger, Connie Stevens, Peter Marshall, Lynn Redgrave, Dina Merrill, Ralph Bellamy, others.

Clockwise from top left: Nathan Coo, James Brolin, Connie Sellecca, Shea Farrell, Michael Spound, Shari Belafonte-Harper, Anne Baxter, and Heidi Bohay.

CAGNEY & LACEY

NUMBER 10, 1983–84

In 1974, a writer named Barbara Corday was dating producer Barney Rosenzweig. In an effort to enlighten her boyfriend about the women's movement, Corday presented Rosenzweig with a book called *From Reverence to Rape: The Treatment of Women in the Movies*, by Molly Haskell. That gesture would change the course of Rosenzweig's life, along with the future of television. After reading the book, Rosenzweig came to the startling conclusion that there had never been a female "buddy" movie, and he became convinced that he should be the one to do it.

Corday heeded her friend's wishes and began developing the project with her writing partner, Barbara Avedon. At first their film was called *Newman & Redford*, referring to the buddy relationship of the two actors in a number of popular movies. The title was soon changed to *Cagney & Lacey*, and it was to be a comedy film set in New York, because, according to Corday, "New York was the funniest city in the world." Not according to the studios in Hollywood, which one by one turned down Rosenzweig's project. The determined producer then pitched it to all three major networks as a potential series. The same rejection happened. In a last-ditch attempt, he pitched it as a made-for-TV movie, and got the nod from CBS.

By now the format had been changed to a straight police drama, but with the two female characters still very central to the concept. Rosenzweig suggested an actress he knew named Sharon Gless for the part of Cagney, but CBS wanted Loretta Swit, who was then committed to a full-time series, "M*A*S*H." "They were blowing me out of the water as a series," complained Rosenzweig, realizing his hopes for a series based on this movie were becoming slimmer. Tyne Daly, daughter of the late James Daly (see "Medical Center," page 178), was signed as Lacey, and the telefeature

aired in October 1981 to a 42 percent share, a huge rating. CBS agreed, and ordered six episodes of a "Cagney & Lacey" series. Of course, Swit wasn't available to do Cagney full-time, so the part would have to be recast; it was, this time with brunette Meg Foster playing Cagney. It debuted in March 1982, airing right after "Magnum, P.I.," and earned a very respectable 24 share.

The following week it earned a 25 share. It was also cancelled at that time by CBS, after only two airings. Rosenzweig was furious. The show had good demographics, i.e., plenty of money-spending females, and he finally convinced the CBS brass to give it one more try, on Sunday, April 25, at 10:00 P.M. Again, the show pulled down good ratings—a 34 share. CBS now placed the new series on its fall lineup. But there was a catch: the role of Cagney had to be recast. Research had shown that viewers found the two women too similar in looks and streetwise mannerisms. Sharon Gless, who had been Rosenzweig's first choice all along, was immediately signed for Cagney.

CREDITS

CREATORS: Barney Rosenzweig, Barbara Corday, Barbara Avedon. EXECUTIVE PRODUCER: Barney Rosenzweig. PRODUCERS: Richard S. Rosenbloom, Steve Brown, P.K. Knelman, Ralph Singleton, Georgia Jeffries, Jonathan Estrin, Shelley List, others. DIRECTORS: various. WRITERS: various. CAST: *Det. Mary Beth Lacey* (Tyne Daly), *Det. Chris Cagney* (Loretta Swit, Meg Foster, Sharon Gless), *Harvey Lacey* (John Karlen), *Harvey Lacey, Jr.* (Tony La Torre), *Michael Lacey* (Troy Slaten), *Charlie Cagney* (Dick O'Neill), *Lt. Bert Samuels* (Al Waxman), *Det. Marcus Petrie* (Carl Bumbly), *Det. Victor Isbecki* (Mark Kove), *Det. Paul LaGuardia* (Sidney Clute), *David Keeler* (Stephen Macht), *Det. Manny Esposito* (Robert Hegyes), others.

EMMYS

Outstanding Lead Actress in a Drama Series—Tyne Daly (1982–83, 1983–84, 1984–85, 1987–88); Outstanding Drama Series (1984–85, 1985–86); Outstanding Directing in a Drama Series—Arthur Karen (1984–85), Georg Stanford Brown (1985–86); Outstanding Writing in a Drama Series—Patricia M. Green (1984–85); Outstanding Lead Actress in a Drama Series—Sharon Gless (1985–86, 1986–87); Outstanding Supporting Actor in a Drama Series—John Karlen (1985–86).

The series bowed in the fall of 1982 with good ratings. But soon ABC began throwing blockbusters like "The Thorn Birds" up against it, and ratings slipped. Again, CBS cancelled the series. Rosenzweig began a round of talk show and press interviews, and a grassroots letter-writing campaign plus four Emmy nominations finally convinced CBS to bring the series back. By March of 1984 it was back on the air with high enough ratings to place it in the top 10 for the season.

While the series was groundbreaking in its coverage of timely issues like date rape, breast cancer, child abuse, drug abuse, alcoholism, and so on, its unique-

Sharon Gless (left) and Tyne Daly.

ness came from the fact that the emphasis was on these problems in its two leads rather than in the criminals they pursued. "Cagney and Lacey are two women who happen to be cops," co-creator Barbara Corday said in *People*. "They are not two cops who happen to be women. We are doing a show about two women who had lives, interests, friendships, lovers, whatever. Being cops put them in more interesting situations, but being cops was never what it was all about."

The show's frankness generated some real-life problems. In 1985, when the Lacey character revealed she had had an abortion as an unwed teenager, the National Right to Life Committee demanded that CBS and its affiliates yank the show or provide opposing

arguments to abortion by showing their 30-minute film *A Matter of Choice* immediately after airing the episode of "C & L" in question. The story had been based on Barbara Corday's own experience as a 19-year-old, and she and Rosenzweig (by then a married couple) refused to back down. "We emphasized the anguish that women go through when they make that decision," he said. There was an unabashed liberal slant to the series; even the initial press release described detectives Mary Beth Lacey and Chris Cagney as women "whose lives embody the very spirit of the Equal Rights Amendment."

During the series' six years, the two main characters never stopped growing and developing. "We surprise ourselves all the time on this show," said Sharon Gless* in the *Hollywood Reporter*, "and the writers surprise us, too, in the development of these characters. The creative doors here are always open to us. As Barney [Rosenzweig] says, 'We are, indeed, the custodians of our characters.'" Tyne Daly agreed. "At the beginning of the series [Lacey's] job was brand-new; she was no longer a street officer and there was a period of adjustment," she pointed out in a 1987 interview. "Now her children are older, she's had another one, she's had a brush with fatal illness, she's killed another human being, and she's still as interesting to me, through all that, as she always was."

In 1987 the series filmed its 100th episode. At that time, Barney Rosenzweig predicted in the *Hollywood Reporter*, "We've come to a place where we see an ending in sight. It will last another year, another two years. Tyne Daly, Sharon Gless and I have more and more come to see that it's a once-in-a-lifetime experience...We all see that this is not going to happen to us again...What that show has meant in terms of its selling, its resurrection, its content, its impact on the rest of television—it's a unique experience."

"Cagney & Lacey" continued through the fall of 1988 and was then seen in syndication. Fans looked forward to reunion movies, which seemed possible due to the series' continuing popularity in syndication. Sharon Gless went on to star in the short-lived Rosenzweig series, "The Trials of Rosie O'Neill."

---

*Rosenzweig's marriage to Barbara Corday eventually broke up; he and Sharon Gless were married in the spring of 1991.

THE COSBY SHOW

NUMBER 3, 1984–85

In 1965, Bill Cosby broke new ground by becoming the first black man to co-star in a TV drama. The network giving him this break was NBC, the show was "I Spy," and Cosby went on to win three Emmys for his performances in the series. In 1984, 19 years, several TV series, and two more Emmys later, "the Cos" returned the favor to NBC. He created the most highly watched series of the decade, which boosted the network's ranking from third to first position. For four years in a row (1985–89) "The Cosby Show" remained on top, a record equalled only by "I Love Lucy," bested only by "All in the Family," and never even approached by an NBC show. In fact, "The Cosby Show" revived the sitcom at a time in television when that genre was a dying species.

It wasn't the most hilarious show ever seen. "Cosby" didn't go for the "I Love Lucy" slapstick yuks, nor was it a Norman Lear iconoclast out to instruct in political correctness. Instead, it was Bill Cosby's attempt to bring a successful family, who happened to be African-American, into the mainstream of television. "The Huxtables were set up to counter some of the minstrel shows Hollywood had set up," said Bill Cosby, co-creator, star, executive producer, creative consultant, and co-author of the show's theme music.

The series revolved around the Huxtable family, headed by Cliff (Bill Cosby), a successful obstetrician ("I had a rough day yesterday. Every child born on the face of this earth, I delivered."). He and his wife Clair, a lawyer, resided with their four children (a fifth one had left for college) in a New York brownstone. They were loving, nurturing, yet strict parents, committed to their careers, but even more so to their family. The show drew a lot of flack from critics, who claimed this was a most atypical black family. A book written by two University of Massachusetts professors claimed the Huxtables' affluence desensitized white Americans to the plight of inner-city blacks.

Authors Sut Jhally and Justin Lewis, who wrote *Enlightened Racism: Audiences, 'The Cosby Show,' and the Myth of the American Dream*, researched their findings in a study partially funded by Bill Cosby. No doubt there will be studies and theses written about "The Cosby Show" for years to come. Meanwhile, most people couldn't have cared less. They watched the Huxtable children grow up over the series' eight years and bonded with their family, a realistic one in the usual land of TV silliness.

Many of the weekly shows seemed to be plotless. Sometimes the family would gather 'round the photo album and reminisce, or spend the evening singing

---

CREDITS

TOP 10 PEAK: No. 1, 1985–86. CREATORS: Ed. Weinberger, Michael Leeson, William H. Cosby, Jr., Ed.D. EXECUTIVE PRODUCERS: Marcy Carsey, Tom Werner. PRODUCERS: John Markus, Carmen Finestra, Gary Kott, Terri Guarnieri, Matt Robinson, Caryn Sneider Mandabach, Matt Williams. DIRECTORS: Jay Sandrich, others. WRITERS: Ed. Weinberger, Michael Leeson, John Markus, Chris Auer, Janet Leahy, Matt Robinson, Gary Kott, Bill Cosby, others. CAST: *Dr. Heathcliff "Cliff" Huxtable* (Bill Cosby), *Clair Huxtable* (Phylicia Rashad*), *Theodore Huxtable* (Malcolm-Jamal Warner), *Vanessa Huxtable* (Tempestt Bledsoe), *Rudy Huxtable* (Keshia Knight Pulliam), *Denise Huxtable Kendall* (Lisa Bonet), *Sondra Huxtable Tibideaux* (Sabrina Le Beauf), *Anna Huxtable* (Clarice Taylor), *Russell Huxtable* (Earl Hyman), *Elvin Tibideaux* (Geoffrey Owens), *Olivia Kendall* (Raven-Symone), others. GUEST STARS: Sammy Davis, Jr., Stevie Wonder, Lena Horne, Tony Orlando, Roscoe Lee Browne, John Amos, Debbie Allen (Phylicia Rashad's sister), Moses Gunn, Jim Valvano, Dick Vitale, others.

EMMYS

Outstanding Comedy Series (1984–85), Outstanding Writing in a Comedy Series—Ed. Weinberger and Michael Leeson (1984–85), Outstanding Guest Performer in a Comedy Series—Roscoe Lee Browne (1985–86), Outstanding Directing in a Comedy Series—Jay Sandrich (1985–86).

---

*Listed as Phylicia Ayers-Allen for the first two seasons, she married NBC sportscaster Ahmad Rashad after he proposed to her on the air during a 1985 broadcast of "NFL Live!"

songs (once, with Stevie Wonder). A typical show found Cliff recalling his college football days when son Theodore (Malcolm-Jamal Warner) made his high school team; another had daughter Rudy (Keshia Knight Pulliam) experiencing something most children go through, when her pet goldfish died and was buried at sea (down the toilet). Whatever the problems, Bill Cosby was usually the one to help resolve them. He came under criticism for being ubiquitous, but hey, that was *his* name in the title, after all.

Although the series was ranked an impressive number five in the 1990–91 ratings, by the 1991–92 season,

station KNBC's decision to carry the final episode of "The Cosby Show." It had been a tough call. If the station carried it, they might be harshly criticized for being too commercial or insensitive and unsympathetic; if they preempted it, they risked criticism from the millions of people *not* involved in the rioting who were expecting this much-ballyhooed climactic episode. Airing it would also help the ratings in that "sweeps" period, when the L.A. viewership was so crucial. Cosby, in fact, had recorded two intros to the show just in case the station *had* preempted his episode. At the conclusion of the hour, another hastily taped statement by

The "Cosby" clan (from left): Sabrina Le Beauf, Malcolm-Jamal Warner, Bill Cosby, Keshia Knight Pulliam, Tempestt Bledsoe, Lisa Bonet, and Phylicia Ayers-Allen.

the cast and crew knew this year would be the show's last. "I ran out of everything I wanted to say with the Huxtables," said Cosby. Rather than let the series just fizzle out, a final episode was planned and heavily promoted. It was the most eagerly awaited episode since Lucy gave birth to Little Ricky. And it met, quite literally, with disaster.

On the afternoon of Thursday, April 30, 1992, the verdicts in the first Rodney King beating trial were announced in Los Angeles. Within hours, the city was beset with arson fires, looting, beatings, and general mayhem. L.A.'s seven VHF television stations immediately preempted all regularly scheduled programming to bring live aerial and ground coverage. There was nothing else to watch. And then, just before eight o'clock, the normal time for airing "The Cosby Show," an announcement was made by Bill Cosby, recorded just moments before air time, which explained local

Cosby was read: "Let us all pray that everyone from the top of the government down to the people in the streets...would all have good sense. And let us pray for a better tomorrow, which starts today." And then it was back to the killing, looting, and fires. Back to reality. A truly sad farewell to such old and dear friends.

The final episode ended with Theo's graduation from New York University. In the concluding scene, Cliff and Clair Huxtable, whose brood (save one) had now all left the nest, danced out the door, breaking that "fourth wall" between the stage and the live studio audience, and waltzed off the set and on to whatever futures awaited them.

"The Cosby Show" won six Emmys, 14 NAACP Image awards, a Peabody, and a Humanitas (writing) award during its eight years and 208 episodes. In 1993, reruns were being "stripped" (shown) daily in syndication, where it continued to bring in good ratings.

FAMILY TIES

The "Family Ties" story is a good example of how a television show can take on a life of its own. When Gary David Goldberg created "Ties" in 1982, the sitcom was to be an ensemble piece and a starring vehicle for actress Meredith Baxter-Birney, blonde-maned daughter of actress/producer Whitney Blake and star of such popular TV series as "Bridget Loves Bernie" (see page 196) and "Family" (1978–80). But before long, one young colt would pull away from the pack to emerge a cult hero and superstar, leaving the others in the dust.

The initial premise of the series had to do with a reverse generation gap. The Keatons had been flower-power '60s hippies; now they were trying to raise their trio of youngsters to admire their values. The kids, however, were products of the Reagan conservative era (not surprisingly, this was Ronald Reagan's favorite program) and considered mom and dad fossils from the Pleistocene. Witness this early banter between mom Elyse (Baxter-Birney) and nine-year-old daughter Jennifer (Tina Yothers) as they looked at a picture of a person with long dark hair, a headband, and a buckskin jacket:

> JENNIFER
> Oh, Mommy, you look so pretty. Like an Indian princess.
>
> ELYSE
> That's your father, dear.

The middle child, Mallory (Justine Bateman), was a 15-year-old, fashion-crazed airhead who blamed the demise of the dinosaurs and polyester leisure suits on the same thing: lack of interest.

And then there was the oldest child, Alex P. Keaton, a dressed-for-success, adolescent yuppie whose pinup of the month was William F. Buckley and who swooned with joy at the mere mention of Richard Nixon. The family

black sheep, to be sure. And yes, the darling of America. As early as the show's seventh episode, which ran 12 minutes overtime in taping because of the actor's show-stopping delivery in an episode in which Alex lost his virginity, it became obvious that Michael J. Fox was on the path to stardom.

The Canadian-born actor almost didn't get the job. Matthew Broderick was everybody's first choice based on the terrific performance he'd just completed in *War Games* (1983). But Broderick was concentrating on a Neil Simon play on Broadway and turned down the idea of working in weekly television. The "Family Ties" casting director recommended a 20-year-old Canadian whose main acting credit had been a series in that country called "Leo and Me," when he was 15. "That's a face you'll never see on a lunchbox," NBC chief Brandon Tartikoff is reported to have said. But the casting director urged them to trust her instincts, and Fox won the role of Alex.

Although Fox insisted he wasn't overplaying the role, it was obvious this young man had star quality. The volume of mail soared at Paramount Studios, where the show was filmed, and soon Michael J. Fox was receiving more letters than anyone on the lot, including Henry "Fonzie" Winkler. In 1985, he made his first feature film, *Back to the Future*, and suddenly Fox was a movie star. He worked hard at his craft, cranking out at least one film per year, yet always insisted on maintaining a loyalty to his "Ties" family. During the shooting of back-to-back *Back to the Future* sequels (*Back to the Future Part II* and *Part III*, released in 1989 and 1990, respectively), Fox worked days on "Ties," then dashed over to Universal to labor on the *Future* films. Other features included *The Secret of My Success* (1987), *Bright*

CREDITS

TOP 10 PEAK: No. 2, 1985–86.
CREATOR/EXECUTIVE PRODUCER: Gary David Goldberg. PRODUCERS: various.
DIRECTORS: various. WRITERS: various.
CAST: *Elyse Keaton* (Meredith Baxter-Birney), *Steve Keaton* (Michael Gross), *Alex P. Keaton* (Michael J. Fox), *Mallory Keaton* (Justine Bateman), *Jennifer Keaton* (Tina Yothers), *Andrew Keaton* (Brian Bonsall), *Skippy* (Marc Price), *Ellen Reed* (Tracy Pollan), *Nick Moore* (Scott Valentine), *Lauren Miller* (Courteney Cox). GUEST STARS: Geena Davis, John Dukakis, Tom Hanks, Barbara Berrie, Jay Tarses, others.

EMMYS

Outstanding Lead Actor in a Comedy Series—Michael J. Fox (1985–86, 1986–87, 1987–88), Outstanding Writing in a Comedy Series—Gary David Goldberg and Alan Uger (1986–87).

Lights, Big City (1988), *Casualties of War* (1989), *Doc Hollywood* (1991), and *The Hard Way* (1991). In 1985, "Family Ties" introduced Tracy Pollan as Ellen, a love interest for Alex. Michael J. Fox found himself smitten, too; he married Pollan a few years later, and the couple had a son, Sam Michael Fox, born in 1989. After taping the final episode of "Family Ties" in 1989, Fox continued his acting as well as a burgeoning directing career. Like most talented hyphenates (actor-directors), he insisted, "I want to direct more."

In an attempt to shift some of the focus away from Fox, the producers incorporated Meredith Baxter-Birney's real-life pregnancy into the series, and in 1984, while she was off delivering twins, the series introduced a new Keaton, baby Andrew, into the cast. The next season the part was played by twin babies (not Baxter-Birney's), as is the Hollywood custom, but in 1986 Brian Bonsall was brought in to play young Andrew, who was supposed to be three now. (Brian was all of four.)

The show continued to garner good ratings, at first because it was piggybacked with "The Cosby Show," but eventually scoring high Nielsens in its own right. At the start of each year there were rumors that it would be the last one; everyone automatically assumed that Fox would cheerfully thumb his nose at his TV family and head off for the lucrative world of full-time feature film making. And Fox always insisted that nothing could be further from his mind. But by 1989 it was apparent to all that the series had run its course. It was decided to have what was now becoming the traditional "final episode" for departing television series. "I know people say that my successful film career killed off the show, but it's just not true," said Fox in an article in *Inside Hollywood*. "My film career started in the fourth season, and the show ended after seven years. We all wanted to stop while it was still good. None of us wanted to see it tail off on a weak note. We wanted to go out on top, and we did." Well, not exactly. The series had finished the 1987–88 season in 17th place. At the end of the 1988–89 season, the series' last one, it was below the Nielsen top 20.

The 176th and final episode of "Family Ties" aired on May 14, 1989. In that episode, Alex graduated and headed off for the Wall Street brokerage career of his dreams. " 'Family Ties' is a section of my life that I wouldn't trade for anything in the world," said Michael J. Fox. "Without this show I'd be digging ditches in Vancouver. It was a complete economic and emotional godsend." At the end of the taping, the cast and crew said farewell to the audience (and their full-time jobs). The moment was taped and shown as part of the episode's conclusion. There were hugs and tears as they took their final bows. No sequels or reunions were planned by the show's creator, Gary David Goldberg, who seemed to have a last moment of hesitation when pulling the plug on this series after seven years. "We don't want to abuse our moment in the sun," he said, "but tonight it does seem like a mistake."

Clockwise from Top left: Justine Bateman, Tina Yathers, Meredith Baxter-Birney, "Baby Andrew," Michael J. Fox, and Michael Gross.

MURDER, SHE WROTE

NUMBER 8, 1984–85

"Murder, She Wrote" was a classic whodunit in the Miss Marple/Agatha Christie vein. In fact, the main character, Jessica Fletcher, was a blending of both, yet was neither. A retired schoolteacher and widow from Cabot Cove, Maine (who moved to Manhattan in 1991), at first she was an amateur sleuth who wrote novels on the side. Later, her mystery writing took a back seat, as Mrs. Fletcher left a trail of bodies everywhere she went—well over 200 by the series' ninth season. Chances are if you were anywhere near this lady, sooner or later a dead body was going to turn up. Of course the police were always inept and usually nabbed the wrong suspect. By paying close attention to details, the audience could play along with Jessica and identify the culprit before the final commercial. It could have been anyone, and red herrings abounded just to keep the audience on its toes. (Hint: watch for details in insert [close-up] shots—tire tracks, lipstick smears on glasses, that sort of thing.) The clues were always there; all you had to do to solve the murder was pay close attention.

And the audience did, year after year, making "Murder, She Wrote" one of the most successful series to span two decades. It went on the air in 1982 and starred Angela Lansbury as Jessica Fletcher. At 59, Lansbury was enjoying the fruits of her long career, which included an Oscar nomination for *Gaslight* (1944) and four Tony Awards for her Broadway musical performances. In 1984 co-creator Peter Fischer approached her to star in "Murder, She Wrote." The part had just been turned down by Jean Stapleton, but Angela wasn't that anxious to do a TV series. "The theater has always had first call on my talents," she said. "I genuinely thrill to the excitement of a live audience, and I have had very little desire to do television or films in recent years."

Yet Lansbury seriously considered the script, along with a different series offer from Norman Lear. She chose "Murder." "It was the first role I could imagine myself doing," she told *People*. "Everything was right there. I could have devised the character of Jessica Beatrice Fletcher myself." She went on to admit that her ego as an actress had a lot to do with her accepting the part. "Attempting to bring off my own show is a great challenge. If I can do it, at the age of 59, it will be a small miracle. I felt that it would have been a gap in my acting experience if I had never done a television series. I wanted to play to that huge audience just once." Actually, she played a lot more than that. In the spring of 1993 she concluded her ninth season as the mystery-prone writer, at the age of 68 (and looking better than when she started nine years before!).

No one expected the series to survive that long. As soon as it was announced, the doomsayers wagged fingers at co-creator Richard Levinson. "At best," he said, "we hoped that it would be a marginal success." But CBS's programming department knew that they had a

---

CREDITS

TOP 10 PEAK: No. 3, 1985–86. CREATORS: Peter Fischer, Richard Levinson, William Link. EXECUTIVE PRODUCERS: Peter S. Fischer, Angela Lansbury. PRODUCERS: Robert F. O'Neill, Robert E. Swanson, Robert Van Scoyk, Bruce Lansbury, Mark Burley, Tom Sawyer, Todd London, others. DIRECTORS: Vince McEveety, others. WRITERS: various. CAST: *Jessica Fletcher* (Angela Lansbury), *Sheriff Amos Tupper* (Tom Bosley), *Grady Fletcher* (Michael Horton), *Dr. Seth Hazlitt* (William Windom), *Mayor Sam Booth* (Richard Paul), *Sheriff Mort Metzger* (Ron Masak), *Dennis Stanton* (Keith Michell), *Robert Butler* (James Sloyan), *Lt. Perry Catalano* (Ken Swofford), *Rhoda* (Hallie Todd), *Dr. Raymond Auerbach* (Alan Oppenheimer). GUEST STARS: Lynn Redgrave, Lance Kerwin, George Maharis, Harry Morgan, Jeffrey Lynn, Martha Scott, Van Johnson, Lloyd Nolan, Arthur Hill, Harry Guardino, Carol Lawrence, Ned Beatty, Jayne Meadows Allen, Robert Culp, Robert Hooks, Jeff Conaway, Gabe Kaplan, David Soul, Mel Ferrer, Dina Merrill, David Birney, Kate Mulgrew, Cesar Romero, James Coburn, Nick Tate, Mitchell Ryan, Robert Vaughn, others.

potential gem of a series on their hands, and set about finding just the right time period in which to berth it. By selecting the Sunday night spot immediately following "60 Minutes," with its intelligent audience, they found that viewers kept their dials right where they were. "Murder, She Wrote" thrived in the time spot, and CBS wisely left it alone for nine years (with the exception of a few months one summer).

On March 11, 1987, a 90-minute episode of "Murder, She Wrote" became the pilot for "The Law & Harry McGraw," a spinoff series starring Jerry Orbach, which ran from September 1987 to February 1988.

By the ninth season (which many said would be the last), Angela Lansbury had been made executive producer of the series. "I realized that after eight years on the job, I knew as much about what makes the show work as anybody else does," she claimed. "Now I'll have the muscle to push through the ideas that I believe in." She voiced a leading role in Disney's *Beauty and the Beast* (1991), as well as starring in a 1992 TV movie, "Mrs. 'Arris Goes to Paris," quite a heavy schedule of work for a woman who was long past the supposed age of retirement, making her a perfect role model for the older generation and an inspiration to the younger set. In 1993, Ms. Lansbury, CBS, and Universal TV reached an agreement for her to star for two additional seasons, providing new murders for Jessica Fletcher to solve through 1995.

Angela Lansbury, with guest star Milton Berle.

KNOTS LANDING

NUMBER 9, 1984–85

Michele Lee and Don Murray.

"Knots Landing" was a spinoff of "Dallas" (see page 260), another one-hour drama from the Lorimar soap factory. According to creator/producer David Jacobs, "Knots" was conceived in 1977, even before its parent series, but was rejected by CBS and later revived as a spinoff. For many years the show was saddled with the "Dallas" connection, which angered Jacobs. "I always hated it. It helped us in the beginning," he said, "but the shows existed on different planes. Our show has always been more middle class."

Then, in 1986, when Val Ewing named her son after his late uncle, Bobby Ewing, only to have Bobby reappear in the infamous shower "dream" scene at the end of the "Dallas" season, Jacobs put his foot down. "After that," said Jacobs, "I said, 'No more crossover plots ever again.'"

Departing "Dallas" in December 1979 for the fictional town of Knots Landing, California, was Gary Ewing (Ted Shackelford), the alcoholic, black sheep, middle Ewing son. In tow was his off-again, on-again wife, the long-suffering Valene Ewing, played by Joan Van Ark (whose biography pointed out that she was named for Joan of Ark). Michele Lee played Karen Fairgate, their neighbor on the cul-de-sac known as Seaview Circle, where much of the action in the early years took place. Back at the beginning, Karen was a housewife/busybody who later took over her deceased husband's business and, later still, eloped to Las Vegas with attorney Mack MacKenzie (Kevin Dobson).

Meanwhile—there's always a "meanwhile" in soap operas—there was enough going on in this town to,

well, to sustain a television series like this for 14 years. To wit: marriages, divorces, murders, kidnappings, brain tumors—every good soap deserves brain tumors—wife swapping, blackmail, conspiracy, adultery, poisonings, and much, much more. Over the years you needed a score card to figure out just who was scoring with whom: Paige slept with Sumner; Linda slept with Sumner; Paige caught Linda sleeping with Sumner; Linda slept with Michael; Anne pretended to sleep with Sumner to irk Paige, who stopped sleeping with Tom, who left town. Val's twins were sold to an illegal adoption ring; Greg got a liver transplant; Chip killed Ciji Dunne and accidentally impaled himself on a pitchfork; Jill died after locking herself in the trunk of Gary's car to frame him for her death; Laura died from the aforementioned brain tumor; and a bullet intended for Mack hit Karen, who was threatened by a serial killer.

In 1988 the series got its first token black couple (why should whites be having all this fun?), played by Larry Riley and Lynne Moody. As unremarkable as this should have been, it was only the second time that blacks had been included in nighttime soapers, with Diahann Carroll having become the first black featured on a prime-time soap a few years back in "Dynasty" (see page 276).

Larry Riley played Frank Williams from 1988 until his death in June 1992 from AIDS. He had been ill during his third season on the show, and it turned out to be his last. According to his wife, Larry hadn't told anyone that the kidney problem he was being treated for was the result of the disease, since he was concerned that his career would be ruined. The whole cast was in shock over the loss of their friend and co-worker.

Joan Van Ark left at the end of the 1991–92 season, leaving Ted Shackelford and Michele Lee as the only two remaining from the original show. When she departed, she left on good terms: "I have loved more than life the 13 years I've had on that show," she said. "The people are my family—we have shared marriages, deaths, divorces. It's far more difficult to leave than I thought."

By 1993 the series' ratings had declined drastically, and no matter what the producers tried—new characters, new relationships, new brain tumors—nothing seemed to help this holdover from the '80s glory days of prime-time soap operas. It was ranked 46th at the end of the 1991–92 season, and by the 1992–93 season had sunk even lower.

In 1993 "Knots Landing" ended its 14-year run. With a total of 344 episodes, the series had become TV's third-longest-running prime-time one-hour drama, right after record holder "Gunsmoke" (406 segments) and "Dallas" (356 episodes). With the demise of "Knots," however, the era of prime-time soaps seemed all washed up.

CREDITS

CREATOR: David Jacobs. EXECUTIVE PRODUCERS: David Jacobs, Michael Filerman, Lee Rich. PRODUCERS: Barbara Corday, Ann Marcus, Mary Catherine Harold, Joel Okmin, Lawrence Kasha, Lynn Marie Latham, Bernard Lechowick. DIRECTORS: Michele Lee, Nicholas Sgarro, Lorraine S. Ferrara, Jerome Courtland, Peter Levin, others. WRITERS: various. CAST: *Gary Ewing* (Ted Shackelford), *Valene Ewing Gibson Waleska* (Joan Van Ark), *Karen Fairgate MacKenzie* (Michele Lee), *Abby Cunningham Ewing Sumner* (Donna Mills), *Lilimae Clements* (Julie Harris), *Mack MacKenzie* (Kevin Dobson), *Gregory Sumner* (William Devane), *Anne Matheson* (Michelle Phillips), *Frank Williams* (Larry Riley), *Julie Williams* (Kent Masters-King). OTHER REGULARS: John Pleshette, Constance McCashin, James Houghton, Kim Lankford, Claudia Lonow, Pat Peterson, Julie Harris, Stephen Macht, Lisa Hartman, Joanna Pettet, Danielle Brisebois, Millie Perkins, Alec Baldwin, Howard Duff, Ava Gardner, Joe Regalbuto, Ruth Roman, Red Buttons, Michael York, Betsy Palmer, Penny Peyser, France Nuyen, others.

CRAZY LIKE A FOX

NUMBER 10 (TIE), 1984–85

"Think: Funny murders." This is the basic instruction executive producers of "Crazy Like a Fox" gave their writers. Think: Nielsen top 10 hit. This was the result of that concept, developed by a team of both comedy and drama writers. The best of both worlds combined to create a hit CBS series.

The premise involved two opposites who did not at all attract. Jack Warden played Harry Fox (the "crazy" one of the title), an old-time detective whose clients ran the gamut from strange to bizarre. His straight-arrow yuppie son, Harrison (John Rubinstein), was a buttoned-down attorney with a family and no desire to help his eccentric dad solve his murder cases. So naturally, each week presented a challenge to find a new way to get son Harrison involved with Harry's cases. "The essence of every show was what we called the 'schmeikel,' says Frank Cardea, one of four executive producers of "Crazy Like a Fox." It was a Yiddish word they used to signify the con that always propelled Harrison into doing Harry's bidding, something he would never do willingly. "So Harry would come into Harrison's house and first compliment him on dinner, then say, 'But wait, there's something in the car you have to come out and see.' He would 'schmeikel' Harrison in, inch by inch," explains Cardea.

"Crazy Like a Fox" was plot-driven action-drama combined with comedic elements, and it didn't get bogged down in revealing psychological dialogue so frequently the essence of modern character-driven series like "thirtysomething" and "L.A. Law." "We always looked for crimes that had a humorous twist to the murder," says George Schenck, another executive producer of the show. "The episodes that were least successful were too intricate. We looked for funny murders, funny crimes, but with a lot of intricate plotting twists and turns."

Neither sitcom nor straight drama, "Crazy" was what is known as a "dramedy"—a hybrid of both. It came on the air when sitcoms were a dying breed, hitting the top 10 in its premiere season (1984–85), a year with only two other comedies making the list. The premise of "funny murders" was the gimmick that turned the trick and gave CBS its only comedy hit for the season.

How could a show about murder be considered funny? Frank Cardea explains, "Even though there was a murder every week, you never saw it; it was always off-camera. I don't think you ever saw blood, per se. There weren't more than half a dozen gun shots in the series' entire 37 hour-long episodes." Schenck concurs. "Our action was car chases played for fun," he says. "We never did the 'A-Team' thing where a car rolls over 15 times and the person walks away. We had car chases and dead bodies, but we didn't go for blood bursting out of people. The show fit Sunday night perfectly—the family could sit there and watch it together."

Jack Warden was selected to play the lead, Harry Fox. A well-known character actor, Warden had appeared in numerous series dating back to "Mr. Peepers" in 1953, along with starring roles in "N.Y.P.D." (1967–69), "Jigsaw John" (1976), and "The Bad News Bears" (1979–80). In 1972 he won an Emmy as Best Supporting Actor for his appearance in the TV movie "Brian's Song." Although noted for his dramatic roles, his flair for comedy garnered him two Academy Award nominations for his work in *Shampoo* (1975) and *Heaven Can Wait* (1978).

John Rubinstein played Harry's son, Harrison Fox. He was not, however, the producers' first choice for the role. They initially auditioned Alec Baldwin, but his reading wasn't what they were looking for. Next they sought Beau Bridges,

---

CREDITS

CREATORS/EXECUTIVE PRODUCERS/WRITERS: Frank Cardea and George Schenck, John Baskin and Robert Shulman. DIRECTORS: Paul Krasny, Gary Nelson, Bob Sweeney, Marc Daniels, Vince McEveety, others. WRITERS: various. CAST: *Harry Fox* (Jack Warden), *Harrison K. Fox* (John Rubinstein), *Cindy Fox* (Penny Peyser), *Josh Fox* (Robby Kiger), *Allison Ling* (Lydia Lei, Patricia Ayame Thomson), *Lt. Walker* (Robert Hanley), *Ernie* (Theodore Wilson), *Nurse Flood* (Della Reese). GUEST STARS: George Kirby, Rue McClanahan, Gene Barry, Cyd Charisse, Dorothy Lamour, June Allyson, Pat Harrington, Alan Hale, others.

Courtesy of George Schenck and Frank Cardera

Jack Warden (left) and John Rubenstein.

but he wanted a "favored nations" contract, giving him the same deal as star Jack Warden. It was Warden who then recommended John Rubinstein, whom he had seen on Broadway in *Children of a Lesser God* (for which Rubinstein won a 1980 Tony Award). Rubinstein had also appeared in numerous television episodes, including "Ironside," "The Mary Tyler Moore Show," "Cannon," "Hawaii Five-O," "The Love Boat," and "Lou Grant," plus others. He won a Best Actor Emmy nomination in 1978 for his role as Jeff on "Family."

The series was blessed with a sizable budget, which allowed for the crew to divide their time between a soundstage in Los Angeles, where interiors were filmed, and the streets of San Francisco for the show's exterior scenes. One of the first buildings selected was the office of Harrison Fox. Although the series wrapped production in 1986, George Schenck claims "If you go to the corner of Sutter and Market, it still says 'Harrison Fox' on the window." The office belonged to a well-known sports attorney, and the building was prominently featured in all the episodes. Another exterior used was Harry's apartment, which turned out to belong to O.J. Simpson at the time they selected it, and

they secured his permission to film the building.

Although the series was an initial smash hit, it succumbed quickly, for a number of reasons. It aired at 9:00 P.M., following "Murder, She Wrote," and was placed opposite NBC's and ABC's two-hour movies beginning at that same hour. Audiences didn't want to split their time—if they watched the one-hour episodes of "Crazy," they'd be joining a movie in progress at 10:00, and in 1986, CBS decided they too would put a two-hour movie in that time slot. In their wisdom, the powers that be at CBS moved "Crazy" to Wednesday nights, opposite "Dynasty," highly popular with the same demographic audience—women over 50 (who found that Harry reminded many of them of their husbands). By September of 1986, the show had been shifted three more times, from Wednesday to Saturday to Thursday (in two different time slots). There was no mystery—'twas CBS that killed this "Fox."

A reunion movie aired on April 5, 1987, called "Still Crazy Like a Fox," with the father-and-son team heading off to England and, of course, getting involved in a murder there. The film was the highest-rated CBS movie that year, but the series did not return to production.

CHEERS

NUMBER 5, 1985–86

Sometimes you want to go
Where everybody knows your name...
——OPENING THEME SONG

The formula for the success of "Cheers" was like that of a potent cocktail that bartender Sam Malone might serve up: one part comedy, one part romance, one part soap opera, add a generous handful of familiar yet somewhat quirky characters, and blend well. Stir in abundant laughter and sip slowly until feeling warm and fuzzy.

"Cheers" first appeared in the Nielsen top 10 after having been on the air for three seasons, and it was never rated lower than number five after 1985 (often topping the list as number one in the weekly Nielsens). Yet for all the show's popularity, it was almost cancelled during the first year due to its low ratings. In the series' first year it frequently appeared near the *bottom* of the chart, hovering around number 60. Fortunately, NBC recognized the potential of this audience pleaser and refused to cancel the series, counting on word of mouth to help the program find its audience. "Cheers" did indeed find its audience. And lucky the audience that managed to find "Cheers."

"Cheers" debuted on September 30, 1982, with a cast of six regulars. Sam Malone (Ted Danson) was the owner of Cheers, a bar with sets patterned after a real-life Boston tavern, the Bull & Finch. For the first five years of the series, Sam—the quintessential woman-izer—was involved with Diane Chambers (Shelley Long), as far above him on the IQ scale as Carl Sagan is above Mickey Mouse.

Another original regular was Nicholas Colasanto as Coach, a bartender with a Gracie Allen-esque outlook on the world:

COACH
I think of smart things and by the time I say them, they come out stupid.

CARLA
That doesn't make any sense.

COACH
Well, you should have heard it before I said it.

Nick once said of his character, "He's innocent and sweet, but not dumb. He may be intelligent, but he's

---

CREDITS
TOP 10 PEAK: No. 1, 1990–91. CREATORS/EXECUTIVE PRODUCERS: Glen Charles, Les Charles, James Burrows. PRODUCERS: Dan O'Shannon, Cheri Eichen, Bill Steinkellner, Phoef Sutton, Peter Casey, David Lee, David Angell, Heide Perlman (Rhea's sister), Tim Berry, Andy Ackerman, Brian Pollack, Mert Rich, Tom Anderson, Larry Balmagia. DIRECTOR: James Burrows. WRITERS: Les Charles, Glen Charles, Heidi Perlman, David Lloyd, Phoef Sutton, others. CAST: *Sam Malone* (Ted Danson), *Diane Chambers* (Shelley Long), *Carla Tortelli* (Rhea Perlman), *Ernie "Coach" Pantusso* (Nicholas Colasanto), *Norm Peterson* (George Wendt), *Cliff Clavin* (John Ratzenberger), *Dr. Frasier Crane* (Kelsey Grammer), *Woody Boyd* (Woody Harrelson), *Rebecca Howe* (Kirstie Alley), *Dr. Lilith Sternin Crane* (Bebe Neuwirth), *Robin Colcord* (Roger Rees), *Eddie LeBec* (Jay Thomas), *Kelly Gaines Boyd* (Jackie Swanson), *Paul* (Paul Willson), *Phil* (Phil Perlman, Rhea's father).

EMMYS
Outstanding Comedy Series (1982–83, 1983–84, 1988–89); Outstanding Lead Actress in a Comedy Series—Shelley Long (1982–83); Outstanding Directing in a Comedy Series—James Burrows (1982–83, 1990–91); Outstanding Writing in a Comedy Series—Glen Charles and Les Charles (1982–83), David Angell (1983–84); Outstanding Supporting Actress in a Comedy—Rhea Perlman (1983–84, 1984–85, 1985–86, 1988–89); Outstanding Guest Performer in a Comedy Series— John Cleese (1986–87); Outstanding Supporting Actor in a Comedy Series—Woody Harrelson (1988–89); Outstanding Lead Actor in a Comedy Series—Ted Danson (1989–90); Outstanding Supporting Actress in a Comedy Series—Bebe Neuwirth (1989–90, 1990–91); Outstanding Lead Actress in a Comedy Series—Kirstie Alley (1990–91); plus eight technical awards. At the end of the 1991–92 season, "Cheers" had amassed more Emmy nominations (109) than any other prime-time series in history, as well as 26 Emmy awards. The 1992–93 season promised to add to the total.

not worldly-wise. He's so positive. That's what makes him funny." Sadly, Nick Colasanto died of a heart attack during the filming of the show's third season.

Razor-tongued waitress Carla Tortelli (Rhea Perlman) spent the first few years of the show having babies (legitimate and otherwise) and hurling verbal spears mainly at the insufferably proper Diane. To wit:

DIANE
Hi, everybody. Guess why I'm here?

CARLA
Generations of inbreeding?

Clockwise from top left: George Wendt, John Ratzenberger, Nicholas Colasanto, Ted Danson, Shelley Long, and Rhea Perlman.

Rounding out the cast (no pun intended) were two permanent fixtures. George Wendt was the beer-bellied, beer-guzzling Norm Peterson. He was the one everybody knew the name of, as in the title song; when he entered, Cheers' patrons always hollered in unison, "NORM!" His drinking buddy was Cliff Clavin (John Ratzenberger), the know-it-all postal worker (now you know why your mail is always late). Cliff and Carla had a mutual hate thing, too:

POSTAL INSPECTOR
Do you have a Clavin here?

CARLA
Yeah, but it hasn't been flushing right lately.

Later additions to the cast included Kirstie Alley as Rebecca Howe, who replaced Shelly Long when she voluntarily left the series in 1987; Woody Harrelson as bartender Woody Boyd, who replaced Coach; Kelsey Grammer as Dr. Frasier Crane, a neurotic psychiatrist (an oxymoron—aren't all TV shrinks?) who was once engaged to Diane; and Bebe Neuwirth as Dr. Lilith Sternin Crane, an erudite ice queen and psychiatrist who eventually married Frasier then left him for another in the 11th season.

"Cheers" was one of the few comedies to have a summer cliffhanger each year, something usually reserved for dramas and soap operas. In fact, there was an underlying soaper feel to "Cheers," since the characters developed and grew during its 11-year run. The biggest cliffhanger of all, however, was: Would "Cheers" return for a 12th season? In December 1992 Paramount announced that the last call had sounded for "Cheers," deciding to terminate production "too early rather than too late." Although the studio tried to pin some of the blame on slipping ratings, the series had in fact finished the 1990–91 season in the number four position, and was still drawing good numbers in the 1991–92 season. Despite NBC's protests that "It was not about money," all facts seemed to indicate otherwise. "Cheers" was believed to be the most expensive show in the history of television, costing NBC $65 million for 26 episodes in 1991–92. And star Ted Danson—who was reportedly in on the decision to pull the plug—earned more than $450,000 per episode.

A final episode, number 275, was planned for May 1993, and like the "M*A*S*H" "Farewell, Goodbye and Amen" finale, it was expected to pull a whopping rating. There were plans for a spinoff series starring Kelsey Grammer as psychiatrist Frasier Crane. And with any luck the "Cheers" cast will all be bellying up to the bar in some future reunion.

THE GOLDEN GIRLS

NUMBER 7, 1985–86

From left: Bea Arthur, Estelle Getty, Betty White, and Rue McClanahan.

NBC-TV's "The Golden Girls" was the highest-rated new series in the 1985–86 season. It also broke ground as the first series to have an all-female cast; in addition, those women were all 50-plus, unusual for a medium that usually gets its strongest audiences for shows with youth appeal. "The Golden Girls," however, managed to draw fans across all lines.

The series concerned four women who were house-mates, all in their golden years—two widows, a divor-cée, and her outspoken mother. It starred Bea Arthur as Dorothy Zbornak, a substitute school teacher who divorced her husband after he left her for a younger woman. (He would attempt to win Dorothy back in later years, to no avail.)

Blanche Devereaux (Rue McClanahan) was a Tennessee Williams-ish southern belle, the owner of the house and the merry widow (she even tried to get a date at her husband's funeral). Determined to hang

onto her youth, her (over)sexuality at times tended to turn her into a one-joke character, but like all the char-acters on this show, she revealed more complexities as the seasons progressed.

Betty White played Rose Nylund, a sweet, lovable, innocent type with a penchant for non sequiturs. She came from the fictional town of St. Olaf, in Minnesota farm country, and she never let anyone forget it. If her stories were to be believed, St. Olaf was actually Gracie Allen-land—a quasi-Scandinavian community that seemed to have come to Earth from the planet Strange. Her character was far and away the series' funniest.

Estelle Getty, a perky sixtysomething redhead, played Dorothy's grey-haired, outspoken mother, Sophia Petrillo, an *eighty*something Sicilian (her part of Sicily could have given St. Olaf a run for its money).

Over the course of the series' seven seasons, audi-ences came to embrace this "family"—and they were a family in nearly every sense of the word—as their own, showering it with consistent top 10 ratings. And each of the gifted actresses playing the "girls" received at least one Emmy.

The series was created by Susan Harris, who had been a writer on "All in the Family" and "Maude," as well as the creator and executive producer of "Soap" and "Benson." Her first idea was to cast Bea Arthur in a role similar to the title character she played in "Maude"—an outspoken, cause-espousing, caustic liberal. While some of those qualities remained, the "Maudiness" was quickly toned down when critics assailed the carbon copy. But she still retained a quick, biting wit, as in this line after their home had been ransacked:

ROSE
They were probably looking for drugs.

DOROTHY
We have Maalox and estrogen. How many thieves have gas and hot flashes?

There had originally been plans to have Betty White play the nymphomaniacal Blanche, a character similar to the Sue Ann Nivens role played by White on "The Mary Tyler Moore Show." And Rue McClanahan was pictured as the spacy Rose, to be played in a manner similar to that of her old role as Vivian, Maude's cheerfully vacant neighbor. But director Jay Sandrich switched the dialogue during an early rehearsal, having the two read each other's parts. It worked, and Betty became Rose while Rue became Blanche.

Although the emphasis was on laughs, there was almost a Norman Lear-like quality to the show in the way it incorporated contemporary issues into many of the story lines—not surprising since Susan Harris had cut her writing teeth on Norman Lear productions. Over the years the "girls" dealt not only with problems of aging gracefully but also with such matters as compulsive gambling, death and the possible afterlife, birthing centers, parents of gay children, lesbianism, HIV and AIDS, heart attacks, and of course sex in the 80s (not the decade—the age!).

In 1991 NBC decided to move "The Golden Girls" to a time slot one hour earlier—from 9:00 P.M. to 8:00 P.M. It was a fatal mistake. The ratings fell off drastically. Then during the course of the year, Walt Disney Productions/Touchstone announced that, in an effort to cut costs, they would no longer produce the series; Warner Bros. soon picked up the ball and agreed to produce episodes the following year. But before that could happen, Bea Arthur announced she would be leaving the series at the end of the 1991–92 season, shocking everyone by claiming, "I love the idea of leaving at the height of its success." (Actually, the show finished the season—its worst—in the number 32 position.) The producers quickly scrambled to find a way to salvage the show, and decided to marry off Dorothy in the finale (to Leslie Nielsen, playing Blanche's uncle Lucas) while creating a spinoff for the other three characters. NBC declined to air the new series, titled "The Golden Palace"; the network wanted more programming with youth appeal, like "Blossom" and "Fresh Prince of Bel Air." Finally, CBS agreed to air the new series.

"The Golden Palace" debuted in the fall of 1992 with Estelle Getty, Betty White, and Rue McClanahan reprising their characters, who now ran a Miami Beach hotel (Cheech Marin was added to the cast to spice things up a bit). Bea Arthur returned to the show for a couple of guest spots as Dorothy Zbornak. But the series, running on Friday nights, didn't seem to be the Nielsen powerhouse its antecedent had been, while critics likened it to the doomed "AfterMASH." Its future after the 1992–93 series did not seem to be that golden.

The glitter may have been gone, but the original remained a 14-carat gem. In 1993 "The Golden Girls" could still be seen in syndication.

CREDITS

TOP 10 PEAK: No. 4, 1987–88. CREATOR: Susan Harris. EXECUTIVE PRODUCERS: Paul Junger Witt, Tony Thomas, Susan Harris. PRODUCERS: Marsha Posner Williams, Terry Grossman, Kathy Speer, Mort Nathan, Barry Fanaro, Winifred Hervey, Jeffrey Ferro, Fredric Weiss, Marc Sotkin, Philip Lasker, Tom Whedon, Gail Parent, Robert Bruce, Marty Weiss, Tracy Gamble, Richard Vaczy, others. DIRECTORS: Jay Sandrich, Paul Bogart, Terry Hughes, others. WRITERS: various. CAST: *Dorothy Zbornak* (Bea Arthur), *Rose Nyland* (Betty White), *Blanche Devereaux* (Rue McClanahan), *Sophia Petrillo* (Estelle Getty), *Stanley Zbornak* (Herb Edelman), *Miles Webber* (Harold Green). GUEST STARS: Polly Holliday, Jerry Orbach, Barbara Babcock, Ken Howard, Cesar Romero, Scott Jacoby, Murray Hamilton, Ruby Dee, Debbie Reynolds, Mitchell Ryan, Lloyd Bochner, Leslie Nielsen, Monte Markham, Michael Ayr, Mel Stewart, Keye Luke, Don Ameche, Howard Duff, Martin Mull, Sonny Bono, Lyle Waggoner, Brenda Vaccaro, Nancy Walker, David Wayne, Paul Willson, others.

EMMYS

Outstanding Comedy Series (1985–86, 1986–87), Outstanding Lead Actress in a Comedy Series—Betty White (1985–86), Outstanding Writing in a Comedy Series—Betty Fanaro and Mort Nathan (1985–86), Outstanding Lead Actress in a Comedy Series—Rue McClanahan (1986–87), Outstanding Directing in a Comedy Series—Terry Hughes (1986–87), Outstanding Lead Actress in a Comedy Series—Bea Arthur (1987–88), Outstanding Supporting Actress in a Comedy Series—Estelle Getty (1987–88).

MIAMI VICE
NUMBER 9, 1985–86

With colors as mellow as those of a tropical Florida sunset, along with a pounding musical score and two symbolically sexy leads in the roles of undercover cops, "Miami Vice" stormed into the 1984 television scene like a hurricane. In its first season it went head-to-head with "Falcon Crest," and having dislodged that show from the Nielsen top 10, it moved on to the war of the cities—"Miami" versus "Dallas." Goodbye Big D. This "Vice" squad was here to stay, at least as long as the Nielsens could stand the heat.

It was a throwback to earlier times of good-and-evil crime shows—our guys were good, the druggies they chased on a weekly basis were bad. Fine, but "Kojak," "Dragnet," and "Mannix" had all had the same premise, yet nobody screamed or swooned when Jack Webb or Telly Savalas strolled down the block. But then, Jack was no Don Johnson in an Armani suit.

Blond, icy-blue-eyed, sandy-voiced Don Johnson was a virtual unknown when cast for the co-lead in this "buddy" series. A Missouri native who had served time in a reformatory during his youth, Johnson attended the University of Kansas on a drama scholarship and later came to Hollywood to star in a series of forgettable B movies (*The Magic Garden of Stanley Sweetheart*, 1970; Harlan Ellison's 1975 cult film, *A Boy and His Dog*) and half a dozen unsold TV pilots. Following his underwhelming success in these ventures, Johnson plunged into a downward spiral of drug use and alcohol abuse. He also had a steady succession of lady friends (one of whom once described him as "drop-dead gorgeous"), including Melanie Griffith (he began dating her when she was only 14, later married and divorced her, and married her again many years later after their relationship was rekindled in a "Miami Vice" episode); Patty D'Arbanville, who gave birth to his son; and even (post-"Miami Vice") Barbra Streisand.

"Miami Vice" creator Anthony Yerkovich had a tough time convincing the NBC brass that Johnson was the right one to play hip undercover cop Sonny Crockett. The network conducted a worldwide search, auditioning dozens of English-speaking actors in the U.S., Canada, and England. Philip Michael Thomas was also initially rejected by the NBC casting people. "I told

my agent they were nuts," he said. "I said, 'No one can do this but me.'" The execs were playing mix and match with acting pairs when, several weeks later, Thomas was called back in to read with fellow reject Don Johnson. The audition, unrehearsed, produced an instant chemical compound. "When I first read with Philip, an electricity struck," Johnson said. "We could feel it, people in the area felt it, and it happens to this day." "We read, and the magic was happening," claimed Thomas. "It was like fire and air."

Thomas, a strikingly handsome man of mixed African-Native American-German-Irish ancestry ("I'm American gumbo"), garnered quite a fan following of his own as Detective Ricardo Tubbs. He also became known as the outspoken, self-promoting member of the cast, given to braggadocio; modesty was not in his vocabulary. "We've become bigger than the Beatles," he

CREDITS

CREATOR: Anthony Yerkovich. EXECUTIVE PRODUCERS: Michael Mann, Anthony Yerkovich. PRODUCERS: various. DIRECTORS: Thomas Carter, Paul Michael Glaser, Edward James Olmos, others. WRITERS: Anthony Yerkovich, Miguel Pinero, Maurice Hurley, others. CAST: *Det. Sonny Crockett* (Don Johnson), *Det. Ricardo Tubbs* (Philip Michael Thomas), *Lt. Martin Castillo* (Edward James Olmos), *Det. Gina Navarro Calabrese* (Saundra Santiago), *Det. Trudy Joplin* (Olivia Brown), *Det. Stan Switek* (Michael Talbott), *Det. Larry Zito* (John Diehl), *Caitlin Davies* (Sheena Easton). GUEST STARS: Gregory Sierra, Jimmy Smits, Jason Robards, Cybill Shepherd, Judith Ivey, Melanie Griffith, Bianca Jagger, Tommy Chong, G. Gordon Liddy (the convicted Watergate felon, in the role of a sneaky real estate dealer), Lee Iacocca (the chairman of Chrysler), Brandon Tartikoff (then president of NBC-TV, in a cameo as a bartender), Glenn Frey, Little Richard, James Brown, Phil Collins.

EMMYS

Outstanding Supporting Actor in a Dramatic Series— Edward James Olmos (1984–85).

once proclaimed (of course, the Beatles had once said the same thing about themselves and Jesus Christ). "I'm like Gandi in a sense," Thomas limned in *People* magazine. "I don't mind walking with the people. I will take off my suits and ties and get down there and work...There are only a few who will be the Fords, the Edisons, the Carnegies, and I think I'm in that number."

The third prominent member of the cast was actor Edward James Olmos, a Tony award winner for his role in the stage play *Zoot Suit*. Olmos went on to win an Emmy as Lieutenant Castillo. "One of the things I have found most exciting about 'Miami Vice' is that they have allowed me to play this character the way I wanted to play him," said Olmos in *Time* magazine. "Castillo is very disciplined, very obsessive in his routines. He is a Ninja warrior. In order to be a very good combatant of crime, you have to understand crime. So Castillo walks a very thin line." Olmos was a product of the Boyle Heights section of the Los Angeles melting pot and spent recent years trying to give something back to the city of his birth. Following the Los Angeles riots in the spring of 1992, Olmos, a well-respected community member, was one of the first on the scene to roll up his sleeves and pitch in to help the city through the healing process.

The series was known for its look as much as for its high-profile cast, with an emphasis on pastel colors—lime green, peach, and mauve—for its backgrounds and clothing. The men's fashion industry was given a shot in the arm when Johnson sported the "Miami Vice" look: loose-fitting linen jackets, pastel T-shirts, pants without a belt, shoes without socks. Macy's, Bloomingdale's, and other large department stores could barely keep up with with the demand for these trendy duds.

And then there was that music score. Besides source music from the likes of Phil Collins, Cyndi Lauper, the Pointer Sisters, the Stones, Lionel Richie, and others, there was the heart-thumping score composed by Czech-born Jan Hammer, whose digital synthesizer cranked out a title theme that shot to the top of the *Billboard* singles chart the week of November 9, 1985. The soundtrack album included Glenn Frey's hit single "You Belong to the City"; the album went on to become the number one soundtrack LP for 11 weeks, the most successful TV soundtrack of all time.

By 1989 the ratings had declined along with America's diminishing attraction to neon, pastels, drug busts, and yes, even Don Johnson and Philip Michael Thomas. The show was consistently over budget, and executive producer Michael Mann (who went on to direct the 1992 film *The Last of the Mohicans*) decided it would be the last season of "Vice." The series had fallen to number 53 by the time production ceased. There was a final episode in which Crockett and Tubbs left the force.

The series was sold into syndication on the USA Cable Network, where it appeared occasionally. And for live-action thrills, Universal Studios, which produced the show, had a popular "Miami Vice" attraction at their Hollywood theme park, with speed boats, helicopters, explosions, and Crockett and Tubbs look-alikes.

Philip Michael Thomas (left) and Don Johnson.

WHO'S THE BOSS?

NUMBER 10, 1985–86

Role reversal was the concept behind the title in "Who's the Boss?," a series that asked the question, Can a single female executive/parent maintain harmony in her own household while supervising a single male/parent housekeeper? It was a burning question for the '80s at a time when women were not only becoming more assertive in daily life but were also assuming their rightful places in the power-struggling corporate world. But the question of who the boss really was in this sitcom, which premiered on ABC in the fall of 1984, was more or less rhetorical. *Both* Angela (Judith Light) and Tony (Tony Danza) were in charge, depending on the situation.

From its inception, the series was tailored for Tony Danza, former co-star of "Taxi" (see page 256). But creators Blake Hunter and Martin Cohan had a difficult time convincing Danza's manager that this was the role of a lifetime for him. "There was a period when we heard that [Danza's manager] Jerry Weintraub was worried that playing a housekeeper was the wrong image for Tony," said Hunter in *TV Guide*. "At that point, we auditioned others, but came to the conclusion that if we couldn't get Tony, it would be pointless to go forward with the project." But after the pot was sweetened financially, Weintraub/Danza saw the benefits of having Tony essentially playing himself, a macho ex-sports star (in "Taxi" it had been boxing; this time it was baseball). His masculinity wouldn't be threatened and his acting capabilities wouldn't be overtaxed. He would play a widower with a young daughter, who worked as a live-in housekeeper for a successful divorcée living in Connecticut with her young son and oversexed, middle-aged mother (was there any other kind?).

In the summer of 1983, when the series was in the early stages of preproduction, the producers had Danza read with several ladies who were contenders for the role of ad exec Angela Bower. No one seemed to click until Judith Light, a star of daytime soaps (five years and two Emmys on "One Life to Live"), was brought in. The producers, none of them soap fans, were ambivalent until, upon completing her reading, Light walked past Danza, who checked out her derrière as she strolled by. Staying in character, Light whirled, held him in her gaze, and demanded, "What are *you* looking at?" The producers broke up laughing, and she got the role. "She just looked so natural," said co-creator/producer Martin Cohan.

The series' third lead was Katherine Helmond as Angela's sex-starved, meddling mother, Mona. Helmond had played the off-center Jessica Tate in Norman Lear's spoof, "Soap" (1977–81). Her expertise at bringing "Boss"'s spunky older lady to life prompted the producers to attempt a spinoff, "Mona," which was presented as an episode of "Who's the Boss?" in May of 1987. A fine cast of TV actors, including Paul Sand, James B. Sikking (as her brother), Joe Regalbuto (later of "Murphy Brown"), and others was assembled, but the material was weak, and "Mona" didn't sell. It was just as well, since much of the success of "Who's the Boss?" could be credited to the byplay between Angela and her constantly critical, wise-cracking mother.

As the years progressed, the characters evolved. Tony bettered himself by completing his education, the kids moved through school, and the relationship between the boss and her employee heated up. After what basically amounted to seven years of foreplay, the couple finally

CREDITS

TOP 10 PEAK: No. 6, 1987–88.
CREATORS: Martin Cohan and Blake Hunter. EXECUTIVE PRODUCERS: Martin Cohan, Blake Hunter, Phil Doran, Danny Kallis. PRODUCERS: Karen Wengrod, Ken Cinnamon, John Anderson, Joe Fisch, Bob Rosenfarb, Clay Graham, Gene Braunstein, Michael Greenspan, John Maxwell Anderson. DIRECTORS: Asaad Kelada, Bill Persky, Tony Singletary, others. WRITERS: various. CAST: *Tony Micelli* (Tony Danza), *Angela Bower* (Judith Light), *Mona Robinson* (Katherine Helmond), *Samantha Micelli* (Alyssa Milano), *Jonathan Bower* (Danny Pintauro), *Billy* (Jonathan Halyalkar).

Clockwise from left: Tony Danza, Judith Light, Katherine Helmond, Alyssa Milano, and Danny Pintauro.

consummated the relationship, and during the final season they became engaged.

In 1992 ABC decided to conclude many long-running series on the same night—Saturday, April 25. That evening was devoted to final episodes of "Who's the Boss?," "Growing Pains," and "MacGyver." In the concluding hour-long "Boss" episode, Tony accepted a year's employment as a teacher/coach in Iowa, and he and Angela resigned themselves to a relationship of weekend commuting. Eventually Angela decided to join Tony in Iowa, which she kept calling Idaho. But when Tony's contract was extended to three years, Angela broke off the engagement and returned to the East; she'd had enough of quilting and coupon clipping and longed for the adrenaline rush of being a type A advertising exec. Of course, the series needed the obligatory sitcom "they all lived happily ever after" finale, so Tony packed up and returned to Connecticut and surprised Angela at her front door. Fresh from shampooing her

hair, Angela arrived at the door clad in the same bathrobe and turban she'd worn when she first greeted Tony in the series opener, eight years earlier. "I hear you're looking for a housekeeper," said Tony. After 199 episodes, the series had come full circle.

The show may have left the prime-time airwaves, but it continued to be a hit in England, where a series called "The Upper Hand" was in its fifth season. The producers there had an arrangement with the American production company whereby they used the original "Who's the Boss?" scripts for their version. The characters were fine-tuned to accommodate the differences between American and British culture (as was the dialogue), but the situation was still that of a successful female advertising executive who hired a widower housekeeper. The series proved so successful that the British group optioned the right to create new scripts when the "Boss" stockpile of 199 runs out. A similar reincarnation was in the works for German television.

NIGHT COURT

NUMBER 7, 1986–87

Approaching the bench (clockwise from top left): Charles Robinson, John Larroquette, Markie Post, and Harry Anderson.

Bowing as a mid-season entry in January 1984, "Night Court" was never a powerhouse or revolutionary sitcom. It was never heavy on issues or messages, and it wasn't particularly craved by the Nielsen family of viewers. Nevertheless it had two aspects that sustained its eight-and-a-half-year tenure on NBC: warm, likable characters and loads of comedic charm.

The original "Night Court" concept was a show similar to "Barney Miller," which had been produced by "Court" creator, Reinhold Weege. The two were cousins, if not brother sitcoms, with similarities that included slightly off-center characters in a fixed location where a profusion of oddballs wandered in and out. (The two shows even had similar theme music by

the same composer.) A nightly parade of hookers, drunks, and domestic brawlers provided passing interest, but the real heart of "Night Court" lay in its quirky characters.

In the pilot, 34-year-old, baby-faced Harry T. Stone was pressed into service as a judge in a typical New York night court when he was the only qualified person available on short notice; he stayed on that bench for more than eight years. The actor who was cast in the part had some uncanny similarities to his character. They were both named Harry. They were both con artists of a sort, and they both did card tricks to relax. Harry Anderson, who had appeared three times on "Cheers" as a con artist/magician, swore (in a

TV Guide interview), "All that was *already* in the script before I even entered the picture. People think they wrote the script especially for me. They didn't. But after I read it, I knew I was that man." In fact, the producers' initial reaction was that Anderson was too young and inexperienced for the role of Judge Stone, but eventually they incorporated some of the elements of Anderson's youth, like wearing blue jeans and sweatshirts under his black judge's robes. Essentially, Anderson played the same character he had played all his life. "I have one character," he said. "He happens to be a judge right now, but he's the same guy I've always been playing. Any magician plays a role. I'm a performer, not an actor."

Anderson was blessed with a gifted cast of fellow performers, although only three of the others would still be there eight years later. Most outstanding of the original players was John Larroquette as Assistant District Attorney Dan Fielding, an arrogant, womanizing sleazeball. Larroquette was first considered for the part of Judge Harry Stone, but after hearing him read, Reinhold Weege, impressed by Larroquette's arrogant smugness and opportunistic attitude (in the reading, not the actor) decided to cast him in the prosecutor's role instead. It was the right choice, and Larroquette's four Emmys proved the point. (He then graciously took himself out of contention for the Emmys to give someone else a chance.) In an interview with E! cable channel's "Behind the Scenes," Larroquette described Dan Fielding as "a fellow with a fairly low self-image, probably a misogynist at heart, but he has an incredible sense of humor and is extremely proficient at his job, but is not very good at social intimacy of any type." Yet despite these drawbacks, Fielding proved to be an even more popular character than Judge Stone, becoming the focal point of the series. Larroquette once called Fielding a "cross between the Marquis de Sade and Barney Fife," and went on to explain his popularity: "I think America just fell in love with that aspect of this man who knew he was a jerk."

Selma Diamond was the original court officer Selma Hacker. The character was aptly named: she chain-smoked and had a voice that sounded like sandpaper in a garbage disposal. The actress who played her also chain-smoked and succumbed to lung cancer in 1985.

She was replaced for one season by Florence Halop as Florence Kleiner; Halop died in 1986 and was replaced by Marsha Warfield as Roz Russell, who stayed with the cast until the finale.

Liz Williams (Paula Kelly) stayed a season as the public defender; she too was twice replaced, first by Ellen Foley as Billie Young (1984–85), and then by Markie Post as Christine Sullivan. Post continued with the cast through the remainder of the series, and a love relationship between Christine and Judge Stone was incorporated into the story line (and out of it, in 1991).

Bull the Bailiff was played by Richard Moll, a shaved-headed, six-foot-eight, incredible hulk of a man who had previously played crazed science fiction monsters in a string of B movies. Bull was originally played for laughs as he scared all who encountered him, but it was quickly established that the only bull Bull had anything in common with was Ferdinand (the one in the children's tale who loved to smell flowers). The big lug was the most sensitive one of the entire bunch.

"Night Court" adjourned for the final time on May 13, 1992. The series had weathered eight and a half years and 10 time-slot changes during the course of its 193 episodes. In the final two-parter, Judge Harry Stone was suddenly inundated with offers: an associate professorship at Columbia; a full partnership in a big law firm; a chance to host a TV talk show ("I'm not taking it too seriously. It's Fox"); an endorsement contract with Nike; and a chance to tour with his idol, Mel Torme. But he made the only choice he could—to stay with his court, his home, where he knew how much he was needed. Christine was elected to Congress (and Markie Post got a new job on CBS's sitcom "Heart's Afire," co-starring John Ritter); Dan Fielding decided he was in love with Christine and set out to pursue her; the court clerk, Mac (Charlie Robinson, who had also been with the show since 1984), got accepted into film school; and the aliens who had been following Bull decided to take him to Jupiter. "Florida?" asked the naïve bailiff. "No, the planet," they replied, and sure enough, they all beamed up to Jupiter. With any luck, Judge Stone will wake up in a shower in some future reunion movie and find out this was all a dream.

CREDITS

CREATOR: Reinhold Weege. EXECUTIVE PRODUCERS: Reinhold Weege, Gary Murphy, Larry Strawther, Chris Cluess, Stuart Kreisman. PRODUCERS: Jeff Melman, Fred Rubin, Bob Underwood, Tim Steele, Kevin Kelton, Nancy Steen, Neil Thompson, Fred Rubin. DIRECTORS: various. WRITERS: various. CAST: *Judge Harry T. Stone* (Harry Anderson), *Assistant D.A. Dan Fielding* (John Larroquette), *Bailiff Bull Shannon* (Richard Moll), *Court Clerk Mac Robinson* (Charlie Robinson), *Christine Sullivan* (Markie Post), *Roz Russell* (Marsha Warfield), *Selma Hacker* (Selma Diamond), *Liz Williams* (Paula Kelly), *Billie Young* (Ellen Foley), *Florence Kleiner* (Florence Halop), others. GUEST STARS: Mel Torme, Charles Levin, Roger Nolan, Fran Ryan, Elayne Boosler, Michael Ross, others.

EMMYS

Outstanding Supporting Actor in a Comedy Series—John Larroquette (1984–85, 1985–86, 1986–87, 1987–88).

GROWING PAINS

NUMBER 8, 1986–87

Alan Thicke had starred in an ill-fated, syndicated late-night talk show from 1983 to 1984. Instead of making him a household word, "Thicke of the Night" as it was called, made the Canadian-born actor/comic/writer the butt of a joke. In other words, the highly-touted but little-watched show (conceived by onetime TV programming whiz Fred Silverman) failed dismally—so badly, in fact, that one night it scored a *zero* in the Philadelphia ratings. As if this weren't enough pain for Thicke, on the same day his series was cancelled, his wife of 13 years filed for divorce.

A year later Thicke was ready to try again, starring in a new series, "Growing Pains," which premiered on September 24, 1985. In a town like Hollywood, known for its "you're only as good as your last project" mentality, it was a wonder he was in the series at all. In fact, he almost wasn't. The executives at ABC, when casting for the lead role of psychiatrist Dr. Jason Seaver, kept auditioning "Alan Thicke types"—over 100 of them—until someone at the network had an original thought: Let's go with the genuine article. When Thicke was told after the tryout that he'd gotten the part, he claimed, "I went to the underground parking lot, got into my car and began to cry. I just let it out. I was so happy."

The series very closely paralleled that NBC success, "The Cosby Show." Both series were about men who were fathers/doctors who worked at home and took care of the kids while mom was off in the business world during the day pursuing her career. Imitation is the sincerest form of flattery, and the Nielsens provided a reward by allowing "Growing Pains" a year to go through its,

um, growing pains, then making way for this "Cosby" wannabe on the ratings chart in the 1986–87 season. The following year it peaked at number five. Thicke could once again hold up his head in La La Land.

Part of the hoopla that attended the series was the attention lavished on the portion of the show that seemed to have been cloned from "Family Ties"—namely a teenage heartthrob, in this case young Kirk Cameron. His character, Mike Seaver, was not the brightest young lad, and he once got himself arrested early in the series. Trouble seemed to follow this as scheming, irksome-yet-lovable walking hormone, but the teens adored him. Actor Kirk Cameron at one time received 15,000 fan letters a week.

The Seavers had two other children: Carol, played by Tracey Gold, and Ben, young Jeremy Miller. In 1988, with these kids rapidly growing up, the producers decided that mom Maggie Seaver should have another child. They played the baby angle for a year, but by 1990, offspring Chrissy Seaver was six years old, a growth rate accelerated even faster than the usual sitcom maturation process.

Over the years, the series tackled a lot of serious topics such as teenage drinking, teen suicide, teen drunk driving, homelessness, and cocaine addiction. Then, at the beginning of the 1991–92 season, the producers and network agreed that it would be the last year for the series. The final episode aired on the night of the ABC farewell marathon — April 25, 1992. It was as if a tornado swept through the network, wiping out whole television shows in its path. That night, viewers said goodbye to "Who's the Boss?" (see page

---

CREDITS

TOP 10 PEAK: No. 5, 1987–88.
CREATOR: Neal Marlens. EXECUTIVE PRODUCERS: Neal Marlens, Michael Sullivan, Dan Guntzelman, Steve Marshall. PRODUCERS: Tom Cherones, Arnold Margolin, David Kendall. DIRECTORS: various. WRITERS: various. CAST: *Dr. Jason Seaver* (Alan Thicke), *Maggie Seaver* (Joanna Kerns), *Mike Seaver* (Kirk Cameron), *Carol Seaver* (Tracey Gold), *Ben Seaver* (Jeremy Miller), *Chrissy Seaver* (Ashley Johnson), *Boner* (Andrew Koenig), *Eddie* (K.C. Martel), *Irma* (Jane Powell), *Wally* (Robert Rockwell), *Ed Malone* (Gordon Jump), *Kate Malone* (Betty McGuire), *Kate MacDonald* (Chelsea Noble), *Luke Brower* (Leonardo DeCaprio). GUEST STARS: Jerry Vale, Dan Lauria, Douglas Seale, Dick O'Neill, Heather Langenkamp, Marius Mazmanian, others.

308), "MacGyver," and "Growing Pains." ABC vice-president Alan Sternfield said, "Like children who have matured and found their own lives, the shows sort of exhausted their story material. We felt we needed fresher shows."

On the set during the final taping in March, the mood was somber. "When we finally [taped the show]," said Thicke, "we all gathered afterward and cried before going out to greet the audience. It was a private moment." Kirk Cameron found his eight-by-ten glossy posted behind the set with the notation, "Available as of 3/20/92. Will act for food and shelter. Please help."

"The end of the show was very sad, but at the same time, it was very satisfying," said Joanna Kerns in the *Orange County Register*. "We had a good, long run and developed great friendships out of it, and you don't get a lot of that in this business. I think every show has a certain

life span, especially one that has children in it, because they grow up and the premise changes in such a way that it's hard to keep things new and fresh."

In the final hour-long episode, Maggie was offered a job as a senator's aide in Washington. As the Seavers left their home forever, they recalled all the good times and bad that were had there over the last seven seasons. And Mike Seaver, now a mature young man, finally popped the question to his girlfriend Kate, played by his real-life wife Chelsea Noble. After 166 episodes in seven seasons, the growing pains had finally stopped.

In 1992, writer/producer/creator Neal Marlens filed a $50 million civil suit against Warner Bros. claiming he was fraudulently denied his share of the profits from the series. The show, which had reportedly earned more than $204 million in gross revenues, was alleged to be over $2.6 million in the hole.

Back row: Joanna Kerns and Alan Thicke; center row: Tracey Gold and Kirk Cameron; front: Jeremy Miller.

313

MOONLIGHTING

NUMBER 9, 1986–87

Bruce Willis and Cybill Shepherd.

"Moonlighting" was an experiment in television that was at once a brilliant success and a dismal failure. Innovative, irreverent, classy, steamily sexy, the series began with a format created by Glenn Gordon Caron about an ex-model named Maddie Hayes (Cybill Shepherd) whose accountant had ripped her off to the tune of millions of dollars, saddling her with a tax write-off—a run-down private detective agency. David Addison (Bruce Willis) was the loser sitting in that saddle, a wisecracking, ain't-life-grand loser reporting for combat duty in what would soon become the battle of the sexes, '80s style.

The series bowed on ABC on March 3, 1985, its two-hour pilot airing as an "ABC Sunday Night Movie." In the beginning, the pair encountered the usual private-eye fare of jewel thieves, psychos, and thugs. But this series soon took on a life of its own, or at least the life of

its creator, who infused each episode with something just a little different, keeping audiences guessing and the Nielsens climbing. If there were cases to be solved, they took a back seat to the real matter at hand: When would Maddie and David *get it on*?

In the beginning, Maddie and David weren't lovers. They were more like haters. Yet there was enough sexual tension between the two to stock an entire year's worth of lab supplies for Chemistry 101. In the tradition of Hepburn and Tracy, Bogie and Bacall, Heckle and Jeckle (well, they did a lot of that)—these two did their share of the verbal joustings so popular in the mid-'80s era of the Big Tease. "Scarecrow & Mrs. King" were into it; so were Sam and Diane on "Cheers" and Tony and Angela on "Who's the Boss?" and Laura and Mr. Steele on "Remington Steele," which also happened to be the previous series on which Glenn Caron had worked.

The foreplay continued for a couple of years; eventually there was a KISS at the end of the 1985–86 season. Viewers inundated the show with letters demanding a consummation of the relationship. In one of the series' gimmicks, in which the actors broke that "fourth wall" and stepped out of character, speaking directly to the home audience (often this was done because the shows ran short), the pair read some of those letters to the camera, then commented:

SHEPHERD
Maybe this season, maybe next. I don't want to be rushed.

WILLIS
Next season! (to camera) Keep those cards and letters coming, folks.

The series prided itself on its innovative episodes. "Our goal is to reinvent ourselves every week," said Glenn Caron. "One week we're comedy, the next week we're fairly serious, and the next week we're a musical." One early episode was a comic spoof of the '40s film-noir era called "The Dream Sequence Always Rings Twice," filmed in glorious black and white. Another time the entire episode was given over to an updated version of Shakespeare's *The Taming of the Shrew*, with David/Bruce as Petruchio and Maddie/Cybill as Kate.

Several were quick to point out that the latter seemed a bit of typecasting. There were reports from the first of on-set bickering between Shepherd and Willis, and Shepherd and Caron, and Willis and Caron, and Shepherd, Willis, and Caron. This wasn't Hollywood's happiest set. The series was also plagued with delays in production, with a new episode becoming a cause for special network announcements practically pleading with the audience (and sponsors) to be patient. In fairness, the "Moonlighting" scripts were probably the most difficult to deliver in all of television, with Caron doing most of the writing for the first couple of years. Although it appeared ad-libbed, the snappy repartee between Maddie and David was very tightly written, often resulting in 100-page, dialogue-laden scripts—nearly twice the average length for scripts of one-hour television series.

Other problems included the show's constantly going over budget. At $1.6 million per episode, it was TV's most expensive hour-long series; "The Taming of the Shrew" episode cost a reported $3 million. On most television series, an episode is shot in seven or eight days; "Moonlighting" consistently took up to 12 days to shoot.

Then, in the third season, the show began to unravel. Success was tampered with. The Maddie-David relationship heated up, then cooled. In 1987 Maddie developed a thing for a yuppie, played by hunky Mark Harmon. Then in March of that year, she and David finally "boinked" (*his* term for making love). By 1988 Maddie was pregnant; coincidentally, so was Cybill Shepherd (she eventually gave birth to twins), and her pregnancy was incorporated into the series. Maddie married—then dumped—a man she met on a train. One weird show had Bruce Willis playing Maddie's unborn baby (which she eventually miscarried).

By the final two seasons, the show's two regulars began showing up for work sporadically. In 1987 Bruce Willis fell in a Sun Valley skiing accident and broke his collarbone, resulting in his absence from the set for several days. That same year, Shepherd missed many weeks' work due to morning sickness from her pregnancy. The season came up short, with only 14 episodes produced, a few starring the *other* detectives from the Blue Moon Detective Agency: Miss Dipesto (Allyce Beasley) and her boyfriend Herbert Viola (Curtis Armstrong). By the final (1988–89) season, the audience had long since departed, fed up with the frequent reruns and format changes. As writer/producer Charles Eglee put it, "The end was a huge relief. It was like having a 97-year-old person who had lived a rich and wonderful life, but now every part of their metabolism is in failure. It's a blessing if they go quietly."

"Moonlighting" was put out of its misery on May 14, 1989; its rating for the final season had sunk to 41st place. After the series left the air, both stars pursued successful careers. Bruce Willis, who was a virtual unknown before "Moonlighting," became a major star of motion pictures, with such hits as *Die Hard* (1988), *Die Hard II* (1991), and *Death Becomes Her* (1992). Cybill Shepherd, whose flagging career was revived by her "Moonlighting" years, went on to do a number of TV movies. Still a sex symbol in her mid-40s, she was frequently seen doing Preference by L'Oreal hair-color commercials.

CREDITS

CREATOR: Glenn Gordon Caron. EXECUTIVE PRODUCERS: Glenn Gordon Caron, Jay Daniel. PRODUCERS: Charles Eglee, others. DIRECTORS: various. WRITERS: Glenn Gordon Caron, Charles Eglee, others. CAST: *Maddie Hayes* (Cybill Shepherd), *David Addison* (Bruce Willis), *Agnes Dipesto* (Allyce Beasley), *Herbert Viola* (Curtis Armstrong), *Virginia Hayes* (Eva Marie Saint), *Alex Hayes* (Robert Webber), *Sam Crawford* (Mark Harmon). GUEST STARS: Rona Barrett, Dr. Joyce Brothers, Ray Charles, others.

EMMYS

Outstanding Lead Actor in a Drama Series*—Bruce Willis (1986–87).

---

* The producers themselves were never quite sure just what genre "Moonlighting" fit into; at first it was described as a romantic comedy, but when it was Emmy time, it was classified as drama.

A DIFFERENT WORLD

NUMBER 2, 1987–88

"A Different World" didn't live up to its title for the first year, but by the second season it would have a bold, new direction. Conceived as a spinoff from Nielsen number one champ "The Cosby Show," the series was immediately panned by critics, who labeled the new series "boring," "unfunny," and "rather shallow." The fact that they were right didn't affect the series ratings, as this child of Cosby clung to its parent's coattails— airing in the 8:30 P.M. spot right after Cos—for a Nielsen blast to number two at the end of the first season (1987–88).

Originally, "A Different World" was to be a starring vehicle for "Cosby" show regular Lisa Bonet, who played daughter Denise Huxtable. She headed off to Hillman College, a fictional, "predominantly black American institution steeped in tradition" (as described in the show's production handouts), which had educated several generations of Huxtables. Two roommates were created for Denise—one black, one white. No explanation was given for the white student, although it would seem her obvious purpose was to attract that portion of the audience that was also white. And in an effort to prevent her from appearing to be the lone white, the background included a lot of white extras.

Susan Fales, one of the original staff writers, later an executive producer, explained the main problem in *Entertainment Weekly*: "We tried to follow the 'Cosby' model: Pretend it's timeless; make no references to current events; make no references to race. And we were under orders from NBC to stay away from anything academic—they felt that was alienating. So we had a show about a black college that wasn't about college and couldn't be black."

By the time there were four episodes in the can, the producers and the NBC executives knew the show was in trouble. In an effort to perk up the yet-unaired new series, they created two new characters and intercut them with the already existing footage. Jasmine Guy was brought in to play Whitley Gilbert, a black Scarlett O'Hara-cum-southern belle/debutante, and Kadeem Hardison was added as Dwayne Wayne, a skirt-chaser who would years later fall in love with and marry Whitley, with most of his sexist attitude toned down.

At the end of the first season, Lisa Bonet was pregnant, and the producers decided to eliminate the character rather than incorporate her pregnancy into the story line (especially since Denise had had no steady boyfriend in the episodes that year). She eventually returned to "The Cosby Show," giving Jasmine Guy's Whitley character a chance to rise to the starring position in "Different World." Although Bonet had taken a lot of blame for the show's dullness, Susan Fales defended the actress, saying, "The character was far more at fault. Denise was not very interesting, and we were asked to make her into Mary Tyler Moore or Tinkerbell, always bringing everyone together. We couldn't."

Then, at the beginning of the second season, an important change took place—a change named Debbie

---

CREDITS

CREATOR: Bill Cosby. EXECUTIVE PRODUCERS: Marcy Carsey, Tom Werner, Anne Beatts, Caryn Mandabach, Susan Fales. PRODUCERS: Thad Mumford, George Crosby, Lissa Levin, Margie Peters, Joanne Curley-Kerner, Cheryl Gard, Gary H. Miller, Debbie Allen, Glenn Berenbeim, Jeanette Collins, Mimi Friedman, Brenda Hanes-Berg. DIRECTORS: Ellen Falcon, Debbie Allen, Kadeem Hardison. WRITERS: Thad Mumford, Lissa Levin, Susan Fales, Jasmine Guy, others. CAST: *Whitley Gilbert Wayne* (Jasmine Guy), *Denise Huxtable* (Lisa Bonet), *Jaleesa Vinson* (Dawnn Lewis), *Dwayne Wayne* (Kadeem Hardison), *Ron Johnson* (Darryl Bell), *Maggie Lauten* (Marisa Tomei), *Millie* (Marie-Alise Recasner), *Walter Oakes* (Sinbad), *Col. Clayton Taylor* (Glynn Turman), *Freddie Brooks* (Cree Summer), *Kim Reese* (Charnele Brown), *Vernon Gaines* (Lou Myers), *Ernest* (Reuben Grundy), others. GUEST STARS: Diahann Carroll, Debbie Allen, Richard Roundtree, Phylicia Rashad, Earle Hyman, Larry Linville, Whoopi Goldberg, Rev. Jesse Jackson, Rosanne Arnold, Tom Arnold, Patti LaBelle, Adele Wayne, others.

Allen, who came aboard as the show's permanent director at the suggestion of Bill Cosby. Allen, a gifted actress/dancer/choreographer who had starred in and helmed the TV series "Fame," assumed the reins with the attitude of a drill sergeant.

"There was no family feeling on the stage, no laughter among the actors," Allen recalled. "Everyone was uptight, like in a prison." One of the first things that the new director did upon taking over was to institute a morning workout for her cast, putting them through paces of sit-ups and stretches "to make them an ensemble company, working together."

Allen herself was a 1971 graduate of Howard University, the prestigious black college in Washington, D.C., so she had the proper background for this series. Hillman was now to be a fully black campus with a proper cafeteria; no servers waited on tables, lots of hot sauce was spread around, and that southern delicacy, grits, would now be served. The writing staff was sent on a field trip (this would become an annual event) to Atlanta's predominantly black colleges, Spelman and Morehouse. "It's appalling that we were allowed to write about black colleges without having done research," said Fales in *Entertainment Weekly*. "There's a spirit of family, intimacy and mission that we didn't know about." Within three more seasons, the series staff would include a largely black behind-the-scenes crew, boosting the feeling of family among those involved.

"A Different World" began to take on some of the issues of the day, while still retaining its comedy focus. Date rape, apartheid, religion, interracial romance, the Persian Gulf crisis, homophobia, and more were dealt with. One of the most serious issues to be tackled was AIDS, the focus of an episode that had guest star Whoopi Goldberg playing a professor. It took more than two years to get that episode made, even with Bill Cosby lending his weight to the effort. "We had to really fight for that story," said producer/director Allen in the *Hollywood Reporter*. "It was postponed three

From left: Lisa Bonet, Marisa Tomei, and Dawnn Lewis.

times. I was going crazy. This is World War III. Babies are dying of the disease." She told *Entertainment Weekly*, "Finally I said, 'If we don't do this, one day we'll look up and 'The Simpsons' will have done it.' " When it was finally made, some of the network's advertisers pulled their commercials, but the episode became the highest-rated one of the series.

In 1992 "The Cosby Show" left the air, leaving "A Different World" to stand on its own. During the 1991–92 season, "World" had often been ranked higher in the ratings than "Cosby," but both series were showing signs of age. In the 1992–93 season, the sixth for "A Different World," ratings were significantly down, and NBC announced in April 1993 that the show would be cancelled following a one-hour finale.

ALF

NUMBER 10 (TIE), 1987–88

He stood three-foot-two, was covered in polyester fur, and had only four fingers on each hand. This unlikely fellow was also the star of his own hit TV series. His nickname was ALF, which stood for Alien Life Form. ALF was part "My Favorite Martian," part E.T., part Mork from Ork, and a 100 percent strange creature from the planet Melmac. One day he crashed his flying saucer—plastic, naturally—through the roof of a "Father Knows Best"-type average American TV family named Tanner. From then on, ALF (who once revealed that his real name was Gordon Shumway) was a family member, sort of like a talking dog or precocious child with a borscht belt graduate's sense of humor and the manners of Archie Bunker. But there was one thing: he loved the family cat. Oh, how he loved cats. Barbequed, sautéed, baked—those were just a few of his favorite ways of enjoying cat *du jour*.

If all this seems like childish nonsense, and perhaps it was, it was serious business to NBC, the network that placed ALF not in their kiddie programming, but smack in the middle of the nightly prime-time schedule. The series was all but ignored at first, but soon the network began a blitz campaign to guarantee public attention would be drawn to their new sitcom, which debuted in September 1986. Promos featured "Golden Girls" Betty White and Bea Arthur cooing and flirting with the little guy; Bryant Gumbel invited him to breakfast on "The Today Show"; ALF hosted "Friday Night Videos" and the Orange Bowl parade, picked winners on "NFL '86," and plopped down in one of the seats on "Hollywood Squares." The network's saturation campaign worked, especially after a special Monday episode of NBC's hit comedy "Family Ties" provided a lead-in. By its second season, ALF was one of the network's hottest new shows.

The character was the brainchild of a former Connecticut high school teacher turned puppeteer for cable and PBS. Paul Fusco had created ALF in 1984 as part of an outer-space program for Showtime, but the project never blasted off. He continued to shop his little creature around town to such animators as Muppeteer Jim Henson and Walt Disney Studios, but without any success. Then his agent sent him to packager Bernie Brillstein, who had helped develop "Saturday Night Live," "Hee-Haw," and "The Muppet Show." Brillstein brought in writer/producer Tom Patchett, and together Patchett and Fusco developed a concept to present to NBC head Brandon Tartikoff. At their pitch meeting, Fusco brought along a green hefty bag with something hidden inside. At just the right moment, he undid the bag and produced ALF, who began rubbing his fuzzy snout on Tartikoff's sleeve. The results, he knew, would either be a one-way ticket back to Connecticut or an instant sale. Fortunately for Fusco, it was love at first sight for Tartikoff and the other NBC brass. "We all loved ALF," said NBC exec Warren Littlefield. "It was the funniest pitch meeting I've ever seen."

ALF was certainly a gimmick show, but one that seemed to transcend age limits. Kids enjoyed the series about a fantasy creature as they would any puppet show, although ALF was somewhat less than the ideal role model from a parent's point of view: he burped loudly, guzzled beer, listened to loud rock music, wolfed food, and generally made himself a nuisance. Adults could relate to ALF's alien point of view as he experienced this bizarre small planet called Earth. The humor was often very adult, with lots of puns (example: on Melmac he played bouillabaiseball). Much of the comedy was of the entertainment industry insider variety, and the writers continued to

CREDITS

CREATORS: Paul Fusco, Tom Patchett. EXECUTIVE PRODUCERS: Bernie Brillstein, Tom Patchett. PRODUCER: Paul Fusco. DIRECTORS: Tom Patchett, Peter Bonerz, Paul Miller, others. WRITERS: Tom Patchett, David Silverman, Stephen Sustarsic, others. CAST: *ALF/Gordon Shumway* (Paul Fusco—voice, Michu Meszaros—body), *Willie Tanner* (Max Wright), *Kate Tanner* (Anne Schedeen), *Lynn Tanner* (Andrea Elson), *Brian Tanner* (Benji Gregory), *Dorothy Halligan* (Anne Meara), *Raquel Ochmonek* (Liz Sheridan), *Trevor Ochmonek* (John La Motta), *Jake Ochmonek* (Josh Blake), *Neal Tanner* (JM J. Bullock).

Clockwise from top left: Benji Gregory, Andrea Elson, Anne Schedeen, ALF, and Max Wright.

sprinkle the dialogue with such gems as "That Scott
Baio, he's the next Tony Danza"; when ALF botched a
babysitting assignment and lost the infant, he piped up
with "Maybe a dingo took your baby—it happened to
Meryl Streep"—a reference to the actress's 1988 film
A Cry in the Dark.

ALF quickly became Brandon Tartikoff's favorite
show, and merchandising ALF became a favorite pas-
time for both network and producers. The little guy's
ugly mug, something of a cross between an aardvark
and Mr. Spock, began appearing on every conceivable
item that could be marketed, to the tune of $250 million
a year. The ALF line of goods included pajamas, trading
cards, games, backpacks, calendars, comic books,
toothbrushes, tricycles, mugs, watches, hats, lunch
boxes, and dolls that spoke in ALF's Rodney
Dangerfield-like voice (provided by creator Paul
Fusco), spouting such ALFisms as "Gimme four," "No
problem," "How about a hug for the Old Alfer?," and

"I *kill* me!" There was an ALF fan club, with 8,000
worldwide members joining from the 50 countries that
aired the series.

The popularity of "ALF" prompted two spinoff
Saturday morning cartoon series, a natural progression
for this life-sized cartoon character. The first was called
simply "ALF," and aired from 1987 to 1990. It featured
the adventures of young 193-year-old ALF on his home
planet as a recent high school grad. In the fall of 1988,
the series, now called "ALF Tales," expanded to an
hour and added spoofs of fairy tales and movies.

By the spring of 1990, "ALF"'s novelty had worn off.
A final episode ended with our furry friend surrounded
by the military, who had finally caught up with the
alien. As cliffhangers go, this one may become the
record holder, since there were no plans to rescue ALF
with any future episodes. His old exploits, however,
continued to be shown in cable reruns on the Family
Channel.

THE WONDER YEARS

NUMBER 10 (TIE), 1987–88

Fred Savage and Danica McKellar.

For husband-and-wife creators Neal Marlens and Carol Black, the late 1960s had been "The Wonder Years," the era today's aging yuppies regard with the nostalgia that members of every generation seem to hold for their preteen and teen years, when one is no longer a child, but not yet an adult. This series, while devoted to both the humorous and sentimental sides of reminiscences, managed to elicit comedy from one of the drearier periods in American history, the Nixon, Vietnam War, political unrest, turn on, tune in, drop out dog days of the late '60s and early '70s. Not a funny or fun time in our nation's past, yet this purported comedy—in actuality a dramedy—sparked the interest of the television audience when it premiered on January 31, 1988, following the Super Bowl; it was then given a late-season premiere on March 15 for a limited six-episode run. It caught fire immediately, burning up the Nielsen charts to land in the tying position of number 10 (with "ALF") for the 1987–88 season, quite an achievement for such a late-season entry.

Part of the reason for the show's authentic feeling was the fact that it was filmed with one camera rather than using the three-camera videotape technique usually designated for sitcoms. The show's young protagonist, Kevin Arnold (Fred Savage), could be filmed outdoors, riding his bike, playing football in the street, sneaking smokes behind the gym, or experiencing his first kiss in the forest. The warm narration by the 20-years-in-the-future Kevin Arnold, looking back in time with the wisdom of the adult he's become, touched just the right chord in each viewer. "I never felt pain like this before in my entire life," the adult Kevin recalled after experiencing his first rejection in love at age 13. "It felt...wonderful."

Bob Brush, the show's executive producer, believed that one of the reasons the series was so popular was the optimism that pervaded the outlook on growing up.

"I think it has to do with the approach we take, the somewhat documentary-like feel that preserves the illusion that it is real life that we're tracking," said Brush in the *Hollywood Reporter*. "This has always been a show that has tried to deal with the basic problems of growing up. They might not be spectacular problems, but they are very real." Some of the serious subjects broached by "The Wonder Years" included the Vietnam War, the counterculture, the space race, puberty, politics, premarital sex, cohabitation, and a number of personal firsts—dates, kisses, beer, and even pimples. One episode, in fact, centered around Kevin and his first zit. Few other series could take such a premise and turn it into warm, human-interest entertainment.

The central character in all this was identified as an average, white, middle-class, suburban boy named Kevin, aged 12 when the story began in the year 1968. His father worked; his mother was a homemaker, an endangered species in this pre-women's-movement era; his older teenage brother was the devil in disguise, bent on making Kevin's awkward early teen years as hellish as possible; and his sister was a typical older sister. But it was Kevin's eyes that provided us with the growing pains he experienced in his junior high, then high school life. ("Growing Pains," in fact, would have made a good title for this series had Neal Marlens not already used it for another series he created.) The fact that there were so many young people at the heart of the series gave it to-die-for demographics: kids, youth, and nostalgic baby boomers longing for the good old days. What's more, the series transcended international boundaries and was seen in more than 50 countries. In 1992 it was playing to a wide-eyed audience in former Eastern Bloc nations of Russia, Poland, Bulgaria, and others anxious to be brought up to speed on America's bygone years.

Fred Savage played Kevin with the sort of acumen usually found only in older, more experienced actors. He became the youngest male ever to be nominated for an Emmy in the Best Actor category, and won the People's Choice Award in which the public voted him 1990's Favorite Young Television Performer.

In 1993, "The Wonder Years" completed its sixth and final season. The series was still doing all right in the ratings, although it was no longer a Nielsen champion (it finished in 38th place for 1991–92). Savage, now 16, was beginning to think about his future—understandable, as his own teen wonder years were slipping away. "I plan to go to college," he said. "It would be great if I also could act then too, but as far as a future in acting goes, I'm just not too sure yet."

CREDITS

TOP 10 PEAK: No. 8, 1989–90. CREATORS: Neal Marlens, Carol Black. EXECUTIVE PRODUCERS: Neal Marlens, Carol Black, Bob Brush, Michael Dinner. PRODUCERS: Jeffrey Silver, Bob Stevens, Ken Topolsky, Matthew Carlson, Jill Gordon, David Chambers, Sy Rosen, Mark Levin, Mark B. Perry, Sy Dukane, Denise Moss, Bruce J. Nachbar. DIRECTORS: Steve Miner, Peter Baldwin, Michael Dinner, others. WRITERS: various. CAST: *Kevin Arnold* (Fred Savage), *Jack Arnold* (Dan Lauria), *Norma Arnold* (Alley Mills), *Wayne Arnold* (Jason Hervey), *Karen Arnold* (Olivia d'Abo), *Winnie Cooper* (Danica McKellar), *Paul Pfeiffer* (Josh Saviano), *Kevin Arnold (Adult)—Voice Only* (Daniel Stern). OTHER REGULARS/GUEST STARS: Robert Picardo, Crystal McKellar, Linda Hoy, Michael Landes, Krista Murphy, Brandon Crane, Michael Tricario, Soleil Moon Frye, others.

EMMYS

Outstanding Comedy Series (1987–88); Outstanding Directing in a Comedy Series—Peter Baldwin (1988–89), Michael Dinner (1989–90); Outstanding Writing in a Comedy Series—Bob Brush (1989–90).

ROSEANNE

Brassy, bold, bulky, and big-mouthed. All these terms have been used to describe the one-woman whirlwind named Roseanne that blew into town one day in 1985 and changed the landscape of television sitcoms three years later. Her series, simply and appropriately named "Roseanne," premiered in the fall of 1988 and was soon grabbing the lioness's share of Nielsen gold. By the end of its first season, it was ranked number two, and by the following year, its 36 million weekly viewers helped cement it to the top of the chart.

Why did Americans find "Roseanne" and Roseanne so appealing? Part of the answer lay in the show's content. Its tell-it-like-it-is attitude presented a picture of working-class America, a blue-collar family who struggled to pay the mortgage and put food on the table. It was the right show for the times in the wake of collapsing Reaganomics and the recession/depression/call-it-what-you-will-depending-on-whether-or-not- you're-working slump that subsequently gripped America. Another part of the answer—a great deal of the answer—lay with the show's star and the excellent cast of supporting players.

Rosanne Barr was a half-Jewish girl from the Mormon enclave of Salt Lake City. That concept alone ought to have given the future standup comic enough material for several routines. She left home in 1971, hitching with a friend to Colorado, where she married a motel night clerk at age 21 and had three kids. Soon she was working as a cocktail waitress, serving up jokes along with martinis, later playing the Denver coffee houses and nightclubs. Eventually she had enough material to take her act to Los Angeles, breezing into town in 1985.

She became a talked-about sensation at the Comedy Store and began appearing on "The Tonight Show," where her routine about a blue-collar housewife caught the attention of the production team of Tom Werner and Marcy Carsey (producers of "The Cosby Show"). A former writer for "Cosby" named Matt Williams had been developing a sitcom about blue-collar working mothers; after meeting Roseanne, he shifted the focus to just one woman.

The story line began with Roseanne Conner working at a factory, but throughout the years she would have (and lose) a succession of jobs, eventually opening her own diner, the Lunch Box. Her husband Dan, played by talented actor John Goodman (*Raising Arizona* [1987], *Babe* [1992]), would also suffer layoffs and financial disasters. They struggled to pay their bills ("You pay the ones marked final notice," said Roseanne, "and you throw the rest away") and to raise their three kids—*real* kids, not the usual television children whose biggest problems are what to wear to the prom. Especially intriguing was daughter Darlene. A brooding, latent beatnik and seeming misfit in this family of lowbrows, Darlene longed to be a writer. She was played by a promising young actress, Sara Gilbert (sister of "Little House on the Prairie" star Melissa Gilbert), a natural who had never had an acting lesson.

The rest of the family—and even the house itself—continued to challenge Roseanne, who once referred to herself as a "domestic goddess." Her home looked like it

---

CREDITS

TOP 10 PEAK: No. 1, 1989–90. CREATOR: Matt Williams. EXECUTIVE PRODUCERS: Roseanne Arnold, Tom Arnold, Jay Daniel, Marcy Carsey, Tom Werner, Bob Myer, Chuck Lorre, Bruce Helford. PRODUCERS: Jeff Abugov, Al Lowenstein, Brad Isaacs, Maxine Lapiduss, others. DIRECTORS: various. WRITERS: various. CAST: *Roseanne Conner* (Roseanne Arnold), *Dan Conner* (John Goodman), *Becky Conner* (Lecy Goranson), *Darlene Conner* (Sara Gilbert), *D.J. Conner* (Michael Fishman), *Jackie Conner Harris* (Laurie Metcalf), *Arnie Merchant* (Tom Arnold), *Crystal Anderson* (Natalie West), *Leon Carp* (Martin Mull), *Bonnie* (Bonnie Sheridan), others. GUEST STARS: Shelley Winters, Estelle Parsons, Morgan Fairchild, others.

EMMYS

Outstanding Performance by a Supporting Actress in a Comedy Series—Laurie Metcalf (1991–92).

John Goodman and Roseanne Arnold.

should be hosed down, dinner was usually macaroni and cheese, the furniture was Early Garage Sale, and hubby Dan's idea of a good time was a six-pack and the remote control. Just another typical day in a typical home.

This wasn't a show about issues. Life was issue enough. There were occasional references to problems with alcoholism and homophobia: in one of Roseanne's jobs she had a gay boss played by Martin Mull; when Roseanne's sister asked her how she would feel if one of her kids was gay, Roseanne replied, "The only thing I want for my kids is that they're happy and outta the house." In season five, part of that wish was granted when 17-year-old daughter Becky eloped with her boyfriend.

In real life, Roseanne Arnold (she changed her name in 1990 after marrying Tom Arnold, one of the show's writers) was one of the most outspoken and controversial actresses/comediennes to come out of television in its history. She became legendary for her antics. It seemed she couldn't sneeze without getting her name in the papers. Roseanne got tattooed; Roseanne sang the Star-Mangled Banner at a Padres baseball game; Roseanne wrote a book; Roseanne announced that she was an incest survivor; Roseanne changed her name; Roseanne lost weight; Roseanne lost the Emmy she longed for (and deserved); and most publicized of all, Roseanne fired her writers every time the leaves changed to autumn gold.

Actually, the studio paint department would have soon run out of supplies if they'd tried to keep up the lettering on the writing staff's office doors. With her name at the top of the show—and the top of the charts —what Roseanne wanted, she got. ABC bowed to her every wish. It may have been hell for those trying to crank out "Roseanne" scripts each week, yet despite the annual march of writers and executive producers on parade, the series was on top for one reason: *it was funny*. Perhaps it succeeded *because of* rather than despite the constant plowing under of the staff, bringing forth fresh, new material each year. As Roseanne said, "I'm not tough to work with, but I care a lot and am real passionate about everything that has my name on it."

By 1990, Roseanne's husband Tom Arnold was acting in the series, as well as executive-producing. The two seemed to be joined at the hip—one continuous entity, as one writer put it, called "Roseanne-and-Tom Arnold." So it wasn't surprising that Tom should get his own series, which debuted in November 1992. It wasn't a spinoff of "Roseanne," but it did have one thing it common with that series—it borrowed its concept from the reality of making "Roseanne." "The Jackie Thomas Show" centered on a temperamental comedy star who drove his writing staff up the wall. Initial ratings were good, thanks to a strong lead-in from "Roseanne." For fans of the Arnolds, this was the perfect pair of his-and-hers comedy series, perhaps another television first. But by the end of the show's first season, ratings for "Jackie Thomas" had slipped to 16th place—too low a number for a show piggybacked with "Rosanne," in ABC's view, raising doubts about its future.

EMPTY NEST

NUMBER 9, 1988–89

"Empty Nest" was a semi-spinoff from "The Golden Girls" (see page 304), the successful NBC sitcom that first aired in 1985. But it was more the setting than the characters that formed the basis of the second series. Created by Susan Harris, who also originated "The Golden Girls" and "Soap," "Empty Nest" debuted in the fall of 1988 and occasionally had Dr. Harry Weston, his daughters, and even their dog, Dreyfuss, paying a visit to Blanche, Rose, and Dorothy, their Miami "Golden Girl" neighbors. But the cross-pollination was very limited. This series was given a strong lead-in by "Golden Girls" but was able to find its own audience, and by the show's second season, 1990–91, it had surpassed its sibling series in the Nielsen ratings, eventually reaching the number seven position.

Dr. Harry Weston (Richard Mulligan) was a widower and eligible bachelor about town. A successful pediatrician, his "nest" was far from empty; his two adult daughters, Carol (Dinah Manoff) and Barbara (Kristy McNichol), took up residence with Daddy while they too searched for spouses. Harry was a Bob Newhart type—the only sane person in a world full of crazies. Barbara was the sensible daughter, although her father would have preferred she wasn't an undercover cop who had to dress like a slut when heading off to work. Carol was the neurotic daughter; her husband had dumped her, and so, it seemed, had every man she ever dated. She and Barbara fought constantly. Poor Harry; he treated children all day at work, then came home to more of the same.

Richard Mulligan played Dr. Weston. He had won an Emmy for his role of Burt Campbell in the

Susan Harris comedy "Soap" (1980) and had appeared in many films, including *S.O.B.* (1981) and *A Fine Mess* (1986). He played the long-suffering pediatrician with a low-key gentleness that was a great part of the show's appeal.

Kristy McNichol, who played daughter Barbara, was a two-time Emmy winner (1977, 1979) for her role of Buddy in "Family," the long-running TV drama. An actress since the age of six, she also appeared in the acclaimed TV movie *Summer of My German Soldier* (1978) and a number of theatrical films, including *Only When I Laugh* (1981) and *Just the Way You Are* (1984). In 1992 McNichol dropped out of "Empty Nest" to deal with reported stress and health problems, and Barbara's absence was explained by her being out of town on a police investigation assignment; a third daughter, Emily (Lisa Rieffel), was introduced in 1993 to fill the interim gap.

Carol was played by Dinah Manoff. The talented daughter of actress Lee Grant, Manoff also wrote and directed some episodes of "Empty Nest." She was a regular on "Soap," and had won a Tony for her role in the comedy *I Ought to Be in Pictures*. She also starred in the 1982 film version of that comedy and co-starred in the Mary Tyler Moore hit film *Ordinary People* (1980). Her portrayal of ditsy Carol evolved the most of any of the characters. Carol's insecurities with men were usually the focus of that characterization, but by 1992 she had landed herself a full-time boyfriend, a sculptor named Patrick who moved into the Weston garage, much to Harry's dismay. In her career, Carol progressed from a nervous librarian

---

CREDITS

TOP 10 PEAK: No. 7, 1990–91. CREATOR: Susan Harris. EXECUTIVE PRODUCERS: Paul Witt, Tony Thomas, Susan Harris, Rod Parker, Hal Cooper, Gary Jacobs. PRODUCERS: Arnie Kogen, Susan Beavers, Roger Garrett, Rob LaZebnik, David Sacks, Harold Kimmel, Gilbert Junger. DIRECTORS: Robert Berlinger, John Bowab, Andy Cadiff, Hal Cooper, Dinah Manoff, Jay Sandrich, Doug Smart, Renny Temple, James Widdoes, Steve Zuckerman. WRITERS: Susan Harris, Susan Beavers, Rod Parker, Rob LaZebnik, Dinah Manoff, others. CAST: *Dr. Harry Weston* (Richard Mulligan), *Barbara Weston* (Kristy McNichol), *Carol Weston* (Dinah Manoff), *Nurse LaVerne Todd* (Park Overall), *Charley Dietz* (David Leisure), *Patrick* (Paul Provenza), *Emily* (Lisa Rieffel), *Dreyfuss* (Bear).

to a nervous caterer, the owner of the Elegant Epicure.

David Leisure played the obligatory next-door neighbor, but rather than being the usual nice guy next door, Charley "The Dietzster" Dietz was a boorish sexist who barged in whenever he felt like it, drank milk from the carton in the Westons' fridge, and put down Carol at every opportunity. Leisure was best remembered for his characterization of Joe Isuzu in automobile commercials.

Park Overall played LaVerne, Dr. Weston's nurse with an attitude, an Ozark-accented, outspoken, but highly efficient professional who sometimes treated Dr. Weston like his youthful patients. Overall had appeared in a number of films, including *Biloxi Blues* (1988) and *Kindergarten Cop* (1991). She received two Golden Globe nominations for her work as LaVerne. "The hard part is...trying to keep her from being a one-note samba," said Overall. In between setups on the show she liked to relax by roller-skating, a habit she said she

substituted for smoking. "To be funny every day of the week is hell," said the Tennessee native, who added with a laugh, "I'm really a very depressed person." Although there was never any office hanky-panky between Dr. Weston and his nurse, the producers had toyed with the idea of kindling a romantic relationship between the two. Overall felt "there could be a whole lot of comedy in that," and added, "People don't know what a smooth, old-fashioned gentleman Richard (Mulligan) is. He's a sweet-talking fox."

One of the most beloved characters on the series was the Weston family dog, Dreyfuss. Dreyfuss was played by a megadog named Bear, and his trainer, Joe Silverman, described the canine in 1992 as a six-year-old mix of golden retriever and Saint Bernard.

"Empty Nest" was renewed by NBC through the 1993–94 season, and in addition to new episodes, reruns were already being stripped in syndication.

Paul Provenza (left) and Richard Mulligan.

ANYTHING BUT LOVE

From left: Holly Fulger, Jamie Lee Curtis, Richard Lewis, Richard Frank, Ann Magnuson, and Bruce Weitz.

"Anything But Love" premiered with a limited run of six episodes on ABC in the spring of 1989 and was an instant hit. So naturally, when the romantic comedy returned in the fall as a full-time series, the producers decided to revamp the format. Go figure.

Jamie Lee Curtis starred as Hannah Miller, a brash, energetic young magazine researcher whose chance meeting on an airplane flight with Marty Gold (Richard Lewis) resulted in her getting a job at *Chicago Weekly*, the fictitious magazine where Gold was a reporter. The series centered on Hannah and her friends at the magazine, and Hannah's love life with Marty, a will-they-won't-they tease of the Maddie-and- David ("Moonlighting") and Sam-and-Diane ("Cheers") variety.

" 'Anything But Love' is smart, original and funny," wrote *Daily Variety*. "In terms of quality, it's already a winner." By the second season, the producers were busily at work tampering with that winner, while ABC did its best to toss this series around like croutons in its scheduling salad. Gone were many of the eccentric friends and co-workers viewers met in the first season; Hannah got a new boss at the magazine (explained by its sale to new owners)—Catherine Hughes, played by Ann Magnuson, a hard-edged, hard-driving dynamo who promoted Hannah to full-fledged writer. When she announced to her staff her plans for the "recontextualization of *Chicago Weekly*—the languaging, the imagistics could all stand to be a good deal more *al dente*," she was met with blank stares until Marty Gold translated: "She wants to stiffen our noodles."

Jamie Lee Curtis's role as Hannah Miller was her second time as a continuing character in a TV series—she'd played Lieutenant Barbara Duran in "Operation Petticoat" from 1977 to 1978—and her first starring role in episodic television. "Curtis is one of the nicest things to happen to sitcoms in a long time," said *Daily Variety*. The daughter of Hollywood actors Tony Curtis and Janet Leigh, she was best known for a number of

horror and "slasher" theatrical features she appeared in during the '70s and '80s, including *The Fog* (1980, with mom Janet Leigh), *Halloween* (1978) and *Halloween II* (1981), and *Prom Night* (1980).

Richard Lewis seemed well matched with Curtis and was able to make the transition from his manically neurotic standup-comedy persona to a completely different TV character, something only a handful of entertainers have done successfully (Robin Williams's Mork was still basically Williams; Rosanne Barr/Arnold's TV character was also an extension of her standup persona, as were Jerry Seinfeld's and Tim Allen's).

Although the series struck Nielsen gold with Marty, Hannah, and her gang of crazies, ABC couldn't seem to get its own act together when it came to airing the series. The original time slot for the 30-minute sitcom was on Tuesdays at 9:30, beginning in March 1989. It aired for the initial six weeks, then returned in August of that year for two weeks; it then appeared in September 1989 and ran through March of 1990 on Wednesdays at 9:30; it again vanished from TV screens until July, when reruns were shown in that same time slot. Then the series pulled another vanishing act, resurfacing in February of 1991 and running until June of that year for the benefit of anyone who still cared. More reruns appeared in August through October, now at 10:00 on Wednesdays. In November, ABC put on new episodes of the series, but by the spring of 1992 it was gone completely, and "Coach" took over its time period. (The last episode aired on June 10, 1992.) With such gaps in the schedule, there was no wondering why the ratings sank so quickly. What had begun with high hopes and exciting casting soon became a mishmash of hit-or-miss programming.

Although there were fewer than the usual 100 episodes needed for syndication, the Lifetime cable channel planned to begin airing the series in January 1993.

CREDITS

CREATOR: Wendy Kout. EXECUTIVE PRODUCERS: Wendy Kout, Peter Noah, Robert M. Myman, John Ritter. PRODUCERS: Janis Hirsch, Dennis Koenig, Barbara Hall, Al Lowenstein, Peter Schindler, Bruce Rasmussen. DIRECTORS: David Trainer, Michael Lessac, others. WRITERS: Wendy Kout, Dennis Koenig, Peter Noah, others. CAST: *Hannah Miller* (Jamie Lee Curtis), *Marty Gold* (Richard Lewis), *Catherine Hughes* (Ann Magnuson), *Jules "Julie" Kramer/Bennett* (Richard Frank), *Robin Dulitski* (Holly Fulger), *Norman Keil* (Louis Giambalvo), *Leo Miller* (Bruce Kirby), *Pamela Peyton-Finch* (Sandy Faison), *Brian Allquist* (Joseph Maher), *Harold* (Billy Van Zandt), *Kelly* (Kate McNeil), *Mike Urbanek* (Bruce Weitz).

AMERICA'S FUNNIEST HOME VIDEOS

NUMBER 5, 1989–90

Bob Saget.

America, America, this is you!
                              —OPENING THEME SONG

In 1989, former "Entertainment Tonight" producer Vin Di Bona bought the rights to a popular Japanese television series called "Fun with Ken and Kato Chan." That series featured a segment in which viewers were invited to send in their homemade videos. The tapes flowed in like sake in Camcorderland, where they'd invented the gizmos in the first place. But when it came time to launch his series in the U.S., Di Bona found himself lacking local videotapes and had to pull favors from his industry contacts back in the U.S.A. "I was a one-man band," says De Bona, who secured eight minutes of time on "Good Morning America" and another bit on his alma mater "Entertainment Tonight" to request videos from viewers. The next day, 25 tapes poured in. He took out ads in *People* and *TV Guide* and on the air, until he and fellow producers finally had about 1,800 tapes, enough of a selection to do the pilot.

"America's Funniest Home Videos" first aired over Thanksgiving weekend in 1989 and was more than an instant hit—it was a sensation. Suddenly America had camcorder fever. By the time the series started its regular run in January 1990, the producers were receiving close to 2,000 tapes a day, with 20 full-time screeners pouring over banks of VCRs choosing the best ones for air. The premise was simple: viewers shot spontaneous, unrehearsed home video footage that was laugh-out-loud funny and mailed in their tapes. If a tape was good, it got on the air. If it was very good, it won a prize of up to $10,000. If it was stupendous, several times a year the studio audience voted a grand prize winner of $100,000, making this the best-paying audience participation program of all time. But it wasn't really about greed. "We find that 50 percent of the people who send in their tapes would like the cash prize," says Di Bona, "and 50 percent would like the fame of being on national TV."

The series was hosted/co-written by funnyman Bob Saget, who simultaneously starred in another top 10 hit, "Full House" (also on ABC), making him the first person since Arthur Godfrey to star in two concurrent series that both made the Nielsen list (although in different years—"America's Funniest Home Videos" in 1989–90, while "Full House" first appeared in the top 10 in 1991–92). According to producer Gary Grossman, Bob Saget personally screened the videos for further refinement and wrote much of his own dialogue. "Bob Saget is a father of three kids," says Grossman, "and he's very, very sensitive to clips where kids get hurt. If he gets a clip that's questionable, he'll say, 'I don't feel comfortable doing the voiceover for this, it's too dangerous; you've

got to kill this clip.' There was a clip where a kid got caught on a refrigerator that tipped over. Bob insisted we had to say that this is dangerous." Grossman cautions against getting that "moment" on tape when someone is in need of help. "*Put the camera down!*" he implores, "and go and help your kid."

With those caveats in mind, here is a basic list of what the series was seeking (from one of their early flyers):

"We're looking for HILARIOUS, AMAZING and UNEXPECTED events YOU'VE captured while shooting home movies.
■ Babies ■ Kids ■ Adults ■ Animals
(all home video formats: VHS, BETA, 8mm accepted)
■ Silly Blunders...At weddings, birthdays, graduations, bar mitzvahs, parties, etc.
■ Unexpected Foul-Ups...Kids at play, kids being kids, baby's first: (step, ice cream, bump, surprise)
■ Animal Antics...Goofy behavior/unusual pet tricks
■ Slip-Ups...During amateur sports, relay races, vacation activities
■ Bloopers...At school plays, recitals, parades, speeches"

In addition to these, viewers were invited to participate in something called "Assignment America" in which the home viewer was given a specific assignment—perhaps a parody of a music video, or a scene from a child's sports event. "Make sure you go to your kid's game with a camera because you never know when something's going to happen," advises producer Grossman.

In the winter of 1992, a milestone was reached as the 250,000th tape came into the production offices. Although they no longer received as large a number as they initially handled, the daily total could average 250 to 300 tapes a day viewed by five full-time screeners, with totals running up to 400 when there was an "Assignment America." As of this writing, the series was still seeking tapes for the coming seasons.

"America's Funniest Home Videos" appeared to be the sort of series that would continue to be revived periodically as long as the popularity of video cameras continued (in 1993 over 30 million Americans owned them). "Candid Camera" (see page 104), a highly rated series with a similar premise, but with the camera in the hands of television professionals (and with more deliberate setups), had been going since the '50s, and it seemed likely that "America's Funniest Home Videos" would enjoy the same kind of longevity.

CREDITS

CREATOR: Vin Di Bona. EXECUTIVE PRODUCERS: Vin Di Bona, Steve Paskay. PRODUCERS: Gary Grossman, Joe Bellon, Greg Bellon, Barbara Bernstein Honig, Melinda Zoldan, Bill Barlow, others. DIRECTORS: Steve Hirsen, others. WRITERS: Todd Thicke, Bob Arnott, Bob Saget, others. HOST: Bob Saget.

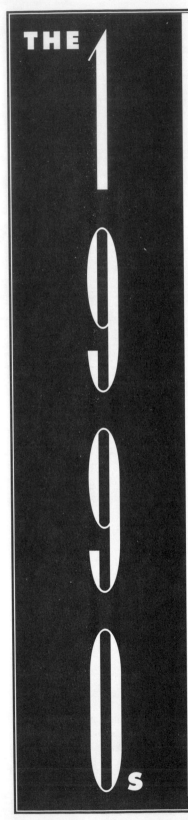

THE 1990s

By 1992, television had become an extension of the American psyche. Ninety-eight percent of the nation's homes had TV sets, and all but one percent of those were color. And television's soul mate, the VCR, was in 77 percent of those homes.

The video revolution was over, but who won the war? The answer would have to be the consumers. With four major networks scrambling to keep up with the proliferation of cable programming, it was clear that ABC, CBS, FBC, and NBC had their work cut out for them. By the end of the decade viewers were expected to be selecting what they wanted to watch and when they wanted to watch it from menus offering hundreds of choices. By 1993, some companies were already gearing up to deliver compressed digital signals that would allow 10 channels to be squeezed into the space once occupied by only one. At least one company was poised to deliver more than 500 channels by 1994, with others rushing to join the new techno-vision breakthroughs that included a fiber-optic cable capable of delivering thousands of channels, and a transmission system via microwave signals. Satellite dishes the size of a magazine would soon be receiving a vast array of special-interest channels. Already waiting in the wings were the Cowboy Channel, the Christian News Network, the Game Channel, the Game Show Channel, the Fitness Channel, the Consumer Channel, the Crime Channel, Talk TV Network, R&B TV, Golden American Network (for the 50-plus viewer), and just about anything else imaginable. Databases would be available to instantly provide users with virtually anything ever put on video, as TV began to allow access to a world of *info*tainment.

What about TV ratings and the Nielsen top 10? Ratings would most likely remain useful to commercial networks as long as they continued to compete in the advertising marketplace. But ratings were probably an endangered species. In the early 1990s, they were already of questionable accuracy, given that many households had multiple VCRs and could watch more than one network offering from the same time period. Whatever the outcome, it would probably become impossible for consumers to turn on their wall-to-wall TVs with their thousands of choices and complain that "There's nothing on!"

MURPHY BROWN

NUMBER 6, 1990–91

"I have sex about as often as we have a Democrat for President." Those words may have once been true, but when a surprised Murphy Brown uttered them in the opening episode of the 1991–92 season of "Murphy Brown," she'd had at least enough of a sex life to find herself pregnant. Soon after that, she gave birth to a political firestorm that straddled the narrow line between fictional television and reality, at least in some people's minds. And not long after that, the United States elected its first Democratic president in 12 years.

"Murphy Brown" began as a satirical program about a feisty Linda Ellerbee-type journalist set among her pals in a Washington, D.C., newsroom where they did a program called "FYI" that was reminiscent of "60 Minutes." But this was not your mother's "Mary Tyler Moore Show" newsroom, and Candice Bergen's Murphy Brown was no perky Barbie doll afraid to stand up to Mr. Grant. Murphy stood up to everyone—including the real vice president of the United States.

Candice Bergen was creator Diane English's first choice for the title character, although there were naysayers who doubted she could pull off the lead in a comedy series. The actress had grown up the privileged daughter of famed ventriloquist Edgar Bergen; from childhood she had had to vie for her father's attention with a former tree—her wooden "brother" named Charlie McCarthy, Bergen's equally famous dummy. Candy survived, though, and landed her first acting role at age 19 in *The Group* (1966). Over the years she appeared in such films as *Carnal Knowledge* (1971), *The Wind and the Lion* (1975), and *Starting Over*, a 1979 movie that brought her an Academy Award nomination. She was also a top model, a globetrotting photojournalist, and the author of a 1985 bestseller about her childhood experiences called *Knock on Wood*. In 1980 she married French film director Louis Malle, and the couple had a child, Chloe, when Candice was 39 years old.

Bergen worked hard at her craft, disproving the CBS brass who were dubious about her comedic abilities; she soon put the doubts completely to rest with what became almost an annual trip to the podium to add to her collection of Emmys (for Best Actress in a Comedy) and a couple of Golden Globe awards. "It was always a dream to do comedy," said the actress in *People*. "This is the one area of acting where I ever felt passion, confidence and joy." But she admitted it wasn't easy. "It's not a show you can phone in. The writing is so meticulous—every comma, every semicolon is worked on...not a preposition gets ad-libbed. The show is demanding and it's fast, and it's a lot to learn in five days, but that's the pace we like."

The others in the cast were an equally worthy ensemble, most of whom would probably go on to shows of their own, like the cast of "Mary Tyler Moore." Broadway veteran Charles Kimbrough played anal-retentive anchor Jim Dial of "FYI." Grant Shaud had held only

CREDITS

TOP 10 PEAK: No. 3, 1991–92. CREATOR: Diane English. EXECUTIVE PRODUCERS: Diane English, Joel Shukovsky, Gary Dontzig, Steven Peterman. PRODUCERS: Tom Seeley, Norm Gunzenhauser, Russ Woody, Barnet Kellman, Frank Pace. DIRECTORS: Barnet Kellman, Peter Bonerz, others. WRITERS: Diane English, others. CAST: *Murphy Brown* (Candice Bergen), *Jim Dial* (Charles Kimbrough), *Frank Fontana* (Joe Regalbuto), *Corky Sherwood-Forrest* (Faith Ford), *Miles Silverberg* (Grant Shaud), *Phil* (Pat Corley), *Eldin Bernecky* (Robert Pastorelli), *Mitchell Baldwin* (Julius Carry), *Carl Wishnitski* (Ritch Brinkley), *John the Stage Manager* (John Hostetter), *Will Forrest* (Scott Bryce), *Gene Kinsella* (Alan Oppenheimer), *Audrey* (Jane Leeves). GUEST STARS: Aretha Franklin, Colleen Dewhurst, Katie Couric, Joan Lunden, Paula Zahn, Mary Alice Williams, Faith Daniels, Darren McGavin, Jay Thomas, Marian Seldes.

EMMYS

Outstanding Lead Actress in a Comedy Series—Candice Bergen (1988–89, 1989–90, 1991–92); Outstanding Guest Actress in a Comedy Series—Colleen Dewhurst (1988–89, 1990–91); Outstanding Writing in a Comedy Series—Diane English (1988–89), Gary Dontzig and Steven Peterman (1990–91); Outstanding Comedy Series (1989–90, 1991–92); Outstanding Guest Actor in a Comedy Series—Darren McGavin (1989–90), Jay Thomas (1990–91); Outstanding Directing in a Comedy Series—Barnet Kellman (1991–92).

From left: Grant Shaud, Joe Regalbuto, Candice Bergen, Charles Kimbrough, and Faith Ford.

a few minor movie roles (*Wall Street*, 1990) before landing the part of the Pepto Bismol-toting Miles Silverberg, the neurotic baby-mogul news producer. Faith Ford, who played former Miss America Corky Sherwood-Forrest (a painfully contrived married name), was hardly the airhead of her alter ego. She had starred in a short-lived (five weeks) 1987 comedy called "The Popcorn Kid," playing another stereotypical dumb blonde. Joe Regalbuto, as Murphy's best pal Frank Fontana, had appeared as a guest star on numerous TV series. Others in the main cast included Robert Pastorelli as Murphy's philosophical housepainter and Pat Corley as the owner of Phil's, the "FYI" watering hole.

Over the years the show poked fun at various newsmaking topics as the characters continued to evolve. Humor came in the form of running gags, like the ever-changing statements on Murphy's office dart board ("I got free checking at BCCI" was one prized example) and the endless parade of Murphy's new secretaries. Then, at the end of the 1990–91 season (the show's first in the top 10), "Murphy Brown" ended with a cliffhanger: our unmarried heroine was pregnant. The 1991–92 season played up the pregnancy and the baby's impending birth, with the season's spring finale (coinciding with the series' 100th episode) culminating in Murphy's giving birth to her baby boy. It became the most watched birth on television since Lucy had had Little Ricky back in 1953. But unlike that fictitious child, Murphy's little Brown became the focus of political attention.

The resulting turmoil began when the vice president of the United States, Dan Quayle, speaking in San Francisco, denounced the "poverty of values" in America's inner cities. Before he was through, he had practically laid the blame for the L.A. riots of April 1992 on Murphy Brown. On Tuesday, May 19, he made the following statement: "It doesn't help matters when prime-time TV has Murphy Brown—a character who supposedly epitomizes today's intelligent, highly paid, professional woman—mocking the importance of fathers by bearing a child alone and calling it just another 'lifestyle choice.'"

Creator/executive producer Diane English was swift in her response to the growing uproar in the press: "If he thinks it's disgraceful for an unmarried woman to bear children, and if he believes that a woman cannot adequately raise a child without a father, then he'd better make sure abortion remains safe and legal."

The score was all tied up when the series returned for its fifth season on September 21, 1992. Over 70 million people tuned in for what amounted to a national event as Murphy prepared to return fire in a one-hour special episode. But the salvo, delivered on "FYI," was anticlimactic, coming close to the end of the hour: "Perhaps it's time for the vice-president to...recognize that, whether by choice or circumstance, families come in all shapes and sizes," said Murphy. Not exceptionally powerful words, but then quite a bit of the press had been given over to Quayle bashing during the summer hiatus, so there was really nothing new to add.

Would the show now focus on Murphy's little baby boy, Avery? English promised that Murphy would remain basically the same. "We're just taking the female W.C. Fields and giving her a child," said English. "She'll be a reporter with a child. Why not challenge a woman in her 40s? I think she's going to reinvent motherhood in a very unconventional way. We're never going to make this a family show or a couch comedy."

DESIGNING WOMEN
NUMBER 10 (TIE), 1990–91

"Designing Women" debuted in the fall of 1986 and immediately gathered a loyal audience of both women and men. Women could relate to the "girl talk" and strong role models provided by the series' quartet of southern belles working at Sugarbakers, an Atlanta interior design firm. Although in the East it ran opposite "Monday Night Football," men took to the series out of curiosity about what women say and do when there aren't men present. Surprise—they talk about men. Not surprisingly, the series dealt with lots of women's issues, but discussions about men's butts, among other things, were also part and parcel of this show.

After a respectable first few weeks' ratings, CBS moved the series from Monday to Thursday nights, giving it a "death slot" opposite NBC's number-seven-ranked "Night Court." Ratings dropped within two weeks from the top 20s to number 63. "We knew that we were doomed," said Dixie Carter, who played Julia Sugarbaker, the design firm's feisty owner. "But what made it so painful was that this was one show that didn't deserve to go down the tubes." Nevertheless, CBS Entertainment president Bud Grant called a halt to the series, putting it on "hiatus," which is more often than not a euphemism for "cancelled."

But viewers were on to CBS. They had brought "Cagney & Lacey" back from the brink of cancellation oblivion in 1984. The same group that had spearheaded that campaign was once again back in action as nearly 1,000 members of a media watchdog organization called Viewers for Quality Television mobilized their legions into writing 50,000 supportive fan letters for the series. They won their case, and by February 1987 "Designing Women" was back on the air, on Sunday nights. A month later it returned to its proper place in the Monday night lineup, where it built a steady audience and rose to a Nielsen top 10 ranking in 1990.

The show was the brainchild of writer Linda Bloodworth-Thomason, and both she and her husband, Harry Thomason, were the executive producers. Both were also southerners, with Bloodworth-Thomason hailing from Little Rock, Arkansas. (The couple became a household name in 1992 as friends of newly elected President Bill Clinton; they even offered their California home as a presidential retreat.) "The show is very southern in tone," said Bloodworth-Thomason, "and we accentuate that tone, but the things we talk about certainly are universal. I think the South gets short shrift on TV—people haven't seen enough of the intelligent, sophisticated South." To maintain that perspective, Bloodworth-Thomason wrote every script for the first two seasons herself.

The original foursome of southern decorators was made up of the two Sugarbaker sisters, Julia and Suzanne, and their two employees, Mary Jo and Charlene. There was also a sole man in this hen house: Anthony, a black ex-convict who served as their assistant (and later, partner). Dixie Carter, a native of McLemoresville, Tennessee, whose own designs once included singing opera, played the older, sensible Sugarbaker sister. In real life she was married to Hal Holbrook, who had played her boyfriend on the series (the character was later killed off). Annie Potts played Mary Jo Shively, a single mother working at Sugarbakers. She was best remembered as the absent-minded

---

CREDITS

TOP 10 PEAK: No. 6, 1991–92. CREATOR: Linda Bloodworth-Thomason. EXECUTIVE PRODUCERS: Harry Thomason, Linda Bloodworth-Thomason, Pamela Norris, Norma Safford Vela, Tommy Thompson, Douglas Jackson. PRODUCERS: E. Jack Kaplan, Emily Marshall, Tommy Thompson, David Trainer. DIRECTORS: Ellen Falcon, Jack Shea, Harry Thomason, David Trainer, David Steinberg, others. WRITERS: Linda Bloodworth-Thomason, Pamela Norris, others. CAST: *Suzanne Sugarbaker* (Delta Burke), *Julia Sugarbaker* (Dixie Carter), *Mary Jo Shively* (Annie Potts), *Charlene Frazier* (Jean Smart), *Anthony Bouvier* (Meshach Taylor), *Reese Watson* (Hal Holbrook), *J.D. Shackleford* (Richard Gilliland), *Bernice Clifton* (Alice Ghostley), *Bill Stillfield* (Doug Barr), *Allison Sugarbaker* (Julia Duffy), *Carlene Frazier Dobber* (Jan Hooks), *Bonnie Jean (B.J.) Poteet* (Judith Ivey), others. GUEST STARS: Scott Bakula, Gerald McRaney, Ann Dusenberry, Barbara Beckley, Jackee, Sheryl Lee Ralph, others.

receptionist in the hit film *Ghostbusters* (1984) and the eccentric record-store manager in *Pretty in Pink* (1986). Like her counterpart, she too was a southern native, hailing from Franklin, Kentucky. Jean Smart played Charlene, the well-meaning but not-altogether-there office manager. Smart, a Seattle native, was the only non-southerner on the show. She met her future husband, Richard Gilliland, on the series when he played Mary Jo's boyfriend. During the 1989–90 season, Smart was pregnant, so her Charlene character was married off, later becoming mother to baby Olivia. Smart elected to leave the series at the end of the following season to spend more time with her family, and Jan Hooks was brought in as her sister, Carlene. Not wishing to tamper with the successful character mix, Carlene was basically the same type as Charlene—dumb but sweet.

The most controversial figure, one of the original sisterhood members, was Delta Burke, who played not-too-bright sexpot Suzanne Sugarbaker. "I'm gonna turn the TV off," announced Suzanne in one episode. "It's just the news and I saw that yesterday." Burke, a native of Orlando, Florida, had been a former beauty queen and Miss America contender (as an 18-year-old Miss Florida). In 1987 one of the show's guest stars was Gerald McRaney, who had played one half of the "Simon & Simon" team before getting his own series, "Major Dad." McRaney played one of Suzanne's ex-husbands, but he soon became Delta Burke's real-life husband when the two were wed in 1989. By 1990, problems were occurring on the set; some blamed McRaney, claiming he was acting as an off-stage Svengali for his new wife. At about the same time, Burke's weight began to increase drastically, giving her character an appearance that was not quite the beauty-queen image originally envisioned by the series' executive producers. Burke insisted the set of "Designing Women" was "not a good workplace, not a good environment," while the Thomasons countered that "We are all mentally exhausted from the daily trials and tribulations of Delta Burke."

Meanwhile, Burke's weight was used to her advantage in a poignant episode called "They Shoot Fat Women, Don't They?" for which she received an Emmy nomination. But by the end of the 1990–91 season, Delta Burke was no longer part of the series; the network had decided not to pick up her option (read: she was fired). Despite the bad, sometimes hurtful publicity, Burke was

Delta Burke (left) and Dixie Carter.

able to overcome the odds and land herself in a new series for the fall of 1992, called simply "Delta." She was taking no chances this time, becoming the co-executive producer as well as the star.

Delta's replacement on "Designing Women" (Suzanne was said to be off visiting her mother in Japan) was Julia Duffy as cousin Allison Sugarbaker, who lasted only a year on the series. The producers claimed her acting was excellent, but her character was dropped because the audience couldn't cotton to this southern-fried bitch.

The following season (1992–93) saw Judith Ivey, winner of two Tony awards, joining the cast as a part owner of Sugarbaker's. Ivey played B.J. Poteet, a rich Texas widow. Meanwhile, Annie Potts announced her intention of leaving the series at the end of that season. "I'm sort of fried," said Potts. "…I just don't think I have anything else to bring to that character, and it's time to move on."

The series, however, would move on, with only Dixie Carter and Meshack Taylor (as Anthony) left from the original group. The series sank to 67th place for the 1992–93 season and was cancelled by CBS, which planned a one-hour final episode for May of 1993.

HOME IMPROVEMENT

NUMBER 5, 1991–92

Tim Allen (left) and Taran Smith.

If it ain't broke, don't fix it. —ANCIENT WISE SAYING
More power!   —TIM TAYLOR

Tim Taylor never met a tool he didn't like—or couldn't use to improve something around his house. Trouble was, his version of "home improvement" (as in the title) usually meant souping up something, adding more power for power's sake. Like the time his wife went off to work and he was supposed to help out around the house by doing the laundry. First, he wired up special dispensers to add just the right amounts of detergent, bleach, and rinse. "Why is the washer in intensive care?" asked his wife, on seeing Tim's IV-like setup. Next, he turbocharged the dryer till it acted like it was on warp power. "Spin dry" took on a new meaning as his kids took turns "riding" the tilt-a-whirl in the garage. Enter Mom. Tim, looking properly sheepish, was contrite, a condition that usually signaled the end of another episode of "Home Improvement."

The only breakout hit of the 1991–92 season, "Home Improvement" starred Tim Allen as Tim Taylor (is there a rule somewhere about stars always using their own first names so audiences won't have to tax their brains?). Tim Taylor was the star of his own TV show, the "show within a show" called "Tool Time," which was a comic send-up of the Bob Vila "This Old House"/ "Home Again" do-it-yourself shows. "Tool Time" wasn't supposed to be comedy, but with Tim Taylor as host, it couldn't be anything else. His assistant, Al (Richard Karn), really had most of the skill (and puppy-dog sex appeal), which aggravated Tim no end. Tim couldn't stand it that Al was better at his job than he was; he played one-upmanship with Al at every opportunity, at times bordering on being abusive. That attitude didn't work at home, however, where Tim's wife, Jill (Patricia Richardson), didn't put up with his shenanigans.

Like Roseanne Arnold in "Roseanne," Tim Allen had been doing a standup-comic routine for a number of years. One evening he was spotted by Walt Disney Studios head Michael Eisner, who asked him if he'd be interested in developing a sitcom with Matt Williams, creator of "Roseanne," using his character. "I wanted to be Bob Vila with a bad attitude," said Allen. The series was fleshed out by Williams, who realized it needed

more than a macho, strutting, tool-toting hero. "Tim blowing up an appliance every week is not going to keep this show running," said Williams. "The relationship between Tim and Jill is a strong one; that's the foundation for the series."

Besides Tim's relationships with his wife, three tow-headed boys, and "Tool Time" partner Al, there were several other layers to this show. As in any good sitcom, there was a next-door neighbor. But this guy was never fully seen from the front. Wilson, the backyard mystic (played by the eyes and hat and occasional nose of Earl Hindman), was usually hidden by the picket fence. "Hi-de-ho, neighbor," he'd chirp, announcing his presence. He never solved Tim's problems, just passed along some words to savor, like "I'm afraid that reality as we know it is someone else's dream," leaving Tim to draw his own conclusions.

Part of the fun of the series was in its technical aspects, such as the "wipes" between scenes. A paintbrush might stroke its way to the next scene, or a tool would jump out of the shot and into the next, all done with computer-enhanced opticals. Also delightful were the closing credits, during which Tim Allen or other cast members could be seen in "bloopers" (outtakes) from the just-viewed episode (a technique creator Matt Williams also used in "Roseanne").

Tim Allen was delighted with the show's success but was concerned about his future as a standup comic. "When I go on the stage, I do 90 minutes of rock-and-roll adult comedy," the show's star said in *TV Guide*. "There's profanity and stuff that I don't think anyone under 18 should hear." He was shocked when he returned to his standup roots during the first summer hiatus and the audience was full of mostly children, who adored his TV show. "I looked out and saw all these little girls, and I thought, my God, even my first joke has gotta go. Instead of my usual four-letter words, I was throwing in expressions like 'Aw, shucks' and 'Golly, darn it.' I felt like such a goof."

Allen needn't have worried about his future for some time to come. In the fall of 1992, ABC made an unprecedented announcement that they were renewing "Home Improvement" for three more years, through the 1995–96 season.

CREDITS

TOP 10 PEAK: No. 3, 1992–93.
CREATORS/EXECUTIVE PRODUCERS: Matt Williams, David McFadzean, Carmen Finestra. PRODUCERS: Gayle S. Maffeo, John Pasquin, Billy Riback, Maxine Lapidus. DIRECTORS: various. WRITERS: various. CAST: *Tim Taylor* (Tim Allen), *Jill Taylor* (Patricia Richardson), *Brad Taylor* (Zachery Ty Bryan), *Randy Taylor* (Jonathan Taylor Thomas), *Mark Taylor* (Taran Noah Smith), *Wilson* (Earl Hindman), *Al Borland* (Richard Karn), *Lisa* (Pamela Denise Anderson).

COACH

The show seemed doomed from the start. Back in 1988, Barry Kemp, who had served as executive producer on "Fresno" and "Newhart" (which he also created) and executive script consultant on "Taxi," approached ABC with an idea for a comedy series about the life of a coach of a small midwestern college town. The idea was met with mixed to unfavorable reaction. ABC didn't like the title, which it felt wouldn't appeal to women, the ones more likely to watch sitcoms. They suggested calling it "My Dad the Coach," or "The Fox." The network also feared that men wouldn't watch because it *was* a comedy. Kemp stuck to his guns. "I felt if we could get enough word of mouth, we could overcome that initial [title] stigma."

Then there was a question about the proposed lead for the series. Kemp wanted Craig T. Nelson, but ABC questioned casting the decidedly unfunny star of heavy dramas like *Poltergeist I* and *II* (1982 and 1986), *Call to Glory* (1984), *The Killing Fields* (1984), and *Silkwood* (1984). But Kemp stood by him, and Nelson got the job even though he himself thought his reading was "absolutely unfunny."

"Coach" began filming in 1988 but didn't debut until February 1989, which was just the wrong time of year to present a show about a football team and its coach. By fall, it was gone from the schedule. Instead, ABC decided to put a new show called "Chicken Soup" in the time slot immediately following "Roseanne." Its ratings weren't bad, but the show generated too much negative publicity because of its over-the-top Jewish ethnicity and controversial lead actor Jackie Mason, and it was cancelled after eight weeks. "Coach" was pressed back into service and was given the dream spot following "Roseanne"; soon it began building up its audience.

"This show took a very long time to develop, not only in terms of an audience, but in our understanding of it," said series star Craig T. Nelson in the *Los Angeles Times*. "It was a very long time for me in developing what an audience would find lovable or acceptable, where [Coach Fox] stood on issues, how he related to his players. What was his attitude? Was he a roughneck? Was he totally gruff? Did he have no intelligence? It was a mixture of a lot of different things."

That mixture was supported by the show's other excellent cast members. Shelley Fabares played a TV news anchor, Coach Fox's long-suffering girlfriend, persevering as their romance heated up and cooled off, only to heat up again. By 1992 the two were headed to the altar when, in a hilarious scene, the bride lost her balance and ended up swinging from the chandelier, landing in the hospital with a broken leg. The amazingly youthful Fabares, who in real life is married to former "M*A*S*H" star Mike Farrell, was best remembered for her childhood role in the old "Donna Reed Show."

Jerry Van Dyke played the dimwitted but lovable assistant coach, Luther Van Dam. Most people recognized him as Dick Van Dyke's brother, and he made occasional appearances on Dick's show. But he was best remembered for starring in what has to have been TV's weirdest program, "My Mother the Car" (1965–66), in which he played a man whose mother had reincarnated as a talking car (you had to be there). *TV Guide* called Jerry Van Dyke the show's "hidden treasure," and the former banjo-playing comic was indeed an asset to the program, as was Bill Fagerbakke as Dauber Dybinski, a hulking perennial student adding to Coach Fox's woes.

No one expected that this show would survive without the "Roseanne" lead-in, and ABC was constantly testing the waters by switching time slots for the series. In the first year alone, it flip-flopped between Tuesday and Wednesday nights five times, eventually settling into Tuesday night, post-"Roseanne."

" 'Coach' will never win the Super Bowl, but it's made it to the playoffs again, which is not a bad record," said *Daily Variety*, referring to the show's perceived inability to capture top 10 ratings. But once again, the prophets of doom were wrong; by the 1991–92 season, "Coach" had attracted men, women, and Nielsen families alike. Coach Hayden Fox and his (mythical) Minnesota State Screaming Eagles were underdog champions where it counted—in the race for the ratings. And in 1992, Craig T. Nelson surprised everyone by walking off with the Emmy Award for Best Actor in a Comedy. Touchdown!

CREDITS

TOP 10 PEAK: No. 6, 1992–93. CREATOR: Barry Kemp. EXECUTIVE PRODUCERS: Barry Kemp, Sheldon Bull, John Peaslee, Judd Pillot. PRODUCERS: Mark Ganzel, Jay Kleckner, Tom Palmer, Neil Scovell, Craig Wyrick, Warren Bell. DIRECTORS: Michael Zinberg, John P. Whitesell II, Alan Rafkin, others. WRITERS: various. CAST: *Coach Hayden Fox* (Craig T. Nelson), *Assistant Coach Luther Van Dam* (Jerry Van Dyke), *Christine Armstrong* (Shelley Fabares), *Dauber Dybinski* (Bill Fagerbakke), *Kelly Fox Rosebrock* (Clare Carey), *Stuart Rosebrock* (Kris Kamm), others.

EMMYS

Outstanding Lead Actor in Comedy—Craig T. Nelson (1991–92).

From left: Craig T. Nelson, Clare Carey, and Shelley Fabares.

FULL HOUSE

NUMBER 8, 1991–92

It wasn't always easy aces for ABC's hit "Full House." When the series premiered in 1987, critics panned the show about three men parenting one of the guys' three young girls, pronouncing the new series "as empty as a sitcom can get...even with a resident comedian, there's nary a laugh in the house." On top of that, *Variety* went so far as to venture, "[The series'] future's not even iffy." Luckily for ABC, they didn't hedge their bets. With three of a kind and a pair of twins, this series' successful future was in the cards.

"We never said that this was a show that was going to cure cancer," proclaimed executive producer Tom Miller, referring to the critical drubbing the show's script content took. Rather than being a message series, this sitcom relied on its emotional appeal for staying power. "A lot of shows come out of the TV and go straight to your head," said John Stamos, who played Uncle Jesse. "This show comes out of the TV and goes straight to your heart."

Admittedly, the premise wasn't the most complex or original one. Danny, a widower (played by Bob Saget), had three young daughters to raise on his own, so his brother-in-law Jesse (John Stamos) and his friend comedian Joey (Dave Coulier) decided to share digs and diapers with the girls' father—yet another untraditional TV family coping with life in the '80s and '90s.

Although nearly cancelled in the first year while still "finding its audience," the series had appeal on many levels, as indicated by its nearly perfect demographics. By 1992, when it finished in the Nielsen top 10 for the first time, "Full House" ranked as one of the top three shows with kids six to 11 years old; it was number eight with teenagers, and even the older folks seemed to like it, ranking the series 17th in the 18-to-34-year-old age group, making this a show for the entire (young) family.

"Full House" was never long on heavy plotting. Most of the episodes had to do with the kids and their problems. Early in the series, a pair of nine-month-old twins, Mary-Kate and Ashley Olsen, were selected to play baby Michelle. As these toddlers grew, they continued alternating in the role of the show's youngest child,

literally growing up before America's eyes. These little scene-stealers kept their poker faces as they made off with the whole pot; by the time they were six and entering first grade, the twins (still alternating in the role of Michelle) were challenging the men in the series for the spotlight and were one (or two) of the reasons for the show's popularity. Occasionally the script called for them to play a scene together, as when a cousin from overseas appeared, or when they played the "good" Michelle and the "bad" Michelle—no need for split-screen opticals here.

Actually, Mary-Kate and Ashley were fraternal, not identical twins, but most couldn't tell them apart. These two six-year-olds had their own talking Michelle doll, providing both kids with enough money from merchandising royalties for their future college educations, and there were plans for a record deal and an album of children's tunes. The girls were just learning to read during the 1992–93 season, so they still had their lines spoon-fed to them by their acting coach.

The oldest sister, D.J., was played by Candace Cameron, sister of Kirk Cameron from "Growing Pains." By the 1992–93 season, she had turned 16, maturing into a promising young actress. Middle daughter, Stephanie, was played by Jodie Sweetin, who began in the role at age five.

In the 1990–91 season, Uncle Jesse (John Stamos) got married, and the couple later became parents of—right—twins. Suddenly the house got fuller with this very extended family all living under one roof. At the same time, John Stamos began talking about the possibility of leaving the show at the end of the 1992–93 season. "I'm not knocking it," said Stamos, "it's a great show—for children. But there's a real ceiling as to what you can do. It's time to go on."

Even without Stamos, the series would certainly find a way to continue, since most of the appeal was to the younger set. "We try to be the most wholesome, sweetest, loving show on television," said executive producer Dennis Rinsler. It was that kind of familiarity that was still attracting viewers to this comfortable "House" as it entered its seventh season in the fall of 1993.

CREDITS

CREATOR: Jeff Franklin. EXECUTIVE PRODUCERS: Jeff Franklin, Thomas L. Miller, Robert L. Boyett, Dennis Rinsler, Marc Warren. PRODUCERS: Don Van Atta, Lenny Ripps, Robert Dames, David Simon, Ellen Guylas, Leslie Gray, Ken Hecht, James O'Keefe, Bonnie Bogard, Jay Abramowitz, Tom Amundsen. DIRECTORS: Joel Zwick, Bill Foster, others. WRITERS: Jeff Franklin, others. CAST: *Danny Tanner* (Bob Saget), *Uncle Jesse Katsopolis* (John Stamos), *Joey Gladstone* (David Coulier), *D.J. (Donna Jo) Tanner* (Candace Cameron), *Stephanie Tanner* (Jodie Sweetin), *Michelle Tanner* (Mary-Kate and Ashley Fuller Olsen), *Rebecca Donaldson Katsopolis* (Lori Loughlin), *Kimmy Gibbler* (Andrea Barber). GUEST STARS: Jack Kruschen, Vera Lockwood, John Aprea, Yvonne Wilder, others.

Back row, from left: David Coulier, Lori Loughlin, and John Stamos; center: Bob Saget; front row, from left: Jodie Sweetin, Mary Kate Olsen, and Candace Cameron.

UNSOLVED MYSTERIES

NUMBER 9, 1991–92

Robert Stack.

What you are about to see is not a news broadcast. Whenever possible, the actual family members and police officers have participated in recreating the events.
　　　　　　　　　　　　—OPENING NARRATION

Missing persons, unsolved crimes, lost loves, the unexplained—all were part and parcel of the mysteries viewers were invited to help solve in this reality-based series that debuted in the fall of 1988 on NBC. There had been a couple of trial runs of the series in previous seasons, hosted by Raymond Burr and Karl Malden, but nobody did it better than permanent host Robert Stack.

Stack, long identified with fighting crime as Eliot Ness of "The Untouchables" (see page 106), now became (in the words of one writer) the "Voice of Doom," as he tolled the various crimes and mysterious happenings reenacted each week. Stack himself was usually seen emerging mysteriously from a fog bank or walking down a vast hallway somewhere, dressed in a trenchcoat while recounting "our toll-free number— 1-800-876-5353" like some reincarnated, detached Rod Serling imploring, "Maybe *you* can help solve a mystery." At 74 years of age (in 1993) he was one of TV's elder statesmen, appearing staid, calm, and above all trustworthy and believable. If he said there was a government cover-up surrounding UFOs, you just knew there was a hangar in New Mexico somewhere with frozen bodies of little silver men from outer space.

Critics deplored the series when it premiered. "Biggest mystery of all remains unsolved," claimed *Variety*, "namely, what viewers see in this sensationalistic tripe." Stack himself found it a mystery that the show eventually became a Nielsen top 10 hit. "To tell the truth, I never thought 'Unsolved Mysteries' would be a hit. But I've learned to expect the unexpected. Life to me is one big unsolved mystery." Spoken like a true host of a series whose future continued to hold no mysteries; this was one of NBC's few hits as the 1992–93 series unfolded.

There was seemingly no end of mysteries to be explained, and in its initial years the show's viewers helped solve approximately one out of four of the cases presented. The season opener was usually a UFO story: that supposed air force cover-up in New Mexico, for instance, and sightings in Pennsylvania, Connecticut, and New York. Extraterrestrial stories were not as prominent as they were in the print tabloids—no one claimed to have given birth to an E.T. baby or to have ridden on a spaceship piloted by Elvis. But those darned wheatfield circles in Britain kept cropping up year after year, even after some farmers claimed to have done the whole thing as a hoax.

But most stories had to do with unsolved murders, disappearances, and the like. Viewers submitted their ideas/quests, and many cases were taken from newspaper accounts or personal experiences of those working on the show. Robert Stack admitted that some of the cases involved friends of his, like the son of oldtime producer Harold Hecht, who disappeared. "The family desperately wants some answers," said Stack. Some recent stories included:

- Unanswered questions in the 1935 shooting of Louisiana senator Huey Long (nicely dramatized);
- The murders of two vacationing Swedish women whose bodies were discovered by deer hunters near Santa Barbara;
- A woman who drew uncanny likenesses of people she'd never met who had died (the mystery, once supposed, was how, or even why?);
- A con game in New York involving fake winning lottery tickets;
- A family reunion of a man and his only living daughter, to whom he planned to bequeath $1 million;
- The search for 17 tons of gold bullion buried since the 1930s atop a mesa in New Mexico;
- A Vietnam veteran's search for the army nurse who gave him the courage to overcome his injuries and recover;
- A search for the Yeti—the Abominable Snowman of the Himalayas.

By the winter of 1992, "Unsolved Mysteries" had reunited over 50 people seeking long-lost relatives or friends.

In the fall of 1992, the show did a special "live" broadcast, with phone lines set to receive calls from across the United States and Canada, as viewers telephoned with hot tips and sightings of missing people or criminals. The producers claimed to have solved about 25 percent of the reports that night; there was an emotional on-air reunion between a woman and her long-lost childhood friend, and a reported location of a man accused of kidnapping.

A spinoff series, also hosted by Robert Stack, premiered in the fall of 1992. It was called "Final Appeal: From the Files of 'Unsolved Mysteries.'" Each week, evidence from both prosecution and defense was presented to the TV audience, leaving it up to them to decide whether or not the criminal, already a convicted felon, deserved a final appeal. But the verdict on this spinoff was that because of the show's narrow scope it had limited appeal, and it was cancelled by October 16, 1992. Meanwhile, reruns of "Unsolved Mysteries" were being syndicated in 1993.

CREDITS

CREATORS/EXECUTIVE PRODUCERS: Terry Dunn Meurer, John Cosgrove. PRODUCERS: Chris Pye, Edward R. Horwitz, Raymond Bridgers, Stuart Schwartz, Shannon McGinn, Kris Palmer, Samuel S. Lucchese. DIRECTORS: John Cosgrove, John C. Joseph, Jim Lindsay, Mike Mathis, others. WRITERS: various. HOST: Robert Stack.

BUT WHAT ABOUT...?

Not all popular series join the ranks of those in the yearly top 10. In checking through the profiles of shows that made it, you may have been surprised to find that at least one of your favorites, or perhaps a classic from TV's so-called Golden Age, didn't appear on the list. Many well-known shows had long track records, ranking just below that magic number 10 for year after year, while other notable series never even came close to a high ranking.

The following non-top-10 television series, presented alphabetically, are listed here for any number of reasons, among them: they are representative of their genre, or are instantly remembered; they had a long initial run on TV; they were revolutionary or innovative, and/or had long runs in syndication. And all will probably be viewed as classics some day; some already are. Among these audience-pleasers that had staying power, if not Nielsen magic, were dozens of other series that could not be listed here due to space limitations.

The Adventures of Ozzie and Harriet.
ABC, October 3, 1951, to September 3, 1966; 435 episodes. They really didn't have many "adventures," unless serving up milk and warm cookies can be considered adventurous. That was Harriet Nelson's job, while Ozzie didn't seem to have one, unless you count raking leaves. Mostly, he was raking in the dough (and not the kind found in Harriet's kitchen) from this long-running TV series (based on his long-running radio series) starring his family—wife Harriet and kids David and Ricky (whose recording career was launched on the series). Ozzie had a job in real life: producer, director, star, and head writer of this domestic sitcom that set a pattern for many future family comedies.

The Bob Newhart Show/Newhart/Bob.
CBS, October 16, 1972, to September 2, 1978; CBS, October 25, 1982, to September 8, 1990; CBS, premiered September, 1992. It's hard to remember a time when Bob Newhart didn't have a series on TV. His first popular show

was called "The Bob Newhart Show" and co-starred Suzanne Pleshette as his wife, Emily. Bob played Bob, a Chicago psychologist. When that show left the air after six years, he showed up as a Vermont innkeeper. Again Bob played Bob; his wife's name was Joanna, played by Mary Frann. A final episode aired after eight years in which Bob woke up in bed with—Emily!—and declared he'd just had the strangest dream. Bob Newhart returned to television in 1992 with a new series, called simply "Bob." (His only remaining title choices were "The," "Show," and "Bob," so, as he put it, "This one had to be 'Bob.' ") This time he played—who else?—Bob, a cartoonist with a young wife named Kaye (Carlene Watkins), a grown daughter who didn't look much younger than mom, and three former head writers from "Cheers" for executive producers.

The Brady Bunch. ABC, September 26, 1969, to August 30, 1974. Here's the story of a man named Brady and his wife and six kids. This extended family started with a widower (Robert Reed) and his three boys, a widow (Florence Henderson) with three girls, a housekeeper (Ann B. Davis), and assorted pets. The couple said "I do," and they did, in a very crowded four-bedroom house. The series became a cult favorite, spawning several spinoffs (including an animated version) and reunion shows. In 1991, a stage production called *The Real Live Brady Bunch* played to capacity crowds in Chicago, New York, and Los Angeles (with other cities set to follow). Adults played all the parts as they read scripts from original episodes of the TV series. In 1992, creator Sherwood Schwartz announced a worldwide talent search to locate a new bunch of kids for his film planned for 1993, *The Brady Bunch—The Movie.*

The Carol Burnett Show. CBS, September 11, 1967, to September 8, 1979. She had a rubber face and a Tarzan yell that sent ripples through the jungle. This was America's all-time best-loved variety show. Carol and her regulars—Harvey Korman, Vicki Lawrence, Lyle Waggoner, and Tim Conway—came up with great comedy sketches, like the long-running soap-opera satire, "As the Stomach Turns," and her renowned movie parodies. Among the most memorable of the latter was *Gone with the Wind*, with Carol playing Scarlett O'Hara dressed in green velvet curtains—and the curtain rod.

The George Burns and Gracie Allen Show. CBS, October 12, 1950, to September 22, 1958. Two of this century's most beloved entertainers, the husband-and-wife team of Burns and Allen started in the '20s in vaudeville, took their act to radio, and entered television in its infancy. George and his ever-present cigar played straight man to Gracie and her ever-present dizziness. She became a television prototype; Betty White, Dick Martin, Woody Harrelson from "Cheers," and Richard Moll from "Night Court" (to name just a few) all paid homage to her in characters they created. The show was a classic but never a Nielsen powerhouse. Gracie died a few years after it left the air, and George ventured out on his own, becoming a major star who, in 1993, was still working at the age of 97.

Get Smart. NBC, CBS, September 18, 1965, to September 11, 1970. This show was created by Mel Brooks and Buck Henry. Agent 86, Maxwell Smart (who wasn't very), was played by Don Adams in this spy spoof conceived during the height of the "secret agent" genre—a genre that grew out of the success of early James Bond movies. Barbara Feldon played his partner, Agent 99. A few years into the show, the pair got married. Smart talked into his shoe telephone (in a parody of James Bond gadgetry) and gave the American lexicon some nifty catch phrases like "Would you believe..." and "Sorry about that, Chief." The supporting cast included Bernie Kopell (later of "The Love Boat") as KAOS agent/bad guy Siegfried and Dick Gautier as Hymie the robot. Agent 13 hid in mailboxes, and agent K-13 was a talking pig. No? Okay then, would you believe a dog named Fang?

Gilligan's Island. CBS, September 26, 1964, to September 4, 1967; 98 episodes. This was a tale about castaways: the Skipper, first mate Gilligan, the millionaire and his wife, the movie star, the Professor, and Mary Ann, all shipwrecked for three years in this silly sitcom that ran ad infinitum even after ceasing production. Creator Sherwood Schwartz explained, "It's from the age of innocence, which there is very little of today." The abuse it took from critics mattered not a whit as the series gave birth to sequels, reunion movies, and, in 1992, *Gilligan's Island—The Musical*, which opened in Chicago to the inevitable negative reviews (and capacity crowds). Set for late 1993: *Gilligan's Island: The Movie.* They're here for a long, long time.

L.A. Law. NBC, premiered October 3, 1986. Completing its seventh season in the spring of 1993, "L.A. Law" may not have been in the top 10, but it deserved to be. The multiple Emmy winner about goings-on at the law firm of McKenzie, Brackman, Chaney & Becker was part soap opera, part courtroom drama. The attorneys may have played "follow the bouncing bed," but the series tackled such contemporary issues as AIDS, child abuse, capital punishment, bisexuality, and environmental pollution—not to mention the Venus Butterfly (watch for it in first-season reruns on the Lifetime cable channel).

Leave It to Beaver. CBS, ABC, October 4, 1957, to September 12, 1963; 234 episodes. One of the few series to present life through the eyes of a child, "Leave It to Beaver" attracted a generation of baby boomers who identified with the Beaver and his brother Wally as they grew up in middle-class suburbia. Mom was a typical '50s mom, like Donna Reed and Margaret Anderson. She did housework in heels and pearls, served cookies, and worried about her boys. Dad had a job (!) as an accountant, and the Beav's older brother was all-wise and all-knowing, the way an older brother should be when his kid brother is a 20th century Tom Sawyer, generating simple problems by refusing to eat Brussels sprouts and giving himself a pre-punk haircut. A reunion movie, *Still the Beaver* (1983), led to a Disney Studios remake of the series, called "The New Leave It to Beaver" (1985–86). It included a new cast (since the boys were now grownups with children of their own) and, of course, Jerry Mathers as the Beaver.

The Man from U.N.C.L.E. NBC, September 22, 1964, to January 15, 1968. A bona fide cult hit, this show began as a spoof of Ian Fleming's James Bond character, with Fleming himself contributing the original outline. U.N.C.L.E. was an acronym for United Network Command for Law Enforcement, a mythical agency whose agents Napoleon Solo and Illya Kuryakin (Robert Vaughn and David McCallum) made the world safe from THRUSH, the international baddies. McCallum, as the sexy Russian good guy (at a time when Russians were decidedly unfriendly cold warriors), created a fashion passion for turtleneck pullovers. One classic episode (now available on videocassette) was "The Project Strigas Affair," with guest stars William Shatner and Leonard Nimoy together for the first time in their pre-"Star Trek" days. Open Channel D!

Mission: Impossible. CBS, September 17, 1966, to September 8, 1973; ABC, October 23, 1988, to June 9, 1990. "Good morning, Mr. Phelps." Long before there was an "A-Team," there was the IMF team—the Impossible Missions Force. This group of top-secret operatives worked for a top-secret government agency (only the 20 million people who watched the show knew of it) that planned and executed secret missions so complex that the actors took a back seat to the schemes and gadgets. Jim Phelps (Peter Graves) headed the team; Martin Landau was their master-of-disguise co-leader; his wife, Barbara Bain, played his wooden associate, Cinnamon; Greg Morris played Barnie, who knew his way around gadgetry better than any M.I.T. graduate; and muscle-bound Peter Lupus as Willie provided—what else?—the muscle. Later additions to the cast were Leonard Nimoy as Paris and Leslie Ann Warren as Dana. In 1988 ABC resurrected the series with a new production filmed in Australia. Peter Graves returned as Jim Phelps, and Greg Morris's son Phil carried on his father's tinkering duties. The series self-destructed in 1990 after the Nielsen families disavowed any knowledge of its actions.

The Monkees. NBC, September 12, 1966, to August 19, 1968; 58 episodes. Hey, hey, they were the Monkees, a "manufactured" group of pseudo-Beatles inspired by the real Fab Four's hit movie *A Hard Day's Night* (1964). Mike Nesmith, Micky Dolenz, Peter Tork, and Davy Jones romped, rather than acted, their way through episodes built around music and gimmicky photography. Only two—Tork and Nesmith—were true musicians, while the others had some acting experience. Nonetheless, after a crash course in music, the group was good enough to score several hit records, like the 1966 number one hits "Last Train to Clarksville" and "I'm a Believer" and 1967's "Daydream Believer." In 1968 the series was cancelled, and a flood of protest mail couldn't convince NBC to reinstate it. The group broke up shortly thereafter. In 1986, three of them (minus Nesmith, heir to the Liquid Paper fortune) returned for a reunion tour, while a year later, Columbia Pictures launched the unsuccessful "The New Monkees" for a quickie 13 episodes.

My Three Sons. ABC, CBS, September 29, 1960, to August 24, 1972. Tapping basketball shoes introduced us each week to the Douglas family: widower Steve, played by the somnambulistic Fred MacMurray, and his three sons, Mike, Robbie, and Chip (Tim Considine, Don Grady, and Stanley Livingston). When Considine left the series, a new son, Ernie (played by Stanley's real-life brother, Barry), was adopted into the family. Maternal nurturing was first provided by grandpa Bub (William Frawley, better known as Fred Mertz on "I Love Lucy"), who died during the fifth season and was replaced by Uncle Charlie (William Demarest). Good things always came in threes for this show; when middle son Robbie married, he obliged by having triplets.

Northern Exposure. CBS, premiered July 12, 1990. Dr. Joel Fleischman (Rob Morrow) was a fish out of water when he landed in Cicely, Alaska (population 813), to fulfill a medical school scholarship obligation. The town was full of quirky types, and Fleischman, who longed to be just another New York Jewish doctor—in New York—soon found himself swimming right along with the rest of the school. This dramedy just kissed the outer limits of the Nielsen top 10, with the characters and bizarre plots making the show an instant cult hit. Where else would viewers see a piano flung in slow-mo by a catapult? But when Morrow quit the show (temporarily) in 1992 with a demand for more money, he soon learned that the other characters—Maggie, Maurice, Chris, Ed, Holling, Shelly, Marilyn, and Ruth-Anne—were becoming just as fascinating in their own right. By fall, Morrow was back in the fold, and viewers placed bets on how long it would be before Joel got it on with Maggie (Janine Turner).

The Simpsons. FBC, premiered December 17, 1989. This animated show first appeared as a series of vignettes during "The Tracey Ullman Show" on Fox in 1988. "The Simpsons" (created by Matt Groening) eventually got their own series even though Ullman's was cancelled. It was fourth network FBC's best-rated show, at one time even challenging "The Bill Cosby Show" and winning several weeks in the ratings race. Audiences loved the antics of Bart (an anagram for "brat"), who at first was the show's centerpiece. But over the years other characters were given equal time, and all were equally intriguing: blue-collar, dumb-but-lovable Homer; long-suffering, blue-beehived Marge; musically talented daughter Lisa; and even baby Maggie, who, in 1992, dropped her pacifier and uttered her first word, "Daddy," in a voice provided by none other than Elizabeth Taylor. In fact, stars fought over the chance to appear as guest voices. Some of the lucky ones: Danny DeVito, Darryl Strawberry, Jackie Mason, Penny Marshall, Larry King, Linda Ronstadt, Hugh Hefner, Leonard Nimoy, Adam West, Johnny Carson, Tom Jones, Sara Gilbert, and (uncredited) Michael Jackson. Emmys have gone to the main characters' voicers: Dan Castellaneta, Julie Kavner, Yeardley Smith, guests Marcia Wallace and Jackie Mason, and Nancy Cartwright as Bart Simpson. Yes, the voice behind Bart was a female. Don't have a cow, man.

Star Trek. NBC, September 8, 1966, to September 2, 1969; 79 episodes. The most popular cult show of all time, the series spawned six feature films as of 1991, two spinoff sequel series, hundreds of fan clubs, and thousands of items of merchandise. Created by Gene Roddenberry, it was his vision of an optimistic future without wars, famine, or prejudice that kept audiences coming back for more. Never a hit in its original prime-time run, "Star Trek" found its first audience in syndicated reruns once the space age really got off the ground with the first moon landing in 1969. William Shatner starred as Captain James T. Kirk, but it was the pointy-eared Vulcan Mr. Spock (Leonard Nimoy) who was the most recognizable character, even to non-Trekkers. In 1987, a new starship Enterprise with a new crew sailed the stars at warp speed and boldly went where no "Star Trek" ratings had gone before—"Star Trek: The Next Generation" became the number one drama show in first-run syndication, still going stronger than ever in its sixth season (1992–93). Scotty, beam us down. There *is* intelligent life on this planet after all.

thirtysomething. ABC, September 29, 1987, to September 3, 1991; 85 episodes. Yuppies—young urban professionals—were the focal point of this ground-breaking series about (and for) middle-aging, angst-ridden baby boomers. But what could have become just another soap opera instead treated its characters and audience with respect, as Michael and Hope, Elliot and Nancy, Ellyn and Gary, and yes, Russell and Peter agonized over their careers, families, relationships, and life's everyday problems. Sensitivity was the operative word for the treatment of subjects like homosexuality, infidelity, ovarian cancer, childbirth, and death (including that of Gary, who died in the final season, making this one of the few series ever to kill off a main character). Although never a Nielsen hit, it quickly gathered an audience that followed the series with cult-like devotion. And its character-driven writing style set a precedent emulated by many quality series of the 1990s. No one remains thirtysomething, however, and the show was cancelled before the stars became fortysomethings. But in reruns on the Lifetime cable channel, viewers could see Gary live again, know that Nancy *would* beat ovarian cancer, and remain thirtysomething in perpetuity.

The Twilight Zone. CBS, October 2, 1959, to September 5, 1965; 151 episodes (134 half-hour, 17 one-hour). This series took us to the "fifth dimension, beyond that which is known to man," a dimension that lurked somewhere in Rod Serling's fertile imagination. He was the creator, frequent writer, executive producer, and host of this classic, quasi-science-fiction series. The stories, laden with plot twists, were generally metaphors, fables, or allegories, and all paid homage to O. Henry with their surprise endings. Quite a number of them had darkly depressing denouements. Too bizarre

to make it into the top 10 or even 20, the series nevertheless remained a perennial cult favorite with a hardcore group of fans, and it reran constantly after cancellation, often with holiday-time day-long marathons in Los Angeles and other cities.

Twin Peaks. ABC, April 8, 1990, to June 10, 1991. "Who killed Laura Palmer?" That was the question on everyone's mind when this offbeat and innovative series from film director David Lynch first took to the air. Fast out of the starting gate, it caught the attention of the media as well as the public, but most of the audience began to drift away as the plot became unbelievably convoluted, the situations increasingly surrealistic. We did eventually learn who killed lovely prom queen Laura—it was her father—but by that time no one but hardcore fans really cared. A spinoff theatrical prequel movie, *Twin Peaks: Fire Walk with Me*, released in 1992, flopped in America but caught fire with the Japanese audience, where Laura Palmer and Agent Dale Cooper were big business. The series itself, although revolutionary in its techniques, couldn't sustain an audience and was cancelled after a little more than a year, even though its characters did serve up cherry pie and damn fine coffee.

You'll Never Get Rich. CBS, September 20, 1955, to September 11, 1959; 138 episodes. A classic from TV's Golden Age, this series played opposite Milton Berle for most of its run and consequently never became a Nielsen top 10 entry, even after winning multiple Emmys. Phil Silvers starred as Master Sergeant Ernest Bilko, master plotter and schemer with a million and one ideas for getting rich quick. Less than a year after the series began, the network changed the title to "The Phil Silvers Show," but most people remember it simply as "Bilko." They also fondly remember his platoon of motor pool characters, like puppy-dog-eyed Private Doberman (Maurice Gosfield), Corporal Henshaw (Alan Melvin), Corporal Barbella (Harvey Lembeck), and the rest of his hapless gang. Of course, Bilko's schemes were almost always foiled by Colonel Hall (Paul Ford), but part of the fun was seeing just how far this quintessential con artist could get before being caught. He made it all the way to 1959—four years of non-stop laughs.

TOP 10 SHOWS BY SEASON, 1950-1993

The following lists show the annual top 10 ratings breakdowns as published in various sources by the A.C. Nielsen Company. Shows new to the list each year are marked with an asterisk (*).

October 1950–April 1951
1. Texaco Star Theater*
2. Fireside Theatre*
3. Philco TV Playhouse*
4. Your Show of Shows*
5. The Colgate Comedy Hour*
6. Gillette Cavalcade of Sports*
7. The Lone Ranger*
8. Arthur Godfrey's Talent Scouts*
9. Hopalong Cassidy*
10. Mama*

October 1951–April 1952
1. Arthur Godfrey's Talent Scouts
2. Texaco Star Theater
3. I Love Lucy*
4. The Red Skelton Show*
5. The Colgate Comedy Hour
6. Arthur Godfrey and His Friends*
7. Fireside Theatre
8. Your Show of Shows
9. The Jack Benny Show*
10. You Bet Your Life*

October 1952–April 1953
1. I Love Lucy
2. Arthur Godfrey's Talent Scouts
3. Arthur Godfrey and His Friends
4. Dragnet*
5. Texaco Star Theater
6. The Buick Circus Hour*
7. The Colgate Comedy Hour
8. Gangbusters*
9. You Bet Your Life
10. Fireside Theatre

October 1953–April 1954
1. I Love Lucy
2. Dragnet

3. Arthur Godfrey's Talent Scouts (tie)
   You Bet Your Life (tie)
5. The Buick-Berle Show*
6. Arthur Godfrey and His Friends
7. Ford Theatre*
8. The Jackie Gleason Show*
9. Fireside Theatre
10. This is Your Life* (tie)
    The Colgate Comedy Hour (tie)

October 1954–April 1955
1. I Love Lucy
2. The Jackie Gleason Show
3. Dragnet
4. You Bet Your Life
5. The Toast of the Town*
6. Disneyland*
7. The Jack Benny Show
8. The George Gobel Show*
9. Ford Theatre
10. December Bride*

October 1955–April 1956
1. The $64,000 Question*
2. I Love Lucy
3. The Ed Sullivan Show
4. Disneyland
5. The Jack Benny Show
6. December Bride
7. You Bet Your Life
8. Dragnet
9. The Millionaire*
10. I've Got a Secret*

October 1956–April 1957
1. I Love Lucy
2. The Ed Sullivan Show
3. General Electric Theater*
4. The $64,000 Question
5. December Bride
6. Alfred Hitchcock Presents*
7. I've Got a Secret (tie)
   Gunsmoke* (tie)
9. The Perry Como Show*
10. The Jack Benny Show

October 1957–April 1958
1. Gunsmoke
2. The Danny Thomas Show*
3. Tales of Wells Fargo*
4. Have Gun Will Travel*
5. I've Got a Secret
6. The Life and Legend of Wyatt Earp*
7. General Electric Theater
8. The Restless Gun*
9. December Bride
10. You Bet Your Life

October 1958–April 1959
1. Gunsmoke
2. Wagon Train*
3. Have Gun Will Travel
4. The Rifleman*
5. The Danny Thomas Show
6. Maverick*
7. Tales of Wells Fargo
8. The Real McCoys*
9. I've Got a Secret
10. The Life and Legend of Wyatt Earp

October 1959–April 1960
1. Gunsmoke
2. Wagon Train
3. Have Gun Will Travel
4. The Danny Thomas Show
5. The Red Skelton Show
6. Father Knows Best* (tie)
   77 Sunset Strip* (tie)
8. The Price Is Right*
9. Wanted: Dead or Alive*
10. Perry Mason*

October 1960–April 1961
1. Gunsmoke
2. Wagon Train
3. Have Gun Will Travel
4. The Andy Griffith Show*
5. The Real McCoys
6. Rawhide*
7. Candid Camera*
8. The Untouchables* (tie)

The Price is Right (tie)
10. The Jack Benny Show

October 1961–April 1962
1. Wagon Train
2. Bonanza*
3. Gunsmoke
4. Hazel*
5. Perry Mason
6. The Red Skelton Show
7. The Andy Griffith Show
8. The Danny Thomas Show
9. Dr. Kildare*
10. Candid Camera

October 1962–April 1963
1. The Beverly Hillbillies*
2. Candid Camera (tie)
   The Red Skelton Show (tie)
4. Bonanza (tie)
   The Lucy Show* (tie)
6. The Andy Griffith Show
7. Ben Casey* (tie)
   The Danny Thomas Show (tie)
9. The Dick Van Dyke Show*
10. Gunsmoke

October 1963–April 1964
1. The Beverly Hillbillies
2. Bonanza
3. The Dick Van Dyke Show
4. Petticoat Junction*
5. The Andy Griffith Show
6. The Lucy Show
7. Candid Camera
8. The Ed Sullivan Show
9. The Danny Thomas Show
10. My Favorite Martian*

October 1964–April 1965
1. Bonanza
2. Bewitched*
3. Gomer Pyle, U.S.M.C.*
4. The Andy Griffith Show
5. The Fugitive*
6. The Red Skelton Hour
7. The Dick Van Dyke Show
8. The Lucy Show
9. Peyton Place*
10. Combat!*

October 1965–April 1966
1. Bonanza
2. Gomer Pyle, U.S.M.C.
3. The Lucy Show
4. The Red Skelton Hour
5. Batman (Thurs.)*

6. The Andy Griffith Show
7. Bewitched (tie)
   The Beverly Hillbillies (tie)
9. Hogan's Heroes*
10. Batman (Wed.)

October 1966–April 1967
1. Bonanza
2. The Red Skelton Hour
3. The Andy Griffith Show
4. The Lucy Show
5. The Jackie Gleason Show
6. Green Acres*
7. Daktari* (tie)
   Bewitched (tie)
9. The Beverly Hillbillies
10. The Virginian* (tie)
    The Lawrence Welk Show* (tie)
    Gomer Pyle U.S.M.C.

October 1967–April 1968
1. The Andy Griffith Show
2. The Lucy Show
3. Gomer Pyle, U.S.M.C.
4. Family Affair* (tie)
   Gunsmoke (tie)
   Bonanza (tie)
7. The Red Skelton Show
8. The Dean Martin Show*
9. The Jackie Gleason Show
10. Saturday Night at the Movies*

October 1968–April 1969
1. Rowan & Martin's Laugh-In*
2. Gomer Pyle, U.S.M.C.
3. Bonanza
4. Mayberry R.F.D.*
5. Family Affair
6. Gunsmoke
7. Julia*
8. The Dean Martin Show
9. Here's Lucy*
10. The Beverly Hillbillies

October 1969–April 1970
1. Rowan & Martin's Laugh-In
2. Gunsmoke
3. Bonanza
4. Mayberry R.F.D.
5. Family Affair
6. Here's Lucy
7. The Red Skelton Hour
8. Marcus Welby, M.D.*
9. Walt Disney's Wonderful
   World of Color*
10. The Doris Day Show*

October 1970–April 1971
1. Marcus Welby, M.D.
2. The Flip Wilson Show*
3. Here's Lucy
4. Ironside*
5. Gunsmoke
6. ABC Movie of the Week*
7. Hawaii Five-O*
8. Medical Center*
9. Bonanza
10. The F.B.I.*

October 1971–April 1972
1. All in the Family*
2. The Flip Wilson Show
3. Marcus Welby, M.D.
4. Gunsmoke
5. ABC Movie of the Week
6. Sanford and Son*
7. Mannix*
8. Funny Face* (tie)
   Adam 12* (tie)
10. The Mary Tyler Moore Show*

October 1972–April 1973
1. All in the Family
2. Sanford and Son
3. Hawaii Five-O
4. Maude*
5. Bridget Loves Bernie* (tie)
   The NBC Sunday Mystery
   Movie* (tie)
7. The Mary Tyler Moore Show
   (tie)
   Gunsmoke (tie)
9. The Wonderful World of Disney
10. Ironside

September 1973–April 1974
1. All in the Family
2. The Waltons*
3. Sanford and Son
4. M*A*S*H *
5. Hawaii Five-O
6. Maude
7. Kojak* (tie)
   The Sonny and Cher Comedy
   Hour* (tie)
9. Cannon* (tie)
   The Mary Tyler Moore Show (tie)

September 1974–April 1975
1. All in the Family
2. Sanford and Son
3. Chico and the Man*
4. The Jeffersons*
5. M*A*S*H

6. Rhoda*
7. Good Times*
8. The Waltons
9. Maude
10. Hawaii Five-O

September 1975–April 1976
1. All in the Family
2. Rich Man, Poor Man*
3. Laverne & Shirley*
4. Maude
5. The Bionic Woman*
6. Phyllis*
7. Sanford and Son (tie)
   Rhoda (tie)
9. The Six Million Dollar Man*
10. ABC Monday Night Movie*

September 1976–April 1977
1. Happy Days*
2. Laverne & Shirley
3. ABC Monday Night Movie
4. M*A*S*H
5. Charlie's Angels*
6. The Big Event*
7. The Six Million Dollar Man
8. Baretta* (tie)
   One Day at a Time* (tie)
   ABC Sunday Night Movie* (tie)

September 1977–April 1978
1. Laverne & Shirley
2. Happy Days
3. Three's Company*
4. 60 Minutes* (tie)
   Charlie's Angels (tie)
   All in the Family (tie)
7. Little House on the Prairie*
8. Alice* (tie)
   M*A*S*H (tie)
10. One Day at a Time

September 1978–April 1979
1. Laverne & Shirley
2. Three's Company
3. Mork & Mindy* (tie)
   Happy Days (tie)
5. Angie*
6. 60 Minutes.
7. M*A*S*H
8. The Ropers*
9. Taxi* (tie)
   All in the Family (tie)

September 1979–April 1980
1. 60 Minutes
2. Three's Company

3. That's Incredible!*
4. Alice (tie)
   M*A*S*H (tie)
6. Dallas*
7. Flo*
8. The Jeffersons
9. The Dukes of Hazzard*
10. One Day at a Time

September 1980–April 1981
1. Dallas
2. The Dukes of Hazzard
3. 60 Minutes
4. M*A*S*H
5. The Love Boat*
6. The Jeffersons
7. Alice
8. House Calls* (tie)
   Three's Company (tie)
10. Little House on the Prairie

September 1981–April 1982
1. Dallas
2. 60 Minutes
3. The Jeffersons
4. Three's Company
5. Alice
6. Too Close for Comfort* (tie)
   The Dukes of Hazzard (tie)
8. ABC Monday Night Movie
9. M*A*S*H
10. One Day at a Time

September 1982–April 1983
1. 60 Minutes
2. Dallas
3. Magnum, P.I.* (tie)
   M*A*S*H (tie)
5. Dynasty*
6. Three's Company
7. Simon & Simon*
8. Falcon Crest*
9. The Love Boat
10. The A-Team* (tie)
    Monday Night Football* (tie)

September 1983–April 1984
1. Dallas
2. 60 Minutes
3. Dynasty
4. The A-Team
5. Simon & Simon
6. Magnum P.I.
7. Falcon Crest
8. Kate & Allie*
9. Hotel*
10. Cagney & Lacey*

September 1984–April 1985
1. Dynasty
2. Dallas
3. The Cosby Show*
4. 60 Minutes
5. Family Ties*
6. The A-Team
7. Simon & Simon
8. Murder, She Wrote*
9. Knots Landing*
10. Crazy Like a Fox* (tie)
    Falcon Crest (tie)

September 1985–April 1986
1. The Cosby Show
2. Family Ties
3. Murder, She Wrote
4. 60 Minutes
5. Cheers*
6. Dallas
7. The Golden Girls* (tie)
   Dynasty (tie)
9. Miami Vice*
10. Who's the Boss?*

September 1986–April 1987
1. The Cosby Show
2. Family Ties
3. Cheers
4. Murder, She Wrote
5. The Golden Girls
6. 60 Minutes
7. Night Court*
8. Growing Pains*
9. Moonlighting*
10. Who's the Boss?

September 1987–April 1988
1. The Cosby Show
2. A Different World*
3. Cheers
4. The Golden Girls
5. Growing Pains
6. Who's the Boss?
7. Night Court
8. 60 Minutes
9. Murder, She Wrote
10. ALF* (tie)
    The Wonder Years* (tie)

September 1988–April 1989
1. The Cosby Show
2. Roseanne*
3. A Different World
4. Cheers
5. The Golden Girls
6. Who's the Boss?

7. 60 Minutes
8. Murder, She Wrote
9. Empty Nest*
10. Anything But Love*

September 1989–April 1990
1. Roseanne
2. The Cosby Show
3. Cheers
4. A Different World
5. America's Funniest Home
   Videos*
6. The Golden Girls
7. 60 Minutes
8. The Wonder Years
9. Empty Nest
10. Monday Night Football

September 1990–April 1991
1. Cheers
2. 60 Minutes
3. Roseanne
4. A Different World
5. The Cosby Show
6. Murphy Brown*
7. Empty Nest (tie)
   America's Funniest Home
   Videos (tie)
9. NFL Monday Night Football
10. The Golden Girls (tie)
    Designing Women* (tie)

September 1991–April 1992
1. 60 Minutes
2. Roseanne
3. Murphy Brown
4. Cheers

5. Home Improvement*
6. Designing Women
7. Coach*
8. Full House*
9. Unsolved Mysteries*
10. Murder, She Wrote

September 1992–April 1993
1. 60 Minutes
2. Roseanne
3. Home Improvement
4. Murphy Brown
5. Murder, She Wrote
6. Coach
7. NFL Monday Night Football
8. Cheers (tie)
   CBS Sunday Movie^ (tie)
10. Full House

PROGRAMS BY TOP-10 LONGEVITY

16 Years in the Top 10
60 Minutes

13 Years
Gunsmoke

10 Years
Bonanza

9 Years
M*A*S*H
The Red Skelton Show

8 Years
The Andy Griffith Show
Cheers

7 Years
All in the Family
The Cosby Show
Dallas
Murder, She Wrote

6 Years
The Danny Thomas Show
The Golden Girls
I Love Lucy

The Lucy Show
Three's Company
You Bet Your Life

5 Years
The Beverly Hillbillies
Gomer Pyle, U.S.M.C.
The Jack Benny Show
Roseanne
Sanford and Son

4 Years
Alice
Arthur Godfrey's Talent Scouts
Candid Camera
The Colgate Comedy Hour
December Bride
A Different World
Dragnet
Dynasty
Fireside Theatre
Have Gun, Will Travel
Hawaii Five-O
I've Got a Secret
The Jackie Gleason Show
The Jeffersons
Laverne & Shirley

Maude
One Day at a Time
The Toast of the Town/
   The Ed Sullivan Show
Wagon Train
Who's the Boss?

3 Years
The A-Team
ABC Monday Night Movie
Arthur Godfrey and His Friends
Bewitched
The Dick Van Dyke Show
The Dukes of Hazzard
Empty Nest
Falcon Crest
Family Affair
Family Ties
Happy Days
Here's Lucy
Marcus Welby, M.D.
The Mary Tyler Moore Show
Monday Night Football
Murphy Brown
Simon & Simon
Texaco Star Theater

ONE-YEAR WONDERS

The following series were in the top 10 for only one year. While most of them ranked below the top 10 before and/or after their top 10 run, a handful of these shows were cancelled after only one season. These series are marked with an asterisk.

The ABC Sunday Night Movie
Adam 12
ALF
Alfred Hitchcock Presents
Angie*
Anything But Love
Baretta
Batman
Ben Casey
The Big Event
The Bionic Woman
Bridget Loves Bernie*
The Buick-Berle Show
The Buick Circus Hour*
Cagney & Lacey
Cannon
Chico and the Man
Combat!
Crazy Like a Fox
Daktari

The Doris Day Show
Dr. Kildare
Father Knows Best
The FBI
Flo*
The Fugitive
Full House
Funny Face*
Gangbusters*
The George Gobel Show
Gillette Cavalcade of Sports
Good Times
Green Acres
Hazel
Hogan's Heroes
Hopalong Cassidy
Hotel
House Calls
Julia
Kate & Allie
Knots Landing
Kojak
The Lawrence Welk Show
The Lone Ranger
Mama
Mannix
Maverick
Medical Center

Miami Vice
The Millionaire
Moonlighting
Mork & Mindy
My Favorite Martian
NBC Saturday Night at the Movies
The NBC Sunday Mystery Movie
The Perry Como Show
Petticoat Junction
Peyton Place
Philco TV Playhouse
Phyllis
Rawhide
The Restless Gun
Rich Man, Poor Man*
The Rifleman
The Ropers*
77 Sunset Strip
The Sonny and Cher Comedy Hour
Taxi
That's Incredible!
This Is Your Life
Too Close for Comfort
The Untouchables
The Virginian
Wanted: Dead or Alive

PROGRAMS THAT BEGAN ON RADIO

In the early days of television, many shows were direct translations of their radio versions, while others were derived from radio shows but had format changes. The following top 10 shows all had radio roots. (If the radio version had a different title, it is shown in parentheses.)

Arthur Godfrey's Talent Scouts
Candid Camera (Candid Microphone)
December Bride
Dr. Kildare
Dragnet
Father Knows Best
The FBI (The FBI in Peace and War)
Ford Theatre
Gangbusters

Green Acres (Granby's Green Acres)
Gunsmoke
Have Gun, Will Travel
Hopalong Cassidy
I Love Lucy (My Favorite Husband)
The Jack Benny Show
The Lawrence Welk Show
The Lone Ranger
The Perry Como Show
Perry Mason
The Red Skelton Show
The $64,000 Question (Take It or Leave It)
Texaco Star Theater (The Milton Berle Show)
This Is Your Life
You Bet Your Life

PRIME-TIME SPINOFFS

Very often a hit series inspires the producers to find a way to keep the magic going, thus producing a spinoff in which characters introduced in the series are given a separate show of their own, or one in which the format of the original is copied with a slight change.

Occasionally, a dramatic segment of an anthology program will become a pilot for a series, although it may not have been planned as such. Among the shows listed below are hit series that were themselves spun off from earlier shows that were not necessarily hits.

Original Show	Spinoff
Adam 12	The New Adam 12
ALF	ALF (animated)
	ALF Tales (animated)
Alice	Flo
All in the Family	Gloria
	The Jeffersons
	Maude
America's Funniest Home Videos	America's Funniest People
The Andy Griffith Show	Gomer Pyle, U.S.M.C.
	Mayberry R.F.D.
The Beverly Hillbillies	Petticoat Junction
Bewitched	Tabitha
The Cosby Show	A Different World
Dallas	Knots Landing
The Danny Thomas Show	The Andy Griffith Show
December Bride	Pete & Gladys
Desilu Playhouse	The Untouchables
Dick Powell's Zane Grey Theater	The Rifleman
	Wanted: Dead or Alive
The Dukes of Hazzard	The Dukes (animated)
	Enos
Dynasty	The Colbys
The Edge of Night	Perry Mason
General Electric Theater	Bachelor Father
The Golden Girls	Empty Nest
	Golden Palace
Growing Pains	Just the Ten of Us
Gunsmoke	Dirty Sally
Happy Days	The Fonz & Happy Days Gang (animated)
	Joanie Loves Chachi
	Laverne & Shirley
	Mork & Mindy
	The Mork & Mindy/ Laverne & Shirley/ Fonz Hour (animated)
	Out of the Blue

Original Show	Spinoff
The Hollywood Palace	The Dean Martin Show
Ironside	Sarge
The Jackie Gleason Show	The Honeymooners
The Jeffersons	Checking In
Little House on the Prairie	Little House: A New Beginning
Love, American Style	Happy Days
The Mary Tyler Moore Show	Lou Grant
	Phyllis
	Rhoda
M*A*S*H	AfterMASH
	Trapper John, M.D.
Maude	Good Times
Maverick	Young Maverick
Murder, She Wrote	The Law and Harry McGraw
Petticoat Junction	Green Acres
The Rifleman	Law of the Plainsman
Roseanne	Little Rosey (animated)
Rowan & Martin's Laugh-In	Letters to Laugh-In
Sanford and Son	Grady
	Sanford
	Sanford Arms
The Schlitz Playhouse of Stars	The Restless Gun
The Six Million Dollar Man	The Bionic Woman
That's Incredible	Those Amazing Animals
Three's Company	The Ropers
	Three's a Crowd
Truth or Consequences	This Is Your Life
Who's the Boss?	Living Dolls

REUNION SHOWS

Producers of hit series will often try to reunite as many of the original cast members as they can into a "reunion" show, usually in the form of a made-for-TV movie. Sometimes the gathering takes the form of a "special," in which the actors reminisce about the original series and present film-clip-filled "scrapbooks" for television.

Original Show	**Reunion Show**
The Andy Griffith Show	Return to Mayberry (1986)
	The Andy Griffith Show Reunion (1993)
Ben Casey	The Return of Ben Casey (1988)
The Beverly Hillbillies	The Return of the Beverly Hillbillies (1981)
	The Legend of the Beverly Hillbillies (1993)
The Bionic Woman	The Return of the Six Million Dollar Man and the Bionic Woman (1987)
	The Bionic Showdown: The Six Million Dollar Man and the Bionic Woman (1989)
Cannon	The Return of Frank Cannon (1980)
Crazy Like a Fox	Still Crazy Like a Fox (1987)
The Danny Thomas Show	Make More Room for Daddy (1967)
	Make Room for Granddaddy (1969)
Dr. Kildare	Young Dr. Kildare (1972)
Dynasty	Dynasty: The Reunion (1991)
Father Knows Best	Father Knows Best Reunion (1977)
	Father Knows Best: Home for Christmas (1977)
Green Acres	Return to Green Acres (1990)
Gunsmoke	Gunsmoke: Return to Dodge (1987)
	Gunsmoke: The Last Apache (1990)
	Gunsmoke III: To the Last Man (1991)
	Gunsmoke: The Long Ride (1993)
Ironside	The Return of Ironside (1993)
Happy Days	The Happy Days Reunion Special (1992)
Kojak	Kojak: The Belarus File (1985)
	Kojak: The Price of Justice (1987)
Little House on the Prairie	Little House on the Prairie: Look Back to Yesterday (1983)
	Little House: Bless All the Dear Children (1983)
	Little House: The Last Farewell (1983)
The Love Boat	The Love Boat: A Valentine Voyage (1990)
Marcus Welby, M.D.	The Return of Marcus Welby, M.D. (1984)
	Marcus Welby, M.D.: A Holiday Affair (1988)
The Mary Tyler Moore Show	The Mary Tyler Moore Show Reunion (1992)
Maverick	The New Maverick (1979)
The NBC Mystery Movie	The Return of Sam McCloud (1985)
Perry Mason	The Return of Perry Mason (1985)
Peyton Place	Return to Peyton Place (1972)
	Murder in Peyton Place (1977)
Rowan & Martin's Laugh-In	Laugh-In's 25th Anniversary Special (1993)
The Six Million Dollar Man	The Return of the Six Million Dollar Man and the Bionic Woman (1989)
	The Bionic Showdown: The Six Million Dollar Man and the Bionic Woman (1987)
The Untouchables	The Return of Eliot Ness (1991)
The Waltons	A Wedding on Walton's Mountain (1982)
	Mother's Day on Walton's Mountain (1982)
	A Day of Thanks on Walton's Mountain (1982)

BIBLIOGRAPHY

Adir, Karin. *The Great Clowns of American Television.* Jefferson, N.C.: McFarland and Company, Inc., Publishers, 1988.

Allen, Steve. *Funny People.* New York: Stein and Day, 1981.

Allen, Steve. *Hi-Ho, Steverino! My Adventures in the Wonderful Wacky World of TV.* Fort Lee, N.J.: Barricade Books, Inc., 1992.

Allman, Kevin. *TV Turkeys.* New York: Perigee Books, 1987.

Andrews, Bart. *The Story of "I Love Lucy."* New York: Popular Library, 1977.

Andrews, Bart, with Cheryl Blythe. *The Official "Cheers" Scrapbook.* New York: New American Library, 1987.

Andrews, Bart, and Thomas Watson. *Loving Lucy.* New York: St. Martin's Press, 1980.

Beck, Ken, and Jim Clark. *The Andy Griffith Show Book.* New York: St. Martin's Press, 1985.

Berle, Milton, with Frankel Haskel. Milton Berle: An Autobiography. New York: Delacorte Press, 1974.

Blythe, Cheryl, and Susan Sackett. *Say Goodnight, Gracie! The Story of George Burns and Gracie Allen.* Rocklin, Calif.: Prima Publishing, 1989.

Bonanno, Margaret Wander. *Angela Lansbury—A Biography.* New York: St. Martin's Press, 1987.

Bowles, Jerry. *A Thousand Sundays—The Story of the Ed Sullivan Show.* New York: G.P. Putnam's Sons, 1980.

Bronson, Fred. *The Billboard Book of Number One Hits, Third Edition.* New York: Billboard Books, 1992.

Brooks, Tim. *The Complete Directory to Prime Time TV Stars, 1946–Present.* New York: Ballantine Books, 1981.

Brooks, Tim, and Earle Marsh. *The Complete Directory to Prime Time Network TV Shows, 1946–Present, Fifth Edition.* New York: Ballantine Books, 1992.

Brown, Les. *Les Brown's Encyclopedia of Television.* New York: Zoetrope, 1982.

Burr, Lonnie. *Two for the Show: Great Comedy Teams.* New York: Julian Mesner, 1979.

Campbell, Robert. *The Golden Years of Broadcasting.* New York: Charles Scribner's Sons, 1976.

Carroll, Diahann, with Ross Firestone. *Diahann: An Autobiography.* Boston: Little, Brown and Company, 1986.

Chandler, Charlotte. *Hello, I Must Be Going: Groucho and His Friends.* New York: Penguin Books, 1979.

Collins, Joan. *Past Imperfect.* New York: Simon and Schuster, 1984.

Cosell, Howard. *Cosell.* Chicago: Playboy Press, 1973.

Crescenti, Peter, and Bob Columbe. *The Official Honeymooners Treasury.* New York: Perigee Books/Putnam Publishing Group, 1990.

Daly, Marsha. *Michael Landon: A Biography.* New York: St. Martin's Press, 1987.

Fireman, Judy. *The TV Book.* New York: Workman Publishing Company, 1977.

Franklin, Joe. *Joe Franklin's Encyclopedia of Comedians.* Secaucus, N.J.: The Citadel Press, 1979.

Greenfield, Jeff. *Television—The First 50 Years.* New York: Harry N. Abrams, Inc., 1977.

Gunther, Marc, and Bill Carter. *Monday Night Mayhem: The Inside Story of ABC's "Monday Night Football."* New York: William Morrow, 1988.

Harris, Jay S. *TV Guide—The First 25 Years.* New York: Simon and Schuster, 1978.

Javna, John. *Cult TV.* New York: St. Martin's Press, 1985.

Javna, John. *The TV Theme Song Sing-Along Song Book.* New York: St. Martin's Press, 1984.

Katz, Ephraim. *The Film Encyclopedia.* New York: Perigee Books/Putnam Publishing Group, 1979.

Maltin, Leonard. *Leonard Maltin's Movie and Video Guide, 1993 Edition.* New York: Penguin Books, 1992.

Martin, Mick, and Marsha Porter. *Video Movie Guide 1988.* New York: Ballantine Books, 1987.

Marx, Arthur. *Everybody Loves Somebody Sometime (Especially Himself): The Story of Dean Martin and Jerry Lewis.* New York: Hawthorn Books, Inc., 1974.

McCoy, Malachy. *Steve McQueen: The Unauthorized Biography.* Chicago: Henry Regnery Company, 1974.

McNeil, Alex. *Total Television: A Comprehensive Guide to Programming from 1948 to the Present, Third Edition.* New York: Penguin Books, 1991.

Mitz, Rick. *The Great TV Sitcom Book.* New York: Richard Marek, 1980.

Morella, Joe and Edward Z. Epstein. *Jane Wyman: A Biography.* New York: Delacorte Press, 1985.

Parish, James Robert, and William T. Leonard. *The Funsters.* New Rochelle, N.Y.: Arlington House, 1979.

Rovin, Jeff. *The Great Television Series.* New York: A.S. Barnes and Company, 1977.

Schuster, Hal. *The Hollywood Death Book.* Las Vegas: Pioneer Books, Inc., 1992.

Schwartz, David, Steve Ryan, and Fred Wostbrock. *The Encyclopedia of TV Game Shows.* New York: Zoetrope, 1987.

Sennett, Ted. *Your Show of Shows.* New York: Macmillan Publishing Co., Inc., 1977.

Settel, Irving. *A Pictorial History of Television.* New York: Frederick Ungar Publishing Co., 1983.

Sherman, Allan. *A Gift of Laughter: The Autobiography of Allan Sherman.* New York: Atheneum Publishers, 1965.

Shulman, Arthur, and Roger Youman. *How Sweet It Was.*

INDEX